2

The Accounting Framework
A Contemporary Emphasis

The Accounting Framework
A Contemporary Emphasis

Ronald Ma
Professor of Accountancy
The University of New South Wales

Russell Mathews
Director, Centre for Research on Federal Financial Relations
The Australian National University

Longman Cheshire

Longman Cheshire Pty Limited
346 St Kilda Road
Melbourne 3004 Australia

Offices in Sydney, Brisbane, Adelaide
and Perth. Associated companies, branches
and representatives throughout the world

© Ronald Ma, Russell Mathews 1979

First Published 1979
based on *The Accounting Framework*
first published 1971

Printed in Singapore by
Kyodo Shing Loong Printing Industries Pte Ltd.

National Library of Australia
Cataloguing-in-Publication data

Ma, Ronald.
  The accounting framework.

  Index
  ISBN 0 582 71077 4

1. Accounting. 1. Mathews, Russell Lloyd, joint
author. II. Title.

657

Contents

Part I: The Accounting System

Accounting classification. The accounting equation. The theory of double entry: underlying assumptions; the interpretation of business transactions. A simplified system of accounts. The recording of business transactions. The trial balance. Summary accounts: (1) the trading account; (2) the profit and loss account. The balance sheet. The funds statement. Accounting reports.

The recording process. Specialized journals. Cash transactions. The classification framework. Balance sheet classification. Profit and loss classification. Chart of accounts. Control accounts and subsidiary ledgers.

Significance of the trial balance. Matching costs and expenses against revenue by periods. The balance-day adjustments. Adjustments to recorded transactions. Recording accrued transactions. Depreciation. Provisions for anticipated revenue, costs, expenses or losses. Closing entries. Preparation and presentation of final reports. Summary and illustration. Using an eight-column trial balance as a worksheet. Preparation of final accounting reports or financial statements.

Valuation of cost of sales and inventories: identified or actual cost; weighted average cost; first-in-first-out; last-in-first-out. Application of 'cost or market' rule. Retail inventory method of accounting for inventories. Depreciation: straight-line depreciation; reducing balance depreciation; sum of the years' digits method of depreciation; depreciation based on output or production. Probability-life approach to depreciation.

Concept of funds as total resources. The conventional funds statement. Form and content of the funds statement. Preparation of the conventional funds statement. Limitations of conventional analysis. The expanded funds statement. Revenue and cost flows. Further application of the external transaction criterion to funds statement analysis. A comprehensive illustration.

Basic assumptions. The accounting unit, accounting period, simple monetary and continuity assumptions. The constant price level and original cost assumptions. The realization and matching assumptions. The allocation problem. Qualitative criteria for judging usefulness of accounting systems: relevance, objectivity; hardness; reliability; comparability. Relevance as the primary quality. Conservatism. Standards and principles.

Structural and trend analysis. Balance sheet structural and trend analysis. Income statement structural and trend analysis. Information analysis by investors. Profitability analysis. Long-run risk analysis. Leverage or gearing. Short-run risk analysis: working capital (or current) ratio; quick asset ratio; fund flow ratios. Information analysis by creditors. Trade creditors. Banks. Ilustration of a cash budget. Long-term creditors. Information analysis by management. Structural and trend analysis. Analysis of overall efficiency. Efficiency in use of working capital: the turnover of book debts; the rate of inventory turnover. Evaluation of management performance by outside parties. Some evidence on the usefulness of ratio analysis: Beaver's study (1966). Limitations of ratio analysis.

Appendix: Analysis of a company's financial statements. Earnings and dividend yields. Market-based rate of return.

Overview of an information system. Objectives of the information system: record keeping; operations and control; integrated planning and policy making. Data processing systems: manual systems; mechanical systems; punched card systems; electronic computer systems. A cost comparison. A computer data processing system. Hardware. Programs, procedures and personnel. Organization of the data processing department. The role of the accountant.

Tools and techniques in system study and design. Organization charts. Flowcharts: basic symbols for flowcharting; system flowchart; logic flowchart. Decision tables. Grid charts. Layout charts. Network diagrams. Steps in new system design: analysis of the existing system; defining the new system requirements; designing and implementing the new system. A case study of a proposed accounts receivable system. Programming languages.

Appendix A: A matrix accounting system.
Appendix B: Running a punched card job on the computer.

Part II: Accounting Entities

Partnership accounts. Formation. Distribution of partnership profits. Revaluation of net assets: change in profit-sharing ratio; admission of new partner; retirement of a partner; dissolution of a partnership.

and by trading enterprises; (c) sale of goods and services by trading enterprises to government and consumers; (d) payment of taxes; (e) sale of securities by the central government to banks; and (f) sale of houses or land by trading enterprises. Summary flow-of-funds statements. National balance sheets and national wealth statements. Business enterprise accounts in relation to national accounting systems. The accounting reports of business enterprises: national income and expenditure accounts; flow-of-funds accounts; national balance sheets. Towards a unified framework of national economic accounts.

Part III: Accounting Measurement and Valuation

of valuation adjustments and their significance. Evaluation of the current distributable income/operating capital maintenance approach to current value accounting; usefulness from viewpoint of the firm; usefulness from viewpoint of the economy. Criticisms of current value accounting.

Business profit/financial capital maintenance approach. Reconciliation of the two approaches to current value accounting. Evaluation of the business profit approach. Are cost savings income? Determination of current values. (1) The Edwards and Bell method. (2) Value to the business. Valuation to the business of inventories. Valuation to the business of fixed assets: what is the replacement cost of a fixed asset; asset valuation and the decision matrix; the use of surrogates; the essentiality criterion. (3) An alternative approach to determining current values.

Relative price change accounting. Relationship between current value and general price level adjustments in relative price change accounting. Evaluation of relative price change accounting. Continuously contemporary accounting (CoCoA). Assumptions underlying CoCoA. Computation of financial position and income under CoCoA: financial position and current cash equivalents; net income measures and current cash equivalents. Method (1): recording CCE measures at the end of the period only. Method (2): continuously updating the CCE measures. Adapting historical record measures to CoCoA; Methods (1) and (2) evaluated. A comparison of CoCoA income and current distributable income. Uses of CoCoA: relevance for decision making; current cash equivalents as measures of net worth, liquidity and risk; economic significance of CoCoA summary measures; consistency with real world events and the allocation problem. Limitations of CoCoA: not a valuation rule for all seasons; the aggregation problem; the problem of markets; effect of zero or minimal current cash equivalents on income measurement.

Recent developments in Australia. The Australian Statement of Provisional Accounting Standards. The Mathews Report. Recent developments in New Zealand. The Richardson Report: the treatment of monetary items. Recent developments in the United Kingdom. The Sandilands Report. The Exposure Draft on CCA. An interim recommendation by the Accounting Standards Committee. Recent developments in the United States. Replacement cost disclosure requirements of the Securities and Exchange Commission. The Conceptual Framework Project of the Financial Accounting Standards Board. Proposed Statement of Financial Accounting Concepts: Objectives of Financial Reporting and Elements of Financial Statements of Business Enterprises. Statement on Accounting Theory and Theory Acceptance.

Part IV: Cost Accounting and Management Decision Making

Cost classifications for income measurement: cost elements; direct and indirect costs;

product costs and period costs; absorption costing v. variable costing methods. Cost classifications for planning and control: variable and fixed costs; controllable and non-controllable costs. Cost classifications for decision making—non-accounting costs: opportunity costs; future costs. Cost classifications for decision making—accounting costs: incremental and sunk costs; avoidable and unavoidable costs.

The cost unit. Integrated cost accounting systems: (1) general ledger control system; (2) dual ledger control system. Accounting for job and process costs. Costs classified by departments. Job cost system. Process cost system. Unit costs: the weighted average method; the FIFO method.

Accounting for materials. Accounting for labour. Accounting for manufacturing overhead—product costing: estimating predetermined overhead recovery rates; normal capacity; overhead allocation to departments; fixed and variable overhead classification. The base for estimating and applying overhead rates. The static manufacturing overhead budget. Accounting treatment of overhead variances. Overhead analysis for cost control in an historical cost system: the flexible manufacturing overhead budget; analysis of manufacturing overhead variances; problems in overhead variance analysis.

Setting standards. Material and labour variances. Causes of variations from standards. Analysis of material and labour variances. Overhead analysis in a standard cost system. Some control aspects of variance analysis. When is a variance significant? Responsibility for variances. Behavioural implications of budgeting and standard costs. Disposition of variances.

Strategic planning. Tactical plans. The multi-period tactical plan. Corporate models. Illustration of corporate model.

Profit planning. Break-even analysis. Profit planning and profit-graph analysis. Profit-graph assumptions. The annual budget and the product-mix problem. Budgets for cost control and planning. The budget period. The budgeted level of activity. The product-mix problem: the multi-product single-constraint case; the two-product multi-constraint case; sensitivity testing; the multi-product multi-constraint case; the interpretation of shadow prices. The master budget.

Significance and problems of capital budgeting. The administration of capital expenditures. Generation of project proposals. Management control over capital expenditures. Relevant costs and benefits. Project evaluation criteria. Crude evaluation techniques: accounting rate of return; payback. Methods of evaluation which involve discounting of cash flows. Cost of capital. Net present value (NPV) method. Internal rate of return (IRR) method. Comparison of NPV and IRR methods. Project ranking under capital rationing. Ranking projects with unequal lives. Technological forecasting and project evaluation. Risk measurement in project evaluation. Shareholders' wealth maximization and project selection. Company's existing portfolio of assets and project selection. Variability of expected return and project selection. Hertz's risk analysis model.

Appendix: Solving for the internal rate of return.

Preface

This book continues the tradition of *The Accounting Framework* by Russell Mathews, which was published in 1971 as a revised edition of the same author's *Accounting for Economists* (1962). The present book has been completely rewritten, blending the best and more enduring features of the earlier books with a wider scope and more comprehensive treatment, a review of the important developments that have been taking place during the past twenty years, and a fresh and critical examination of the major issues that have emerged in accounting theory and practice.

Although written primarily for students, this book is not restricted to an account of settled doctrine and established procedures. Rather it adopts a questioning approach to accounting orthodoxy, and in many key subject areas it makes what the authors believe to be useful contributions to accounting thought. These areas include income measurement and valuation theory, public sector and national economic accounting, financial planning and capital budgeting.

In seeking to explain and evaluate the vast and interlocking complex of theory and practice that has recently been developed, the authors have been concerned to show how the accounting framework can most effectively achieve its primary purpose of providing information as a basis for decision making, planning and control by those who must take responsibility for these activities in the private and public sectors of the economy. The book thus seeks to show how contemporary thought and methodology may be applied to the economic choices that have to be made in a complex and rapidly changing world.

The book also differs from standard texts in its somewhat encyclopaedic approach. The intention has been not to provide a text for a single course in accounting, but rather to develop a compendium of structural studies that may be used as a continuing source of reference by students of accounting in both introductory and advanced courses. This approach has its problems and, because the degree of difficulty differs from chapter to chapter (and in some cases within individual chapters), the book must be used selectively. The authors have it in mind that teachers and students will use the different parts and chapters as building blocks in designing courses that meet their own particular needs, orientation and level. Nevertheless, each of the four parts of the book has been designed as a comprehensive unit in itself and as an integral component of the overall design. The book should therefore serve the needs of accounting, business and economics students in universities and colleges in a variety of ways, and at the same time give teachers and experienced practitioners of accounting a fresh perception of contemporary developments in the art.

The four parts of the book are concerned respectively with: the accounting system; accounting entities; accounting measurement and valuation; and cost accounting, planning and decision making. Parts I and II are designed to provide an introductory course in accounting, which will develop a sound knowledge of the principles of double entry, accounting methodology and accounting for business groups and public authorities. Accounting method must be leavened with theory, and the basic accounting system which is developed in Parts I and II reflects a conceptual approach to accounting problems. Chapter 6 in Part I and the whole of Part III are concerned with accounting measurement and valuation theory. Chapters 8 and 9 provide an introduction to information systems and the computer.

Part II is concerned with the application of the double-entry principles and procedures developed in Part I to different kinds of business and non-business entities. Chapters 14 and 15, on public authority and national economic accounting respectively, will be useful to accountants, economists and students with interests in the public sector.

Although many of the chapters (or sections of chapters) in Parts III and IV may be read by first-year students with understanding and benefit, the second half of the book is intended primarily for advanced students. Competing accounting valuation models are explained and evaluated in Part III, while Part IV is concerned with selected aspects of management accounting (with special reference to planning, control and decision making).

The authors are very grateful to Pramond Pandey for writing Chapters 8 and 9 on accounting information systems. Wal Burke, Vic Levy, John Macmullen, Malcolm Miller, Richard Morris and Pramond Pandey took a continuing interest in our work, and we benefited from their generous help and criticism. Bob Jay, Brian Booth, Murray Wells, Ted Bloomfield and Mark Scott read and commented on various sections of the book. Malcolm Miller has kindly permitted us to use material from a joint article with one of the authors in *Accounting and Business Research*. We are also obliged to the editors of the following journals for permission to draw on our writings in these journals: *Abacus, Accountants' Journal, Accounting and Business Research, The Accounting Review, Journal of Accounting Research* and *The Economic Record*. We have inevitably drawn on the ideas of many other writers. Although we have attempted to acknowledge these in the 'References' and 'Additional Reading' at the end of each chapter, there is such a vast literature that it is possible that on occasions we have been unwittingly remiss in this respect; if so, we hope that our lapses will be forgiven. The usual disclaimers of course apply.

To assist students and teachers in their use of *The Accounting Framework*: *A Contemporary Emphasis,* a *Students' Companion* and a *Teachers' Manual* have been prepared, which offer suggested solutions to the exercises provided in the book and supplement those exercises with additional problems.

Nina Kingston was responsible for the production of the *Students' Companion* and the *Teachers' Manual* in respect of Parts I (except for Chapters 8 and 9), II and III; and Pramond Pandey was responsible for the *Students' Companion* and the *Teachers' Manual* in respect of Chapters 8 and 9 and Part IV.

We are grateful to the University of Adelaide, the Australian National University and our colleagues in these universities for permitting us to reproduce some of the discussion questions and exercises that were originally set as test or examination questions. We have also made use of three questions taken from *Some Questions in Graduate Accounting Theory* published by the University of Oregon. The authors are especially indebted to Michelle Jones for her loyal and efficient help in typing, proof reading and generally facilitating the production of this book. Lastly, we dedicate this book to our wives, Ursula and Joan, for lightening the arduous burden of authorship through their tolerance and support.

R.M. and R.M.
June 1978

Part I

The Accounting System

Introduction to Part I: The Accounting System

Accounting involves the systematic recording, measurement and interpretation of economic transactions and activities, and communication of the results to decision makers. The accounting field is wider in scope than book-keeping, which is concerned solely with the recording aspect. Historically, the need to keep financial records has been associated with the imposition of taxes on the one hand and the growth of trade and commerce on the other. The development of a systematic method of book-keeping—double-entry book-keeping—occurred during the great expansion of trade initiated by the Italian city-states in the 14th and 15th centuries. As trading ventures became too large to be financed by an individual trader, a new form of business organization—the partnership—was introduced. Partners required full financial records to be maintained in order that their rights and obligations might be clearly defined, and by the end of the 15th century these records were frequently in double-entry form. During the next 400 years, the double-entry or 'Italian' method of book-keeping spread to other countries of Europe and is now used universally. The industrial revolution of the 19th and 20th centuries, and the change in business organization that resulted from the joint-stock company legislation introduced in this period, led to many new developments in the field of accounting; but double-entry book-keeping has adapted itself to all these changes. It has proved to be as suitable for the company form of organization as for the partnership; as useful and necessary for the giant manufacturing enterprise as for the small trader. The double-entry method has also proved adaptable to the needs of non-trading clubs and societies, governments and government enterprises. Even the recording of the nation's economic transactions, in the form of national or social accounts, depends on the application of double-entry methods.

Double-entry book-keeping has thus proved to be the most suitable medium for the recording of all economic transactions. An important complementary development has been the ingenious integration of *asset and capital accounts* (i.e. accounts of assets and financial obligations [or, as financial obligations are often called, equities]) and *operating accounts* (i.e. accounts of revenues, costs and expenses). Thus the interrelationship of the investment in resources and the return on the investment is disclosed in what has been referred to as 'Italian capital-income accounting'.

The major purpose of accounting is to provide information to decision makers about the nature and significance of economic transactions. The proprietors or shareholders of a business enterprise, for example, wish to know the financial results of operations in a given period, or the financial position of the business at a given point of time. Management seeks information from the accounting records to be used as a basis for controlling the activities of the business, or for making decisions on operating policy. In order to provide this information several accounting processes are necessary. The first task is to arrange for the *collection* of the information which is to be recorded, and for its expression in monetary terms. The *recording* or book-keeping process follows in two steps; a chronological record is made in a book known as the journal, and this is followed by entries in a classifying medium known as the ledger, which groups together (in ledger 'accounts') transactions of similar significance. The next process involves the *summarizing* of all transactions in two statements, the profit and loss statement which records the total revenue and total expenses of the business during a given period, and the balance sheet which summarizes the sources of the funds used and shows how these funds have been applied to the purchase of assets.

The *presentation* or reporting of the information contained in the summary statements is also an important accounting function, since the results of operations only acquire meaning when they are communicated to interested parties. Finally, *analysis* and *interpretation* of the accounting reports must be undertaken in order to emphasize significant features and explain the technical limitations inherent in the accounting processes.

1 Basic Accounting Method: A Simplified System of Accounts

Accounting Classification

The processes of collecting and recording information, the presentation of accounting reports and their analysis and interpretation are influenced by the bases of *classification* that are adopted in order to distinguish the different classes of business transactions. Therefore, classification is itself an important accounting function. Indeed, there is a sense in which the whole process of accounting may be regarded as a system of classification. In a business enterprise, the main classes of transactions are buying and selling goods and services, acquiring assets and incurring financial obligations. More particularly the following principal groups of transactions may be distinguished:

(a) the earning of revenue from the sale of trading inventory, which may be designated as *sales*;

(b) the cost of acquiring the trading inventory which is sold, which may be designated as *cost of sales*;

(c) the expenses incurred in the course of earning revenue, which may be designated as *expenses*;

(d) the acquisition of funds or the incurring of financial obligations by the business:

    (i)   in the form of the funds contributed by the proprietor himself, which may be designated as *proprietorship equity*,

    (ii) in the form of funds borrowed from outside creditors, which may be designated as *liabilities*;

(e) the accumulation of resources (money, claims to money or material resources), which may be designated as *assets*.

All business transactions may be assumed to fall within one or other of these six groups. The relationships between the different groups may be expressed as follows:

$$\text{Sales} - \text{Cost of sales} = \text{Gross profit}$$
$$\text{Gross profit} - \text{Expenses} = \text{Net profit}$$
$$\text{Assets} - \text{Liabilities} = \text{Proprietorship equity}$$

On the basis of the foregoing classification and having regard to these relationships, the accountant is able to answer the following important questions relating to the income and wealth of the enterprise:

(a) What are the results of business operations during any period? That is to say, what revenue has been earned, and what costs and expenses have been incurred?

(b) What is the financial position of the business at any point of time? That is to say, what are its financial obligations and its assets?

The answer to the first question is derived from a summary statement called the *profit and loss statement*, which takes the following form:

Profit and Loss Statement for the Year Ended 31 December 1985

Sales	$ ...
Less: Cost of sales	...
Gross profit	...
Less: Expenses	...
Net profit (or loss*)	$ ...

* A loss is a negative profit.

The answer to the second problem is obtained by reference to the *balance sheet*, which takes the following form:

Balance Sheet as at 31 December 1985

Assets	$ ...
Less: Liabilities	...
Proprietorship equity	$ ...

The Accounting Equation

The two summary statements are linked through net profit, which represents an increase in proprietorship equity. As a corollary, transactions affecting the profit and loss statement are always reflected in changes in assets or liabilities; revenue from sales is matched by an increase in assets, while the incurring of costs and expenses involves a reduction in assets or an increase in liabilities. The relationship between the profit and loss statement and the balance sheet may be expressed more precisely by reference to the following fundamental balance-sheet equation, sometimes called the accounting equation:

$$\text{Assets } (A) = \text{Financial obligations (or equities)}$$
$$= \text{Proprietorship equity} (P) + \text{Liabilities} (L)$$

Strictly, this is an identity, in which the left side of the expression represents the resources under the control of the accounting entity, and the right side represents the sources of funds utilized for the acquisition of these resources.

From the last expression it follows that:

$$A - L = P \tag{1}$$

This equation holds good continuously, so that an increase in proprietorship (ΔP) must always be reflected by an equivalent increase in assets (ΔA) or reduction in liabilities ($-\Delta L$):

i.e.
$$\Delta A - \Delta L = \Delta P \tag{2}$$
and
$$(A + \Delta A) - (L + \Delta L) = P + \Delta P \tag{3}$$

Since net profit represents an increase in proprietorship equity, the earning of profit must always be accompanied by an increase in assets or a reduction in liabilities. Revenue earned from sales (R) may be regarded as a temporary increase in proprietorship equity (out of which costs and expenses (C) have to be recovered before net profit is determined), and it follows from the accounting equation that the earning of revenue must always be accompanied by an identical increase in assets or reduction in liabilities. The incurring of costs and expenses, on the other hand, may be regarded as a temporary reduction in proprietorship equity, which must be offset by an identical reduction in assets or increase in liabilities. Other factors affecting proprietorship equity are new investment or contributions by the proprietor (I) and withdrawals by the proprietor (W). Thus $\triangle P$ may be expanded as follows:

$$\triangle P = R - C + I - W \tag{4}$$

The debit and credit recording rules are illustrated in (5), which is obtained by substituting (4) in (3) and rearranging. *Debit items are shown on the left-hand side and credit items on the right-hand side of expression (5) below*:

$$(A + \triangle A) + C + W = (L + \triangle L) + (P + I) + R \tag{5}$$

Rearranging (5), the expanded balance sheet equation is derived:

$$(A + \triangle A) - (L + \triangle L) = (P + I - W) + (R - C) \tag{6}$$

The equilibrium which the book-keeping record achieves through the accounting equation is an essential feature of double entry. The creation of assets within an enterprise is always accompanied by the incurring of identical financial obligations, either to the proprietors of the enterprise (proprietorship equity) or to outside creditors (liabilities). The derivation of profit is always accompanied by an identical increase in the net assets (i.e. assets *minus* liabilities) of the enterprise. It is now possible to see how double-entry book-keeping produces this equilibrium of results by ensuring that the equation holds good at all times.

The Theory of Double Entry

Underlying Assumptions

The theory of double-entry book-keeping may be explained by reference to the six major classes of transactions that have been distinguished. At this stage, mention should be made of three important assumptions underlying accounting method. The first relates to the *accounting unit* or *accounting entity*. For purposes of exposition, the accounting unit is identified with the business enterprise, but there may be other forms of accounting units, e.g. clubs, trusts, governments. What is important, however, is the assumption that each business enterprise has a separate entity for accounting purposes; the transactions that are classified into the above groups are the transactions affecting a particular business. As a corollary, it is assumed that the business unit has an entity quite distinct from that of its owners. It follows that transactions between the business and its proprietors must be accounted for in the same way as transactions between the business and outside parties.

The entity assumption defines the area of the accounting record. The next assumption relates to the period covered in the record. Business operations are continuous and results may only be determined with accuracy over the whole life-time of the business. For the purposes of accounting, however, it is assumed that the life-time of the business may be broken up into arbitrary periods of fixed length, usually one year. This is the *accounting period*.

The third assumption relates to the unit of measurement. It is necessary to express transactions of all kinds in terms of a common unit of measurement, the *monetary unit*; as a corollary it is usually assumed that changes in the value of money may be ignored for accounting purposes.

The accounting period assumption and the monetary assumption do not correspond with reality, and later it will be necessary to consider some of the limitations and problems that result from their use.

The Interpretation of Business Transactions

Double-entry book-keeping is based on the dual aspect of business transactions. Business transactions always involve an element of exchange, and the act of exchange involves two distinct aspects *for each party* to the exchange—the aspect of receiving and the aspect of giving. When A sells goods to B in return for cash, for example, the transaction may be described from A's viewpoint by saying that A has received cash in return for the goods he has given up; while from B's viewpoint the transaction represents the receipt of goods and the giving of cash. Other transactions may be similarly analysed into a receiving aspect and a giving aspect.

Double-entry book-keeping recognizes the dual nature of business transactions by providing that every transaction shall be recorded twice in the accounting records of the accounting entity. The first entry records the receiving aspect, and the second the giving aspect. The essential record in which the double entry is made is the *ledger*, which comprises a number of ledger *accounts*. Every ledger account is divided into two sides, and each side has columns in which may be recorded the date, narrative or description, and monetary value of transactions. The left-hand side is conventionally described as the *debit* (*dr.*) side of the account, and records the receiving aspect of transactions. The right-hand side of the account is called the *credit* (*cr.*) side, and records the giving aspect of transactions. Figure 1—A illustrates the form of a ledger account.

Figure 1—A
The Ledger Account

| | | | | | | Name of Account | | | | Account Number | |

Dr.											Cr.
Date	Narrative		Folio	$		Date	Narrative		Folio		$

The narrative column records the name of the other ledger account affected by the transaction, and the folio column is used as a cross-reference to the other book, known as the *journal*, which (as will be seen later) provides the original accounting record of the transaction.

In any accounting system, a separate account is maintained for each group of transactions of similar significance. When a transaction takes place, it is recorded by making an entry on the debit side of an account (to record the receiving aspect of the transaction), and a second entry, of equal monetary value, on the credit side of another account (to record the giving aspect of the transaction). Thus for every debit entry in an accounting system there must be a corresponding credit entry, and the sum of the debit entries in the ledger must always equal the sum of the credit entries.

All transactions must be interpreted from the viewpoint of the business enterprise itself, and not from that of the proprietor. This follows from the entity assumption. Perhaps the best method of interpreting transactions is to consider their effect on the accounting equation. From the viewpoint of the business, the receiving aspect of a transaction is always reflected by an increase in assets or a reduction in financial obligations, while the giving aspect corresponds to a reduction in the assets or an increase in the financial obligations of the business. Increases in assets or reductions in financial obligations are therefore recorded by means of debit entries in the appropriate accounts; while reductions in assets or increases in financial obligations are recorded by credit entries. Transactions affecting profit and loss, i.e. transactions involving the earning of revenue or the incurring of costs and expenses, are interpreted in accordance with their influence on proprietorship equity. Such transactions affect the financial obligations of the business to its proprietors. Revenue from sales may be regarded as temporarily increasing proprietorship equity, thereby increasing the financial obligations of the enterprise to its proprietors. Such transactions are therefore recorded by means of credit entries in revenue or sales accounts. Costs and expenses, on the other hand, temporarily diminish proprietorship equity, and are recorded by debit entries in cost or expense accounts.

Irrespective of the method of interpretation, however, it is necessary to remember the basic rule of double-entry book-keeping; every transaction involves two entries in the accounting records, a debit entry in one account with a corresponding credit entry in another account.

A Simplified System of Accounts

A simple framework of accounts may be constructed by reference to the six major classes of transactions that have already been distinguished. For purposes of exposition let us assume that the accounting system comprises the following accounts:

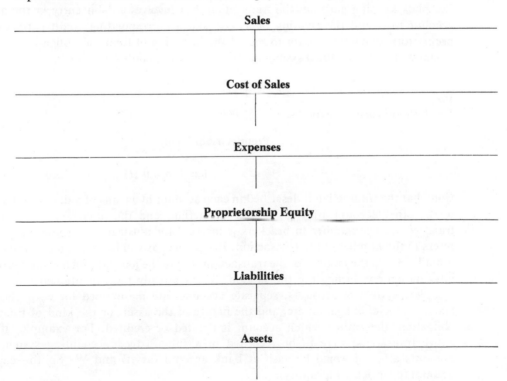

Sales

Cost of Sales

Expenses

Proprietorship Equity

Liabilities

Assets

In practice, the classification of transactions needs to be expanded. Instead of one account for expenses, for example, it may be necessary to maintain twenty or thirty accounts, each recording a particular class of expense. The position is the same with the other groups. However, every account used in practice represents a category of transactions similar to one of the six groups of transactions that have been distinguished, and the simple framework of six accounts may be used to illustrate the way in which an accounting system operates.

The Recording of Business Transactions

The recording of a number of representative transactions in the books of account of a hypothetical business will now be considered by reference to the simplified system of six accounts.

Transaction 1—Assets and proprietorship equity: Let us assume that W. Smith decides to establish himself in business as a grocer. On 1 January 1985 he pays $1 000 into a bank account to finance the operations of the business. From the point of view of the accounting equation, this transaction may be interpreted as having the following two-fold significance for the business:

(a) Creation of assets (cash at bank)	$1 000
(b) Incurring of financial obligations (funds contributed by proprietor)	$1 000

For book-keeping purposes the transaction thus involves a debit entry in the assets account to record the creation of assets; and a corresponding credit entry in the proprietorship equity account to record the incurring of financial obligations by the business. In our simplified system the transaction is recorded as follows:

Assets

1985	
Jan. 1 Proprietorship equity (*1*) $1 000	

Proprietorship Equity

	1985
	Jan. 1 Assets (*1*) $1 000

Note that the transaction is described in each account by means of a date, a reference to the other account affected by the transaction, and the monetary value of the transaction. The number in brackets is inserted for illustrative purposes only, and refers to the number of the transaction. In practice, as will be seen later, a reference is made, not to the number of the transaction, but to the journal which is the source of information concerning the transaction. It has already been mentioned that, in a complete system of accounts, separate accounts are maintained for each class of asset, financial obligation etc. and the nature of the asset, or the kind of financial obligation, determines which account is debited or credited. For example, if the above transaction were to be recorded in a fully-fledged accounting system the accounts affected would be cash at bank account (asset) and W. Smith—capital account (proprietorship equity).

Transaction 2—Assets and liabilities: All other transactions may be similarly recorded, having regard to their significance from the viewpoint of the business and their effect on the accounting equation. Let us assume that Smith borrows $200 from T. Thomas to provide additional funds for the conduct of operations. If this amount is paid into the enterprise's bank account on 1 January, the transaction may be interpreted as having the following effect on the accounting equation:

(a) Increase in assets (cash at bank)	$200
(b) Increase in financial obligations (loan from T. Thomas)	$200

For accounting purposes, the receiving aspect of the transaction is similar to that in Transaction 1 and is recorded by means of a debit entry in the assets account (cash at bank); while a credit entry in the liabilities account (T. Thomas—creditor) records the fact that the funds or financial obligations of the business have been increased by the loan received from Thomas:

Assets

1985		
Jan. 1 Proprietorship equity (*1*)	$1 000	
Liabilities (*2*)	200	

Liabilities

	1985	
	Jan. 1 Assets (*2*)	$200

The double entry for Transaction 2 is thus completed, and three accounts—assets, proprietorship equity and liabilities—have been established to record the two transactions considered so far.

Transaction 3—Balancing an account: At this stage it is convenient to describe a technical operation known as *balancing* an account. Where there is more than one entry in an account (remember that both debit and credit entries may appear in the one account), the net effect of transactions affecting that account may be determined by calculating the balance of the account. This is the difference between the sum of the debit entries and the sum of the credit entries. If the sum of the debit entries exceeds the sum of the credit entries, the balance is described as a *debit balance*; if the sum of the credit entries exceeds the sum of the debit entries, the balance is a *credit balance*. In balancing an account with a debit balance, a credit entry is made in the account for the amount of the balance, which is said to be carried down (c/d); the two sides of the account are added up and the totals inserted (if the correct balance has been struck the total will be the same on each side); and a debit entry is made on the next line to record the amount of the balance brought down (b/d) and to preserve the principle of double entry.

The assets account, for example, may be balanced as follows:

Assets

1985		1985	
Jan. 1 Proprietorship equity (*1*)	$1 000	Jan. 1 Balance c/d (*3*)	$1 200
Liabilities (*2*)	200		
	$1 200		$1 200
1985			
Jan. 1 Balance b/d (*3*)	$1 200		

The balance of $1 200 represents the sum of the debit entries, $1 200, *minus* the sum of the credit entries, nil; and it is a debit balance. In the case of a credit balance the balancing procedure is reversed. The balance of an account is simply the residual amount necessary to bring both sides of the account into equilibrium. The significance of the balance is that it shows at a glance the effect of all transactions affecting the account. The balance of the assets account thus shows the total assets of the enterprise at the date the balance is struck. If there is only one entry in an account, that entry constitutes the effective balance and the formal balancing procedure is unnecessary.

The following balances therefore appear in the ledger at this stage:

Proprietorship Equity

	1985	
	Jan. 1 Assets (*1*)	$1 000

Liabilities

	1985	
	Jan. 1 Assets (*2*)	$200

Assets

1985	
Jan. 1 Balance b/d (*3*)	$1 200

It has already been noted that the sum of the debit entries in a double-entry system always equals the sum of the credit entries. It will now be seen that the sum of debit balances in the system equals the sum of credit balances. Likewise the accounting equation is confirmed as follows:

Proprietorship equity ($1 000) = Assets ($1 200) − Liabilities ($200)

At the close of business on 1 January 1985, if it is assumed that no other transactions are entered into on that day, it is possible to summarize the enterprise's financial position by preparing a balance sheet in the form illustrated on page 6. The balance sheet lists the balances of the ledger accounts relating to proprietorship equity, liabilities and assets, and thus gives formal expression to the accounting equation:

W. Smith
Balance Sheet as at 1 January 1985

Assets	$1 200
Less: Liabilities	200
Proprietorship equity	$1 000

Transaction 4—Payment of expenses: The transactions recorded to this stage relate only to assets and financial obligations, but other types of transactions may also be interpreted by reference to the accounting equation. Let us assume that Smith rents a shop, complete with fittings and equipment, at $10 per week, and pays a week's rent in advance on 2 January. The rent represents an expense of the business, which will ultimately have to be taken into account in determining the profit or loss for the period. Since the profit made, or loss suffered, in effect augments or diminishes the funds contributed to the business by the proprietor, the expense may be interpreted as a temporary reduction in proprietorship equity, which must be offset against revenue

earned in order to measure the net increase or reduction in proprietorship equity resulting from trading operations. From the point of view of the accounting equation, therefore, the transaction may be interpreted as follows:

(a) (Temporary) reduction in proprietorship equity (expense incurred)	$10
(b) Reduction in assets (cash at bank)	$10

The expenses account is debited to reflect the temporary reduction in proprietorship equity (in practice an expense account, shop rent account, would be established to identify the kind of expense incurred), and the assets account (cash at bank) is credited to record the reduction in assets:

Expenses

1985	
Jan. 2 Assets *(4)*	$10

Assets

1985		1985	
Jan. 1 Balance b/d *(3)*	$1 200	Jan. 2 Expenses *(4)*	$10

The double entry for Transaction 4 is thereby completed.

Transaction 5—Cash purchases: Smith is now in a position to commence trading, and on 2 January he buys goods for resale at a cost of $500, making payment in cash. From the viewpoint of the accounting equation the transaction may be interpreted in the following way:

(a) (Temporary) reduction in proprietorship equity (cost incurred)	$500
(b) Reduction in assets (cash at bank)	$500

Purchases or costs of this nature, like expenses, represent a temporary diminution in proprietorship equity which must ultimately be offset against revenue earned, in order to determine the net change in proprietorship equity resulting from trading operations. For book-keeping purposes the transaction is described by debiting the cost of sales account, to reflect the temporary fall in proprietorship equity, and crediting the assets account, to record the reduction in assets (cash at bank). For the time being, it will be assumed that the cost of purchases is synonymous with the cost of sales, i.e. that all goods bought in any accounting period are sold within the same period. It will be seen later that this assumption is unrealistic to the extent that goods bought during a period remain unsold at the end of the period, and that the accounting procedure described here must be expanded in order to make allowance for unsold purchases, or inventories as they are called.

Cost of Sales

1985	
Jan. 2 Assets *(5)*	$500

Assets

1985		1985	
Jan. 1 Balance b/d *(3)*	$1 200	Jan. 2 Expenses *(4)*	$10
		Cost of sales *(5)*	500

Transaction 6—Cash sales: If, on 3 January, cash sales are made to the value of $250, the transaction may be interpreted as an increase in assets (cash at bank), matched by a temporary increase in proprietorship equity resulting from the revenue earned:

(a) Increase in assets (cash at bank)	$250
(b) (Temporary) increase in proprietorship equity (revenue earned from sales)	$250

The revenue earned from sales will ultimately be compared with costs and expenses incurred, in order to ascertain the net change in proprietorship equity resulting from operations of the period. For the time being it may be regarded as an increase in proprietorship equity.

For book-keeping purposes the transaction is recorded by debiting the assets account (cash at bank), and crediting the sales account:

Assets

1985			1985		
Jan. 1	Balance b/d (3)	$1 200	Jan.2	Expenses (4)	$10
3	Sales (6)	250		Cost of sales (5)	500

Sales

		1985		
		Jan. 3	Assets (6)	$250

Transaction 7—Credit purchases: So far every transaction has involved the payment of cash by one of the parties to the exchange. However, business accounting is not normally confined to the recording of cash transactions, and it is now necessary to introduce transactions involving the purchase or sale of goods and services on credit.

Apart from single-entry records maintained by many small business enterprises, there are three different kinds of accounting systems in use:

(a) Systems which record only cash transactions. Many governments, for example, maintain accounting records which consist of little more than single-entry records of cash receipts and cash payments. Some public authorities, on the other hand, have complete double-entry accounts but only record cash transactions in the system.

(b) Systems which record cash transactions only during the accounting period, but which incorporate outstanding or accrued claims (i.e. debts owed to or by the enterprise) at the end of the accounting period, when the profit statement and balance sheet are being prepared. Although the recording of transactions is incomplete when this sytem is used, double-entry procedures may be employed in respect of those transactions which are recorded. A reasonable measure of results for each accounting period may be obtained by this method, which is often employed by non-profit-making clubs and associations.

(c) Systems which record all transactions, whether or not they involve cash, at the time they occur. Business enterprises must employ this kind of system if they are to measure results accurately and maintain effective control over their operations, and it is this system which is described in this chapter.

The interpretation of credit transactions and the recording of such transactions in the accounting system raise no fresh problems; all that is necessary is the application of the theory of double entry that has been outlined above.

Let us assume that, on 4 January, Smith makes a credit purchase of $300 worth of trading inventory from Wholesale Suppliers Ltd. Although the business does not pay cash for the goods, the transaction must be recorded immediately in its books. Like the previous transactions considered, it may be interpreted by reference to the accounting equation, as follows:

(a) (Temporary) reduction in proprietorship equity (cost incurred)	$300
(b) Increase in liabilities (amount owing to Wholesale Suppliers Ltd)	$300

The reduction in proprietorship equity is recorded by debiting the cost of sales account and the increase in liabilities by crediting the liabilities account (in a complete system of accounts the credit entry would be recorded in a creditor's account, Wholesale Suppliers Ltd—creditor):

Cost of Sales

1985		
Jan. 2 Assets (5)	$500	
4 Liabilities (7)	300	

Liabilities

	1985	
	Jan. 1 Assets (2)	$200
	4 Cost of sales (7)	300

It will be observed that for accounting purposes the only difference between a cash purchase transaction (Transaction 5) and a credit purchase transaction (Transaction 7) lies in the fact that the former, involving as it does the payment of cash by the business, is recorded by means of a credit entry in an asset account; whereas the latter, which creates a liability for the business, is recorded by means of a credit entry in a liability account. In both cases the debit entry is made in the cost of sales account, and in both cases the transaction is recorded in the books of account as soon as it takes place.

Transaction 8—Credit sales: Finally, let us assume that on 6 January, at the end of the first week's trading, Smith sells all his remaining trading inventories to B. Brown for $600, allowing Brown credit for the amount of the sale.

This transaction may be interpreted as follows:

(a) Increase in assets (amount owing by Brown)	$600
(b) (Temporary) increase in proprietorship equity (revenue earned)	$600

The transaction is recorded by debiting the assets account (B. Brown—debtor), and crediting the sales account to complete the double entry.

Assets

1985		1985	
Jan. 1 Balance b/d (3)	$1 200	Jan. 2 Expenses (4)	$10
3 Sales (6)	250	Cost of sales (5)	500
6 Sales (8)	600		

Sales

	1985	
	Jan. 3 Assets (6)	$250
	6 Assets (8)	600

It would be possible to illustrate the interpretation and recording of other transactions, but those illustrated above may be regarded as typical of the transactions of trading enterprises. To sum up, it may be said that each transaction requires two entries in the accounts, one (the debit entry) to record increases in assets, or decreases in liabilities and proprietorship equity, resulting from the transaction; and the other (the credit entry) to record decreases in assets, or increases in liabilities and proprietorship equity, resulting from the transaction. Costs and expenses tend to diminish proprietorship equity, and are therefore recorded by means of debit entries (in the cost of sales account and the expenses account, respectively), while the earning of revenue increases proprietorship equity and is the basis of a credit entry (in a sales account).

The Trial Balance

If it is assumed that no other transactions take place, it is now possible to summarize the week's activities. As a first step in the summarization process, it is usual to construct a *trial balance* or list of ledger account balances as at the end of the period. Since the sum of debit balances in the system must equal the sum of credit balances, a comparison of total debit balances in the trial balance with total credit balances enables the double-entry aspect of the recording process to be checked.

Before the trial balance can be compiled the accounts must be balanced by the procedure that has already been illustrated (Transactions 9, 10, 11 and 12):

Sales

1985			1985		
Jan. 6 Balance c/d (9)		$850	Jan. 3 Assets (6)		$250
			6 Assets (8)		600
		$850			$850
			1985		
			Jan. 6 Balance b/d (9)		$850

Cost of Sales

1985			1985		
Jan. 2 Assets (5)		$500	Jan. 6 Balance c/d (10)		$800
4 Liabilities (7)		300			
		$800			$800
1985					
Jan. 6 Balance b/d (10)		$800			

Expenses

1985		
Jan. 2 Assets (4)		$10

Proprietorship Equity

			1985		
			Jan. 1 Assets (1)		$1 000

Liabilities

1985			1985		
Jan. 6	Balance c/d (*11*)	$500	Jan. 1	Assets (*2*)	$200
			4	Cost of sales (*7*)	300
		$500			$500
			1985		
			Jan. 6	Balance b/d (*11*)	$500

Assets

1985			1985		
Jan. 1	Balance b/d (*3*)	$1 200	Jan. 2	Expenses (*4*)	$10
3	Sales (*6*)	250		Cost of sales (*5*)	500
6	Sales (*8*)	600	6	Balance c/d (*12*)	1 540
		$2 050			$2 050
1985					
Jan. 6	Balance b/d (*12*)	$1 540			

The trial balance lists these balances in the following way, and establishes the arithmetical accuracy of the book-keeping records:

W. Smith
Trial Balance as at 6 January 1985

	Dr.	Cr.
Sales		$850
Cost of sales	$800	
Expenses	10	
Proprietorship equity		1 000
Liabilities		500
Assets	1 540	
	$2 350	$2 350

The trial balance does not act as a complete check on the work that has been carried out in the book-keeping process. For example, faulty interpretation of transactions, involving an entry in a wrong account, or failure to record a transaction at all will not be picked up by the preparation of a trial balance. It will, however, help to reveal errors caused by failure to complete the double entry, the recording of a transaction on the wrong side of an account, or faulty additions when balancing.

Summary Accounts

1 *The Trading Account*

When the double entry has been checked by means of the trial balance, it is possible to summarize the transactions of the period. In a trading enterprise, profit and loss transactions are usually summarized in two accounts, both of which are included as essential components in the double-entry system. The first of these accounts is the *trading account*, which records net sales during the period and the cost of those sales. In our simple example the net sales of the enterprise are represented by the balance of the sales account, and the cost of sales is represented by the balance of the cost of sales account.

The balances of these two accounts are therefore 'transferred' to the trading account. This is done by debiting the sales account and crediting the cost of sales account with their respective balances, the corresponding credit and debit entries being made in the trading account (Transactions 13 and 14). The sales and cost of sales accounts have then fulfilled their function in the accounting records, and are said to be closed. For accounting purposes the closing of an account is indicated by drawing a horizontal line under the amount on each side (or, if several figures are involved, by totalling both sides and inserting each total between horizontal lines, with of course no balancing figure below):

Sales

1985		1985	
Jan. 6 Trading account (*13*)	$850	Jan. 6 Balance b/d (*9*)	$850

Cost of Sales

1985		1985	
Jan. 6 Balance b/d (*10*)	$800	Jan. 6 Trading account (*14*)	$800

Trading

1985		1985	
Jan. 6 Cost of sales (*14*)	$800	Jan. 6 Sales (*13*)	$850

The information contained in the sales and cost of sales accounts has now been transferred to the trading account, where the net effect of the enterprise's trading operations may be calculated. Sales minus cost of sales by definition equals gross profit, so that the balance of the trading account represents gross profit on trading during the period.

2   *The Profit and Loss Account*

The gross profit is transferred from the trading account to the second summary account, the *profit and loss account* (Transaction 15), and at the same time the balance of the expenses account is transferred to the profit and loss account (Transaction 16):

Trading

1985		1985	
Jan. 6 Cost of sales (*14*)	$800	Jan. 6 Sales (*13*)	$850
Profit and loss account			
(gross profit) (*15*)	50		
	$850		$850

Expenses

1985		1985	
Jan. 2 Assets (*4*)	$10	Jan. 6 Profit and loss account (*16*)	$10

Profit and Loss

1985		1985	
Jan. 6 Expenses (*16*)	$10	Jan. 6 Trading account	
		(gross profit) (*15*)	$50

After this operation all the accounts recording revenue, costs and expenses, as well as the trading account itself, have been closed. Ali the information relating to the enterprise's profit earning activities has been summarized in the profit and loss account. Since gross profit minus expenses equals net profit, the balance of the profit and loss account represents net profit. It remains to transfer this balance to the credit of the proprietorship equity account (Transaction 17), thereby recognizing the fact that the proprietor ultimately benefits from the profit earned by the operations of the enterprise. (In a complete system, a separate proprietorship account, W. Smith—current account, is likely to be established to record profits earned and other non-capital transactions affecting the proprietor, such as profit withdrawals.) The proprietorship equity account may now be balanced (Transaction 18):

Profit and Loss

1985			1985		
Jan. 6	Expenses (*16*)	$10	Jan. 6	Trading account	
	Proprietorship equity			(gross profit)	$50
	(net profit) (*17*)	40			
		$50			$50

Proprietorship Equity

1985			1985		
Jan. 6	Balance c/d (*18*)	$1 040	Jan. 1	Assets (*1*)	$1 000
			6	Profit and loss account	
				(net profit) (*17*)	40
		$1 040			$1 040
			1985		
			Jan. 6	Balance b/d (*18*)	$1 040

The trading and profit and loss accounts are usually combined into a narrative statement, described as a *profit and loss statement* or *income statement*, for the purposes of presentation:

W. Smith
Profit and Loss Statement for Period 2—6 January 1985

Sales	$850
Less: Cost of sales	800
Gross profit	50
Less: Expenses	10
Net profit	$40

The Balance Sheet

The profit and loss account is now closed, and only the proprietorship equity, liability and asset accounts remain open in the ledger:

Proprietorship Equity

	1985		
	Jan. 6	Balance b/d (*18*)	$1 040

Liabilities

	1985	
	Jan. 6 Balance b/d (*11*)	$500

Assets

1985		
Jan. 6 Balance b/d (*12*)	$1 540	

The final step is to list these balances in a statement called a *balance sheet*, which may take the following form:

W. Smith
Balance Sheet as at 6 January 1985

Assets	$1 540
Less: Liabilities	500
Proprietorship equity	$1 040

In this form the balance sheet reflects the accounting equation $P = A - L$. An alternative, more conventional, form reflects the equation $A = P + L$:

W. Smith
Balance Sheet as at 6 January 1985

Proprietorship equity	$1 040	Assets	$1 540
Liabilities	500		
	$1 540		$1 540

When the two-sided form is used, assets are usually recorded on the right-hand side of the balance sheet, and liabilities and proprietorship equity on the left-hand side. Apart from tradition there is no particular significance attached to this fact. It is emphasized that, unlike the trading account and the profit and loss account, the balance sheet is not itself part of the double-entry recording system, but is derived from the balances of the accounts in that system.

The Funds Statement

It is now possible to assess the effect on the accounting equation of introducing profit and loss transactions into the system. This may be done by comparing the balance sheet prepared on 1 January, before any profit and loss transactions took place, with the balance sheet prepared on 6 January:

	1 January	6 January	Change
Assets	$1 200	$1 540	+$340
Less: Liabilities	200	500	+ 300
Proprietorship equity	$1 000	$1 040	+ $40

Proprietorship equity has increased by the net profit earned, $40. This profit has been reflected in the other balance sheet items by an increase in assets, $340, less an increase in liabilities, $300. The temporary changes in proprietorship resulting from revenue, cost and expense transactions are finally reflected in proprietorship equity as a result of the compilation of the summary trading and profit and loss accounts.

Thus the trading and profit and loss accounts explain the change in proprietorship equity at the end of the period as a result of trading activities.

The corresponding changes that occurred in assets and liabilities are, of course, not affected by the summarization process. The changes in assets and equities during a particular accounting period are clearly significant, and may be disclosed in a statement known as a *funds statement*, or statement showing the sources and disposition of funds in a given period. One part of the funds statement records the funds which became available to the enterprise during the period, which must have been provided either by increases in liabilities (i.e. borrowing) and proprietorship equity, or reductions in assets (i.e. proceeds from the sale or realization of assets). The other part of the funds statement records the uses to which the additional funds were put, viz. reductions in liabilities and proprietorship equity or increases in assets. The following statement thus records the movement of funds and assets during the period 2-6 January:

W. Smith
Funds Statement for Period 2—6 January 1985

Funds acquired	
Increase in proprietorship equity—profit earned from operations	$40
Increase in liabilities	300
	$340
Funds applied	
Increase in assets	$340

Accounting Reports

In this way the end-products of the recording processes have been compiled. The two essential statements are the profit and loss statement, showing the results of operations during the period, and the balance sheet, showing the financial position at the end of the period. However, the funds statement, showing as it does changes in the financial position of the enterprise, is hardly less important. It has been observed that the trading account and the profit and loss account actually form part of the double-entry system, whereas the balance sheet and the funds statement do not. The profit and loss statement which is prepared for purposes of presentation should, however, be distinguished from the accounts in the ledger, and the three summary statements—the profit and loss statement, the balance sheet and the funds statement—may be most conveniently regarded as accounting reports derived from an analysis of the ledger.

The accountant's function is by no means completed when these reports have been prepared. The profit and loss statement, balance sheet and funds statement are technical documents which need to be interpreted before they can be fully comprehended by those not familiar with the processes and the assumptions underlying their preparation. Before the problems of analysis and interpretation are considered, however, it will be necessary to show how the simple framework of accounts may be expanded to meet the complex needs of modern business.

Discussion Questions

1 Why do business enterprises need to maintain accounting records?

2 In a business enterprise what individuals or groups have an interest in the information portrayed by the accounting record, and what kind of information are they likely to need?

3 Briefly describe the main steps in the accounting process.

4 What are the main classes of business transactions? What are the relationships between them and how are they summarized in accounting reports?

5 In what sense does the accounting system maintain (a) duality of record, and (b) equilibrium of results? What is the significance of the entity assumption in achieving these effects?

6 What is the accounting equation, and how is it affected by revenue, cost and expense transactions?

7 Discuss the significance for accounting purposes of the accounting period and the monetary assumptions.

8 Under what circumstances are transactions affecting (a) assets, (b) liabilities and (c) the profit and loss account, recorded by means of debit entries, and when do transactions involving these items require the use of credit entries?

9 (a) Describe the procedure of balancing an account.
   (b) What is the significance of the trial balance, and how is it prepared?

10 Business enterprises do not usually restrict their accounting records to cash transactions. Explain why, and indicate what other kinds of transactions are usually recorded in their accounting systems. Do other accounting entities follow business enterprises in this regard?

11 Discuss the following concepts: (a) liabilities; (b) cost of sales; (c) assets; (d) gross profit; (e) proprietorship equity; (f) net profit.

12 Discuss the significance of the three main accounting reports and indicate how they are related to the ledger.

Exercises

1 Record the transactions 1-8 listed in the text in a complete system of double-entry accounts, in which are distinguished the different classes of assets, financial obligations, revenue, costs and expenses. Prepare relevant accounting reports for presentation to the proprietor.

2 The following comprise all the items recorded in financial statements drawn up for Jones Grocery Store at the close of the year ending 31 December 1985. Fill in the missing figures and show how the information may be presented in a profit and loss statement and balance sheet.
Net profit (   ); shop fittings ($4 550); G. Jones—capital ($10 000); gross profit ($6 450); sales ($19 800); cash at bank (   ); G. Jones—current account (Cr.

$1 100); shop rent ($750); inventory ($6 250); shop wages ($2 650); debtors ($2 700); cost of sales (   ); creditors ($3 700).

3 Complete the following table:

Transaction	Effect on Accounting Equation			Account	
	A	*L*	*P*	Debited	Credited
(a) Bought shop fittings for cash	+			Shop fittings	
	−				Cash at bank
(b) Sold goods to S. Smith on credit					
(c) Received cash loan from Investment Finance Ltd					
(d) Paid wages					
(e) Proprietorship withdrawal of cash for personal use					

4 (a) Record the following transactions in a detailed system of ledger accounts, prepare a trial balance as at 7 January 1985, transfer the balances of the revenue, cost and expense accounts to the trading and profit and loss accounts in the ledger, transfer the net profit to A. Dexter's capital account, and prepare a profit and loss statement for the week ended 7 January and a balance sheet as at that date. It may be assumed that all trading inventories purchased during the week were sold, i.e. that there were no unsold inventories at the end of the week.

1985	
Jan. 2 A. Dexter paid capital into bank account	$10 000
3 Paid shop rent for week ending 7 January	200
Purchased goods for cash	3 400
Purchased shop fittings for cash	1 450
Paid newspaper advertising charges	50
4 Sold goods for cash	4 300
Credit purchases from S. Borrie	630
5 Cash sales	450
Credit sales to D. Lamble	740
Purchased goods from P. West on credit	80
6 Paid S. Borrie on account	400
Cash purchases	780
7 Paid wages for week	240
Withdrew cash from bank for household expenses	220
Cash sales	800

(b) Interpret each of the above transactions from the point of view of its effect on the accounting equation.

5 On the basis of the following information, prepare a funds statement for the Capitol Teashop for the year ended 31 December 1985:

	Balance Sheets as at	
	31 December 1984	31 December 1985
Bank	$100	$100
Inventory	50	200
Shop fittings	750	800
Kitchen equipment	2 300	2 400
Total assets	3 200	3 500
Less: Creditors	1 200	1 000
Proprietorship equity—S. Beaton	$2 000	$2 500

Assuming that S. Beaton withdrew $2 000 in anticipation of profits during the year, what conclusions would you draw about the profitability of the teashop and about the reasons for changes in its financial position during the year?

6 At 30 June 1985, John Barnes owned the following assets:

House	$25 000
Shares in XYZ Co. Ltd	3 100
Furniture and household effects	6 350
Motor car	2 500
Savings bank balance	450

A loan of $10 000 from the Mutual Life Assurance Company was secured by a mortgage over the house, and Barnes also had a personal overdraft of $300 with City Bank Ltd. In addition, he was the sole proprietor of two businesses which had the following assets and liabilities at 30 June 1985:

Barnes Wine Cellars		Barnes Sports Store	
Utility truck	$2 500	Premises	$14 000
Wine stocks	7 350	Fittings	1 150
Shop fittings	1 400	Owing to creditors	1 000
Owing to suppliers	650	Owed by customers	250
Cash at bank	900	Inventories	3 350
		Bank overdraft	400
		Loan from father (P. Barnes)	4 000

Prepare balance sheets at 30 June 1985 for the three accounting entities involved (Barnes' proprietorship interests in the two businesses should be recorded as assets in his personal or household balance sheet). Is Barnes in a sound financial position?

7 S. Nixon set himself up in business as a restaurateur on 1 January 1985 with $10 000 of his own capital and $5 000 borrowed from a friend. He invested $10 000 in premises and $5 000 in other assets (including cash at bank). At the end of 1985, his other assets had increased to $6 000, but he had not repaid any of the amount owing to his friend and he now also owed suppliers $2 500. The restaurant premises were still considered to be worth $10 000. During the year Nixon had paid himself a salary of $6 000.

(a) How would you assess the performance of the business in its first year of operations and its financial position at 31 December 1985?

(b) Nixon had apparently been relying on his cash position, as reflected in his bank statement, as his main source of information about the profitability and financial position of the business. What advice would you give him about this practice and about the information which he needs if he is to manage the business effectively?

8 The balance sheet of the Speedit Carrying Company at 30 June 1985 recorded the following information:

Assets	
Cash at bank	$500
Debtors	420
Diesel fuel stocks	1 270
Trucks	14 380
Office furniture	340
Land and buildings	3 260
	20 170
Less: **Liabilities**—Creditors	530
Proprietorship equity—A. Adam, capital	$19 640

The following transactions took place during the first week in July 1985:

Cash received from debtors	$130
Cash on delivery received for services to customers	190
Invoices sent to customers for services provided on credit	1 220
Diesel fuel purchased for cash	530
Diesel fuel used	480
Paid creditors	170
Paid wages	310

Prepare a balance sheet as at the end of the period (6 July) and a funds statement for the week 30 June-6 July.

2 Basic Accounting Method: Expanding the Accounting System

In practice the accounting system that has been described in Chapter 1 needs to be expanded in three areas:

(a) *The recording process*. The book-keeping processes must be extended by introducing other records besides the ledger.

(b) *The classification framework*. A more detailed classification of ledger accounts is required and other bases of classification have to be superimposed on the fundamental division of transactions described in Chapter 1.

(c) *Control accounts and subsidiary ledgers*. The ledger itself usually needs to be subdivided into a general ledger and subsidiary or supporting ledgers. The general ledger is thereby simplified so that it records in summary form the large numbers of transactions of similar significance which are recorded in detail in the subsidiary ledgers.

The Recording Process

There are essentially three steps that have to be carried out before the recording aspect of accounting is completed. First, it is necessary to collect the original documents which provide evidence that a transaction has taken place. These *evidence records*, as they are called, comprise documents such as invoices and receipts, which are the basis of the entries that appear in the books of account. For example, a sales invoice given by the seller of goods to the buyer is evidence, so far as the buyer is concerned, that the purchase of goods occurred, and it is this document which provides the information for the entries in the buyer's books of account. Likewise, a copy of the sales invoice will be retained by the seller and used in writing up his accounts. Evidence of the subsequent settlement by the buyer will be provided, so far as the buyer is concerned, by the receipt he receives (and by the entry in his cheque-butt); a copy of the receipt will be used by the seller as the basis of the entry in his books of account. Every transaction in which a business engages must be supported in a similar way, and the collection of the necessary documents or evidence records is essentially the first task in the book-keeping process.

The next step involves the recording of transactions chronologically in the journal. The journal is the first formal book-keeping record, and for that reason is sometimes described as the book of original entry. It is written up from the evidence records and its significance is three-fold. It serves as a diary of business transactions, recording each transaction as it occurs in chronological order; it acts as a preliminary classifying medium by showing how each transaction is to be interpreted for accounting purposes (that is to say, it indicates which ledger account is to receive the debit entry and which account is to receive the credit entry); and finally it provides, for reference purposes, a brief summary of the nature of the transaction (called the narration). The form of the conventional journal entry may be illustrated by reference to Transaction 1 in Chapter 1. If it is assumed that a detailed system of ledger accounts is employed in practice (in place of the simplified system outlined in Chapter 1), this transaction is recorded in the journal in the manner illustrated in Figure 2—A.

Figure 2—A
The Journal   Folio No. 1

Date	Particulars of Transaction	Ledger Folio	Dr.	Cr.
1985				
Jan 1	Cash at bank		$1 000.00	
	W. Smith—Capital			$1 000.00
	Proprietor's capital paid into bank			

It can be seen that the journal records the date of the transaction; it indicates that cash at bank account (one of the asset accounts) is to be debited and W. Smith—capital account (in the proprietorship equity group of accounts) is to be credited with the amounts shown in the respective money columns; and it describes the nature of the transaction in the brief narration which follows the names of the accounts affected. The ledger folio column is used for purposes of cross-reference to the ledger, and will subsequently record the numbers of the ledger folios or accounts to which the information contained in the journal is transferred.

This transferring of information from the journal to the ledger, or 'posting' as it is called, constitutes the final step in the recording process, and for this reason the ledger is sometimes described as the book of final entry. Posting from the journal to the ledger involves making a debit entry in the appropriate ledger account to correspond with the debit entry in the journal, and a credit entry in the other ledger account to correspond with the credit entry in the journal. The procedure is illustrated in Figure 2—B.

Figure 2—B
The Ledger

Cash at Bank   Account No. 1

Date	Narrative	Folio	$	Date	Narrative	Folio	$
1985							
Jan. 1	W. Smith—Capital	1	1 000.00				

W. Smith—Capital   Account No. 15

				1985			
				Jan. 1 Cash at bank		1	1 000.00

The entry in the folio column in the ledger refers to the number of the journal folio in which the original entry was made, and the posting is completed by making the appropriate cross-reference to the ledger account number in the ledger folio column in the journal.

When the ledger has been posted the formal record is complete. It will be observed that the transaction, which was recorded chronologically in the journal, has been recorded again in the ledger in appropriate groupings in accordance with its accounting significance; that is to say, the information has been classified into ledger accounts. The information relating to the transaction is then stored in the ledger accounts, along with the information concerning other transactions, until such time as it is needed, e.g. when the summarizing process begins.

Specialized Journals

At this stage it should be noted that, although the book-keeping records theoretically conform to the pattern that has been illustrated above, influences associated with the growing scale of business organization and the use of accounting machines and computers are tending to break down the rigidity of conventional accounting forms and procedures. In the modern world, for example, a business of any size enters into so many transactions that the use of a single journal would impose intolerable restrictions on its ability to maintain adequate records. It is therefore usual to break down or subdivide the journal into a number of specialized journals, each being used to record transactions of a certain kind. In particular, it is likely that all transactions involving credit sales will be recorded in a separate journal known as the sales journal; transactions involving credit purchases of goods in a purchase journal; receipts of cash in a cash receipts journal; and cash payments in a cash payments journal. Separate journals may also be maintained for other groups of transactions which occur frequently, such as returns or allowances in respect of goods bought (returns outward journal) or sold (returns inward journal), bills of exchange receivable (bills receivable journal) or payable (bills payable journal), leaving the general journal to record only those transactions not included elsewhere.

For reasons which will be explained shortly, the conventional journal form has been discarded in the specialized journals, which are best regarded, perhaps, as chronological lists of transactions of a similar kind. The sales journal, for example, may take the form of Figure 2—C (the entries refer to hypothetical transactions).

Figure 2—C
Sales Journal   Folio No. 1

Date	Debtor	Ledger Folio	Amount
1985			
Feb. 1	W. Johnson		$100.00
	T. Barton		50.00
	M. Malone		75.00
			$225.00

Since all transactions recorded in the journal by definition represent credit sales, involving a credit entry to the sales account, it is unnecessary to have a second line in the particulars column or a second money column. The particulars column, sometimes headed 'Debtor' or 'Account Debited', simply records the name of the debtor to whom the sale was made (and whose account is to be debited by posting from the sales journal). The use of the specialized sales journal thus saves time and effort in making the original entry. It also facilitates posting to ledger accounts, since it is no longer necessary to make a separate credit entry to the sales account for each credit sales transaction—it is sufficient to post the total value of the transactions for a given period, say a day, to the credit of the sales account. In the example that has been given, the sales journal would be posted to the ledger at the conclusion of the day's transactions on 1 February by debiting the accounts of W. Johnson, T. Barton and M. Malone with the respective amounts of their purchases, and by crediting the sales account in total with $225, representing the total of the day's credit sales transactions:

Ledger

					W. Johnson—Debtor		Account No. 8

1985							
Feb. 1	Sales	S1	$100.00				

					T. Barton—Debtor		Account No. 9

1985							
Feb. 1	Sales	S1	$50.00				

					M. Malone—Debtor		Account No. 10

1985							
Feb. 1	Sales	S1	$75.00				

					Sales		Account No. 27
				1985			
				Feb. 1	Debtors	S1	$225.00

In the folio columns of the ledger the reference S1 refers to the sales journal, page 1; since several journals are now used, a separate code is required for each journal. As in the case of the general journal, the posting operation will be completed by inserting, in the folio column of the sales journal, the numbers of the ledger accounts to which the postings have been made.

In a large business, such as a retail store, in which hundreds or thousands of credit sales transactions take place daily, the use of a specialized sales journal results in an obvious saving in clerical effort. Moreover, the subdivision of the journal in this way facilitates the division of clerical labour in writing up the books of account, because one book-keeper may record credit sales transactions, while another records credit purchases, and so on.

The form of the purchase journal (see Figure 2—D) is similar to that of the sales journal.

Figure 2—D
Purchase Journal   Folio No...

Date	Creditor	Ledger Folio	Amount

It should be noted that the form which a particular journal takes, and the manner in which it is prepared, depend very much on the nature and circumstances of the business for which it is designed. It is often possible, for example, to simplify the recording process by introducing additional columns into journals for the purpose of recording transactions of a similar kind. Thus, in a departmental organization, the sales journal (and the purchase journal) may have a number of columns to record the sales (and purchases) attributable to each of the departments.

Cash Transactions

The recording of cash transactions particularly lends itself to the use of specialized journals. The cash receipts journal (and the cash payments journal), in addition to the columns recording cash receipts (and cash payments), may have separate columns for similar kinds of receipts (or payments) which it is desired to classify separately, or for transactions such as cash discounts allowed or received which are commonly associated with the receipt or disbursement of cash. A typical cash receipts journal is illustrated in Figure 2—E.

Figure 2—E
Cash Receipts Journal   Folio No. 1

Date	Particulars	Ledger Folio	Debtors	Discount Allowed	Amount Received	Bank
1985						
Feb. 2	W. Johnson		$100.00	$2.00	$98.00	
	T. Barton		50.00	1.00	49.00	$147.00
3	M. Malone		75.00	1.50	73.50	73.50
	Total		$225.00	$4.50	$220.50	$220.50

For purposes of exposition it has been assumed that the hypothetical credit sales transactions recorded in the sales journal above have now been followed by cash settlements, and that the debtors have been allowed cash discounts for prompt payment of their accounts. The entries in the 'Debtors' column represent the amounts that are to be posted to the credit of the debtors' accounts (thereby recording the extinction of their debts). At the same time the totals of the columns 'Discount Allowed' and 'Amount Received' are to be posted to the debit of the discount allowed account (an expense account) and the cash at bank account (an asset account) respectively. The effect of the transaction is thus to credit one group of asset accounts (debtors) with $225.00, in order to record the reduction in those assets; to debit another asset account (cash at bank) with $220.50, to record the increase in that asset; and to debit an expense account (discount allowed) with $4.50, to record the temporary diminution in proprietorship equity that is matched by the net reduction in assets. Note how the principle of double entry is preserved. The final column in the cash receipts journal ('Bank') has no accounting significance, but is used to record bank lodgements and to provide a link between the cash receipts journal and the statement, or pass book, which is received periodically from the bank. If, as is the usual practice, cash receipts are banked daily, there will be one entry in the bank column for each day's transactions. Entries in the bank column can thus be checked against the record of deposits appearing in the bank statement or pass book. The posting from the cash receipts journal to the ledger is illustrated below.

In the folio columns of the ledger, the reference CR1 refers to the cash receipts journal, page 1. Once again the posting operation is completed by making the appropriate cross-references in the folio column of the cash receipts journal.

Ledger

	Cash at Bank			Account No. 1
1985				
Feb. 3 Cash receipts	CR1 $220.50			

	W. Johnson—Debtor			Account No. 8
1985		1985		
Feb. 1 Sales S1 $100.00		Feb. 2 Bank and discount CR1 $100.00		

T. Barton—Debtor   Account No. 9

1985					1985			
Feb. 1	Sales		S1	$50.00	Feb. 2	Bank and discount	CR1	$50.00

M. Malone—Debtor   Account No. 10

1985					1985			
Feb. 1	Sales		S1	$75.00	Feb. 3	Bank and discount	CR1	$75.00

Discount Allowed   Account No. 39

1985				
Feb. 3	Debtors		CR1	$4.50

The form of the cash payments journal is similar to that of the cash receipts journal, with money columns for creditors, discount received, amount paid and bank. In addition to the cross-reference to the ledger which is made in the ledger folio column, it is useful to include another column after the date, headed 'Cheque Number', to provide a cross-reference to the original document which is the source of the information appearing in the journal (see Figure 2—F).

Figure 2—F
Cash Payments Journal   Folio No. 1

Date	Cheque Number	Particulars	Ledger Folio	Creditors	Discount Received	Amount Paid	Bank

The 'Bank' column in this case contains a separate entry for each cheque paid, so that it is possible to check the record of cash payments appearing in the cash payments journal against the entries appearing in the statement, or pass book, received from the bank.

Bank Reconciliation Statements

The checking of entries in the cash receipts and cash payments journals against corresponding entries in the bank statement, or pass book, illustrates the possibility of using an external document to check the accuracy of the firm's internal accounting records. The use of such checks is an essential feature of the internal audit or internal control procedures which need to be incorporated in the design of accounting systems. In turn the internal records provide a check of the bank statement. The reconciliation of the cash receipts and cash payments journals with the bank statement, or pass book, is effected by means of the following procedures:

(a) Check the individual entries in the 'Bank' column in the two cash journals against the entries in the bank statement made up to the date of the reconciliation, ticking the corresponding entries in each record. Unticked items in the preceding reconciliation statement should have been recorded in the current bank statement. The bank statement, representing as it does the firm's ledger account in the bank's ledger, records transactions from the opposite viewpoint to that which is reflected in the firm's ledger, so that debit entries in the bank statement correspond to credit entries in the firm's cash journals and vice versa.

(b) Unticked entries in the bank statement represent transactions (such as bank charges, interest on overdraft and dishonoured cheques) that have not yet been recorded in the firm's own accounting records. It is therefore necessary to record these transactions in the cash journals and the bank account in the firm's ledger, using the bank statement itself as the evidence record (subject to such further verification as may be necessary).

(c) Errors excepted, unticked entries in the cash journals represent transactions that have not been recorded by the bank up to the time of the reconciliation, in particular deposits not yet credited or unpresented cheques, and these form the basis of a bank reconciliation statement which takes the following form:

A. B. Collins
Bank Reconciliation Statement at 31 January 1985

Bank balance as recorded on bank statement		Cr. $...
Deduct: Unpresented cheques—		
Cheque no. ...	$...	
...	...	
...	...	...
		...
Add: Deposits not credited—31 January		...
Bank balance as recorded in bank account in firm's ledger		Dr. $...

(d) Note that an amount on deposit with the bank is recorded in the bank statement as a credit balance (or liability of the bank), whereas an overdraft is recorded as a debit balance. If the bank statement records a credit balance, the subsequent presentation of unpresented cheques will have the effect of reducing the balance; it is therefore necessary to deduct them in order to arrive at the figure recorded in the bank account in the firm's ledger. Similarly the subsequent recording of deposits not credited will have the effect of increasing a credit balance as recorded in the bank statement, and it is necessary to add such amounts in order to arrive at the figure recorded in the bank account in the firm's ledger. If the bank statement records an overdraft, the two sets of arithmetical operations described above need to be reversed. Care is necessary if the credit balance recorded in the bank statement is less than the aggregate amount of the unpresented cheques; the deduction of the latter will make the adjusted bank statement balance an overdraft, and deposits not credited must be deducted from this in order to arrive at the balance as recorded in the bank account in the firm's ledger.

(e) Discrepancies revealed by failure to reconcile the two records must of course be investigated.

Example: The bank statement which Concrete Constructions received from its bank at the end of March 1985 recorded a credit balance of $123.43. The debit balance in its own bank account at the same date was $168.88. A check with the company's cash journals revealed that bank charges amounting to $5.00 appearing in the bank statement had not been recorded in the cash payments journal, that cheques amounting to $48.70 had been recorded in the cash payments journal but had not been presented to the bank by 31 March, and that a deposit of $89.15 recorded in the cash receipts journal on 31 March had not been credited in the bank statement. You are asked to prepare a bank reconciliation statement as at 31 March 1985. After recording the bank charges of $5.00 in the cash payments journal and posting to the bank account in the firm's ledger, the balance on the latter becomes $163.88, and the bank reconciliation statement takes the following form:

Concrete Constructions
Bank Reconciliation Statement at 31 March 1985

Bank balance as per bank statement	Cr. $123.43
Deduct: Unpresented cheques—	
Cheque no. ... $...	
... ...	
... ...	48.70
	74.73
	89.15
Add: Deposit not credited 31 March	
Bank balance as per bank account in ledger	Dr. $163.88

Petty Cash Transactions

Another specialized journal, one that is in almost universal use, should be mentioned at this stage. This is the petty cash journal. A useful working procedure is to pay *all* cash receipts, whether currency or cheques or other forms of money, into the enterprise's bank, thereby passing them through the cash receipts journal and the cash at bank account. It would be possible, similarly, to make all payments by cheque, thereby making the cash payments journal a complete record of all cash disbursements. In practice, however, it is convenient to keep a small amount of actual currency on hand to pay for small items of expenditure, such as bus fares, newspapers and postage stamps, for which it is inconvenient to pay by cheque. In this way a distinction is drawn between cash transactions passed through the bank and those involving actual currency; the latter, confined to cash payments of small individual amounts, are recorded in the petty cash journal.

The petty cash advance is made in the first instance by drawing and cashing a cheque for an amount, say $50, considered sufficient to cover the minor items of expenditure in a given period, say a week. This transaction is recorded in the cash payments journal in the usual way (see Table 2—1):

Table 2—1
Cash Payments Journal Folio No. 1

Date	Cheque Number	Particulars	Ledger Folio	Creditors	Discount Received	Amount Paid	Bank
1985 Feb. 1	001	Petty cash advance				$50.00	

When the cash payments journal is posted a debit entry is raised in an asset account, the petty cash advance account, with the corresponding credit appearing in the cash at bank account. An increase in the asset, petty cash advance, that is to say, has been offset by a reduction in the asset, cash at bank.

At the same time, the receipt of the petty cash advance is recorded in another specialized journal, the petty cash journal. This journal is drawn up in a way which records petty cash receipts on the one hand and petty cash expenditures, classified according to the main heads of expenditure, on the other. The petty cash journal is shown in Table 2—2 with the receipt of $50.00 recorded therein as the first entry.

Petty cash expenditure is then recorded *only* in the petty cash journal—no entry is made in the cash payments journal at this stage. Each payment should be supported by a voucher, or receipt, verifying that the transaction has taken place, and the petty cash journal is in effect written up from the petty cash vouchers. In addition to entries in the 'Date', 'Particulars', 'Voucher Number' columns, payments are recorded in both the 'Total Expenditure' and the appropriate 'Analysis of Expenditure' columns, depending on their nature. (It is important to note, for reasons that will presently be apparent, that the headings of the 'Analysis of Expenditure' columns correspond to actual expense accounts in the ledger.) Several hypothetical petty cash payments are recorded in the petty cash journal illustrated in Table 2—2.

At the end of the week, or whenever the petty cash advance needs replenishing, the total expenditure and analysis columns are added up and the totals inserted. The balance of petty cash, which corresponds to the amount of currency remaining on hand, is then carried forward for use during the succeeding period, and another cheque is drawn and cashed to reimburse petty cash for the amount spent. The whole procedure, which is known as the *imprest system* of recording petty cash transactions, is illustrated in Table 2—2.

Table 2—2
Petty Cash Journal

Folio No. 1

Date	Particulars	Voucher No.	Total Receipts	Total Expenditure	Travelling Expenses	Postage	Printing and Stationery	General Admin. Expenses
							Analysis of Expenditure	
1985								
Feb. 1	Cheque no. 001	CP1	$50.00					
	Telegrams	V1		$5.00		$5.00		
2	Train fares	V2		6.25	$6.25			
3	Stationery	V3		7.50			$7.50	
4	Newspapers	V4		2.25				$2.25
5	Stamps	V5		4.50		4.50		
6	Taxi fares	V6		7.25	7.25			
				32.75	$13.50	$9.50	$7.50	$2.25
Feb. 7	Balance c/d			17.25				
			$50.00	$50.00				
Feb. 7	Balance b/d		$17.25					
	Cheque no. 007		32.75					

The cashing of the reimbursing cheque brings the unspent balance up to the original amount of the petty cash advance, $50.00. The cheque drawn to reimburse the petty cash advance for the amount spent is recorded in the cash payments journal in accordance with the totals of the 'Analysis of Expenditure' columns in the petty cash journal, which together with the supporting vouchers is the authority for the drawing of the cheque (see Table 2—3).

Table 2—3
Reimbursing Petty Cash
Cash Payments Journal   Folio No. 2

Date	Cheque Number	Particulars	Ledger Folio	Creditors	Discount Received	Amount Paid	Bank
1985							
Feb. 7	007	Travelling expenses				$13.50	
		Postage				9.50	
		Printing and stationery				7.50	
		General administrative expenses				2.25	$32.75

Postings from the cash payments journal are thus made to the debit of the several expense accounts concerned, the corresponding credit entry being absorbed in the total of the 'Amount Paid' column, which is ultimately posted to the credit of the cash at bank account. Note that under the imprest system, the reimbursing cheque does not result in an entry being posted to the petty cash advance account in the ledger. The balance of this account remains at $50.00 unless the amount of the advance is changed, or the advance is repaid. At any point of time the balance of the petty cash advance account is represented either by actual currency, or by vouchers representing expenditure that will subsequently be recorded in the cash payments journal and the appropriate expense accounts in the ledger.

So much for the use of specialized journals; the main points to remember are first, that they need to be adapted to the needs of the particular business for which they are designed; and second, that they should only be introduced into the system when the number of transactions is sufficient to warrant their use. All transactions not covered by one or other of the specialized journals will continue to be recorded in the general journal.

The Classification Framework

The simplified system of accounts described in Chapter 1 involves a classification of transactions into the following main groups: assets, liabilities, proprietorship equity, sales revenue, cost of sales and expenses. This classification, based as it is on the accounting equation, may be regarded as the fundamental accounting classification. As has already been indicated, however, it is necessary in practice to expand the classification system in order to permit a more detailed grouping of transactions. It is not sufficient, for example, to record an increase in assets or financial obligations generally. If there has been an increase in assets as a result of a particular transaction, the accounting system needs to show what kind of asset is involved; likewise if the financial obligations of the business have been increased, it is necessary to record the nature of the change. This means that all transactions must be classified according to their inherent nature or economic significance; in effect, a separate ledger account is established for each class of transaction which, for accounting purposes, it is desired to group together. Thus, in place of one account for assets, a large number of asset accounts, such as petty cash advance, cash at bank (or XYZ Bank Ltd), various accounts for debtors, and accounts for different kinds of trading inventory and equipment would normally be required. The ultimate, i.e. most detailed, act of classification thus corresponds to the ledger account grouping itself—each ledger account represents a separate kind of transaction. Superimposed on this 'natural' classification (as it is called) is not only the fundamental accounting equation grouping, but a number of other bases of classification intended to facilitate the usefulness of the accounting record. Of course the methods of classifying transactions in any business depend very much on the kind of information which is required concerning those transactions, and the purposes for which that information is to be used. With this in mind some of the commonly used bases of classification will now be considered.

Balance Sheet Classification

Assets

Taking the accounting equation grouping as the starting point, one can begin with assets, which may be defined as economic resources that are under the control of the accounting entity and which are expected to yield valuable services or benefits to the entity through subsequent use or exchange. In general these resources are legally owned by the entity, but the control criterion may be expanded in some circumstances, e.g. to cover leased assets or assets under hire purchase.

For purposes of financial analysis, assets are usually classified according to their liquidity, i.e. in accordance with their convertibility into cash. In this way light is thrown on the capacity of the business to meet its financial obligations and it is possible to assess its financial stability. The conventional grouping which results from this basis of classification is as follows:

(a) *Current assets.* These are described as cash and other assets which are regularly converted into cash or consumed during the normal operating cycle of the business. The normal operating cycle is defined as the period covered by the conversion of cash into trading inventories and their reconversion into cash (cash → trading inventories → cash). Current assets are often subdivided into.
    (i) *monetary assets*, which are cash and claims to cash fixed in dollar terms; and
    (ii) *non-monetary current assets,* which include short-term investments, trading inventories and prepayments (prepayments are described in Chapter 3).
(b) *Non-current or fixed assets.* These are usually described as assets held by the business in order that it may carry out its revenue-earning activities, but which are not ordinarily traded in. They are intended primarily for use rather than exchange. Fixed assets are sometimes further subdivided on the basis of their so-called tangibility:
    (i) *fixed tangible assets*, which are physical resources such as land and buildings, plant and machinery, shop fittings and furniture; and
    (ii) *fixed intangible assets*, or rights acquired by the business which do not reflect physical resources. Examples are goodwill (the benefits arising from the established reputation of the business) and patent rights.

In many respects this conventional classification is unsatisfactory. The division into current and non-current, although it theoretically ensures that the groups are mutually exclusive, does not always provide a clear and unambiguous basis of division. Thus investments owned by the business may be either current or non-current, depending not only on the nature of the investments but also on the purpose for which they are held. This difficulty may be overcome by applying time and intention tests to the act of division. Thus assets which can be, and are intended to be, converted into cash within a certain arbitrary time, conventionally one year, are usually regarded as current assets; while assets which do not meet these tests are classified as non-current. This means that investments such as short-term government securities which meet the time and intention tests are classified with the current group; while investments such as shares in subsidiary companies, which it is not intended to realize in the foreseeable future, are classified as non-current assets. The criterion of the normal operating cycle or one year, whichever is the longer, is sometimes advocated.

Another difficulty results from the inclusion of trading inventories in the current group. It is true that in the ordinary course of events, inventories, whether raw materials or partly processed or finished goods, are turned over and converted into more liquid assets, such as debtors or cash. There is a sense, however, in which some or all of the inventories of a business are more closely related to fixed assets than to current, since there is at least a minimum level below which inventories cannot be allowed to fall if the business is to continue its operations. And for purposes of financial analysis, as will be seen later, it is unwise to regard inventories as relatively liquid assets, for the reason that whenever liquidity becomes a matter of extreme importance, e.g. because of a sudden trade recession, their sale usually becomes more difficult. In most business enterprises, inventories exert a dominating financial influence, and it is therefore a wise policy to record them as a separate group. If the current/non-current basis of division is retained, this means dividing the current group into a number of sub-groups: financial assets, inventories and others. Financial assets then comprise all cash and money claims which meet the current asset criterion, including bank balances, debtors, amounts owing to the entity on hire purchase contracts, and other accounts receivable. Current financial assets are sometimes described by the term 'quick assets', a useful reminder of the fact that such assets are expected to be quickly converted into cash. Inventories include stock-in-trade and, in the case of manufacturing enterprises, raw materials, finished goods and partly-processed goods (usually described as work-in-process). Items such as prepaid expenses may be classified in a further sub-group.

In the non-current group the division between fixed tangible assets and fixed intangible assets is also rather artificial, especially as intangible assets, such as goodwill, are only recorded in the books of account when consideration has been paid for them (e.g. as the result of the acquisition of another business). For practical purposes a division of non-current assets into (a) long-term financial assets, (b) property and equipment, and (c) other capital expenditure, is probably more useful. Financial assets which fail to meet the current asset criterion, such as shares in subsidiary companies, are then included as a separate sub-group. Property and equipment, which may also be described as 'fixed capital assets', include such assets as freehold and leasehold property, plant and machinery, equipment and furniture. This leaves 'other capital expenditure' as a residual sub-group, comprising all capital expenditure (e.g. expenditure involving the creation of assets as distinct from expenditure involving the incurring of costs or expenses to be written off in the current period) not included elsewhere in the non-current asset grouping. 'Other capital expenditure' thus includes goodwill and the capital expenditure involved in establishing a new company (usually described as preliminary expenses). To the extent that items in this sub-group do not have a use or exchange value which is separable from that of the business in general, there is a case for not regarding them as assets at all and for treating them in the balance sheet as a deduction from proprietorship equity.

The classification of assets which results from the adoption of the above suggestions is illustrated in Figure 2—G, where typical account titles (corresponding to the natural or detailed basis of classification) are included under each sub-group that has been distinguished. The order of accounts in the ledger normally follows the scheme of classification which has been adopted, and the adoption of a numerical code helps to fix the position of each account in the ledger and to identify its place in the classification framework. The numbering system which is followed in Figure 2—G is known as the decimal system. It involves numbering the major divisions in sequence, beginning with 1 for assets, 2 for liabilities and so on; adding a second series of numbers in sequence to identify the groups within each division, so that current assets become 11 and non-current assets 12, while the first group of liabilities is numbered 21 and the second group 22; and continuing to add numbers in this way for each subsequent act of division. Thus within the current assets group, quick assets are numbered 111 and inventories 112; while in the quick assets sub-group the account, petty cash advance, is given the number 1111, 'XYZ' bank account is numbered 1112, and so on. This system enables the place of any account in the classification framework to be easily determined, since all asset accounts have numbers beginning with 1, all current assets have numbers beginning with 11 and so forth; and it has the advantage of being sufficiently flexible to permit new accounts to be added, or even new bases of classification superimposed, without upsetting the system.

Financial Obligations

Just as assets are usually classified in accordance with their relative liquidity so, to facilitate financial analysis, the financial obligations of a business are usually classified on the basis of their relative urgency, that is to say in the order in which the obligations have to be discharged. Since outside liabilities have to be met before the proprietor has any claim on the assets of the business, liabilities will be dealt with first.

Liabilities, or the financial obligations of the business to its creditors, are usually classified into two main groups:

(a) *Current liabilities*, or obligations to outside creditors which have to be met in the ordinary course of business either on demand or within a period not exceeding one year. Examples are bank overdraft, trade creditors and other accounts payable. Sometimes a further distinction is made between so-called 'quick' liabilities, or all current liabilities other than the bank overdraft, and the bank overdraft which for some purposes may be regarded as having greater permanence.

(b) *Non-current or deferred liabilities,* or obligations to outside creditors of a relatively long-term nature, such as loans on mortgage.

As in the case of assets, the division between current and non-current liabilities is usually made on an arbitrary time basis; current liabilities are defined as those liabilities which have to be discharged within one year, and non-current liabilities are all other liabilities. For disclosure purposes, a further classification of non-current liabilities by their redemption periods is often desirable.

Figure 2—G
Classification of Assets

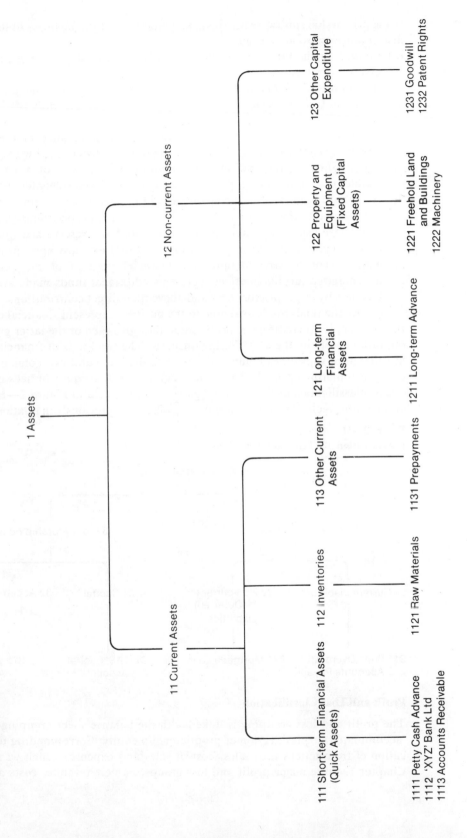

Proprietorship equity, or the financial obligations of the business to its proprietors, also comprises two main groups:

(a) *Capital,* or the funds contributed by the proprietor through the commitment of assets to the business.

(b) *Accumulated surplus*, or the funds which have been accumulated in the business as a result of the earning of profits that have not been fully distributed to the proprietor, or by reason of asset revaluations. In an unincorporated business, accumulated surplus is represented by the credit balance of the proprietor's current account, which is the account that is usually credited with profits earned and debited with proprietorship withdrawals. The use of a current account enables the proprietor's capital account to be employed solely for the recording of contributed capital. In a company, as will be seen later, accumulated surplus is represented by the balances of the profit and loss appropriation account (to which profits are usually transferred for distribution) and reserve accounts (which are established by transfers of profit from the profit and loss appropriation account with a view to strengthening the financial position of the company). The accumulated surplus in effect represents additional funds made available to the business by its proprietors over and above their direct contributions.

Because the funds made available to the business represent financial obligations of the business to its creditors or proprietors, they give each of the latter groups a claim on, or an equity in, the assets of the business. The two kinds of financial obligations are therefore sometimes combined and described as equities. Total proprietorship equity is sometimes described as owner's equity, residual equity or net worth.

The classification of financial obligations is illustrated in Figure 2—H, which also employs the decimal system of numbering described previously in relation to assets.

Figure 2—H
Classification of Financial Obligations

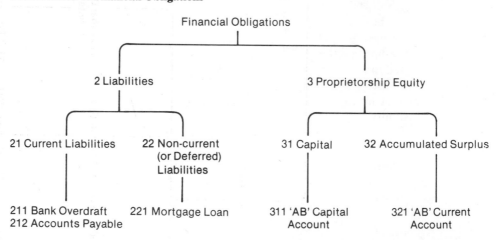

Profit and Loss Classification

The profit and loss grouping is linked with the balance sheet grouping through the 'accumulated surplus' section of proprietorship equity. Corresponding to the classification of transactions into sales, cost of sales and expenses which was observed in Chapter 1, three major profit and loss groups, namely revenue, costs and expenses may be distinguished, and for purposes of classification it is convenient to consider costs and expenses as one group. The classification of revenue, costs and expenses is, in general, influenced by managerial requirements, and is intended to assist management in its control and policy-making functions.

Revenue

Revenue is defined as the gross earnings of the business resulting from the sale of goods and services. It includes both revenue from sales of inventory and revenue from other sources, e.g. fees or commissions. Although revenue is sometimes defined as the increase in the net assets of the business which results from its sales, it is more appropriate to regard the inflow of assets as a concomitant of the earning of revenue. Revenue is normally subdivided into:

(a) *Operating revenue,* which is the normal revenue earned from the major activities of the business during the period in question. In a trading business, as has been seen, sales revenue is the most important item of operating revenue. In a professional business, such as an accountancy firm, operating revenue takes the form of fees; in an agency business it is represented by commission earned, and so on.

(b) *Non-operating revenue,* which is all revenue which fails to meet the operating revenue criteria.

In effect three different bases of classification, or three tests, help to distinguish operating revenue from non-operating revenue. These are: (i) normality—is the transaction a normal one for this kind of business? (ii) relation to major activities—is the transaction related to the major purposes for which the business was formed? and (iii) relation to the current accounting period— is the transaction relevant to the current period's operations? If a negative answer is given to any one of these questions the transaction concerned must be classified as non-operating.

Obviously, the distinction between operating and non-operating revenue in any particular business depends on the nature and object of the business. Interest received is operating revenue in an investment company, for example, but needs to be classed as non-operating revenue in an ordinary trading enterprise. Capital gains usually fail to meet one or other of the operating revenue criteria.

Other bases of classification may be applied to revenue; thus it is desirable, for purposes of managerial control, to make a division on the basis of administrative responsibility wherever it is possible to distinguish different departments, branches, etc. Note also that there are certain transactions, which at first sight appear to be costs or expenses, which more appropriately are regarded as negative revenue items and, accordingly, are classified within the revenue group. Such transactions are returns inward(sales returns and allowances), cash discounts allowed and possibly the uncollectable proceeds of sales (usually described as 'bad debts').

Costs and Expenses

Although costs and expenses are often treated as synonymous, conceptually a distinction may be made between them. Costs represent the financial sacrifices which are involved in acquiring or producing assets; costs become expenses as the assets are used and transformed in the process of generating revenue. Strictly, the item 'cost of sales' in the trading account is therefore an expense, the amount of which is measured by the cost of the goods which are recorded as having been sold. Of course, not all expenses flow directly from the consumption of physical assets such as inventories or fixed capital assets. Certain expenses, such as salesmen's wages, represent the utilization of services which are recorded directly as expenses at the time the services are received. (As a further complication, however, it may be noted that some forms of wages, e.g. manufacturing wages, may be embodied in the cost of assets and hence will not be recorded as expenses until the assets themselves generate revenue.) Irrespective of their form, expenses do of course involve a reduction in the net assets of the business. For example, cost of sales reflects a decrease in trading inventories while advertising expense is accompanied by a reduction in cash or an increase in liabilities (representing amounts payable to the agency providing the advertising services). Expenses may therefore be defined as the financial sacrifices involved in consuming assets or utilizing services in the process of earning revenue.

Despite the conceptual difference between costs and expenses, the need to combine cost of sales and expenses makes it convenient to continue to use the term 'costs and expenses' in classifying the resources used in earning revenue.

Costs and expenses, like revenue, may be subdivided into:

(a) *operating costs and expenses;* and

(b) *non-operating costs and expenses.*

The same criteria of normality, relation to major activities and relation to the current accounting period, which were used to distinguish operating from non-operating revenue, may be used to distinguish operating from non-operating costs and expenses.

Operating costs and expenses are invariably classified on a functional basis, i.e. according to the purpose they serve or the administrative divisions of the business in which they are incurred. Classification on this basis permits the cost of each administrative division or function to be established and related to the performance of that function, thereby helping to control costs and ensuring that efficiency is achieved. In a trading enterprise, typical functional groups of costs and expenses are:

(a) *cost of sales*: those costs incurred in buying the goods which have been sold and preparing them for sale;

(b) *selling expenses*: expenses incurred in publicizing, selling and delivering the goods traded in by the business;

(c) *administrative expenses*: general expenses of administration, supervision and control; and

(d) *finance expenses*: expenses incurred in obtaining financial resources, e.g. interest on borrowed funds.

The classification of costs and expenses must obviously be related to the needs of the particular business. Where a business is organized into branches or departments, for example, the classification of costs and expenses must conform to this horizontal division of administrative responsibility as well as to the vertical functional grouping. The functional divisions themselves vary from business to business. In the case of a large retail store, for example, there may be separate groups for occupancy expenses, publicity expenses and perhaps delivery expenses as well as those specified above. A manufacturing business, on the other hand, needs to classify the costs of its manufacturing activities in separate groups.

Other important bases of cost and expense classification will be considered later but some should be briefly mentioned here. The first classifies costs and expenses according to the way they are affected by changes in the volume of activity, i.e.

Figure 2—I
Classification of Revenue, Costs and Expenses

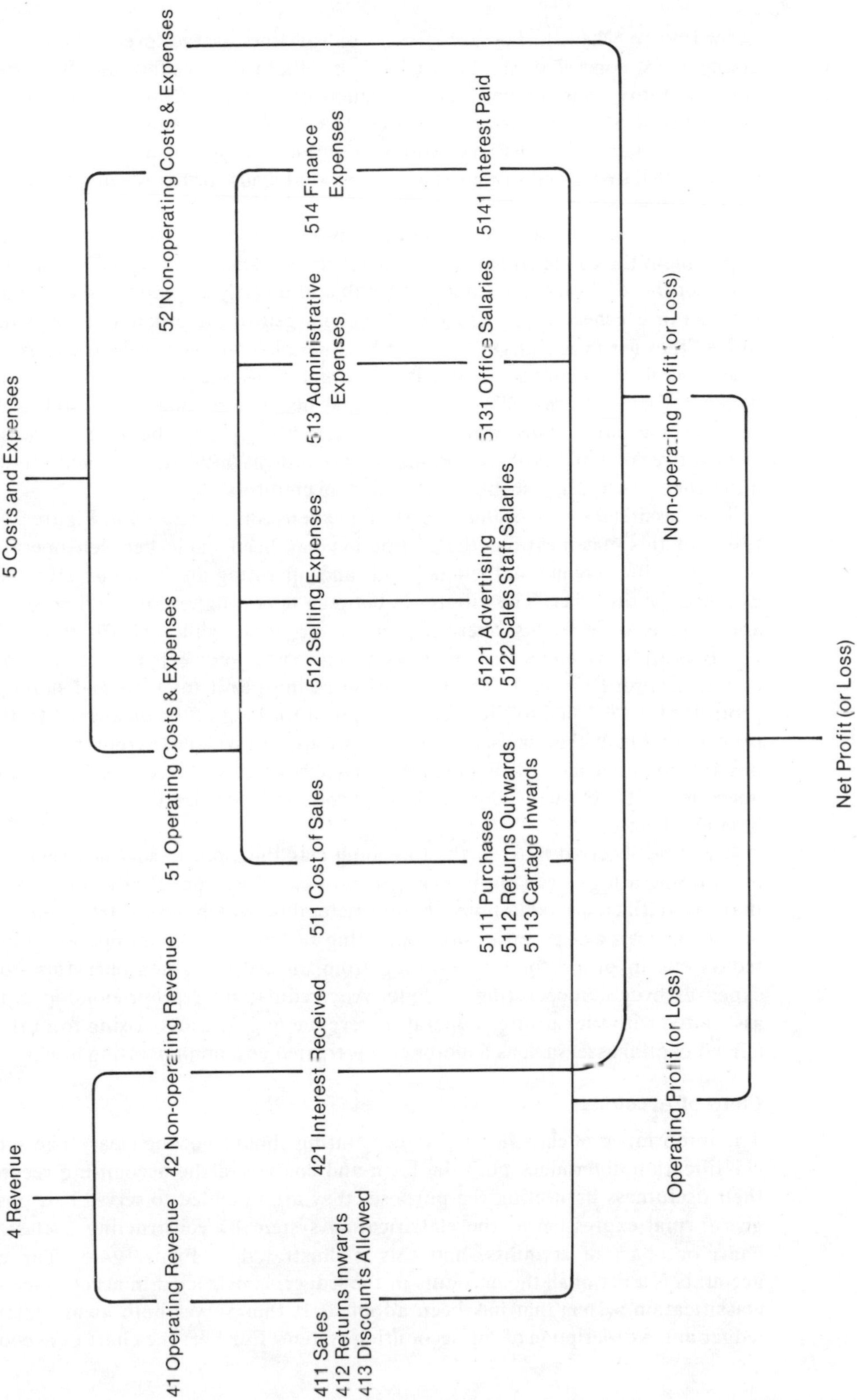

according to whether they are 'fixed' or 'variable' as the level of sales or output changes. A somewhat similar division is obtained by adopting the criterion of controllability, in which the test is whether or not the costs or expenses in question can be controlled (it will be seen later that some costs and expenses result from decisions taken in the past and cannot be influenced by current decisions—these are the so-called uncontrollable costs which are analogous for many purposes to the fixed costs distinguished by the variability criterion). Finally, costs and expenses are classified according to their relationship to the cost unit, i.e. the product or department the cost of which is being determined. This results in a division into direct costs, or those which can be identified with and directly assigned to the cost unit, and indirect or overhead costs, which must be charged to the product or department—if indeed they are to be charged to the cost unit at all—on some arbitrary basis.

Just as it was observed that it is sometimes convenient to classify certain items, which at first sight are costs and expenses, as negative revenue items, so it is useful to regard some transactions, which might reasonably appear to be revenue transactions, as negative costs and expenses. Examples are returns outwards (purchase returns and allowances) and cash discounts received from creditors.

The classification of revenue, costs and expenses is illustrated in Figure 2—I. As a result of this classification, the distinction has been made between operating and non-operating revenue on the one hand, and operating and non-operating costs and expenses on the other. The difference between operating revenue and operating costs and expenses represents operating profit (or loss); while the difference between non-operating revenue and non-operating costs and expenses represents non-operating profit (or loss). The sum of operating profit (or loss) and non-operating profit (or loss) is equal to the overall net profit (or loss) of the business. By deducting proprietorship withdrawals (such as drawings or dividends) from net profit, it is possible to derive the addition to accumulated surplus which results from the period's operations. It is this item which links the profit and loss classification with that of the balance sheet.

It will be observed that, in the foregoing classification, losses—whether operating or non-operating—are simply negative profits. More specifically, operating losses may be defined as reductions in proprietorship which result from an excess of operating costs and expenses over operating revenue, while non-operating losses are reductions in proprietorship resulting from an excess of non-operating costs and expenses over non-operating revenue. Any reduction in proprietorship equity not associated with the earning of operating revenue (e.g. the loss arising from the sale of a fixed capital asset such as a motor car) is treated as a non-operating loss.

Chart of Accounts

The importance of classification in accounting should now be clear. The scheme of classification determines both the form and content of the accounting records, and their usefulness in meeting the purposes they are intended to serve. It is possible to give formal expression to the classification system by constructing a classification chart or chart of accounts, and this is illustrated in Figure 2—J. The chart of accounts is a list of all the accounts in the ledger, constructed in accordance with the classification system that has been adopted. It thus serves both as an index to the ledger and a description of the accounting system. Further, the chart of accounts sets

Figure 2—J
Chart of Accounts

1 Assets

    11 Current Assets
        111 Short-term Financial Assets
            1111 Petty Cash Advance
            1112 'XYZ' Bank Limited
            1113 Accounts Receivable
        112 Inventories
            1121 Raw Materials
        113 Other Current Assets
            1131 Prepaid Expenses

    12 Non-current Assets
        121 Long-term Financial Assets
            1211 'M' Limited—Long-term Advance
        122 Property and Equipment
            1221 Freehold Land and Buildings
            1222 Machinery
        123 Other Capital Expenditure
            1231 Goodwill

2 Liabilities

    21 Current Liabilities
        211 Bank Overdraft
        212 Accounts Payable

    22 Non-current Liabilities
        221 'Finance Corporation'—Mortgage Loan

3 Proprietorship Equity
    31 Capital
        311 'AB' Capital Account

    32 Accumulated Surplus
        321 'AB' Current Account

4 Revenue

    41 Operating Revenue
        411 Sales
        412 Returns Inwards

    42 Non-operating Revenue
        421 Interest Received

5 Costs and Expenses

    51 Operating Costs and Expenses
        511 Cost of Sales
            5111 Purchases
            5112 Returns Outwards
        512 Selling Expenses
            5121 Advertising
            5122 Sales Staff Salaries
        513 Administrative Expenses
            5131 Office Salaries
        514 Finance Expenses
            5141 Interest Paid

    52 Non-operating Costs and Expenses

6 Determination of Profit
    61 Trading Account
    62 Profit and Loss Account

the pattern of the final accounting reports (the profit and loss statement, and the balance sheet) and thereby acts as a link between these statements and the ledger.

In Figure 2—J the items in italics correspond with actual account titles in the ledger (the list is illustrative and not intended to be exhaustive). It will be seen that a place must be found in the classification system for all ledger accounts, including such accounts as the trading account and the profit and loss account. In Figure 2—J these accounts are incorporated in a separate group, as accounts necessary in connection with the 'determination of profit'.

Control Accounts and Subsidiary Ledgers

The expansion of the accounting system which has just been described, because it has the effect of providing a separate ledger account for each class of transaction, may obviously result in a very large number of accounts in a business of any size. In a large retail store, for example, there may be hundreds of creditors' accounts and thousands or tens of thousands of debtors' accounts, imposing an immense book-keeping problem simply through weight of numbers. From the point of view of the business, all the accounts of, say, trade debtors have similar significance, i.e. they record amounts which are owed to the business by its customers and which it is expected will shortly be paid. For certain purposes, in the preparation of the balance sheet for example, it is sufficient for clarity to record only the total amount owed by debtors under the general heading 'trade debtors'. It is nevertheless necessary, if management is to be in a position to maintain effective control over amounts owing, for a separate account to be kept for each debtor. How may this need for detailed information in the ledger be reconciled with the task of facilitating understanding and providing information for balance sheet purposes in summary form? The solution lies in the adoption of an important accounting technique, involving the use of what are known as control accounts and subsidiary ledgers, which simplifies the handling of large numbers of accounts of similar significance.

The control account technique is really an extension of a procedure that has already been noted in connection with the journal. It was observed that, where the number of transactions to be recorded is very large, it is convenient to subdivide the journal into a number of specialized journals in order to simplify the work in making journal entries and permit posting to ledger accounts by total. The control account technique extends this principle a stage further and results in the subdivision of the ledger as well as the journal. It should be noted that the successful application of the technique in fact depends on the installation of a system of specialized journals such as were described above. In describing the use of control accounts, attention will be confined to debtors' accounts but, as will be seen later, the principle is capable of general application.

When the number of, say, debtors' accounts is inconveniently large they may be removed to another ledger, known as the debtors' ledger. The ledger is in effect subdivided into the general ledger and the subsidiary debtors' ledger. In place of the debtors' accounts which have been removed to the debtors' ledger, the general ledger contains only one summary account, the debtors' ledger control account, and this records in total the transactions which are recorded in detail in the debtors' accounts in the debtors' ledger. In this way the principle of double entry is preserved in the general ledger. The debtors' ledger does not form part of the double-entry system, and its accounts are best regarded as memorandum records.

The subdivisions of the journal must be planned in such a way as to facilitate posting to the debtor's ledger control account in total. The sales journal and the cash receipts journal illustrated (pages 28-30) do not require any adaptation for this purpose. The individual entries in the sales journal are posted to the debit of individual accounts in the debtors' ledger in the way that has already been described; but the total sales, as recorded in the sales journal for any particular period, are posted to the general ledger as follows:

Debtors' ledger control account	Dr.	$...
Sales	Cr.	$...

If a separate returns inwards or sales allowances journal is kept, the individual entries are likewise posted to the credit of debtors' accounts in the debtors' ledger, while the total is posted to the debit and credit of the appropriate general ledger accounts:

Returns inwards	Dr.	$...
Debtors' ledger control account	Cr.	$...

Remittances from debtors and cash discounts allowed, after being recorded in the cash receipts journal in the usual way, are posted to the credit of individual accounts in the debtors' ledger. The total of the 'Debtors' column in the cash receipts journal is posted to the credit of the debtors' ledger control account in the general ledger; the total of the 'Discount Allowed' column is posted to the debit of the discount allowed account in the general ledger; and the double entry in the general ledger is maintained by debiting the cash at bank account with the total of the 'Amount Received' column:

Cash at bank	Dr.	$...
Discount allowed	Dr.	$...
Debtors' ledger control account	Cr.	$...

Where a system of control accounts and subsidiary ledgers is in operation, the general journal must be designed in such a way as to ensure that entries are posted both to the subsidiary ledger and to the appropriate control account in the general ledger. One method of achieving this result is to add a third money column to the general journal, in which to record amounts to be posted to subsidiary ledger accounts (the original money columns are reserved for the debit and credit entries to be posted to the general ledger). In recording a particular transaction, it is then necessary to supplement the normal entry with a line indicating the name of the subsidiary ledger account concerned, the way it is affected (debit or credit) and the amount of the transaction (recorded in the third money column). The procedure is illustrated below by reference to a hypothetical transaction, in which it is assumed that a debtor's account is settled by his acceptance of a bill of exchange drawn in favour of the business. (If there are many such transactions, it is desirable to set up a separate bills receivable journal, but if bill transactions are relatively infrequent they may conveniently be recorded in the general journal.)

General Journal

			General Ledger		
Date	Particulars	Ledger Folio	Dr.	Cr.	Subsidiary Ledger
1985	Bills receivable		$50.00		
Mar. 1	Debtors' ledger control			$50.00	
	S. Smith (debtors' ledger) Cr.				$50.00
	Acceptance of bill payable one month after date				

Posting to ledger accounts would involve, first, posting to the two general ledger accounts concerned and, finally, posting to the credit of the subsidiary ledger account which is indicated in the 'Particulars' column.

Example: The general application of the control account technique may be illustrated by assuming that the following transactions have been recorded in the sales journal and cash receipts journal respectively:

Sales Journal Folio No. 1

Date	Debtor	Ledger Folio	Amount
1985			
Sept. 1	A. Anderson		$75.00
2	J. Johnson		56.00
3	M. Myer		104.00
4	A. Anderson		63.00
5	T. Thomson		48.00
	Total		$346.00

Cash Receipts Journal Folio No. 1

Date	Particulars	Ledger Folio	Debtors	Discount Allowed	Amount Received	Bank
1985						
Sept. 2	A. Anderson		$75.00	$3.00	$72.00	$72.00
4	J. Johnson		20.00		20.00	20.00
5	M. Myer		104.00	4.00	100.00	
	Sales (cash)				30.00	130.00
	Total		$199.00	$7.00	$222.00	$222.00

These entries are posted to ledger accounts in the following way. First the debtors' ledger accounts are posted by the usual method as the transactions occur, an appropriate reference being made in the 'folio' column of the journal as each entry is posted (to indicate that it is the debtors' ledger to which the posting has been made, the code letters 'DL' may be inserted before the folio or account number). It is emphasized that the debtors' ledger is a subsidiary ledger which constitutes a memorandum record and is not part of the double-entry framework.

Debtors' Ledger

A. Anderson   Account No. DL1

1985				1985			
Sept. 1	Sales	S1	$75.00	Sept. 2	Bank and discount	CR1	$75.00
4	Sales	S1	63.00	4	Balance	c/d	63.00
			$138.00				$138.00
Sept. 4	Balance	b/d	$63.00				

J. Johnson   Account No. DL2

1985				1985			
Sept. 2	Sales	S1	$56.00	Sept. 4	Bank	CR1	$20.00
					Balance	c/d	36.00
			$56.00				$56.00
Sept. 4	Balance	b/d	$36.00				

M. Myer   Account No. DL3

1985				1985			
Sept. 3	Sales	S1	$104.00	Sept. 5	Bank and discount	CR1	$104.00

T. Thomson   Account No. DL4

1985			
Sept. 5	Sales	S1	$48.00

Insofar as the general ledger is concerned, any transactions which do not affect control accounts (such as the cash sale transaction on 5 September) are posted in the usual way, the appropriate reference (to a GL folio or account number) being made in the 'folio' column of the journal. Transactions affecting control accounts are posted in total, at the end of the period, in the manner described above (cross-references to GL folios being made in the 'folio' column of the journal, opposite the totals and in the order of the accounts affected):

General Ledger

Bank   Account No. GL 1112

1985			
Sept. 5	Cash receipts	CR1	$222 00

Debtors' Ledger Control   Account No. GL 1113

1985				1985			
Sept. 5	Sales	S1	$346.00	Sept. 5	Bank and discount	CR1	$199.00
					Balance	c/d	147.00
			$346.00				$346.00
Sept. 5	Balance	b/d	$147.00				

				Sales				Account No. GL 411

1985					1985			
Sept. 5	Balance	c/d	$376.00		Sept. 5	Debtors	S1	$346.00
						Bank	CR1	30.00
			$376.00					$376.00
					Sept. 5	Balance	b/d	$376.00

			Discount Allowed		Account No. GL 413

1985			
Sept. 5	Debtors	CR1	$7.00

The balancing of the general ledger accounts and the listing of the balances in a partial trial balance confirm that the double entry is complete:

Trial Balance as at 5 September 1985

		Dr.	Cr.
1112	Bank	$222.00	
1113	Debtors' ledger control	147.00	
411	Sales		$376.00
413	Discount allowed	7.00	
		$376.00	$376.00

The balances of the individual debtors' ledger accounts do not appear in the trial balance (or the balance sheet) but are listed in a separate schedule:

Schedule of Debtors' Ledger Balances at 5 September 1985

1.	A. Anderson	$63.00
2.	J. Johnson	36.00
3.	M. Myer	—
4.	T. Thomson	48.00
		$147.00

It will be observed that the total of the debtor's ledger balances is equal to the balance of the debtors' ledger control account. Because all transactions which are recorded in detail in the subsidiary ledger are recorded in total in the corresponding control account, the aggregate balances of the accounts in the subsidiary ledger must, at any time, be equal to the balance of the control account. It is in this sense that the latter provides a 'control' over the subsidiary ledger.

The control account technique which has been described may be applied similarly to transactions with creditors and other groups of related accounts, detailed information concerning which is not required in the general ledger. It is particularly useful, for example, in accounting for inventories, fixed capital assets or expenses, and has general application to the accounts of manufacturing enterprises and organizations consisting of a head office and one or more branches. It is merely necessary, in deciding to transfer a group of accounts from the general ledger to a subsidiary ledger, to substitute a control account in the general ledger and to adapt the relevant journals (e.g. by introducing an additional analysis column therein) in order to facilitate the posting of totals to the control account.

It will be seen that the use of the control account technique enables the general ledger to be confined to the basic information necessary for a broad understanding of the operating results and the financial position of a business. It also permits the same advantages of specialization and division of labour that resulted from the subdivision of the journal. One book-keeper may be made responsible for the debtors' ledger, another for the creditors' ledger, and so on, and the more important general ledger may be maintained by a senior member of the accounting staff as a more or less confidential record. Since the subsidiary ledgers and the control accounts in the general ledger are entered independently from the same source, they each provide a check on the accuracy of the other. In this way the use of control accounts forms a valuable part of the system of internal check which is an essential feature of a well-designed accounting system. Finally, it is possible to prepare short-term accounting reports from the relatively few general ledger balances at any time, without extracting the balances of the individual accounts in subsidiary ledgers. Time may thus be saved, and managerial control facilitated, in this important operation.

Discussion Questions

1 What are the main components of an accounting system and what are their purposes?

2 (a) What is the significance of evidence records in relation to the book-keeping process? Which documents would provide evidence of the following transactions: (i) payments of amounts owing to creditors; (ii) purchase of shop premises; (iii) credit sales; (iv) wages payable to salesmen; (v) reimbursement of petty cash advance; and (vi) cash withdrawals by proprietor?

(b) What function is served by the journal in an accounting system?

3 (a) An accounting system should be designed in such a way as to facilitate two kinds of control: (i) managerial control intended to achieve operating efficiency; and (ii) internal control intended to ensure the accuracy of the accounting records and reports themselves. Give examples of each.

(b) Indicate the action you would take, in designing an accounting system for a wholesale butcher, to provide effective control over the cash transactions of the enterprise.

4 (a) What is the significance of classification in relation to the problem of planning an accounting system? Discuss.

(b) What is the purpose of functional classification of costs and expenses?

(c) What functional groups would you expect to be relevant to: (i) a large retail department store; and (ii) an advertising agency?

(d) In which functional group would each of the following transactions be recorded: (i) rent from houses let to employees; (ii) freight inward; (iii) payroll tax on salesmen's salaries; and (iv) directors' fees.

(e) Indicate the balance sheet or profit and loss statement group in which each of the following items would normally be included: (i) advertising costs incurred to launch a new product; (ii) interest on government bonds (held temporarily by a manufacturing company); (iii) income tax payable; (iv) bank loan secured by mortgage and repayable in nine months' time; (v) sales allowances; (vi) trading inventories held for sale; (vii) cash discounts from creditors; (viii) amounts owing by debtors in respect of hire purchase contracts; (ix) amount temporarily advanced by partner; (x) premium paid for mineral lease; and (xi) insurance on shop premises.

5 (a) Define the following accounting concepts and indicate in what ways, if any, the accounting definitions differ from popular usage of the same terms: (i) assets; and (ii) profit.

(b) Define: (i) current liabilities; (ii) operating revenue; (iii) short-term financial assets; and (iv) accumulated surplus.

6 Distinguish between costs and expenses. To what extent does the distinction arise out of differences in the kinds of economic activity which are represented by the two kinds of transactions?

7 (a) Discuss the relationship between (i) revenue and assets, and (ii) expenses and assets.

(b) Do you acquire an asset when you obtain (i) a rail ticket to Sydney; (ii) a stock of advertising literature; (iii) a grazing lease; (iv) a new managing director; and (v) a contract for services to be performed?

(c) Is it possible for a firm to have assets which are not recorded in its balance sheet? Explain.

8 (a) Identify the expense incurred in the following transactions: (i) 1 000 litres of petrol are ordered from XYZ Petroleum Company; (ii) the petrol is delivered; (iii) an invoice is received from XYZ Petroleum Company; (iv) the amount owing to XYZ Petroleum Company is paid; (v) 10 litres of petrol are pumped into a salesman's car; (vi) the salesman travels 200 kilometres and receives orders for $1 000 worth of merchandise; the merchandise is (vii) delivered and (viii) paid for by the customers concerned.

(b) Would you expect the accounting records to recognize the expense at the time it is incurred in earning revenue? Would failure to do so invalidate the information provided by the accounting system?

9 (a) Indicate which of the following transactions you would expect to be recorded as expenses at the time they take place: (i) paid salesman's salary; (ii) purchased motor car; (iii) paid electricity account for shop lighting and heating; (iv) paid advertising agency for supply of advertising literature; and (v) purchased trading inventories.

(b) What other action, if any, may need to be taken in respect of each of the foregoing items in order to ensure that correct amounts are charged to expenses?

10 For some purposes, the accounting process may be characterized as a cash conversion cycle. Indicate the main steps in the cycle and consider its significance in relation to the classification of transactions.

11 In designing an accounting system for a retail departmental store what use would you make of: (a) a chart of accounts; and (b) the control account technique? Illustrate your answer by reference respectively to: (i) a pro forma chart of accounts; and (ii) illustrative general and subsidiary ledger accounts which record a number of hypothetical transactions relating to debtors.

12 Design an accounting system suitable for a small wholesale grocery business operated by a sole proprietor, indicating:

(a) the classification scheme you propose (in the form of a chart of accounts);

(b) a brief outline of the accounting procedures you recommend for purposes of accounting for cash, credit sales and credit purchases (showing in particular the journals and ledgers considered necessary); and

(c) the nature of the relationship between the general ledger and the recommended subsidiary ledgers.

13 (a) Under what circumstances should the journal and the ledger be subdivided, and how might the act of subdivision be expected to facilitate the book-keeping processes of the firm?

(b) Briefly describe the accounting procedures you would employ in order to operate a system of control accounts and subsidiary ledgers for debtors and creditors.

(c) In what sense does the adoption of the control account technique help to achieve control within an enterprise?

Exercises

1 (a) Record the following transactions of Albert Pupil, a wholesale grocer, in the form of general journal entries, post to ledger accounts and take out a trial balance as at 31 March 1985.

1985			
March	2	Paid into the bank as capital	$3 900
	3	Bought office furniture for cash	500
		Bought shop fittings for cash	700
	4	Bought goods from Cassell & Co.	250
	5	Sold goods to H. Hoole on credit	50
		Sold goods to G. Grace on credit	70
	6	Paid rent for premises	50
	8	Bought goods from Cassell & Co.	150
	9	Sent Cassell & Co. a cheque	200
	11	Sold goods to E. Hart	85
	12	Received cheque from H. Hoole,	
		$49, discount allowed him being $1	
	13	Paid wages in cash	110
	17	Sold goods for cash	40
	18	Bought goods from I. Gee	500
	20	Drew cheque for private expenses	50
	22	Sold goods to G. Grace on credit	170
	24	Cash sales	150
	27	Paid wages in cash	110
	28	Received a cheque from G. Grace for $68,	
		discount allowed him being $2	
	29	Paid electricity charges	30
	31	Cash sales	75

(b) Indicate briefly the documentary evidence you would expect to support each of the above transactions.

2 (a) Give general journal entries for the following transactions relating to Jones Fashion Boutique:

(i) February 10—Petty cash advance, $50.00.

(ii) February 20—Cheque drawn for reimbursement of petty cash, $34.50.
The petty cash records are kept on the imprest system, and the expenditure columns in the petty cash journal record the following amounts: travelling expenses, $15.25; postage, $4.50; stationery, $10; and flowers, $4.75.

(iii) February 26—Fashion goods taken by proprietor (N. Jones) for personal use (at cost), $45.

(iv) February 28—Returned cash to a customer for defective goods supplied, $10.

(b) What documents would provide evidence of the foregoing transactions?

3 Post the following transactions to appropriate accounts in the general ledger and the debtors' ledger, balance the accounts and prepare a trial balance and supporting schedule of debtors' balances:

Sales Journal

Date	Particulars	Ledger Folio	Amount
1985			
Jan. 3	B. Bray		$250
4	M. Bible		190
5	L. Gore		210
6	B. Bray		120
7	N. Smith		150
			$920

Cash Receipts Journal

Date	Particulars	Ledger Folio	Debtors	Discount Allowed	Amount	Bank
1985						
Jan. 3	Sales				$50	$50
5	B. Bray		$150	$3	147	
	M. Bible		90	2	88	235
7	L. Gore		210	5	205	205
			$450	$10	$490	$490

4 On 1 July 1985 the following balances were recorded in the debtors' ledger of J. Anson: Samson, $130; Byron, $218; Chaucer, $150; Browning, $118; and Everett, $196. During the month of July the following transactions took place:

1985	
July 2	Sold goods to Everett, $172
	Received cash from Browning for balance of account
4	Received cheque, $150, from Byron and allowed him $5 discount
	Sold goods to Samson, $203
5	Sold goods to Chaucer, $146 and received his cheque on account for $75
6	Sold goods to Byron, $185 and also to Browning, $136
8	Everett returned goods, $50
	Samson sent a cheque for $130
	Cash sales, $100
9	Byron returned goods, $56
13	Received cash on account from Chaucer, $100 and allowed him $3 discount
18	Sold goods to Samson, $216
22	Byron sent a cheque for $211 and was allowed $7 discount
24	Received a cheque from Browning, $120 and allowed him $4 discount
25	Sold goods to Byron, $140

You are required:
- (a) to record the above transactions in a system of specialized journals;
- (b) to write up the debtors' ledger and extract a list of balances; and
- (c) to set out the control account that would appear in the general ledger.

5 (a) The bank statement of Jones Stores discloses a debit balance of $193.40 at 30 June 1985. A check with the cash journals shows that cheques amounting to $273.74 have not yet been presented, and that a deposit of $86.31 recorded in the cash receipts journal on 30 June was not credited in the bank statement until 1 July. What should the balance of the bank account in the ledger of Jones Stores be at the close of business on 30 June? Present your answer in the form of a bank reconciliation statement.

(b) The bank account in the ledger of Stonehenge Quarries recorded a debit balance of $304.32 at 30 June 1985. A comparison of the cash journals and the bank statement as at the same date revealed the following discrepancies:

(i) Items recorded in bank statement but not in cash journals:

Bank charges	$5.00
Interest collected by bank on government bonds held on behalf of Stonehenge Quarries	53.50
Cheques received from S. Smith dishonoured on presentation	13.37

(ii) Items recorded in cash journals but not in bank statement:

Deposit, 30 June	$193.06
Cheque no. 71, 28 June	43.14
Cheque no. 74, 29 June	14.73
Cheque no. 75, 30 June	33.29

Make appropriate entries in the cash journals and the bank account of Stonehenge Quarries and, by means of a bank reconciliation statement, calculate the balance that would need to appear in the bank statement in order that the two sets of records may be reconciled.

6 At 31 October 1985, the bank account in the ledger of Radio and Television Services had recorded a debit balance of $143. The bank statement made up to the same date recorded a credit balance of $174, and a reconciliation revealed that the difference in the two balances represented cheque no. 131, which had been drawn on 30 October but had not been presented by the time the bank statement was prepared.

During November, cash receipts and cash payments transactions were recorded as follows:

Cash Receipts Journal

1985		Debtors	Discount	Amount	Bank
Nov. 1	Cash sales			$18	$18
2	B. Cooke	$117	$3	114	
	Cash sales			4	118
3	C. Drew	71	1	70	70
7	Cash sales			19	
	D. Egan	64		64	83
10	Sale of motor car			650	650
13	Cash sales			19	19
15	K. Francis	79	1	78	78
17	Cash sales			90	
	B. Cooke	14		14	104
20	Commission received			45	45
21	Cash sales			23	23
22	R. Dixon	91	2	89	89
23	Cash sales			34	34
24	K. Francis	14		14	14
27	Cash sales			91	91
29	Cash sales			24	24
30	Commission received			20	
	D. Egan	15	1	14	
	Cash sales			29	63
		$465	$8	$1 523	$1 523

Cash Payments Journal

1985		Chq. No.	Creditors	Discount	Amount	Bank
Nov. 1	Wholesale Suppliers	134	$143	$3	$140	$140
3	Wages	135			75	75
7	Advertising	136			21	21
10	Electricity	137			34	34
13	Postage				4	
	Administrative expenses	138			7	
	Travelling expenses				4	15
14	Subscription to trade association	139			10	10
15	P. Mott	140	94	2	92	92
17	Wages				75	
	Drawings—S. Smith	141			50	125
20	Advertising	142			14	14
21	Newvision Ltd	143	240	4	236	236
22	Office furniture	144			24	24
24	Wholesale Suppliers	145	73		73	73
27	Postage	146			11	11
29	Radio Parts Ltd	147	114	2	112	112
30	Donations	148			20	20
	Wages	149			75	75
			$664	$11	$1 077	$1 077

The following bank statement was received from Australian Bank Ltd at the end of November:

Australian Bank Ltd
In Account with Radio and Television Services

1985		Dr.	Cr.	Balance
Oct. 31				$174
Nov. 1	Deposit		$18	192
2	Deposit		118	
	Cheque 131	$31		279
3	Cheque 135	75		
	Deposit		70	
	Cheque 134	140		134
7	Deposit		83	
	Cheque 136	21		196
11	Deposit		650	
	Cheque 137	34		812
13	Cheque 138	15		797
14	Deposit		19	816
15	Service charge	10		806
16	Deposit		78	884
17	Deposit		104	
	Cheque 141	125		863
18	Cheque C. Drew returned NSF (not sufficient funds)	70		793
20	Cheque 142	14		
	Deposit		45	
	Cheque 140	92		732
21	Deposit		23	755
22	Deposit		89	
	Cheque 143	236		608
23	Deposit		34	642
24	Deposit		14	
	Cheque 145	73		583
27	Deposit		91	
	Cheque 146	11		663
29	Deposit		24	
	Cheque books	2		685
30	Cheque 147	112		
	Cheque 144	24		
	Cheque 149	75		474

You are required to take whatever action is necessary to complete the relevant accounting records of Radio and Television Services to the end of November and to prepare a bank reconciliation statement as at 30 November 1985.

7 Set out below are the cash receipts and cash payments journals (bank column only) of A. Southan:

Cash Receipts Journal

Date	Particulars	Amount
1985		
March 5	Rogers & Co.	$281
10	J. Laws	137
12	Carlton United	163
16	A. McRae	37
24	A. Hunter	120
31	Lastex Ltd	163

Cash Payments Journal

Date		Particulars	Cheque No.	Amount
1985				
March	3	Wages	121	$179
	4	Self	122	220
	6	J. Royce	123	157
	7	R. Gray	124	139
	10	C. Forbes	125	87
	17	Wages	126	123
	27	Sales tax	127	87

The following is the statement of his account with the Bank of New South Wales.

R. Southan
In Account with Bank of New South Wales

1985			Cheque No.	Dr.	Cr.	Balance
March	3	Cheque	121	$179		$179 Dr.
	4	Cheque	122	220		399 Dr.
	6	Deposit			$281	118 Dr.
	10	Cheque	124	139		257 Dr.
	11	Cheque	125	87		344 Dr.
	12	Deposit			137	207 Dr.
	14	Deposit			163	44 Dr.
	15	Australian Consolidated				
		Loan Interest			45	1 Cr.
	17	Cheque	126	123		122 Dr.
		Cheque book		5		127 Dr.
	18	Deposit			37	90 Dr.
	21	Bank fee		3		93 Dr.
	24	Deposit			120	27 Cr.
	29	Cheque	127	87		60 Dr.
	31	Cheque dishonoured				
		(A. McRae)		37		97 Dr.

You are required to prepare a bank reconciliation statement as at 31 March 1985.

8 (a) Give entries in the cash payments journal to record the following transaction: reimbursement of petty cash, $18.30. The petty cash records are maintained on the imprest system, and the expenditure columns in the petty cash book record the following amounts:

Stationery	$2.70
Travelling expenses	5.41
General administrative expenses	10.19

(b) Record the following transactions by means of appropriate entries in a cash payments journal and a petty cash journal (the latter is maintained on the imprest system):

1985			
Jan.	1	Established petty cash advance	$10.00
	2	Purchased stamps	1.50
	3	Paid for stationery	0.75
	4	Telegram charges	1.30
		Donation to charitable appeal	1.00
	5	Fares	0.45
	8	Purchased stamps	1.45
		Paid for 3 bottles of ink	0.40
	9	Manila folders purchased	0.70
	10	Paid newsagent for newspapers	1.20
	11	Reimbursed office boy for bus fares	0.45
		Drew reimbursing cheque	

It may be assumed that there are ledger accounts for postage and telegraphic expenses, stationery and office supplies, travelling expenses and general administrative expenses.

9 S.T. Peters, who conducts a wholesale grocery business, maintains an accounting system which includes a general journal, a cash payments journal, a purchase journal, a general ledger and a creditors' ledger. During the week ended 10 September 1985, he enters into the following transactions with suppliers:

1985		
Sept.	5	Credit purchases from Burnside Biscuits Ltd, $330.44; Prospect Preserving Company, $191.20
	6	Credit purchases from C. Cliff, $88.15
	7	Cash purchases, $207.32
	8	Credit purchases from Prospect Preserving Company, $125.01; credit note received from C. Cliff—allowance for case of olive oil short supplied, $14.69
	9	Paid amount owing to Burnside Biscuits Ltd, less $2\frac{1}{2}\%$ cash discount
	10	Paid Prospect Preserving Company $120.00 on account

Assuming there are no other transactions, you are required:
    (a) to record the above transactions in appropriate journals and ledgers;
    (b) to balance all the accounts as at 10 September 1985; and
    (c) to prepare a list of general ledger balances at that date (in the form of a trial balance), supported by a schedule of creditors' balances.

10 Describe the imprest system of recording petty cash transactions. Illustrate your answer by means of a specimen form of petty cash journal and a number of hypothetical entries, and show clearly the relationship between the petty cash book and the cash payments journal.

11 You have been asked to install an accounting system for a wholesale fruit business operated by a sole proprietor. Describe the steps you would take in planning the system, and prepare a chart of accounts in a form that will reflect the scheme of classification which you decide to adopt.

12 The following entries appear in the books of original entry of A. Retailer during a week in November 1985:

(a) Purchase Journal

Date	Particulars	Folio	Amount
1985			
Nov. 1	A. Woodley		$76
	T. Croft		34
2	T. Johnson		20
	G. Tucker		72
	M. Copeland		18
3	A. Woodley		55
	T. Johnson		6
4	H. Spring		8
	G. Tucker		95
	T. Croft		17
5	A. Woodley		69
			$470

(b) Sales Journal

Date	Particulars	Folio	Amount
1985			
Nov. 1	J. Bray		$82
	S. Hepburn		19
	M. Stevenson		4
2	T. Bourke		60
	L. Moore		17
	F. Herring		19
3	M. Stevenson		9
	H. Spring		18
	W. Cumming		30
	S. Hepburn		18
4	J. Bray		63
	T. Bourke		13
	F. Herring		27
5	J. Bray		19
	L. Moore		62
	S. Hepburn		15
	T. Bourke		40
	M. Stevenson		39
			$554

(c) Cash Payments Journal

Date	Particulars	Folio	Creditors	Discount Received	Amount	Bank
1985						
Nov. 1	Cash purchases				$13	$13
	Rent				20	20
2	Cash purchases				62	62
4	T. Johnson		$26	$1	25	25
	Cash purchases				15	15
	A. Woodley		131	3	128	128
5	Cash purchases				15	15
	Wages				26	26
	T. Croft		34	1	33	33
			$191	$5	$337	$337

(d) **Cash Receipts Journal**

Date	Particulars	Folio	Debtors	Discount Allowed	Amount	Bank
1985						
Nov. 1	Cash sales				$30	$30
2	Cash sales				19	19
3	J. Bray		$82	$2	80	
	Cash sales				40	120
5	Cash sales				14	
	S. Hepburn		37		37	
	L. Moore		17	1	16	
	F. Herring		46	1	45	
	H. Spring		10		10	
	W. Cumming		15		15	137
			$207	$4	$306	$306

(e) In addition to the above, the following transactions have been recorded in the general journal:

(i) November 5—allowance to T. Bourke for returns inward, $5.

(ii) November 5—settlement by contra with H. Spring, $8.

A. Retailer's ledger is subdivided into a general ledger, a debtors' ledger and a creditors' ledger (the general ledger containing control accounts in respect of the two subsidiary ledgers). You are required:

(1) to show how the transactions listed under (e) above would be recorded in the general journal;

(2) to post all the entries listed to appropriate accounts in the ledgers; and

(3) to balance the accounts and prepare a trial balance of general ledger accounts as at 5 November, supported by schedules of individual debtors' and creditors' balances.

3 The Financial Reports: Profit and Loss Statement and Balance Sheet (A)

Significance of the Trial Balance

The expanded system of accounting that was described in the previous chapter carries the book-keeping or recording process through to its final stage, the preparation of the trial balance. Previous chapters have described how evidence of transactions is collected; how the transactions are recorded in the journals and ledgers; and how the methods of recording transactions and organizing the ledger accounts necessarily depend on the scheme of classification which is adopted. When all the transactions for a particular period have been duly recorded in ledger accounts, the accounts may be balanced and the general ledger balances listed in a trial balance in the manner illustrated in Chapter 1 (the trial balance being supported by schedules of subsidiary ledger balances where a system of control accounts and subsidiary ledgers is in operation). The trial balance not only provides a rough check on the arithmetical accuracy of the recording process, and helps to ensure that the double entry is complete; it also serves as a convenient starting point for the next major accounting procedure, the summarizing process, which ends with the preparation of the final accounting reports or financial statements: the profit and loss statement, the balance sheet and the funds statement.

Matching Costs and Expenses against Revenue by Periods

The process of profit determination which is carried out in the trading account and the profit and loss account depends, as has been seen, on the comparison of the revenue earned in the period covered by the accounts with the costs and expenses incurred in producing that revenue. Profit is derived as the difference between total revenue and total costs and expenses. There are thus really two ideas or assumptions which underlie the preparation of the trading and profit and loss accounts and the determination of profit. The first is that costs and expenses may appropriately be compared with (or 'matched' against) revenue in order to ascertain profit; and the second, which is of course related to the first, is that the results (the revenue earned and the costs and expenses incurred) may be satisfactorily measured by *periods*.

With respect to the first assumption, accountants themselves have traditionally upset the logic of the 'matching' concept by insisting that revenue should not be brought into account until it is realized, whereas costs and expenses may, under certain circumstances, be anticipated. The second assumption, that of the accounting period, was mentioned briefly in Chapter 1. It implies that for profit measurement purposes the life of the business may be arbitrarily divided into periods of a fixed length, e.g. one year, to which revenues, costs and expenses may be assigned. The two assumptions give rise to some difficult measurement problems, which are treated in Chapter 6.

The preparation of financial reports at the end of an accounting period necessitates making a number of adjustments to recorded transactions and these will now be considered.

The Balance-day Adjustments

The application of the accounting period assumption makes it necessary for certain adjustments to be made to the items of revenue, cost and expense which have been recorded in ledger accounts during the accounting period. These adjustments are made after the accounts have been balanced and the trial balance prepared at the end of the accounting period (they are therefore sometimes known as the 'balance-day adjustments') but before the balances of the revenue, cost and expense accounts are transferred to the trading and profit and loss accounts. They are designed to ensure that the trading and profit and loss accounts (and the profit and loss statement which is subsequently derived from them) include all those items of revenue, cost and expense which are relevant to the current period, but exclude items of revenue, cost and expense which relate to past or future accounting periods. In effect the accounting period assumption results in a classification of transactions into current and capital; transactions or parts of transactions not related to the current period are capitalized.

The main problem which arises in making balance-day adjustments is that many of the ordinary transactions of a business involve a continuous sequence of activities that cannot be easily associated with one accounting period rather than another. For example, a fixed capital asset, such as a machine, is purchased with the intention that it will provide services to the business over a number of accounting periods. It is therefore considered appropriate to allocate part of the cost of the machine, as an expense, to each of the accounting periods in question. But on what basis should this allocation (which is known as 'depreciation') be made? The answer is that the best possible estimate must be made of the expense which is attributable to each accounting period. Matching costs and expenses against revenue for a given period is thus not always a clear-cut process; it involves estimating, by the best means available, the revenue which has been earned in the period, and the costs and expenses which have been incurred during that period and which may reasonably be associated with the revenue earned.

Balance-day adjustments are of four main kinds:
(a) transactions which have been recorded in the books of account during the current period, but which relate wholly or partly to subsequent accounting periods;
(b) transactions which have occurred during the current period, but which for some reason have not been recorded in the books of account prior to balance day;
(c) allocations to the current period of its share of the original cost of fixed capital assets—depreciation; and
(d) provisions for anticipated revenue, costs or losses arising out of the current period's operations, the exact amounts of which cannot be determined at balance-day.

These adjustments are recorded in the general journal, by means of what are known as 'adjusting entries', on the last day of the period. The posting of these entries to appropriate accounts in the ledger means that the adjusted balances of revenue, cost and expense accounts reflect accurately the results of operations in the current period, and the transfer of these balances to the trading account and the profit and loss account may be undertaken without further delay. Before this procedure is illustrated, each of the main classes of balance-day adjustments will be considered in some detail.

Adjustments to Recorded Transactions

The first kind of adjustment relates to transactions that have been recorded in the books of account during the current period, but which are attributable wholly or partly to subsequent accounting periods. Examples are purchases of trading goods (or supplies or materials) which have not all been sold (or used up) during the current period, and expenses paid in advance (or revenue received in advance) for a period that extends beyond the balance-day.

(a) Inventories

In Chapter 1 the problem of profit measurement was deliberately over-simplified by leaving out of account any stocks of trading goods which remain on hand at the end of the accounting period. After gross profit had been defined as sales *minus* cost of sales, cost of sales was identified with the cost of trading goods purchased. It was possible to do this in our simple example, because it was explicitly assumed that all the goods which had been purchased were sold prior to the end of the accounting period, i.e. that there were no unsold stocks to be taken into account. In compiling the trading account in Chapter 1, the item cost of sales was represented by the cost of purchases made during the period, as shown on page 16.

In practice, it is usually necessary to distinguish between the cost of purchases and the cost of sales by recording goods purchased in a separate purchases account, the balance of which may be transferred to the cost of sales account at the end of the accounting period, instead of recording them directly in the cost of sales account. This involves expanding the ledger accounts as follows:

Sales

1985			1985		
Jan. 6 Trading account		$850	Jan. 6 Balance	b/d	$850

Purchases

1985			1985	
Jan. 6 Balance	b/d $800		Jan. 6 Cost of sales	$800

Cost of Sales

1985		1985	
Jan. 6 Purchases	$800	Jan. 6 Trading account	$800

Trading

1985		1985	
Jan. 6 Cost of sales	$800	Jan. 6 Sales	$850
Profit and loss account			
(gross profit)	50		
	$850		$850

Physical or periodic inventory method: The assumption that all the goods purchased during the period are sold before the end of the period is seldom justified in reality and must now be dropped. A trading business invariably finds it necessary to keep a quantity of inventories on hand at all times. This means that at the end of the accounting period, when the trading account is drawn up, not all the goods bought during the period have been sold. It is these unsold inventories which need to be introduced into the system by means of a balance-day adjustment, the purpose of which is to estimate the cost of sales attributable to the current period's operations. Using the above figures for sales and purchases, let us now assume that at the end of the week the value of unsold goods, or closing inventories as they are usually called, is $50. (The value of inventory on hand at the end of the period may be estimated by taking a physical count.) These closing inventories are introduced into the system by debiting an asset account, the inventory account, with the value of closing inventories (as determined by the physical stocktaking), the corresponding credit entry being made in the cost of sales account:

1985			
Jan. 6	Inventory	Dr.	$50
	Cost of sales	Cr.	$50
	Closing inventory as per physical stocktaking		

As a result of this general journal entry, which is the balance-day adjustment or adjusting entry, the cost of sales account is relieved of those purchases which should not be included in the cost of sales because the goods remain unsold and are still held in the form of inventories. Part of the cost of purchases is being recorded as an asset. The balance of the cost of sales account then represents the cost of goods actually sold during the period.

After the balance-day adjustments have been recorded, the balance of the cost of sales account (representing as it does cost of sales for the period) is transferred to the trading account in the usual way. Provided there are no deductions from sales, the difference between the cost of sales and the balance of the sales account, which is also transferred to the trading account, represents gross profit. The following ledger accounts set out the position after the relevant journal entries have been posted:

Inventory

1985				
Jan. 6 Cost of sales	$50			

Sales

1985			1985			
Jan. 6 Trading account	$850		Jan. 6 Balance	b/d	$850

Purchases

1985				1985		
Jan. 6 Balance	b/d	$800		Jan. 6 Cost of sales		$800

Cost of Sales

1985			1985		
Jan. 6 Purchases	$800		Jan. 6 Inventory		$50
				Trading account	750
	$800				$800

Trading

1985			1985	
Jan. 6	Cost of sales	$750	Jan. 6 Sales	$850
	Profit and loss account (gross			
	profit)	100		
		$850		$850

It will be observed that, as a result of the action in bringing closing inventories into account, profits (and thus proprietorship equity) have increased by $50. Assets have increased by a corresponding amount through the creation of the asset inventory account, the balance of which is recorded in the balance sheet and carried forward into the accounts of the next period. What has been done, in effect, is to capitalize a portion of the recorded cost of purchases and treat it as an asset.

Although the balance-day adjustment for closing inventory has now been completed, it is convenient at this stage to consider the problem of accounting for inventory in the next accounting period, which begins on, say, 8 January. The closing inventory of the previous period becomes the opening inventory of the new period. If it is assumed for the time being that it is sold in the new period, this opening inventory may be charged to the cost of sales account (by transferring the balance of the inventory account that has been brought forward, thereby closing the inventory account):

1985				
Jan. 8	Cost of sales		Dr.	$50
	Inventory		Cr.	$50
	Opening inventory (reversing entry)			

This entry in effect reverses the adjusting entry made on 6 January, and is therefore described as a 'reversing entry'. Reversing entries, like adjusting entries, are recorded in the general journal. If it is assumed that sales in the new week amount to $950 and purchases $850, and that inventory on hand at the end of the week is valued at $75 (whether closing inventory comes from new purchases or opening inventory need not matter for the time being), the relevant accounts for the period take the following form:

Inventory

1985				1985		
Jan.	6 Balance	b/d	$50	Jan.	8 Cost of sales	$50
Jan.	13 Cost of sales		$75			

Purchases

1985				1985		
Jan. 13 Balance		b/d	$850	Jan. 13 Cost of sales		$850

Cost of Sales

1985			1985		
Jan.	8 Inventory (opening)	$50	Jan. 13 Inventory (closing)		$75
	13 Purchases	850		Trading account	825
		$900			$900

Sales

1985			1985		
Jan. 13 Trading account		$950	Jan. 13 Balance	b/d	$950

Trading

1985			1985		
Jan. 13 Cost of sales		$825	Jan. 13 Sales		$950
Profit and loss account					
(gross profit)		125			
		$950			$950

It will be seen that in the new period opening inventory and purchases have been brought into cost of sales, while closing inventory has been excluded therefrom by means of an adjusting entry made at the end of the period. The balance of the cost of sales account which is transferred to the trading account thus again represents the cost of goods actually sold in the period. Opening inventory has been absorbed into costs while closing inventory is taken into the balance sheet at the end of the new period as an asset.

A question arises as to how closing inventory should be valued for purposes of the balance-day adjustment. Since the goods concerned were originally included among purchases at cost price, it is logical to value them at cost price also for purposes of the balance-day adjustment, and for the time being this may be regarded as the procedure to be followed. This general statement greatly over-simplifies the problem of inventory valuation, however, and different aspects of the question will be discussed in greater detail in Chapter 4 as well as in Part III of the book.

Perpetual inventory method: The method of accounting for inventories which has been described is known as the physical or periodic inventory method, because it necessitates a physical stocktaking or count of inventories at the end of each accounting period in order to make the appropriate balance-day adjustment. There is an alternative system of accounting for inventories, based on the control account technique described in Chapter 2, which avoids the need to make balance-day adjustments in respect of closing inventories. Briefly, this alternative procedure involves recording purchases of goods in an asset account, the inventory account, as soon as they are bought, and crediting the asset account (and debiting the cost of sales account) with the cost of sales at the time the goods are disposed of. This system, which is known as the perpetual inventory method, thus provides a continuous record of movements of goods into and out of inventories, so that at any time during the accounting period the asset account should record inventories actually on hand. Likewise, under this method the balance in the cost of sales account at any time records the cost of the goods which have been sold up to that time. In order to operate the perpetual inventory system, it is necessary to ascertain, in relation to each sales transaction, the cost of the goods sold. Two sets of entries are made to record sales. The first is in terms of selling price and records the increase in the asset debtors (or bank), and the revenue earned:

Sundry debtors (or bank)	Dr.	$x
Sales	Cr.	$x

Simultaneously another entry (this one in terms of cost price) records the expense associated with the sale and the reduction in assets as a result of the movement of the goods:

Cost of sales	Dr.	$x
Inventory	Cr.	$x

At the end of the accounting period, the balance of the cost of sales account is transferred to the trading account without adjustment, while the balance of the inventory account represents the amount that is recorded in the balance sheet. The foregoing transactions for the week ending 6 January would be recorded as follows in a perpetual inventory system:

Sales

1985			1985		
Jan. 6	Trading account	$850	Jan. 1-6 Customers		$850

Inventory

1985				1985			
Jan. 1-6	Suppliers		$800	Jan. 1-6 Cost of sales			$750
				Jan. 6	Balance	c/d	50
			$800				$800
Jan. 6	Balance	b/d	$50				

Cost of Sales

1985			1985		
Jan. 1-6	Inventory	$750	Jan. 6	Trading account	$750

Trading

1985			1985		
Jan. 6	Cost of sales	$750	Jan. 6	Sales	$850
	Profit and loss account				
	(gross profit)	100			
		$850			$850

The inventory account in a perpetual inventory system may usefully serve as a control account controlling subsidiary inventory accounts (or perpetual inventory stock cards) which record movements and balances in respect of each line of inventory. The detailed inventory records may be thought of as subsidiary ledger accounts, with debit entries recording receipts of inventory (purchases) and credit entries recording issues (sales), but they usually also contain supplementary information designed to facilitate control over inventories, such as a description of the goods and their location in the store, information concerning quantities and prices and the reorder level, and a record of orders placed. Figure 3—A is an example of a typical perpetual inventory stock card.

Stock cards are written up from copies of orders placed, invoices received from suppliers in respect of purchases, and copies of invoices for goods sold. Insofar as the inventory control account in the general ledger is concerned, information regarding purchases (the source of debit entries) is obtained from suppliers' invoices in the usual way. Credit entries (recording the cost of goods sold) are made on the basis of summaries of sales invoices or requisitions, in respect of which the necessary cost information has been derived from the stock cards.

Figure 3—A
Perpetual Inventory Stock Card

Code No.:   Description: Maximum: Order Point:
Bin No.:   Unit: Minimum: Order Quantity

Ordered		Received				Sold				Balance		
Date	Order No.	Invoice No.	Quantity	Unit Cost	Amount	Invoice No.	Quantity	Unit Cost	Amount	Quantity	Unit Cost	Amount

The direct calculation of cost of sales at the time goods are sold poses a number of valuation problems which are examined in Chapter 4. It may be seen, however, that the perpetual inventory method in effect reverses the procedure of the physical inventory method. The latter records the cost of goods purchased as an expense in the first instance, crediting the expense account (cost of sales account) and debiting an asset account (inventory account) in respect of inventories unsold at the end of the accounting period. The perpetual inventory method, on the other hand, initially records the cost of goods purchased as an asset, crediting the asset account (inventory account) and debiting an expense account (cost of sales account) with the cost of inventories that are sold. In theory, the two systems should result in the same amounts for cost of sales and closing inventories, but each system makes implicit valuation assumptions which carry implications with respect to the measurement and control of inventory movements and balances.

The physical inventory method results in a direct estimate of closing inventory, and it is assumed that inventory not seen to be on hand when the physical inventory is taken has been sold. If opening inventories are $1 000, purchases for the period are $9 000, and closing inventories (as revealed by the physical stocktaking) are $750, the assumed cost of sales is calculated as follows:

Opening inventory	$1 000
Purchases	9 000
	10 000
Less: Closing inventory	750
(Assumed) Cost of sales	$9 250

The disadvantage of this method, from the point of view of profit measurement and control, lies in its assumption that inventory not on hand at the end of the period has entered cost of sales. In practice some of the inventory assumed to have been sold may have been stolen or lost.

Under the perpetual inventory system of accounting for inventories, on the other hand, a direct estimate is made of the cost of sales, and the value of inventory remaining on hand is estimated as a residual item. If opening inventories and purchases are $1 000 and $9 000 respectively, as in the above example, but the cost of sales is calculated at $9 000, the assumed value of closing inventory is estimated in the following way:

Opening inventory	$1 000
Purchases	9 000
	10 000
Less: Cost of sales	9 000
(Assumed) Closing inventory	$1 000

It would appear that the perpetual inventory system, used by itself, is also unsatisfactory, because the assumed closing inventory may not correspond with actual inventory on hand (and does not do so in the above example). However, this apparent defect in the perpetual inventory system is easily rectified. The adoption of the perpetual method of recording does not preclude the need to check that the recorded inventory in the books is consistent with the physical inventory in the warehouse—indeed business prudence would counsel a physical check from time to time. A physical stocktaking needs to be undertaken at the end of the period to establish the value of the closing inventory. If the value of inventory on hand, as given by the perpetual inventory accounting records, does not agree with the value disclosed by the physical stocktaking, the difference is an inventory loss to be recorded separately from cost of sales, by debiting a loss of inventory account and crediting the inventory account as follows:

Loss of inventory	Dr.	$250
Inventory	Cr.	$250

Loss of inventory appears as a separate item in the profit and loss statement, either in the trading section if the loss is a normal one, e.g. anticipated obsolescence or wastage, or as an extraordinary item in the profit and loss section, e.g. loss by fire. The reasons for inventory losses must of course be carefully investigated; this is an essential requirement if the accounting records are to play their part in facilitating cost control.

The perpetual inventory system has the advantage that it is not necessary to await the end of the accounting period before undertaking the physical stocktaking. Stock cards may be checked by a physical stocktaking at any time, so that the inconvenience of a huge annual stocktaking is avoided and more effective control over inventories is achieved throughout the year. Another important benefit is that information on inventory on hand is readily available, facilitating the preparation of interim accounting reports.

(b) Supplies and Materials

Where inventories of supplies or materials, which have previously been recorded as expenses, remain on hand at the end of the accounting period, the balance-day adjustment is similar to that for inventories illustrated above in relation to the physical inventory system. If, for example, fuel which has been purchased during the accounting period has not been fully used up by the end of the period, it is necessary to make an adjusting entry debiting the fuel inventory account and crediting the fuel expense account (to which the cost of fuel purchases has previously been charged):

Fuel inventory	Dr.	$x
Fuel expense	Cr.	$x

The diminished balance of the fuel expense account is transferred to the profit and loss account as the expense attributable to the period. Fuel inventory is recorded in the balance sheet as an asset, and the balance of the account is carried forward to the next accounting period. As in the case of trading inventories, a reversing entry (debiting fuel expense account, crediting fuel inventory account) is made on the first day of the new period with the object of transferring this balance to the fuel expense account in the new period.

(c) Prepayments

Essentially the same procedure is followed with other expenses which have to be paid in advance for a period that extends beyond the current accounting period. These are known as prepaid expenses or 'prepayments'. Insurance premiums, for example, usually have to be paid in advance, and if the period covered by the premium overlaps two accounting periods, a balance-day adjustment must be made at the end of the period in which payment is made. If the accounting period is a year (ending on 31 December) and a premium of $120 has been paid on 1 December for the period ending 30 November in the following year, the following balance-day adjustment must be made on 31 December of the current year:

1985				
Dec. 31	Prepayments		Dr.	$110
	Insurance		Cr.	$110
	Adjustment for insurance paid 1 December for period			
	1 December 1985—30 November 1986			

The entry has the effect of relieving the insurance expense account, to which the original payment has been debited, of that part of the expense which is attributable to the subsequent accounting period. The debit to the prepayments account recognizes the existence of an asset, namely the right (to insurance cover in the next period) which has been paid for during the current period. The balance of the prepayments account is therefore recorded in the balance sheet as an asset (in the current asset section) and carried forward in the ledger into the next period, when it is transferred to the insurance expense account by means of a reversing entry debiting the insurance account and crediting prepayments. It will be clear that the net effect of the adjusting and reversing entries, when considered in relation to the original payment, is to allocate the cost of the insurance premium to the two accounting periods according to the time in each for which cover has been secured. The relative time period forms the basis for many allocations in the recording of prepayments as well as other transactions.

As with trading inventories, the method of recording prepayments may be reversed by debiting an asset account, prepayments, with the full amount of $120 at the time the payment is made and transferring an appropriate amount to the expense account for insurance at the end of each accounting period, until the cover expires. (In the period ending 31 December the amount so transferred, by means of an adjusting entry debiting the insurance account and crediting the prepayments account, would be $10.) No reversing entry is needed when this method is used, as the adjustment procedure outlined will automatically give the same allocation to expenses in each accounting period as the other method which has been discussed above.

(d) Revenue Received in Advance

If a receipt has been previously recorded as revenue, this must also be adjusted with respect to that portion of the revenue that relates to the subsequent accounting period. For example, if rent due to the business has been received in advance for a period extending beyond balance-day, an adjusting entry must be made whereby the amount attributable to the subsequent period is credited to the rent received in advance account and debited to the revenue account, rent received, which has previously been credited with the full amount received:

Rent received	Dr.	$x
Rent received in advance	Cr.	$x

The balance in the rent received account then records the net revenue derived from rent in the current period. Rent received in advance is recorded in the balance sheet as a current liability, representing the obligation of the business to provide services in the ensuing period. The balance of the rent received in advance account is transferred at the beginning of the new period to the rent received account, by means of a reversing entry debiting the rent received in advance account (thereby closing this account) and crediting the new period's rent received account. As a result of these entries it will be observed that the revenue received from rent is allocated to the two accounting periods according to the respective times covered by the tenant's payments.

Recording Accrued Transactions

The second kind of balance-day adjustment relates to transactions which have taken place during the current accounting period but which have not been recorded prior to the end of the period. Payment is made for certain expenses and revenue in arrears, and if no record is made of such transactions until payment is effected it is necessary to make provision at the end of the accounting period for the expenses or revenue which may be said to have 'accrued'.

(a) *Accrued Expenses*

Suppose, for example, that the end of the accounting period (31 December) falls on a Wednesday, and that wages are usually paid weekly at the close of business on Fridays. At the time the trial balance is drawn up, the wages due for the period extending from the last pay-day to balance-day (Monday to Wednesday) have not been recorded, and it is necessary to make an adjusting entry to bring them into account. If the weekly payroll is $100, and $60 of this represents wages chargeable to the period Monday to Wednesday, the following balance-day adjustment must be made:

1985			
Dec. 31	Wages	Dr.	$60
	Accrued expenses	Cr.	$60
	Wages accrued to 31 December 1985		

The debit to the wages account increases the expense which is to be transferred to the profit and loss account, and thereby reduces profit (and proprietorship equity). The credit entry, by recognizing the amount owing by the business, creates a liability in respect of accrued expenses. This appears among current liabilities in the balance sheet, and the balance of the account is carried into the ledger of the next accounting period. At the beginning of the new period a reversing entry is made debiting the accrued expenses account (thereby closing the account) and crediting the wages expense account. The effect of the latter entry is to offset, against the $100 paid on the first Friday of the new period and debited to the wages account, the $60 attributable to the previous period. The balance of $40 in the wages account of the new period thus reflects the wages chargeable to that period, and the effect of all the entries taken together is to allocate wage payments to their appropriate accounting periods.

(b) *Accrued Revenue*

Revenue earned during the current accounting period, but not received until the subsequent period, is recorded similarly as a balance-day adjustment by debiting an asset account, accrued revenue account, and crediting the appropriate revenue account (thereby increasing recorded profits and proprietorship equity). If, for example, interest on investments has accrued prior to balance-day, the amount accrued is brought into account by means of the following adjusting entry:

Accrued revenue	Dr.	$x
Interest received	Cr.	$x

After the adjustment, the balance of the interest received account is transferred to the profit and loss account in the usual way, while the balance of the accrued revenue account, after being recorded in the balance sheet as a current asset, is carried forward into the ledger of the next accounting period. The reversing entry made at the beginning of the new period, debiting interest received and crediting accrued revenue, closes the latter account and provides an offset in the former against the interest which will ultimately be paid into the account in respect of the overlapping period. Accrued revenue is normally not recorded unless the future receipt is relatively certain, e.g. interest on government bonds.

Depreciation

The third kind of balance-day adjustment is conventionally designed to allocate to the current accounting period its share of the cost of fixed capital assets.[1] When a fixed asset (such as a machine) is purchased, its cost is recorded by a debit entry in an appropriate asset account, say a machinery account. The purpose in acquiring the machine, however, is not to hold it idle but rather to use it as a means of producing revenue; the initial cost of the machine may therefore be regarded as a cost which is subsequently to be treated as an expense incurred in producing revenue. This cost differs from other costs and expenses in that the machine will be used over a period of many years; in order to match the cost of the machine with the revenue that will be derived from its use, therefore, it is necessary to allocate the cost as an expense among all the accounting periods during which the machine will be used, i.e. over its expected working life. This cost allocation is known as depreciation, and depreciation is recorded by means of a balance-day adjustment designed to charge the current accounting period with its share of the original cost of the machine. The accounting concept of depreciation differs from the common language meaning of the word. In common usage, depreciation means the physical using up or wear-and-tear of an asset. In its traditional accounting sense, depreciation is a financial charge which is made in the accounts to reflect the cost of using an asset in a given accounting period or, more specifically, to reflect that portion of the original money cost of the asset which may be regarded as having been used up in producing revenue in a particular accounting period.

A simple example may serve to explain why it is necessary to regard part of the initial cost of a fixed asset as an expense incurred in producing revenue in each period in which it is used. Suppose a machine is purchased at the beginning of Year 1, with an estimated working life of five years and a zero residual value, at a cost of $10 000. If $10 000 revenue is earned during each year and $7 500 expenses (other than depreciation) are incurred, the data may be set out as follows:

---

[1] It will be seen later that depreciation may sometimes be regarded as a decline in the value of an asset as opposed to an allocation of its original cost. In this chapter the conventional accounting cost-allocation notion of depreciation will be adhered to.

Year (accounting period)	Revenue	Expenses (excl. depreciation)	Cost of Machine
1	$10 000	$7 500	$10 000
2	10 000	7 500	—
3	10 000	7 500	—
4	10 000	7 500	—
5	10 000	7 500	—
6	10 000	7 500	10 000*

*Assumed cost of a new machine.

If the cost of the machine is not regarded as a cost or expense at all for profit measurement purposes, a profit of $2 500 per annum is recorded and this obviously overstates the true profit earned. At the end of Year 5 the machine will have been used up, although it will still be recorded at $10 000 in the books of account. It will then be necessary to write it off as a capital loss, and this will have the effect of reducing proprietorship by $10 000. There will, incidentally, be a financial crisis in Year 6, when funds will have to be raised to buy a new machine (which will presumably be needed to replace the old one that has worn out). Clearly the cost of the machine has to be taken into account in measuring profit.

It is inequitable, however, to regard the cost of the asset as an expense appropriate to the year of purchase only. When the same revenue is earned and the same expenses are incurred in each of the five years, and the machine is used throughout, it is clearly a distortion of profit trends to suggest that a loss of $7 500 is incurred in Year 1 and a profit of $2 500 earned in each of the next four years.

These difficulties can be overcome by spreading the initial cost of the machine over the five years of its life, e.g. by making an annual depreciation charge of $2 000. When this additional expense is brought into account the recorded profit on each year's operations is $500, and this seems to be a reasonable interpretation of the results of the business over the whole period. By setting off the depreciation charged each year against the original cost of the machine, the net recorded value of the machine in the balance sheet is reduced year by year. At the end of Year 1, for example, the net value of the machine in the balance sheet is $10 000 less the depreciation charged ($2 000), or $8 000; at the end of Year 2 the net value is $6 000, and so on. This balance sheet value at any time represents that part of the original cost of the machine which still has to be charged against future accounting periods. At the end of Year 5 the balance sheet value of the machine will be nil, and the whole of its original cost will have been recouped. Provided they have not been used or are not required for some other purpose, funds will now be available for the replacement of the machine. It will be clear from what has been said, however, that the purpose of the depreciation charge is not to provide funds for replacement (although this result may be achieved indirectly under the conditions postulated); it is rather to prevent capital being unwittingly withdrawn for consumption by the proprietors through the understatement of expenses and the overstatement of profits.

The foregoing example has over-simplified the problem of accounting for depreciation, because the productive life of an asset is usually not precisely known in advance. Depreciation can therefore seldom be other than an estimate. To make this estimate one needs to know the original cost of the asset (C), its estimated working life in accounting periods (n), and its estimated residual or scrap value (S). Given this information, there are several methods of calculating depreciation, each depending on a different assumption, but for the time being the straight-line method will be used. (Other depreciation methods are explained in Chapter 4.)

The formula for calculating depreciation in any period by the straight-line method is $\frac{C-S}{n}$. That is to say, the depreciation charge in any period is determined by dividing the estimated number of periods of productive use into the original cost of the asset less its estimated scrap value. Under this formula, the depreciation charge is the same in each period of the asset's life. If, for example, a motor car costs $1 100, and it is expected to last five years before being sold for $100, the annual depreciation charge by the straight-line method is $\frac{\$1\ 100 - \$100}{5}$ or $200 per annum. In effect, a fixed percentage is applied to the original cost of the asset less its estimated scrap value, the percentage (which depends on the life of the asset) being given by the formula $\frac{100}{n}$ per cent (in this example $\frac{100}{5}$ or 20 per cent).

The method of recording depreciation in the accounts reflects the fact that it is only an estimate. It would be perfectly feasible to debit a depreciation expense account and to make the corresponding credit entry in the appropriate asset account, so that the balance of the asset account at any time represents the original cost of the asset less depreciation charges to date. If this course of action is taken, however, valuable information relating to the asset, namely its original cost and its accumulated depreciation charges, is not recorded in the balance sheet; only the written-down value of the asset appears, and without knowing anything about the reliability of the depreciation estimates it is difficult to say just how much this information is worth.

To overcome this difficulty and to emphasize the provisional nature of the depreciation estimate, the procedure is adopted of recording the credit entry, not in the asset account, but in another account known as the provision for depreciation or accumulated depreciation account. The asset account only records the original cost of the asset, and no other entry is made therein until such time as the asset is disposed of. In the case of the above motor car, for example, the following entry is made as a balance-day adjustment at the end of the first year (assuming the accounting period is a year, that the car was purchased at the beginning of the year, and that straight-line depreciation is appropriate):

1985			
Dec. 31	Depreciation of motor car	Dr.	$200
	Provision for depreciation of motor car	Cr.	$200
	20% on original cost ($1 100) less estimated scrap value ($100)		

The debit entry records the expense which is posted to a depreciation of motor car account, and the balance of this account is transferred to the trading account or the profit and loss account along with other costs and expenses. The provision for depreciation of motor car account, on the other hand, is a negative asset account which remains open so long as the motor car is recorded in the books, being augmented by the new provision made at the end of each subsequent accounting period. For balance sheet purposes the balance of the provision for depreciation of motor car account is deducted from the balance of the motor car account (which records the original cost of the motor car) in the following way (say, at the end of Year 2):

Motor car (at cost)	$1 100	
Less: Provision for depreciation	400	$700

Reversing entries are not made in respect of depreciation, because the balance-day adjustment itself is intended to bring about the correct cost allocation.

Although not strictly relevant to the problem of balance-day adjustments, it is convenient to consider what happens after the adjusting entries have been made in Year 5. The motor car and the provision for depreciation of motor car accounts will then contain balances of $1 100 (debit) and $1 000 (credit) respectively, and if the original estimates concerning the life of the motor car and its scrap value have proved correct the car will be sold to the second-hand dealer for $100. The balances of the motor car and the provision for depreciation of motor car accounts are then transferred (thereby closing these accounts) to a new account, the sale of motor car account, which is also credited with the cash received from the sale:

Motor Car

Balance	b/d	$1 100	Sale of motor car		$1 100

Provision for Depreciation of Motor Car

Sale of motor car		$1 000	Balance	b/d	$1 000

Sale of Motor Car

Motor car	$1 100	Provision for depreciation of motor car		$1 000
		Bank (proceeds of sale)		100
	$1 100			$1 100

The car then ceases to be recorded in the books of account. If, as is more likely, the original estimates are not exactly borne out by events, the sale of motor car account records a profit, or loss, on sale which is transferred to the profit and loss account as a non-operating profit or loss. If, for example, only $60 is realized from the sale, there is a residual debit balance of $40 in the sale of motor car account. This represents a non-operating loss which must be transferred to the profit and loss account, as illustrated below. The loss arises, in effect, because the depreciation charges during the five years' life of the asset (based on an expected scrap value of $100) have been $200 per annum when they should really have been $208 per annum, i.e. $\frac{(\$1\ 100 - \$60)}{5}$.

Sale of Motor Car

Motor car	$1 100	Provision for depreciation		
		of motor car		$1 000
		Bank (proceeds of sale)		60
		Balance	c/d	40
	$1 100			$1 100
		Profit and loss account		
Balance	b/d	$40	(loss on sale of motor car)		$40

Separate depreciation and provision for depreciation accounts need to be maintained for each class of asset. If a system of control accounts is employed, the detailed accounts may be incorporated in a form of subsidiary ledger, known as a *fixed asset register*. This records, in respect of each asset, financial information including initial cost, the basis of providing for depreciation and the provisions made, and profit or loss resulting from proceeds of sale or disposal, as well as a physical description (serial number, type, model, name of supplier, etc.) and such information as is needed for insurance and taxation purposes. The financial section of the fixed asset register enables the register to be used as a subsidiary ledger controlled by summary accounts for fixed capital assets and depreciation provisions in the general ledger.

Depreciation expense must in any case be classified under appropriate functional groupings. Thus if the motor car is a traveller's car the depreciation thereon needs to be included among selling expenses; depreciation on office furniture is included with administrative expenses, and so on.

Although depreciation is conventionally recorded as a balance-day adjustment, it is clear that the expense really accrues continuously throughout the accounting period. It will also be seen from the foregoing discussion that the difference between outlay on fixed capital assets and outlay on expenses is not as clear-cut as may appear at first sight; it is merely one of degree. Both fixed assets and expenses are recorded by means of debit entries in the accounts; and in a sense the debit balances in fixed asset accounts merely represent the long-term prepayment of costs and expenses, ultimately to be matched against revenue.

Provisions for Anticipated Revenue, Costs, Expenses or Losses

The final group of balance-day adjustments is concerned with the need to make allowance for anticipated revenue, costs, expenses or losses arising out of transactions in the current accounting period, where the exact values of the transactions cannot be determined at balance-day.

(a) Provision for Doubtful Debts

An example is the anticipated loss or expense arising out of non-payment of a debtor's account. Where a debt or part thereof is known to be uncollectable, e.g. because of bankruptcy, it should be written off immediately. This is done by debiting a bad debts account and crediting the debtors' ledger control account. At the same time the individual debtor's account in the (subsidiary) debtors' ledger is credited, thereby ceasing to regard the debtor's account as an asset. It is good management policy to set up a register of bad debts, in which documentary evidence of the indebtedness is retained. The entries in the general journal are shown below:

	General Ledger Dr.	General Ledger Cr.	Subsidiary Ledger
Bad debts	$x		
Debtors' ledger control		$x	
W. Williams (debtors' ledger)	Cr.		$x

At balance-day all debtors' accounts need to be scrutinized to estimate doubtful debts and a provision for doubtful debts account set up (if one has not been established previously) by means of the following entry. Suppose that it is desired to establish a provision for doubtful debts of $700:

1985			
Dec. 31	Bad debts	Dr.	$700
	Provision for doubtful debts	Cr.	$700
	Provision for doubtful debts account established		

The provision for doubtful debts is a *valuation account*, i.e. it serves the purpose of revaluing the asset represented by total debtors outstanding, giving due allowance to the probability of some debtors not meeting their financial obligations. The credit balance in the provision for doubtful debts account is recorded in the balance sheet as a deduction from debtors:

Debtors		$x
Less: Provision for doubtful debts	x	$x

It will be observed that no entry is made in the debtors' ledger control account or any debtor's account when provision is made for doubtful debts. The balance in the provision for doubtful debts account remains unaltered until the end of the next period, when it is adjusted upwards or downwards to revalue the balance of debtors outstanding at that date, the corresponding entry being in the bad debts account. Suppose it is estimated that a provision of $625 is appropriate to revalue total debtors outstanding at the end of the following period:

1986			
Dec. 31	Provision for doubtful debts	Dr.	$75
	Bad debts	Cr.	$75
	Provision for doubtful debts adjusted downwards by $75 to $625		

The balance in the bad debts account, comprising bad debts actually incurred and written off (with the corresponding credit entry in the debtors' ledger control account) during the year and the entry corresponding to the adjusting entry in the provision for doubtful debts account made at the end of the year, is transferred to the profit and loss account, and shown therein as bad debts expense (or bad and doubtful debts expense). Whether bad and doubtful debts are in the nature of losses (in which case they are recorded in the non-operating section of the profit and loss statement) or revenue offsets or expenses (in which case they are recorded as deductions from sales or, if they are regarded as expenses incurred by making finance available to debtors, as finance expenses), depends on whether they relate to debts established in past accounting periods (in which case they are non-operating), or to debts incurred during the current period, and the view taken of the nature of the loss.

In the case of a large business it is probable that statistical procedures, in addition to the individual scrutiny of significantly large accounts, will be employed to estimate doubtful debts. Thus a percentage of debtors, or of credit sales in the current period, may be regarded as doubtful on the basis of past experience and provision made accordingly. Because it is reasonable to infer that the longer a debt has been outstanding the less likely it is to be collected, an age distribution of debtors' balances may be used to facilitate the estimation of doubtful debts. In the following illustration, a separate percentage is applied to the debts outstanding in each age group in order to estimate the amount which past experience suggests is likely to be uncollectable:

Age	Debtors' Balances	Estimated Percentage Uncollectable	Provision for Doubtful Debts
	$	%	$
1-30 days	20 000	1	200
31-60 days	10 000	2	200
61-90 days	2 500	5	125
91 days-1 year	500	20	100
Over 1 year	—	100	—
	$33 000		$625

On this basis doubtful debts are estimated at $625 and provision will be made accordingly. The age schedule will incidentally help in the calculation of cash discounts allowable (see below). If debtors' balances are classified by age at the end of each month, information is also available which will facilitate the task of credit management. Changes in the age distribution over time may thus be expected to throw light on the effectiveness of credit policy and collection procedures. The age schedule of debtors' balances, and hence the provision for doubtful debts, will automatically reflect changes in economic conditions affecting the ability of debtors to meet their obligations, but under some circumstances (e.g. financial stringency affecting the building industry in the case of a firm supplying builders' hardware), it may be advisable to make additional provision for loss. In any case, large debts should be carefully scrutinized and any additional information which is available (e.g. advice to the effect that a debtor for a large amount is bankrupt) should be utilized in estimating the charge for doubtful debts.

(b) Provision for Discounts

Other anticipated expenses or losses arising out of the current period's operations may be dealt with in the same way. For example, estimated cash discounts allowable on book debts recorded in the trial balance may be brought into account by means of the following adjusting entry (since the revenue resulting from the corresponding sales has been recorded in the current period):

Discount allowed	Dr.	$x
Provision for discount allowable	Cr.	$x

Discount allowed, although sometimes regarded as an expense associated with the provision of finance to customers, is more appropriately treated as a negative item of revenue, i.e. an offset against sales revenue. Depending on the treatment adopted, the balance of the discount allowed account is transferred to the profit and loss account or the trading account. Provision for discount allowable, like provision for doubtful debts, is a negative asset and is deducted from debtors in the balance sheet.

Accountants are traditionally reluctant to bring unrealized revenue into account, but anticipated revenue arising out of the current period's operations may be provided for in the same way. Provision may thus be made for expected cash discounts receivable from creditors by debiting the provision for discount receivable account (a negative liability account, the balance of which is deducted from sundry creditors in the balance sheet) and crediting the discount received account, a revenue account.

It will be apparent that reversing entries are not made at the beginning of the new period in respect of provisions for anticipated revenue, expenses or losses. The balances of such accounts are carried forward until such time as they are needed. Thus a provision for discount receivable (or allowable) is carried forward until the anticipated discount is received (or allowed). The latter is then credited (or debited) to the provision account; because it has been recorded as revenue (or expense) in the previous period it does not affect the profit and loss account in the period in which the discount is actually received (or allowed). Likewise the balance of the provision for doubtful debts account is carried forward until such time as the debt proves uncollectable and is written off.

Discount Receivable: A Control Device

On the principle that more effective control over operations is achieved if action is taken to highlight losses, a procedure may be employed to record cash discounts receivable which is quite different from that described above. At the time of purchase, the supplier's account is credited with the full purchase price of the goods, but only the net cost (the quoted price *minus* the cash discount which is available), is debited to the purchases account. The difference is debited to an unclaimed cash discount receivable account, the balance of which at any time is a potential loss since it represents cash discounts receivable which have not so far been claimed. Thus the purchase on credit of goods priced at $200, subject to a cash discount of $2\frac{1}{2}$ per cent if payment is made within a stated period, may be recorded in the books of the purchaser as follows:

Supplier (Creditor's Account)

	Purchases and unclaimed cash discount receivable	$200

Purchases

Supplier	$195	

Unclaimed Cash Discount Receivable

Supplier	$5	

If payment is subsequently made within the discount period, the supplier's account is debited with the $195 paid, and the extinction of the debt is achieved by transferring $5 from the unclaimed cash discount receivable account:

Cash at Bank

	Supplier	$195

Supplier

Bank	$195	Purchases and unclaimed cash discount receivable	$200
Unclaimed cash discount receivable	5		
	$200		$200

Purchases

Supplier	$195	

Unclaimed Cash Discount Receivable

Supplier	$5	Supplier	$5

If, for financial or other reasons, advantage is not taken of the discount receivable, the supplier's account subsequently has to be paid in full and the amount of the loss must be transferred from the unclaimed cash discount receivable account to a cash discount lost account. At the end of the accounting period, the balance of the cash discount loss account needs to be transferred as a separate item to the profit and loss account:

Cash at Bank

		Supplier	$200

Supplier

Bank	$200	Purchases and unclaimed cash discount receivable	$200

Purchases

Supplier	$195	

Unclaimed Cash Discount Receivable

Supplier	$5	Cash discount lost	$5

Cash Discount Lost

Unclaimed cash discount receivable	$5	

The effect of adopting the above procedure is thus to record the net value of purchases as a cost, while the amount of cash discount receivable *forgone* (if any) is recorded as a loss. This method of recording cash discounts receivable assumes, in effect, that finance ought to be available to enable advantage to be taken of the discount terms (normally based on exceedingly generous interest rates).[2] It implies that a loss of discounts is due to inefficiency. It is, therefore, more likely to ensure that appropriate remedial action is taken to eliminate such losses, so that it has particular merit from the point of view of managerial control.

When cash discounts are recorded in this way, it is necessary to ensure that all cash discounts lost through failure to take advantage of the discount terms are transferred to the cash discount lost account at balance-day, so that the balance of the unclaimed

[2] Consider the following cash discount terms: 3% discount allowed on payment within 15 days and no discount allowed thereafter (the credit period is 30 days). One way of looking at the problem is to assume a loan of, say, $97 from the *purchaser* to the *vendor* 15 days after the purchase transaction, and a repayment of $100, representing principal plus interest, by the vendor to the purchaser at the end of a further 15 days. The interest on this notional transaction is about 75% p.a.

cash discount receivable account represents only amounts that may still be claimed within the discount terms. In the balance sheet, the balance of the unclaimed cash discount receivable account may then be shown as a separate deduction from creditors.

Closing Entries

When the appropriate balance-day adjustments have been made, the balances of the accounts recording revenue, costs and expenses should reflect accurately the transactions attributable to the current accounting period, and all assets and liabilities existing at the end of the period should have been brought into account. It remains to complete the book-keeping process by closing the revenue, cost, expense and loss accounts. This is done by transferring their balances to the trading and profit and loss accounts in the ledger. These 'closing entries', as they are called, are recorded in the general journal whence they are posted to the ledger. They involve, first, transferring the balance of the sales account (and other accounts, e.g. returns inward or discounts allowed, related thereto) and the cost of sales account, to the trading account:

1985			
Dec. 31	Sales	Dr.	$x
	Trading account	Cr.	$x
	Balance transferred (closing entry)		
	Trading account	Dr.	x
	Cost of sales	Cr.	x
	Balance transferred (closing entry)		

Next, the balance of the trading account, which represents gross profit on trading, is transferred to the profit and loss account along with the balances of other revenue, expense and loss accounts:

1985			
Dec. 31	Trading account	Dr.	$x
	Profit and loss account	Cr.	$x
	Gross profit for year transferred		
	Profit and loss account	Dr.	x
	Advertising	Cr.	x
	Sales staff salaries	Cr.	x
	Office salaries	Cr.	x
	...		
	...		
	...		
	Balances transferred (closing entry)*		
	Interest received	Dr.	x
	Profit and loss account	Cr.	x
	Balance transferred (closing entry)		

* In this entry the amount of the debit entry equals the sum of the credit entries. In the journal it is obviously unnecessary to record a separate debit to the profit and loss account for each expense account balance transferred thereto.

Finally, the balance of the profit and loss account, which represents net profit for the period, is transferred to a proprietorship account such as, in the case of a single proprietor, his current account. (Later it will be seen that in a multiple proprietorship such as a partnership or company the net profit is transferred to an 'appropriation account' in which its subsequent distribution is recorded.)

1985			
Dec. 31	Profit and loss account	Dr.	$x
	Proprietor's current account	Cr.	$x
	Net profit for year transferred		

The only accounts now remaining open in the ledger are the asset, liability and proprietorship accounts, which provide the information required in compiling the balance sheet. These accounts are not closed; they record the assets and financial obligations with which the business commences the next period. As stated earlier, the balance sheet, unlike the trading account and the profit and loss account, is not part of the double-entry system.

Preparation and Presentation of Final Reports

When all the adjusting and closing entries have been recorded, the way is clear for the preparation of the final accounting reports, the profit and loss statement (or income statement), the balance sheet and, at a subsequent stage, the funds statement. In this chapter, our attention will be confined to the profit and loss statement and balance sheet, leaving the special problems of the funds statement to be dealt with in Chapter 5. It is necessary to present the information contained in the profit and loss statement and the balance sheet in such a way as to highlight significant features and facilitate subsequent analysis. Obviously the classification system in use plays an important role in determining the arrangement and grouping of the information presented in the profit and loss statement and the balance sheet. The profit and loss statement is based on the information contained in the trading account and the profit and loss account and records, as separate groups, transactions relating to sales, cost of sales, functional groups of expenses and non-operating items. The balance sheet is derived from the balances of accounts remaining open in the ledger after the closing entries have been posted, and groups assets and financial obligations in accordance with their relative liquidity or permanence. The accounting reports may take either the narrative (or statement) form or the two-sided account form. The narrative form of presentation is tending to replace the two-sided form, at least insofar as the profit and loss statement is concerned, partly because the narrative form is more readily understood by laymen and partly because it assists analysis, e.g. by making it easier to include comparative figures for other accounting periods.

Summary and Illustration

The sequence of accounting operations associated with the preparation of accounting reports is thus, *first*, the preparation of the trial balance at the end of the period; *second*, the recording in the general journal and ledger of the balance-day adjustments, thereby ensuring that revenue, cost and expense accounts record all current transactions and only current transactions (transactions affecting subsequent periods being, in effect, capitalized); *third*, as a result of closing entries in the general journal, the transferring of revenue, cost and expense account balances to the summary trading account and profit and loss account in the ledger; *fourth*, on the basis of information contained in these two summary accounts and the balances of the remaining ledger accounts, the preparation of the profit and loss statement, the balance sheet and, later, the funds statement; and *fifth*, at the beginning of the new accounting period, the recording in the general journal and the ledger of the reversing entries, and the closing of the temporary asset and liability accounts established as a result of the balance-day adjustments. These procedures will now be illustrated by reference to a simple example.

At the close of the year ending 30 June 1985, the following trial balance has been extracted from the general ledger balances in the accounts of Economic Stores (J. Clapham, proprietor):

	Dr.	Cr.
Petty cash advance	$10	
Bank	793	
Debtors' control	8 749	
Provision for doubtful debts		$300
Inventory	2 727	
Shop fittings	2 000	
Provision for depreciation on shop fittings		600
Creditors' control		2 345
Capital—J. Clapham		7 500
Current account—J. Clapham	1 200	
Sales		29 336
Purchases	18 000	
Advertising	330	
Salesmen's salaries	2 473	
Shop rent	780	
Delivery expenses	649	
Office salaries	756	
Office general expenses	1 374	
Bad debts	240	
	$40 081	$40 081

Note: Assume that the reversing entry with respect to the inventory account has not been made.

Prior to preparing the final accounting reports, adjustments are to be made in respect of the following:

(a) Closing inventory, 30 June 1985	$2 140
(b) Amounts owing but unpaid at 30 June 1985:	
Salesmen's salaries	56
Office salaries	48
(c) Rent prepaid at 30 June 1985	30
(d) Depreciation on shop fittings (10% p.a. on original cost)	200
(e) Provision for doubtful debts to be increased to	400

These adjustments are recorded in the general journal and posted to general ledger accounts (which already record the balances listed in the trial balance) in the manner illustrated:

General Journal   Folio 10

			General Ledger		Sub-sidiary Ledgers
			Dr.	Cr.	
1985					
June 30	Cost of sales	511	$20 727		
	Inventory	1121		$2 727	
	Purchases	5111		18 000	
	Opening balances transferred				
	Inventory	1121	2 140		
	Cost of sales	511		2 140	
	Closing inventory as per physical stocktaking				
	Salesmen's salaries	5122	56		
	Office salaries	5131	48		
	Accrued expenses	212		104	
	Salaries accrued to 30 June 1985				
	Prepayments	1115	30		
	Shop rent	5123		30	
	Rent prepaid at 30 June 1985				
	Depreciation on shop fittings	5124	200		
	Provision for depreciation on shop fittings	122		200	
	10% p.a. on original cost				
	Bad debts	5141	100		
	Provision for doubtful debts	1114		100	
	Increased provision at 30 June 1985				
			$23 301	$23 301	

General Ledger

	Petty Cash Advance			Account No. 1111
1985				
June 30	Balance	b/d	$10	

	Bank			Account No. 1112
1985				
June 30	Balance	b/d	$793	

	Debtors' Control			Account No. 1113
1985				
June 30	Balance	b/d	$8 749	

Provision for Doubtful Debts   Account No. 1114

				1985			
				June 30	Balance	b/d	$300
					Doubtful debts	GJ10	100

Prepayments   Account No. 1115

1985			
June 30	Shop rent	GJ10	$30

Inventory   Account No. 1121

1984				1985			
June 30	Cost of sales		$2 727	June 30	Cost of sales	GJ10	$2 727
1985							
June 30	Cost of sales	GJ10	$2 140				

Shop Fittings   Account No. 121

1985			
June 30	Balance	b/d	$2 000

Provision for Depreciation on Shop Fittings   Account No. 122

				1985			
				June 30	Balance	b/d	$600
					Depreciation on shop fittings	GJ10	200

Creditors' Control   Account No. 211

				1985			
				June 30	Balance	b/d	$2 345

Accrued Expenses   Account No. 212

				1985			
				June 30	Salesmen's salaries	GJ10	$56
					Office salaries	GJ10	48

Capital—J. Clapham   Account No. 311

				1985			
				June 30	Balance	b/d	$7 500

Current Account—J. Clapham   Account No. 312

1985			
June 30	Balance	b/d	$1 200

Sales   Account No. 411

				1985			
				June 30	Balance	b/d	$29 336

Cost of Sales   Account No. 511

1985				1985			
June 30	Inventory (opening)	GJ10	$2 727	June 30	Inventory (closing)	GJ10	$2 140
	Purchases	GJ10	18 000				

Purchases   Account No. 5111

1985				1985			
June 30	Balance	b/d	$18 000	June 30	Cost of sales	GJ10	$18 000

Advertising   Account No. 5121

1985			
June 30	Balance	b/d	$330

Salesmen's Salaries   Account No. 5122

1985			
June 30	Balance	b/d	$2 473
	Accrued expenses	GJ10	56

Shop Rent   Account No. 5123

1985					1985			
June 30	Balance	b/d	$780		June 30	Prepayments	GJ10	$30

Depreciation on Shop Fittings   Account No. 5124

1985			
June 30	Prov. for depreciation on shop fittings	GJ10	$200

Delivery Expenses   Account No. 5125

1985			
June 30	Balance	b/d	$649

Office Salaries   Account No. 5131

1985			
June 30	Balance	b/d	$756
	Accrued expenses	GJ10	48

Office General Expenses   Account No. 5132

1985			
June 30	Balance	b/d	$1 374

Bad Debts   Account No. 5141

1985			
June 30	Balance	b/d	$240
	Provision for doubtful debts	GJ10	100

Trading   Account No. 61

Profit and Loss   Account No. 62

The next task is to balance the accounts and, by means of the closing journal entries, to transfer the balances of the revenue, cost and expense accounts to the trading account and the profit and loss account:

General Journal   Folio 11

| | | | General Ledger | | Sub- |
			Dr.	Cr.	sidiary Ledgers
1985					
June 30	Sales	411	$29 336		
	Trading account	61		$29 336	
	Balance transferred (closing entry)				
	Trading account	61	18 587		
	Cost of sales	511		18 587	
	Balance transferred (closing entry)				
	Trading account	61	10 749		
	Profit and loss account	62		10 749	
	Gross profit for year transferred				
	Profit and loss account	62	6 976		
	Advertising	5121		330	
	Salesmen's salaries	5122		2 529	
	Shop rent	5123		750	
	Depreciation on shop fittings	5124		200	
	Delivery expenses	5125		649	
	Office salaries	5131		804	
	Office general expenses	5132		1 374	
	Bad debts	5141		340	
	Balances transferred (closing entry)				
	Profit and loss account	62	3 773		
	Current account—J. Clapham	312		3 773	
	Net profit for year transferred				
			$69 421	$69 421	

General Ledger

Petty Cash Advance   Account No. 1111

1985				
June 30	Balance	b/d	$10	

Bank   Account No. 1112

1985				
June 30	Balance	b/d	$793	

Debtors' Control   Account No. 1113

1985				
June 30	Balance	b/d	$8 749	

Provision for Doubtful Debts   Account No. 1114

1985				1985			
June 30	Balance	c/d	$400	June 30	Balance	b/d	$300
					Doubtful debts	GJ10	100
			$400				$400
				1985			
				June 30	Balance	b/d	$400

Prepayments   Account No. 1115

1985			
June 30	Shop rent	GJ10	$30

Inventory   Account No. 1121

1985			
June 30	Cost of sales	GJ10	$2 140

Shop Fittings   Account No. 121

1985			
June 30	Balance	b/d	$2 000

Provision for Depreciation on Shop Fittings   Account No. 122

1985				1985			
June 30	Balance	c/d	$800	June 30	Balance	b/d	$600
					Depreciation on		
					shop fittings	GJ10	200
			$800				$800
				1985			
				June 30	Balance	b/d	$800

Creditors' Control   Account No. 211

				1985			
				June 30	Balance	b/d	$2 345

Accrued Expenses   Account No. 212

1985				1985			
June 30	Balance	c/d	$104	June 30	Salesmen's salaries	GJ10	$56
					Office salaries	GJ10	48
			$104				$104
				1985			
				June 30	Balance	b/d	$104

Capital—J. Clapham   Account No. 311

				1985			
				June 30	Balance	b/d	$7 500

Current Account—J. Clapham   Account No. 312

1985				1985			
June 30	Balance	b/d	$1 200	June 30	Profit and loss		
	Balance	c/d	2 573		account	GJ11	$3 773
			$3 773				$3 773
				1985			
				June 30	Balance	b/d	$2 573

Sales   Account No. 411

1985				1985			
June 30	Trading account	GJ11	$29 336	June 30	Balance	b/d	$29 336

Cost of Sales   Account No. 511

1985				1985			
June 30	Inventory			June 30	Inventory		
	(opening)	GJ10	$2 727		(closing)	GJ10	$2 140
	Purchases	GJ10	18 000		Trading account	GJ11	18 587
			$20 727				$20 727

Advertising   Account No. 5121

1985				1985			
June 30	Balance	b/d	$330	June 30	Profit and loss		
					account	GJ11	$330

Salesmen's Salaries   Account No. 5122

1985				1985			
June 30	Balance	b/d	$2 473	June 30	Profit and loss		
	Accrued expenses	GJ10	56		account	GJ11	$2 529
			$2 529				$2 529

Shop Rent   Account No. 5123

1985				1985			
June 30	Balance	b/d	$780	June 30	Prepayments	GJ10	$30
					Profit and loss		
					account	GJ11	750
			$780				$780

Depreciation on Shop Fittings   Account No. 5124

1985				1985			
June 30	Provision for			June 30	Profit and loss		
	depreciation on				account	GJ11	$200
	shop fittings	GJ10	$200				

Delivery Expenses   Account No. 5125

1985				1985			
June 30	Balance	b/d	$649	June 30	Profit and loss		
					account	GJ11	$649

Office Salaries				Account No. 5131			
1985				1985			
June 30	Balance	b/d	$756	June 30	Profit and loss		
	Accrued expenses	GJ10	48		account	GJ11	$804
			$804				$804

Office General Expenses				Account No. 5132			
1985				1985			
June 30	Balance	b/d	$1 374	June 30	Profit and loss		
					account	GJ11	$1 374

Bad Debts				Account No. 5141			
1985				1985			
June 30	Balance	b/d	$240	June 30	Profit and loss		
	Provision for doubtful				account	GJ11	$340
	debts	GJ10	100				
			$340				$340

Trading				Account No. 61			
1985				1985			
June 30	Cost of sales	GJ11	$18 587	June 30	Sales	GJ11	$29 336
	Profit and loss						
	account	GJ11	10 749				
			$29 336				$29 336

Profit and Loss				Account No. 62			
1985				1985			
June 30	Advertising	GJ11	$330	June 30	Trading account	GJ11	$10 749
	Salesmen's salaries	GJ11	2 529				
	Shop rent	GJ11	750				
	Depreciation on						
	shop fittings	GJ11	200				
	Delivery expenses	GJ11	649				
	Office salaries	GJ11	804				
	Office general						
	expenses	GJ11	1 374				
	Bad debts	GJ11	340				
	Current account						
	—J. Clapham	GJ11	3 773				
			$10 749				$10 749

This completes the recording process in the books of account so far as the current year is concerned, and it remains merely to prepare the final reports on the basis of the information contained in the trading account, the profit and loss account and the balances of the accounts recording assets, liabilities and proprietorship equity.

At the beginning of the next accounting period, the following reversing entries are recorded in the general journal and posted to the ledger accounts concerned:

General Journal   Folio 1

		General Ledger		Sub-sidiary
		Dr.	Cr.	Ledgers
1985				
July 1	Cost of sales	$2 140		
	Inventory		$2 140	
	Reversing entry			
	Accrued expenses	104		
	Salesmen's salaries		56	
	Office salaries		48	
	Reversing entry			
	Shop rent	30		
	Prepayments		30	
	Reversing entry			
		$2 274	$2 274	

Using an Eight-column Trial Balance as a Worksheet

The foregoing illustration has shown how final accounting reports may be prepared after the necessary adjusting and closing entries have been made in the general journal and the ledger. The organization of the data represented by the trial balance and the balance-day adjustments, in a form which will facilitate the preparation of the financial statements, may be conveniently carried out on a worksheet known as an eight-column trial balance. This is illustrated in Table 3—1, using the data from the example. The eight-column trial balance is particularly useful as a working paper when accounting reports need to be prepared at frequent intervals, e.g. monthly. Although management will almost certainly need such interim reports, it is not usually necessary or desirable to record month-end adjustments relating thereto in the journal and the ledger.

In preparing an eight-column trial balance the following steps need to be carried out. *First*, the ledger balances at the end of the accounting period (before making any balance-day adjustments) are recorded in the first two money columns. These constitute the trial balance and it is necessary to establish the fact of balance in the usual way. *Second*, the necessary balance-day adjustments are recorded in the third and fourth columns, introducing such additional account names as may be necessary. It will be seen that these adjustments correspond to the adjusting entries recorded on page 86; the letters in brackets refer to the adjustments listed on page 85. Double entry must be preserved in the usual way, and the two adjustment columns are totalled as a check against omissions. *Third*, the figures in the first four columns are transferred to their appropriate places in the last four columns, profit and loss statement items appearing in the fifth and sixth columns, and balance sheet items in the seventh and eighth columns. Where two amounts appear opposite an account name (as is the case with provision for doubtful debts), the aggregate amount (or the net amount in the case of one debit and one credit entry) is transposed. It will be seen that the amounts transferred to the profit and loss statement columns represent, in effect, the closing entries. *Fourth*, the profit or loss for the period is calculated as the balancing figure in the profit and loss statement columns, the corresponding entry

Table 3—1
Economic Stores
Eight-column Trial Balance, 30 June 1985

	Trial Balance		Adjustments		Profit and Loss Statement		Balance Sheet	
	Dr.	Cr.	Dr.	Cr.	Dr.	Cr.	Dr.	Cr.
Petty cash advance	$10						$10	
Bank	793						793	
Debtors' control	8 749						8 749	
Provision for doubtful debts		$300		$100(e)				$400
Shop fittings	2 000						2 000	
Provision for depreciation on shop fittings		600		200(d)				800
Creditors' control		2 345						2 345
Capital—J. Clapham		7 500						7 500
Current account—J. Clapham	1 200						1 200	
Sales		29 336				$29 336		
Purchases	18 000			18 000				
Cost of sales			$20 727	2 140(a)	$18 587			
Advertising	330				330			
Salesmen's salaries	2 473		56(b)		2 529			
Shop rent	780			30(c)	750			
Delivery expenses	649				649			
Office salaries	756		48(b)		804			
Office general expenses	1 374				1 374			
Bad debts	240		100(e)		340			
Inventory	2 727		2 140(a)	2 727			2 140	
Accrued expenses				104(b)				104
Prepayments			30(c)				30	
Depreciation on shop fittings			200(d)		200			
Net profit					3 773			3 773
	$40 081	$40 081	$23 301	$23 301	$29 336	$29 336	$14 922	$14 922

being made in the appropriate balance sheet column (whence it is taken into account in calculating proprietorship equity, being credited to the proprietor's current account in the example). *Finally*, the two balance sheet columns are totalled to ensure that they agree. The last four columns in the eight-column trial balance now provide the information which is needed in the preparation of the profit and loss statement and the balance sheet.

Presentation of Final Accounting Reports or Financial Statements

Tables 3—2 and 3—3 illustrate the form of presentation of the profit and loss statement and the balance sheet by reference to the data contained in the example. The following points should be noted:
(a) The use of clear, descriptive headings, which indicate the name of the accounting entity and the date of, or the period covered by, the report.
(b) The important role played by classification in the presentation of the reports. Both the profit and loss statement and the balance sheet reflect a scheme of classification similar to that described in Chapter 2, with the profit and loss statement emphasizing operating, non-operating and functional groupings, while the balance sheet throws light on the relative liquidity or permanence of assets and relative urgency or permanence of financial obligations. It will be seen that credit balances representing negative assets, such as provision for doubtful debts or provision for depreciation, are offset against the assets to which they relate. Note also how figures have been inset in such a way as to provide group totals.

Table 3—2
Economic Stores
Profit and Loss Statement for Year Ended 30 June 1985 (Figures for previous year in brackets)

Sales (21 299)			$29 336
Less: Cost of sales* (13 868)			18 587
Gross profit (7 431)			10 749
Less: **Selling expenses** (3 421)			
Advertising (247)	$330		
Salesmen's salaries (1 820)	2 529		
Shop rent (750)	750		
Depreciation on shop fittings (200)	200		
Delivery expenses (404)	649	$4 458	
Administrative expenses (1 346)			
Office salaries (745)	804		
Office general expenses (601)	1 374	2 178	
Finance expenses (215)			
Bad and doubtful debts (215)		340	
Total operating expenses (4 982)			6 976
Net profit (2 449)			$3 773

* In practice it may be desirable to show the composition of cost of sales, e.g. in the following manner:

Opening inventory		$2 727
Purchases		18 000
		20 727
Less: Closing inventory		2 140
		$18 587

being made in the appropriate place the balance is taken into account in retaining proprietorship equity, being credited to the proprietor's current account in the example. Finally, the two balance sheet columns are totalled to ensure that they agree. The last four columns of the twelve-column trial balance now provide the information which is needed for preparation of the profit and loss statement and the balance sheet.

Presentation of Final Accounting Reports or Financial Statements

Tables 3—2 and 3—3 illustrate the form of presentation of the profit and loss statement and the balance sheet by reference to the data contained in the example. The following points should be noted:

Table 3—3
Economic Stores
Balance Sheet as at 30 June 1985 (Figures for previous year in brackets)

Current liabilities (2 304)			
Sundry creditors (2 140)	$2 345		
Accrued expenses (164)	104		
		$2 449	
Proprietorship equity (8 106)			
Capital—J. Clapham (7 500)	7 500		
Current account — J. Clapham (606)	2 573		
		10 073	
		$12 522	

Current assets (9 010)			
Short-term financial assets (7 029)			
Petty cash (10)		$10	
Bank (483)		793	
Sundry debtors (6 836)	$8 749		
Less: Provision for doubtful debts (300)	400		
		8 349	
			$9 152
Inventory (1 960)			2 140
Prepayments (21)			30
			11 322
Non-current assets (1 400)			
Shop fittings (at cost) (2 000)	2 000		
Less: Provision for depreciation (600)	800	1 200	
			$12 522

(c) The use of the narrative form for the profit and loss statement and the two-sided form for the balance sheet. Alternatively, as stated earlier, the balance sheet could have been presented in narrative form as follows:

Assets	$x
Less: Liabilities	x
Proprietorship equity	$x

(d) The provision of comparative figures for the previous period. The usefulness of accounting reports is enhanced if figures in respect of one or more previous years are provided as a basis of comparison, and with this in view hypothetical figures for the preceding year are recorded in brackets in the profit and loss statement and the balance sheet, alongside each item in the reports. In practice such figures may conveniently be recorded in separate columns in distinctive colouring.

Discussion Questions

1 What is the significance of the accounting period in relation to the matching of costs and expenses against revenues? Does the matching approach to profit measurement necessarily imply adherence to the accounting period assumption?

2 Why is it necessary to make balance-day adjustments? Distinguish between the main kinds of balance-day adjustments and briefly examine the problems of accounting measurement associated with each.

3 Discuss the role played in profit measurement by the concept of 'matching costs with revenues', with particular reference to the major kinds of balance-day adjustments.

4 Why is it possible to record transactions involving inventories in two different ways and still derive the same figures in the profit and loss statement and the balance sheet? What assumptions underlie the two methods, and which method is likely to be most conducive to effective managerial control?

5 Explain the reason for reversing entries and indicate: (a) which balance-day adjustments give rise to reversing entries; and (b) which adjustments do not.

6 Discuss the accounting concept of depreciation with special reference to: (a) the purpose of providing for depreciation; and (b) the straight-line method of calculating and recording depreciation in the accounts.

7 Why is it necessary to record depreciation expense in the accounts? What factors are relevant in calculating depreciation charges? How does depreciation differ from other expenses? Why is the offsetting credit entry in respect of depreciation made in an account other than the appropriate asset account?

8 What is the relationship between depreciation charged in respect of an asset and the profit or loss which is recorded when it is disposed of? How would you deal with such a profit or loss (a) in the ledger, and (b) in the profit and loss statement?

9 One of the major functions of the accounting system is to provide information that may be used to facilitate managerial control over operations. With this in mind, advise on appropriate procedures for accounting for: (a) inventories; (b) debtors; and (c) cash discounts receivable.

10 (a) Why is it necessary to provide for doubtful debts?

(b) Explain how you would use an age distribution of debtors' balances to estimate the amount of the provision which should be made.

(c) Under what circumstances should charges for doubtful debts be treated as offsets to revenue? as finance expenses? as non-operating losses?

11 Are balance-day adjustments necessary in a cash accounting system, e.g. a government accounting system which records only transactions involving cash receipts or payments? Examine the relationship between balance-day adjustments and the system of accrual accounting which is normally employed by business enterprises.

12 Discuss the significance of: (a) the trial balance, (b) balance-day adjustments, and (c) closing entries, in the preparation of final accounting reports.

Exercises

1 Give general journal entries to record the following:

(a) Sale of motor car for $1 250. The car had originally cost $4 600 and the balance in the provision for depreciation account at the time of sale was $3 600.

(b) Wages accrued at balance-day, 30 June 1985, $45. Give (i) adjusting entry, (ii) reversing entry.

(c) Insurance paid in advance. $600 was paid on 1 November for the year commencing 1 December and charged to the insurance expense account. Give (i) adjusting entry, (ii) reversing entry. The balance day is 31 December.

(d) Straight-line depreciation on a motor car for month of June 1985. Motor car cost $2 500 on 1 June, and it was estimated that its resale value after four years would be $580.

(e) Cash discount receivable lost through non-payment within discount period, $2\frac{1}{2}\%$ on purchases of $500. Give entries (i) at time of purchase, (ii) at time of payment.

(f) Rates assessed by municipal council for year ending 30 September 1985, $56. The accounting period for the business ended on 30 June 1985, at which date the rates had not been paid. Give (i) adjusting entry, (ii) reversing entry.

2 (a) Illustrate, by reference to the following data, two methods of accounting for inventories (ledger accounts only are required):

Inventory, 1 January	$4 800
Purchases, 10 January	1 400
Sales, 15 January—cost	4 700
—selling price	6 100
Inventory, 31 January	1 500

(b) If a physical stocktaking at 31 January revealed that only $1 400 worth of the inventories referred to in (a) remained on hand, what inference would you draw? How would you account for the discrepancy?

3 (a) Illustrate the physical inventory and perpetual inventory methods of accounting for inventories by means of ledger entries recording the following data:

Inventory, 1 January	$1 800
Purchases, January	2 400
Sales, January—cost	3 500
—selling price	5 000
Inventory, 31 January	700

(b) Indicate how (i) cost of sales, and (ii) closing inventory would be ascertained under each method. What assumptions underlie each method, and to what extent are the assumptions valid?

(c) What action would you recommend as a means of ensuring effective control over inventories at all times?

4 At 31 December 1985, Carpet-laying Services prepared a trial balance as follows (transactions related to a six-month period):

Carpet-laying Services
Trial Balance at 31 December 1985

	Dr.	Cr.
Cash	$340	
Investments (shares in Carpet Manufacturing Ltd)	3 000	
Accounts receivable	480	
National Bank Ltd		$400
Capital—A. Persian		2 000
Current account—A. Persian	3 200	
Revenue from services		8 470
Administrative expenses	1 150	
Assistant's salary	2 700	
	$10 870	$10 870

Balance-day adjustments were necessary as follows: accrued salary, $100; accrued office rent, $50; interim dividends receivable in respect of shares for six months ending 31 December, $120; accrued interest on bank overdraft, $10; accounts receivable not yet recorded or invoiced to customers, $300.

You are required to prepare (a) an eight-column worksheet; (b) a profit and loss statement for the six months; and (c) a balance sheet as at 31 December.

5 The general ledger of Smith and Company records the following balances at the end of the firm's first year of operation, 30 September 1985:

	Dr.	Cr.
Cash	$4 000	
Debtors	11 000	
Inventory	21 400	
Land and buildings	10 000	
Equipment	24 000	
Creditors		$4 300
Capital—J. Smith		40 000
Mortgage loan		5 000
Sales		85 400
Cost of sales	43 000	
Selling expenses	14 300	
Administrative expenses	7 000	
	$134 700	$134 700

Additional information: depreciation on buildings, $500; depreciation on equipment, $2 500; interest accrued on mortgage loan, $50; accrued selling expenses, $300; prepaid administrative expenses, $150.

You are required:

    (a) to set up ledger accounts and enter therein balances at 30 September 1985;

    (b) to record balance-day adjustments in the general journal and post to the ledger;

    (c) to record closing entries in the general journal and post to the ledger;

    (d) to prepare financial statements for presentation to the proprietor;

    (e) to record reversing entries at 1 October 1985.

6 The trial balance of C.Ross at 30 April 1985 is given below:

C. Ross
Trial Balance at 30 April 1985

	Dr.	Cr.
Cash at bank	$1 261.14	
Debtors' control	176.17	
Inventory (opening)	484.98	
Shop fittings	80.00	
Creditors' control		$874.54
Sales revenue		1 426.95
Purchases	1 000.00	
Rent expense	40.00	
Advertising expense	42.00	
Office expense	20.74	
Wages expense	133.55	
Discount allowed	8.91	
Discount received		6.00
Capital—C. Ross		1 000.00
Drawings—C. Ross	60.00	
	$3 307.49	$3 307.49

You are required to set up an eight-column worksheet and after taking account of the following adjustments, complete the worksheet, make necessary entries in the general journal and the ledger, and prepare appropriate accounting reports for presentation to the proprietor, C. Ross, at the end of April:

    (a) inventory 30 April, $433.10;

    (b) advertising material still on hand, $14.50;

    (c) accrued wages, $14.30;

    (d) depreciation on shop fittings to be provided for at the rate of $1 per month.

7 The trial balance of Luxury Import Stores at 31 December 1985 is given in the following worksheet:

Luxury Import Stores
Eight-column Trial Balance, 31 December 1985

Account	Trial Balance		Adjustments		Income Statement		Balance Sheet	
	Dr.	Cr.	Dr.	Cr.	Dr.	Cr.	Dr.	Cr.
Bank	$4 310							
Debtors	4 420							
Provision for doubtful debts		$200						
Inventory, 1 January 1985	7 490							
Warehouse fittings	4 880							
Accumulated depreciation on warehouse fittings		1 464						
Creditors		6 316						
Capital—S. Liu		10 000						
Current account—S. Liu	1 360							
Sales		31 500						
Sales returns	500							
Purchases	18 330							
Purchase returns		430						
Cartage inwards	430							
Selling expenses	4 320							
Administrative expenses	3 870							
Total	$49 910	$49 910						

The following additional information is available:

(a) A bankrupt debtor's balance previously considered doubtful (and allowed for in provision for doubtful debts) is now considered uncollectable, $180.

(b) Remaining debtors' balances have been analysed by age as follows: under one month, $2 400; one to six months, $1 600; over six months, $240. Past experience suggests that these groups result in bad debts of one per cent, five per cent and 50 per cent respectively.

(c) Warehouse fittings are depreciated at the rate of 10 per cent on the straight-line method.

(d) Warehouse rent (apportioned $\frac{3}{4}$ to selling expenses and $\frac{1}{4}$ to administrative expenses) paid on 28 November for three months ending 28 February 1986, $1 200.

(e) Salaries for the last half of December (salesmen $180, office $140) have not yet been recorded or paid.

(f) Inventory at 31 December 1985, $4 720.

You are required to complete the worksheet and prepare appropriately classified financial statements for presentation to Mr Liu. In what way may the worksheet be used to facilitate the recording process in the firm's journal and ledger?

8 From the following information prepare appropriate accounting reports for the proprietor of the North Terrace Trading Company:

(a) Ledger balances as at 30 June 1985:

Petty cash advance	$10	
Bank	826	
Debtors' control	9 163	
Provision for doubtful debts		$200
Inventory, 1 July 1984	2 751	
Investments (government bonds)	1 000	
Office equipment	450	
Provision for depreciation on office equipment		90
Showroom fittings	880	
Provision for depreciation on showroom fittings		176
Creditors' control		4 504
Capital—S. Smith (1 July 1984)		6 500
Drawings—S. Smith	1 050	
Sales		27 231
Sales returns	95	
Purchases	17 063	
Purchase returns		136
Cartage inward	83	
Freight outward	169	
Sales staff salaries	2 783	
Advertising	620	
Office staff salaries	965	
Rent	450	
Lighting	56	
General office expenses	149	
Discount allowed	260	
Bad debts	69	
Discount received		25
Interest		30
	$38 892	$38 892

(b) Adjustments required:

(i)   Inventory on hand, 30 June 1985, $2 390.

(ii) Interest at 4% p.a. on government bonds has been received to 31 March 1985 only.

(iii) Amounts owing but unpaid at 30 June 1985:

Sales staff salaries	$36
Office staff salaries	30
Cartage inward	15
Rent	30

(iv) Telephone rental prepaid (included in general office expense), $9.

(v)   Depreciation is to be charged on office equipment and showroom fittings at the rate of 10 per cent per annum on cost.

(vi) Provision for doubtful debts is to be $250.

(vii) Discount of $2\frac{1}{2}$ per cent is allowed on accounts paid within 30 days, and it is desired to make provision for the payment of discount on total June sales, $2 440.

(viii) Rent and lighting are to be apportioned $\frac{7}{8}$ to selling and $\frac{1}{8}$ to administration.

9 As newly-appointed accountant to Front End Motor Repair Workshops you are proposing to recommend to the proprietor, Mr M. Dodge, that the accounting system should be modified to enable income statements and balance sheets to be presented at monthly intervals in future. Before your appointment Mr Dodge received reports only once each year after a comprehensive and time-consuming physical stocktaking. Write a report setting out the reasons for your recommendation, indicating any difficulties that are likely to be encountered in implementing it, and describing the accounting procedures that you propose in order to achieve your aims.

10 The following transactions relate to a new business established by J. Smith on 1 February. You are required to record these transactions in appropriate journals (cash receipts, cash payments, sales, cost of goods sold, purchases, general journal), post to accounts in the general ledger, accounts receivable ledger and accounts payable ledger, prepare trial balance and schedules of accounts receivable and accounts payable balances at the end of each week, and prepare an income statement and a balance sheet at the end of the fourth week:

Transactions—First Week

Feb. 1 Deposited $5 000 capital in bank
Paid January rent $200
Purchased shop fittings $1 200 for cash

2 Purchased trading inventories as follows (credit purchases):

T. Thompson	$600	
S. Stewart	450	
B. Barker	575	
G. Grace	365	
H. Howard	420	
M. Moss	785	$3 195

Credit sales (cost of goods sold $195):

J. Jackson	85	
P. Parker	20	
W. Williams	40	
N. Norton	95	
C. Carter	45	285

Cash sales (cost $590) | | 1 100 |

3 Credit sales (cost $106):

J. Jackson	40	
C. Carter	15	
W. Williams	95	150

Cash sales (cost $100) | | 140 |

4 Credit purchases:

M. Moss	283	
G. Grace	203	
H. Howard	141	
S. Stewart	290	917

Cash sales (cost $141) | | 204 |

5 Credit sales (cost $114):

J. Jackson	94	
N. Norton	43	
W. Williams	49	186

Purchase returns—M. Moss	48
Wages paid	190
Proprietor's drawings	60

Transactions—Second Week

Feb. 8	Paid advertising expenses		$24
	Credit sales (cost $140):		
	C. Carter	$48	
	N. Norton	42	
	P. Parker	115	
	R. Royce	40	
			245
9	Credit purchases:		
	B. Barker	148	
	T. Thompson	280	
	M. Moss	115	
	H. Howard	319	
			862
	Donations		10
10	Credit sales (cost $314):		
	J. Jackson	142	
	N. Norton	206	
	W. Williams	140	
			488
	Cash sales (cost $231)		410
11	Credit purchases:		
	G. Grace	213	
	T. Thompson	194	
	S. Stewart	84	
			491
12	Wages paid		190
	Proprietor's drawings		60
	Credit sales (cost $320):		
	C. Carter	145	
	P. Parker	40	
	R. Royce	89	
	N. Norton	175	
			449

Transactions—Third Week

Feb. 15	Credit purchases:		
	H. Howard	$49	
	B. Barker	180	
	M. Moss	247	
	T. Thompson	96	
			$572
	Cash sales (cost $181)		274
16	Credit sales (cost $184):		
	W. Williams	141	
	N. Norton	69	
	J. Jackson	74	
	R. Royce	38	
			322
17	Cash sales (cost $243)		324
	Paid advertising expenses		49
18	Credit sales (cost $194):		
	N. Norton	49	
	P. Parker	68	
	C. Carter	43	
	W. Williams	130	
			290
19	Cash sales (cost $284)		401
	Wages paid		190
	Proprietor's drawings		60
	Credit sales (cost $48):		
	R. Royce		81

	Transactions—Fourth Week		
Feb. 22	Credit purchases:		
	G. Grace	$143	
	S. Stewart	92	
	M. Moss	202	
	B. Barker	41	$478
	Cash sales (cost $248)		342
23	Credit sales (cost $199):		
	C. Carter	49	
	W. Williams	86	
	R. Royce	68	
	J. Jackson	104	307
24	Cash receipts:		
	J. Jackson	125	
	C. Carter	60	185
	Cash sales (cost $246)		351
	Credit sales (cost $100):		
	N. Norton	140	
	P. Parker	34	174
25	Cash payments:		
	B. Barker	575	
	G. Grace	568	
	H. Howard	420	
	Electricity Commission	43	1 606
26	Wages paid		190
	Proprietor's drawings		60
	Credit sales (cost $248):		
	R. Royce	148	
	C. Carter	48	
	W. Williams	204	400
26	Depreciation on fittings		10

Practice Set

11 You are appointed accountant of Tropical Fruit Sellers (a wholesale fruit market) by the proprietor of the business, Robinson Crusoe, who instructs you that your duties include the maintenance of the book-keeping records and the preparation of monthly accounting reports.

The books of original entry maintained by the business are the general journal, cash receipts journal, cash payments journal, sales journal, purchase journal and petty cash book (kept on the imprest system). There are three ledgers, the general ledger, debtors' ledger and creditors' ledger, the last two being controlled by control accounts in the general ledger.

The following chart of accounts illustrates the classification system in use, and the amount shown after each account title represents the balance of the account at 1 June 1985, the date of your appointment.

Enter these balances in appropriate ledger accounts, and record the transactions listed. All cash receipts are banked daily, and all cash payments except those under $2 are made by cheque. Credit terms are monthly.

Tropical Fruit Sellers
Chart of Accounts

	Balance, 1 June 1985	
	Dr.	Cr.
1 Assets		
10 Current Assets		
101 Petty cash advance	$10.00	—
102 Cash at bank	7 926.83	—
103 Debtors control	4 657.14	—
104 Provision for doubtful debts	—	$483.89
105 Provision for discount allowable	—	200.00
106 Bills receivable	385.56	—
107 Inventory	2 089.05	—
108 Prepayments	—	—
109 Accrued revenue	—	—
11 Non-current Assets		
111 Investments (Commonwealth bonds)	2 000.00	—
112 Motor truck	2 500.00	—
113 Provision for depreciation of motor truck	—	500.00
114 Store equipment	1 136.42	—
115 Provision for depreciation of store equipment	—	240.00
116 Office furniture	491.00	—
117 Provision for depreciation of office furniture	—	174.00
118 Freehold property	9 000.00	—
119 Provision for depreciation of freehold property	—	1 050.00
2 Liabilities		
20 Current Liabilities		
201 Creditors control	—	3 098.17
202 Bills payable	—	1 060.89
203 Accrued expenses	—	—
3 Proprietorship		
301 Capital—R. Crusoe	—	16 000.00
302 Current account—R. Crusoe	—	3 371.59
303 Drawings—R. Crusoe	2 200.00	—
4 Operating Revenue		
401 Sales	—	38 836.52
402 Returns inward	123.45	—
c/f	$32 519.45	$65 015.06

			b/f $32 519.45	$65 015.06
5	**Operating Expenses**			
	50	Cost of Goods Sold		
		501 Purchases	25 873.33	—
		502 Returns outward	—	284.44
		503 Buying expenses	327.12	—
		504 Freight inward	42.32	—
		505 Cost of sales	—	—
	51	Selling Expenses		
		511 Salesman's salary	1 700.00	—
		512 Motor truck running expenses	376.35	—
		513 Driver's wages	1 237.05	—
		514 Depreciation of motor truck	—	—
		515 Depreciation of store equipment	—	—
		516 Packing cases	334.00	—
		517 Trade promotion and advertising	35.20	—
		518 Sundry selling and delivery expenses	14.80	—
	52	Administration Expenses		
		521 Office salaries	1 818.00	—
		522 Printing and stationery	73.08	—
		523 Postage, telephone, telegrams	89.67	—
		524 Depreciation of office furniture	—	—
		525 Sundry administrative expenses	50.60	—
		526 Rates and land taxes	499.56	—
		527 Fire insurance	71.42	—
		528 Depreciation of freehold buildings	—	—
	53	Finance Expenses		
		531 Bad and doubtful debts	35.07	—
		532 Discounts allowed	436.30	—
		533 Discounts received	—	189.18
		534 Interest payable	15.46	—
6	**Non-operating Revenue**			
		601 Interest receivable	—	100.00
7	**Non-operating Expenses**			
		701 Donations	39.90	—
8	**Determination of Profit**			
		801 Trading account	—	—
		802 Profit and loss account	—	—
			$65 588.68	$65 588.68

Debtors' Ledger

103-1	Adams, A.	$126.94
103-2	Cooper, D.J.	398.92
103-3	Costa, S.	457.24
103-4	Harrison, K.	626.97
103-5	Keith, M.	342.48
103-6	Lawson, T.S.	178.38
103-7	McKay, T.	412.11
103-8	Nilssen, S.	1 020.47
103-9	Ozone Cafe	—
103-10	Percival, N.	—
103-11	Plaza Fruit Shop	—
103-12	Ross, M.	346.82
103-13	Wallace, N.J.	—
103-14	Young, E.	589.20
103-15	Tait, J.	157.61
		$4 657.14

Creditors' Ledger

201-1	Banana Growers' Co-operative Company	$486.32
201-2	Christopherson, S.	—
201-3	Davis, M.T.	—
201-4	Johnson, K.	267.80
201-5	Mason & Thomas	511.05
201-6	Pineapple Plantations Ltd	—
201-7	Ricci, P.	363.82
201-8	Sanderson, M.J.	—
201-9	Sherwin, S.	641.60
201-10	Watson, P.	827.58
		$3 098.17

The balance in the bills receivable account arises from a promissory note for $385.56 payable one month after sight received by Tropical Fruit Sellers from E. Young on 13 May 1985.

Assume no new non-current assets have been purchased since 1 January 1985.

System of recording to be followed: After recording transactions in the books of original entry, debtors and creditors ledgers should be posted daily, for the reason that the balance of a debtor's or creditor's account should be available at any time. Entries should not be posted to the general ledger, however, until the books of original entry have been totalled and ruled off at the end of each month. This practice reduces the risk of figures being altered in the journals after the general ledger has been posted, and helps to locate errors that may show up in the trial balance, which should be taken out immediately following the month's postings to the general ledger.

Record the following transactions for June in Tropical Fruit Sellers' books of original entry and subsidiary ledgers, and at the end of the month post the general ledger and compile a trial balance:

1985
June   1   Cheque no. 94—Petrol and oil $5.70
           Credit sales:
               Invoice no. 168—A. Adams, $230.42
                         169—S. Costa, $159.31
                         170—K. Harrison, $191.22
                         171—M. Keith, $302.22
                         172—N. Percival, $99.32
                         173—Plaza Fruit Shop, $208.39
           Petty cash disbursements: newspaper 4c, telegram 30c, fares 40c, stamps $1
       2   Cash sales: $67.41
           Credit purchases:
               Banana Growers' Co-op. Company, $217.32
               M.T. Davis, $35.49
               Mason & Thomas, $119.31
               S. Sherwin, $167.42
               P. Watson, $169.22
           Cheque no. 95—Paid freight inward, $26.75
           Cheque no. 96—Bought packing cases, $130
           Petty cash disbursement: office stationery, $1.34
       3   Credit sales:
               Invoice no. 174—D.J. Cooper, $38.32
                         175—T. S. Lawson, $178.10
                         176—T. McKay, $29.83
                         177—Ozone Cafe, $116.29
                         178—M. Ross, $36.20
                         179—N. J. Wallace, $175.20
                         180—E. Young, $263.36
       4   Cheque no. 97—Paid salesman's salary $40, driver's wages $30, office salaries $40
               (all net of tax), R. Crusoe $60
           Cheque no. 98—Purchased tax stamps with wage and salary deductions:
               salesman $10, driver $4, office staff $16
           Cash sales: $38
           Credit sales (invoice 181): J. Tait, $28.31
           Ozone Cafe returned fruit bought 3 June, $11 (credit note sent)
       7   Cheque no. 99—Petrol and oil $3.35
           Credit purchases:
               S. Christopherson, $87.91
               M. T. Davis, $125.13
               Pineapple Plantations Ltd, $407.91
               M. J. Sanderson, $129.32
           Petty cash disbursements: window cleaning $1
       8   Credit sales:
               Invoice no. 182—A. Adams, $28.32
                         183—K. Harrison, $146.93
                         184—T. McKay, $165.78
           Credit purchases:
               K. Johnson, $35.42
               Mason & Thomas, $165.10
               P. Ricci, $150.90
               S. Sherwin, $182.18
           Petty cash disbursements: office supplies 78c

June   9   Credit note received from Mason & Thomas—allowance on case of mouldy fruit purchased 29.5.1985, $11

Receipt no. 37—Cheque received from D. J. Cooper, $70.93

Credit sales:

   Invoice no. 185—M. Keith, $155.75

            186—T. McKay, $46.19

            187—N. Percival, $166.85

            188—Plaza Fruit Shop, $207.91

10   Cheque no. 100—Petrol $4

Credit purchase: peppers received from E. Young, $29.05 (establish new creditor's account)

Credit sales:

   Invoice no. 189—K. Harrison, $202.37

            190—M. Ross, $109.32

Petty cash disbursements: registered letter 20c

11   Cheque no. 101—Paid salesman's salary $40, driver's wages $30, office salaries $40 (all net of tax), R. Crusoe, $60

Cheque no. 102—Purchased tax stamps with wage and salary deductions: salesman $10, driver $4, office staff $16

Credit purchases: P. Watson, $342.27

14   Cheque no. 103—Paid advertising, $156.32

Cheque no. 104—Purchased packing cases, $65.05

Cheque no. 105—Paid advertising agent, $35

Credit purchases:

   M. T. Davis, $139.14

   S. Sherwin, $31.92

Petty cash disbursements: staff tea $1.15

15   E. Young's promissory note met at maturity and his cheque paid into bank, $385.56

Credit sales:

   Invoice no. 191—A. Adams, $174.44

            192—T. McKay, $39.95

Petty cash disbursements: stamps $1.50, telegram 35c

16   Credit sales:

   Invoice no. 193—D.J. Cooper, $67.42

            194—M. Keith, $79.41

            195—N. Percival, $159.42

Cheque no. 106—Reimbursed petty cash

17   Cheque no. 107—Petrol $4.05

Cash sales: $65.11

Credit purchases:

   Banana Growers' Co-op. Company, $159.39

   K. Johnson, $121.18

   Pineapple Plantations Ltd, $387.43

Petty cash disbursements: ink 30c, typewriter ribbons $1.20

18   Cheque no. 108—Paid salesman's salary $40, driver's wages $30, office salaries $40 (all net of tax), R. Crusoe $60

Cheque no. 109—Purchased tax stamps with wage and salary deductions: salesman $10, driver $4, office staff $16

Cheque no. 110—Donation to United Nations Appeal for Children, $21

June 21 Credit purchases:
      S. Christopherson, $151.40
      M.T. Davis, $125.19
      Mason & Thomas, $103.47
      M.J. Sanderson, $65.23
    Petty cash disbursements: fares 15c, stationery $1.40

   22 Credit sales:
      Invoice no. 196—A. Adams, $228.27
             197—K. Harrison, $203.91
             198—T.S. Lawson, $158.04
             199—Ozone Cafe, $56
    Credit purchases: S. Sherwin, $98.29
    Petty cash disbursements: biscuits for staff tea $1

   23 S. Nilssen paid $20.47 (receipt no. 38) and gave 90 days' bill for $1 000, plus interest at 4% p.a. ($9.86) in settlement of balance of account
    Credit purchases:
      S. Christopherson, $143.32
      K. Johnson, $203.10
      Pineapple Plantations Ltd, $230.50
      Mason & Thomas, $120.55
    Petty cash disbursements: newspapers 20c, fares 50c

   24 Credit sales:
      Invoice no. 200—J. Smithson (new customer), $147.90
             201—M. Keith, $98.20
             202—T. McKay, $53.43
    Petty cash disbursements: typist's notebooks, $1.25, pencils 75c

   25 Cheque no. 111—salesman's salary $40, driver's wages $30, office salaries $40 (all net of tax), R. Crusoe $60
    Cheque no. 112—Purchased tax stamps with wage and salary deductions: salesman $10, driver $4, office staff $16
    Cheque no. 113—Buying agent's commission $49

   28 Cheque no. 114—Petrol $3.70
    Receipt no. 39—T. McKay paid $401.81, allowed discount $10.30
    Receipt no. 40—J. Tait paid $153.67, allowed discount $3.94
    Cash sales: $7.12
    Credit sales:
      Invoice no. 203—D.J. Cooper, $101.15
             204—K. Harrison, $99.32
    Credit purchases:
      Banana Growers' Co-op. Company, $501.30
      S. Sherwin, $131.90
      P. Watson, $195.75
      P. Ricci, $196.82

   29 Cheque no. 115—Paid Banana Growers' Co-op. Company, $474.16, and received discount $12.16
    Cheque no. 116—Paid K. Johnson $261.11, received discount $6.69
    Cheque no. 117—Paid Mason & Thomas $487.55, received discount $12.50
    Cheque no. 118—Paid P. Ricci $354.73, received discount $9.09
    Cheque no. 119—Paid S. Sherwin $641.60
    Cheque no. 120—Paid P. Watson $827.58
    Petty cash disbursements: fares 45c, stationery 89c

June 30   Cheque no. 121—Paid City Motors $65.35 (servicing $5.35, construction of stand for canopy on truck $40, tarpaulin $20)

    Receipt no. 41—A. Adams paid $123.78, allowed discount $3.16

    Receipt no. 42—S. Costa paid $445.81, allowed discount $11.43

    Receipt no. 43—K. Harrison paid $611.29, allowed discount $15.68

    Receipt no. 44—Cheque received from E. Young $574.47, allowed discount $14.73, contra settlement $29.05

    Cheque no. 122—Reimbursed petty cash

    Credit sales:

    Invoice no. 205—A. Adams, $167.90

            206—S. Costa, $156.19

            207—T.S. Lawson, $247.92

            208—Ozone Cafe, $29.25

            209—N. Percival, $61.40

            210—Plaza Fruit Shop, $140.38

            211—M. Ross, $79.22

            212—N.J. Wallace, $102.22

            213—J. Tait, $58.30

Note: Before ruling off and posting the cash receipts and cash payments journals, check against the following bank statement, make any additional entries necessary and prepare a bank reconciliation statement:

Tropical Fruit Sellers
In Account Current with
The South Australian Bank Limited

			Dr.	Cr.	Balance
June 1	Balance Forward				$7 332.36Cr.
		66	$2.00		7 330.36Cr.
		82	2.60		7 327.76Cr.
	C/C			3 009.78	10 337.54Cr.
2		88	301.89		10 035.65Cr.
		90	455.53		9 580.12Cr.
		76	9.90		9 570.22Cr.
	CSH			67.41	9 637.63Cr.
3		94	5.70		9 631.93Cr.
		89	1 166.51		8 465.42Cr.
		91	344.92		8 120.50Cr.
		95	26.75		8 093 75Cr.
4		97	170.00		7 923.75Cr.
		98	30.00		7 893.75Cr.
	CSH			38.00	7 931.75Cr.
7		92	75.98		7 855.77Cr.
		93	55.98		7 799.79Cr.
		96	130.00		7 669.79Cr.
8		99	3.35		7 666.44Cr.
9	CHQ			70.93	7 737.37Cr.
11		101	170.00		7 567.37Cr.
		102	30.00		7 537.37Cr.
14		100	4.00		7 533.37Cr.
15	FEE		2.25		7 531.12Cr.
		103	156.32		7 374.80Cr.
16	CHQ			385.56	7 760.36Cr.
		106	8.06		7 752.30Cr.
17		107	4.05		7 748.25Cr.
	CSH			65.11	7 813.36Cr.
18		108	170.00		7 643.36Cr.
		109	30.00		7 613.36Cr.
23	CBK		6.00		7 607.36Cr.
		105	35.00		7 572.36Cr.
	CHQ			20.47	7 592.83Cr.
25		111	170.00		7 422.83Cr.
		112	30.00		7 392.83Cr.
		110	21.00		7 371.83Cr.
28	C/C			562.60	7 934.43Cr.
29		114	3.70		7 930.73Cr.
30		122	8.09		7 922.64Cr.

Explanation of abbreviations:
FEE — Bank charge for keeping account   CSH — Cash
CBK — Cheque book   CHQ — Cheques
C/C — Cash and cheques

Record the following adjustments in the books of Tropical Fruit Sellers, and close the nominal accounts by transferring their balances to the trading account and the profit and loss account (adjusting and closing entries should be posted from the general journal). Formally balance the remaining accounts in the three ledgers, and prepare final accounting reports for the six months ending 30 June 1985. The balance of the profit and loss account, representing profit for the period, and the balance of drawings account—R. Crusoe, should be transferred to current account—R. Crusoe.

Inventory, 30 June 1985: $3 861.26
Packing cases on hand, $131
Depreciation:
　Motor truck 20% p.a. on cost
　Store equipment 10% p.a. on cost
　Office furniture 10% p.a. on cost
　Freehold buildings $2\frac{1}{2}$% p.a. on cost ($7 000)
Interest 5% p.a. for 6 months receivable on Commonwealth bonds, 15 September
Fire insurance includes $52 for year ending 31 March 1986
Rates and land taxes are for 6 months ending 30 June 1985
Discount allowable: make provision for 3% discount on balances of debtors' accounts representing June sales, and offset existing provision against discounts allowed in current period
Salaries accrued—3 days at $140 per week
Provision for doubtful debts—to be raised to $550

---

4 The Financial Reports: Profit and Loss Statement and Balance Sheet (B)

This chapter deals with two sets of accounting valuation problems that are closely related to the balance day book-keeping adjustments explained in Chapter 3. Both sets of problems directly affect income measurement and asset valuation in the profit and loss statement and the balance sheet, respectively.

The first problem area is that of inventory valuation, involving the valuation of sales or issues of inventory and closing inventories, the application of the 'cost or market' rule, and the retail inventory method. The problem of valuing inventory sales or issues is of course readily evident in a perpetual inventory system, but a little reflection shows that it is also germane to periodical inventory accounting. The second set of valuation problems is concerned with the depreciation and valuation of fixed assets.

Valuation of Cost of Sales and Inventories

It has been seen that, in accounting for inventories, there are two main problems:

(a) to ascertain, for balance sheet purposes, the value of inventory unsold at the end of the accounting period; and

(b) to establish the cost of sales for the period under review, an essential step in the process of profit measurement.

The valuation of inventories for these purposes presents certain difficulties. In the first place, even under a system of historical record accounting, the concept of cost is by no means unambiguous, and cost may in fact be interpreted in several different ways. Suppose that a number of lots of a particular class of commodity has been purchased during a period, each lot at a different unit price. In these circumstances how is the cost of goods sold or issued from these lots assessed, and how is the inventory remaining on hand valued for balance sheet purposes? Suppose, for example, that 10 units are purchased on Day 1 at a price of $10 each, and five units are bought on Day 2 at a price of $13 each. If 10 units are sold on Day 3, what cost value is placed upon them in the 'sold' column of the stock card and in the entry in the general ledger debiting the cost of sales account and crediting the inventory account; and, turning to the other side of the coin, how is the remaining inventory valued?

Several methods of determining the cost of goods sold tend to be adopted in practice, depending on the kinds of inventories concerned and the assumptions that are made regarding their disposal. The most common methods are:

(a) *Identified or actual cost*: Where the commodities sold are easily recognizable, it is possible to identify each unit sold with the actual lot whence it came. The unit price of that lot is then used to determine the cost of sales. Likewise, the cost of the units remaining on hand at any time may be identified with particular lots purchased. This method of interpreting cost, which accords strictly with the original cost assumption, is known as the identified or actual cost method, and its use is naturally limited to inventories of large or valuable commodities such as motor cars and jewellery.

(b) *Weighted average cost*: More frequently, goods purchased go into bulk store and it is not possible to identify particular lots. In these circumstances it is necessary to make some assumptions regarding the movement of goods into and out of the store. One such assumption is that all goods purchased go into a common pool, the cost of different lots being averaged to determine the unit price both of goods sold and of goods remaining in stock. This method is known as the average cost method and uses a weighted average, whereby the values of the different lots purchased are taken into account in determining the average cost to be used for pricing issues. In the above example, the weighted average cost after the purchases on Day 2 is $\dfrac{\$100 + \$65}{15}$ or $11 per unit. This figure is used to determine both cost of sales and the value of unsold inventories, until such time as new purchases are made, when a new average cost figure is calculated. The method can become rather complicated if frequent purchases are made. The effect of the average cost method, it will be clear, is to smooth out fluctuations in the cost of sales and the value of unsold inventories arising out of changes in purchase price.

(c) *First-in-first-out*: Another method of pricing inventory issues, known as the first-in-first-out (or FIFO) method, assumes that goods are sold in the order in which they have been acquired. (This is a valuation assumption only and does not necessarily reflect the physical movement of goods.) Goods sold, in other words, are assumed to be those that have been in stock the longest time, while goods still on hand are assumed to be those that have been most recently purchased. In the above example, the 10 units sold on Day 3 are assumed by the FIFO method to be the 10 units purchased on Day 1, so that the cost of goods sold is $10 per unit; while the unsold inventories, which are assumed to be those purchased on Day 2, are valued at $13 per unit. This method of pricing inventory issues assumes special importance when prices rise or fall continuously over a period. Under such circumstances the FIFO assumption results in the balance sheet values of unsold inventories being reasonably close to current replacement prices; while cost of sales, on the FIFO assumption, is lower in times of rising prices, and higher in times of falling prices, than under the average cost assumption or that of last-in-first-out (or LIFO) which will now be considered.

(d) *Last-in-first-out*: The last-in-first-out method makes the valuation assumption that goods sold are those that have been most recently acquired, and that goods still on hand are those that have been in stock the longest time. In the foregoing example, the 10 units sold on Day 3 are assumed to come from those acquired on Day 2 until they are all used up and it is assumed to be necessary to draw on the units acquired on Day 1. Thus five are issued at the cost price of Day 2's acquisitions, viz $13 per unit, and five are issued at the cost price of the goods bought on Day 1, viz. $10 per unit. The value of the five units remaining on hand is determined by reference to the cost price of the oldest units, viz. $10 per unit. When prices are rising or falling continuously over a period, the LIFO assumption gives a figure for cost of sales that approximates current replacement prices. The balance sheet values of unsold inventories are higher than under FIFO or average cost when prices are falling, and lower when prices are rising, and in a period of steadily rising or falling prices LIFO balance sheet values become progressively unrealistic in relation to current replacement prices.

Table 4—1
Pricing Inventory Issues Under Various Assumptions
Stock Card

No: 31
Description: Cement

Unit: Bag
Bin No: 3 East

Date	Ordered Order No.	Ordered Quantity	Received Invoice No.	Received Quantity	Received Price	Received Value	Sold Invoice No.	Sold Quantity	Sold Price	Sold Value	Balance Quantity	Balance Price	Balance Value
1. Weighted average cost													
Day 1				10	$10	$100					10	$10	$100
Day 2				5	13	65					15	11	165
Day 3								10	$11	$110	5	11	55
2. FIFO													
Day 1				10	$10	$100					10	$10	$100
Day 2				5	13	65					{10	10	100}
											5	13	65}
Day 3								10	$10	$100	5	13	65
3. LIFO													
Day 1				10	$10	$100					10	$10	$100
Day 2				5	13	65					{10	10	100}
											5	13	65}
Day 3								{5	$13	$65}	5	10	50
								5}	10	50}			

The effect of different assumptions on (a) cost of sales, and (b) balance sheet values, is illustrated in the stock card presented in Table 4—1. The figures which are reflected in the profit and loss statement as cost of sales, and in the balance sheet as closing inventory values, are given, in effect, in the stock card in the values of the 'sold' and 'balance' columns respectively. The following summary clearly shows the effect of the different assumptions on cost of sales and the value of unsold inventories at the end of the period when prices are rising (as in the example):

	Cost of Sales	Value of Unsold Inventory (at end of period)
Weighted average cost	$110	$55
FIFO	100	65
LIFO	115	50

Although company legislation, income tax regulations and pronouncements by professional accountancy bodies require the effects of any change in inventory valuation assumptions by an individual firm to be clearly disclosed in financial statements, the lack of uniformity between firms makes it difficult to interpret the significance, with respect to either profit measurement or balance sheet valuation, of inventory movements. Even within a single firm which adheres consistently to either the FIFO or the LIFO assumption, moreover, financial statements lack consistency. This is because, if prices are changing, it is only possible for either the profit statement or the balance sheet, but not both, to reflect the current prices of inventories. The average cost assumption produces hybrid figures the significance of which depends on the units purchased and the rate of price change. If, as will be suggested below, information about the effects of price changes needs to be recorded in the accounts, this should be done explicitly and not indirectly and haphazardly as a result of valuation assumptions.

The alternative methods of inventory valuation which have been discussed may serve satisfactorily as a means of inventory control, but for purposes of income measurement, balance sheet valuation and current operating policy, they do not meet certain important criteria of accounting information, discussed in Chapter 6. To the extent that historical record accounting continues to be used, however, it would seem desirable, both in the interest of uniformity and in order to adopt an inventory valuation assumption that is consistent with the historical record approach, for all firms to adopt the FIFO assumption. [1]

Application of 'Cost or Market' Rule

There is a further difficulty in accounting for inventories arising out of the almost universal application of the 'cost or market' rule. Under this rule, inventories are not always valued on the basis of cost, but are brought into account at market value when this is lower than cost. As usually applied, the cost or market rule means the lower of cost or net realizable value. The cost or market rule is an example of the operation of a policy of conservatism, since it implies that prospective losses on unsold inventories

[1] The Australian professional accounting standards require that costs be assigned to inventories by one or more of the following methods: identified or actual cost, weighted average cost, FIFO, and standard cost, and specifically states that the LIFO method should not be used. The LIFO method is not acceptable for income tax purposes in Australia. Standard cost is discussed in Chapter 26.

need to be taken into account before determining profit on goods that have been sold. Like other applications of accounting conservatism, the rule as normally applied distorts operating results, by failing to distinguish between cost of sales and anticipated losses on unsold inventories.

It is possible to reconcile the application of the cost or market rule with a logical method of accounting for inventory, which also accords with the historical record approach. The following example shows how this may be done. Suppose that the following accounts set out the relevant information in respect of inventory, cost of sales and sales in a particular period:

Inventory

Balance b/d	$2 000	Cost of sales	$5 500
Purchases	5 000	Balance c/d	1 500
	$7 000		$7 000
Balance b/d	$1 500		

Cost of Sales

Inventory	$5 500	

Sales

	Debtors, etc.	$10 000

Suppose further that although closing inventories are valued at $1 500 in terms of cost their estimated net realizable value is only $1 000. Provision may be made for this anticipated loss, i.e. the cost or market rule may be applied, by making the following adjusting entry:

Anticipated loss on inventory realization	Dr.	$500
Provision for anticipated loss on inventory realization	Cr.	$500

This results in the creation of two new accounts:

Anticipated Loss on Inventory Realization

Provision for anticipated loss on inventories	$500	

Provision for Anticipated Loss on Inventory Realization

	Anticipated loss on inventories	$500

The balance of the anticipated loss on inventory realization account may be transferred to the profit and loss account as a separate charge against profits, being treated as a deduction from gross profit. Strictly, however, it should be regarded as a non-realized loss and recorded in a separate non-operating section of the profit and loss account. If the former procedure is adopted the profit and loss statement takes the following form:

Profit and Loss Statement for Year Ended 31 December 1985

Sales		$10 000
Less: Cost of sales—		
Opening inventory (at cost)	$2 000	
Purchases	5 000	
	7 000	
Less: Closing inventory (at cost)	1 500	
		5 500
Gross profit		4 500
Less: Anticipated loss on inventory realization		500
Adjusted gross profit		$4 000

The balance of the provision account is carried forward and offset against inventory in the balance sheet as follows:

Balance Sheet as at 31 December 1985

Inventory (at cost)	$1 500	
Less: Provision for anticipated loss on inventory realization	500	
		$1 000

When the inventories are subsequently sold, the balance of the provision account is transferred to the profit and loss account as an adjustment to gross profit (offsetting the loss that is suffered when opening inventories are brought into account at cost), or as an item of non-operating revenue.

The adoption of the foregoing procedures means that the effects of the application of the cost or market rule are clearly disclosed both in the profit and loss statement, and in the balance sheet. In particular, the anticipated loss on unsold inventory is clearly distinguished from the cost of inventories sold.

Retail Inventory Method of Accounting for Inventories

There is another method of accounting for inventories which differs fundamentally from those already considered, and because it is frequently used by large retail stores it is worth while devoting some attention to it. This is the retail inventory, or estimated gross profit margin, method of estimating cost of sales and closing inventory values. Under this method the need to maintain detailed stock records is avoided, but original cost information cannot be used to price issues of inventory in the manner described above. Instead the cost of sales is estimated by reference to selling price. If the selling price in a retail store is always determined by adding a constant percentage mark-up to cost, then it is possible to estimate the cost of sales by deducting the gross profit margin equivalent from the value of sales. Suppose, for example, that goods are always marked up by $33 \frac{1}{3}$ per cent on cost (i.e. selling price is $133 \frac{1}{3}$ per cent of cost price). Then if sales in a given period are $10 000, the cost of sales may be estimated at $\frac{100}{133 \frac{1}{3}} \times \$10\ 000 = \$7\ 500$. The cost of closing inventory is ascertained as a residual value by deducting estimated cost of sales from the cost value of opening inventory plus purchases. The estimated closing inventory should be verified by a physical stocktaking.

It is obvious that if the retail inventory method is to be used there must be a more or less constant relationship between costs and selling prices, i.e. a reasonably constant mark-up. If the mark-up varies between departments, a separate calculation needs to be performed in respect of each department. It is possible to make allowance for special mark-ups and mark-downs, discounts to employees, etc. by keeping a record of such variations, making appropriate adjustments to the recorded value of sales in order to find the originally intended selling value, and estimating cost of sales by reference to the latter.

Suppose, for example, that a firm normally operates on a mark-up of 25 per cent; its opening inventory and purchases have been recorded in terms of cost at $2 000 and $8 000 respectively, and in terms of selling value at $2 500 and $10 000 respectively; the recorded value of sales for the period is $7 500, and special discounts or mark-downs to the value of $500 have been allowed on sales. It is clear that goods have been sold that were originally intended to have a selling value of $7 500 + $500 = $8 000, and that the $\frac{\text{cost price}}{\text{selling price}}$ relationship of $\frac{100}{125}$ or 80 per cent needs to be applied to this figure of $8 000 in order to determine the cost of sales, $6 400. The whole position is set out in the following table:

	Cost Price		Selling Price
Opening inventory b/f	$2 000		$2 500
Purchases	8 000		10 000
Inventory available for sale	10 000		12 500
Recorded sales		$7 500	
Add: Special discounts		500	
Sales at cost and intended selling value	6 400*		8 000
Closing inventory c/f	$3 600		$4 500

* $\frac{100}{125}$ x $8 000

It will be seen that, in making the above calculation, it has been assumed that the special discounts or mark-downs apply only to goods sold during the period. In most circumstances this is probably a reasonable assumption, as discounts or mark-downs are usually made only when sales are recorded (e.g. discounts to staff) or with the express intention of clearing inventories (e.g. bargain sales).

Suppose, however, that because of poor trading conditions it is decided that mark-downs are to apply both to goods sold during the period and to goods remaining on hand at the end of the period. Since goods with an intended selling value of $8 000 were sold for $7 500, inventory available for sale with an intended selling value of $12 500 would be correspondingly marked down to $\frac{7\ 500}{8\ 000}$ x $12 500 or about $11 720.

When this is compared with the cost price of inventory available for sale of $10 000, it is seen that the revised mark-up is 17.2 per cent (which becomes the mark-up that will be applied to purchases in the succeeding period). The new position is as follows:

	Cost Price	Selling Price
Opening inventory b/f	$2 000	$2 500
Purchases	8 000	10 000
Inventory available for sale	10 000	12 500
Less: Policy mark-downs	—	780
Inventory available for sale	10 000	11 720
Sales	6 400*	7 500
Closing inventory c/f	$3 600	$4 220

* $\dfrac{100}{117.2}$ x $7 500

A change in the original mark-up is more likely to be treated as permanent when the mark-up is revised upwards. In any case management doubtless knows whether revisions upwards or downwards affect only goods sold during the period or are to apply to unsold inventories at the end of the period as well, and can adopt the appropriate method for estimating cost of sales and closing inventories depending on circumstances.

The chief significance of the retail inventory method is that it facilitates managerial control and enables financial statements to be prepared easily and at frequent intervals without reference to detailed stock records. Perpetual inventories may be very difficult and costly to maintain in a large retail establishment engaged in hundreds or thousands of transactions daily.

Depreciation

The other important input item that poses a valuation problem in a system of historical record accounts is depreciation, or the cost of using fixed assets. It has already been shown that a fixed asset has the distinguishing characteristic that it is held with a view to earning revenue and in the normal course of events is not intended for resale. It was also seen that, under the historical record approach, its balance sheet valuation is not intended to measure realizable or current replacement value, but simply reflects the original cost of the asset after allowance has been made for the amounts previously absorbed into cost by way of depreciation charges.

It follows that the depreciation provision is not intended to constitute a fund for the replacement of the asset, although this result may be achieved indirectly in a time of stable prices and little technological change. If, as was suggested in Chapter 3, the original purchase of a fixed capital asset is best regarded as a cost to be allocated over the accounting periods during which the asset is used, the depreciation to be charged in any period depends on the original money cost of the asset (less any cost expected to be recovered when the asset is finally disposed of), the estimated working (or service) life of the asset, and the allocation method adopted. The original money cost of the asset is usually known, so that the valuation problem in respect of depreciation is essentially that of estimating the asset's working life and its residual or scrap value, and of determining the allocation method. The estimates depend not only on the physical capacity of the asset, but also on any obsolescence (whether technical or economic) which is expected to occur. To the extent that the depreciation charge is based on estimates of future events, in particular the expected working life of the asset and its expected scrap value, there is of course a departure from historical record and a loss of objectivity and reliability. Some allocation methods often found in practice are briefly discussed below.

Straight-line Depreciation

The estimate of the asset's working life may be made on the basis of either time or output. In Chapter 3, a method of allocating depreciation on the basis of time, called the straight-line method, was described. It was seen that the straight-line method involves spreading the original cost of the asset (less its estimated scrap value, if any) in equal instalments over the periods of the asset's expected use. Given the original cost of the asset (C), its estimated working life in accounting periods (n), and its estimated scrap value (S), the straight-line depreciation charge in any accounting period is equal to $\dfrac{C-S}{n}$. In the case of a motor car, which originally cost $1 100 and is estimated to have a scrap value of $100 at the end of its expected life of five years, the annual depreciation charge calculated by the straight-line method is $200. When the straight-line method is used the net balance sheet value (i.e. the book value) of the asset also is reduced by equal instalments; thus the book value of the motor car (original cost less accumulated provisions for depreciation) falls to $900 at the end of the first year, $700 at the end of the second year, and so on until at the end of the fifth year the book value is equal to the estimated scrap value, $100.

Reducing Balance Depreciation

A second method of accounting for depreciation on the basis of time is known as the reducing balance method. This involves writing off in each period a fixed percentage of the asset's residual book value or net balance sheet value, i.e. its original cost less accumulated provisions for depreciation representing amounts charged in previous periods. In the first period the fixed percentage is applied to the original cost of the asset (and not to original cost minus scrap value as in the case of the straight-line method) and the object is to fix the percentage at the rate that will reduce the net balance sheet value of the asset to its scrap value at the end of its estimated working life.

A little reflection will show that, given the same estimated life and scrap value, a larger percentage write-off is necessary under the reducing balance method than under the straight-line method. The reducing balance method results in greater amounts being written off in earlier years of the asset's life and smaller amounts in later years; and gives a smaller net balance sheet value until the very end of the asset's expected life, when the book value is reduced to its expected scrap value.

When the reducing balance method is used, the formula for the depreciation rate, r, may be derived as follows:

$$S = C(1 - r)^n$$
$$(1 - r)^n = S/C$$
$$1 - r = \sqrt[n]{S/C}$$
$$r = 1 - \sqrt[n]{S/C}$$

Expressed as a percentage, $\quad 100r = 100\,(1 - \sqrt[n]{S/C}\,)$

If scrap value is expected to be zero, a nominal scrap value, say $1, must be used to derive the depreciation rate.

In the example of the motor car, the required rate is approximately 38.1 per cent and the application of this rate results in the following depreciation being written off each year (figures rounded):

Year	Depreciation			Net Balance Sheet Value at End of Year			
1	38.1% of $1 100 =	419		$1 100 —	$419 =	$681	
2	38.1% of	681 =	259	681 —	259 =	442	
3	38.1% of	422 =	161	422 —	161 =	261	
4	38.1% of	261 =	99	261 —	99 =	162	
5	38.1% of	162 =	62	162 —	62 =	100	
	Total	$1 000					

It is clear that the two methods of allocating depreciation charges to accounting periods—straight-line and reducing balance—imply different assumptions concerning the time-pattern of fixed asset cost-absorption. The reducing balance method is more complicated than the straight-line method, and the arguments put forward to justify its use are usually more concerned with practical or financial considerations (e.g. minimizing tax liability) than with the allocation of depreciation on some logical accounting pattern. It is sometimes claimed to be an advantage to have the heaviest depreciation charge recorded in the earlier years, when the cost of repairs to the asset is presumably low, and vice versa. To the extent that the higher rate of depreciation in earlier years is based on the honest expectation that the asset will yield more services or that obsolescence will be heavier in those years, there can be an accounting justification for a reducing charge. However, if the heavier charges in earlier years are merely designed to provide for unexpected obsolescence, they suffer from the usual disadvantages of the doctrine of conservatism.

Sum of the Years' Digits Method of Depreciation

There are numerous variants of the reducing balance method, all designed to accelerate the rate of depreciation in the earlier years of the asset's life. One such method, known as the 'sum of the years' digits' method, determines the proportion to be written off each year by dividing the expected number of years' life remaining at the beginning of the year by the sum of the corresponding figures for every year of the asset's life. In the case of an asset with an expected overall life of three years, for example, the life (in years) remaining at the beginning of each year is 3, 2 and 1 respectively, a sum of 6, and the proportion of the cost of the asset (less estimated scrap value if any) to be written off is $\frac{3}{6}$ in the first year, $\frac{2}{6}$ in the second year, and $\frac{1}{6}$ in the third year. When the sum of the years' digits method is used the formula for the depreciation rate, r, may be derived as follows:

Let s be the sum of the series of consecutive natural numbers $(1, 2, \ldots, n)$, where n is the economic life in years of the asset.

$$s = \frac{n(n + 1)}{2}$$

For Year 1, $r_1 = \frac{n}{s}$

Year 2, $r_2 = \frac{n - 1}{s}$

Year t, $r_t = \frac{n - t + 1}{s}$

In general, the same considerations apply to the use of variants of the reducing balance method, such as the sum of the years' digits method, as to the use of the reducing balance method proper. To the extent that they result in arbitrary, rapid, write-offs they fail to satisfy certain important criteria of accounting information, discussed in Chapter 6.

Depreciation Based on Output or Production

Alternatively, the estimate of the asset's working life may be based on output instead of time. In the example of the motor car used above, the estimate of working life may thus be in terms of a distance travelled, say 50 000 kilometres, instead of a life of five years. The depreciation charge in each accounting period and the net balance sheet value at the end of the period then depend on the distance travelled in that period. Thus, if the distances travelled over a five-year period are 5 000, 8 000, 10 000, 15 000 and 12 000 kilometres respectively, the depreciation charges are calculated as follows (the same figures for original cost, $1 100, and estimated scrap value, $100, are assumed as previously):

Year	Distance in Kilometres	Depreciation
1	5 000	$\frac{5\ 000}{50\ 000} \times (\$1\ 100 - \$100) = \$100$
2	8 000	160
3	10 000	200
4	15 000	300
5	12 000	240
	50 000	$1 000

Where it can be applied, this method of calculating depreciation probably results in a more reasonable allocation than the time basis, although it is usually just as difficult to make accurate estimates of working life and residual scrap value.

The choice between the different methods of measuring depreciation and asset values should be made in accordance with a judgement about which method most accurately reflects the consumption or expiration of asset services. But the diversity of depreciation methods that may be adopted impairs the usefulness of financial statements. The operating results and balance sheet values of different firms lack comparability to the extent that they reflect different methods of charging depreciation.

Probability-life Approach to Depreciation

As noted above, the historical cost depreciation figure in a particular year is determined by a number of factors—the cost of the fixed asset, estimates of working (or service) life and scrap value, and the selected depreciation method. Several writers have pointed out that the use of average asset life to compute depreciation can give a bias to the charge made in individual years, compared with the figure that would result from using the entire probability distribution of possible working lives.

Suppose a machine costs $600, estimated scrap value is nil, straight-line depreciation is appropriate and estimates of possible service lives and their associated probabilities (given in parentheses) are: 1-year (0.25), 2-year (0.5) and 3-year (0.25).

If the conventional method is used, the expected or average life will be estimated at two years and the depreciation charges will be $300 in Year 1 and $300 in Year 2.

The use of the entire probability distribution of service lives will give a different depreciation pattern, as follows:

Possible Service Life	Year 1	Year 2	Year 3
1-year	$600		
2-year	300	$300	
3-year	200	200	$200

If the probabilities of the three outcomes are taken into account, the depreciation charge in Year 1 will be calculated at $600 (0.25) + $300 (0.5) + $200 (0.25) or $350. On the basis of the original probabilities, the depreciation charges will be $200 and $50 in Year 2 and Year 3 respectively.

The probability-life approach can facilitate the making of revisions to depreciation expense in the light of hindsight experience. For example, if the machine is in working condition by the end of the first year, the probabilities may be redistributed as follows: 1-year (0.0), 2-year (0.67) and 3-year (0.33). The depreciation charges then are revised to $267, $267 amd $66 in the three respective years.

Conventional methods make use of only one value, i.e. the expected or mean life, in an entire probability distribution of values and treat that figure as deterministic. They are, therefore, theoretically inferior methods of estimating the depreciation expense. For long-lived assets and for distributions of service lives in which the possible outcomes are clustered closely around the mean outcome, conventional depreciation calculations in individual years will approximate closely to measures of depreciation obtained under the probability-life approach. Where these conditions do not hold, conventional methods distort the depreciation expense and hence the measures of income and balance sheet values in the years in which the asset is employed.

References

Ijiri, Y. and Kaplan, R.S., 'Probabilistic Depreciation and Its Implications for Group Depreciation', *Accounting Review*, October 1969, pp. 743-56.

Jen, F.C. and Huefner, R.J., 'Depreciation by Probability-Life', *Accounting Review*, April 1970, pp. 290-8.

Discussion Questions

1 You have been appointed accountant in a wholesale business which trades in bicycle parts, and one of your first tasks is to install a satisfactory system of accounting for inventories. Outline the accounting procedures you would consider necessary to achieve the following general objectives:

(a) the maintenance of continuous physical and financial control over inventories;

(b) the determination of cost of goods sold as part of the process of periodic measurement, having regard to the need to distinguish between cost on the one hand and actual or anticipated losses on the other; and

(c) the valuation of inventories for balance sheet purposes, having regard to the need for disclosure of the effects of financial policies such as conservatism.

2 In accounting for inventories, what action would you take to distinguish between cost of goods sold, losses actually incurred (e.g. losses due to theft) and anticipated losses arising out of the application of the 'cost or market' rule? Briefly describe the accounting procedures you would employ, and illustrate your answer by reference to a hypothetical trading account.

3 To what extent do you consider that alternative bases of inventory valuation should be permitted in company financial statements?

4 State how each of the following bases for pricing inventories, under the economic conditions indicated, would affect:
    (a) the cost of goods sold, and
    (b) the ending inventory:

Basis	Price Level
(i) Average Cost	Rising
(ii) FIFO	Rising
(iii) LIFO	Rising
(iv) Lower of Cost or Market	Falling

5 Explain briefly what the periodic depreciation charge is supposed to represent, under the historical record accounting system.

6 Explain the rationale underlying (a) a production basis, and (b) a time basis for charging depreciation.

7 Indicate whether the following statements are true or false:
    (a) Reducing balance depreciation always results in a higher depreciation charge than straight-line depreciation.
    (b) In historical record accounting, depreciation is a process of allocation, not of valuation.
    (c) The loss on sale of a fixed asset may be regarded as an adjustment to depreciation charges previously recorded in respect of the assets.
    (d) Depreciation provides the cash needed to replace assets as they wear out.
    (e) The historical record book value of a fixed asset may be used by management as a guide to the insurance cover needed in respect of the asset.

8 In historical record accounting, what part do the following factors play in the calculation of depreciation:
    (a) the original cost of the asset;
    (b) the current replacement value of the asset;
    (c) obsolescence;
    (d) the flow of services which the asset yields;
    (e) the life of the asset;
    (f) the asset's disposal or scrap value?

9 By reference to the depreciation of fixed assets, show how the application of conservatism as an accounting doctrine may lead to the undervaluation of assets and the creation of secret reserves on the one hand, and the distortion of operating results as disclosed in the profit and loss statement on the other.

10 Examine the historical record accounting concept of depreciation with special reference to:

(a) the purposes of providing for depreciation;

(b) methods commonly used by accountants for purposes of calculating and recording depreciation in the accounts.

To what extent do you consider that the use of alternative methods of calculating depreciation may be justified?

11 Trans-Universe Airline makes the following statement in an information brochure for passengers:

Trans-Universe Aircraft Never Grow Old

They are kept as fit and new as when they left the manufacturer. During day-to-day operation, thorough checks are made before each take-off and after each landing. At regular intervals, according to a prescribed number of flying hours, each aircraft is stripped down for thorough inspection and overhaul in Trans-Universe Airline's vast workshops.

Its wings, control systems, turbines, pressurization systems, instruments, landing gear and other component parts are submitted to rigorous tests. If they are found wanting in the slightest degree, they are replaced immediately. In turn, the new parts are tested. When the aircraft is finally reassembled, extensive flight tests are undertaken before it is ready to go back into operation.

The managing director, conscious of this policy, told the airline's chief accountant that he could see no reason for making an annual depreciation charge for aircraft when, in the words of the brochure, 'they are kept as fit and new as when they left the manufacturer'. 'Since the accounts have to record the costs of maintaining them in this condition,' he argued, 'it would be double-counting to include depreciation expense as well.' As chief accountant of Trans-Universe Airline, how would you reply?

Exercises

1 A perpetual inventory stock card records the following balances:

15 units at	$1.00 each	$15
10 units at	1.10	11

If five units are sold, what would be the recorded cost of sales and the balance sheet value of the remaining inventories, assuming that issues are priced in accordance with (a) the FIFO assumption, (b) the LIFO assumption, and (c) the weighted average cost assumption?

2 By reference to hypothetical figures on perpetual inventory stock cards, contrast the effects on (a) profit measurement and (b) balance sheet valuation of the use of the following assumptions in pricing inventory issues:

(i) weighted average cost; (ii) LIFO; and (iii) FIFO.

3 (a) Record the following transactions in a perpetual inventory stock card on the FIFO assumption, in such a way as to show clearly the cost of sales and the value of closing inventories:

Jan. 15	Purchases	50 units at $1.00
16	Purchases	80 units at $1.10
18	Sales	60 units
19	Purchases	40 units at $1.20
20	Sales	80 units

(b) How would the application of the cost or market rule affect the perpetual inventory stock card?

4 A. Lamb, who sells sheepskin rugs, maintains perpetual inventory stock records for each grade of rug in his store and determines the cost of the rugs he sells on the basis of the first-in-first-out (FIFO) assumption.

(a) Write up a stock card to report the following transactions relating to a particular type of rug in March, 1985:

> Inventory:
> > 1   March—10 rugs which cost $5.50 each
>
> Purchases:
> > 3   March—20 rugs   at $5.00 each
> > 11 March—15 rugs   at $4.60 each
> > 23 March—18 rugs   at $4.50 each
>
> Sales:
> > 2   March— 2 rugs
> > 9   March—10 rugs
> > 14 March—10 rugs
> > 21 March—15 rugs
> > 26 March—10 rugs

(b) How would the cost of sales and the balance sheet value of closing inventories have been affected in the above situation if Lamb had used the last-in-first-out (LIFO) method of determining cost?

5 The manager of a retail enterprise desires to know, with reasonable accuracy, the results of trading activities for the month of July. A physical stocktaking is not contemplated, but the following information is available:

Inventory at 1 July, at cost	$2 250
Inventory at 1 July, at retail prices	3 150
Gross sales charged to debtors	6 250
Cash sales (net of any discount)	1 800
Returns from customers	250
Freight inwards	120
Purchases, at cost	6 730
Purchases, at retail	9 500
Selling and administration expenses	1 100
Mark-ups	350
Mark-downs	550
Discounts to staff	150

Some goods marked up are still in stock at the end of July, but all goods marked down have been sold.

Calculate by use of the retail inventory method the value at which inventory on hand at 31 July would be shown in a balance sheet as at that date, and prepare an operating statement for the month of July.

6 Clarkson Ltd purchased a motor delivery truck from Commercial Motor Co. Ltd on 1 January 1983, for $4 500. At that time, its working life was estimated at three years and its disposal value at $900. On 30 June 1985, the truck was traded in on a new vehicle for $1 200.

By means of entries in ledger accounts, record the above transactions and depreciation charges during the period 1 January 1983 to 30 June 1985. It may be assumed that the firm uses straight-line depreciation and that its accounting period is the calendar year.

7 (a) What depreciation charge would have been recorded each year if the firm in Exercise 6 had used the sum of the years' digits methods of calculating depreciation?

(b) If Clarkson Ltd had estimated the working life of the truck in Exercise 6 at 60 000 kilometres, and depreciated it on the basis of the following distances travelled, what depreciation charge would have been recorded each year?

	Kilometres
1983	20 000
1984	30 000
1985	10 000

5 The Financial Reports: Funds Statement

Subject to important limitations which will be discussed in subsequent chapters, the balance sheet of a business purports to show the financial position of the business at a point of time. Information on the changes in assets and financial obligations that have taken place in the past period can be obtained by comparing two successive balance sheets (referring to the beginning and end of the period respectively). But such a comparison will not indicate what factors have *caused* the changes. The profit and loss statement, which is often called the connecting link between the two balance sheets, is of course a statement of change. But it describes the change in only one section of the balance sheet, i.e. the change in proprietorship equity resulting from operations in the period. It does not show changes in assets, liabilities and proprietorship equity which have been occasioned by capital transactions (e.g. the sale and purchase of fixed assets), incurring or discharge of debt, or changes in proprietorship equity resulting from contributions of capital or distributions of profit.

The funds statement, on the other hand, reports on changes in *all* of the balance sheet items, both from operations (as revealed in the profit and loss statement) and from other causes. The funds statement thus complements the profit and loss statement and the balance sheet, and in a sense provides a link between the two statements.[1]

The Concept of Funds as Total Resources

Before the form and content of the funds statement and the procedures involved in its preparation are examined, it is necessary to consider the nature of the funds concept. Text-books usually devote a considerable amount of space to a discussion of the kinds of financial resources which are included in funds, so that the concept is described sometimes in terms of cash resources (implying that movements in funds represent movements in cash), sometimes in terms of liquid resources generally (implying that movements in funds represent changes in liquid resources and in the uses of liquid resources) and sometimes in terms of working capital (i.e. the excess of current assets over current liabilities). An analysis of cash flows may be expected to throw useful light on the liquidity of the business (and cash flow statements will be examined in this context in later chapters), but it fails to provide information about other movements of funds which cannot be ignored when reviewing changes in the firm's

[1] Companies in Australia and New Zealand are not required to publish a funds statement as part of their annual financial statements, although the professional accounting bodies in both countries have recommended its publication. Listed public companies in Australia must include a funds statement in their published accounts in order to comply with stock exchange regulations. In the United States of America, Opinion No. 19 issued by the Accounting Principles Board has required companies to include a 'statement of changes in the financial position' as a basic financial statement since 1971. Funds are interpreted as total resources and the statement is not required to be audited. In the United Kingdom, Statement of Standard Accounting Practice No. 10, issued by the professional accounting bodies, has required companies to publish a funds statement (funds are defined as 'net liquid funds') as part of the audited financial statements since 1976.

overall financial structure. Similar limitations attach to statements which record only flows of liquid resources or working capital. For example, the purchase of property through a long-term loan issue would not be reflected in the funds statement, if these relatively narrow views on funds were adopted. Attempts to restrict funds statement analysis to partial approaches of this kind therefore demonstrate a lack of understanding of the significance of the funds concept, which is best regarded in the light of the balance sheet notion of funds which has been developed in earlier chapters, i.e. the financial obligations associated with the total resources of the enterprise. Just as the balance sheet constitutes a record of the funds available to the enterprise at a particular point of time (its financial obligations) and the manner in which those funds are employed (the assets of the business), the funds statement provides a record of movements in funds available and funds employed during a particular period.

One difference between the balance sheet and the funds statement results from the fact that the movements in financial obligations and assets which are reported in the latter may be negative as well as positive, so that funds may become available through reductions in specific assets as well as through increases in financial obligations, while funds may be applied to reductions in financial obligations as well as to increases in assets. Quite apart from this, however, there is an important difference in the way in which the funds concept is interpreted in the two statements, and an understanding of this difference is necessary to an appreciation of the significance of the funds concept as it applies to the funds statement. The difference results from a restriction which is placed on the interpretation of the funds concept for purposes of funds statement analysis but which does not operate in relation to the balance sheet. Movements in funds as reported in the funds statement are restricted to changes in financial obligations and assets *which result from external transactions of the enterprise.* It has been seen that this is not necessarily true of the balance sheet, which takes account of book entries (such as those made to record depreciation charges) which are made for internal accounting purposes and which do not record transactions between the enterprise and outside entities.

The Conventional Funds Statement

Form and Content of the Funds Statement

In its conventional form, the funds statement shows the sources of funds which have become available to the enterprise during the accounting period, and the ways in which those funds have been applied, distinguishing between the following groups:

1 *Sources of Funds*

(a) Increases in proprietorship equity resulting from:
   (i) profits earned from trading operations;
   (ii) new capital contributions by proprietors.
(b) Increases in financial obligations resulting from:
   (i) increases in long-term liabilities;
   (ii) increases in short-term (i.e. current) liabilities.
(c) Reduction in assets resulting from:
   (i) reduction in short-term financial assets;

(ii)   reduction in inventories;
(iii) reduction in long-term financial assets;
(iv)   proceeds from sale of fixed assets.

2 *Uses of Funds*

(a) Reduction in proprietorship equity resulting from:
   (i)   losses on trading operations;
   (ii) dividend payments or withdrawals of capital.
(b) Reduction in financial obligations resulting from:
   (i)   reduction in long-term liabilities;
   (ii) reduction in short-term liabilities.
(c) Increases in assets resulting from:
   (i)   increases in short-term financial assets;
   (ii)   increases in inventories;
   (iii) increases in long-term financial assets;
   (iv)   purchase of fixed assets.

Total sources of funds in any period must, of course, equal total uses of funds. Items recording changes in current assets and current liabilities, viz. 1(b) (ii), 1(c) (i), 1(c) (ii), 2(b) (ii), 2(c) (i) and 2(c) (ii), are sometimes removed from the main body of the statement and recorded in a separate schedule of working capital movements. Since (as will be seen later) working capital is measured by the difference between current assets and current liabilities, the substitution of one short-term item 'net change in working capital' for the several items recording changes in current assets and current liabilities serves to maintain the over-all balance of the funds statement. In any case the short-term sources and uses of funds should be distinguished always from the long-term items, to facilitate the use of the funds statement for financial analysis and for management planning and control.

Preparation of the Conventional Funds Statement

In order to derive the funds statement from the other accounting reports it is necessary, as a first step, to set up comparative balance sheets as at the beginning and end of the period and to record the change in each balance sheet item during the period. On the basis of this information, a simplified statement may be prepared recording, as sources of funds, increases in the book value of financial obligations and reductions in the book value of assets; and recording, as uses of funds, reductions in the book value of financial obligations and increases in the book value of assets. (Book value is defined as the balance sheet value net of provisions.) This simplified statement records only net changes in some important items, e.g. it includes profits only to the extent that they have not been distributed. It therefore requires elaboration in respect of such items with a view to recording gross rather than net movements of funds. Finally, adjustments to the simplified statement are necessary in order to eliminate the effect of book entries, such as depreciation charges, which do not record transactions between the business and outside entities.

A simple example will serve to illustrate the procedure and methods of handling some of the problems involved. Suppose that summary comparative balance sheets of Smith's Retail Store at the beginning and end of a period provide the information set out in Table 5—1, which also records profit and loss statement data for the period.

Table 5—1
Illustrative Data for Purposes of Funds Statement Preparation

Smith's Retail Store
Balance Sheets at 31 December

		Year 1984		Year 1985	Change
Short-term financial assets		$1 000		$1 000	—
Inventories		1 000		1 300	+ $300
Shop fittings	$1 000		$1 200		
Less: Provision for depreciation	100	900	200	1 000	+100
		$2 900		$3 300	+$400
Short-term liabilities		1 000		1 200	+200
Proprietor's capital account		1 000		1 100	+100
Proprietor's current account		900		1 000	+100
		$2 900		$3 300	+$400

Smith's Retail Store
Profit and Loss Statement for Year Ended 31 December 1985

Sales		$3 000
Less: Cost of sales		1 900
Gross profit		1 100
Less: Depreciation on shop fittings	$100	
Other expenses	400	
		500
Net profit		$600

Assume that, with the exception of the depreciation charge, all items recorded in the profit and loss statement record transactions with outside parties, that the increase in the shop fittings account represents purchases of new shop fittings, and that the increase in the proprietor's current account reflects the profit earned, $600, *less* proprietorship withdrawals, $500.

On the basis of the comparative balance sheets a simplified funds statement, which may be considered a first approximation to the conventional funds statement, may be prepared in the form of Table 5—2.

Table 5—2
Simplified Funds Statement: A First Approximation

Sources of funds	
Undistributed profits (increase in proprietor's current account)	$100
New capital contribution by proprietor	100
Increase in short-term liabilities	200
Total funds acquired	$400
Uses of funds	
Increase in short-term financial assets	—
Increase in inventories	300
Increase in shop fittings	100
Total funds applied	$400

This simplified statement may now be expanded in order to take account of profit and loss statement data. With the conventional approach to the problem this means substituting two items for the item 'undistributed profits'. The item 'net profit earned, $600' is recorded among the sources of funds, and the item 'proprietorship withdawals, $500' is recorded among uses of funds. It is, of course, necessary to ensure that the overall balance of the statement is maintained, and in effect this has been done by adding $500 to each section of the statement (i.e. to both the source side and the use side).

One other adjustment needs to be made to the simplified funds statement. Since the depreciation charge recorded in the profit and loss statement (and reflected in the book value of shop fittings as recorded in the balance sheet) represents a book entry which has not involved the enterprise in any movement of funds, it is necessary to eliminate the effect of this entry from the funds statement. Conventionally, this is done by adding back an item 'charge not requiring funds' to the recorded net profit figure in order to derive the total funds obtained from trading operations, and at the same time eliminating the effect of the entry on the movement in fixed assets, by ignoring the change in depreciation provisions and confining the recorded change in fixed assets to the funds involved in purchasing (or selling) such assets. In the example, this involves adding $100 to the sources of funds as a charge not requiring the use of funds, and $100 to the uses of funds by recording the cost of fixed assets purchased, $200, in lieu of the change in the book value of such assets, $100. After these adjustments have been made, the completed funds statement may be prepared in the form of Table 5—3.

Table 5—3
Funds Statement—Conventional Form

Smith's Retail Store
Funds Statement for Year Ended 31 December 1985

Sources of funds		
Net profit earned	$600	
Add back: Charge not requiring funds—depreciation	100	
Funds from trading operations		$700
New capital contribution by proprietor		100
Increase in short-term liabilities		200
Total funds acquired		$1 000
Uses of funds		
Proprietorship withdrawals		500
Increase in short-term financial assets		—
Increase in inventories		300
Purchase of shop fittings		200
Total funds applied		$1 000

Since the funds statement serves as a tool for financial analysis and planning, there can be no standard arrangement of the component items. Some users of funds statements may prefer a highly condensed report which presents a bird's eye view of the major funds flow or a focus on the change in working capital, as illustrated in Table 5—4. The change in working capital can be explained in a supporting schedule detailing changes in the individual current asset and current liability items.

Table 5—4
Funds Statement—Conventional Form (Condensed)

Smith's Retail Store
Funds Statement for Year Ended 31 December 1985

Sources of funds	
Funds from trading operations	$700
New capital contribution by proprietor	100
Total funds acquired	**$800**
Uses of funds	
Purchase of shop fittings	200
Proprietorship withdrawals	500
Increase in working capital	100
Total funds applied	**$800**

Limitations of Conventional Analysis

There are two reasons why the conventional method of preparing and presenting the funds statement is unsatisfactory for purposes of understanding and analysis. The first stems from the negative treatment which is accorded to book entries, such as charges for depreciation. In effect, such charges are allowed to reduce the recorded figure of funds obtained from profits, and are then added back to the profit figure in order to obtain the total funds derived from trading operations (see Table 5—3). The adding back of deductions which should not have been made in the first place is confusing, especially to non-accountants who are not familiar with the rationale behind the procedure. The second reason for dissatisfaction with the usual form of funds statement is that, by recording only net profits, it deals inadequately with movements in funds resulting from trading operations. If the effect of these operations on the financial structure of the enterprise is to be properly assessed, the gross flows affecting the profit and loss statement, and not merely the net results, need to be recorded in the funds statement. In a real sense it is sales revenues, and not profits, that generate funds.

The Expanded Funds Statement

Revenue and Cost Flows

Both these weaknesses in the conventional treatment of funds statements may be overcome simultaneously by recording revenue derived from external transactions as a separate item among sources of funds, and costs and expenses incurred through external transactions as a separate item among uses of funds. By this means, revenue and cost items which result from book entries are not recorded in the funds statement at any stage, but gross revenue and cost flows between the business and outside entities are recorded in full, along with the other flows affecting assets and financial obligations.

If this procedure is adopted, the funds statement may be expanded to provide information in respect of the following fund flows:

1 *Sources of Funds*

(a) revenue from sale of inventories or services;
(b) capital contributions by proprietors;
(c) increases in long-term liabilities;
(d) increases in short-term liabilities;
(e) reduction in short-term financial assets;
(f) reduction in long-term financial assets;
(g) proceeds from sale of fixed assets.

2 *Uses of Funds*

(a) costs and expenses incurred through external transactions—purchase of inventories, other expenses;
(b) withdrawal of profits or capital by proprietors;
(c) reduction in long-term liabilities;
(d) reduction in short-term liabilities;
(e) increases in short-term financial assets;
(f) increases in long-term financial assets;
(g) expenditure on fixed assets.

Purchases of inventories need to be recorded in full, thereby combining purchases included in cost of sales and purchases resulting in increased stocks. This is because costs incurred, and not costs charged against revenue in the matching process, are significant for purposes of the funds statement. Likewise, it is expenditure on fixed assets, and not the depreciation charge made for profit measurement purposes, which needs to be recorded in the funds statement.

Table 5—5 shows how the funds statement in respect of Smith's Retail Store (Table 5—3) may be recast to give effect to this classification of fund flows.

Table 5—5
Funds Statement—Expanded Form

Smith's Retail Store
Funds Statement for Year Ended 31 December 1985

Sources of funds			
Revenue from sale of inventories			$3 000
New capital contribution by proprietor			100
Increase in short-term liabilities			200
Total funds acquired			$3 300
Uses of funds			
Costs and expenses incurred through external transactions—			
Purchases of inventories—			
In cost of sales	$1 900		
Added to stocks	300	$2 200	
Other expenses		400	2 600
Withdrawals of profits by proprietor			500
Expenditure on shop fittings			200
Total funds applied			$3 300

Table 5—5 may be reconciled with Table 5—3 by considering how the item 'funds from trading operations' has been expanded in Table 5—5. It will be recalled that in Table 5—3 this item was shown as a source of funds, $700, while there was a separate item among uses of funds in respect of 'increase in inventories', $300. In Table 5—5 these two items, which record a net source of funds of $400, are expanded and combined in the two items 'revenue from sale of inventories', $3 000 (which is recorded as a source of funds), and 'costs and expenses incurred through external transactions', $2 600 (which is recorded as a use of funds), again a net source of funds of $400.

Further Application of the External Transaction Criterion to Funds Statement Analysis

The foregoing example illustrates the kinds of problems which are encountered in the preparation of funds statements, but two other transactions involving book entries are worthy of special mention. The first is the sale of fixed assets and the second is the making of provisions for anticipated revenue, costs, expenses or losses of the kind discussed in Chapter 3.

Since, as has already been emphasized, only external transactions are recorded in funds statements, only the actual proceeds derived from the sale of fixed assets are recorded as sources of funds. This means that any profits or losses resulting from the sale of fixed assets need to be ignored for purposes of the funds statement, along with the corresponding reduction in the book value of the assets concerned in the balance sheet. Such profits or losses may best be regarded as adjustments to previous depreciation provisions, resulting from the fact that such provisions were only estimates which, being based on expected scrap or disposal values that differed from the actual proceeds, proved to be wrong. Profits or losses on the sale of fixed assets, and the changes in asset values that accompany such profits or losses, are therefore omitted from the funds statement in a manner which is consistent with the treatment of depreciation. Suppose, for example, that an asset which cost $1 000, and in respect of which a depreciation provision of $500 has been accumulated, is sold for $600 cash. As a result of this transaction the book profit of $100 appears in the non-operating section of the profit and loss statement, and is reflected in undistributed profits in the balance sheet, while the book value of fixed assets is $500 lower than before and cash is $600 higher than it otherwise would have been. For purposes of the funds statement however, the profit on the sale and the reduction in the book value of the asset have no significance; the only items which need to be recorded are the proceeds derived from the sale, $600 (a source of funds) and the increase in cash, $600 (a use of funds).

If the funds statement is derived by reference to balance sheet changes as suggested on pages 133-5, the profit on sale needs to be eliminated from the recorded change in undistributed profits, and the reduction in the book value of the asset resulting from the sale needs to be eliminated from the recorded change in the book value of fixed assets. Since the sum of these two items is equal by definition to the proceeds of the sale, they may be replaced in the funds statement by the latter item without affecting the balance of the statement. The increase in cash resulting from the sale is automatically recorded in the funds statement by taking account of changes in the cash position. The sale of other assets, e.g. investments, may be dealt with in the same way as the sale of fixed assets.

In deciding on the appropriate funds statement treatment of provisions for anticipated revenue, costs, expenses or losses, the test is again the extent to which external transactions are involved. The problem may be illustrated by reference to provisions for doubtful debts. The arguments underlying two *alternative* treatments are given below.

Charges in respect of doubtful debts have the effect of reducing book profits and the net book values at which debts owing to the business are recorded in the balance sheet. Because they do not affect the legal liability of debtors for the amounts owing, there is a case for arguing that no external transaction is involved; it would follow that the charge for doubtful debts should not be recorded as an expense involving the use of funds, and that the fall in net balance sheet values resulting from the provision should not be recorded as a source of funds. Similarly with bad debts; the writing-off of bad debts does not involve any movement of external funds, even though the amount recorded as owing by particular debtors is reduced. If the writing-off of bad debts were to be interpreted as an external transaction, the amount written-off would be recorded as a use of funds like any other expense item, while the corresponding diminution in debtors would be recorded as a source of funds. It is difficult to attach a sensible meaning to such a procedure, because no funds have in fact flowed into the enterprise from the debtors concerned, and the diminution in the book value of debtors has been achieved only by earmarking revenue for the purpose.

However, there is another way of looking at the problem of bad and doubtful debts, which has the attraction of simplicity and which is not inconsistent with the use of the external transactions criterion. This is to regard bad and doubtful debts in the profit and loss statement as offsets to past external transactions which were originally (and as it turns out, wrongly) recorded as providing funds in the form of sales revenue. Likewise, reductions in the net book value of debtors resulting from charges for bad and doubtful debts may be treated as offsets to external transactions which were thought at the time (and as it turns out, wrongly) to have absorbed funds in the form of debts owing to the business. If this interpretation is adopted, only net revenue from sales (i.e. gross sales less amounts deemed to be irrecoverable as a result of charges for bad and doubtful debts) needs to be recorded as a source of funds, while the amount recorded as a use of funds may be restricted to the increase in the net book value of debtors (i.e. debtors less provision for doubtful debts). In effect, this procedure results in the elimination of irrecoverable sales from the funds statement; they are deemed not to be effective external transactions. On balance, this approach appears to be the more logical one (at least insofar as bad and doubtful debts resulting from the current period's sales are concerned) and it is adopted in the illustration that follows.

Revaluations of other assets, such as inventories or fixed assets, intended to bring the balance sheet values of the assets concerned into line with realizable values or other bases of valuation, do not meet the external transactions criterion and the effect of all such revaluations must be eliminated from the funds statement.

Provisions designed to record estimated liabilities do meet the external transaction test and need to be recorded in the funds statement. The provision made by a company for its estimated income tax liability in the current year is therefore recorded in the funds statement as a use of funds, while the corresponding increase in short-term liabilities, which results from the recognition of the income tax liability, is recorded as a source of funds. This procedure is adopted because the liability for tax accrues as soon as profits are made, so that even though the exact amount of the liability may not be known at the time the charge is recorded, the provision has the same effect as any other external transaction. The subsequent payment of tax is recorded as a source of funds (the reduction in cash) accompanied by a use of funds (the reduction in the short-term liability to the taxation authorities).

A Comprehensive Illustration

Information relating to the balance sheets as at 30 June 1984 and 1985 and the profit and loss statement for the year ended 30 June 1985 of Austral Enterprises are presented below:

Balance Sheet Items at 30 June	1984		1985	
	Dr.	Cr.	Dr.	Cr.
Sundry creditors		$6 253		$5 916
Bank overdraft		4 390		12 432
Capital—P. Rossini		30 000		40 000
Current account—P. Rossini		9 382		12 971
Petty cash advance	$25		$25	
Sundry debtors	6 537		10 975	
Provision for doubtful debts		500		1 000
Inventory	18 258		30 289	
Freehold land and buildings	4 200		4 200	
Vehicles	20 700		30 000	
Provision for depreciation of vehicles		2 745		5 570
Furniture	5 000		3 900	
Provision for depreciation of furniture		1 450		1 500
	$54 720	$54 720	$79 389	$79 389

Revenue and Expense Items for Year Ended 30 June 1985			
Sales			$105 021
Less: Cost of sales—			
Opening inventory		$ 18 258	
Purchases		90 802	
		109 060	
Closing inventory		30 289	78 771
Gross profit			26 250
Less: Administrative expenses—			
Depreciation of furniture		250	
Other expenses		6 960	
Selling expenses—			
Depreciation of vehicles		2 825	
Bad and doubtful debts		800	
Other expenses		7 876	18 711
Net operating profit			7 539
Profit from sale of furniture			50
Net profit for the year			$7 589

During the year, the proprietor, P. Rossini, had withdrawn $4 000 from his current account. Furniture which had originally cost $1 100, and on which depreciation provisions amounting to $200 had been accumulated, had been sold during the year for a profit of $50.

Table 5—6
Austral Enterprises
Worksheet for Funds Statement

	Balance Sheet Changes Dr.	Cr.	Adjusting Entries Dr.	Cr.	Funds Flow Summary Uses	Sources
Balance sheet changes:						
Sundry creditors		$8 042				$8 042
Bank overdraft		10 000				10 000
Capital account		3 589	$7 539(a) 50(b)	$4 000(c)		—
Current account*	$337				$337	—
Sundry debtors (net)	3 938				3 938	
Inventory	12 031				12 031	
Vehicles (net)	6 475		2 825(a)		9 300	
Furniture (net)		1 150	250(a) 1 100(b)	200(b) 950(b)		950
	$22 781	$22 781				
Funds from operations				10 614(a)		10 614
Profit withdrawn by proprietor			4 000(c)		4 000	
			$15 764	$15 764	$29 606	$29 606

Adjusting entries:

Funds from operations—

Net operating profit	Dr.	$ 7 539(a)
Add back:		
Depreciation—Furniture	Dr.	250(a)
Vehicles	Dr.	2 825(a)
Funds from operations	Cr.	$10 614(a)

Proceeds from sale of asset—

Proceeds from sale of furniture	Cr.	950(b)
Depreciation	Cr.	200(b)
Furniture	Dr.	1 100(b)
Profit on sale	Dr.	50(b)
Profit withdrawn by proprietor		4 000(c)

* The proprietor's current account (or retained earnings account) is always closed off in the worksheet, i.e. total debits always equal total credits for this row.

Note: Letters in parentheses are used to identify debits with corresponding credits.

The profit from the sale of furniture is merely a book profit which did not generate funds. It represents the difference between the depreciated value of the asset and the cash proceeds. The total proceeds of the sale are, of course, a source of funds. The relevant ledger accounts are shown to demonstrate how the sales proceeds and the profit (or loss) on the sale are arrived at:

Furniture			
Balance b/f	$5 000	Sale of furniture	$1 100
		Balance c/d	3 900
	$5 000		$5 000
Balance b/d	$3 900		

Provision for Depreciation of Furniture			
Sale of furniture	$200	Balance b/f	$1 450
Balance c/d	1 500	Profit and loss	250
	$1 700		$1 700
		Balance b/d	$1 500

Sale of Furniture			
Furniture	$1 100	Provision for depreciation of furniture	$200
Profit on sale	50	Cash	950
	$1 150		$1 150

Funds statements in both the conventional and expanded forms for the year ended 30 June 1985 are presented in Tables 5—7 to 5—9. A simple worksheet is illustrated in Table 5—6.

Table 5—7
Funds Statement—Conventional Form

Austral Enterprises
Funds Statement for Year Ended 30 June 1985

Sources of funds		
Net profit earned	$7 539	
Add back: Charge not requiring funds—depreciation	3 075	
Funds from trading operations		$10 614
New capital contribution by proprietor		10 000
Increase in short-term liabilities		8 042
Proceeds from sale of fixed assets		950
Total funds acquired		$29 606
Uses of funds		
Proprietorship withdrawals		4 000
Reduction in short-term liabilities		337
Increase in short-term financial assets		3.938
Increase in inventories		12 031
Purchase of vehicles		9 300
Total funds applied		$29 606

Table 5—8
Funds Statement—Conventional Form (Condensed)

Austral Enterprises
Funds Statement for Year Ended 30 June 1985

Sources of funds	
Funds from trading operations	$10 614
New capital contribution by proprietor	10 000
Proceeds from sale of fixed assets	950
Total funds acquired	**$21 564**
Uses of funds	
Proprietorship withdrawals	4 000
Purchase of vehicles	9 300
Increase in working capital*	8 264
Total funds applied	**$21 564**

* Schedule explaining increase in working capital:	
Increase in debtors	$3 938
Increase in inventories	12 031
Reduction in creditors	337
	16 306
Less: Increase in bank overdraft	8 042
Increase in working capital	$8 264

In preparing the expanded funds statement, the revenue and cost flows underlying the source of funds from operations must be separately identified, as follows:

Sales (gross)	$105 021	
Less: Bad and doubtful debts	800	$104 221
Purchases	(90 802)	
Less: Increase in inventories	12 031	(78 771)
Administrative expenses		(6 960)
Selling expenses		(7 876)
Funds from operations		$10 614

Note: Figures in parentheses are negative items.

Table 5—9 may be interpreted as follows. The table shows that the sales revenue fell short of purchases and other expenses in the period, partly on account of increased holdings in inventories. Additional capital funds introduced by the proprietor were not sufficient to meet the deficit, profit withdrawals and increased investments in debtors and fixed assets. Table 5—9 indicates that over-investment had created an illiquid situation, resulting in a substantial increase in short-term indebtedness of the business to its bankers.

Table 5—9
Funds Statement—Expanded Form

Austral Enterprises
Funds Statement for Year Ended 30 June 1985

Sources of funds			
Net revenue from sale of inventories			$104 221
New capital contribution by proprietor			10 000
Increase in short-term liabilities			8 042
Proceeds from sale of fixed assets			950
Total funds acquired			**$123 213**
Uses of funds			
Costs and expenses incurred through external transactions—			
Purchases of inventories—			
In cost of sales	$78 771		
Added to stocks	12 031		
		$90 802	
Other expenses		14 836	
			105 638
Withdrawal of profits by proprietor			4 000
Reduction in short-term liabilities			337
Increase in short-term financial assets			3 938
Purchase of vehicles			9 300
Total funds applied			**$123 213**

Summary

The significance of the funds statement in the accounting process will now be apparent. By recording the changes in financial structure that have resulted from the enterprise's trading and other activities, and at the same time indicating the reasons for those changes, it serves the dual role of an accounting report and an analytical tool. It indicates the way in which the revenue and cost flows have been reflected in changes in the financial position of the business; how capital contributions by proprietors have been applied to the reduction of liabilities or to the accumulation of assets; how purchases of inventories or fixed assets have been financed; or why changes have taken place in the liquidity position of the business as reflected in its short-term financial assets and liabilities.

There are a number of qualifications on the interpretation which may be drawn from the funds statement. The statement shows, in effect, a 'circular flow of resources'. Funds derived from a particular source contribute to the total pool of funds generated and usually cannot be separately identified and traced to a particular use. Similarly most uses draw from the general pool of funds available. Further, the analysis of the funds statement of a particular year needs to be related to the pattern of resource movements over time as well as to a complementary analysis of the other two financial reports (see Chapter 7).

If these qualifications are borne in mind, certain useful assumptions on how the business has generated and applied financial resources in past periods can be drawn, and past performance can be compared with planned performance. The use of the funds statement is, however, not confined to the analysis of historical changes in the financial structure of a business. It will be seen in a later chapter that funds statement analysis may also be used for purposes of forecasting the financial requirements of a business as part of the budgeting process.

The preparation and presentation of the accounting reports completes the more mechanical aspect of the accountant's function. Recent developments in computer technology have important implications for the recording and reporting processes of accounting, which have so far been our main concern; these will be examined in Chapters 8 and 9.

Discussion Questions

1 Contrast the funds statement and the cash flow statement, with special reference to their respective contents and their roles in the analysis of changes in a firm's financial structure.

2 By means of a *pro forma* funds statement, list the main sources and uses of funds likely to appear in the funds statement of a business enterprise. How should these items be arranged in a funds statement in which it is desired to emphasize movements in working capital?

3 What criterion may be used in deciding whether or not a transaction or event involves movements in funds and needs to be recorded in the funds statement? Consider the application of the criterion to: (a) depreciation; and (b) doubtful debts.

4 Distinguish the relevant fund flows which result from the following transactions: (a) old motor car traded in for new model; (b) first and final dividend recorded from the trustee for the creditors of a bankrupt debtor, in respect of whose debt no prior provision for loss has been made; and (c) withdrawal of goods by a proprietor for his personal use.

5 In what sense is the funds statement derived from the profit and loss statement and the balance sheet? Would it be (a) conceptually possible, and (b) practically feasible, to prepare a funds statement directly from transaction data?

6 Would it be possible for a firm's short-term financial assets to increase during a period in which it operated at a loss? What light would a funds statement throw on this situation?

7 What is the principal purpose of the funds statement and in what ways does it supplement the other main financial statements?

8 Do you consider that a statement of changes in balance sheet items between the beginning and end of the accounting period contains all the essential data on movements in funds during the period? Comment.

9 It is sometimes said that depreciation allowances constitute one of the main sources of funds available to an enterprise. Critically examine this notion of depreciation allowances as a source of funds.

10 Define 'funds' and consider the funds concept from the point of view of its significance in relation to (a) the funds statement, and (b) the balance sheet.

11 Consider, with special reference to fixed assets, inventories, revenues and expenses, some of the difficulties involved in preparing a funds statement from information contained in the published financial statements of a public company which does not present a separate funds statement.

12 It is often the rapidly growing and profitable firm, rather than the stagnating and relatively unprofitable one, which encounters financial difficulties through a shortage of working capital. How is this situation likely to be represented in the funds statement, and what remedial action is indicated?

13 The managing director of Southern Cross Enterprises Ltd complained, in his annual report to shareholders, about the high rate of company taxation; it had been necessary, he said, for the company to borrow $1 000 000 during the past year in order to meet its company tax liability. Comment.

Exercises

1 On the basis of the following information, prepare a funds statement for the North Terrace Teashop for the year ended 30 June 1985:

Balance Sheet at 30 June	1984	1985
Current assets	$100	$150
Fixed assets	750	900
	$850	$1 050
Current liabilities	250	200
Capital—T. Thomsom	600	850
	$850	$1 050

Apart from the profit earned during the period, the only transaction recorded in T. Thomson's capital account was drawings, $750.

2 The balance sheets of Widescreen Cinemas recorded the following information relating to projection equipment at the beginning and end of 1985:

	Beginning		End	
Projection equipment (at cost)	$14 500		$16 300	
Less: Provision for depreciation	3 700	$10 800	4 100	$12 200

Further enquiries reveal that equipment which had cost $2 000, and which had accumulated depreciation provisions of $1 400, was sold for $350 during the year, and that new equipment was purchased to replace it. You are required to show how the relevant fund flows would be recorded in a funds statement.

3 Prepare a funds statement for the year ended 30 June 1985 from the following information supplied by the Pacific Tiles Co.
  (a) Information from the income statement for the year ended 30 June 1985:

Sales	$56 000
Cost of goods sold	28 000
Operating expenses	10 000
Profit on sale of plant and machinery	1 000

(b) Balance sheets as at 30 June 1984 and 30 June 1985:

	1984		1985	
	Dr.	Cr.	Dr.	Cr.
Cash at bank	$20 000			$12 000
Accounts receivable	16 000		$24 000	
Inventory	32 000		36 000	
Plant and machinery	44 000		44 000	
Provision for depreciation		$20 000		16 000
Accounts payable		64 000		32 000
Capital		28 000		44 000
	$112 000	$112 000	$104 000	$104 000

(c) Plant and machinery which had cost $20 000 and had been depreciated by $12 000 was sold during the year.

4 In successive balance sheets of the Henderson Corporation, the book value of the item 'land and buildings' was $69 000 calculated as follows:

Land (at valuation) and buildings (at cost)	$103 500	
Less: Provision for depreciation on buildings	34 500	$69 000

The directors had asked the secretary (Mr Freport) to explain a substantial build-up in cash balances which had occurred during the year, and the secretary said to the accountant (Mr Deutry): 'Well, it seems clear enough that, on the basis of these figures, the explanation cannot be sought in transactions affecting buildings.' Mr Deutry was not so sure. He looked at the relevant ledger accounts (as follows) and produced figures which indicated that there had indeed been substantial movements in funds affecting land and buildings during the year. You are required to summarize these movements as they would be recorded in a funds statement.

Land and Buildings

Jan. 1	Balance b/d	$103 500	Mar. 4	Sale of buildings	$48 300
Aug. 15	Bank—new buildings	14 000	June 21	Fire loss—buildings	2 200
Nov. 1	Land revaluation reserve*	36 500	Dec. 31	Balance c/d	103 500
		$154 000			$154 000

* Book entry to record increase in market value of land.

Provision for Depreciation on Buildings

Mar. 4	Sale of buildings	$7 300	Jan. 1	Balance b/d	$34 500
June 21	Fire loss—buildings	1 400	Dec. 31	Depreciation on buildings	8 700
Dec. 31	Balance c/d	34 500			
		$43 200			$43 200

Sale of Buildings

Mar. 4	Land and buildings	$48 300	Mar. 4	Provision for depreciation	
	Profit and loss account			on buildings	$7 300
	(profit on sale)	9 000		Bank (proceeds of sale)	50 000
		$57 300			$57 300

Fire Loss—Buildings

June 21 Land and buildings	$2 200	June 21 Provision for depreciation on buildings		$1 400
		Oct. 3 Bank (settlement of claim on Insurance Underwriters Ltd)		400
		Profit and loss account (unrecouped loss from fire)		400
	$2 200			$2 200

5 S. Forbes conducts a wholesale grocery business. He asks you to explain why, despite a satisfactory profit during the year, the liquid position of the enterprise has deteriorated to the extent that a substantial bank balance at 30 June 1984 has been replaced by an overdraft at 30 June 1985.

Your investigation reveals the following information:

	Year ended 30 June 1985
Sales	$16 000
Cost of goods sold	11 500
Anticipated loss on unsold inventories	500
Selling and administrative expenses	2 000
Net profit	2 000

	As at 30 June	
	1984	1985
Bank	$3 250	(Cr.) $1 000
Debtors	5 000	6 500
Inventory	10 000	14 000
Fixed assets (at cost)	7 500	7 500
Provision for depreciation on fixed assets	750	1 000
Creditors	4 000	5 000
Proprietor's capital	21 000	21 000

You ascertained that the anticipated loss on unsold inventories represented the writing down of closing inventories, which had cost $14 500, to $14 000 as a result of flood damage in the storeroom. You are required to write a report to Forbes showing the reasons for the deterioration in the liquid position. Your report should incorporate a funds statement showing the purposes for which new funds were required and the sources of finance which became available to the firm during the year.

6 The Top Grade Cleaning Company earned an operating profit of $15 500 during the year ended 31 December 1985. The following is the income statement for that year:

Charges for cleaning services		$65 000
Less:		
Cleaners' wages	$45 000	
Cleaning materials used	1 000	
Depreciation on equipment	250	
Depreciation on motor van	750	
Office expenses	2 500	49 500
Operating profit		$15 500

Comparative financial data for the Top Grade Cleaning Company as at the end of 1984 and 1985 are shown below:

	31 December 1984		31 December 1985	
Cash	$100		$75	
Bank	1 500		2 200	
Debtors	2 500		2 400	
Inventory of cleaning materials	1 500		1 800	
Motor van	7 500		7 500	
Cleaning equipment	2 000		2 500	
Creditors		$1 250		$1 500
Loan from finance company		3 250		2 550
Accumulated depreciation on motor van		1 500		2 250
Accumulated depreciation on cleaning equipment		600		650
Capital		8 500		9 525
	$15 100	$15 100	$16 475	$16 475

During the year cleaning equipment was bought for $1 000 and old equipment was sold for $100. Prepare a funds statement for the year ended 31 December 1985.

7 Starsky and Hutchinson are partners in De Luxe Frozen Food Company. The partnership provides that all profits and losses will be shared equally. At the beginning of the financial year on 1 July 1985, the partners agreed to leave part of their current account balances in the business by increasing their agreed capital contributions to $39 000 each.

During July, new plant was purchased at a cost of $36 000. The old freezing plant was sold for cash, and realized a profit of $1 500 on the written-down value.

The following financial statements were prepared as a summary of operations for the six months ended 31 December 1985:

De Luxe Frozen Food Company
Income Statement for the Six Months Ended 31 December 1985

Revenue from sale of frozen foods		$44 000
Less: Expenses—		
Cost of goods sold	$20 000	
Wages	2 400	
Amortization of lease	3 000	
Depreciation of plant	7 200	
Electricity	750	
General expenses	675	
Repairs to machinery	525	
Water rates	300	34 850
Net operating profit		9 150
Profit on sale of freezing plant		1 500
Net profit		$10 650

Comparative Balance Sheets

	30 June 1985		31 December 1985	
Cash at bank		$5 250		$585
Accounts receivable		1 860		975
Inventory of frozen goods		3 390		3 420
Lease on premises	$9 000		$9 000	
Less: Amortization	1 500	7 500	4 500	4 500
Freehold land and buildings		45 000		45 000
Plant and machinery	30 000		48 000	
Less: Accumulated depreciation	10 800	19 200	11 100	36 900
Total assets		$82 200		$91 380
Accounts payable		3 240		3 360
Loan from finance company		—		3 000
Starsky—Capital		30 000		39 000
Current account		9 600		3 600
Hutchinson—Capital		30 000		39 000
Current account		9 360		3 420
Total equities		$82 200		$91 380

You are required to prepare a funds statement for the De Luxe Frozen Food Co. for the six months ended 31 December 1985 and to show your workings in the form of completed ledger accounts for the partners' current accounts and accounts relating to plant and machinery.

6 Assumptions, Qualitative Criteria and Standards in Historical Record Accounting

This chapter is concerned with the descriptive theory underlying the historical record accounting system that is the subject matter of Parts I and II of this book. Descriptive theory explains 'what is' (i.e. present-day accounting practice) and may be distinguished from normative theory concerned with 'what should be', which is discussed in Part III. But many of the features of the descriptive theory described below would be present also in descriptive theories of other accounting systems (in particular current purchasing power accounting and current value accounting), with certain important exceptions such as the price level assumption.

Basic Assumptions

The descriptive theory comprises *basic assumptions* and *qualitative criteria* (i.e. desirable qualities of accounting information) as well as *principles* and *standards* issued by the professional bodies. Since accounting practice is based on these assumptions, qualities and standards, which are often subjective in character and do not always correspond with reality, it is necessary to consider the limitations which they introduce into the accounting record. Basic assumptions are the building blocks of the descriptive theory. It is therefore necessary to begin by examining the effect which the assumptions have on profit measurement and balance sheet valuation. Assumptions in the first group discussed below (accounting unit, accounting period, simple monetary and continuity assumptions) are common to all accounting valuation systems; those in the second group (constant price level and original cost assumptions) are unique to historical record accounting, while those in the third group (realization and matching assumptions) belong in the historical record and current value accounting systems.

The Accounting Unit, Accounting Period, Simple Monetary and Continuity Assumptions

Some of the limiting assumptions of historical record accounting, which this system shares with other accounting valuation systems, have been mentioned briefly in previous chapters. The *accounting unit* or *accounting entity assumption*, which defines the accounting entity and emphasizes the distinction between the entity and its proprietors, is fundamental to double-entry accounting in a business enterprise, since it is necessary to record transactions between the business and its proprietors in the same way as other transactions. Likewise, the accounting period assumption, which postulates that the lifetime of the business may be broken up into arbitrary time periods, and the simple monetary assumption, which permits the recording process to be carried out in terms of the monetary unit, are necessary for the practical performance of the accounting function. Some pertinent criticisms of the latter two assumptions may be offered.

The application of the *accounting period assumption* results in the balance-day adjustments and the estimating of profits by periods. However, periodical profit measurement is difficult and involves many compromises. Since the operations of the modern business are continuous, only lifetime profit can be accurately determined, by comparing total revenues with total costs and expenses over the whole life of the enterprise. Revenues, costs and expenses for a particular period can only be estimated, so that the consequence of applying the accounting period assumption is to introduce a subjective element into the process of profit measurement. First, the periodical revenue needs to be determined and, second, costs and expenses must be matched with the revenues to which they relate, by periods. From the point of view of balance sheet valuation, the assumption likewise imposes limitations. As a result of the balance-day adjustments, certain balance sheet values are, in effect, by-products of the profit measurement process; the recorded value of funds employed thus also reflects the estimates made in assigning revenues, costs and expenses to periods. Both the profit and loss statement and the balance sheet are only partly factual; they are also partly expressions of opinion. Unfortunately the periodical estimation of profit (or some alternative measure of performance) cannot be avoided since interested parties, i.e. management, owners, creditors, etc., rely on periodical reports for their decision making.

The application of the *simple monetary assumption* means that different kinds of transactions—transactions involving different kinds of goods and services—are all recorded in terms of a common unit of measurement. This assumption is clearly necessary if there is to be any kind of systematic accounting record, but it results in certain limitations inherent in the measurement of profit and funds employed. As a result of the monetary assumption, accounting is merely a statistical approximation to reality. Heterogeneous transactions cannot be made homogeneous simply by expressing them in terms of the same unit of measurement. They retain their heterogeneity, and the accounting record is merely a financial approximation to the real flows of goods and services which are taking place.

The *continuity* (or *going concern*) *assumption* postulates indefinite continuing existence (at least up to the planning horizon) of the accounting entity and, like the other three assumptions in this group, is common to all accounting valuation systems. However, the concept is given specific interpretations in different contexts. In the context of the historical record accounting system, it is assumed that the 'going-concern' value of assets is their original cost to the business, modified in the case of fixed capital assets by allowances for depreciation. No attempt is made to estimate the current replacement or realizable values of assets, although in special circumstances (e.g. imminent or actual bankruptcy), the assumption is sometimes abandoned.

On the other hand, in a replacement cost or current cost accounting system[1] the going concern assumption is extended to postulate not only continuing existence of the entity but also the maintenance of the scale of its operations. This implies a particular capital maintenance concept, and is a normative statement advocating a particular valuation approach, i.e. one which relates to the replacement costs of assets employed in the business, or the current costs of equivalent services.

---

[1] A replacement cost or current cost system is a sub-system in current value accounting, as explained in Chapters 19 and 20.

The Constant Price Level and Original Cost Assumptions

The *constant price level* (or *extended monetary*) *assumption* highlights the most fundamental defect of historical record accounting. Whereas the simple monetary assumption is based on the use of the monetary unit as the unit of account, the extended monetary assumption postulates that the monetary unit may also be accepted as a measure of value. Accountants implicitly assume that the dollar possesses constant purchasing power; alternatively, that price level changes do not affect the financial statements significantly, or at least that when prices change they will eventually return to their original level. The constant price level assumption and the associated original cost assumption distinguish historical record accounting from accounting systems based on different approaches to the valuation problem.

The *original cost assumption* postulates that purchase transactions, and events flowing from those transactions, are to be recorded in terms of their original exchange prices. This assumption relates to transactions involving assets purchased or services acquired, costs and expenses resulting from the use of those assets or services, and financial obligations incurred as a result of the transactions. It implies that the transactions themselves, and subsequent events flowing from them, may all be recorded as factual events, the values of which are to be based on the original purchase prices paid for the assets or services.

Such an assumption is reasonably straightforward in relation to the original transactions themselves, since the values are given by the easily identified exchange prices of the transactions. But to the extent that costs and expenses reflect operations which are carried out internally within the enterprise, such as the using up of fixed capital assets or the processing of raw materials in the course of manufacture, valuation difficulties arise. These internal operations are recorded and valued on the basis of the original external transactions. It follows that the values ascribed to such costs and expenses are merely apportionments of past exchange values, so that a subjective element is introduced into the process of profit measurement and the reliability of the resulting information is open to question. There is an even more fundamental criticism. The original cost assumption, by restricting the accounting record to historical values or approximations thereto, also carries the implication that current values are ignored in the profit and loss statement and the balance sheet.

To the extent that information about current values is needed for purposes of decision-making, therefore, accounts prepared in accordance with the constant price level and original cost assumptions fail to provide information which meets the needs of decision-makers.

The Realization and Matching Assumptions

The realization and matching assumptions govern income determination in the historical record and current value accounting systems.[2] The *realization assumption* results in revenue generally being recognized at the point of sale, an objective criterion for revenue recognition since the value of assets in exchange has been determined by external transactions of the business entity itself. The assumption is a product of periodical reporting; it assigns revenue to the particular period in which a sale occurs. But this distorts reality, because the economic activity of a business

[2] Except where asset values are based on net realizable values, as in the system advocated by Professor Chambers (see Chapter 21).

enterprise is a continuous process from planning and manufacturing to sale of the finished goods and collection of the proceeds, in which all stages jointly contribute to the generation of revenue.

There is an alternative and widely held view, sometimes encountered in practice, that revenue may be recognized when the most critical function (or the last critical function when there are more than one) in the revenue earning process is performed. This critical event could occur early or late in the operating cycle. For example, where the sale of the output is certain, as in some mining and agricultural operations which are the basis of pre-determined fixed-price contracts, the critical events may be the winning of the ore and the reaping of the harvest, respectively. In the case of most industrial and commercial businesses there is no certain market for their output, and sale is generally the critical function. The critical event concept proposes the reduction of uncertainty in the revenue earning process as the criterion of revenue recognition. Thus the concept provides a rationale for recognizing revenue at the point of sale in many industrial and commercial situations, and in a few instances it provides justification for recognizing revenue at earlier stages in the operating cycle, due allowance being made for costs and expenses which still need to be incurred.

In historical record accounting, the realization assumption implies that certain external events which may be of significance or relevance to the enterprise, such as an increase in the market price of inventories on hand, are ignored. While the realization assumption is retained in a replacement cost or current cost accounting system, an important limitation—the failure to recognize an important dimension of external value changes (i.e. replacement costs)—is overcome. It is of interest to note that in a current value accounting system based on realizable (or so-called exit) values, in which assets are valued at selling price, the realization assumption is discarded entirely.

The *matching assumption* arises out of the necessity of accounting for periodical income. The assumption postulates that costs and expenses incurred in earning revenues can be charged against revenues in the period in which the revenues are recognized. For convenience, those expenses which cannot be associated directly with revenues are assigned to the periods in which the expenses are incurred. Matching embraces the important accounting principles of accrual and deferment. Accrual accounting is held to be superior to cash accounting. In the cash system only cash receipts and payments are recorded; not only are accrued items ignored but cash receipts and payments relating to other periods may, by inadvertence, be treated as income or expense of the period in which the cash flows occur. By contrast, accrual accounting recognizes revenues earned (whether received in cash or not) and expenses incurred (whether paid in cash or not) in the associated financial period. Deferment constitutes another way of looking at depreciation expense; a fixed asset is conceived of as a bundle of deferred charges, to be associated with the services it renders in each successive period of its economic life.

Unfortunately the matching principle is beset with difficulties in its application. For example, an outlay may give rise to a benefit or a loss. A loss can be defined as an expiration of value for which there is no return or compensation, and is normally written-off in the period in which the loss is discovered. Often, as with advertising, it may not be possible to distinguish clearly whether the outlay has given rise to a benefit or a loss (and so conservatism counsels writing-off the outlay immediately).

Where an outlay gives rise to a future benefit or a series of future benefits, the expense normally is capitalized and carried forward to be matched against future revenues. Departures from this principle are encountered widely, e.g. where it is not possible to measure objectively the future benefits, or there are tax advantages in writing-off the total outlay in the period in which the outlay takes place. Examples are found in the practice of the immediate charging, as expenses, of advertising and research and development outlays.

There is a more fundamental criticism. Matching involves an allocation procedure which is arbitrary in nature and often cannot be justified, as discussed below.

The Allocation Problem

The earning of revenue is a joint process attributable to all stages in the operating cycle, including purchasing, handling and storage of materials, production, advertising, sales, collection of proceeds, after-sales services and a variety of administrative functions. For convenience, revenue is reported as earned at one point (or a number of points) in the operating process. The measurement of periodical revenue is thus a case of arbitrary allocation, in the sense that no single allocation method can be justified as the *only* proper allocation method.

Thomas has argued that the entire matching process may also be seen as one of allocation. Some examples of the arbitrary nature of allocations in accounting are given below. Consider a simplistic situation in which an asset is purchased for x and has an expected life of three years, and expected sales of the output from use of the asset are valued at a, b and c, respectively. As explained above, revenue recognition on sale of the output is itself arbitrary. In order to match associated costs with revenue in each period, some accountants would favour relating the annual depreciation charge in some systematic manner to the pattern of revenues. But the depreciation problem is similar to a joint cost problem,[3] and there is no way of identifying the relationship, on a period by period basis, between the consumption of services flowing from an asset and the quantity or value of the output which results from its use. To put the problem in another way, the periodical flow of asset services is immeasurable, and it is impossible to determine the pattern of depreciation charges by reference to an unambiguous theory of depreciation based on the consumption of asset services. Thus depreciation expense by its very nature is arbitrarily determined.[4]

There is a further difficulty. In real life situations the asset (e.g. a machine in a factory) is likely to be part of a complex of assets. Interaction between several assets is present in most production processes. The gross revenues from sale of the output are attributable to the joint use of the assets, and it is not possible to allocate the revenues to individual production units, except in arbitrary fashion; this is another illustration of a joint cost problem.

Similar problems occur with other transactions, e.g. when expenses of a large advertising campaign are capitalized and recorded as an asset which is then treated as a periodical expense to be charged against sales in succeeding years.

It is not possible to formulate methods of measuring enterprise revenue and associated expenses in discrete time periods, in such a way as to avoid arbitrary allocation of some of the constituent items of revenue or expense. The allocation

---

[3] A joint cost is a common cost incurred in producing two or more products as a group, where no part of the cost can be assigned to any one individual product except in arbitrary fashion.

[4] A measurement method is said to be arbitrary if it cannot be defended logically and conclusively against all alternative methods.

problem is seemingly intractable, and is present and widespread in the historical record as well as other accounting systems. The seriousness of the problem is accentuated by the long-term nature of capital formation in modern industry. The commitment to long-run projects means that periodical income measurement becomes correspondingly less precise and less meaningful for decision making. The resultant ambiguity of accounting information is believed by some critics to deprive financial statements of much of their usefulness for readers.

Thomas doubts that a solution to the allocation problem will be found. Since allocation is part and parcel of income measurement and reporting, one response to the problem is to avoid allocation altogether by eschewing income measurement. Thomas has recommended that the income statement be replaced by a net-quick-asset funds statement in external reporting. [5]

Other accountants, however, believe that the critics of arbitrariness in allocation methods may have overstated their case. Admittedly it may not be possible to defend any particular allocation, e.g. charging a particular depreciation expense in the period, as the only valid allocation method. But machines do wear out (or become obsolete) and the cost of this wear and tear (or obsolescence) must be matched with the associated revenue earned in each period if a measure of periodical income is to be derived. The accountant's task is to develop a depreciation method which will achieve this matching of revenue and expense in the fairest way possible. Many accounting allocations are essential to periodical reporting within the historical record (or other) accounting framework, and therefore useful for this purpose. In the light of the theoretical limitations which have been discussed, the important issue is not whether an allocation method can be regarded as definitive and unambiguous, but whether allocation effects are so profound as to render the accounting system misleading, or at least less effective than some other means of disclosing information to interested parties. These are empirical issues, and to date the charges have not been supported by available evidence.

Qualitative Criteria

Qualitative criteria are evaluative tools for judging what constitutes good accounting practice. They have a normative flavour in contrast with the basic assumptions which are imperatives. Nonetheless the criteria are part of the descriptive theory, because they are concerned with guiding accounting practice. In the past, these criteria were sometimes known as doctrines, e.g. doctrines of conservatism, consistency and materiality. In recent years the criteria have come to be regarded as qualities of accounting information which govern the usefulness of financial statements for decision-makers. Thus they are used to evaluate competing accounting methods as well as competing accounting valuation systems.

Qualitative Criteria for Judging Usefulness of Accounting Systems

In particular, the qualities of relevance, objectivity, hardness, reliability and comparability, which are all in some degree interrelated, have considerable merit and serve as appropriate criteria for judging the usefulness of historical record accounting

---

[5] It will be seen in Part IV that an allocation problem is present in cost accounting as well as in financial accounting.

as well as other accounting valuation systems.[6] As with information systems generally, relevance is of particular significance, while the other four criteria are intended to reduce measurement and communication imperfections to a minimum.

Relevance

Relevance is the most important quality of accounting information. The output of an accounting system must have relevance for users' needs. This is not as straightforward a proposition as may appear at first sight, since it is necessary to identify the users of accounting information and specify the decision models they employ.[7] These users are often taken to be management (internal users) and owners and creditors (external users), but in addition the information needs of employees, customers, governments and the public at large may need to be considered. Unfortunately, little is known about users' decision models and their information requirements. Some writers support the view that accountants should supply information relevant to *normative* decision models, i.e. decision models which are considered to be appropriate by those providing the information. In any case, there needs to be a two-way flow of information about users' needs and the value-data considered relevant to those needs (so-called positive and negative feed-back), between the accountants who provide accounting information and the decision-makers who use it.

Value in accounting has many dimensions, e.g. value in exchange, value in use or value for income tax purposes. Value-data which are relevant for one purpose will not necessarily be suitable for another. Likewise, value-data which are relevant at one point of time will not necessarily be pertinent at another. There are two considerations. First, since accounting must serve many purposes, a strong case can be made for the adoption of an accounting valuation system that facilitates the measurement of different values in accordance with the purposes to be served.

Second, the accountant should specify the purpose or purposes intended to be served by a set of accounting data, and the limitations of the information for other purposes. This applies both to a particular set of financial statements which have relevance for certain broad purposes (but not for others), and to specific information which is highly relevant for use in a particular context (and could be misleading outside that context).

Objectivity

Objectivity in accounting measurement may be interpreted in a number of ways, requiring, for example, independence or freedom from personal bias, verifiability by another competent measurer or a degree of consensus among a given group of qualified measurers. In discriminating between different accounting valuation systems or different accounting measurement methods, the role of objectivity as a qualitative criterion is enhanced if objectivity is interpreted as a degree of consensus, since this can be subjected to empirical testing.

The degree of consensus achieved in practice may be measured statistically by reference to the variability of the values which different measurers ascribe to an item.

---

[6] There are other qualities of accounting information, such as verifiability, freedom from bias, quantifiability, understandability, timeliness and materiality. Many of these are incorporated to a large extent in the more significant qualities discussed in this chapter, e.g. timeliness and materiality are implicitly present in relevance.

[7] A decision model is a set of rules employed by a decision-maker in choosing among alternative courses of action.

Suppose there are n accountants or measurers, and that x_i is the quantity reported by the ith measurer ($i = 1, 2, \ldots, n$), then a statistical measure of objectivity, which may be called V, is:

$$V = \frac{1}{n} \sum_{i=1}^{n} (x_i - \bar{x})^2$$

where $\bar{x}$ is the average of x_is reported by all measurers. The smaller the value of V, the greater is the degree of objectivity of the measurement system under which the accountants operate.

Hardness

Ijiri has proposed that *hardness* is a useful characteristic of financial statements, which may be employed as a criterion to choose between competing measurement methods or accounting valuation systems. A relatively hard measure is one about which there is little disagreement, but hardness is not the same as objectivity. Objectivity is the characteristic of a measure made in a neutral environment, while hardness assumes a competitive environment. A measure is said to be hard if it is rigid and resistant to bias when the measurer is motivated to manipulate the measure in one direction or the other.[8] Ijiri provides the following illustration. A group of independent assessors agree that the value of a house is about $100 000. This measure is said to be highly objective. Now suppose that some of the assessors are employed by the seller and some by a potential buyer. The assessors in the former group are motivated to justify a higher price, and those in the latter group a lower price. It is in these competitive circumstances that the hardness of a measure is determined. Hardness, like objectivity, is a relative rather than an absolute characteristic. But the two qualities must be carefully distinguished. In evaluating accounting measures, a more objective measure is not necessarily also harder.

The financial statements represent reports by management on its own performance; they are also a means for calculating the firm's liability to income tax. Because there is always an incentive for management or proprietors to seek to introduce an upward or downward measurement bias into the external reports, the accountant needs to employ hard measures. The provision of relatively hard data is important also for resolving the conflicting interests of management, proprietors, creditors, employees or other groups, because such data are less open to dispute.

Reliability

Reliability implies dependability in relation to the purposes to be served, so that users of financial statements can depend on the information contained therein with a degree of confidence. The objectivity and hardness of a measure are independent of the purpose which the measure may serve but, like relevance, reliability is a function of purpose. An accounting measure or the information provided by an accounting system in general may be highly reliable for one purpose, while lacking relevance or reliability for other purposes. But reliability is different from relevance. For example, the present (or capitalized) value of a future earnings stream is a highly relevant measure with respect to investment decisions, but because of the difficulty of estimating future earnings it may not meet the accountant's standard of reliability.

---

[8] A measure may be relatively hard in one direction and relatively soft in the other.

Reliability has several dimensions, some of which are reflected in objectivity (freedom from personal bias in a neutral environment) and hardness (resistance to bias in a competitive environment). Reliability also has an independent meaning of special significance in relation to valuation, namely fidelity. One interpretation of this requirement is that the values which are recorded in the accounting system should represent accurately the economic events to which they relate. The difficulty here lies in the notion of 'economic reality', which can only be defined by reference to information relevance. Another interpretation is that an accounting system is reliable if its output can be used for *predictive* purposes with confidence, e.g. if dividend payments or share prices can be predicted from accounting measures of income. Here reliability can at least be tested *ex post*, but caution needs to be exercised because the test perforce is a joint test of the system's reliability and the user's decision model.

Although reliability is an important qualitative criterion of accounting information, its use in evaluating accounting information in practice may be severely circumscribed by the fact that the concept cannot be clearly and unambiguously defined in operational terms.

Comparability

Comparability is a further criterion by which accounting information may be judged. Comparability has a number of aspects. The first is inter-firm comparability, which implies that the financial statements of firms should be based on similar accounting principles and methods. The second is temporal comparability, which implies that a given entity should employ the same accounting procedures over time. The first type of comparability requires that the valuation procedures and accounting practices adopted by different accounting entities be relatively uniform. This is often important for investors' decisions. Because firms report under very different conditions, it is held by some writers that some degree of diversity in reporting procedures cannot be avoided. We believe that uniformity is particularly important for firms in the same industry, if meaningful evaluation by investors is to be possible. Given the differences in operating risks and other factors that exist between industries, comparability between firms in different industries is often not possible. The second type of comparability requires consistency in accounting procedures employed within a given entity over time. Consistency facilitates the analysis of trends in a firm's financial statements (see Chapter 7), and is necessary in order that the reporting of results in consecutive years does not mislead the reader. Where a change in accounting procedures takes place, full disclosure of its effects on the financial statements should be made.

There is a further consideration. Comparability also implies consistency in the meaning of the information to users. This is an important requirement, because uniform valuation procedures may nonetheless produce data to which a consistent meaning cannot be attached by those using the data, e.g. the reporting of inventories at the lower of cost or market value. (However, the use of the cost or market rule may more appropriately be regarded as a multiple valuation procedure than as a uniform procedure.)

Relevance as the Primary Quality

The important qualities that all accounting information should have — relevance, objectivity, hardness, reliability and comparability — have now been discussed. In practice accounting information possesses these desirable qualities in different degrees. To some extent, therefore, the choice between different accounting methods and systems is a matter of the accountant's judgement on possible trade-offs between these qualities. These trade-offs are also dependent on the purpose for which the accounting information is required, e.g. information for tax purposes needs to be relatively objective and hard, whereas information for purposes of internal management may emphasize other qualities. Relevance is the primary quality which all accounting standards *must* have, but even this is a matter of degree. Where conflict exists between two or more qualities, it is probable that relevance for user needs is the dominant consideration. However, some degree of relevance may be forgone in favour of incorporating a higher degree of some other quality. For example, in external reporting a relatively objective market price may be preferred to a more relevant but subjectively determined measure. Further, the most relevant measure is often not the most appropriate measure given the accounting objectives; it may not be readily understandable by users (e.g. a probabilistic estimate) or the increased cost of obtaining more relevant information may not be justified by the additional benefits which may be expected to flow from that information.

It is important to note that the qualitative criteria only bear on the benefits of information. The generation of information incurs costs and, because different accounting methods and accounting systems are associated with different information costs, the overall criterion for accounting choice must be a cost-benefit measure. Generally a particular accounting method or system is preferred over its competitor if, and only if, the incremental benefits of the additional information exceed the incremental costs of obtaining it.

Conservatism

Conservatism is an observable quality of most published accounting statements, but we do not view it as a desirable quality, let alone as a criterion for accounting choice. Until recent years, the so-called doctrine of conservatism has had at least as great an impact on conventional accounting practice as the foregoing assumptions and qualities, some of which, indeed, it has conflicted with and been allowed to over-ride. The doctrine reflects financial caution and expresses the belief that, because much of the information which appears in accounting reports is based on estimates and opinions rather than economic facts, accountants should ensure that profits and assets are not overstated, and that losses and liabilities are not understated. In practice, however, this bias towards conservatism has frequently meant that profits are deliberately understated and losses are overstated, and this has obviously affected the accuracy and validity of the profit and loss statement and the balance sheet. Indeed accounting conservatism carried to excess can be said to offend against all the qualitative criteria of accounting information discussed earlier.

The doctrine of conservatism is applied in a number of ways:

(a) Revenues are recorded in accordance with the realization assumption only when realized, but losses are provided for as soon as there is any possibility that they will be incurred. This introduces an obvious bias into the accounts and distorts the profit measurement process.

(b) Unsold inventories at the end of the accounting period are valued according to the cost or market rule, i.e. at cost price or net realizable value, whichever is the lower. The application of this rule means that closing inventories are recorded (for purposes of both profit measurement and balance sheet valuation) at current market value, if this should be lower than cost, in order to make provision for the loss which it is anticipated will result when the inventories are subsequently sold. The cost or market rule conflicts with the original cost assumption (of historical record accounting), and distorts the measurement of profit and assets by recognizing some value changes but not others. Zealous proponents of the doctrine of conservatism sometimes even value inventories below cost or market values, thereby destroying any pretence of accuracy in the accounting reports.

(c) Estimates in respect of accrued revenue and accrued expenses are biased towards conservatism.

(d) The charging of depreciation is 'accelerated' by making excessive depreciation charges in respect of a fixed capital asset during the earlier years of its life, or writing it off over a period considerably less than its useful working life. Suppose, for example, that a machine is purchased for $1 000, and that it is expected to have a working life of 10 years and no scrap value at the end of that time. If the straight-line method of calculating depreciation is employed, a depreciation charge of $100 per annum is recorded each year until at the end of 10 years the book value of the machine is reduced to nil. If, however, as a result of applying the doctrine of conservatism the annual depreciation charge is increased to $200, the recorded value of the asset is reduced to nil at the end of five years. That is to say, the machine ceases to be recorded as an asset in the books of account (or in the balance sheet), even though it still has an estimated working life of a further five years.

The above example of accelerated depreciation illustrates some possible consequences from applying a doctrine of conservatism. These consequences are: first, the distortion of operating results in the profit and loss statement, since in the first five years expenses are overstated and profits understated, and in the second five years expenses are understated (there is no depreciation charge) and profits are correspondingly overstated; and second, the under-valuation of assets and net worth, and the creation of so-called secret reserves,[9] in all years. Similarly, understating the closing inventory results in profit being understated in the current year and overstated in the following year.

There have been influences operating in recent years to reduce the importance of the doctrine of conservatism. In particular, authoritative pronouncements by the accountancy profession, insisting on the need for consistency and disclosure in accounting reports, have by implication condemned conservatism as an accounting procedure. The overthrow of conservatism as an appropriate accounting policy in a system of historical record accounting does not necessarily mean that it should cease to operate as a commercial or financial policy. In its own financial sphere, conservatism is a perfectly legitimate procedure.

However, where a policy of conservatism is adopted in the interests of financial prudence, its effects should be clearly disclosed in the accounts. The application of a conservative financial policy may then be recorded in the profit and loss statement (preferably in the non-operating section), by making the same kind of provision that is made for other anticipated losses. In the balance sheet, assets may be recorded at their gross book values, with separate deductions in respect of the provisions that have been established for anticipated losses. This technique has been illustrated in

---

[9] Secret reserves are funds employed by the business which are not disclosed in the accounts. They may be created by the understatement of profits or the under-valuation of assets.

detail in Chapter 4, when the cost or market rule was discussed in relation to the problem of inventory valuation.

Standards and Principles

While the assumptions and qualitative criteria have a fundamental influence on developments in accounting practice, the latter are governed directly by principles and standards emanating from the professional accounting bodies. Standards are pronouncements of the professional bodies which lead to the establishment of accounting principles. Principles are authoritative and must be complied with.[10] The standards and principles that have been issued by the professional bodies embrace important areas of accounting practice, such as disclosure of accounting policies and methods, profit reporting, inventory valuation and depreciation accounting. (An example of the role of accounting standards in profit reporting can be found in Chapter 11.) In order that the financial statements should disclose 'a true and fair view', sometimes it is necessary for the accountant to employ a method which is inconsistent with a standard or principle; such departures should of course be fully disclosed.

Unfortunately, some standards and principles condone a certain degree of permissiveness in the choice of accounting methods as, for example, in the valuation of inventories and the depreciation of fixed assets. This is often understandable in the context of the complex environment in which businesses operate. Nonetheless, the existence of alternative accounting methods conflicts with some of the foregoing qualitative criteria and has been criticized accordingly. Alternative accounting methods provide management with a means of influencing the financial statements through a judicious selection of methods. The corollary, of course, is that users of financial statements may be deceived. As has been seen, reports based on different accounting methods lack comparability.

Conclusion

Because accounting is largely concerned with the measurement of operating results and financial position, the central concepts of accounting are those of periodic surplus and capital employed. It has been noted that the traditional accounting concept of periodic surplus, which is based on historical record assumptions, is that of profit, and that the measurement of accounting profit involves a comparison or matching of costs and revenues for a given period. More explicitly, accounting profit was seen as the arithmetical difference between the revenue earned in a given period and the costs and expenses incurred in producing that revenue. Problems of profit measurement are thus essentially problems of measuring revenue, costs and expenses, and it was noted that in recording these transactions accountants have traditionally made a number of limiting assumptions, the significance of which was considered at some length. It must be emphasized that accounting profit expresses periodic surplus only in terms of historical money values. For some accounting purposes, this may be reasonable, but the accounting concept of profit frequently fails to satisfy the

[10] In the United States, principles are sometimes referred to as 'generally accepted accounting principles' (GAAP).

qualitative criteria which have been discussed earlier in this chapter. Such a concept should therefore not be regarded as a unique measurement of periodic surplus—one which is suitable for all purposes. This is so for two closely related reasons.

The first is that the historical record accounting profit figure is a measure of periodic surplus in terms of historical money values. If the unit of measurement—the monetary unit, i.e. the dollar—changes in value, then revenues, costs and expenses, which have been recorded at different points of time, are not being measured in terms of the same unit, and it is difficult to say how significant the profit figure is or what it means.

The second limitation of accounting profit as a measure of periodic surplus is that it is calculated in a way which, in periods of changing prices, fails to preserve the value of the enterprise's capital (as represented by its proprietorship equity) in terms of its command over goods and services. Adherence to historical money values in the profit measurement process merely maintains the money value of proprietorship capital. During inflation, the money capital commands a diminishing volume of operating assets (the most important of which are fixed capital assets and inventories). This effect, which is produced by conventional procedures in times of inflation, has been described as the 'capital erosion' effect. It may be possible to augment the money capital by withholding profits from distribution or by raising fresh capital, but unless this is done the business must reduce its scale of operations, or face the danger of insolvency as its capital resources may no longer be adequate to support the existing volume of transactions (the business is said to be 'under-capitalized').

The limitations of the historical record assumptions thus extend to the concept of capital employed and the maintenance of this capital. These limitations mean that the historical record approach is unlikely to be suitable for purposes of evaluating performance, determining business policy or securing effective managerial control over operations. Nevertheless, the historical record accounting concepts of revenue, costs, expenses, profit and capital employed may still have their uses. Because accounting profit is based on actual events, it is relatively easy to calculate; so long as historical money values are adhered to, a measure of surplus is derived which is reasonably free from the bias of subjective estimates and opinions. Moreover, a money concept of surplus has a definite meaning in a society where financial relationships are necessarily expressed in monetary terms, and it is a legitimate purpose of accounting to measure such a concept.

In Part III alternative approaches to accounting valuation will be examined, to see to what extent they can be used to overcome the limitations which the historical record assumptions introduce into the accounting information system.

References

American Accounting Association, *A Statement of Basic Accounting Theory*, 1966, Chapter 2.

Ijiri, Y., *Theory of Accounting Measurement*, Studies in Accounting Research No. 10, American Accounting Association, 1975, Chapter 3.

Thomas, A.L., *The Allocation Problem in Financial Accounting Theory*, Studies in Accounting Research No. 3, American Accounting Association, 1969.

Additional Reading

Hendriksen, E.S., *Accounting Theory*, Irwin, Homewood, Ill., 1977, Chapter 4.

Myers, J.H., 'The Critical Event and Recognition of Net Profit', *Accounting Review*, October 1959, pp. 528-32.

Paton, W.A. and Littleton, A.C., *An Introduction to Corporate Accounting Standards*, American Accounting Association, 1960, Chapter 2.

Thomas, A.L., *Financial Accounting: The Main Ideas*, Wadsworth, Belmont, Calif., 1972, Chapters 6 and 13.

Discussion Questions

1 Examine the principal assumptions of historical record accounting with particular reference to their effects on income determination and balance sheet valuation.

2 What are the principal criteria which may be used in evaluating accounting information systems? To what extent are these criteria applicable to information systems in general?

3 Consider the proposition that, in the evaluation of accounting information systems, relevance is the primary criterion. How successful is historical record accounting in meeting the relevance criterion?

4 Critically examine the realization assumption in historical record accounting, with special reference to its implications for income measurement and asset valuation.

5 Consider the problem of recognizing revenue in an historical record accounting system by reference to hire purchase sales. In what circumstances, if any, would you consider it necessary to restrict the recognition of revenue to hire purchase instalments received in cash? Under generally accepted accounting principles, how is the procedure of recognizing hire purchase revenue at the time of sale reconciled with the probability of losses resulting from non-payment of instalments?

6 As well as dealing with problems of sources of data about transactions and values, accountants need to consider problems of recognizing the stage at which events need to be recorded in the accounting system. Discuss these problems.

7 Except to a limited extent in respect of certain classes of assets (e.g. debtors), balance sheets usually present information about different kinds of assets without differentiating between the probabilities of items being realized or converted into cash. Is this desirable or necessary?

8 'The process of profit measurement in an historical record accounting system provides a measure of periodic surplus which is unsuitable as a basis for distribution policy.' Discuss.

9 Is it true that, under historical record accounting, accountants always restrict their attention to historical record data and refuse to incorporate current values into the accounting record? Under what circumstances is the substitution of current values for historical costs likely to be considered an acceptable or even a necessary procedure under generally accepted accounting principles? What implications do these departures from the historical record assumption have from the point of view of (a) the relevance, and (b) the objectivity of the accounting record?

10 How does the accountant's concern with measurement affect his concept of income?

11 Should accountants measure real income or money income? Why?

12 What are the major problems the accountant faces in his attempts to measure income?

13 Since there is ample evidence that many businesses fail, how can accountants justify a going-concern concept?

14 Does the use of the consistency assumption in accounting mean that an accounting method, once adopted, cannot be changed?

15 The matching assumption tends only to undo the damage caused by adhering to the realization assumption. Do you agree with this statement?

16 Ideally, there is only one measure of the income of an entity for a specific period of time. Discuss.

17 What, if any, is the relationship between the assumptions of realization, original cost and matching costs with revenues? Justify your opinions in non-technical language; i.e. write as though to an intelligent layman who knows nothing about accounting.

7 Analysis and Interpretation of Financial Reports

A major objective of accounting is to provide quantitative financial information about the accounting entity to various interested parties to assist them in making decisions concerning that entity. Users of accounting reports are a diverse and heterogeneous group, with different information needs (about which little is known) and, often, conflicting interests. The internal user is management, which employs both financial statements and special-purpose accounting reports (relevant for specific control and decision situations), but even here conflicting interests may exist between, say, top and middle level managers or between managers of divisions within the firm. External users comprise existing and potential owners (shareholders in the case of companies), creditors and potential creditors, employees, suppliers, customers, governments and the public at large. Among external users, owners and creditors in particular have a need for financial information relevant for investing and lending decisions respectively. At the same time, shareholders and creditors often do not have access to information other than that contained in the published financial statements. Thus the three main financial statements—the profit and loss statement, the balance sheet and the funds statement—have always been oriented strongly to meeting the information needs of these two user groups. In this chapter, the analysis and interpretation of financial statements and other accounting information are considered from the viewpoints of the main user groups, namely owners, creditors and management. In addition to the financial statements, external analysts also make use of other publicly available information (such as share prices and industry surveys), while management has recourse to a considerable amount of data contained in the firm's books and records that are not usually available to outside parties.

Analysis of the financial statements proceeds from the measurement of certain financial relationships (ratios or percentages), their comparison with appropriate standards, [1] and their interpretation to provide insight on the performance and financial position of the business. A financial ratio or percentage is a number which expresses the relationship of one financial magnitude to another, e.g. that of profit to invested funds. A number by itself, of course, can be neither good nor bad. Therefore a ratio or percentage is compared with an explicit or implicit standard, in order to determine to what extent it differs from the standard. If it is significantly different, further investigation is justified in order to ascertain the cause of variation and take remedial action. The standard used may be the corresponding figures for competitor firms or the corresponding industry average in respect of the current period; such comparisons are described as cross-sectional analysis. Alternatively, the standard may be the corresponding figure for the same firm in respect of past periods; these comparisons are described as trend or time-series analysis. Both cross-sectional and trend comparisons should be employed, since they complement one another in the interpretation of the financial data. Cross-sectional and trend analyses may also be combined, e.g. when trends of relationships for the firm are compared with corresponding trends for the industry.

---

[1] The term 'standard' is used here to denote something that can serve as a basis for comparison. It has no relation to the standards of accounting practice promulgated by the professional bodies, as discussed in Chapter 6.

Structural and Trend Analysis

Tables 7—1 and 7—2 present comparative balance sheets and income statements respectively of XYZ Traders for the three years 1983, 1984 and 1985 and provide the data for illustrating the forms of analysis discussed in this chapter. In practice, financial statements relating to a longer period (say, 5—10 years) would be employed for purposes of trend analysis, while relationships representing the industry averages for the current year would also be presented if cross-sectional analysis was desired. For simplicity, it is assumed that book values recorded in Table 7—1 and 7—2 reflect current market values (thus enhancing the usefulness of the analysis).

Table 7—1
XYZ Traders
Structural Analysis of Balance Sheet Data

Balance Sheets as at 31 December	1983		1984		1985	
	$	%	$	%	$	%
Short-term financial assets	2 000	20.0	2 000	16.0	3 000	20.0
Inventories	2 000	20.0	3 000	24.0	4 000	26.7
Current assets	4 000	40.0	5 000	40.0	7 000	46.7
Fixed capital assets (net of depreciation)	6 000	60.0	7 500	60.0	8 000	53.3
Total assets	10 000	100.0	12 500	100.0	15 000	100.0
Current liabilities	1 000	10.0	3 000	24.0	3 500	23.3
Long-term liabilities	1 000	10.0	1 000	8.0	1 500	10.0
Proprietorship equity	8 000	80.0	8 500	68.0	10 000	66.7
Total equities	10 000	100.0	12 500	100.0	15 000	100.0

Table 7—2
XYZ Traders
Structural Analysis of Profit and Loss Statement Data

Income Statements for Year Ended 31 December	1983		1984		1985	
	$	%	$	%	$	%
Gross sales	10 400		11 160		12 000	
Less: Sales returns and other sales deductions	400		1 160		1 000	
Net sales	10 000	100.0	10 000	100.0	11 000	100.0
Less: Cost of sales	6 550	65.5	6 500	65.0	6 800	61.8
Gross profit	3 450	34.5	3 500	35.0	4 200	38.2
Less: Selling expenses	1 500	15.0	1 700	17.0	1 720	15.6
Administrative expenses	550	5.5	550	5.5	550	5.0
Interest expense	100	1.0	100	1.0	150	1.4
Net operating profit	1 300	13.0	1 150	11.5	1 780	16.2
Add: Non-operating revenue (net of non-operating expenses)	250		400		530	
Net profit (before tax)	1 550	15.5	1 550	15.5	2 310	21.0
Less: Income tax payable	450		420		660	
Net profit (after tax)	1 100	11.0	1 130	11.3	1 650	15.0

Balance Sheet Structural and Trend Analysis

For purposes of assessing the financial stability of a business, a convenient starting point is the presentation of comparative balance sheets in which the main items and groups of assets and equities are expressed as percentages of total assets and total equities.[2] This form of analysis, which is analogous to cross-sectional analysis within the firm, may be described as structural analysis because it throws light on the relationships between different items and groups in each financial statement. In the hypothetical figures in Table 7—1, only the major groups are included, but in practice greater detail is likely to be necessary.

The analysis carried out in Table 7—1 serves to direct attention to changes that have taken place in the financial structure of the business and the purposes to which its funds have been applied. It is evident from the figures that the company has increased its reliance on current liabilities relative to long-term funds for the financing of its operations and that, although short-term financial assets, inventories and fixed capital assets have all increased in terms of absolute money values, an increasing proportion of the company's funds is being absorbed by inventories.

Structural analysis of this kind may be supplemented by an analysis of balance sheet trends. Successive balance sheet values for each item or group may be expressed as percentages of its value in a base year, say 1983 in the example. A comparison of the relative changes as between different items or groups then throws light on developing strengths or weaknesses in the financial position. The earliest year in the series is usually chosen as the base year, but there are advantages in employing a normal year as the base. Sometimes the data of a number of years (say, three years) are combined and averaged to smooth out irregular fluctuations and serve as a 'normalized' base year. It will be clear that trend analysis is likely to lead to essentially the same conclusions regarding movements in financial stability as result from comparisons of structural changes, and for this reason it is usually sufficient to confine the calculation of trend relationships to one or two important items, such as inventories, current assets and liabilities (see Table 7—3).

Table 7—3
XYZ Traders
Analysis of Balance Sheet Trends

Balance Sheet Trends for Year Ended 31 December	1983 $	1983 %	1984 $	1984 %	1985 $	1985 %
Inventories	2 000	100	3 000	150	4 000	200
Current assets	4 000	100	5 000	125	7 000	175
Current liabilities	2 000	100	3 000	150	3 500	175

A comparison of the trends indicates that inventories rose more rapidly than current assets, in general, between 1983 and 1984, but less rapidly in the following year. Likewise, current liabilities increased at a faster rate during the first year, and at a slower rate during the second year, than current assets. This comparison carries important implications with respect to the liquidity or short-term financial position of the business, and shows that, during 1984, the company was incurring short-term

---

[2] A word of caution is needed here. Other things being equal, an absolute increase in a component item will lead to an increase in its proportionate value and corresponding decreases in the proportionate values of all other items in the set.

debts more rapidly than it was building up its short-term assets. In view of the relative trends which have been noted, the short-term financial stability of the business may thus be said to have deteriorated in 1984. (A comparison of the absolute figures for inventories and current assets further indicates that the increase in current assets was wholly attributable to the relatively illiquid inventory item.) These adverse trends have been reversed during 1985, but not to the extent of restoring the 1983 position.

Income Statement Structural and Trend Analysis

In looking at the profitability of a business, consideration has to be given to structural and trend relationships affecting the income statement and to inter-statement relationships. Revenue, cost and profit figures, taken in isolation, cannot reveal very much. A profit of, say, $20 000 for a particular year may represent an adequate return for a small corner shop in the suburbs, but is obviously not a satisfactory return for a large department store in the city. Income therefore needs to be related to other items, such as sales turnover, previous income figures, budgeted income for the period or funds employed, in order to determine whether or not operating results are satisfactory. Costs and expenses may be related to the revenues with which they are associated; individual items or groups of costs, expenses and revenue may be related to corresponding figures in past profit statements or budgets.

Operating profit and net profit may be expressed as percentages of sales revenue (i.e. turnover) and at the same time the relationship between different cost and expense groups and sales revenue may be measured by calculating structural relationships in comparative income statements. Each cost and expense group, as well as gross profit, net operating profit and net profit (before and after tax) may thus be expressed as a percentage of sales by presenting the relevant income statements in the form illustrated in Table 7—2. Hypothetical figures are given for three years, but in practice a longer period is desirable. Much of the detail of the individual income statements has been eliminated in order to simplify the exposition and concentrate attention on the major groups. In interpreting the movements that have occurred, however, reference back to the detailed statements is certain to be necessary. For this reason, in practice it will usually be necessary to present the comparative statements in greater detail.

A number of observations may be made about these structural relationships and the light they throw on changes in the profitability of the firm. It will be observed that the base to which cost, expense and income items have been related is net sales, after deductions, and not gross sales. Substantial variations may be recorded in gross sales which have no significance in relation to the profitability question. The percentages of cost of sales to net sales, and gross profit to net sales, provide an indication of the profit potential of the business before charges are made for selling and administrative expenses. The relationship between gross profit and sales (the gross profit ratio) is a particularly important indicator of profitability. Increases in this ratio, such as occur in the example, may be due to relatively greater increases in selling prices than in the cost of sales, or relatively greater reductions in cost of sales than in selling prices. Where prices have to be reduced to maintain turnover, or where increases take place in the cost of sales due to rising purchase prices, inadequate inventory control or ineffective buying policy and it is not possible to pass these on through higher selling prices, the gross profit ratio may be expected to fall. A more detailed analysis of the gross profit ratio is given in the following section.

The percentages of the functional groups of expenses (selling, administrative and interest expenses in the example) to net sales provide an indication of the effect of the different functions on profitability, but some care is needed in interpreting changes in the percentages of these groups. To the extent that such groups consist of expenses which, being relatively fixed or constant in amount, are not affected by changes in turnover, reductions (or increases) in percentages result merely from increases (or reductions) in the sales figure on which the percentages are based. This seems to be the explanation of the fall in the percentage of administrative expenses to net sales which has occurred in 1985 in the example (see Table 7—2). The increase in the percentage of selling expenses to net sales in 1984, on the other hand, seems to reflect increased selling efforts which may have contributed to the increased revenue in 1985.

The percentage of net operating profit to net sales indicates the profitability of the operating sections of the business, while the percentage of net profit after tax to net sales indicates the ability of the business to earn distributable income. It will be observed that percentages of non-operating revenue, or income tax, to net sales have not been calculated, because no meaningful relationships exist between these items.

These are the important income statement structural relationships which may be used to analyse the operating results of a business. They may be supplemented by income statement trend relationships, which indicate the significance of changes over time by expressing items or groups as percentages of corresponding items or groups in a base period (e.g. 1983 in the example). It is not usually necessary to calculate trend relationships for all items or groups; to a large extent such analysis merely provides a similar explanation of the observations which result from a comparison over time of the structural relationships. If the trends of net sales and cost of sales are compared, for example, it can be seen that the improvement in the gross profit ratio in 1985, which was noticed when comparing structural relationships, may be explained by the fact that sales have increased at a faster rate than cost of sales, as shown in Table 7—4.

Table 7—4
XYZ Traders
Analysis of Income Statement Trends

Income Trends for Year Ended 31 December	1983		1984		1985	
	$	%	$	%	$	%
Net sales	10 000	100.0	10 000	100.0	11 000	110.0
Cost of sales	6 550	100.0	6 500	99.2	6 800	103.8

The items or groups for which trend relationships may be worth calculating are:

(a) net sales (because of the dominating influence which turnover exerts on profitability);

(b) the various items or groups which, because they are not considered to have a close relationship with sales, do not figure prominently in the structural analysis. If administrative expenses are relatively constant or fixed in relation to turnover, for example, trends in such expenses need to be watched more carefully than changes in their percentages on sales; and

(c) the different income measures such as net operating profit and net profit before and after tax.

Some simple illustrations of structural and trend analyses which are of general interest to users of financial statements have been presented above. The following sections describe some financial relationships and other analytical tools which are tailored to the needs of specific user groups. Only the more significant and useful ratios or percentages are considered, and all computations in the following pages are based on data contained in Tables 7—1 and 7—2. Figure 7—A sets out some important user groups and their information needs.

Figure 7—A
Analysis of Accounting Information by Decision Makers

Decision Maker	Decision Variables	Ratios or Percentages and Other Analytical Tools
Investor or potential investor	Profitability	Structural and trend analyses of income statements (1) gross profit/net sales (2) net profit/net sales (3) net profit/average proprietorship equity (4) net profit/average total equities
	Risk: long-run—Financial stability	Structural and trend analyses of balance sheets
	Other	(5) earnings variability (6) debt/debt plus proprietorship equity (7) net operating profit (before interest and tax)/ interest expense (7c) net operating profit (before interest and tax)/ interest expense plus principal repayment
	Risk:short-run	(8) current assets/current liabilities (9) quick assets/quick liabilities (10) quick assets/operating cash outlays per day
Creditor or potential creditor	Return	(11) bond yield
	Risk	Relationships (5) to (10), as above Cash budget
Management	Financial stability	Structural and trend analyses of balance sheets
	Profitability and efficiency	Structural and trend analyses of income statements Profitability relationships (1) to (4) (12) du Pont formula (13) book debts/average daily credit sales (14) cost of sales/cost of average inventory

Notes: (a) The relationships in Figure 7—A are broadly defined, e.g. relationship (6) above embraces both (6) and (6a) in the subsequent text.
(b) The relationships discussed in the Appendix to this chapter are not included above.

Information Analysis by Investors

The decisions that face an investor or owner in a business relate to whether he should increase or decrease his investment in the business and whether he should seek to retain or replace the present management. [3] In turn these decisions depend on his evaluation of management performance and the profit potential of the business. Investors typically are concerned with two main characteristics of their investment: profitability and risk. [4] To some extent these two factors are inter-related. Since all or most investors may be assumed to be averse to risk, investors will expect higher returns for bearing greater risks. Generally, in comparing two investments, the one which promises a higher return for the same level of risk or the same return for less risk will be preferred.

Profitability Analysis

There are several profitability measures, of which some have been mentioned earlier—the ratios of gross profit and net profit respectively to sales. The *gross profit ratio* (or *gross profit margin*) is calculated as a percentage as follows:

$$\frac{\text{net sales} - \text{cost of sales}}{\text{net sales}} \times 100 \tag{1}$$

On the basis of the figures in Table 7—2, the gross profit ratio is thus 34.5, 35.0 and 38.2 per cent in 1983, 1984 and 1985 respectively.

There are two useful net profit ratios that may be computed. One is the *ratio of net operating profit to net sales,* which is 13.0, 11.5 and 16.2 per cent in the respective years. The other is the *net profit ratio* (or *net profit margin*), which measures the relationship to sales of the after-tax net profit, calculated by reference to operating profit *plus* or *minus* any non-operating items (such as interest income). If the analyst is interested in short-term fluctuations in profits, all non-operating items need to be included in the profit figure. But if he is interested in the long- or medium-term profit trend, only those non-operating items normally accruing to the business should be included, and any non-recurring non-operating items (such as gains or losses on currency devaluation) should be excluded. The net profit ratio is calculated as follows:

$$\frac{\text{net profit (after tax)}}{\text{net sales}} \times 100 \tag{2}$$

= 11.0, 11.3 and 15.0 per cent in the respective years.

For many businesses the gross profit ratio tends to be relatively stable and a significant change in this figure should be investigated. Some possible causes have been suggested when structural relationships were discussed earlier. Another possibility is a change in the sales-mix when profit margins vary between different product lines. For example, suppose that XYZ Traders sell two product lines, *A* and *B*, which have mark-ups on their respective selling price of 40 per cent (for *A*) and 30 per cent (for *B*). The following illustration shows how a change in the sales-mix may affect the gross profit margins reported in different years:

---

[3] In many business situations investors may have little influence on the appointment of management.

[4] Thus they would be interested in the structural and trend analyses of income statements (with respect to profitability) and balance sheets (with respect to financial stability, i.e. the firm's long-term risk structure), as discussed earlier. See also Figure 7—A.

Product Line	1983	1984	1985
Proportion in total net sales:			
A	0.45	0.50	0.82
B	0.55	0.50	0.18
	1.00	1.00	1.00
Contribution to gross profit margin:	%	%	%
A	18.0	20.0	32.8
B	16.5	15.0	5.4
	34.5	35.0	38.2

A tentative explanation can now be provided for the fall in the net operating profit margin in 1984 and the increases in sales, and both gross and net profit margins in 1985. It may be hypothesized, for example, that increased selling efforts in 1984 (the expense of which led to the decline in net operating profit) focused on product line *A* on account of its greater profit potential, and that this, in turn, led to the dominance in sales of product *A* in 1985 and the favourable improvement in the gross profit margin in that year. As was explained earlier, financial statement analysis both reveals the problem areas and initiates the search for appropriate remedial action. However, a correct interpretation depends on detailed investigation into the relevant facts underlying the financial statements.

Other measures of profitability are given by rates of return on investment, i.e. relationships of earnings to funds employed. Of direct interest to owners is the *rate of return on proprietorship equity*, which is computed as follows:[5]

$$\frac{\text{net profit (after interest and tax)}}{\text{average proprietorship equity}} \times 100 \qquad (3)$$

= 13.8, 13.7 and 17.8 per cent in 1983, 1984 and 1985 respectively.

From the owner's viewpoint this ratio may reasonably be regarded as the ultimate test of profitability and efficiency, since it indicates the distributable profit potential of the business. A low or declining percentage may be due to a number of factors—inefficient management, poor tax planning, unfavourable business conditions, excessive investment in assets or undue reliance on proprietorship rather than debt funds. The last factor indicates that this ratio is not always suitable for comparing the performance of different companies, which may vary in the extent to which funds are provided by owners and creditors. A broader based measure for evaluating profitability is the *rate of return on total equities* (or *total assets employed*), as computed below; interest is added back in order to remove the effect of financing charges on net profit, while tax payable is adjusted by the tax deductibility component in the interest charges:[6]

[5] Average proprietorship equity is taken as $8 000 in 1983 (since the preceding year's figure is not available), $8 250 (the average of $8 000 and $8 500) in 1984, and $9 250 (the average of $8 500 and $10 000) in 1985.

[6] Assuming a tax rate of 40 per cent, the tax deductibility component in the interest payments is $40, $40 and $60 in 1983, 1984 and 1985, respectively. Net profit before interest and after tax adjusted for the interest component is $1 160, $1 190 and $1 740. The corresponding figures for average total equities (computed in the same way as average proprietorship equity) are $10 000, $11 250 and $13 750.

$$\frac{\text{net profit (before interest and after tax adjusted for the interest component)}}{\text{average total equities}} \text{ x } 100 \text{ (4)}$$

$$= 11.6, 10.6 \text{ and } 12.7 \text{ per cent in the respective years.}$$

Where a firm is decentralized into a number of operating divisions, departments or branches, profits expressed as percentages on sales or funds employed in the individual sections may be computed to throw light on the profitability of those sections. Care must be taken to include in the analysis only those revenues and expenses which can be traced directly to the individual sections (as explained in Chapter 13).

Long-run Risk Analysis

Past and current earnings may be used by investors to predict expected future profitability. Since investors are risk-averse, there is an inverse relationship between expected profitability and risk—the higher the level of risk the greater the return investors expect. Risk has many dimensions, of which two are of special interest to owners. These are the quality of earnings [7] and the long- and short-term financial position of the business.

The quality of earnings relates to the degree of variability (i.e. the extent of fluctuations) in a firm's earnings stream over time. Attention is usually concentrated on net profit variability, but variability in sales or operating profit may also be relevant. Variability may be expressed in terms of average deviation from the arithmetic mean of the series, given by the variance or standard deviation. Where possible the analyst should employ data for an entire business cycle, covering say eight to twelve years. In comparing the variability in earnings of two or more businesses of different sizes, a special ratio—the *coefficient of variation*—may be employed. Other things being equal, the earnings stream with greater stability is preferred. The measures may be computed as follows:

$$\text{Mean earnings } (\overline{X}) = \frac{1}{n} \sum_{t=1}^{n} X_t$$

$$\text{Variance } (s^2) = \frac{\Sigma(X_t - \overline{X})^2}{n}$$

$$\text{Standard deviation } (s) = \left[\frac{\Sigma(X_t - \overline{X})^2}{n} \right]^{\frac{1}{2}}$$

$$\text{Coefficient of variation } (V) = \frac{s}{\overline{X}} \tag{5}$$

where X_t denotes earnings (sales or profit) in year t ($t = 1, 2, ..., n$).

The soundness and stability of the long-term financial position of the business depend on a satisfactory relationship between borrowed funds and proprietorship funds. This relationship can be expressed in a number of ways, but a useful, easily understood, measure is the *debt-equity ratio*. This may be computed as follows:

$$\frac{\text{total liabilities}}{\text{total liabilities + proprietorship equity}} \text{ x } 100 \tag{6}$$

$$= 20.0, 32.0 \text{ and } 33.3 \text{ per cent in the respective years.}$$

---

[7] The quality of earnings refers to the riskiness of those earnings. However, some investment analysts use the term to refer to earnings of companies which adopt conservative accounting practices.

Alternatively, attention may be directed to the relationship between long-term debt and proprietorship equity:

$$\frac{\text{long-term debt}}{\text{long-term debt} + \text{proprietorship equity}} \times 100 \qquad (6a)$$

= 11.1, 10.5 and 12.0 per cent in the respective years.

While both of the above ratios are commonly used, ratio (6a) is to be preferred because it focuses on the relatively permanent funds employed in the business. Since firms in the same industry face similar business risks, they tend to have similar long-term capitalization structures. Thus a significant deviation in a firm's dependence on outside funds from the accepted practice in its industry indicates *prima facie* that the firm is employing either relatively insufficient debt funds or insufficient equity funds.

A more direct measure of the risk of using debt funds is the *interest cover ratio*, i.e. the number of times interest charges are covered by net operating income (before interest and tax). It is important to note that the stability of this ratio is as important as the size of the cover; the market will accept a much smaller margin of cover if earnings are relatively secure and stable. The interest cover ratio is computed as follows:

$$\frac{\text{net operating profit (before interest and tax)}}{\text{interest expense}} \qquad (7)$$

= 14.0, 12.5 and 12.9 times in the respective years.

Since the firm's debt servicing capacity (i.e. its ability to pay interest and repay principal as these amounts fall due) relates more closely to cash flows than to profits, some writers have suggested that the numerator in the above expression should be: net operating profit (before interest and tax) *plus* depreciation.

Different creditors may be interested in different measures of interest cover. Assume that in 1985 the interest expense comprises interest of $100 on a first mortgage of $1 000 and interest of $50 on a second mortgage of $500. Since the first mortgage interest constitutes a senior charge, the respective interest cover in respect of the first mortgage is:

$$\frac{\text{net operating profit (before interest and tax)}}{\text{interest on first mortgage}} \qquad (7a)$$

= 19.3 times.

The interest cover in respect of the second mortgage is:[8]

$$\frac{\text{net operating profit (before interest and tax)}}{\text{interest on first mortgage} + \text{interest on second mortgage}} \qquad (7b)$$

= 12.9 times.

The use of the interest cover ratio implicitly assumes that the long-term loan will be redeemed eventually out of new capital contributions or a new loan issue, and not out of profits. Where both loan interest and the periodical repayment of principal are met out of current earnings, the appropriate ratio is:

[8] It would be misleading to compute the interest cover in respect of the second mortgage as $\frac{1\,930 - 100}{50}$ or 36.6 times.

$$\frac{\text{net operating profit (before interest and tax)}}{\text{interest} + (\text{repayment of principal x } T)} \tag{7c}$$

where T is a tax factor.[9]

Leverage or Gearing

The use of loan funds increases the risk of insolvency, but it also enhances the return on proprietorship equity. In considering these questions of risk and return on proprietorship equity, it is necessary to look at what is called the *leverage* or *gearing* of the firm's financial structure. Leverage or gearing may be illustrated by contrasting two firms with different kinds of financial structure:

(a) Firm A whose funds comprise $4 000 in outside liabilities, consisting wholly of bank overdraft on which five per cent per annum interest is payable, and $1 000 in proprietorship equity; and

(b) Firm B whose funds comprise bank overdraft of $1 000 at five per cent per annum and proprietorship equity of $4 000.

The relative weights of the different forms of finance are assumed to be reversed in the two firms. If it is assumed that the profit earned by each firm, before any charge is made for interest on bank overdraft, is $500, and that the whole of the $500 is to be distributed, the amounts paid out to the different groups providing finance are as set out in Table 7—5.

Table 7—5
Effect of Gearing on Rates of Return

	Funds Provided	Interest or Dividend	Rate of Return on Funds Provided
Firm A	$	$	%
5% bank overdraft	4 000	200	5.00
Proprietorship equity	1 000	300	30.00
Total	5 000	500	
Firm B			
5% bank overdraft	1 000	50	5.00
Proprietorship equity	4 000	450	11.25
Total	5 000	500	

It will be observed that Firm A, because it relies more on relatively cheap outside funds, is able to achieve a much higher rate of profit distribution than Firm B (30 per cent as against 11.25 per cent). So long as the average rate of profit (before interest) on total funds is greater than the rate of interest payable on the borrowed funds, it is possible to increase the rate of profit distribution in this way. Action of this kind is described as 'trading on the equity', and a business with a high proportion of debt in its capitalization structure is said to be highly geared.

But increasing the gearing not only increases the yield on proprietorship equity, it also increases the risks of proprietorship interests, of outside creditors and ultimately of the business itself. If profits (before interest) fall to $200 in the above example, the profit distribution cuts out in the high-geared Firm A, whereas Firm B is still able to

[9] Since the principal repayment (unlike the interest expense) is not tax deductible, the amount is adjusted by the tax factor T, where $T = \dfrac{1}{1-\text{tax rate}}$. Suppose the tax rate is 40%, then $T = \dfrac{1}{1-0.4} = 1.67$.

make a distribution of $\frac{150}{4\,000}$ or 3.75 per cent. If profits (before interest) fall to \$100, the highly geared Firm *A* cannot even cover its interest commitment, while Firm *B* can meet its interest liability and still have something ($\frac{50}{4\,000}$ or 1.25 per cent) left over for distribution to its owners. This means that the degree to which the financial structure can be safely geared depends on the risk of profit fluctuations in relation to the level of profits which is expected to be earned. (See ratio (5) for a measure of this risk.) If profits are not expected to vary significantly over time, a relatively high-geared financial structure may be employed safely and, from the viewpoint of the owners, profitably. If, on the other hand, the business is operating under risky conditions and profits are likely to show substantial fluctuations from year to year, a highly geared structure is undesirable even if outside funds can be obtained. In general, the owners of a business are expected to shoulder the risks of the enterprise in return for the possibility of large returns if it is successful, while outside creditors accept a lower return in the expectation that they are safe from the risks of non-payment of interest or loss of capital. In a highly geared company subject to profit fluctuations, however, the outside creditors are forced to shoulder the risk-bearing function which rightly belongs to the owners, and this of course carries the added implication that the business itself may fail if profits (before interest) fall below the level needed to meet the interest commitment. A business in a highly speculative industry should therefore be content with a low gearing ratio.

Short-run Risk Analysis

The risk relating to the firm's solvency, i.e. its ability to meet its long-term commitments, has been discussed in the preceding section. Owners are also interested in the risk relating to liquidity, i.e. the firm's ability to meet its short-run obligations.

Working Capital (or Current) Ratio

Measures of liquidity often employed include the *working capital* (or *current*) *ratio*, which is computed as follows:

$$\frac{\text{current assets}}{\text{current liabilities}} \tag{8}$$
$$= 4.0, 1.7 \text{ and } 2.0 \text{ in the respective years.}$$

The working capital ratio attempts to weigh the advantages arising out of the availability of the short-term funds represented by current liabilities (in particular their cheapness and convenience) against the risks involved in relying unduly on this source of finance (in particular the risk that the business will not be able to repay the debts when they fall due). This means that the working capital ratio should be neither too high nor too low. A very high working capital ratio may mean that short-term funds are not being profitably employed; because they are invested in unduly large holdings of cash, financial assets with low yields or trading inventories, the overall rate of return in the business is lower than it should be. If the working capital ratio is too low, on the other hand, it implies that the business has insufficient funds to carry on its operations at a satisfactory level. This may mean, in the extreme case, that the business cannot meet its maturing short-term financial obligations, with the result that it may be forced into liquidation by its creditors. Even if this plight is avoided, a firm with insufficient working capital is likely to find its profitability adversely affected by its inability to replace fixed assets when they wear out or become obsolete, or to purchase trading inventories on the most profitable terms, or to take steps to expand production or increase turnover. It needs to be emphasized, perhaps, that it is frequently the prosperous and rapidly expanding business which is faced with a shortage of working capital, simply because its earning capacity has outgrown the initial asset structure and capital resources of the enterprise. In these circumstances, the business is said to be under-capitalized, and additional long-term funds are required. [10]

Unfortunately, it is not possible to specify a working capital ratio which is appropriate for all firms and industries. The accepted doctrine points to a ratio of 2, but this figure has little justification because so much depends on trade practice, credit terms, the timing of cash flows and other factors. One cannot even say a decreasing ratio is always a bad sign; it may be a symptom of economies of scale or more efficient use of assets associated with business expansion. However in the example, the drastic fall in the ratio in 1984 needs to be investigated.

Quick Asset Ratio

Because current assets include prepayments and inventories (the latter may not be readily convertible into cash, especially in a time of financial crisis), and current liabilities include bank overdraft (which may be regarded as a revolving fund of somewhat greater permanence than other short-term liabilities), the working capital ratio needs to be supplemented by the *quick asset* (or *liquidity*) *ratio*, computed as follows (it is assumed bank overdraft amounts to $0, $1 000 and $1 500 in the three respective years): [11]

$$\frac{\text{quick assets}}{\text{quick liabilities}} = \frac{\text{current assets} - (\text{inventories} + \text{prepayments})}{\text{current liabilities} - \text{bank overdraft}} \tag{9}$$
$$= 2.0, 1.0 \text{ and } 1.5 \text{ in the three years.}$$

The quick asset ratio indicates the capacity of the business to meet its immediate financial obligations. It is sometimes called the acid test of financial viability, because it throws light on the firm's ability to cope with a sudden financial emergency from its own liquid resources, without having to realize trading inventories and other non-financial assets, or to rely on the forbearance of creditors. It will be seen from the above figures that the liquidity of the firm deteriorated sharply during 1984, so that by the end of that year it could barely meet the acid test. Coinciding with the improvement in the working capital position that has already been noted, the liquidity of the business has recovered somewhat in 1985.

There are certain weaknesses in using the working capital and quick asset ratios as measures of liquidity. First, the current assets and current liabilities are recorded at the date of the balance sheet, and the financial position may be quite different at other times. There is also a possibility of 'window dressing' or manipulation by management. Thus a working capital ratio greater than unity can be increased if some current liabilities are paid off, while a ratio less than unity can be increased by

[10] The usage of the terms 'under-capitalization' and 'over-capitalization' tends to be somewhat loose. Thus a firm is said to be under-capitalized if it is employing relatively insufficient equity funds. Over-capitalization usually refers to a surplus of funds not being efficiently used.

[11] Bank overdraft should be excluded only if the stated assumption (i.e. its relative permanence) is valid.

purchasing inventory on credit. [12] Disposal of inventories increases the quick asset ratio. Secondly, the ratios of expanding firms typically display a falling trend, rendering interpretation difficult. Lastly, the two ratios portray a static relationship, a criticism that is relevant to much of ratio analysis. The claims of creditors are not necessarily met out of existing assets, but may be met from new funds generated by sales.

Fund Flow Ratios

Because of the weaknesses of the working capital and quick asset ratios as measures of liquidity, other ratios which focus on fund flows have been proposed. One such measure is the ratio of funds generated by operations in the accounting period to current liabilities at the end of the period. Another liquidity measure is the ratio of quick assets (so-called defensive assets) to average out-of-pocket expenditures per day on operations. This is a measure of the firm's defensive position, i.e. the average number of (working) days' cover provided by quick assets for operating out-of-pocket outlays (expenses excluding depreciation and bad debts). This ratio, called the *basic defensive interval*, is computed as follows (assuming 300 working days in the year):

$$\frac{\text{quick assets}}{\text{estimated operating out-of-pocket outlays in year}} \times 300 \tag{10}$$

Information Analysis by Creditors

A person or firm that has lent money or supplied goods to a business has recourse only to legal remedies if the borrower does not comply with the terms of the contract entered into. In some cases, these terms may include the maintenance of a specified maximum debt-equity ratio (see ratios (6) and (6a)). The analysis of financial statements is more likely to be undertaken by a potential trade creditor or potential lender of money, with the object of acquiring information on the advisability or otherwise of providing the credit or the loan. The information analyses undertaken by various creditors and potential creditors—trade creditors, banks and two classes of long-term creditors—are discussed below. As will be seen, some creditors are in a stronger position than others, with respect to both their access to information and their financial options.

Trade Creditors

In deciding on credit terms in supplying goods to purchasers, potential trade creditors normally rely on the advice of credit agencies and their past experience of the customers. Insofar as trade creditors employ financial statement analysis, they are concerned with short-term risk ratios, e.g. ratios (8), (9) and (10), as indicators of the prospective debtors' liquidity position.

Banks

Banks have a preference for granting self-liquidating short-term loans, e.g. loans for the purchase of trading inventories, and borrowers are required to provide adequate

---

[12] Suppose that in 1985 current liabilities to the value of $1 000 were redeemed. The working capital ratio in that year would increase from 2.0 to 2.4 $\left(\text{i.e. from } \frac{7\,000}{3\,500} \text{ to } \frac{6\,000}{2\,500}\right)$.

collateral as well as evidence of credit-worthiness. The quality of earnings (5), long-term solvency ratios such as (6), (6a), (7), (7a), (7b) and (7c), as well as short-term liquidity ratios such as (8), (9) and (10), based on the borrower's financial statements for the most recent years, may be employed in evaluating risk. Banks also conduct their own valuations of assets underlying the financial statements, in particular of assets offered as collateral for the loan. But the best indication of the borrower's debt servicing capacity is a cash budget covering the period of the loan, and the bank, unlike the trade creditor, is often in a position to require a cash budget to be submitted in support of the loan application.

Illustration of a Cash Budget

Suppose that ABC Co. has a credit bank balance on 31 December of $800 and applies to the bank for a loan of $10 000 at 10 per cent interest per annum payable monthly, the principal amount to be repaid at the end of a three-month period. The company submits the cash budget reproduced in Table 7—6 in support of its loan application.

Long-term Creditors

Long-term debts are usually secured, and may be negotiable or non-negotiable. Where debts are non-negotiable (e.g. mortgages) potential creditors are influenced by return and risk considerations, but they have a different viewpoint from that of owners. The fixed interest income offered must be equal to or greater than an acceptable rate of return on loan funds, given the level of risk. The degree of risk in turn is a function of the margin of safety afforded by the collateral, i.e. the market value (the selling price) of the security relative to the amount of the loan, and of the financial position of the borrower, which may be evaluated by reference to the ratios of earnings variability (see ratio (5)), solvency and liquidity discussed above. Of particular significance are the ratios denoting the borrower's debt servicing capacity (ratios (7), (7a), (7b) and (7c)), and the presence of any senior secured claims in respect of the collateral.

Most negotiable long-term loans are secured (e.g. debentures),[13] although in recent years some well-established companies have successfully issued unsecured negotiable long-term debt instruments called 'unsecured notes'. The latter naturally carry a higher interest rate. Another example of a negotiable debt is a bond issued by a government authority. Basically the same considerations and objectives apply to the holders of negotiable and non-negotiable debt instruments, but the former class of creditors has a distinct advantage in the ready transferability of the investments in the market place.

Suppose a municipality has issued bonds which have a face value of $100, coupon rate [14] of 10 per cent per annum and are redeemable at par in 10 years time. If the current market price of the bond is $88.70, its *yield* (equivalent to the internal rate of return explained in Chapter 16) *r* is given by:

---

[13] A debenture is a long-term loan, usually secured, issued by a company.
[14] The coupon rate is the nominal interest rate payable on the face value of the bonds.

Table 7—6
ABC Co.
Cash Budget for the First Quarter 1985

	January	February	March
Cash balance, first of month	$800	$3 657	$5 489
Budgeted receipts as per Schedule A	48 000	55 875	52 200
Loan from bank	10 000		
	$58 800	$59 532	$57 689
Less: Budgeted disbursements as per Schedule B	$55 060	$53 960	$44 560
Interest on bank loan	83	83	83
Repayment of bank loan			10 000
	$55 143	$54 043	$54 643
Budgeted cash balance, end of month	$3 657	$5 489	$3 046

Schedule A
Budgeted Collections on Accounts Receivable

Month of Sales	Sales Value	Collections January	Collections February	Collections March
November (actual)	$40 000	$6 000		
December (actual)	52 500	42 000	$7 875	
January (estimated)	60 000		48 000	$9 000
February (estimated)	54 000			43 200
		$48 000	$55 875	$52 200

Note: All sales are on credit, no collections are made in month of sales, 80 per cent of sales are collected in the following month, 15 per cent in the month after and five per cent are uncollectable.

Schedule B
Budgeted Disbursements

	January	February	March
Month of purchases:			
December (actual)	$30 000		
January (estimated)		$20 000	
February (estimated)			$20 000
Payments to creditors	$30 000	$20 000	$20 000
Wages and salaries	18 500	18 000	18 000
Insurance		7 200	
Advertising	2 000		
Other expenses	4 560	4 560	4 560
Dividends			2 000
Purchase of vehicle		4 200	
	$55 060	$53 960	$44 560

Note: Purchases are paid for in the following month at the full cost price, and all other expenses are paid for in the month in which they are incurred.

$$V = \sum_{t=1}^{n} \frac{B_t}{(1 + r)^t} + \frac{P}{(1 + r)^n} \tag{11}$$

where V = market price of bond
B_t = interest payment in year t
P = principal repayment at end of bond's life
n = bond's life in years

$$\text{Thus } \$88.70 = \frac{\$10}{(1 + r)} + \frac{\$10}{(1 + r)^2} + \ldots + \frac{\$10}{(1 + r)^{10}} + \frac{\$100}{(1 + r)^{10}}$$

The above equation gives a yield of 12 per cent. If this rate is lower than that obtainable elsewhere, given the level of risk, the lender will sell the bond and invest the proceeds in a more attractive alternative. The same analysis may be applied to a holding in company debentures. Indeed, expression (11) may be used to determine the return on any loan investment (or its cost from the debtor's viewpoint), where the return is not readily evident.

Information Analysis by Management

Management decisions are governed by diverse motives, and management goals and owners' goals are not always congruent, e.g. management may strive for growth at the expense of profitability. Like owners and creditors, management makes use of accounting information analysis for a number of purposes, such as profit planning and budgeting, evaluating its own efficiency overall and in specific functional areas, and preparing reports on its performance to external users of financial statements, in particular, owners and creditors.

Structural and Trend Analyses

It is evident that a careful analysis of structural relationships and past trends disclosed by the financial statements must underlie the setting of targets in operating budgets and budgeted financial statements. The preparation of budgets and their role in the financial planning and control functions of management are treated in Chapters 28 and 29. For example, the cash budget is the most direct and reliable measure of the firm's current and expected liquidity position. Budgets serve one other important function. Generally, budget targets provide management with appropriate standards for evaluating its own performance.

Analysis of Overall Efficiency

Two ratios—operating profit to sales and sales to total assets—are often combined to provide a measure of overall management efficiency. This is the so-called *du Pont formula*, and its calculation and application to the data for XYZ Traders are shown as follows:

$$\left(\frac{\text{profit}}{\text{net sales}} \times 100 \right) \times \frac{\text{net sales}}{\text{investment}} = \left(\frac{\text{profit}}{\text{investment}} \times 100 \right) \qquad (12)$$

1983	14.0%	x	1.00	=	14.0%
1984	12.5%	x	0.89	=	11.1%
1985	17.6%	x	0.80	=	14.1%

where profit = net operating profit before interest and tax, and
investment = average total equities or total assets. [15]

The essence of the formula is that the effects of sales, operating profit and total assets employed are considered together in appraising management performance. It is particularly useful in comparing the results of decentralized divisions of different sizes. Secondly, the comparison indicates what action is required to improve management efficiency and profitability. For example, the results of XYZ Traders in 1985 are not greatly superior to those in 1983. There is an impressive reduction in operating costs, but the asset turnover ratio $\left(\frac{\text{net sales}}{\text{investment}} \right)$ has deteriorated; possibly the investment base is too large relative to the scale of operations, i.e. there may be over-capitalization.

Efficiency in Use of Working Capital

The investment base comprises two components: plant and working capital. The efficient use of fixed assets and the related problem of achieving the most economical production process are the responsibility of the works manager and the production engineer. But the accountant's financial data can throw light on the question of the efficient use of working capital. The major uses of working capital are to provide trade credit to customers and to finance the holding of inventories. Management efficiency in these areas may be measured by the rate of turnover of book debts and the rate of inventory turnover respectively.

The Turnover of Book Debts

The *rate of turnover of book debts* is represented by the number of days' *credit* sales represented by sundry debtors (before making any provisions for doubtful debts or discounts allowable). If credit sales in a particular year are valued at $9 000, book debts (before provisions) at the end of the year are $1 200, and it is estimated that there are 300 working days in the year, the number of working days' credit sales represented by the book debts may be calculated as follows: [16]

$$\frac{\text{book debts (before provisions)}}{\text{average daily credit sales}} = \frac{\$1\ 200}{\$30} = 40 \text{ working days} \qquad (13)$$

This figure may be compared with the normal credit terms of the business with a view to ascertaining whether undue credit is being extended. If sales are spread evenly over the month and the credit terms are monthly, i.e. the customer is not required to pay until the end of the following month, the average turnover period may be

---

[15] Sometimes investment is defined as total operating assets before deducting accumulated depreciation allowances.

[16] This assumes credit sales are evenly spread throughout the year. Otherwise the figure of average daily credit sales should be based on sales in the most recent months.

expected to be in the region of $1\frac{1}{2}$ months (or $37\frac{1}{2}$ working days on the basis of 25 working days a month). This is because the range of credit extended is between two months (in respect of sales made at the beginning of a month which are not due for payment until the end of the following month) and one month (in respect of sales made at the end of a month which are still due for payment at the end of the following month). If, as in the example, actual turnover of book debts is slower than the theoretical limit, action may be needed to speed up collections. On the other hand, if the average collection period is considerably less than $37\frac{1}{2}$ working days, consideration may need to be given to a relaxation of credit terms to encourage sales. Trends in the turnover of book debts are significant in deciding whether or not credit is being effectively controlled.

A more direct measure of efficiency in the collection of receivables is provided by an *age schedule of debtors* prepared at the end of each month, as explained in Chapter 3. Changes in the age distribution of debtors over time give insight into the effectiveness of credit policy and collection procedures. Since an age schedule imparts more information than the average collection period summary figure, the use of the age schedule is to be preferred.

The Rate of Inventory Turnover

The *rate of inventory turnover* in a period is calculated by dividing the cost of sales for the period by the cost of average inventory held during the period, the result being expressed as the number of times the inventory has turned over. It is desirable that both cost of sales and inventory figures are expressed in terms of current cost; if this is not done variations in selling margins or in methods of valuing inventories can distort the calculation. As a rough approximation, average inventory may be taken to be the average of opening and closing inventories for the year, but in practice it is preferable to take the average of monthly or even weekly figures, and to calculate rates of inventory turnover in respect of periods of less than a year. If the current cost of sales in the year 1985 is $6 800 and the current cost of average inventory held is $3 500, the number of times the stock has turned over may be calculated as follows:

$$\frac{\text{cost of sales}}{\text{cost of average inventory}} = \frac{\$6\ 800}{\$3\ 500} = 1.9 \text{ times} \tag{14}$$

Obviously, the higher the rate of inventory turnover the more effective is the use of funds. Different calculations may be made for different departments or different categories of inventories with a view to reducing the volume, or accelerating the flow, of slow-moving lines. Reductions in the rate of inventory turnover may be due to deliberate policy (e.g. where inventories are held in anticipation of price increases); or to circumstances beyond the control of management (resulting for example from depressed business conditions); or to managerial inefficiency (resulting from such causes as lack of control over the ordering and holding of inventories, the buying of lines which prove difficult to sell, or poor salesmanship). Trends in the rate of inventory turnover need to be carefully watched and the causes of deterioration ascertained and, if within the control of management, remedied.

Ratios of inventory turnover tend to vary markedly between industries, e.g. they are very high for fishmongers and low for firms selling grand pianos. These ratios are therefore not appropriate for purposes of inter-firm comparisons, unless the firms are in the same industry and catering for a similar clientele.

Evaluation of Management Performance by Outside Parties

There is a further aspect of accounting information analysis by management which can be briefly mentioned. Management is judged by the owners, creditors and the capital market generally, in many cases through the reports on its performance as displayed in the financial statements. Insofar as management is motivated to improve its performance and thereby to present a more favourable report, this can only be beneficial to all parties concerned. But management may also be motivated to mislead those to whom it is reporting, e.g. by manipulating figures or 'window-dressing', to reveal a more favourable liquidity or profitability position than really exists. Management may also modify its plans and budgets in order to make achieved results appear favourable to outsiders, e.g. it may delay the purchase of plant in order to display a more favourable liquidity position or rate of return on investment in the current period. Investors, creditors and other external users of financial statements need to complement their analysis with an extensive knowledge of the firm and its industry.

The principal tests that may be used to assess the significance of the results recorded in financial statements or accounting reports have now been examined. The performance of these tasks of analysis and interpretation marks the completion of the basic accounting process.

Some Evidence on the Usefulness of Ratio Analysis

A number of empirical studies of the usefulness of ratio analysis has been carried out in recent years. One such study, which focused on the differences between financial ratios of failed and non-failed companies, is that of W.H. Beaver (1966).

Beaver's study is based on data in the financial statements of 79 failed[17] and 79 non-failed American companies reported in *Moody's Industrial Manual,* covering the period 1954 to 1964. Each failed company was matched with a non-failed company of approximately the same size from the same industry. The financial data of each failed company relate to each of the five years before failure, and the data of the matching non-failed company relate to the same fiscal years.

Beaver examined the differences between the average values of 30 financial ratios for failed and non-failed companies, for each of the five years preceding the failures. Average values for six of the ratios are depicted in the charts of Figure 7—B.[18] The charts, which need to be read from right to left, reveal a consistent pattern of increasing divergence between ratio mean values for failed and non-failed companies as time to failure shortens. However, without knowledge of the distributions of mean values of financial ratios for failed and non-failed companies, no significance can be attached to these observations.

---

[17] Beaver defines a failed company as one which is unable to meet its financial obligations as they mature. His sample of 79 failed companies comprises failures from the following events: bankruptcy (59 companies), non-payment of dividends on preference shares (16), bond, i.e. debenture, default (3), and overdrawn bank account (1).

[18] The no-credit interval ratio is defined as: (defensive or quick assets *minus* current liabilities)/out-of-pocket expenditures for operations.

Figure 7—B
Comparison of Mean Ratios of Failed and Non-Failed Companies

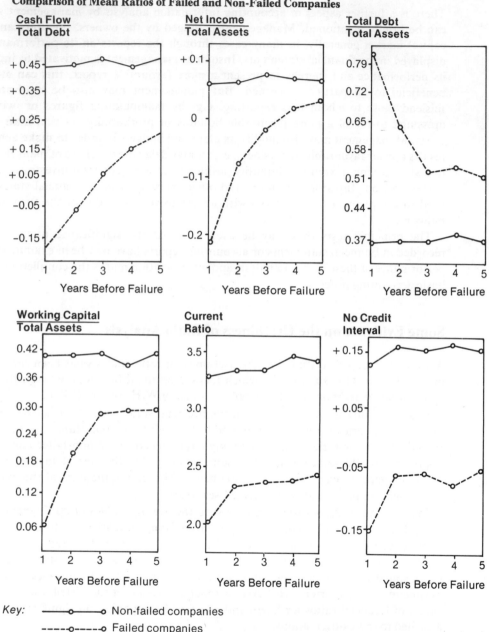

Key: —o——o Non-failed companies
        ----o----o Failed companies

Source: W.H. Beaver, 'Financial Ratios as Predictors of Failure', p.82.

In a test designed to determine whether individual financial ratios were useful as predictors of subsequent company failure, Beaver randomly divided his sample into two sub-samples, an 'estimation' sample and a 'validation' sample. For each financial ratio and for each of the five years, the companies in the estimation sample were ranked in order of ratio value and a cut-off point determined. The cut-off point for each ratio in each year was chosen to minimize the total number of incorrect classifications in the estimation sample. The cut-off points were then used to predict failed and non-failed companies in the validation sample, and the percentage of incorrect classifications was calculated (for each ratio in each year). The percentages of companies incorrectly classified on the basis of the two ratios with the least incorrect classifications were as follows:

	Year Before Failure				
	1	2	3	4	5
Cash flow to total debt	13	21	23	24	22
Net income to total assets	13	21	23	29	28

In a subsequent analysis, Beaver (1968) showed that some ratios performed consistently better than other ratios in predicting failure. The two ratios shown above (which Beaver calls non-liquid asset ratios) had a lower percentage error in each of the five years than any of the liquid asset ratios tested. For example, corresponding percentage errors associated with the working capital and quick asset ratios were as follows:

	Year Before Failure				
	1	2	3	4	5
Current assets to current liabilities	20	32	36	38	45
Quick assets to current liabilities	24	32	40	34	37

This evidence suggests (somewhat surprisingly) that ratios relating cash flows or income to debts or assets perform considerably better than liquid asset ratios in predicting failure.

Empirical studies of the usefulness of financial ratios need to be interpreted with caution, not least because of the lack of an adequate theoretical basis for the approaches adopted in the studies. In univariate prediction models, such as Beaver's, different ratios may give conflicting signals. Some studies have used a multivariate approach in an attempt to discover an optimal combination of financial ratios for the prediction of company failure, but to date results obtained have not been markedly superior to those obtained with univariate models.

Another interesting application of ratio analysis is developed in the study by Beaver, Kettler and Scholes. This study shows that accounting ratios may be used to obtain good estimates of the risk of a company as perceived by investors in the stock market.

Limitations of Ratio Analysis

Certain limitations generally associated with the use of ratio analysis are discussed below. Because of the limitations, financial statement analysis has a restricted, although nonetheless useful, role in decision making. Ratios are not intended to provide solutions. They are not the answers to questions; rather they suggest the questions that should be asked and the need to seek answers to these questions. They indicate areas of further investigation and the directions which the investigations should take. Further, individual ratios should be evaluated in the context of a comprehensive analysis of the financial statements and other available information. Each ratio contributes a small part to the understanding of the overall picture of profitability and financial conditions presented in the financial statements.

In the late 19th century, analysts employed the current ratio, i.e. the ratio of current assets to current liabilities, to assess the liquidity of firms. Since then a large number of ratios have come into use in *ad hoc* fashion, each purporting to measure some significant economic relationship. Thus it is not surprising that a unified theory of ratio analysis has not developed, and this lack of a general theory is perhaps the most fundamental limitation affecting the interpretation of financial statements. A large number of financial ratios is commonly used, but many have little or dubious significance (such as the ratio of sales to fixed assets when leased assets are important and are not included in the analysis), while other ratios merely duplicate one another with respect to the information they impart (such as the ratios of debt to proprietorship equity and debt to total equities).

Generally, it is difficult to determine unambiguously whether a particular ratio is good or bad in relation to a firm's profitability or financial position. Increased sales may be bad if costs have been increased disproportionately. Even increased net profits may be bad if the increase has been brought about at the expense of future profits, e.g. by cutting back on research and development expenditures.

A ratio expresses a relationship between two financial magnitudes. Where these two magnitudes have an economic link, interpretation may be relatively straightforward, as in the ratio of gross profit to sales or of return on investment. Where there is no clear-cut functional relationship, as in the current ratio, it is often difficult to say whether a particular value or a change therein is good or bad. The essence of ratio analysis is comparison with a standard, which theoretically represents an ideal circumstance. As this ideal is not known, it is customary to employ an industry average or the past experience of the firm as a standard. The danger here is that one may be comparing one inefficient set of circumstances with another. An industry average thus includes the experiences of both the efficient and the inefficient firms in the industry. Some writers recommend that the industry average should be the median rather than the arithmetic mean (which is affected by extreme outlying values), but it is difficult to be enthusiastic about a policy of judging performance by reference to average performance. Where data relating to the firm's most efficient competitors are available, an effective standard for comparison is given by the range of values which reflect the experience of efficient competitors. *Prima facie*, a bad ratio may be defined as one which lies outside the range, but the information is rarely obtainable and the guideline itself is imprecise. For example, is the distribution of values important or is deviation in either direction equally undesirable?

A fundamental limitation of ratio analysis relates to the monetary assumption discussed in earlier chapters. For example, the use of the current ratio as an index of liquidity is only meaningful when current assets are stated at their current market values and, strictly, these values should be given by the market resale price. With other ratios, such as the ratio of gross profit to sales, current replacement cost of inventories is often the appropriate valuation measure to employ. Generally, cross-sectional analyses need to be based on current values for purposes of meaningful interpretation. Changes in the value of the dollar over time (as measured by a general price index) do not vitiate cross-sectional analysis (which relates to a point of time), although they may have to be taken into account in trend analysis. For example, when a comparison of absolute magnitudes (such as sales figures) over a series of years is undertaken, they should be deflated by a relevant price index (such as the consumer price index or one of its components). On the other hand, ratios such as the ratio of gross profit to sales can be compared one year with another, without needing adjustments for price changes. Many writers believe that current market prices should be used in the construction and use of ratios for both cross-sectional and trend analyses. If the financial statements are based on historical costs they should be recast in current value terms, as demonstrated in Chapter 19, in order that more meaningful analysis can be undertaken.

There is a further consideration relating to the element of permissiveness in accounting methods. Financial statements need to be standardized before a useful comparison of the information contained therein can be made. For purposes of trend analysis, financial statements for different years need to be prepared on a consistent basis, while for purposes of cross-sectional analysis the financial statements of different firms need to be based on a uniform accounting system. If necessary, the statements must be recast before an analysis is undertaken, so as to ensure comparability. It is difficult to draw valid conclusions from a comparison of the financial statements of different firms, or of the same firm in different years, when alternative accounting methods (e.g. different inventory valuation and depreciation methods, different treatments of exploration outlays or of leases) or different accounting classification systems are employed.

Lastly, the reader needs to be cautioned that the basic objective of his analysis is not primarily to reveal the past but rather to influence or predict the future. Even if the analysis is undertaken as a means of evaluating past performance, its real purpose is to facilitate control and thereby improve future performance. If the analysis is intended to facilitate planning or decision making by management, investors or creditors, the link with the future is direct. Since the future is unknown, prediction is always a hazardous business. Knowledge of past event is needed as a basis for predictions (as otherwise they will merely be guesswork), but the most careful predictions must be based on assumptions regarding the projection of past trends and relationships into future periods. Many accountants would claim that prediction is not an accounting function, but it cannot be denied that the prediction of future outcomes is an important goal of those who submit the accounting system's output to close scrutiny and analysis.

Appendix

This appendix is included in order to round off the discussion on ratio analysis. The reader is advised to defer study of the appendix until after he has read Chapter 11 on company accounts.

Analysis of a Company's Financial Statements

The analysis of a company's financial statements is basically similar to that of an unincorporated firm or sole trader. However, there are certain items relating to shareholders' equity in a company's balance sheet and profit and loss statement, the treatment of which needs to be explained.[19] The shareholders' equity of Australasia Traders Ltd in Table 11—1 of Chapter 11 is shown below in summary form. It is assumed that goodwill and other intangible assets do not represent productive

---

[19] The analysis of debentures and unsecured notes in a company's balance sheet does not differ from that for other long-term debts. The analysis of long-term debts has been explained earlier.

resources and hence are treated as a reduction of shareholders' equity in the balance sheet.

50 000, 6% preference shares of $1 each		$50 000
100 000 ordinary shares of $1 each		100 000
		150 000
Reserves	$75 400	
Retained earnings (or unappropriated profits)	5 410	
		80 810
Total share capital and reserves		230 810
Less: Goodwill and other intangible assets not written off		4 000
Shareholders' equity		$226 810

Certain revenue items in Table 11—2 of Chapter 11 follow. Data from Tables 11—1 and 11—2 are employed to illustrate ratios in this appendix.

Net profit for year after tax	$17 400
Dividends on preference shares	3 000
Dividends on ordinary shares	6 000

Generally, holders of preference shares are entitled to certain privileges, including the payment of dividends at a *fixed* rate (six per cent in the above illustration) before any dividends are paid on ordinary shares, but preference dividends can only be paid out of profits and may not be paid if profits of the company are inadequate. Thus preference shares occupy a half-way position between long-term debt and ordinary share capital. For example, for the purpose of examining the effect of gearing on the return on ordinary shareholders' equity (see Table 7—5), preference shares should be treated as analogous to debt funds; this is because the preference dividend is at a fixed rate. However, the risk of insolvency is not increased by the use of preference capital because the fixed dividend, unlike the interest on debt, is payable only if profits are earned. Thus in computing the debt-equity ratios (6) and (6a) in order to evaluate the long-term financial position, preference shares are treated as part of proprietorship equity.

Because management performance is judged by the ordinary shareholders, of particular interest to the ordinary shareholders and to management is the *return on ordinary shareholders' equity*. This is computed as follows:

$$\frac{\text{net profit after tax} - \text{preference dividends}}{\text{average shareholders' equity } less \text{ average par value of preference shares}} \times 100$$

$$= \frac{\$17\ 400 - \$3\ 000}{\$226\ 810 - \$50\ 000} \times 100 = 8.1\% \ [20]$$

Another measure of the return on ordinary shares is that of *earnings per share*, computed as follows:

$$\frac{\text{net profit after tax} - \text{preference dividends}}{\text{number of ordinary shares}}$$

$$= \frac{\$14\ 400}{100\ 000} = 14.4 \text{ cents}$$

[20] Strictly the denominator is an average of the respective book value figures at the beginning and end of the period.

A particular version of earnings per share is based on earnings after adding back depreciation expense, to give an approximation to the operating cash flow for the year. Caution is needed in interpreting this ratio, because in the long run a company must recover its fixed capital costs:

$$\frac{(\text{net profit after tax} - \text{preference dividends}) + \text{depreciation}}{\text{number of ordinary shares}}$$

$$\approx \frac{\text{operating cash flow generated}}{\text{number of ordinary shares}}$$

Earnings and Dividend Yields

The market value of a share represents the present value of the company's expected future cash flows (discounted at the appropriate market-determined rate). Clearly the future cash flows are stochastic and the share price is an equilibrium price that reflects an average of the expectations and risk preferences held by all market participants.

An individual investor will form his own assessment of what the shares of a particular company are worth, and he will compare this assessment with the market's assessment for the purpose of his decision whether to buy, hold or sell. He may do this by comparing either: (a) the earnings or the dividend yield with his subjective or required rate of return; or (b) the share's market price with his subjective value of the share. The two methods (a) and (b) are the same and give the same answer. This is because the subjective value of the share is calculated as the relationship of net profit per share to the subjective or required rate of return. The equivalence of the two methods may be illustrated by assuming that the earnings yield is equal to the subjective rate of return. The first method then involves the following comparison:

$$\frac{\text{net profit per share}}{\text{market price per share}} = \text{required earnings rate of return}$$

while the second method involves the following comparison:

$$\frac{\text{net profit per share}}{\text{required earnings rate of return}} = \text{market price per share}$$

It will be seen that the two equations are the same.

The current earnings and dividends used in the analysis are taken to be indicators of future earnings and dividends, but the data should be adjusted in the light of publicly available information about future earnings and dividend levels.

Example: Australasia Traders Ltd currently earns 14.4 cents per ordinary share. Because of financial prudence, dividend pay-outs have been low, averaging 6 cents per share, but the directors have announced that dividends will be in the region of 10 cents per share in future years. The market price of the share is $1.08, and on an investment of this risk class you require either an earnings return of 14 per cent or a dividend return of 11 per cent.

(a) Evaluation based on earnings:

$$\text{Earnings yield} = \frac{\text{net profit per share}}{\text{market price per share}} \times 100$$

$$= \frac{\$0.144}{\$1.08} \times 100$$

$$= 13.3\%$$

$$\text{Subjective value of share} = \frac{\text{net profit per share}}{\text{required earnings rate of return}} \times 100$$

$$= \frac{\$0.144}{14} \times 100$$

$$= \$1.03$$

(b) Evaluation based on dividends:

$$\text{Dividend yield} = \frac{\text{dividend per share}}{\text{market price per share}} \times 100$$

$$= \frac{\$0.10}{\$1.08} \times 100$$

$$= 9.3\%$$

$$\text{Subjective value of share} = \frac{\text{dividend per share}}{\text{required dividend rate of return}} \times 100$$

$$= \frac{\$0.10}{11} \times 100$$

$$= \$0.91$$

In the above illustration, both earnings and dividend tests indicate a sell (or do not buy) decision. The two tests do not always give the same signal, since the relative importance of earnings and dividends as viewed by the individual investor may be different from that of the market. For example, a particular investor may have a preference for capital gains rather than dividend income because of tax considerations, and therefore he will place greater emphasis on the earnings yield test.

A ratio much favoured by investment counsellors is the price-earnings ratio, which is the inverse of the earnings yield and is computed as follows:

$$\frac{\text{market price per share}}{\text{net profit per share}}$$

$$= \frac{\$1.80}{\$0.144} = 7.5$$

A reason for the ratio's popularity is that it is readily understood, e.g. the above says that the shareholder is buying 7.5 years of current earnings. The measure gains no special merit by being stood on its head and is subject to all the qualifications attributed to the earnings yield noted above. Like the earnings yield, it needs to be interpreted with care.

Market-based Rate of Return

Where the company's shares are traded on the stock exchanges, the most appropriate comparison is a market-based rate of return with the investor's required rate of return for shares in that risk class. The market-based return includes a capital gain component and a dividend component, and is computed as follows:

$$R(e)_t = \frac{P_t - P_{t-1} + D}{P_{t-1}} \times 100$$

where
$R(e)_t$ = return on ordinary equity in period t,

P_{t-1}, P_t = share price at the beginning and end of the current period respectively, [21] and

D = dividend paid in the period.

Suppose a share sold for \$7 on 1 January and for \$8 (*ex dividend*) on the following 31 December, on which day a dividend of \$0.50 was paid. Its marked-based rate of return is $\frac{\$8 - \$7 + \$0.50}{\$7} \times 100$ or 21 per cent approximately. [22]

Some Conclusions

In the case of a listed company, investors can compare their subjective assessments of its value with that implied by the earnings or dividend yield or market-based rate of return, as explained above. However, it should be made clear that the share price is a market-determined equilibrium price reflecting the buying and selling decisions of all market participants. Given this and the considerable evidence that the market is efficient in using publicly available information (i.e. information is rapidly and fully reflected in the share price), it seems reasonable to conclude that the individual investor cannot out-perform the market (unless he has insider information). The assessment of a particular share's intrinsic worth by the methods of analysis discussed in this chapter, for purposes of making investment decisions, has been questioned by some writers.

The most appropriate policy for the individual investor would appear to be to invest in a diversified portfolio of shares, in which the risks that are peculiar to individual shares are minimized. The investor's objective should be to maximize his portfolio return subject to his preferred level of portfolio risk.

References

Beaver, W.H., 'Financial Ratios as Predictors of Failure', *Empirical Research in Accounting: Selected Studies, 1966 (Supplement to Journal of Accounting Research)*, 1966, pp. 71-111.

Beaver, W.H., 'Alternative Accounting Measures as Predictors of Failure', *Accounting Review*, January 1968, pp. 113-22.

Beaver, W.H., Kettler, K. and Scholes M., 'The Association between Market Determined and Accounting Determined Risk Measures', *Accounting Review*, October 1970, pp. 654-82.

Additional Reading

Anthony, R.N., *Management Accounting, Text and Cases*, Irwin, Homewood, Ill., 1970, Chapter 11.

[21] Due allowances should be made for any share splits and bonus and rights issues.

[22] Whether the investor bases his analysis on the experience of the most recent period or a number of recent periods will depend on his knowledge or belief about the return generating process.

Beaver, W.H., 'Financial Statement Analysis', in S. Davidson, *Handbook of Modern Accounting*, McGraw-Hill, New York, 1970, Chapter 5.

Van Horne, J.C., *Financial Management and Policy*, Prentice-Hall, Englewood Cliffs, N.J., 1974, Chapter 26.

Discussion Questions

1 Describe and examine the significance of the following relationships in the analysis of company financial statements: (a) gross profit ratio; (b) inventory turnover; (c) working capital ratio; (d) interest cover ratio; and (e) rate of return on funds employed.

2 Critically examine the working capital ratio as an indicator of a firm's short-term financial strength.

3 (a) What is the significance of (i) the rate of inventory turnover, and (ii) the turnover of book debts, in assessing a firm's efficiency in using the funds under its control? Explain how each may be measured.

(b) What light can annual accounting reports throw on the question whether funds invested in fixed assets are being effectively used? What other information might management seek in assessing a firm's efficiency in utilizing its fixed assets?

4 It has been said that, for many firms, inventories represent the most important item in the balance sheet. Comment on why this may be so and discuss problems which arise in interpreting the significance of movements in inventories.

5 You have recently been asked to advise a wholesale trading company which finds itself financially embarrassed by a large overdraft, which the bank is pressing the company to reduce. It appears to you that investment in inventories is abnormally large and that insufficient attention is paid by management to the control of inventories.

(a) Discuss the measures you would employ to determine whether or not funds invested in inventories are being effectively used.

(b) Assuming that you find that investment in inventories is excessive, what remedial measures would you suggest?

6 Explain how different classes of creditors and potential creditors can make use of financial statement analysis for their own needs.

7 Consider the role of the funds statement in relation to the assessment of a firm's financial strength.

8 Discuss the limitations of financial statement analysis.

9 Discuss some of the empirical evidence on the usefulness of ratio analysis.

10 Explain how increased gearing of a company's financial structure may raise the rate of return on ordinary capital. Under what circumstances may such action be justifiable? What are its disadvantages from the viewpoint of (a) ordinary shareholders, (b) debenture holders, and (c) other creditors.

11 To what extent can an investor proposing to buy shares in a company evaluate effectively the profitability and financial strength of the company by reference to its published profit and loss statements and balance sheets?

12 In analysing and interpreting the financial statements of a retail department store with a view to possible investment in the enterprise (which is a limited liability company whose shares are quoted on the stock exchange), what relationships would you examine to throw light on the following:

(a) the profitability of the enterprise;

(b) the efficiency with which funds are employed; and

(c) the extent to which financial stability is being maintained?

What other information would you seek to obtain to supplement the data available from accounting reports?

13 Examine the view that, because they are backward-looking, indicators of profitability and financial stability derived from a company's published financial statements are of limited usefulness in assessing the company's performance prospects. What other means of assessment are available to (a) the managers of the company, and (b) investors contemplating the purchase of shares in the company?

14 Smithson Ltd is a department store operating in the main retail district of a rapidly growing capital city. Its land, which was purchased nearly 50 years ago, and its buildings, which were constructed 15 years ago, are recorded in the firm's balance sheet at original cost less accumulated depreciation provisions. The balance sheet also records substantial inventory holdings (valued at cost or market, whichever is the lower) and debtors, and the current ratio is approaching 3:1. There are no long-term liabilities. During the last 10 years, the company has achieved an average rate of return, as measured by net profits in relation to shareholders' equity, of 9.3 per cent; the rate for the last year was 9.7 per cent. The dividend on ordinary capital has been maintained at 10 cents per 50 cents share for eight years. The ordinary shares are quoted on the stock exchange at $2.20.

A financial analyst, in his weekly column in a national business journal, has recommended the shares of Smithson Ltd as an excellent investment. Comment on this advice with respect to:

(a) the company's earning power in relation to the resources at its command; and

(b) the attractiveness of the company as a prospective take-over target.

Exercises

1 Calculate significant relationships from the following information, and comment briefly on changes in the firm's operating results and financial position as revealed by your analysis:

(a) Summary of Income Statements for Year Ending:

	30 June 1983	30 June 1984	30 June 1985
Sales	$40 000	$48 000	$50 000
Cost of sales	30 000	34 000	36 000
Gross profit	$10 000	$14 000	$14 000
Selling expenses	2 000	2 400	4 000
Administration expenses	1 400	1 800	2 200
Financial expenses	200	200	600
Net profit	$6 400	$9 600	$7 200

(b) Summary of Balance Sheets as at:

	30 June 1983	30 June 1984	30 June 1985
Current liabilities	$ 8 000	$ 6 400	$20 000
Proprietorship equity	32 000	34 000	32 400
	$40 000	$40 400	$52 400
Current assets	22 000	20 000	26 000
Fixed assets	18 000	20 400	26 400
	$40 000	$40 400	$52 400
Bank	5 800	800	Cr. (12 000)
Accounts receivable	7 400	8 000	7 600
Inventories (at cost)	8 000	10 000	18 000

(c) *Additional information*:

Inventory at 1 July 1982 (at cost), $6 000. All sales were credit sales.

2 Analyse and interpret the following information relating to a trading enterprise, with particular reference to profitability, the effectiveness with which funds are being used, and the financial stability of the business. Your answer should include:

(a) comparative accounting reports which highlight significant relationships bearing on the above questions;

(b) a funds statement for the year ended 30 June 1985.

	Year Ended 30 June	
	1984	1985
Sales	$36 000	$43 200
Cost of goods sold	25 200	27 000
Selling and administrative expenses	5 400	9 000

	As at 30 June	
	1984	1985
Cash at bank	$3 780	—
Accounts receivable	5 400	$7 200
Inventories	8 640	16 380
Fixed assets (at cost)	12 600	14 400
Provision for depreciation	6 300	8 820
Accounts payable	4 320	3 960
Bank overdraft	—	4 500
Proprietor's capital	18 000	18 000
Proprietor's current account	1 800	2 700

Inventories at 1 July 1983, $7 200. All sales were made on monthly credit terms. No fixed assets were sold during the year.

3 The following information has been extracted from the books of a small retail organization:

Income Statements

	1984		1985	
Sales		064 000		$80 000
Cost of sales		48 000		64 000
Gross profit		16 000		16 000
Depreciation of fixtures and fittings	$1 600		$1 920	
Selling expenses	1 600		2 880	
Depreciation of office furniture	800		800	
Administrative expenses	5 600	9 600	5 600	11 200
Net operating profit		6 400		4 800
Loss on sale of office furniture		—		160
Net profit		**$6 400**		**$4 640**

Balance Sheets

	End 1984		End 1985	
Bank		$2 400		$320
Accounts receivable		6 400		8 160
Inventories		9 600		12 960
Fixtures and fittings	$16 000		$19 200	
Less: Accumulated depreciation	6 400	9 600	8 320	10 880
Office furniture	8 000		7 200	
Less: Accumulated depreciation	4 000	4 000	4 320	2 880
Total assets		**$32 000**		**$35 200**
Accounts payable		5 760		9 280
B. Cummings—Capital		24 000		24 000
B. Cummings—Current account		2 240		1 920
Total equities		**$32 000**		**$35 200**

Additional information:
    (a) it may be assumed that all sales were credit sales;
    (b) inventories on 1 January 1984 were valued at $6 400;
    (c) fixtures and fittings costing $3 200 were bought on 1 January 1984;
    (d) office furniture (which originally cost $800 and had a net book value of $320) was sold for $160 at the end of 1985.

You are required to write a report to the proprietor, B. Cummings, analysing changes in profitability and financial position which occurred during 1985. Your report should include a funds statement for 1985 and also any other measures which may explain the changes which have occurred.

4 The manager of the Edgeware China Co. submitted the following information for your perusal:

(a) Balance Sheets as at 31 December

	1984		1985	
Cash at bank		$5 200		$6 000
Accounts receivable		39 600		40 000
Inventories		71 800		84 000
Buildings and equipment	$98 200		$108 000	
Less: Accumulated depreciation	38 800	59 400	44 200	63 800
Land		22 800		22 800
Total assets		$198 800		$216 600
Accounts payable		13 200		16 800
Notes payable		31 000		34 200
Estimated tax liability		4 200		4 800
Mortgage		23 400		27 200
Paid-up capital		79 200		79 200
Retained earnings		47 800		54 400
Total equities		$198 800		$216 600

(b) Income Statements for Year Ended 31 December

	1984		1985	
Sales		$210 400		$213 400
Cost of sales		115 400		117 400
Gross profit		95 000		96 000
Depreciation	$5 000		$5 400	
Selling and administrative expenses	66 000	71 000	67 400	72 800
Income before interest and tax		24 000		23 200
Interest expense		2 800		3 000
Income before tax		21 200		20 200
Estimated tax		9 700		9 300
Net income after tax		11 500		10 900
Dividends		4 300		4 300
Retained earnings		$7 200		$6 600

You are required to report to:
(i)   the manager on the profitability and financial stability of the company;
(ii) a potential investor on the advisability of investing in the company; and
(iii) a potential creditor on the advisability of making a loan to the company.

5 Your client wishes to invest in the Exclusive Gift Shop Co. and asks you to advise him on the profitability and financial position of the company. You are supplied with the income statement and balance sheet of the company as well as selected ratios relating to the financial statements of previous years. In your report to your client you should also indicate what additional information you require to help you in your analysis of the business.

(a) Income Statement for Year Ended 31 December 1985

Sales		$300 000
Cost of sales:		
Operating inventory	$60 000	
Purchases	120 000	
	180 000	
Closing inventory	90 000	90 000
Gross profit		210 000
Selling and distribution expenses	30 000	
General and administrative expenses	45 000	
Financial expenses	15 000	90 000
Net profit before tax		120 000
Estimated tax		60 000
Net profit after tax		60 000
Retained earnings 1 January 1985		72 000
		132 000
Proposed final dividend		21 000
Balance of retained earnings 31 December 1985		$111 000

(b) Balance Sheet as at 31 December 1985

Shareholders' equity		
Paid-up capital	$159 000	
Retained earnings	111 000	$270 000
Non-current liabilities		
Loan		78 000
Current liabilities		
Bank overdraft	$6 000	
Estimated tax liability	60 000	
Accounts payable	18 000	
Proposed dividend	21 000	105 000
		$453 000
Current assets		
Accounts receivable	30 000	
Inventory	90 000	120 000
Non-current assets		
Motor vehicles	24 000	
Land and buildings	203 000	
Fixtures and fittings	37 000	
Office equipment	18 000	
Leasehold premises	51 000	333 000
		$453 000

(c) Selected Ratios from Previous Years' Financial Statements

	1982	1983	1984
Gross profit ratio (%)	60	68	65
Net profit (before tax) to sales ratio (%)	46	47	45
Net profit (before tax) to shareholders' equity (%)	50.1	49.5	50
Debt-equity ratio (%)	15	11	9
Working capital ratio	1.3	1.5	1.6
Quick asset ratio	1.1	1.15	1.05
Rate of inventory turnover (times p.a.)	3.6	4.1	3.2

6 The Dynamic Manufacturing Co. Pty Ltd is a long-established firm which manufactures machinery to customers' orders. The company wishes your firm to supply them with materials valued at $4 480 on 30-day terms.

From the following information you are asked to submit a report on the financial condition of the company and recommend whether your firm should supply goods on credit to the company. Support your arguments with ratio and other analyses.

Balance Sheets as at 30 June

	1984		1985	
Current assets				
Petty cash advance	$224		$224	
Accounts receivable	13 440		14 560	
Work-in-process	8 400		16 800	
Inventory of raw materials	10 080		8 960	
Prepaid expenses	336	$32 480	336	$40 880
Non-current assets				
Plant and machinery (at cost)	23 520		26 880	
Less: Accumulated depreciation	11 200		11 760	
	12 320		15 120	
Factory building (cost)	33 600	45 920	33 600	48 720
		$78 400		$89 600
Shareholders' equity				
Paid-up capital		28 000		28 000
Retained earnings		3 360		(2 240) Dr.
		31 360		25 760
Non-current liabilities				
Mortgage		11 200		28 000
Current liabilities				
Bank overdraft	10 080		11 200	
Accounts payable	25 760	35 840	24 640	35 840
		$78 400		$89 600

You are also informed that annual sales amounted to $67 200 and $75 600 in 1984 and 1985, respectively.

7 The following information relates to the operations and financial position of the O.P.R. Trading Co. Ltd:

(a) Income Statements for Year Ended 30 June

	1984		1985	
Credit sales		0012 000		$390 000
Less: Cost of sales				
Opening inventory	$57 200		$52 000	
Purchases	244 400		312 000	
	301 600		364 000	
Closing inventory	52 000	249 600	39 000	325 000
Gross profit		62 400		65 000
Expenses		43 680		45 500
Net profit before tax		18 720		19 500
Estimated tax		6 500		7 800
Net profit after tax		12 220		11 700
Retained earnings brought forward		—		3 120
		12 220		14 820
Proposed dividend		9 100		10 400
Retained earnings carried forward		$3 120		$4 420

(b) Balance Sheets as at 30 June

	1984		1985	
Current assets	$2 600		—	
Bank	26 000		$39 000	
Accounts receivable	52 000		39 000	
Inventories		$80 600		$78 000
Fixed assets (net)		130 000		182 000
		$210 600		$260 000
Shareholders' equity	130 000		135 200	
Paid-up capital	3 120		4 420	
Retained earnings	22 880	156 000	22 880	162 500
Reserves				
Non-current liabilities		15 600		32 500
10% debentures				
Current liabilities				
Bank overdraft	—		26 000	
Estimated tax liability	6 500		7 800	
Proposed dividend	9 100		10 400	
Accounts payable	23 400	39 000	20 800	65 000
		$210 600		$260 000

(c) There were 300 trading days in each year. The terms of credit for both purchases and sales were 10 days.

(d) Funds Statements for the Year Ended 30 June 1985

Sources of funds	
Revenue from sales	$390 000
Use of cash funds and bank overdraft	28 600
Issue of shares	5 200
Issue of debentures	16 900
Increase in income tax payable	1 300
	$442 000
Uses of funds	
Purchases of inventory for sale	312 000
Expenses incurred	
(not including depreciation of $6 500)	39 000
Fixed assets purchased	58 500
Appropriation of profits to income tax	7 800
Dividend paid	9 100
Additional credit allowed to customers	13 000
Reduction of amounts owing to suppliers	2 600
	$442 000

Although the sales volume has increased, profits and the financial position of the company remain unsatisfactory.

You are required to write a report:

(i)   suggesting reasons why profits have not increased;

(ii) setting out trends in the financial position and explaining what these trends mean; and

(iii) giving your recommendation for future management action.

Your arguments should be supported by trend and ratio analyses.

8 Information Systems, Data Processing and the Role of the Accountant

Traditionally, man, material, money and machines have been considered the main resources of an organization, but in recent years there has been a growing awareness that *information* is an additional important resource without which organizational objectives cannot be achieved. In general terms, information is produced by converting raw data into a more useful and refined form. The volume of data in modern organizations has grown to such proportions that information production has become a specialized activity. Increasingly, attention is being paid to the design of an effective information system and this itself has become a specialized task. Although accountants in the past have been involved in the production of information for management, their traditional role is changing with the emergence of a new technology of information production and information system design. This chapter presents an overview of the information system and discusses the main data processing techniques used in practice. The electronic data processing system is treated in some detail because of its wide acceptance in commerce and industry, and the role of the accountant in the design and operation of a computerized information system is discussed.

Overview of an Information System

The information system of an organization can be subdivided into two groups: (a) an informal information system; and (b) a formal information system.

In an informal information system, data are collected and processed and information disseminated in an unstructured way. The source of the data is often varied and indiscriminate, e.g. trade journals, newspapers, government announcements and business discussions. There are no set procedures for the selection of relevant data, there is no predetermined frequency for processing the data and there are no definite report formats for the output. Examples of informal information are the memoranda on various matters received from time to time by the managing director or general manager of a company from his executive assistant.

A formal information system is characterized by a set of procedures for the selection of relevant data and input preparation, a predetermined frequency of processing, and a well defined report format for the output. The weekly inventory status reports distributed to the department heads in a retail store are examples of formal information. While the informal information system often has an important role within an organization, our main concern is with the formal information system, which hereafter will be referred to as the information system.

The information system comprises a data processing system and input preparation at different sections of the organization. The structure of an information system differs between business organizations. Figure 8—A illustrates the information flow in a business organization which operates a central data processing system and has a number of departments—accounting and finance, production, personnel and marketing. Inputs are received by the accounting and finance, production, personnel and marketing departments from various sources, such as debtors, creditors, warehouse, employment agencies and the sales force. These inputs are edited for use in the central data processing department. Other inputs, such as environmental constraints and forecasts, are also received by the central data processing department from management itself. The output produced by the central data processing department is disseminated to general management and the various departments in the organization as well as to outside parties. In practice, the nature of the business differs significantly between organizations; therefore the amount of information related to each of the activities also can be expected to differ.

Figure 8—A
An Overview of a Hypothetical Formal Information System in Business Organizations

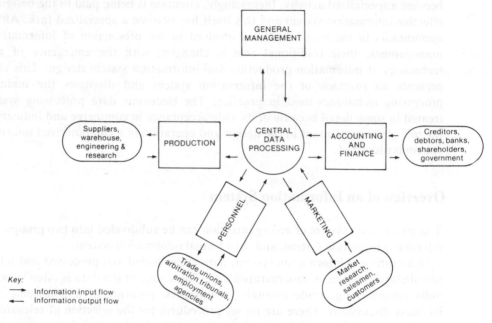

Key:
→ Information input flow
← Information output flow

Figure 8—B
Specialized Information Requirements for Different Organizations

Nature of Business	Examples of Firms or Departments	Specialized Functions of the Information System
Industrial	Manufacturing companies	Sales forecasting, purchases and inventory management, production scheduling and control
Commercial	Insurance companies	Preparing notices of premiums due, commission and dividend calculations, processing claims
	Banks	Processing cheques, updating current and savings accounts, reporting to the Reserve Bank
Service	Electricity, tele-communications and gas corporations	Resources management, preparation of monthly bills
	Airlines	Passenger bookings and reservations
Government	Income tax department	Income tax processing
	Social security department	Social security payments

For the purpose of analysing these differences, organizations may be classified into four groups: (a) industrial, (b) commercial, (c) service, and (d) government organizations. There are some common applications, such as personnel, payroll, accounts receivable, accounts payable and general ledger accounting, which are extensively used by all types of organizations. But specialized information systems have been developed to match the specific requirements of organizations, as shown in Figure 8—B.

Objectives of the Information System

Some specialized information systems are limited to the handling of a large volume of data, e.g. the preparation of monthly bills by an electricity corporation, while others are designed to assist in day-to-day operations, such as production scheduling in a manufacturing firm. Specialized information systems are limited and sectional in nature, reflecting only a segment of the organization's activities. Since the organization is an integrated entity with interdependent functions, the information system should also be an integrated whole encompassing the overall activities of the organization. [1] The objectives of an information system will depend on the view management takes about its information requirements; these may include one of the following: record keeping, operations and control, and integrated planning and policy making.

Record Keeping

In many organizations, the volume of transactions is so great that the handling of information with efficiency, accuracy and economy represents a difficult problem. In these organizations, the processing of routine information becomes the first priority in mechanization. The information system is designed either to assemble the evidence of transactions or simply to give a summarized historical report. The provision of information for decision making in these situations, while important, is not the main objective of the system.

Examples of the output of information systems oriented to record keeping are historical financial statements, customer billings, inventory status reports, income tax returns and social security payment listings.

Operations and Control

The information system may be designed to assist employees in their day-to-day operations, and to exercise control over the implementation of short-run plans. An airline passenger booking system and a production scheduling system are examples of information systems oriented to operations. An airline booking system is designed to give instantaneous reports on the status of seats available on particular flights, so that passenger bookings can be confirmed on the spot. A production scheduling system is used to determine the allocation of machine time to various jobs, so that delivery schedules can be met at the least cost.

Variance reports on financial, sales and production plans are examples of information systems oriented to control. These reports compare actual performance with planned performance, so that corrective measures may be taken on the basis of differences disclosed.

---

[1] Some segments of the organization may be relatively independent and operate their own information systems, which relate to their separate activities.

Integrated Planning and Policy Making

At the general management level, the problems of concern are the performance of the entire organization and the formulation of long-term plans. [2] These problems are relatively broad in scope, usually involving the overall activities of the organization. The information system designed for the needs of general management may comprise a mathematical model of the entire operation. By representing the entire operation in the form of a mathematical model and by manipulating the model, it is often possible to predict the likely outcome of alternative decisions. These mathematical models are usually called corporate models. They provide an example of an information system oriented to integrated planning and policy making. Corporate models are discussed in Chapter 27.

Two conclusions can be drawn from the above discussion. First, the volume of information related to the various functions in an organization depends upon the relative importance of these functions. For example, a marketing-oriented organization is more likely to have a greater proportion of marketing-oriented information in the information mix than production, personnel or accounting information (although this is not necessarily the case). Second, the information system may have a wide range of objectives. In the simplest form, these objectives may be limited to record keeping and historical reporting, while in a more complex form the objectives may relate to the overall operation of the entire organization. The concepts of 'information mix' and 'information objectives' have an important bearing upon the role of the accountant in the design and operation of the information system. This will be examined later in this chapter.

Data Processing Systems

Figure 8—A shows that the data processing system is a part of the total information system. All data processing systems go through a common data processing cycle which has three steps: input, processing or manipulation, and output. During each of these steps, a set of tasks is performed, as illustrated in Figure 8—C. Data storage is connected to all three steps of the cycle, the reason being that data storage represents a temporary repository for data that may be used over and over again, and in different ways.

Data processing systems differ in the extent to which they are mechanized and may be classified into manual, mechanical, punched card and computerized systems.

Manual Systems

Manual data processing systems are predominant in small organizations where all functions are performed manually. The traditional tools used in conjunction with manual systems are pencils, pens, printed forms, journals, ledgers, worksheets, files, etc. Manual systems are easy to set up and the initial establishment costs are low. The system is flexible and therefore changes can be introduced at any stage without encountering serious difficulty. On the other hand, variable costs per transaction are high and the system output is prone to errors.

---

[2] Long-term plans may be strategic or tactical. We refer here to management's tactical multi-period plans. See Chapter 27.

Figure 8—C
Common Features of a Data Processing System

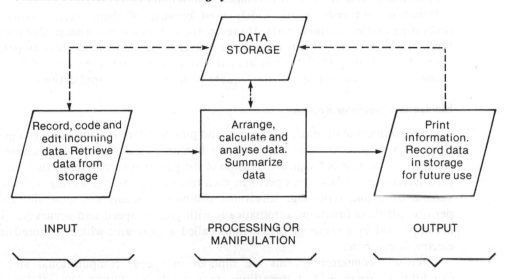

Mechanical Systems

In mechanical systems, manual effort is assisted by mechanical devices such as typewriters, calculators, accounting machines and cash registers. The set-up cost of mechanical systems is higher than that for manual systems, but data processing is relatively error free. Another advantage is that control figures (such as total accounts receivable) are produced automatically. A disadvantage of mechanical systems is that the capacity of each machine is limited by the speed of the operator, because the operation itself is performed manually. As a result, operator speed is critical and a bottleneck can occur in the system as the volume of transactions increases.

Punched Card Systems

A punched card system makes use of a combination of machines, most of which require only a minimum amount of manual effort and supervision in order to perform their tasks. The operations performed automatically in a punched card system are: recording, sorting, comparing, calculating, summarizing and reporting. However,

Figure 8—D
A Punched Card System

Machine	Function
Card punch	Records source data in punched cards
Verifier	Verifies the accuracy of source data recorded by the card punch machine
Sorter	Arranges a single file in pre-determined order (such as alphabetical, numerical or any other classification)
Collator	Merges and matches two punched card files
Calculator	Performs calculations from data on punched cards, and records the results of calculations
Accounting machine	Reads, summarizes and prints from data recorded on punched cards
Reproducer	Reproduces punched cards for storage and future use

the card punch and verifier must be operated manually. A typical punched card system, comprising seven basic machines, is shown in Figure 8—D.

Punched card systems are widely used because of their speed, accuracy of processing and low variable costs. However, the system has two undesirable features. First, the files of the system need to be converted to and maintained as punched cards. Second, the calculator has limited mathematical and logic capability, which makes the punched card system inadequate for more complex applications.

Electronic Computer Systems

The development of manual, mechanical and punched card systems reflects a general trend in data processing to eliminate the human element as far as possible. The electronic computer is a logical extension of the punched card system. In a punched card system several machines perform such tasks as recording, sorting, calculating, summarizing and reporting. Electronic computer systems are generally able to perform all these functions automatically with greater speed and accuracy. This is accomplished by a series of instructions called a program, which is stored in the electronic computer.

Electronic computer systems are superior in speed, computational and logic capabilities, accuracy and versatility. As a result computers are gaining wider acceptance in both large and small organizations.

A Cost Comparison

A cost comparison of the four main data processing systems may be made by identifying the fixed and variable costs associated with each of the systems. [3] The fixed costs are the costs of equipment and the set-up costs, the level of which does not vary with the volume of data to be processed. The set-up costs include system study,

Figure 8—E
A Cost Comparison of Four Data Processing Systems

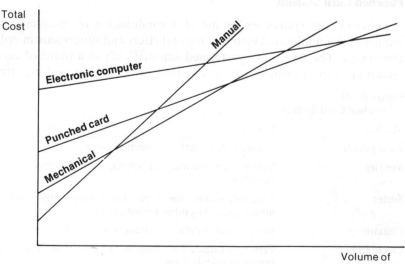

[3] See Chapter 23 for a discussion of the fixed-variable cost dichotomy.

procedure design, programming and implementation costs. The variable costs are the costs of converting data into a form in which they may be processed by the machine or computer, the costs of supplies and the system operating costs. A cost comparison based on the fixed-variable cost classification is illustrated in Figure 8—E. As can be seen, cost criteria favour increasing mechanization of the data processing system (i.e. from manual to mechanical to punched card to the electronic computer) as the volume of transactions progressively increases. There is a further consideration. Recent developments in computer technology suggest that the fixed costs associated with electronic computers will continue to fall in future years, so that the resulting total cost comparison will increasingly favour the computer as against other data processing systems. Computer installations are currently within the reach of a relatively large number of organizations. A description of a computer data processing system is presented in the following section.

A Computer Data Processing System

Five basic functions are performed by a computer system: (a) preparation of data; (b) preparation of input; (c) computation, logic and control; (d) storage; and (e) output (see Figure 8—F). This configuration is similar to the common features of the data processing system presented in Figure 8—C, except that the input function is split into two steps. The functions of a computer system are performed by the interaction of machines (known as hardware),[4] a set of instructions for the computer (known as a program), a set of procedures and personnel.

Figure 8—F
Basic Functions of a Computer System

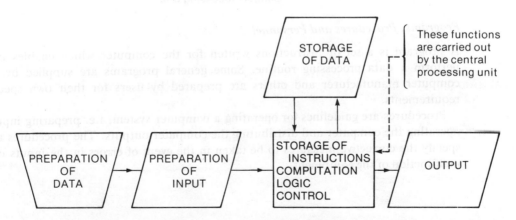

[4]Software comprises those items in a computer system that are not hardware, e.g. programs, files and documents.

Hardware

A summary of the equipment which can be used for performing the basic functions of a computer system is presented in Figure 8—G.

Figure 8—G
Computer Hardware

Function	Equipment
Preparation of input	Key driven card punch, key driven card verifier, paper tape, other magnetic tape unit, key-to-disc equipment, voice recognizer, optical character recognizer, conversion devices, etc.
Instructions, computation, logic and control	Central processing unit
Storage	Magnetic tape, magnetic disc, magnetic drum, magnetic card or strip, etc.
Output	Card punch, paper tape punch, printer, visual display unit, etc.

The central processing unit is usually referred to as the *computer*. It has a section for the storage of instructions and programs, carries out computation, performs logical operations and controls the entire system, as shown in the following schematic diagram:

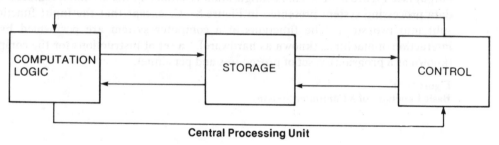

Central Processing Unit

Programs, Procedures and Personnel

A program is a set of instructions written for the computer which enables it to perform a data processing routine. Some general programs are supplied by the computer manufacturer and others are prepared by users for their own specific requirements.

Procedures are guidelines for operating a computer system, i.e. preparing inputs, operating the computer and distributing the computer outputs. The procedures also specify the corrective measures to be taken in the event of errors in the inputs or a malfunction of the equipment.

The personnel involved in computer systems can be classified into three groups: system analysts, programmers and operators. Their job descriptions are given in Figure 8—H.

Figure 8—H
Computer Personnel

Job Title	Job Description
System analyst	Studies and designs the information system, and prepares specifications for the data processing system
Programmer	Writes computer programs based on system design and specifications
Operator	Operates computer equipment

A large data processing department is likely to employ personnel in all three categories, but a smaller unit may need only operators. If punched cards are used as inputs, key punch machine operators are required for input preparation.

Organization of the Data Processing Department

When computers were first introduced in large organizations, the data processing system was usually placed under the supervision of the chief accountant or the treasurer. This was a logical step because initially most computer applications were related to the accounting information system. Even today this practice is followed by many organizations. In more complex data processing installations, it is common practice for a data processing executive to occupy a relatively high position in the organization. Figure 8—I shows the data processing organization of a large computing installation, headed by a controller—management information system, who reports directly to a chief executive (see Chapter 9 for an explanation of an organization chart).

The Role of the Accountant

Three factors influence the accountant's role in the design and operation of the information system: information objectives, information mix and the organizational structure of the data processing department. If the information objectives are specialized and sectional in nature, and there is a dominant accounting and financial segment in the information mix, the accountant has a leading role in the design and operation of the information system. Once the information system departs from a sectional approach and becomes a fully integrated system, then specialists are likely to become responsible for the design and operation of the system.

If the chief accountant is head of the data processing department, it is essential for him to have a specialization in the field of data processing. In fact, his role is no longer that of an accountant. Where the system design and operation are entrusted to specialists, it will still be necessary for the accountant to have a general understanding of the information system design and operation. Specifically, the accountant will be expected to:
(a) communicate his requirements to the specialists;
(b) understand the system design documentation prepared by the system designer;
(c) supervise the preparation of the input data for processing; and
(d) suggest modifications to the existing system.

Figure 8—I
Typical Organization Chart
of a Data Processing Installation

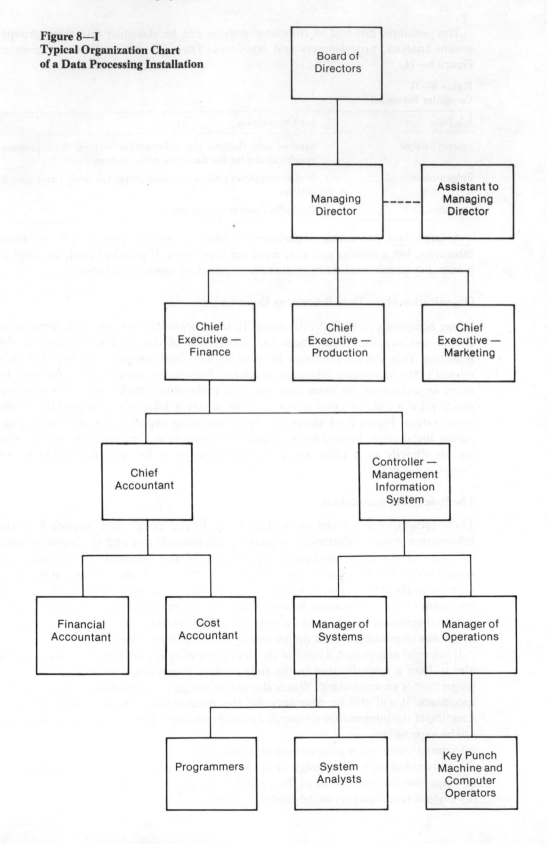

Summary

There has been a growing awareness that information is an important resource of an organization. Information systems may differ significantly from one organization to another, depending upon the nature of operations. Information objectives may also differ significantly. In a simple form, the system may relate to a section of the organization; in the ultimate form it will represent the entire organization. If the chief accountant is supervising the information system, it is essential that he should have a specialized training. If the design and operation are carried out by specialists, it will be necessary for the accountant to have a general understanding of information system design and operation.

Information system design and operation will be dealt with in the following chapter.

Discussion Questions

1 Distinguish between informal and formal information systems, citing examples of each. Which system is the more important?

2 Briefly describe the information system within a business organization. Why is it necessary to differentiate between types of organizations when discussing information systems? What are the different classifications used when making these differentiations?

3 Discuss the possible objectives of an information system. Give examples of information systems designed to achieve each of the objectives.

4 Outline the common features of all data processing systems.

5 Compare and contrast the four main types of data processing systems. Include in your analysis a comparison of costs.

6 What basic functions must a computerized system be able to carry out? What are the components of a computer that enable it to perform these tasks? Give a brief description of each of the various components.

7 Should the accountant always be given control over the data processing system? Explain, giving reasons.

8 What factors must be taken into consideration when defining the role of the accountant within the information system? How should a firm decide whether to leave the accountant with responsibility for the data processing, or bring in a specialist to fill the role? If a specialist is employed what responsibilities must the accountant assume?

Exercises

1 Are the following sources of information part of the informal information system or the formal information system of your company?

(a) The gossip of visiting salesmen.

(b) A variance report.

(c) Announcement of a currency devaluation.

(d) Minutes of a weekly Chamber of Commerce meeting.

(e) Your company's monthly income statement.

(f) A hired management consultant's report.

(g) The Bank of New South Wales Annual Survey of the Manufacturing Industry.

(h) The Statement of Provisional Standards on Current Cost Accounting.

(i) The annual federal government budget.

(j) A market survey conducted by the company's marketing department.

(k) A market survey conducted because of perceived problems with a new product.

(l) An announcement by the Reserve Bank of a reduction in interest rates.

(m) A special newspaper report entitled 'The State of the Economy'.

(n) The quarterly national wage case decision.

(o) A proposal for an advertising campaign from an advertising agency.

(p) A government announcement of increased tariffs for the manufacturing industry.

2 Classify the following organizations into the categories used in Figure 8—B, on page 204:

(a) the Department of Agriculture; (b) Woolworths; (c) a management consulting firm; (d) the Reserve Bank; (e) BHP; (f) a liquor store; (g) Institute of Chartered Accountants; and (h) Joe's Corner Factory.

3 You have recently been hired as Chief Accountant by a medium-sized department store and given control of the complete information system, including data processing. It is obvious that there has never been an attempt to integrate the firm's information system. List the objectives that the information system should seek to achieve, and the specific information required to fulfil these objectives.

4 Under what circumstances would a firm change from a mechanical to a computerized information system even if the cost of the new system was greater? Explain.

9 Design and Operation of an Accounting Information System

The objective of this chapter is to prepare the accountant to function effectively in an environment where modern data processing systems are employed. First, the tools and techniques used in system study and design are explained. Second, the steps that should be followed in system study and design are discussed and, third, an example of system design documentation, which is typical of what the accountant is required to evaluate in practice, is presented.

Tools and Techniques in System Study and Design

Some of the tools and techniques used by system designers are organization charts, flowcharts, decision tables, grid charts, layout charts and network diagrams. These tools serve two purposes: (a) to organize thinking about the problem of system design in a systematic manner; and (b) to present the facts, analyses and conclusions in a visual manner, so that these can be comprehended readily by management.

Organization Charts

An organization chart is a graphical representation of the hierarchical relationships among key employees in the company. It shows clearly the responsibilities of the key employees and the persons reporting to them. Each position is represented by a box, which is joined by a solid line to another box if a direct reporting relationship exists between the two positions. A broken line usually represents an advisory relationship. A typical organization chart was illustrated in Figure 8—I in Chapter 8.

The organization chart indicates:
(a) who is responsible to whom and for what function; and
(b) what manpower resources are at the disposal of the key employees.

The first piece of information, (a), is used by the system analyst to design report formats consistent with the information required by each of the key employees. The second piece of information, (b), is used in estimating manpower requirements and availability at different locations in the organization. This information also facilitates planning for the preparation within departments of data input for central data processing.

Flowcharts

Flowcharts are pictorial representations of data flows and the sequence of operations in an information system, whereby the overall operation can be visualized readily. To maintain uniformity, standard symbols prepared by the International Organization for Standardization are used in presenting flowcharts. These symbols will be used in this chapter.

There are two kinds of flowcharts: (a) a system flowchart; and (b) a logic flowchart. The system flowchart illustrates broadly the flow of data and operations. The main emphasis is on the inputs and outputs produced by operations, while the detailed logic involved in transforming data during the operations is ignored. The details omitted by a system flowchart are the main concern of a logic flowchart. The logic flowchart shows how an operation is performed, what data manipulation is carried out, and how data are transformed into a useful form. The distinction between a system and a logic flowchart will be clarified later by illustrations.

Basic Symbols for Flowcharting

There are four basic symbols by which any flowchart can be presented. These are the input/output, process, annotation and flowlines symbols, as shown in Figure 9—A.

Figure 9—A
Basic Symbols for Flowcharting

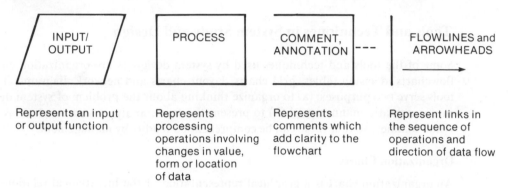

INPUT/OUTPUT	PROCESS	COMMENT, ANNOTATION	FLOWLINES and ARROWHEADS
Represents an input or output function	Represents processing operations involving changes in value, form or location of data	Represents comments which add clarity to the flowchart	Represent links in the sequence of operations and direction of data flow

System Flowchart

A system flowchart of an accounts receivable system is presented in Figure 9—B. There are three classes of data input: sales invoices, credit adjustments and cash receipts issued for payments by customers. The numerals 1 and 2 between the symbols in the figure indicate the sequence of operations. The processing relating to the operation 'Prepare Accounts Receivable Report' is carried out by the data processing department. The input files (Credit Sales, Credit Adjustments and Payments by Customers), and the output files (Updated Accounts Receivable File and Accounts Receivable Report), are clearly shown in relation to the processing operation.

The advantage of a flowchart using the basic symbols lies in its simplicity. However, there are also certain limitations. The use of additional and specialized symbols to overcome some of these limitations is illustrated in Figure 9—C and explained below:

(a) If the system flowchart extends to the next page, there is no basic symbol to denote this situation. Therefore a connector symbol is used to represent the junction at which the flowchart extends to, or is continued from, another page, e.g. (B) in Figure 9—D. A connector symbol may also be employed to indicate linkages between different points in a flowchart presented on the same page, e.g. (A) in Figure 9—D.

Figure 9—B
System Flowchart of Accounts Receivable System

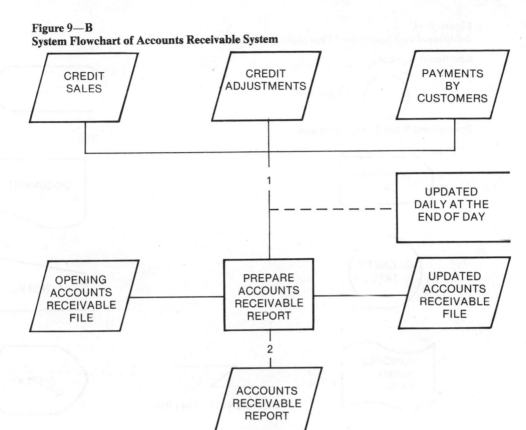

(b) The basic symbols flowchart cannot show clearly the start, interruption or end of operations. A terminal symbol is used for this purpose.

(c) The basic symbol used to indicate input/output, a parallelogram, fails to specify the form of input and output media. For example, input may be in the form of a source document, punched card, drum or disc. Similarly, output may be in the form of a printed report, punched card, drum or disc. Specialized symbols are used to represent various forms of input and output storage media.

(d) The basic symbol which indicates processing does not specify whether the process is manual, mechanical, etc., nor does it specify whether the process represents a decision or not. Specialized symbols are used to specify the processing mode.

In summary, the connector and terminal symbols are additional symbols which are used to make it easier to follow the flow of data and operations. The symbols described in (c) and (d) above are specialized symbols used to specify the input/output media and processing mode. Figure 9—D shows how the system flowchart in Figure 9—B can be improved and made more meaningful by the use of the additional and specialized symbols. Flowlines show the sequence of the steps to be performed. An explanation of the steps involved is included.

Figure 9—C
Additional and Specialized Flowchart Symbols

Additional Symbols

CONNECTOR

TERMINAL

Specialized Input/Output Symbols

PUNCHED
CARD

DOCUMENT

MAGNETIC
TAPE

KEYBOARD

PUNCHED
PAPER
TAPE

COMMUNICATION LINK

DISPLAY

MAGNETIC
DISC

MAGNETIC
DRUM

Specialized Input/Output (Storage) Symbols

ON-LINE
STORAGE

OFF-LINE
STOR-
AGE

Specialized Processing Symbols

DECISION

AUXILIARY
OPERATION

PREDEFINED
PROCESS

MANUAL
OPERATION

Logic Flowchart

In system flowcharts, the process of data transformation is not illustrated in detail. For example, Step 9 of the system flowchart in Figure 9—D simply states 'Update run'. A system flowchart may have several such statements. A detailed logical presentation of the statement 'Update run' is presented in a logic flowchart, as illustrated in Figure 9—E. The logic flowchart breaks down the operation of the updating run into a number of steps. The main points to be noted are:

(a) 'Start' and 'Stop' statements define the beginning and end of the operation.

(b) Execution instructions denoted by rectangular or parallelogram boxes describe individual steps which need to be performed. These steps may take the form of reading data inputs (Step 4), performing computations (Step 7) or printing output (Step 8).

(c) A decision operation (e.g. Step 2) tests the conditions to be satisfied. The result of the test determines the next step to be carried out. In this case if the answer to 'End of file?' is positive, the computer is instructed to perform 'Stop run'; otherwise it continues the operation by reading the master file for validation of the input data.

Decision Tables

Decision tables are tabular representations of problems and their solutions. Problems are displayed as a set of conditions and their solutions given as a set of actions to be taken. Decision tables take the form of:

If ...	Condition statement	Condition entry
Then ...	Action statement	Action entry

Consider the example of a retail company that sells goods on credit. The company requires a customer to pay the balance on his account on the receipt of a payment notice. When the account becomes overdue, a reminder is sent. But if the account is overdue for more than 60 days, the action to be taken depends on whether the customer has been with the company for at least two years.

The analyst in the above example has three alternatives: (a) he can give a written description of the problems and associated solutions; (b) he can present the problems and solutions by means of a logic flowchart; or (c) he can present the problems and solutions in a decision table. For a complex set of problems the use of a decision table is considered by some people to be the best choice, because of its ability to present the relationships between problems and solutions in a compact manner. These relationships are captured at the appropriate decision points in the computer program.

The problems and associated actions are presented in a logic flowchart in Figure 9—F and a decision table in Figure 9—G.

Grid Charts

Grid charts are tabular representations of relationships between two sets of factors. One set of factors is given in the columns of the table, while the other set is given in the rows. Thus the table is analogous to a matrix, as can be seen in Figure 9—H. An entry of 'x' in the figure depicts that a *relationship* exists between the corresponding column and row element.

Figure 9—D
System Flowchart of Accounts Receivable System Using Additional and Specialized Symbols

Step 1: Documents from various sources (i.e. other departments) arrive in the data processing department.

Step 2: The data processing department checks the source documents for accuracy. If the documents are unacceptable, these are sent back to the point of origin. Otherwise, processing continues.

Step 3: Totals are accumulated for the debtor numbers (a so-called 'hash' total, i.e. one without mathematical significance) and dollar amounts. These totals are used to ensure that all the transactions entering the system are processed at later points in the system.

Step 4: The source documents are key punched, key verified, and then stored in a history file.

Step 5: The punched cards are read into the computer and a proof listing is prepared. The totals for debtor numbers and amounts are printed for each source of origin.

Step 6: The control totals from the proof listing are compared with the totals accumulated at Step 3. If the control totals for any department (source of origin) are out of balance, the input batch is sent back to the key punch centre for checking.

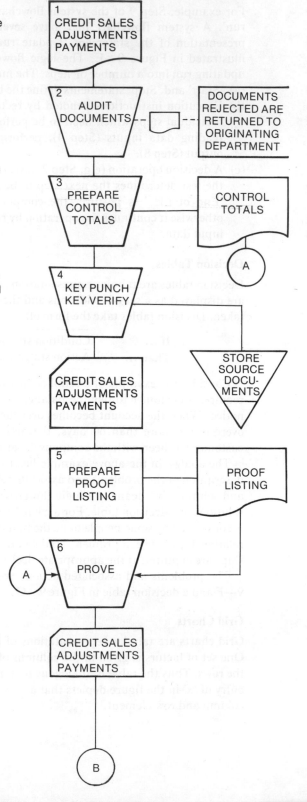

Figure 9—D (contd)

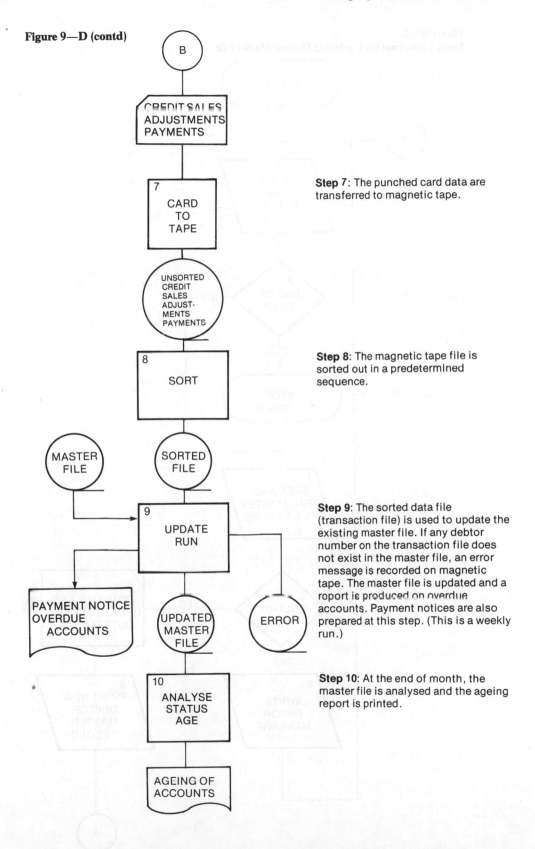

Step 7: The punched card data are transferred to magnetic tape.

Step 8: The magnetic tape file is sorted out in a predetermined sequence.

Step 9: The sorted data file (transaction file) is used to update the existing master file. If any debtor number on the transaction file does not exist in the master file, an error message is recorded on magnetic tape. The master file is updated and a report is produced on overdue accounts. Payment notices are also prepared at this step. (This is a weekly run.)

Step 10: At the end of month, the master file is analysed and the ageing report is printed.

Figure 9—E
Logic Flowchart for Updating Debtor Master File

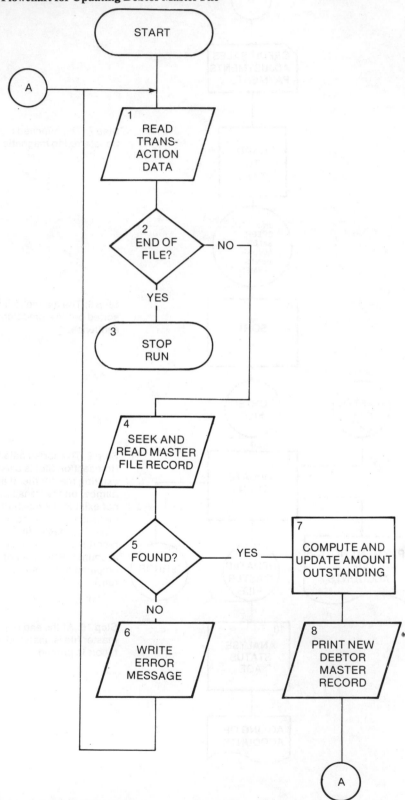

Figure 9—F
Logic Flowchart for Overdue Accounts

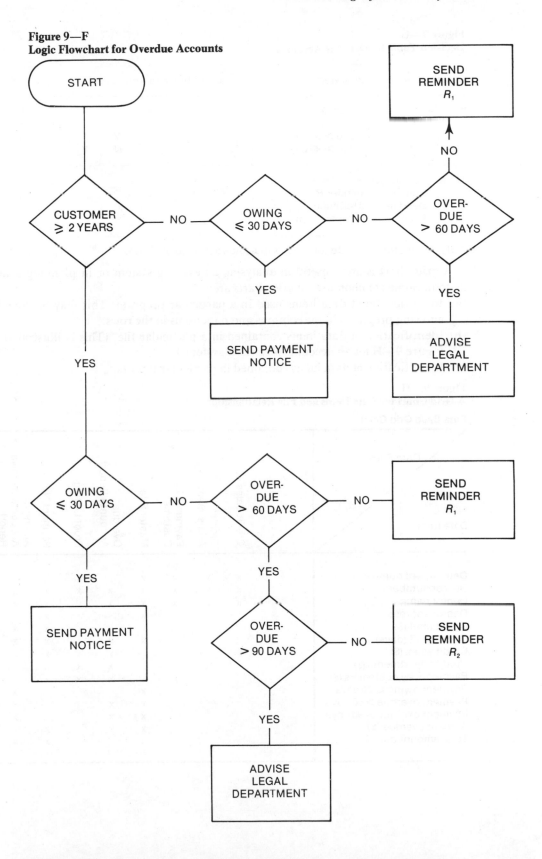

Figure 9—G
Decision Table for Overdue Accounts

Condition and Action Statements	Condition and Action Entries						
If . . . Customer for at least 2 years	Y	Y	Y	Y	N	N	N
Payment owing ≤ 30 days	Y	N			Y	N	
Payment overdue > 60 days		N	Y			N	Y
Payment overdue > 90 days			N	Y			
Then . . . Send payment notice	x				x		
Send first reminder R_1		x				x	
Send second reminder R_2			x				
Refer to legal department				x			x

Note: Y denotes Yes; *N* denotes No; x indicates action to be taken.

A grid chart is often useful in analysing an existing system or in planning a new system. Some common uses of grid charts are:

(a) Identification of data items used in a particular program. This may be done by entering programs in the columns and data items in the rows.

(b) Identification of data items contained in a particular file. (This is illustrated in Figure 9—H for an accounts receivable system.)

(c) Identification of data items contained in particular reports.

Figure 9—H
A Grid Chart for Data Items and File Relationships

Data Base Grid Chart

Data Items \ Data Files	Credit Sales	Credit Adjustments	Payments by Customers	Master File	Overdue Accounts Report	Proof Listing	Payment Notice	Ageing of Accounts Receivable Report
Department number	x	x	x	x		x		
Debtor number	x	x	x	x	x	x	x	x
Debtor name	x	x	x	x	x		x	x
Debtor address				x			x	
Credit limit ($)				x	x		x	x
Credit limit (days)				x	x		x	x
Credit sales ($)	x			x	x	x		
Credit adjustments ($)		x		x	x	x		
Payments by customers ($)			x	x	x	x		
Payment owing ≤ 30 days				x				x
Payment overdue > 60 days				x	x			x
Payment overdue > 90 days				x	x			x
Amount overdue ($)				x	x		x	
Total amount due ($)				x			x	x

Figure 9—I
Printed Layout Worksheet: Ageing of Accounts Receivable Report

ACCT NO | NAME OF CUSTOMER | LIMIT $ | LIMIT DAYS | 1 TO 30 DAYS | 31 TO 60 DAYS | 61 TO 90 DAYS | EXCEEDS 90 DAYS | TOTAL ACCTS RECEIVABLE

SUMMARY

OWING 30 DAYS OR LESS

OVERDUE 31 TO 60 DAYS

OVERDUE 61 TO 90 DAYS

OVERDUE MORE THAN 90 DAYS

FINAL TOTAL

DOLLAR AMOUNT

PER CENT OF TOTAL

Layout Charts

Layout charts are displays of the actual format of source documents, inputs or report outputs. Before a system is put into operation, the user can visualize how the source documents, inputs or outputs will appear by reference to the layout charts. A layout format of an accounts receivable report is displayed in Figure 9—I.

Network Diagrams [1]

Network diagrams are basically flow diagrams indicating the steps and linkages involved in the completion of a project. Two main characteristics of a network diagram are: (a) the logical sequence of events is disclosed clearly, and (b) the interdependence of events is reflected. A simplified network diagram is illustrated in Figure 9—J.

Figure 9—J
Critical Path Analysis of an Accounts Receivable System

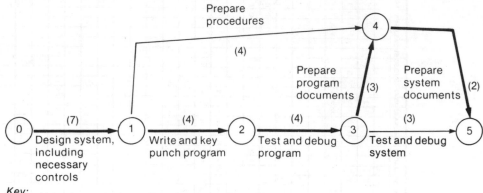

Key:

- x Number in circle represents activity number
- (Y) Number in parentheses represents number of days required for completion of activity
- ——— Critical path
- ——— Path with slack

In Figure 9—J, a number within a circle represents an activity number, and a number in parentheses represents the duration time required for completion of the activity. For example, activity 0-1 is 'Design system' which takes seven days, and activity 1-2 is 'Write and key punch program' which takes four days. The diagram indicates that activity 1-2 cannot commence until activity 0-1 has been completed. The circles are known as nodes and each activity is represented by uniquely defined beginning and ending node numbers. The path (there may be more than one in some instances) taking the longest time in the network is known as the critical path and this is represented by the thick line in Figure 9—J.[2] The activities shown on the top of the following page represent critical activities in the network.

Network diagrams are useful in controlling the implementation of computerized information system projects. The diagram focuses on the critical activities and an

[1] Network analysis in various forms is also referred to as Program Evaluation and Review Technique (PERT), Critical Path Method (CPM), or Project Control System (PCS).

[2] Sometimes the critical path can be 'crashed', i.e. its duration may be reduced at an additional cost. It is then possible for a new critical path to be established, comprising a different sequence of activities.

Node Numbers	Activity	Estimated Time to Accomplish Activity
0-1	Design system, including necessary controls	7 days
1-2	Write and key punch program	4
2-3	Test and debug program	4
3-4	Prepare program documents	3
4-5	Prepare system documents	2
Total time		20 days

overview of the entire project is available to the user in a compact manner. The diagram show here is a simplified one; a detailed diagram in practice may embrace hundreds of activities and complex network relationships.

Steps in New System Design

System design relates to the development of new systems or the improvement of existing systems. The main objectives usually are to increase the effectiveness of operations and to accomplish greater economy in data processing. There are five major steps in designing and implementing a new system:

(a) study and analyse the existing system;
(b) define the requirements of the new system;
(c) design a system that meets the specified requirements;
(d) propose the equipment, procedures, costs and time-table necessary for implementing the new system; and
(e) implement the new system.

After the new system has been designed and implemented, periodical reviews should be made to ascertain that the system is operating efficiently and the specified objectives are being achieved. A brief explanation of the steps involved in system design and implementation is given below.

Analysis of the Existing System

The merits, limitations and drawbacks of the existing system may be revealed by an analysis of the inputs, resources, outputs and procedures of the system. Analysis of the inputs of the present system involves consideration of the data source and frequency of input preparation. Resources include equipment, personnel, facilities and supplies used by the system. A study of the resources will also throw light on the system's current operating cost. The system output is analysed by studying the format, content, frequency and uses of the reports produced. In the study of procedures, an overall system flowchart, showing the operations of the entire system from source documents to the final report format, is useful to depict the information flows.

Personnel interviews are an important part of the analysis. The analyst should interview participants in the present system to confirm the use made of existing system output, and current and future information requirements.

Defining the New System Requirements

The new system will be defined and influenced by three factors: (a) information objectives; (b) information mix; and (c) resource commitment. The first two factors have been discussed in the previous chapter. An analyst can study the critical areas of a business enterprise and propose the objectives of its information system. But the objectives will be constrained by the amount of resources management is willing to commit to the task of developing a new information system. Once the resource commitment has been determined, the new system can be broadly defined to include: (a) input requirements, (b) output requirements, and (c) resource requirements. Within this broad framework, the information system can be developed and designed in greater detail.

Designing and Implementing the New System

In designing the new system, a detailed analysis of the input, processing and output alternatives is made. There are several possible configurations embodying input and output media, and processing methods. The best combination consistent with the system definition should be selected.

Input media can take one of several forms. For example, data from source documents may be recorded on punched cards, magnetic tapes or paper tapes, and then read by the computer. Alternatively, data can be directly entered into computer-controlled files. Processing can be performed in a number of ways, such as the use of manual, mechanical or electronic processing methods. The output alternatives are also numerous, and include printed reports, punched cards, magnetic media and data transmission to a remote terminal.

After the new system has been designed and the input, processing and output details specified, equipment must be selected. The selection of equipment depends on a number of factors, such as the volume of data, computational complexities, future expansion program, timeliness of information and cost considerations. At this stage all relevant factors have been considered and the analyst is able to present a comprehensive proposal for approval. The entire process may take a few weeks in the case of a simple system, or several months or years where the system is complex. It is also possible that the process needs to be recommenced at any stage in response to feedback from system users.

The accountant will be involved with the implementation of the new system, as well as directly or indirectly with its operations, depending on how the data processing department is organized and on the nature of the application. It is virtually impossible to design a new system which is free of shortcomings. After the system is in operation, any inherent deficiencies will become apparent to the accountant, provided he monitors the system performance carefully. It is essential to observe the system during the operating phase, with particular attention to the following:
(a) the accounting information system should accomplish the objectives for which it has been designed; and
(b) the procedures and processes should be efficient under operating conditions.

If the accounting information system falls short of expectations, modifications and change will be necessary. At this point the accountant has to communicate his requirements to professional system designers.

A Case Study of a Proposed Accounts Receivable System

A simplified example relating to an accounts receivable system is presented as follows to illustrate how actual system documentation is prepared, and how some of the tools and techniques described in this chapter are applied to a practical situation.

PROPOSAL

FOR

AN

ACCOUNTS

RECEIVABLE

SYSTEM

Contents

1

1   Introduction
This is a description of an accounts receivable (A/R) system for Kensington Retailers Ltd.

2   General Description
The A/R system is designed to calculate and age the amounts outstanding on debtors' accounts.

3   Basic Objectives
The system has two main objectives:
3.1   to maintain a record of debtor accounts;
3.2   to provide a basis for collecting overdue accounts.

4   System Scope
The A/R system comprises two separate sub-systems:
4.1   The A/R system for new customers, i.e. customers known to the company for less than two years.
4.2   The A/R system for old customers, i.e. customers known to the company for two or more years.
   This documentation describes the A/R system for the new customers.

5   Basic Steps
The basic steps required to process A/R are as follows:
5.1   Data records are created for three kinds of transactions: (a) the amounts for which goods are sold on credit, (b) adjustments for returns and errors, and (c) payments on account.
5.2   The data records are entered into the system and controls incorporated, so that the input data can be matched with the source document data.
5.3   The daily transaction file is sorted into debtor number order and matched with the corresponding debtor record in the master file. Thereafter the master file is updated with the current transactions.
5.4   The debtor listing with amount outstanding, payment notices, and ageing of A/R is printed.
5.5   Information on the current period is made available to the credit collection, accounts and legal departments. The ageing report is forwarded to management.
5.6   Data from the current period are retained for use in the next processing.

6   Relationship to Other Systems
The A/R system is directly related to the credit collection and the accounts systems.
6.1   Credit collection system: The credit department provides all permanent information on new debtors to the A/R system. It also provides information about changes in status of the present debtors.
6.2   Accounts system: The accounts system merges data from the A/R system with expense, budget and balance sheet items to provide accounting and financial information.

2

7   File Description

The files utilized by the A/R sub-system are described below:

7.1   Source documents: Three source documents are used — credit sales documents from the sales department, payment documents from the accounts department and adjustment documents from the sales or accounts department.

7.2   Punched card files: This is the punched card record created from the source documents.

7.3   Magnetic tape files: The debtor master file is on magnetic tape. It holds the main data required by the A/R system. The data record should be added to the file upon acceptance of a new credit customer, deleted upon termination and updated upon change of status.

7.4   Printed files: There are four printed files in the system.

7.4.1   Batch totals: The purpose of the batch total is to provide a base for comparison with the original data, to ensure that all source documents are correctly converted to the punched card file.

7.4.2   Overdue accounts: This file provides a listing of overdue accounts.

7.4.3   Payment notices: Payment notices are sent to customers within the first 30 days.

7.4.4   Ageing of A/R: This report breaks down the A/R into three age groups: 30 days or less, 31 to 60 days and over 60 days.

The content of each file is shown in the Data Base Grid Chart below.

Data Base Grid Chart

Data Items / Data Files	Credit Sales	Credit Adjustments	Payments by Customers	Master File	Overdue Accounts Report	Proof Listing	Payment Notice	Ageing of Accounts Receivable Report
Department number	x	x	x	x		x		
Debtor number	x	x	x	x	x	x	x	x
Debtor name	x	x	x	x	x		x	x
Debtor address				x			x	
Credit limit ($)				x	x		x	x
Credit limit (days)				x	x		x	x
Credit sales ($)	x				x	x	x	
Credit adjustments ($)		x			x	x	x	
Payments by customers ($)			x		x	x	x	
Payment owing ≤ 30 days					x			x
Payment overdue > 60 days					x	x		x
Payment overdue > 90 days					x	x		x
Amount overdue ($)					x	x	x	
Total amount due ($)					x		x	x

3

8   System Flowchart

The System Flowchart below shows the details and sequence of the data flow.

System Flowchart

Step 1: Documents from various sources (i.e. other departments) arrive in the data processing department.

Step 2: The data processing department checks the source documents for accuracy. If the documents are unacceptable, these are sent back to the point of origin. Otherwise, processing continues.

Step 3: Totals are accumulated for the debtor numbers (a so-called 'hash' total, i.e. one without mathematical significance) and dollar amounts. These totals are used to ensure that all the transactions entering the system are processed at later points in the system.

Step 4: The source documents are key punched, key verified, and then stored in a history file.

Step 5: The punched cards are read into the computer and a proof listing is prepared. The totals for debtor numbers and amounts are printed for each source of origin.

Step 6: The control totals from the proof listing are compared with the totals accumulated at Step 3. If the control totals for any department (source of origin) are out of balance, the input batch is sent back to the key punch centre for checking.

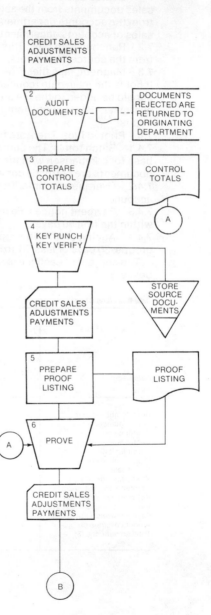

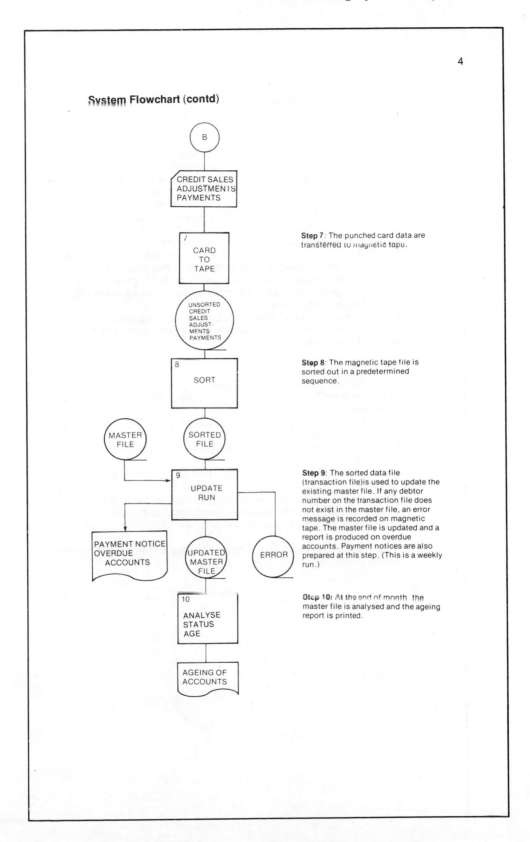

System Flowchart (contd)

4

B

CREDIT SALES
ADJUSTMENTS
PAYMENTS

CARD
TO
TAPE

Step 7: The punched card data are transferred to magnetic tape.

UNSORTED
CREDIT
SALES
ADJUST-
MENTS
PAYMENTS

8
SORT

Step 8: The magnetic tape file is sorted out in a predetermined sequence.

MASTER
FILE

SORTED
FILE

9
UPDATE
RUN

Step 9: The sorted data file (transaction file) is used to update the existing master file. If any debtor number on the transaction file does not exist in the master file, an error message is recorded on magnetic tape. The master file is updated and a report is produced on overdue accounts. Payment notices are also prepared at this step. (This is a weekly run.)

PAYMENT NOTICE
OVERDUE
ACCOUNTS

UPDATED
MASTER
FILE

ERROR

10
ANALYSE
STATUS
AGE

Step 10: At the end of month, the master file is analysed and the ageing report is printed.

AGEING OF
ACCOUNTS

9   Equipment and Hardware

The existing equipment will be utilized for the proposed A/R system.

10   Control Requirements

Three control mechanisms are incorporated.

10.1   Control totals: Control totals are established for each batch of source documents, as shown in Step 3 of the System Flowchart. The control totals include debtor number (a 'hash' total), total credit purchases, total payments and total adjustments. These are balanced against similar totals from the control total listing produced in Step 5 of the System Flowchart.

10.2   Validity checks: When the weekly processing is carried out in Step 9 of the System Flowchart, the debtor numbers from the source documents are checked for validity to ensure that these are legitimate numbers. For example, if a debtor number 12–5492 is read from the source document and no such number exists in the debtor master file, it is an invalid number.

10.3   Error conditions: When error conditions are detected on validation, it is written on a magnetic tape as shown in Step 9 of the System Flowchart.

11   Program Specifications

There are four programs in the system:

11.1   Preparation of proof listing, as shown in Step 5 of the System Flowchart.

11.2   Sorting of transactions in a sequence, as in Step 8 of the System Flowchart.

11.3   Updating and printing of report, as in Step 9 of the System Flowchart.

11.4   Analysis of ageing, as in Step 10 of the System Flowchart.

   Program 11.3 is described briefly below.

11.3.1   Program description: the program carries out four functions: (a) it validates the source document input data; (b) it updates the master file; (c) it carries out calculations; and (d) it prints out payment notices and reports.

11.3.2   Logic flowchart: The program is based on the Logic Flowchart shown on page 6.

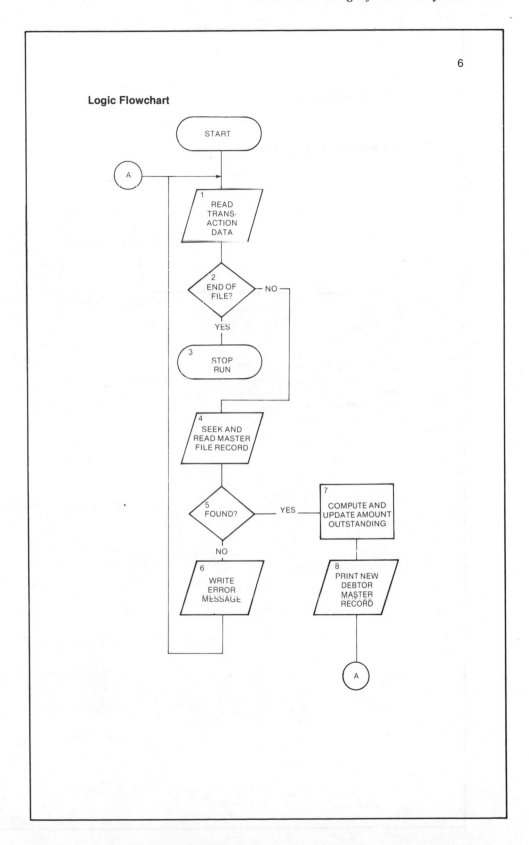

Logic Flowchart

7

12   Implementation

The proposed A/R system can be made operational in 20 days. A network diagram for the project is shown below:

Network Flow Diagram

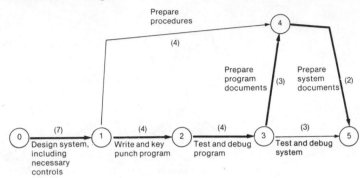

Prepare procedures
(4)

Prepare program documents (3)   Prepare system documents (2)

(7)   Design system, including necessary controls

(4)   Write and key punch program

(4)   Test and debug program

(3)   Test and debug system

Key:

ⓧ   Number in circle represents activity number

(Y)   Number in parentheses represents number of days required for completion of activity

▬▬▬   Critical path

───   Path with slack

Programming Languages

Once a logic flowchart has been prepared to show the detailed steps of data transformation, a series of instructions is written for the computer to perform these operations. As explained in Chapter 8, a series of instructions to complete a given routine, procedure or computation is called a program, and the development of the series of instructions is referred to as programming. Languages in which the programs are written are known as programming languages.

Programming languages can be classified into two groups: (a) machine oriented languages, and (b) problem oriented languages. A machine oriented language is designed to make the best use of the special features and capacity of a particular make of computer, and its use is restricted to that particular computer. Machine oriented languages have certain disadvantages: (a) the programmer has to learn a new language for each type of computer, if he is required to write a program in machine oriented language; and (b) any significant additions to, or changes in, the equipment will usually require considerable reprogramming. On the other hand, problem oriented languages are universal in nature and are generally independent of a particular make or type of computer. The focus is on problem solving rather than on maximizing the use of specialized computer features or computer capacity. For these reasons, problem oriented languages are more widely used than machine oriented languages.

The most commonly used problem oriented languages are: COBOL (acronym for COmmon Business Oriented Language; and FORTRAN (acronym for FORmula TRANslator).[3] These programming languages specify a set of rules to be followed by programmers. The rules used for COBOL resemble English, while FORTRAN notations resemble the language of mathematics. Only a specified set of numbers, letters and special characters may be used in writing a program. There are also special rules for punctuation and the use of blank spaces. Two programs are reproduced in Figures 9—K and 9—L. One of these programs is in COBOL, and the other in FORTRAN.

The COBOL program is designed to calculate the total amount outstanding on a debtor's account. Only the procedure division of the program has been shown. The FORTRAN program is designed to calculate total savings after five years on a sum invested now at 10 per cent per annum compounded at half-yearly intervals. Both examples have been simplified for illustrative purposes.

---

[3] In business information systems, other languages that are commonly used are PL1, RPG, Basic and Algol.

Figure 9–K
An Illustration of a COBOL Program

```
       PROCEDURE DIVISION.
       START.
           OPEN INPUT ACREC TO OUTPUT PRINT-FILE.
           MOVE SPACES TO PRINT-LINE.
       READ-A-CARD.
           READ ACREC AT END GO TO FINISH.
           ADD AMT-I-OVERDUE TO WORKING-COUNTER.
           ADD CR-I-SALES TO WORKING-COUNTER.
           ADD CR-I-ADJ TO WORKING-COUNTER.
           SUBTRACT PAYMENT-I FROM WORKING-COUNTER.
           MOVE WORKING-COUNTER TO NEW-I-BALANCE.
           ADD WORKING-COUNTER TO TOTAL-COUNTER.
           MOVE ZEROS TO WORKING-COUNTER.
           MOVE ACT-NUMBER-I TO PRT-ACT-NUMBER.
           MOVE DESCRIPTION-I TO PRT-DESCRIPTION.
           WRITE PRINT-LINE AFTER ADVANCING 1.
           MOVE SPACES TO PRINT-LINE.
           GO TO READ-A-CARD.
       FINISH.
           MOVE TOTAL-COUNTER TO PRT-TOTAL.
           WRITE PRINT-LINE AFTER ADVANCING 1.
           CLOSE ACREC PRINT-FILE.
           STOP RUN.
```

Figure 9–L
An Illustration of a FORTRAN Program

```
C     THIS PROGRAM CALCULATES TOTAL SAVINGS AFTER 5 YEARS AT 10%
C     INTEREST COMPOUNDED TWICE A YEAR FOR SUM INVESTED NOW.
10    READ(1,2) SUM
2     FORMAT(F10.0)
      TOTAL = SUM*(1.0+.05)**10
      PRINT(3,4) SUM, TOTAL
4     FORMAT(9H A SUM OF,F10.2, 7H YIELDS,F10.2)
      GO TO 10
      END
```

Summary

The accountant should gain familiarity with the tools and techniques used in system design and operation, and with the steps involved in system design, in order to operate effectively in an environment where modern data processing systems are used. Some of the tools and techniques used by system designers are organization charts, flowcharts, decision tables, grid charts, layout charts and network diagrams. The steps involved in system design are: (a) studying and analysing the existing system; (b) defining new system requirements; (c) designing a new system; and (d) proposing the detailed system.

The accountant will be involved in all these stages, as well as in the implementation and operation of the system. The tools and techniques discussed in this chapter will be useful to the accountant in gaining a better understanding of the information system, of which accounting is an important part.

A Study Guideline

While this chapter provides a general background knowledge of the tools and techniques used in system design and operation, accountants who wish to gain a specialized knowledge of information systems should carry out further studies in the following main areas:

(a) mechanical, punched card and electronic data processing systems;
(b) input, output and storage devices used in data processing;
(c) computing equipment;
(d) programming languages; and
(e) electronic data processing operations.

A selected bibliography is given at the end of the chapter.

Appendix A

A Matrix Accounting System

Double entry is the commonly used method of accounting record keeping. An alternative method involves the recording of transactions in an accounting matrix instead of a double-entry system of disaggregated accounts. While this represents a drastic modification to the conventional form, it does not depart from the notion of duality of record and equilibrium of results, which are essential features of the accounting system. Each transaction in a matrix system is recorded by means of a single entry in the accounting matrix. This replaces the dual entries in conventional ledger accounts. A description of a matrix accounting system follows.

A matrix accounting system may take several forms, but it may be viewed essentially as a table of inter-related rows and columns, of which the rows represent accounts to be debited while the columns represent accounts to be credited. A transaction is then recorded in the matrix by means of a single entry in the cell formed by the intersection of the row for the account to be debited and the column for the account to be credited.

Table 9—1 shows how Transactions 1-8 described in Chapter 1 might be recorded in a matrix accounting system. Transaction 1, representing the payment of the proprietor's capital contribution into the firm's bank account, thus results in an entry in the cell formed by the first row, which records debits to assets, and the third column, which records credits to proprietorship equity. The transactions recorded in Table 9—1 may be identified by means of the figures in parentheses. The process of balancing an account (Transaction 3) does not require an entry in the matrix.

Table 9—1
An Accounting Matrix

W. Smith
Ledger Matrix for Period 2-6 January 1985

($)

Debit \ Credit	Assets	Liabilities	Prop. equity	Sales	Cost of sales	Expenses	Total debits
Assets	—	200(2)	1 000(1)	250(6) 600(8)	—	—	2 050
Liabilities	—	—	—	—	—	—	—
Prop. equity	—	—	—	—	—	—	—
Sales	—	—	—	—	—	—	—
Cost of sales	500(5)	300(7)	—	—	—	—	800
Expenses	10(4)	—	—	—	—	—	10
Total credits	510	500	1 000	850	—	—	2 860

Where the matrix takes the form of Table 9—1 and opening balances have to be taken into account, they may be recorded as separate entries in the cells 'Debit Assets/Credit Proprietorship Equity' and 'Debit Proprietorship Equity/Credit Liabilities' respectively. The total debits and total credits may then be used to establish the trial balance as follows:

	Total Debits	Total Credits	Net Balances Dr.	Net Balances Cr.
Assets	$2 050	$510	$1 540	—
Liabilities	—	500	—	$500
Proprietorship equity	—	1 000	—	1 000
Sales	—	850	—	850
Cost of sales	800	—	800	—
Expenses	10	—	10	—
	$2 860	$2 860	$2 350	$2 350

Calculation of profit and preparation of financial statements may then proceed in the usual way.

Alternatively, the form of the matrix may be varied to include rows and columns for opening balances, closing entries and closing balances (see Table 9—2).

Table 9—2

An Accounting Matrix Expanded to Record Opening and Closing Balances and Closing Entries

W. Smith

Ledger Matrix for Period 2-6 January 1985

($)

Debit \ Credit	Assets	Liabil-ities	Prop. equity	Sales	Cost of sales	Expenses	Opening balances	Total debits	Closing entries	Closing balances
Assets	—	200	1 000	250 600	—	—	—	2 050	—	1 540
Liabilities	—	—	—	—	—	—	—	—	—	—
Prop. equity	—	—	—	—	—	—	—	—	—	—
Sales	—	—	—	—	—	—	—	—	850	—
Cost of sales	500	300	—	—	—	—	—	800	—	—
Expenses	10	—	—	—	—	—	—	10	—	—
Opening balances	—	—	—	—	—	—	—	—	—	—
Total credits	510	500	1 000	850	—	—	—	2 860	—	—
Closing entries	—	—	40	—	800	10	—	—	850	—
Closing balances	—	500	1 040	—	—	—	—	—	—	1 540

It will be seen that, in order to arrive at the closing balance for each item, total credits in respect of that item have been offset against total debits. Net profit has been calculated as the balancing closing debit entry and credited to proprietorship equity. The closing entries in effect provide the information needed to compile the income statement, while the closing balances form the basis of the balance sheet, as follows:

W. Smith

Income Statement for Period 2-6 January 1985

Sales	$850
Less: Cost of sales	800
Gross profit	50
Less: Expenses	10
Net profit	$40

W. Smith

Balance Sheet as at 6 January 1985

Assets	$1 540
Less: Liabilities	500
Proprietorship equity	$1 040

A Logic Flowchart for a Matrix Accounting System

Figure 9—M illustrates a flowchart that has been constructed to assist with the writing of the computer program. It will be seen that the first step involves the establishment of matrices for each ledger. KASYS may be thought of as a code name, which the computer will interpret as the general ledger, while IREC and IPAY represent the accounts receivable and accounts payable ledgers. Then follows so-called initialization, in order to set values in all cells of the matrices equal to zero. (There are no opening balances in the example.) Another matrix (IASYS) is needed for posting transaction data to the general ledger matrix (KASYS) which accumulates and stores the data, but it is not strictly necessary to initialize this because the reading of data into the matrix will automatically cancel any information which has been previously recorded in the matrix.

After noting the number of weeks (N) for which transaction data are to be recorded, the system provides for a 'Do loop' which ensures that the computer will keep reading in transaction data for each week from the posting matrix (IASYS), and adding these to the accumulating matrix (KASYS) until the number of repetitive operations (being counted by K) equals the number of weeks (N). By this means the ledger matrix (KASYS) receives a cumulative record of the transactions affecting each cell in the matrix. The subsidiary ledger matrices (IREC and IPAY) are then posted.

The totals of the columns and rows of the general ledger matrix (KASYS) may now be computed and converted to account balances which form the basis of the trial balance. A simple decision operation tests the accuracy of the trial balance, producing an error message if necessary. If the trial balance agrees, the processing continues with the computation of the closing balances in the subsidiary ledger matrices (IREC and IPAY); the aggregate balances in each subsidiary ledger are compared, in a further test instruction, with the appropriate control account balance in the general ledger.

It remains to instruct the computer to print the general ledger matrix, the trial balance and the subsidiary ledger matrices in respect of each week's transactions. Another test instruction tells the computer to proceed, if the end of a four-week period has been reached (i.e. if N = 4), to define income statement and balance sheet values by reference to previously calculated trial balance figures and, after testing to confirm the balance sheet equation, to print the income statement and balance sheet.

A computer program can be written on the basis of the logic flowchart presented in Figure 9—M.

Appendix B

Running a Punched Card Job on the Computer

Most universities and other tertiary institutions have computing facilities for students where punched card inputs can be used for problem solving. A general description of punched cards as input media and the procedure for running a punched card job on a computer are presented below.

Eighty-column Punched Card

The standard punched card has 80 vertical card columns, as shown in Figure 9—N. Each column is divided into 12 rows. Ten of these rows are marked as 0,1,2, ..., 8 and 9. The other two rows are positioned above row 0 and are referred to as Y and X (also called rows 12 and 11). The sequence of the 12 rows is then: Y, X, 0, 1, ..., 8 and 9. The top two rows, i.e. Y and X, are known as zone punches, and rows 1 to 9 inclusive are known as digit punches. The row 0 serves the role of both a zone punch and a digit punch.

Figure 9—M
A Logic Flowchart for a Matrix Accounting System

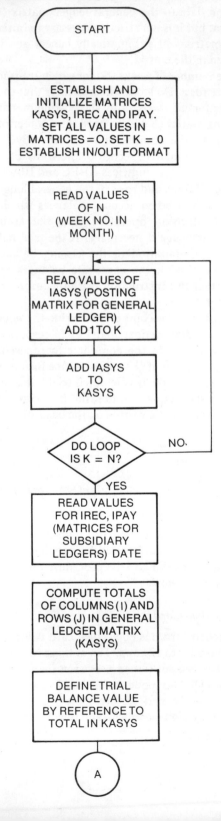

Figure 9—M (contd)

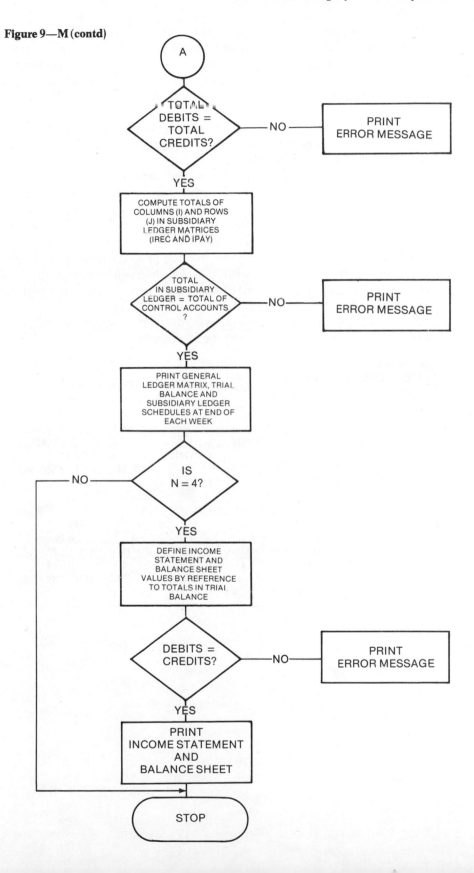

The punched card can accommodate three types of inputs: digits, alphabets and special characters. Digits are recorded by holes punched in appropriate positions in the digit punch area only. The alphabets and special characters are recorded by a combination of holes in the same column in both the zone punch and digit punch areas. For example, digit '1' is recorded by punching a hole in row 1, the letter 'A' is recorded by punching a hole in row 12 and a hole also in row 1, and the special character '$' by holes in rows 11, 3 and 8, relating to the respective individual column. These positions are punched automatically by selecting the appropriate key, i.e. '1' 'A' or '$', on the key punch machine.

To run a job on the computer, the punched card input must be prepared and arranged as shown in Figure 9—0. The cards are classified and arranged into five categories. The first group of cards contains details of user name, account number, the computer language in which the program is written, input devices and output devices to be used during the run. The second group contains the computer program. The third group instructs the computer that the program reading is completed and that the next cards are the data cards. The fourth group comprises the data cards, and the fifth category (a single card) instructs the computer that the inputs have been completely read by the computer and that the job can be processed.

After the card reader has read the input cards (all five categories), the processing is completed and the output is printed by the line printer.

Figure 9—N
An Eighty-column Punched Card

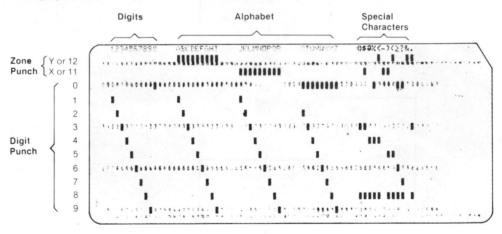

Figure 9—O
Running a Punched Card Job on the Computer

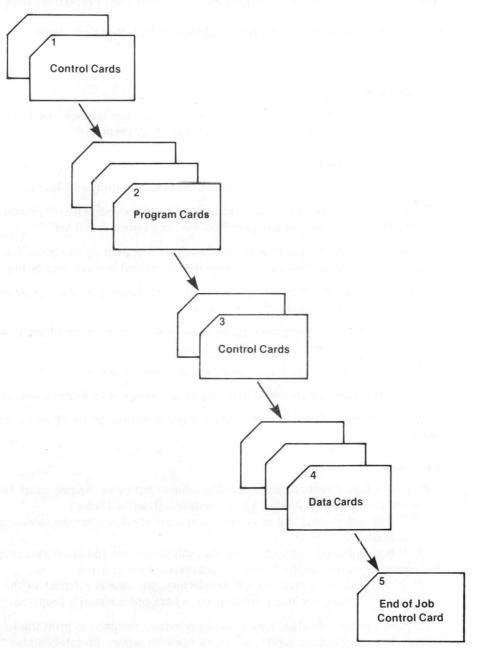

Note: The cards are read in the sequence 1, 2, 3, 4 and 5. The 'End of Job Control Card' is the last card to be read.

References

Arnold, R.R., Hill, H.C. and Nichols, A.V., *Modern Data Processing*, John Wiley, New York, 1972.

Davis, G.B., *Computer Data Processing*, McGraw-Hill, New York, 1969.

Forkner, I. and McLeod, R., *Computerized Business Systems,* John Wiley, New York, 1973.

Additional Reading

Carrington, A.S., Battersby, G.B., and Howitt, G., *Accounting, An Information System,* Whitcombe and Tombs, Christchurch, N.Z. (in press).

Discussion Questions

1 What are the main tools and techniques used in system study and design?

2 What are flowcharts? What is the difference between a system flowchart and a logic flowchart? Describe the four basic symbols used in a system flowchart.

3 What are the advantages of a system flowchart prepared by using the four basic symbols? What are the limitations of these flowcharts and how can they be improved?

4 Define a program. Why are problem oriented languages more popular than machine oriented languages?

5 Most problems can be represented by either a decision table or a logic flowchart. When would a decision table be preferred?

6 Describe a grid chart and its role in information system design.

7 Discuss the main steps involved in the study and design of an information system.

8 Discuss the role of the accountant during the operating phase of an information system.

Exercises

1 Prepare a logic flowchart and a decision table to represent the procedure required to process customer sales orders. The procedure is described below:

(a) The inventory level and customer's credit are checked after the sales order has been received.

(b) If both are satisfactory a packing slip, shipping ticket and invoice are prepared. The customer record and the inventory master record are updated.

(c) If the customer's credit is not satisfactory, the case is referred to the credit manager. If the inventory level is inadequate, a back order record is prepared.

2 Prepare a system flowchart for an inventory system designed to print the following reports: inventory reorder report; inventory stockout report; inventory status report; and inventory usage report. The inventory master file is on a magnetic tape and the inputs are prepared on the punched cards.

3 The inventory system of Exercise 1 includes a daily updating run which produces a purchase report. Draw a logic flowchart to prepare this purchase order report.

Part II   Accounting Entities

Introduction to Part II: Accounting Entities

The accounting system that was described in Chapters 1-5 was concerned essentially with the activities of a sole proprietor. It is now necessary to consider some of the special problems that arise in accounting for other kinds of entities. In Part II the accounts and reports of different kinds of group entities will be examined. In particular, the distinction between business groups and public authorities will be made. This distinction is useful, partly because the two kinds of group entity have differing financial objectives and partly because they tend to employ different kinds of accounting systems. Business groups (partnerships and companies) are usually concerned with the earning of profits, and their accounts are normally maintained on an accrual basis in accordance with the general principles that have been outlined in previous chapters. Public authorities, on the other hand, do not usually set out to make profits; their objectives are rather to provide collective services on the basis of compulsory membership. As was indicated in Chapter 1, moreover, public authorities frequently employ different systems of accounting from the accrual method which is used by business enterprises. Many governments, for example, confine their accounting record to cash transactions.

It should, perhaps, be emphasized that there is no theoretical reason why public authorities should not adopt the accrual basis of accounting used by business enterprises, and in practice many do. They then need to substitute a revenue account (recording a residual surplus or deficit in lieu of a profit or loss) for the trading and profit and loss accounts in a business system; and an accumulated fund account in place of the capital account of a business enterprise. With this exception, their accounting systems can be similar to the one described in earlier chapters. Business undertakings run by public authorities are especially likely to adopt business accounting methods.

Whether or not they use different kinds of accounting systems, governments are likely to require different bases of classification from those used by business enterprises. Apart from this, the main complication that arises in accounting for any group entity is the need to record transactions affecting the relationships between the different members of the group. In the case of a business group, this involves accounting for the capital contributed by members of the group (partners or shareholders) and for the appropriate distribution of the profits earned. In the case of a government, it involves accounting for the accumulated funds of the government and for the surplus or deficit that results from each period's activities.

In the following chapters, the special accounting problems posed by partnerships, companies, company combinations, divisions of business enterprises in the form of departments or branches, and public authorities will be considered in more detail. The final chapter of Part II takes the form of an introduction to national accounting systems, in which the transactions of all entities in the economy as a whole are recorded for different purposes in different ways. Although national accounting systems record exchange transactions in a way that reflects the dual nature of transactions, it will be seen that national accounting systems use different accounting frameworks and classification systems from those of business enterprises and public authorities.

10 Partnerships

Partnership has been defined as 'the relationship which subsists between persons carrying on business in common with a view to profit'. The business must be carried on in common, and the objective must be the earning of financial gain. While it is desirable for a partnership agreement to take the form of a written contract, an oral contract is also valid. Further, the Courts have ruled that, in the absence of any explicit agreement, the existence of a partnership may be implied from the conduct of the parties concerned.

Usually the relationship between partners is governed by the terms of the partnership agreement. This agreement covers such matters as the proportions in which capital is contributed, interest on partners' capital contributions and advances, the profit and loss sharing ratio, partners' salaries, restrictions (if any) on the powers of partners, and the termination of the partnership. If the agreement is silent on any matter affecting the rights and responsibilities of partners, or if there is no agreement, the provisions of the relevant Partnership Act apply.[1] These usually stipulate that, in the absence of an agreement, profits and losses are to be divided equally, no salaries are to be paid to partners and no interest is to be allowed on capital or charged on withdrawals of funds (drawings); but that interest is to be allowed on advances at a specified rate. Where an agreement to continue the partnership does not exist, the partnership must terminate on the death of any one of the partners.

A special feature of the partnership form of enterprise is that the act of any one of the partners binds the firm where the act is in the ordinary course of the firm's business, while a contract with the firm is a contract with all individual partners. The liability of partners towards the firm's creditors is said to be 'joint'. This means that although debts are normally met out of the firm's assets, if these are insufficient every partner is liable for the debts of the firm to the full extent of his personal assets.

Two important differences between a partner and a shareholder in a limited company are: first, subject to agreement a partner has an equal right with his co-partners to share in the management of the firm, whereas a shareholder does not participate in the management of the company; and second, a partner's liability for the firm's debts is unlimited, whereas the liability of a shareholder in a limited liability company is limited to the par value of his shares. The holder of a fully paid-up share in such a company has no further liability.

Partnerships are formed for a number of reasons. In some professions, such as medicine, law and public accounting, the company form of business organization is prohibited for public policy considerations. In industry and commerce, the partnership form of organization provides the opportunity for members of the group to pool their capital resources and specialized skills, and at the same time retain management control. There may be a tax advantage insofar as the partnership is not liable to company income tax, although individual partners are liable to personal income tax on their respective shares of the firm's profits.

---

[1] The States of Australia have separate Partnership Acts, which are substantially similar.

Partnership Accounts

Formation

On the formation of a partnership, a separate capital account needs to be established for each partner, to which is credited the value of the cash or other assets contributed by the partner to the firm (the corresponding debit entries are, of course, made in appropriate asset accounts). Advances (as distinct from agreed capital contributions) made by a partner to the firm also need to be recorded separately, by crediting the partner's advance account and debiting, say, the bank account. Finally, a separate current account needs to be established for each partner, in which are recorded other transactions between the partner and the firm, such as profit distribution, salary earnings, withdrawals of funds from the partnership (drawings), and interest allowed on capital and advances or charged on drawings.

Distribution of Partnership Profits

Business transactions are recorded in the accounts of a partnership in the same way as for a single proprietor, and the preparation of the trading and profit and loss accounts follows a similar course. When the net profit has been determined, however, it is transferred from the profit and loss account proper to the credit of an account called the profit and loss appropriation account which, as its name suggests, records the way in which the profit is appropriated or distributed among the partners. In addition to the net profit, the appropriation account is credited with interest charged on partners' drawings, and it is debited with interest allowed to partners on capital or advances, with partners' salaries (if these are notional amounts and therefore have not been charged to the profit and loss account proper) and with the partners' respective shares of residual profits. The corresponding double entry in each case is made to the current account of the partner concerned, which meanwhile has been debited with any withdrawals made by the partner in anticipation of profits or other earnings.

Suppose, for example, that Adams and Black are in partnership sharing profits and losses in the ratio 3:2. Their respective capital contributions are $10 000 and $6 000 and, under the partnership agreement, interest is allowed on capital at five per cent per annum. No interest is charged on drawings. Black is allowed a salary of $1 000 per annum, and the net profit on business operations for the first year of the partnership (before charging Black's salary) is $5 000. If their respective drawings during the year have been $1 600 and $1 400, the profit and loss appropriation account and the partners' current accounts take the following form:

Profit and Loss Appropriation

Salary—Black		$1 000	Profit and loss account		
Interest on capital—			(net profit)		$5 000
Adams	$500				
Black	300				
		800			
Share of residual profit—					
Adams	1 920				
Black	1 280				
		3 200			
		$5 000			$5 000

Current Account—Adams

Bank (drawings)	$1 600	Profit and loss appropriation	
Balance c/d	820	account—	
		Interest on capital	$500
		Share of residual profit	1 920
	$2 420		$2 420
		Balance b/d	$820

Current Account—Black

Bank (drawings)	$1 400	Profit and loss appropriation	
Balance c/d	1 180	account—	
		Salary	$1 000
		Interest on capital	300
		Share of residual profit	1 280
	$2 580		$2 580
		Balance b/d	$1 180

In the partnership balance sheet, proprietary interests are recorded in the order of priority of claim against assets, namely: (a) partners' advances; (b) capital contributions; and (c) current account balances. The proprietorship section of the balance sheet in the foregoing example therefore appears as follows:

Capital—			
Adams		$10 000	
Black		6 000	$16 000
Current accounts—			
Adams		820	
Black		1 180	2 000
			$18 000

Revaluation of Net Assets

There are certain situations in partnership accounting in which the historical record assumptions, in particular the monetary postulate, are relaxed. Specifically the net worth of a partnership must be revalued when any change in the partners' relationships takes place, in order to bring book values of individual assets into line with agreed current values and to take a goodwill element into account. Goodwill may be defined as the capitalized value of that portion of future profits which exceeds a normal return on investment. For the present purpose it may be assumed that goodwill is measured as the difference between the value of the firm as a going concern and the sum total of the current values of individual net assets. The situations discussed below include changes in the profit-sharing ratio of existing partners, admission of a new partner, retirement of an old partner and dissolution of the partnership.

Change in Profit-sharing Ratio

Suppose that Adams and Black agree to share profits equally in future, and that a valuation indicates that various asset accounts need to be revalued upwards by $1 000 and that goodwill is valued at $6 000. Since the change in the profit-sharing ratio is to relate to future profits, the gain of $7 000 on revaluation should be credited to the partners' capital accounts in the *old* profit-sharing ratio of 3:2, as shown in the following journal entries:

1985	Asset accounts (various)	Dr.	$1 000	
	Goodwill	Dr.	6 000	
	Partnership revaluation account	Cr.		$7 000
	Asset revaluations, including the setting up of goodwill account			
	Partnership revaluation account	Dr.	7 000	
	Capital—Adams	Cr.		4 200
	Capital—Black	Cr.		2 800
	Gain on asset revaluations, including goodwill, taken to partners' capital accounts			

If the new values of assets and goodwill are to remain in the books, no further entries are necessary.

Although an amount of $6 000 has been brought into account for goodwill in order to adjust the partners' capital accounts before the new profit-sharing arrangements operate, accountants are usually reluctant to record goodwill in the accounts. This is because the value of goodwill depends essentially on a subjective assessment of the firm's profitability or earning power in relation to some standard notion of profit. The value of goodwill depends on a comparison of the relationship between the return on funds employed (see Chapter 7) and corresponding returns in other firms and industries. Funds employed for this purpose must be interpreted as equal to the current values of individual, tangible operating assets less liabilities. [2]

If, for this reason, it is decided to write off goodwill after the revaluation has taken place, this may be done by debiting the partners' capital accounts in accordance with the *new* profit-sharing ratio, as shown:

1985				
	Partnership revaluation account	Dr.	$6 000	
	Goodwill	Cr.		$6 000
	Goodwill account written off			
	Capital—Adams	Dr.	3 000	
	Capital—Black	Dr.	3 000	
	Partnership revaluation account	Cr.		6 000
	Write-down of goodwill charged to partners' capital accounts			

[2] It would be misleading to include goodwill in the asset base for the purpose of determining a value for goodwill.

The abridged balance sheet of Adams and Black after the above entries have been made is as follows:

Capital—			Net assets	$19 000
Adams	$11 200			
Black	5 800	$17 000		
Current accounts—				
Adams	820			
Black	1 180	2 000		
		$19 000		$19 000

Admission of a New Partner

On the admission of a new partner where the partnership has been in existence for some time, the old partners may reasonably require to be compensated for the goodwill resulting from the established earning power and reputation of the business. In addition, the old partners' capital accounts must be credited (debited) with the gain (loss) on restating assets at their current values. This may be arranged in one of two ways:

(a) By debiting the goodwill account (with the agreed value of goodwill) and the various asset accounts (with the gain on revaluation) and crediting the partner-ship revaluation account, thereby ensuring that the old partners' capital accounts are credited with their shares of goodwill and gain on revaluation. If this procedure is adopted, the total value of the cash and other assets brought into the partnership by the new partner is credited to his capital account.

(b) By regarding part of the cash or other assets contributed by the incoming partner as a premium payable for goodwill, which is credited to the revaluation account (or directly to the existing partners' capital accounts). The new partner's capital account is then credited only with the balance of the assets he brings into the partnership, and no goodwill account is raised in the firm's books of account.

Suppose that Chapman joins the partnership of Adams and Black. Assets are already recorded at current values of $19 000, and the agreed value of goodwill is $6 000. Chapman is to contribute capital of $8 000. Profits and losses are to be shared equally among the three partners.

The value of the existing firm is thus $25 000 (net assets $19 000 *plus* goodwill $6 000). The following entries record the admission of the partner under (a), the first procedure:

Partnership Revaluation

Capital—Adams	$3 000	Goodwill	$6 000
Capital—Black	3 000		
	$6 000		$6 000

Bank

Capital—Chapman	$8 000		

Goodwill

Partnership revaluation account	$6 000		

Capital—Adams

Balance c/d	$14 200	Balance b/d	$11 200
		Partnership revaluation account	3 000
	$14 200		$14 200
		Balance b/d	$14 200

Capital—Black

Balance c/d	$8 800	Balance b/d	$5 800
		Partnership revaluation account	3 000
	$8 800		$8 800
		Balance b/d	$8 800

Capital—Chapman

		Bank	$8 000

If it is decided to write off the balance of the goodwill account, the three partners' capital accounts will be debited in accordance with their profit-sharing ratios:

1985			
Capital—Adams	Dr.	$2 000	
Capital—Black	Dr.	2 000	
Capital—Chapman	Dr.	2 000	
Partnership revaluation account	Cr.		$6 000
Goodwill written off, taken to partners' capital accounts			

If the second procedure, (b), is adopted, the partners need to agree on how much of Chapman's contribution of $8 000 is to be regarded as a premium for goodwill and how much represents capital. The amount of the premium represents Chapman's share of the goodwill, on the assumption that the total value of goodwill is first written up in the books and is then written off against the partners' capital accounts in accordance with their profit-sharing ratios. In this case the premium is $2 000, i.e. one-third of $6 000. Under this procedure the partnership books take the following form:

Partnership Revaluation

Capital—Adams	$1 000	Bank (premium for goodwill)	$2 000
Capital—Black	1 000		
	$2 000		$2 000

Bank

Partnership revaluation account (premium for goodwill)	$2 000	Balance c/d	$8 000
Capital—Chapman	6 000		
	$8 000		$8 000
Balance b/d	$8 000		

Capital—Adams

Balance c/d	$12 200	Balance b/d	$11 200
		Partnership revaluation account	1 000
	$12 200		$12 200
		Balance b/d	$12 200

Capital—Black

Balance c/d	$6 800	Balance b/d	$5 800
		Partnership revaluation account	1 000
	$6 800		$6 800
		Balance b/d	$6 800

Capital—Chapman

		Bank	$6 000

Irrespective of whether the first or the second procedure described above is adopted, the partners' interests in the business are maintained in a similar manner. If the partnership is dissolved soon after Chapman's admission, and the agreed net worth of the business has been correctly assessed (i.e. the sale of the business realizes $33 000, including Chapman's contribution), the pattern of distribution of the proceeds among the partners is the same under both methods of recording, and Chapman will recover $8 000, the amount of his original contribution.

Retirement of a Partner

The retirement of a partner likewise usually requires the revaluation of assets and the making of adjustments in respect of goodwill, the gains or losses on revaluations being taken to all partners' capital accounts in the agreed profit-sharing ratios. The procedures for asset (including goodwill) revaluations to be followed are often laid down in the partnership agreement. The retiring partner is then entitled to the total of the balances outstanding in his capital and current accounts; this amount constitutes a liability of the business to the retiring partner.

Where a retiring partner, with the consent of the other partners, sells his interest to an outside party, a journal entry is made to debit the retiring partner's capital and current accounts and to credit the new partner's corresponding accounts accordingly. The new partner stands in the shoes of the retiring partner and no other entry in the partnership's books is necessary.

Dissolution of a Partnership

When a partnership is dissolved it is necessary to establish a partnership realization account, to which are transferred the balances of all asset accounts (other than the bank account) and related provisions, such as provisions for depreciation and doubtful debts. As the assets are sold, the realization account is credited and the bank account debited with the proceeds of the sale. If any of the assets are taken over by the partners, their capital accounts are debited and the realization account credited with the agreed values. The realization account is debited with the expenses of dissolution (agent's commission, valuer's fees, etc.), and the balance of the account represents the surplus or deficit on realization which, in the absence of agreement to the contrary, is allocated to the partners in the proportions they share profits and losses. Any balances in the partners' current accounts are transferred to their capital accounts, after which the remaining claims are met in the following order: (a) liabilities to outside creditors, (b) partners' advances and (c) partners' capital. The resulting debit entries in the liability and capital accounts, and the credits in the bank account, close the accounts remaining in the ledger.

The procedure may be illustrated by assuming that the partnership of Adams, Black and Chapman is to be dissolved after several years' operations, and that at the date of dissolution the firm's balance sheet reveals the following information:

Creditors		$5 000	Bank		$6 500
Partners' equity:			Debtors	$9 000	
Capital—			*Less*: Provision for		
Adams	$14 200		doubtful debts	1 000	
Black	8 800				8 000
Chapman	8 000		Inventory		10 000
		$31 000	Fixed assets	15 000	
Current accounts—			*Less*: Provision for		
Adams	2 500		depreciation	3 500	
Black	1 500				11 500
Chapman	2 000	6 000	Goodwill		6 000
		37 000			
		$42 000			$42 000

Black agrees to take over the debtors at their net book value, and the inventory and fixed assets are sold for $11 000 and $14 000, respectively. Expenses of dissolution are $500. Because the assets are sold separately nothing is realized on the firm's goodwill. Under these circumstances the dissolution is effected in the following way:

Realization

Debtors	$9 000	Provision for doubtful debts		$1 000
Inventory	10 000	Provision for depreciation		3 500
Fixed assets	15 000	Capital—Black (debtors)		8 000
Goodwill	6 000	Bank (proceeds for inventory)		11 000
Bank (expenses of dissolution)	500	Bank (proceeds for fixed assets)		14 000
		Loss on realization—		
		Capital—Adams	$1 000	
		Capital—Black	1 000	
		Capital—Chapman	1 000	
				3 000
	$40 500			$40 500

Capital—Adams

Realization loss	$1 000	Balance b/d	$14 200
Bank	15 700	Current account—Adams	2 500
	$16 700		$16 700

Capital—Black

Realization account (debtors)	$8 000	Balance b/d	$8 800
Realization loss	1 000	Current account—Black	1 500
Bank	1 300		
	$10 300		$10 300

Capital—Chapman

Realization loss	$1 000	Balance b/d	$8 000
Bank	9 000	Current account—Chapman	2 000
	$10 000		$10 000

Bank

Balance b/d	$6 500	Realization account—	
Realization of assets—		(expenses of dissolution)	$500
Inventory	11 000	Creditors	5 000
Fixed assets	14 000	Capital—Adams	15 700
		Capital—Black	1 300
		Capital—Chapman	9 000
	$31 500		$31 500

If, as a result of realization losses or for other reasons, a partner's capital account ends up with a debit balance, the partner must make good the deficiency by a payment of cash. If the partner is insolvent and in the absence of any agreement to the contrary, many writers are of the opinion that the decision of an English Court prescribes that the deficiency be borne by the remaining partners in proportion to their respective capital contributions. But there is considerable doubt and confusion concerning the solvent partners' obligations in this situation.

Discussion Questions

1 Explain how the distribution of net profit to owners is dealt with in the accounts of (a) sole traders, and (b) partnerships. What happens to profits not distributed?

2 Under what circumstances will goodwill appear in the books of a partnership following the admission of a new partner?

3 What are the important differences between a partner and shareholder in a limited liability company?

4 What factors will lead to the termination of the legal life of a partnership?

5 What are the principal clauses relating to the accounts which should be contained in a partnership agreement, and in the absence of such an agreement how are the interests, rights and duties of the partners determined?

6 The ownership equity of a partnership, although similar to the equity of a sole proprietor, is classified according to the interests of each of the partners. Discuss the significance of the classification.

Exercises

1 Alan Ladd and Fred MacMurray have decided to form a partnership. Ladd is to invest $150 000 and MacMurray $100 000. It is agreed that Ladd is to work full-time in the business and MacMurray is to work only half-time. The following plans for the division of income are being considered:

(a) equal division;

(b) in the ratio of the partners' capital contributions;

(c) in the ratio of hours per week employed in the business;

(d) interest of eight per cent to be charged on capital and remaining profits to be shared in the ratio of 3:2;

(e) interest of eight per cent to be charged on capital, salaries of $20 000 to be paid to Ladd and $10 000 to MacMurray, and the remaining profits to be shared equally; and

(f) as in (e), except that Ladd is also to be allowed a bonus equal to 10 per cent of the amount by which net income exceeds salary allowances.

You are required to ascertain the amount of net income each partner will receive with each of the above plans, under the following assumptions: (i) net income is $55 000, and (ii) net income is $30 000.

2 Warren Grant and John Sullivan form a partnership on 1 July 1985. Grant, who has been trading as sole trader, is to invest certain business assets at agreed valuations, transfer his business liabilities and contribute sufficient cash to bring his total capital to $75 000.

Details of Grant's assets and liabilities, and agreed valuations are set out below:

	Book Value in Grant's Ledger	Agreed Valuation
Accounts receivable	$31 800	$31 800
Allowance for doubtful debts	1 500	2 400
Inventories	50 000	40 000
Plant and machinery (net)	20 000	25 000
Accounts payable	18 000	18 000
Notes payable	12 000	12 000

Sullivan agrees to bring in inventories with a value of $36 500 and $23 500 in cash.

The partners have agreed that the capital accounts are to be fixed, interest to be allowed on capital at eight per cent, salaries of $10 000 and $15 000 are to be paid to Grant and Sullivan respectively, and the remaining profits are to be shared in the ratio of 5:4.

(a) You are required to:

(i) give the journal entries necessary to set up the books of the partnership; and

(ii) prepare a balance sheet of the partnership as at 1 July 1985.

(b) One year later, the accounts show that net profit (before payment of partners' interest and salaries) for the year ended 30 June 1986 is $70 000. The current accounts of Grant and Sullivan have debit balances of $12 000 and $16 000 respectively. You are required to record the distribution of profits, as it will appear in the appropriation account and the partners' current accounts.

3 Harris Bros. have been trading for many years as manufacturers of exclusive bathroom fixtures and fittings. On 30 June 1985 their trial balance was:

Petty cash advance	$50	
Bank overdraft		$2 000
Inventories on hand	19 500	
Accounts receivable	10 500	
Accounts payable		2 200
Allowance for doubtful debts		750
Patents	1 750	
Prepayments	300	
Motor vehicles	6 000	
Plant and machinery	18 900	
Office furniture	3 500	
Accumulated depreciation:—		
Motor vehicles		1 500
Plant and machinery		7 560
Office furniture		740
Buildings	30 000	
Mortgage on buildings		15 750
Capital—M. Harris		30 000
Capital—T. Harris		30 000
	$90 500	$90 500

On 1 July 1985 it was decided to admit A. Jones to the partnership on the following terms:

(a) goodwill of Harris Bros. to be brought into the accounts at $10 000;

(b) bad debts of $300 to be written-off and the allowance for doubtful debts to be increased to $950;

(c) patents to be written off;

(d) inventories to be revalued at $21 750; and

(e) the new partner Jones to contribute the following assets:

Accounts receivable	$5 000
Inventories	7 000
Motor vehicles	1 500
Plant	7 500

In addition, Jones agreed to contribute sufficient cash to make his capital equal to that of each of the other partners.

Give the journal entries necessary to record the above transactions in the books of the partnership and present the balance sheet of the new firm.

4 A. Oliver and B. Twist have been in business for many years sharing profits and losses in the ratio of 4:3. On 31 December 1985 they agreed to dissolve the partnership. A statement of their financial position on that date was as follows:

Balance Sheet as at 31 December 1985

Partners' equity			Current assets		
Capital—			Cash at bank	$1 000	
Oliver		$16 000	Accounts receivable	20 000	
Twist		10 800	Inventories	17 800	$38 800
		26 800			
Current accounts—			**Fixed assets**		
Oliver	$1 600		Plant and machinery (net)	7 800	
Twist	800	2 400	Fixture and fittings (net)	2 000	
		29 200	Goodwill	5 000	14 800
Current liabilities					
Accounts payable	18 500				
Loan account—					
Oliver	5 900	24 400			
		$53 600			$53 600

In the course of realization, plant and machinery and fixtures and fittings were sold for $6 000 and $1 000 respectively. The debtors paid their accounts except for a bad debt of $1 000, and inventories realized $16 000. Dissolution expenses amounted to $350. On 1 March 1986 when cash was received on the above sales, the creditors were settled in full for $18 000 and the partnership accounts were closed off.

You are required to show the realization account, the bank account and the partners' capital and current accounts to close the books of the partnership.

5 Brown, White and Grey who have been in partnership, agree to dispose of their business to the ABC Company. Brown and Grey wish to retire and White has decided to go into a new business on his own. The partnership balance sheet was made up of the following items at the date of dissolution:

Cash at bank	$4 800	
Accounts receivable	7 350	
Inventories on hand	25 200	
Plant and machinery (net)	4 860	
Furniture and fittings (net)	2 160	
Accounts payable		$5 520
Loan—Brown		7 500
Capital—Brown		12 000
Capital—White		9 000
Capital—Grey		6 600
Current account—White		2 100
Current account—Grey		1 650
	$44 370	$44 370

The ABC Company took over the inventories, plant and machinery, and furniture and fittings and gave the partners 20 000 shares, which have a nominal value of $1 each and a market value of $1.75 each, in full settlement. The company also took over the accounts receivable at an agreed value of $7 240, this sum being paid into the partnership bank account. Brown and Grey agreed to accept 12 000 and 8 000 shares respectively, and pay into the partnership any cash that may be required to settle their accounts, so that White could be paid his share in cash. All partners shared profits and losses equally.

Show the ledger accounts required to record the dissolution of partnership.

11 Companies

Companies as Business Organizations

A company is essentially a means of mobilizing financial resources for the purpose of undertaking business activity. The company form of organization has other distinguishing characteristics—limited liability, continuity of existence, transferability of ownership, separation of management from ownership, and special statutory and taxation responsibilities—but it has been developed primarily to serve a financial purpose. Companies existed before the nineteenth century, being established by Royal Charter or Act of Parliament for the purpose of promoting specific projects, usually in the field of foreign trade. But just as the partnership organization evolved as a means of providing the venture capital needed to finance the great upsurge in economic activity associated with the commercial revolution of the Middle Ages, so the corporate structure developed in response to the enormous financial demands that were generated by the industrial revolution of the nineteenth and twentieth centuries. As the scale of business operations expanded, it became impossible for individuals— or even groups of individuals organized in partnerships—to provide funds in the quantities required by many of the larger enterprises, and a new pattern of financing evolved around the corporate structure. Parliaments recognized the situation by enacting legislation, in the form of Companies Acts, governing the conditions under which companies could be established and the standards of conduct to which they were required to conform. Companies have proved such effective and efficient modes of harnessing and utilizing capital that they have become the dominant form of enterprise in most non-communist industrialized countries.

Today a company is invariably formed whenever a business is established on such a scale, or grows to such a size, that it is beyond the capacity of its promoters or owners to provide the capital required from their own resources. In these circumstances, other persons are invited to contribute the required capital funds in return for shares in the company. Companies may be either *public* or *proprietary* companies. If the invitation to contribute funds is extended to the public at large, the company is said to be a *public company*; and, further, if its shares are transferable through one or more of the stock exchanges, it is known as a *listed public company*. A *proprietary company* is prohibited from inviting public subscriptions of equity or loan capital, and is limited to fifty or fewer shareholders whose right to transfer shares is restricted; an *exempt proprietary company* basically is a proprietary company whose shares are not held by a public company. Proprietary companies are exempted from certain disclosure requirements, while additional exemptions apply to exempt proprietary companies.

In deciding whether to seek public or proprietary company status, the promoters of a new company will generally be guided by the capital requirements of the business. However, other considerations may affect the choice. Because of imperfections in the capital market or because the shares are not sufficiently attractive, it may not be possible to arrange or float a successful public issue, even if it is desired to do so. On the other hand, the promoters or owners of the business may not wish to surrender control over its activities to the extent that would be required by the formation of a public company; or they may desire to avoid public disclosure of the company's affairs, and may be willing to forgo the advantages of a greater capital-raising potential and of ready transferability of shares, for the sake of maintaining effective management control in a proprietary company.

By contrast with the members of a partnership, shareholders of both public and proprietary companies have the privilege of limited liability. That is, they are liable for the debts of their companies only up to the amounts, if any, unpaid on their shares (except that acceptance of a share in a no-liability company, invariably a mining enterprise, does not even involve this liability).[1] Both public and proprietary companies are required to appoint directors to manage their affairs. Directors are formally responsible to the shareholders who appoint them and must act in the shareholders' interests. Unfortunately, in public companies where ownership is widely diffused, this is not always seen to be the case. Shareholders are not informed of what management is doing (at least not until the next annual general meeting), and are often not in a position to exercise any effective control.

For income tax purposes, companies are classified on a different basis into public or private companies. A public company for company law purposes is not necessarily a public company for tax purposes. A public company for tax purposes basically is one in which the public is substantially interested; the most common examples are listed companies and (generally but not necessarily) their subsidiaries. A private company basically is one in which the public is not substantially interested and is so designated by the Tax Commissioner. The private company is subject to an undistributed profits tax on all undistributed profits in excess of a specified retention allowance.

The use of the terms public, proprietary and private companies in Australia differs from that in other English-speaking countries. The classifications 'public' and 'proprietary' employed in Australia are equivalent to the classifications 'public' and 'private' employed elsewhere. The purpose of classifying companies in Australia into 'public' and 'private' companies for tax purposes is to prevent closely held companies from retaining excessive amounts of profits in order that their owners may derive (non-taxable) capital gains from the eventual sale of their shares. Similar tax legislation exists in other countries, such as the United Kingdom.

Like a partnership, a company is a separate accounting entity, but it differs from a partnership in that it also is a legal entity which is quite distinct from its members. The name of a company must end in the words 'Limited' (usually abbreviated to 'Ltd'), Proprietary Limited ('Pty Ltd') or No Liability ('N.L.') depending on the kind of company and the relevant statutory requirements.

The activities of a company are governed by legislation in the form of a Companies Act,[2] and by two documents known as the Memorandum of Association and the Articles of Association. These are drawn up when the company is being established and filed with a statutory authority (the Registrar of Companies), whose responsibility it is to administer the Companies Act and with whom the company must be registered. The memorandum of association records: the name of the company; the objects for which it is formed; a declaration that the liability of members is limited; the amount of nominal or authorized share capital and how it is divided into shares.

[1] There is also a small number of companies limited by guarantee and unlimited companies, which are relatively unimportant.
[2] The States of Australia have separate Companies Acts, which are more or less uniform.

The objects clause is important, as it sets out at length the types of activities which the company may undertake. The articles of association set out the rules governing the internal affairs and the management of the company.

A company is required to keep certain non-accounting records, such as a share register, minute books for meetings of shareholders and directors, and registers recording transfers of shares and other dealings with individual shareholders; but these need not concern us in this book. Of more importance for the purposes of this book are the accounts which must be maintained by the company and the accounting reports which must be presented periodically to shareholders.

Accounting for Share Capital

The recording of day-to-day business transactions follows the same pattern in a company as in any other kind of entity, but special accounts are needed to record share capital transactions.

For this purpose it is necessary to distinguish between the following terms:

(a) *Nominal or authorized capital*—the total capital which the company is authorized to issue under its memorandum of association.

(b) *Unissued capital*—the amount of nominal capital which remains unissued.

(c) *Issued capital*—the amount of nominal capital which has been issued or allotted to shareholders.

(d) *Uncalled capital*—the amount of issued capital which has not been 'called', i.e. which shareholders have not yet been asked to pay.

(e) *Called-up capital*—the amount of issued capital which has been called up.

(f) *Unpaid calls*—the amount of called-up capital which has not yet been paid.

(g) *Paid-up capital*—the amount paid up on issued capital.

Accounts are required for authorized capital, unissued capital, uncalled capital and calls. The absence of a paid-up capital account (as is used in the United Kingdom), disclosing the total of shareholders' contributed funds, renders it necessary to measure paid-up capital by a series of deductions, as in the following statement:

Authorized capital	$...
Less: Unissued capital	...
Issued capital	...
Less: Uncalled capital	...
Called-up capital	...
Less: Unpaid calls	...
Paid-up capital	...

In practice, companies usually confine the substantive entry in the balance sheet to 'issued and paid-up capital' or, where issued capital is not fully paid up, to a summary statement such as the following: 'Paid-up capital: ...... $1 shares paid up to 50 cents, $......'.

Accounting for Share Capital—An Illustration

The method of accounting for share capital may be illustrated by a simple example. Suppose that a company, Australasia Traders Ltd, is registered with an authorized capital of $100 000, composed of 100 000 shares of $1 each. The potential capital of the company is $100 000 and this is matched by a potential asset in the unissued shares which it is hoped to convert into cash or other assets. On registration of the company, therefore, the existence of the potential asset and potential capital may be recorded in the books of the company by means of a debit entry in the unissued capital account and a credit entry in the authorized capital account, respectively:

Unissued Capital		Authorized Capital	
Authorized capital $100 000			Unissued capital $100 000

Since the issuing power has not yet been converted into actual assets, a balance sheet of the company at this stage must be purely notional, but it may be conceived of as taking the following form:

Shareholders' equity:			
Authorized capital	$100 000		
Less: Unissued capital	100 000		
Issued capital	—	**Assets**	—

Issue of Shares

The next step is to record the issue of shares. Suppose that the directors decide to issue 50 000 shares and invite applications accordingly. They are converting one potential asset, the issuing power represented by the unissued shares, into another potential asset, the calling power represented by the amount they can call up on the shares they hope to issue. The increase in one potential asset and the reduction in another may be recorded by means of a debit entry in the uncalled capital account and a credit entry in the unissued capital account respectively:

Unissued Capital			Authorized Capital	
Authorised capital $100 000	Uncalled capital $50 000			Unissued capital $100 000
	Balance c/d 50 000			
$100 000	$100 000			
Balance b/d $50 000				

Uncalled Capital	
Unissued capital $50 000	

A notional balance sheet at this stage may take the following form:

Shareholders' equity:			
Authorized capital	$100 000		
Less: Unissued capital	50 000		
Issued capital	50 000		
Less: Uncalled capital	50 000		
Called-up capital	—	**Assets**	—

Application, Allotment and Calls

It is usual for the directors to ask that applications for shares be accompanied by an amount of cash payable on application, and sometimes a further amount is payable when the shares are allotted. Suppose that $0.25 per share is payable on application and $0.25 on allotment. Part of the potential asset, uncalled capital, is in effect being converted into another potential asset, the right to receive application and allotment moneys. This may be recorded by debiting the application and allotment accounts (which may be regarded as unpaid call accounts) and crediting the uncalled capital account:

Unissued Capital				Authorized Capital		
Authorized capital	$100 000	Uncalled capital	$50 000		Unissued capital	$100 000
		Balance c/d	50 000			
	$100 000		$100 000			
Balance b/d	$50 000					

Uncalled Capital			
Unissued capital	$50 000	Application	$12 500
		Allotment	12 500
		Balance c/d	25 000
	$50 000		$50 000
Balance b/d	$25 000		

Application	
Uncalled capital	$12 500

Allotment	
Uncalled capital	$12 500

When future calls are made, they may be recorded in the same way as amounts payable on application and allotment, by debiting the Call No... account and crediting the uncalled capital account with the amount of each call.

Again a notional balance sheet may be drawn up to illustrate the net effect of the transactions to date:

Shareholders' equity:			
Authorized capital	$100 000		
Less: Unissued capital	50 000		
Issued capital	50 000		
Less: Uncalled capital	25 000		
Called-up capital	25 000		
Less: Unpaid calls	25 000		
Paid-up capital	—	**Assets**	—

Payment of Application and Allotment Moneys, and Calls

As the application and allotment moneys are received, they are debited to the bank account and credited to the application or allotment accounts. This reflects the fact that the potential assets represented by the balances in the application and allotment accounts have been converted into actual assets, and the increase in the asset, cash at bank, is automatically matched by an increase in paid-up capital representing actual funds contributed by shareholders. Assume that applications have been received for 60 000 shares, of which 50 000 have been allotted, and that an amount of $5 000 out of allotment moneys has also been received. The ledger accounts of the company appear as follows:

Unissued Capital

Authorized capital	$100 000	Uncalled capital	$50 000	
		Balance c/d	50 000	
	$100 000		$100 000	
Balance b/d	$50 000			

Authorized Capital

Unissued capital	$100 000

Uncalled Capital

Unissued capital	$50 000	Application	$12 500
		Allotment	12 500
		Balance c/d	25 000
	$50 000		$50 000
Balance b/d	$25 000		

Application

Uncalled capital	$12 500	Bank	$15 000
Balance c/d	2 500		
	$15 000		$15 000
		Balance b/d	$2 500

Allotment

Uncalled capital	$12 500	Bank	$5 000
		Balance c/d	7 500
	$12 500		$12 500
Balance b/d	$7 500		

Bank

Application	$15 000	Balance c/d	$20 000
Allotment	5 000		
	$20 000		$20 000
Balance b/d	$20 000		

The credit balance in the application account represents amounts oversubscribed which need to be returned to unsuccessful applicants. It is a liability and should be recorded as such in the balance sheet (unless excess application moneys received from successful applicants are to be credited in respect of amounts due on allotment or future calls, in which case the application account is debited and, say, the allotment account credited with the amounts held for this purpose).

The paid-up capital is then composed of the application and allotment moneys received in respect of the shares that have been allotted. If it is assumed that the amounts oversubscribed are to be refunded, a balance sheet may now be drawn up as follows:

Shareholders' equity:		Current assets:	
Authorized capital	$100 000	Bank	$20 000
Less: Unissued capital	50 000		
Issued capital	50 000		
Less: Uncalled capital	25 000		
Called-up capital	25 000		
Less: Unpaid calls (allotment)	7 500		
Paid-up capital	17 500		
Current liabilities:			
Application moneys refundable	2 500		
	$20 000		$20 000

The share capital accounts thus record how potential funds and assets are converted, by a series of steps, into actual financial obligations and assets of the company.

Share Issues, Payments and Transfers

Shares Issued at a Premium or Discount

The foregoing example assumes that shares are issued at par or nominal value. After a company has been in operation for some time the directors may have the power to issue shares at a premium. They are especially likely to adopt this course of action if the shares are being traded on the stock exchange at prices in excess of their nominal value. If a company issues, say, 10 000 $1 shares at a premium of $0.25 per share, persons to whom shares are allotted are required to pay $1.25 for each share. In the share accounts the issue of shares at a premium may be recorded by:
(a) debiting the uncalled capital account with the full amount payable on the shares;
(b) crediting the unissued capital account with the face value of the shares; and
(c) crediting the difference (the total premiums payable) to a separate account, the share premium reserve account.

The calling up of application and allotment moneys and calls may then proceed in the usual way. The balance in the share premium reserve account represents a capital reserve, i.e. it is not available for distribution as dividends, and it is recorded in the shareholders' equity section of the balance sheet.[3] From the point of view of the company, the significance of the share premium is that it represents funds which it has been able to acquire without incurring a nominal obligation to shareholders through the issue of additional securities.

Subject to certain legal restrictions (and again provided the company has been in operation for a specified time), shares may sometimes be issued at a discount, in which case the amount of the discount is debited to the discount on shares account (a negative capital item which needs to be deducted from shareholders' equity in the

[3] The concepts of capital and revenue reserves are considered later in this chapter.

balance sheet). The uncalled capital account is debited with the reduced amount payable on the shares (reflecting the reduced calling power that results from the discount), while the unissued capital account is credited with the full face value in the usual way.

Payment in Full on Application

The amounts payable on shares are not always called up by stages. The practice of requiring part of the amount payable to be lodged on application and allotment, and part on calls as determined by the directors, is common among new companies undertaking development that needs to be financed progressively over a period. It is wasteful of resources for such companies to call up amounts prematurely and hold idle cash balances. Old established companies making new issues, on the other hand, frequently have an immediate use for the whole of the funds represented by the shares being issued, and may require payment in full on application. In these circumstances, the use of the uncalled capital account may be dispensed with, and the issue may be recorded by debiting the application account directly and crediting the unissued capital account with the amount of issued capital.

Shares Issued for a Consideration other than Cash

Shares may be allotted for a consideration other than cash, e.g. where a company is formed to take over an established business from a proprietor, who is allotted fully paid-up shares in the company (and perhaps paid some cash also) in return for his interest in the business. The unissued capital account is credited with the nominal value of the shares issued to the proprietor; the bank account is credited with any cash payment made to the proprietor; and appropriate asset accounts are debited with the value of the assets taken over by the company. If the purchase price (shares issued plus cash) exceeds the aggregate value of the individual assets taken over, the difference is debited to the goodwill account, or an account expressly titled 'excess of cost of investment over net assets purchased account'. This represents, in effect, the price paid for the established reputation and earning power of the business being acquired by the company. In the reverse case, the difference is credited to the 'excess of net assets purchased over cost of investment account', which is classified as part of shareholders' equity.

Share Transfers

When a shareholder disposes of shares, e.g. by selling them on the stock exchange, the transfer is recorded in the company's transfer and share registers, and on the share certificates, but no entry is made in the double-entry accounting records. This is because the share capital of the company is not affected by the transfer of shares. The purchaser of the shares naturally assumes all the obligations attaching to the shares, including the responsibility to meet future calls.

Forfeiture of Shares

If power is given in the company's Articles of Association, a shareholder's failure to meet allotment or call moneys may result in his shares being forfeited. The shareholder then ceases to be a member of the company and forfeits any claim to the amounts he has already paid on his shares. Except in the case of a no-liability company, however, he remains liable for the unpaid balance of the shares until the company receives payment in full for them.

The forfeiture of shares is recorded by:

(a) debiting the unissued capital account with the nominal value of the shares (this has the effect of withdrawing the forfeited shares from the issued capital of the company, i.e. of restoring the company's issuing power in respect of the shares);

(b) crediting the uncalled capital account with the amount uncalled on the forfeited shares (the future calling power is thereby regarded as having lapsed);

(c) crediting the allotment or call accounts with the amounts called but unpaid (unpaid allotment and call moneys are also regarded as having lapsed when the shares are forfeited); and

(d) crediting a new account, forfeited shares reserve account, with the amounts paid on the shares prior to forfeiture. (Any share premiums or share discounts in respect of the forfeited shares should be debited to the share premium reserve account or credited to the discount on shares account to complete the double entry.)

The net result of these entries, it may be observed, is to reverse all the entries previously made in share capital accounts in respect of the forfeited shares; and to leave just two entries, the debit previously made in the bank account and the credit now made in the forfeited shares reserve account, to record the cash received on the shares before they were forfeited. In effect, the amounts paid prior to forfeiture are transferred from paid-up capital to a capital reserve account; they are still part of shareholders' equity but no longer represent a nominal obligation to particular shareholders that has been incurred through the issue of securities.

An Illustration

An extension of the previous example may serve to illustrate the accounting effects of share forfeiture. Suppose that Australasia Traders Ltd, having received all application and allotment moneys (and having returned excess application moneys to unsuccessful applicants), subsequently makes a first call of $0.20 per share. Payment is received on all except 1 000 shares which, in accordance with the company's articles of association, the directors decide to forfeit.

Prior to forfeiture, a balance sheet of the company may be drawn up as follows:

Shareholders' equity:		Current assets:	
Authorized capital	$100 000	Bank	$34 800
Less: Unissued capital	50 000		
Issued capital	50 000		
Less: Uncalled capital	15 000		
Called-up capital	35 000		
Less: Unpaid calls (No. 1)	200		
Paid-up capital	$34 800		$34 800

An amount of $0.50 per share ($0.25 for application and $0.25 for allotment), i.e. $500, has already been received on the 1 000 forfeited shares, and $300 of the balance of the uncalled capital account and the whole of the balance of Call No. 1 account relate to the forfeited shares. The journal entries to record the forfeiture are as follows:

Unissued capital	Dr.	$1 000	
Uncalled capital	Cr.		$300
Call No. 1	Cr.		200
Forfeited shares reserve	Cr.		500

Forfeiture of 1 000 shares (nominal value $1)
for default in payment of first call of 20 cents

After these entries are posted, the ledger takes the following form:

Unissued Capital

Authorized capital	$100 000	Uncalled capital	$50 000
Uncalled capital	300	Balance c/d	51 000
Call No. 1	200		
Forfeited shares reserve	500		
	$101 000		$101 000
Balance b/d	$51 000		

Authorized Capital

		Unissued capital	$100 000

Uncalled Capital

Unissued capital	$50 000	Application	$12 500
		Allotment	12 500
		Call No. 1	10 000
		Unissued capital	300
		Balance c/d	14 700
	$50 000		$50 000
Balance b/d	$14 700		

Forfeited Shares Reserve

		Unissued capital	$500

Application

Uncalled capital	$12 500	Bank	$15 000
Bank	2 500		
	$15 000		$15 000

Allotment

Uncalled capital	$12 500	Bank	$12 500

Call No. 1

Uncalled capital	$10 000	Bank	$9 800
		Unissued capital	200
	$10 000		$10 000

Bank

Application	$15 000	Application	$2 500
Allotment	12 500	Balance c/d	34 800
Call No. 1	9 800		
	$37 300		$37 300
Balance b/d	$34 800		

A new balance sheet may be drawn up as follows:

Shareholders' equity:		Current assets:	
Authorized capital	$100 000	Bank	$34 800
Less: Unissued capital	51 000		
Issued capital	49 000		
Less: Uncalled capital	14 700		
Called-up capital	34 300		
Less: Unpaid calls	—		
Paid-up capital	34 300		
Forfeited shares reserve	500		
	$34 800		$34 800

Reissue of Forfeited Shares

The forfeited shares may be reissued on such terms as the directors (within their powers) decide. The reissue of shares is recorded in the same way as when they were originally issued. If the new holder is allotted the shares at a price which is less than their paid-up value, the shares are, in effect, being issued at a discount, but in this case the amount of the discount (the difference between the paid-up value and the amount paid for the shares) may be offset against the forfeited shares reserve account. As already indicated, if the company is unable to dispose of the shares at a price which covers the total amount unpaid on them at the time of forfeiture, the original holder is liable for the difference (except in the case of a no-liability company).

Suppose that the 1 000 forfeited Australasia Traders Ltd shares are reissued by the directors for an amount of $0.60 per share payable on allotment, in return for which the shares are to be regarded as paid up to $0.70. The uncalled capital account is debited, and the unissued capital account is credited, with the full nominal value of the reissued shares of ($1 000) in the usual way. The allotment account is debited with the amount now payable (1 000 x $0.60 = $600); the forfeited shares reserve account is debited with the difference between the paid-up value and the amount now payable ($700—$600 = $100); and the uncalled capital account is credited with the paid-up value of the shares (1 000 x $0.70 = $700).

Provided that the $600 payable on allotment of the reissued shares is duly paid, the full story is recorded in the ledger and the balance sheet in the following way:

Unissued Capital				Authorized Capital			
Balance b/d $51 000		Uncalled				Balance	
		capital	$1 000			b/d	$100 000
		Balance c/d	50 000				
	$51 000		$51 000				
Balance b/d $50 000							

Uncalled Capital				Forfeited Shares Reserve			
Balance b/d $14 700		Allotment	$600	Uncalled		Balance b/d.	$500
Unissued		Forfeited		capital	$100		
capital	1 000	shares reserve	100	Balance c/d	400		
		Balance c/d	15 000				
	$15 700		$15 700		$500		$500
Balance b/d $15 000						Balance b/d	$400

Allotment

Uncalled capital	$600	Bank	$600

Bank

Balance b/d	$34 800	Balance c/d	$35 400
Allotment	600		
	$35 400		$35 400
Balance b/d	$35 400		

Balance Sheet as at ....

Shareholders' equity:			Current assets:	
Authorized capital	$100 000		Bank	$35 400
Less: Unissued capital	50 000			
Issued capital	50 000			
Less: Uncalled capital	15 000			
Called-up capital	35 000			
Less: Unpaid calls	—			
Paid-up capital	35 000			
Forfeited shares reserve	400			
	$35 400			$35 400

An Alternative Method of Accounting for Share Capital

There is an alternative method of accounting for share capital, in which a memo-randum record only of authorized capital is made, and the ledger accounts in respect of all share capital items reflect only funds receivable. For example, in the Australasia Traders Ltd illustration the issue of 50 000 shares of $1 each, payable $0.25 on application, and $0.25 on allotment, is recorded in the journal as follows:

Application	Dr.	$12 500	
Allotment	Dr.	12 500	
Issued and called-up capital	Cr.		$25 000
Issue of 50 000 shares of $1 each, payable $0.25 on application and $0.25 on allotment.			

The journal entry below is made to record Call No. 1:

Call No. 1	Dr.	$10 000	
Issued and called-up capital	Cr.		$10 000
First call of $0.20 per share.			

The receipt of application, allotment and call moneys is recorded in the usual way as shown in the earlier pages. The amount of paid-up capital is given by the difference between the credit balance in the issued and called-up capital account and the debit balances (if any) in the allotment and call accounts which represent unpaid calls. When shares are forfeited, the balance in the allotment or call account is transferred to the debit of the forfeited shares reserve account. The forfeited shares reserve account is credited with an amount transferred from the issued and called-up capital account which is equal to the total called-up value of the shares being forfeited. On the reissue of the shares, the reissue of forfeited shares account is debited, and the issued and called-up capital account credited, with the original called-up value of the shares (thus restoring the balance in the issued and called-up capital account to its value before the forfeiture). The reissue of forfeited shares account is credited with the cash proceeds from the sale of the forfeited shares, and the account is closed off by posting any balance in it to the forfeited shares reserve account.

The ledger accounts and balance sheet under this method are shown below:

Application

Issued and called-up capital	$12 500	Bank	$15 000
Bank	2 500		
	$15 000		$15 000

Issued and Called-up Capital

Forfeited shares reserve	$700	Application and allotment	$25 000
Balance c/d	35 000	Call No. 1	10 000
		Reissue of forfeited shares	700
	$35 700		$35 700
		Balance b/d	$35 000

Allotment

Issued and called-up capital	$12 500	Bank	$12 500

Forfeited Shares Reserve

Call No. 1	$200	Issued and called-up capital	$700
Reissue of forfeited shares	100		
Balance c/d	400		
	$700		$700
		Balance b/d	$400

Call No. 1

Issued and called-up capital	$10 000	Bank	$9 800
		Forfeited shares reserve	200
	$10 000		$10 000

Reissue of Forfeited Shares

Issued and called-up capital	$700	Bank	$600
		Forfeited shares reserve	100
	$700		$700

Bank

Application	$15 000	Application	$2 500
Allotment	12 500	Balance c/d	35 400
Call No. 1	9 800		
Reissue of forfeited shares	600		
	$37 900		$37 900
Balance b/d	$35 400		

Balance Sheet as at ...

Shareholders' equity:		Current assets:	
Authorized capital	$100 000	Bank	$35 400
Issued and called-up capital	35 000		
Less: Unpaid calls	—		
Issued and paid-up capital	35 000		
Forfeited shares reserve	400		
	$35 400		$35 400

Classes of Equities

Ordinary and Preference Shares

So far no distinction has been made between the different classes of shares which may be issued by a company. There are two main classes:

(a) *Ordinary shares*, the holders of which are entitled to a share of the residual profits in the form of dividends (as recommended by the directors) after all other claims have been met. Ordinary shares usually carry the main voting rights and hence the ultimate control of the company, and because of their residual claim over profits they are sometimes described as 'equity' shares. The return payable to holders of ordinary shares, known as the 'ordinary dividend', depends on the level of profits and the need to retain funds in the company. If profits are inadequate, or if losses are incurred, the dividend may be 'passed' (i.e. missed) altogether.

(b) *Preference shares*, the holders of which are entitled to special privileges, such as *prima facie* priority in the payment of dividends. Holders of shares carrying preferential dividend rights are entitled to dividends at a fixed rate (e.g. six per cent on the paid-up value of the shares) before any dividends are paid on ordinary shares. Even so, however, preference dividends may not be paid if the profits of the company are inadequate. Because of this possibility, preference shares are sometimes given cumulative preferential rights, which make any unpaid preference dividends a first charge on all future profits earned by the company. Preference shareholders may be entitled to priority in the return of capital on the liquidation of the company, if this privilege is provided in the memorandum or articles of association.

Although ordinary shares carry more risk than preference shares, it will be observed that the residual claim of ordinary shares over profits carries with it the possibility of a higher return, compared with the fixed dividend payable on preference shares, if the company prospers.

For accounting purposes, the chief significance of the different classes of shares is that separate capital accounts are needed for each class. If a company has both six per cent cumulative preference shares and ordinary shares, for example, it requires both a six per cent cumulative preference authorized capital account and an ordinary authorized capital account; both a six per cent cumulative preference unissued capital account and an ordinary unissued capital account, and so on. The different classes of shares must be recorded separately in the balance sheet. Separate non-accounting records (share registers, dividend registers, etc.) must of course also be maintained.

Reserves

Reserves are part of shareholders' equity. Reserves comprise, first, surpluses which originate in capital transactions such as a share premium reserve (in a sense analogous to shareholders' capital) or a forfeited shares reserve and, second, amounts appropriated from profits to strengthen the financial position of the company.

Reserves should be carefully distinguished from provisions. Reserves are, in all cases, an element of proprietorship equity. Provisions, on the other hand, relate to expenses charged against current profits to provide for known liabilities or diminutions in the value of assets, the exact amounts of which cannot be determined with substantial accuracy at the time the accounting record is made. Examples of provisions are provision for depreciation, provision for doubtful debts and provision for long service leave.

It is generally considered useful to classify reserves into two types:

(a) *Revenue reserves* are derived from trading profits, which normally have been appropriated to the reserve account by a transfer from the profit and loss appropriation account (to which the net profit of a company is transferred prior to its distribution). Revenue reserves are legally available for distribution to shareholders as dividend, but a transfer from the profit and loss appropriation account to a revenue reserve account implies that the directors have set aside resources to finance current operations and do not intend to use these resources for dividend purposes unless exceptional circumstances arise. Typical examples of revenue reserves are a general reserve (set up to strengthen the general financial position) and a dividend equalization reserve (set up for a specific purpose). Although not altogether consistent with the above description, the balance outstanding on the profit and loss appropriation account is classified as a revenue reserve.

(b) *Capital reserves* represent amounts which are not available for distribution as cash dividends because of legal reasons or because of the financial policy of directors. Capital reserves may result from surpluses on account of capital transactions, such as share transactions or the revaluation of capital assets. The revaluation reserves described in Chapter 19 constitute a special class of capital reserve. Other capital reserves are set up through profit appropriations, such as a capital redemption reserve and a reserve for increased cost of asset replacement. A capital redemption reserve represents profit appropriations legally required, where redeemable preference shares are redeemed otherwise than out of the proceeds of a new share issue. When the shares are eventually redeemed, the preference capital account is debited (thus closed off) and, say, the bank account credited. The capital redemption reserve is maintained indefinitely as a capital (non-distributable) reserve which may be applied only towards certain (non-distributive) purposes, as specified in the Companies Act.

The classification of reserves into revenue and capital reserves, while useful, contains a number of grey areas because availability for distribution may depend on financial policy as well as legal constraints. For example, the surplus on the sale of a fixed asset may be distributable or may need to be taken to capital reserve, depending on a number of circumstances. Briefly, a share premium reserve and a capital redemption reserve are legally not distributable, while other capital reserves, such as a forfeited shares reserve, debenture redemption reserve and asset revaluation reserve may be legally distributable by way of cash dividends, but are as a rule classified as non-distributable for financial policy reasons.

Secret Reserves

Secret reserves may be created by companies which deliberately overstate expenses and understate assets (particularly land and buildings). It is sometimes held that secret reserves are a source of financial strength and enable the company to cope with unforeseen contingencies. The principle runs counter to the basic accounting objective of disclosing all relevant information to decision makers and cannot be justified. Unfortunately the system of historical record accounting is conducive to the creation of secret reserves in periods of inflation, to the extent that the historical values of expenses and assets understate their current values.

Bonus Shares

In discussing share transactions, it has so far been assumed that all the shares issued by the company are in consideration for cash or other assets acquired by the company. It is now necessary to recognize another possibility, namely the issue of *bonus shares*, i.e. shares which are issued to shareholders for no consideration at all.

Bonus shares may be issued out of:
(a) current profits;
(b) accumulated profits or revenue reserves; or
(c) capital reserves.

If bonus shares are issued out of current profits, a 'dividend' is being paid, in effect, in the form of shares instead of cash. In this way the company retains the use of the funds represented by the shares (just as it does when profits are transferred to reserve) but incurs an obligation to pay future dividends on the bonus shares.

If bonus shares are issued out of accumulated profits or revenue reserves, the effect is to capitalize the reserves and prevent them from ever being distributed as dividends. Bonus share issues from reserves (revenue or capital) are frequently made prior to a new issue of shares by an established company, the intention being to protect the equity of existing shareholders in the company (by converting the reserves into paid-up shares which are distributed to existing shareholders) before the new shares are issued to the public. Companies contemplating new issues frequently revalue their assets and thereby create revaluation reserves which are used to finance the issue of bonus shares. This procedure, which is analogous to that recommended in Chapter 19 as a routine method of accounting for current values, implies a relaxation of the conventional price level assumption in historical record accounting.

The description of a bonus issue as a non-cash dividend can be confusing. In a sense all capital reserves can be 'distributed' to existing shareholders through an issue of bonus shares. The essence of such a transaction is the conversion of reserves into permanent capital. An issue of bonus shares out of current or past profits, or out of revenue reserves, can be conceptualized in a similar way.[4]

---

[4] A bonus issue from profits is subject to tax. This tends to strengthen the impression that a bonus issue is a distribution of profits.

The issue of bonus shares may be recorded in two journal entries as follows:

Reserve (or profit and loss appropriation account)	Dr	$...
Shareholders' bonus account	Cr.	$ ...
(This entry records the total amount of the bonus issue.)		

Shareholders' bonus account	Dr.	$...
Unissued capital account	Cr.	$ ...
(This entry records the issue of shares to an amount corresponding to the bonus.)		

The credit and debit entries made in the shareholders' bonus account exactly offset each other, so that the net effect of all the entries is to record a diminution in reserves on the one hand and a corresponding increase in paid-up capital on the other. The following example makes this clear.

Example: Suppose a company's balance sheet, prior to a bonus share issue, takes the following form:

Shareholders' equity:		Assets:	$100 000
Authorized capital	$100 000		
Less: Unissued capital	50 000		
Issued and paid-up capital	50 000		
General reserve	50 000		
	$100 000		$100 000

The directors decide to make a bonus issue of one new share for each two shares held. The transaction is recorded in ledger accounts as follows:

Unissued Capital

Balance b/d $50 000	Shareholders' bonus	$25 000
	Balance c/d	25 000
$50 000		$50 000
Balance b/d $25 000		

Authorized Capital

	Balance b/d $100 000

Shareholders' Bonus

Unissued capital $25 000	General reserve $25 000

General Reserve

Shareholders' bonus $25 000	Balance b/d $50 000
Balance c/d 25 000	
$50 000	$50 000
	Balance b/d $25 000

After the bonus issue, the balance sheet records the following information:

Shareholders' funds:		Assets:	$100 000
Authorized capital	$100 000		
Less: Unissued capital	25 000		
Issued and paid-up capital	75 000		
General reserve	25 000		
	$100 000		$100 000

The practice of issuing bonus shares results from the statutory requirement that all shares should have a stated par or nominal value. If, as is already the case in some countries, it were to become legally possible to issue shares without attaching a specified par value to them, bonus share issues would be unnecessary and a source of much confusion among shareholders and investors would be avoided. The holder of 1 000 shares in a company which has issued 100 000 shares owns a hundredth part of the company; if, as a result of a 1 for 2 bonus issue, he then holds 1 500 shares of a total of 150 000 shares, he still owns a hundredth part of the company. His equity in the company is only affected if a new share issue is made to outsiders on terms more favourable than the current worth of his equity as reflected, say, by the prevailing market value of the company's shares.

Debentures and Other Fixed-interest Securities

Companies are in a position to raise funds by the issue of other types of securities besides shares, or even to accept funds on deposit. Apart from liabilities incurred in the course of trading and borrowing from banks, the main kinds of fixed-interest liabilities which a company may incur are obligations arising out of the issue of debentures or notes and the acceptance of deposits.

Debentures are securities issued in return for fixed-interest bearing loans to the company. Such loans are usually repayable after a specified interval of time (the debentures are then described as 'redeemable' debentures), but the principal sums are sometimes not repayable so long as the company continues in existence ('irredeemable' debentures). Irredeemable debentures thus have some of the attributes of preference shares but, like other debentures, they rank before preference shares in the payment of interest and the return of capital on liquidation, and interest is payable whether or not profits are earned by the company. Interest payable on debentures is therefore recorded in the accounts as an expense, and appears among finance expenses in the profit and loss account. Debenture holders are not members of the company and do not share in profits. Provision is, however, sometimes made for debentures or notes to be convertible into ordinary shares after a specified period has elapsed.

Debentures may be secured by a fixed charge over particular assets of the company ('mortgage' debentures), or by a floating charge on all the assets of the company in whatever state they happen to be from time to time.

The issue of debentures may be accounted for in roughly the same way as share issues. If debentures are issed at par, payable in full on application, it is necessary to:

(i) debit debenture holders application account (a potential asset); and
(ii) credit debentures account (a potential liability) with the full nominal value of the debentures. The bank account is debited and the debenture holders application account credited with the cash received from debenture holders, so that the net effect of the issue is to record an increase in assets (bank) matched by an equivalent increase in liabilities (debentures).

If debentures are issued at a premium, the difference between the amount payable (which is debited to the debenture holders application account) and the nominal value of the debentures (which is credited to the debentures account), must be credited to a debenture premium account (the balance of which should be amortized against the interest cost over the life-time of the debentures). If the amount payable by debenture holders (and debited to the debenture holders application account) is less than the nominal value of the securities (credited to the debentures account), the difference is debited to a debenture discount account, the balance of which must be recorded as a capitalized loss and amortized as an additional charge against revenue over the term of the debentures. In the balance sheet, the unamortized balance of the debenture premium account or debenture discount account should be added to, or subtracted from, the balance of the debentures account. The net amount will then, in effect, represent the present value of the liability discounted at the effective, as opposed to the nominal, rate of interest payable on the debentures.

If the amounts due on the debentures are payable by instalments, separate accounts for debenture holders application, debenture holders allotment, debenture instalment no. 1, etc. may be debited with the amounts payable under the respective instalments, and the debentures account credited with the full nominal value of the debentures.

The paid-up nominal value of debentures is recorded in the balance sheet (as deferred or long-term liabilities, if redeemable debentures, and as fixed liabilities if irredeemable) in the following way:

1 000   6% mortgage debentures of $100 paid to $50 ...... $50 000

Well-established companies may be able to raise long- or medium-term loans without mortgaging their assets, by issuing unsecured or registered *notes* or accepting *deposits*. The issue of notes may be recorded in the same way as debentures, and the lodgement of deposits has the effect of increasing both the company's assets (bank) and liabilities (deposit liabilities) by equivalent amounts. Interest payable on notes and deposits is recorded in the same way as interest on debentures. Whether note and deposit liabilities are recorded in the balance sheet as current or deferred liabilities depends on their term. Deposits withdrawable on demand are clearly current liabilities, whereas notes with a currency beyond one year are deferred or long-term liabilities.

Company Profit Reporting and Statutory and Professional Requirements

The Profit and Loss Statement

The preparation of the trading and profit and loss accounts of a company at the end of the accounting period follows the normal procedure outlined in earlier chapters. Net profit or loss is then transferred to the profit and loss appropriation account which, as in the case of partnerships, records the distribution or appropriation of profits. A company's published income statement is usually divided into two sections: a profit and loss statement proper and a profit and loss appropriation statement. The profit and loss statement may be presented in the usual form in which sales, cost of sales and expenses (appropriately classified) are reported, but many companies disclose only the minimum information required by statute. The Companies Act requires companies to disclose certain revenue and expense items, including: trading profit, investment income, interest expense, depreciation, bad and doubtful debts, directors' fees, audit fees, and profit or loss on sale or revaluation of non-current assets.

However, professional accounting standards in Australia require additional disclosure in the profit and loss statement, of what are called operating profit, abnormal items, income tax charged in arriving at operating profit, and extraordinary items (and the income tax applicable thereto).[5] This is illustrated in the following *pro forma* profit and loss statement:

Trading profit before including items below	$x
Normal operating items (not shown elsewhere)	x
Abnormal items	x
Net operating profit before tax	x
Income tax applicable thereto	x
Net operating profit after tax	x
Extraordinary items (net of income tax applicable thereto)	x
Net profit after tax	$x

Note: Items in a group, e.g. individual abnormal items, must be stated separately.

Abnormal items are defined as revenue and expense items of the period which are highlighted in the report because of their unusual size and effect on the results for the period, e.g. major losses arising from bad debts, write-downs of inventory, or write-offs of research and development expenditure. *Extraordinary items* are those which fall outside the ordinary operations of the business, such as gains and losses arising from a currency revaluation or from the sale of a major segment of the business or of long-term investments, or write-offs of goodwill and other intangible assets which are not in accordance with a systematic amortization program. Prior period adjustments are treated as operating items (abnormal items, if the adjustments are large) where they relate to the ordinary operations of the business, and as extraordinary items otherwise.[6]

Under the Australian professional accounting standards, *company income tax* is treated as an expense, and deducted from net operating profit before tax to arrive at net operating profit after tax, in the profit and loss statement. Since the amount of tax payable is usually not known with certainty at the time the accounts are finalized, it is necessary to estimate the tax payable and make the following entries:
(i) debit the profit and loss account with 'income tax expense'; and
(ii) credit the estimated company tax liability account (or the provision for company tax account).

Estimated company tax liability appears among current liabilities in the balance sheet. When the tax is subsequently paid in the new accounting period, the estimated company tax liability account is debited and the bank account credited with the amount paid. Any balance in the estimated company tax liability account, resulting from a difference between actual and estimated tax, may be held in the estimated company tax liability account and taken into account when the tax liability for the new period is being estimated.

Certain complex problems are covered by the above disclosure requirements, such as the nature of tax payments, the principles underlying the amortization of goodwill and other intangible assets, and the method of disclosing prior period adjustments.

[5] It will be observed that the definitions of items which must be disclosed to conform to Australian accounting standards differ from the definitions of operating and non-operating items suggested in Chapter 2.
[6] An example of a prior period adjustment is the settlement of a litigation claim relating to events in the past.

The accounting profession has cut the Gordian knot, as it were, and declared that a number of diverse and controversial items are all determinants of the profit for the current period. Some pertinent comments with reference to the treatment of income tax, capitalized expenses and prior period adjustments follow.

Income tax. We believe that it is wrong to treat income tax as an expense. An expense is an expired resource used up in producing the profit for the period. But profits first must emerge and be known before a liability for tax arises. It is sometimes argued that the tax is a payment for services provided by the government. This is mere rationalization. Income tax is a compulsory levy by the government on profits earned by the business, and is properly treated, not as an expense incurred in earning those profits, but as an appropriation of profits.

If tax is regarded as a government imposition, the amount (or estimated amount) of appropriation for the period is given by the actual tax payable to the government. The treatment of tax as an expense, however, has given rise to a problem known as 'tax allocation' or 'tax effect accounting'. Tax allocation is concerned with the differences between accounting income and taxable income of companies, when certain revenue and expense items are recognized in the financial reports and in the tax returns in different periods. The accounting problem is whether these timing differences lead to the creation of a liability (asset), when the tax payable is less (greater) than the *prima facie* tax based on accounting income. It is beyond the scope of this chapter to evaluate the pros and cons of the arguments in the literature, but we believe that the case for recording deferred taxes in the accounts is difficult to justify, and will not be considered further in the text.

Capitalized expenses. When a company takes over an existing business, it usually has to pay something for the goodwill (or the capitalized value of its established reputation and profit potential) of the business and the amount so paid is debited to the goodwill account, which appears in the balance sheet under the heading 'other capital expenditure'. Likewise, the establishment of a company involves the incurring of numerous expenses such as promoters' fees, registration expenses and underwriters' commission. These expenses, known as 'preliminary expenses', are capital expenses in the sense that they are properly attributable to the whole lifetime of the company, and not merely to its first year of operations. For this reason they are usually capitalized; the various expenses are debited to a preliminary expenses account, the balance of which is recorded separately among 'other capital expenditure' in the balance sheet.

There is a special difficulty with goodwill, in that only purchased goodwill is recorded in the books of account, while self-developed goodwill is not recorded. Thus it is difficult to interpret the significance of a goodwill figure in the balance sheet. As noted in Chapter 10, the value of goodwill depends on a subjective assessment of the firm's profitability as given by the relationship between profits and proprietorship equity, where proprietorship equity is defined as tangible operating assets less liabilities. An objective value for goodwill can only be determined when the ownership of a company changes hands. At other times, no meaning can be attached to any balance in a company's goodwill account.

The general problem with so-called intangible assets is whether they embody future service potential. Where the capitalized expenses do not represent productive resources, they should be written off immediately. On the other hand, if they represent benefits which stretch into the indefinite future, the amounts to be written off each year would be infinitely small.

However, most companies have a policy of writing off goodwill and other capitalized expenses over a fixed period, say, 10 years. This is partly for reasons of financial conservatism, and partly because it is difficult to interpret the significance of capitalized expenses in a balance sheet for the reasons given above. It is evident that the writing off of capitalized expenses does not reflect expenses incurred in earning the current period's profit, rather it constitutes an act of financial prudence. Therefore it should be carried out by means of profit appropriations in the profit and loss appropriation account and not by charges against revenue in the profit and loss account, which would distort the profit measurement process.

Prior period adjustments. There is no ideal method of dealing with prior period adjustments. One method would be to make the adjustment relating to a prior period directly against the opening balance of retained earnings, but this in itself is insufficient disclosure for purposes of time series analysis. Adequate disclosure of prior period adjustments can be made in a number of ways, e.g. by including in the notes to the accounts for the current year three profit series—net operating profit before and after tax, and net profit—which contain the *adjusted* profit figures of prior periods as part of the series. But to bring prior period adjustments into account in the manner required by the accounting standards (as either operating or extraordinary items of the current period), defeats a prime objective of the profit and loss statement, *i.e. to report the net operating profit and net profit for the current period.*

The Distribution of Company Profits

As noted above, the net profit for the period is transferred from the profit and loss account proper to the profit and loss appropriation account, which records the distribution or appropriation of profits. Profits may be appropriated in the following ways:[7]

(a) by providing for the payment of dividends; and

(b) by setting aside amounts to reserves.

(a) *Dividends.* Dividends payable are recorded as follows:

　(i)   debit the profit and loss appropriation account; and

　(ii) credit the dividend liability account (or provision for dividend account).

Separate entries (and accounts) are required for each class of shares. Since the dividends recommended by the directors require the ratification of shareholders, they are in the nature of a provisional appropriation until they are formally declared. The balance of the dividend liability account appears in the balance sheet as a current liability. When the dividends are paid in the new accounting period, the dividend liability account is debited and the bank account credited.

Directors are sometimes empowered to declare 'interim' dividends after the results are known for part of the year, say six months. Such dividends are paid before the end of the year, and are recorded by debiting the interim dividend account and crediting the dividend liability account when the dividends are declared, and debiting the dividend liability account and crediting the bank account when the dividends are paid. At the end of the accounting period, the balance of the interim dividend account is transferred to the profit and loss appropriation account, where it appears as a separate profit allocation. Where

---

[7] Here, and in the example which follows, it is assumed that estimated income tax payable is debited to the profit and loss account and not, as the authors recommend, to the profit and loss appropriation account.

interim dividends are paid, the dividends provided for at the end of the accounting period are described as 'final' dividends.

(b) *Transfers to reserves*. As explained earlier, reserves are part of shareholders' equity. Transfers from profits to reserves are recorded as follows:
(i) debit the profit and loss appropriation account; and
(ii) credit the reserve account.

The term 'reserve fund' is sometimes used to describe a reserve which is represented by specifically earmarked investments.[8] Two journal entries are employed. The first journal entry records the transfer of profits to the reserve fund, as follows:
(i) debit the profit and loss appropriation account; and
(ii) credit the reserve fund account.

The second journal entry records the accompanying injection of cash into the investment account, as shown:
(i) debit the reserve fund investment account; and
(ii) credit the bank account.

Profit and Loss Appropriation Account Balance

Any balance which is left in the profit and loss appropriation account, after these transfers and appropriations have been made, is carried forward and appears as a separate item in the balance sheet among shareholders' equity. The appropriation account balance is, of course, a revenue reserve, as stated earlier. The profit and loss appropriation account may take the following form in the ledger:

Profit and Loss Appropriation

Dividend liability	$ ...	Balance b/d	$ ...
General reserve	...	Net profit (transferred from	
Balance c/d	...	profit and loss account)	...
	$ ...		$ ...
		Balance b/d	$ ...

The profit and loss appropriation statement, compiled from the information contained in the ledger account, constitutes one of the essential accounting reports or financial statements presented to shareholders at the end of each accounting period. The Companies Act requires that all transfers to and from reserves, and the amount of dividends paid and proposed for the period, be disclosed.

An Illustration of the Financial Statements of a Limited Company

A specimen balance sheet of Australasia Traders Ltd after several years of operations is presented in Table 11—1 to illustrate points discussed above. For illustration purposes, it is assumed that approval has been given for the company to increase its capital by an issue of 50 000 redeemable preference shares of $1 each at par, and that a redemption reserve fund has been set up for periodical appropriations from profits, to provide for the eventual redemption of the preference shares.

[8] Normally, earnings from the investments are reinvested in the fund.

Table 11—1
Australasia Traders Ltd
Balance Sheet as at 30 June 1985

Shareholders' Equity			Non-current Assets			
					Provision for deprecia-tion	Net book value
Authorized, issued and fully paid share capital				Cost		
Ordinary shares of $1 each		$100 000				
Redeemable 6% cumulative preference shares of $1 each		50 000	Freehold land	$120 000	—	$120 000
			Building	80 000	$20 000	60 000
			Plant	60 000	30 000	30 000
		150 000	Vehicles	20 000	8 000	12 000
				$280 000	$58 000	222 000
Capital reserves						
Share premium reserve	$25 000		**Capital Redemption Reserve Fund**			
Capital redemption reserve fund	30 000		**Investment** (market-value of investment $31 200)			30 000
Forfeited shares reserve	400					
		55 400				
Revenue reserves			**Current Assets**			
General reserve	20 000		Inventory		50 000	
Unappropriated profits	5 410	25 410				
Total share capital and reserves		230 810	**Short-term financial assets**			
Less: Goodwill	$8 000		Trade debtors $9 200			
Less: Provision for amortization	5 000	3 000	*Less*: Provision for doubt-ful debts	400 $8 800		
Preliminary expenses	2 000		Cash	3 180		
Less: Amounts written-off	1 000	1 000	4 000		11 980	
Shareholders' Equity		226 810				61 980
Non-current Liabilities						
1 000 6% mortgage debentures of $100 paid to $50	50 000					
10% unsecured notes	10 000					
		60 000				
Current Liabilities						
Trade creditors	8 920					
Provision for company tax	12 000					
Provision for interest	750					
Provision for dividends on:						
Preference shares	1 500					
Ordinary shares	4 000					
		5 500				
		27 170				
		$313 980				$313 980

Notes: (1) Comparative figures relating to the preceding year must be shown in the financial statements.

(2) In practice, information on the bases of valuation and details of many balance sheet items, e.g. share capital and non-current assets, are often given in notes to the accounts which form an integral part of the financial statements. The modern trend is to simplify the presentation of financially significant totals.

A specimen profit and loss appropriation statement is shown in Table 11—2.

Table 11—2
Australasia Traders Ltd
Profit and Loss Appropriation Statement for Year Ended 30 June 1985

Balance of unappropriated profits b/f from preceding year		$6 010
Net profit for year after tax		17 400
Profits available for appropriation		23 410
Dividends paid and proposed:		
Preference shares	$3 000	
Ordinary shares	6 000	
Transfer to: Capital redemption reserve fund	5 000	
General reserve	4 000	18 000
Balance of unappropriated profits c/f to following year		$ 5 410

Note: As in the case of the balance sheet, comparative figures relating to the preceding year must be given in the profit and loss statement.

Liquidation of Companies

Apart from the special problems posed by share capital transactions and profit appropriations, accounting for the day-to-day operations of companies follows the same pattern as accounting for other kinds of business enterprise. Certain other events affecting share capital, such as alterations, reconstructions and amalgamations, need not concern us here, and it is also not necessary to spend much time in considering the accounting problems that arise when a company goes into liquidation (i.e. when it is wound up and ceases to have any legal existence). The accounting procedure on liquidation roughly follows a similar course to that of the dissolution of a partnership. A liquidator is appointed to take over the company's affairs from its directors, realize its assets and discharge its liabilities. If the liquidation is a compulsory one (i.e. if it has been ordered by the Court), the liquidator must draw up a statement of affairs (the first part of which records the company's liabilities and the expected proceeds of assets; and the second part of which records the different classes of paid-up capital) and a deficiency account (which records the results of trading operations since the company's incorporation or such later date as the liquidator may decide, and expected losses or profits arising out of the realization of assets).

In both compulsory and voluntary liquidations, the liquidator has certain other statutory duties to perform, including the periodical return of a detailed statement of his receipts and payments. So far as the ledger itself is concerned, a liquidation account takes the place of the realization account in a partnership. The balances of asset accounts (other than the bank account) and the expenses of liquidation are transferred to the debit side of the liquidation account, and the proceeds resulting from the sale of the assets are credited to the account, the difference being a profit or loss on liquidation. Accumulated profits or losses on trading or other operations (which are reflected in the balances of the reserve and profit and loss appropriation accounts) are also transferred to the liquidation account, and the net surplus or deficiency is transferred to a shareholders' distribution account, which is also credited with the paid-up capital (by means of appropriate transfers from the share capital accounts) and any calls due. The balance of the shareholders' distribution account, if a credit balance, records the amount due to shareholders (after all liabilities have been paid); if a debit balance, it records the deficiency in the amount of cash available to meet outside liabilities. It is naturally important that claims on the company's assets should be met in accordance with the statutory rights of creditors and the rights conferred on the different classes of shareholders by the company's memorandum and articles of association. However, this whole problem of company liquidation is the preserve of the professional accountant and the detailed accounting procedures relating thereto fall outside the scope of this book.

Discussion Questions

1 Compare and contrast ordinary shares, cumulative preference shares and unsecured notes from the viewpoint of (a) the holders of the securities, and (b) the company which issued the securities.

2 Distinguish between liabilities, revenue reserves and capital reserves by reference to: forfeited shares reserve; provision for dividends; share premium reserve; provision for company income tax; dividend equalization reserve; fixed asset revaluation reserve; and profit and loss appropriation account.

3 What is the accounting significance of a bonus share issue? Illustrate by reference to hypothetical balance sheets before and after the issue.

4 Examine the case for permitting the issue of no-par-value shares. How would the adoption of a system of current value accounting affect your arguments?

5 What is the accounting significance of the items goodwill and preliminary expenses in a company's balance sheet? What action is taken to deal with them in accordance with generally accepted accounting principles?

6 The professional accounting standards in Australia require disclosure of items additional to those required by the Companies Act. What are these items?

7 Explain the following: tax allocation; capitalized expenses; prior period adjustments; reserve fund; and debentures.

Exercises

1 (a) ABC Co. Ltd was formed with an authorized capital of $200 000, consisting of 100 000 ordinary shares of $2 each, of which 80 000 were issued on the following terms:
 25c on application,
 25c on allotment,
 50c on first call one month after allotment,
 50c on second call two months after allotment.
The amounts due on application and allotment were paid in full, and $35 000 was received in respect of the first call and $30 000 was received in respect of the second call.
Record the above transactions in the general journal and show how they would appear in the company's balance sheet.

(b) The Titan Plant Hire Co. had an authorized capital of $1 000 000, consisting of 2 000 000 shares of 50c each. The company had issued 800 000 shares which were fully paid up. As the company had accumulated considerable reserves, directors decided to issue bonus shares to the existing shareholders out of the general reserve on the basis of one new share for every four shares held, and also issued 100 000 new shares at $1 each payable in full on application. Give the general journal entries to record these transactions.

2 The Lollipop Co. Ltd was formed on 1 April 1985 with an authorized capital of $250 000, divided into 50 000 ordinary shares of $5 each. On 15 April, 20 000 shares were offered to the public, the terms of issue being $1.50 per share payable on application and $1.50 per share on allotment, and the balance in two calls of $1 each as and when required.

By 15 May applications had been received for 25 000 shares, together with amounts payable on application. The directors allotted 20 000 shares on 20 May. Surplus application money on 2 000 shares was applied in payment of allotment and the balance was returned to the unsuccessful applicants.

All allotment money was received by 15 June. On 1 August, the directors resolved to make a call of $1 per share and on 30 August, $23 000 was received, 5 000 shareholders having paid for their second call as well as their first call. On 15 September the shares on which the first call was due were forfeited and on 1 November these shares were reissued as paid to $4 per share on the payment of $3.50 per share.

You are required to enter these transactions in the general journal and the cash receipts and payments journals, and to prepare a balance sheet in statement form as at 1 November 1985.

3 You are given the following information relating to Snuggle Bedding Co. Ltd:

1984

June 1   The Snuggle Bedding Co. Ltd was registered with an authorized capital of $700 000, divided into 100 000 preference shares of $2 each and 500 000 ordinary shares of $1 each.

    2   50 000 preference shares and 200 000 ordinary shares were offered to the public, the preference shares being payable $1 on application and $1 on allotment. The ordinary shares were offered at a premium of 10c per share, being payable 40c on application (including the premium of 10c), 20c on allotment and two calls of 25c each to be made as and when required.

July 2   Applications and application moneys were received for 50 000 preference shares and 220 000 ordinary shares. The preference shares were allotted in full. With respect to the ordinary shares, the directors returned application moneys received on 10 000 shares and applied the balance of the surplus application moneys in payment of allotment.

   10   All allotment money was received on shares allotted.

Oct. 1   A first call of 25c was made on the ordinary shares.

   21   $50 000 was received from shareholders. However, one shareholder who held 2 000 shares failed to pay this call and another shareholder paid for both first and second calls.

Dec. 1   Since no money was received on the outstanding first call, the shares were forfeited.

1985

Jan. 2   Shares previously forfeited were reissued as fully paid on payment of 70c per share. Costs of forfeiture and reissue of these shares amounted to $50.

You are required to:
(a) record these transactions in the company's general ledger; and
(b) prepare a balance sheet for the company as at 2 January 1985.

4 You are required to record the following transactions in the form of general journal entries:

(a) (i) On 1 May, the MYM Co. Ltd declared and paid an interim dividend of 6% on 1 000 000 fully paid up shares having a nominal value of 50c per share and a market value of $1.70 per share.

(ii) At the end of the financial year, 30 September, the directors of MYM Co. Ltd recommended that a final dividend be paid to the shareholders, so that the total annual dividend would be 15% on fully-paid shares. The market value of these shares had remained fairly steady throughout the financial year.

(b) The ZYX Co. Ltd had made considerable profits during its financial year ending 30 June 1985, and had also accumulated considerable reserves. In view of this the directors of the company decided to make an issue of bonus shares to the holders of 500 000 50 cent shares, the bonus to be met out of accumulated profits. The shareholders received one 50c share for every five shares already held.

(c) The QPO Co. Ltd made an issue of 10 000 9 per cent debentures of $10 each at a discount of 50c, payable $4.50 on application and one instalment of $5 to be paid three months after application.

5 Adam West, who started out in business as a fibreglass fabricator, decided to convert his business into a limited liability company, as it had grown extensively over the past few years and further expansion was anticipated. The FGI Co. Ltd was registered with an authorized capital of $250 000 of 50 000 ordinary shares of $5 each. The vendor, A. West, was to receive 12 000 fully paid shares in return for the assets and liabilities of the business. A summary of A. West's balance sheet as at 1 July 1985 is given below:

Accounts receivable	$8 550	
Inventories	14 560	
Plant and machinery	37 500	
Prepayments	250	
Petty cash advance	50	
Office furniture	2 750	
Allowance for doubtful debts		$500
Accumulated depreciation—		
Plant and machinery		7 500
Office furniture		825
Bank overdraft		1 750
Accounts payable		7 500
Capital—A. West		45 585
	$63 660	$63 660

As additional capital was required to finance the expected expansion of the business, 10 000 shares were offered to the public, $1 on application, $1 on allotment and three calls of $1 each to be made as and when further funds were required. Applications were received for 8 000 shares and these shares were allotted. All allotment moneys were duly received.

Give the general journal entries to record the transactions in the books of the company and the balance sheet of the company on completion of the transactions.

6 From the following information relating to the Global Trading Co. Ltd prepare appropriate accounting reports for submission to the directors of the company:

Trial Balance as at 30 June 1985

Authorized capital (225 000 ordinary shares of $1 each)		$225 000
Unissued capital	$ 80 000	
Uncalled capital	20 000	
Retained earnings		11 400
Advertising	4 500	
Discount received		550
Audit fees	750	
Calls in arrears	1 250	
Bank		2 500
Investment (10% debentures acquired on 30 June 1985)	5 000	
Directors' fees	1 520	
Discount expense	524	
Interim dividend paid	5 000	
Fixtures and fittings	7 500	
Interest expense	1 250	
Goodwill	8 500	
Insurance	520	
Accounts receivable	19 520	
Accounts payable		12 550
Inventory on hand (1 July 1984)	45 615	
Interest income		250
Heat and lighting	675	
Mortgage on buildings		20 000
Land and buildings	65 000	
Motor vehicles	25 750	
Office furniture	3 570	
Petty cash advance	50	
Office expenses	415	
Office salaries	6 500	
Salesmen's salaries	15 000	
Accumulated depreciation—		
Fixtures and fittings		2 500
Office furniture		357
Motor vehicles		5 155
Buildings		3 000
Rates and taxes	2 100	
General reserve		5 000
Sales returns	1 560	
Purchases returns		525
Sales		157 907
Purchases	124 625	
	$446 694	$446 694

The following adjustments are required:
  (a) Inventory on hand at 30 June 1985 is $69 066.
  (b) Expenses accrued at 30 June 1985:

Office expenses	$45
Office salaries	50
Salesmen's salaries	300
Interest expense	25
Heat and lighting	75

(c) Expenses paid in advance at 30 June 1985:

Rates and taxes $175

Insurance $130

(d) Interest revenue accrued $20

(e) Depreciation charges on the straight line method are to be made at the following rates:

Furniture and fittings	$7\frac{1}{2}\%$ p.a
Office furniture	$7\frac{1}{2}\%$ p.a
Motor vehicles	15% p.a
Buildings	$2\frac{1}{2}\%$ p.a

(f) An amount of $6 600 is to be provided for income tax, $2 000 is to be written off goodwill and the directors have recommended a final dividend of 5c per share.

7 The accounts in the ledger of the Marine Accessories Ltd had the following balances as at 31 December 1985:

Cash at bank	$2 525	
Accounts receivable	35 000	
Allowance for doubtful debts		$1 000
Inventory on hand 31 December 1985	34 500	
Prepaid insurance	2 050	
Plant and machinery	55 000	
Accumulated depreciation on plant and machinery		13 500
Accounts payable		24 085
Authorized capital (150 000 shares of $1 each)		150 000
Unissued capital	70 000	
Uncalled capital	40 000	
Premium on shares		10 000
Retained earnings		12 250
Cost of goods sold	175 750	
Estimated tax liability		10 500
Sales		271 600
Income tax paid	9 500	
Interim dividend	5 000	
Petty cash advance	100	
Formation expenses	1 200	
Fixtures and fittings	3 600	
Accumulated depreciation on fixtures and fittings		540
Salaries expense	18 500	
Office expense	10 350	
Insurance expense	1 000	
Rates and taxes	3 700	
Selling expenses	25 000	
Interest expense	700	
	$493 475	$493 475

You are given the following additional data:

(a) Depreciation to be provided on plant and machinery at 10 per cent per annum on cost and on fixtures and fittings at 7½ per cent per annum on cost.

(b) Expenses accrued at 31 December 1985:

Rates and taxes $375

Salaries $1 150

(c) It is the company's policy to make a provision for bad debts equal to one per cent of sales.

(d) Unexpired insurance is $1 200 at 31 December 1985.

(e) Estimated income taxes for the year are $12 500.

(f) The directors have recommended a final dividend of $2 500.

(g) Formation expenses are to be written off.

You are required to prepare suitable accounting reports for presentation to management.

12 Company Combinations

Holding Companies and Consolidated Statements

A holding company exercises control over a subsidiary company not by taking over its assets directly, but by acquiring its shares. It is not necessary, however, for the holding company to own all the shares of the subsidiary. By law a company is usually regarded as a holding company when it holds a majority of the issued shares of another company, or has more than 50 per cent of the voting power, or has the power to appoint a majority of the directors. It is essentially the power to control the activities of another company which characterizes the holding company. The principle is extended to include as a subsidiary what amounts to a grandchild; for example, where P Co. is the parent of S Co. and S Co. is the parent of T Co., then T Co. is deemed also to be a subsidiary of P Co. While a company may form subsidiary companies for the express purpose of taking over existing divisions of the business (e.g. departments or branches) or developing new products or services, holding companies more commonly are created as a result of mergers among or take-overs of existing companies.

There is a number of reasons for the rapid development of the parent-subsidiary group structure in recent years. First, it facilitates company growth through acquisitions. A holding company content with less than 100 per cent ownership of other companies in the group is often able to deploy limited financial resources to control a relatively large financial empire. Such a method of gearing or leverage, sometimes called pyramiding, is illustrated as follows:

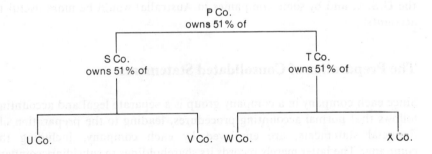

Cross-ownership relationships are also common.

Second, a company planning to embark on a venture fundamentally different from its traditional line of business may acquire (or establish) a subsidiary company for this purpose. An important advantage to the parent company is the protection afforded by limited liability in the new and possibly risky venture. Lastly, the parent-subsidiary relationship enables the subsidiary to retain its individual identity, which may be necessary to protect the goodwill of the subsidiary or to enable the subsidiary to operate effectively in a foreign country.

A holding company is required to present group accounts at the end of each financial period and these are usually in the form of a set of consolidated statements (i.e. a consolidated profit and loss statement and a consolidated balance sheet) for the whole group of companies. It is uncommon for the group accounts to comprise a number of consolidated statements relating to two or more sub-groups, or a set of individual accounts for each company in the group. Cases of less than full consolidation may occur in situations where companies within the group operate in basically diverse fields, such as manufacturing and finance, or where exchange or other restrictions exist with respect to foreign subsidiaries.

The objective of consolidated statements is to show the operating results and financial position of the group as if it were a single entity, *from the viewpoint of the shareholders of the holding company*. The total resources deployed by the group are disclosed, while potential returns in future periods to shareholders in the holding company can be more accurately assessed. The accounts of the holding company are in many cases virtually useless for these purposes. There is another important advantage. By engaging in inter-company transactions and transfers of funds, companies within a group could easily report misleading information on operations and financial position in their individual financial statements. Consolidated statements prevent this form of abuse of the accountability function.

There are, however, severe limitations to the usefulness of consolidated statements. The company group is not a separate legal entity, and consolidated statements are in the nature of statistical statements. The assets and liabilities of subsidiary companies stated therein are not legally the property or liabilities of the holding company. Also, creditors of individual companies in the group have recourse only to the assets of their companies. Furthermore, from the viewpoint of disclosing information on return and risk, segmented reports (i.e. reports on important lines of business covered by the operations of a company or a group, such as those presented by large companies in the U.S.A. and by some companies in Australia) would be more useful than group accounts.

The Preparation of Consolidated Statements

Since each company in a company group is a separate legal and accounting entity, it follows that normal accounting procedures, leading to the preparation of the usual financial statements, are employed by each company, including the holding company. The latter merely records its shareholdings in subsidiary companies among its non-current assets in the balance sheet. In order to assess the significance of the operations of the whole group of companies, it is necessary to bring the accounting reports of the individual companies together by means of consolidation techniques.

For purposes of consolidation, the group as a whole needs to be regarded as the accounting entity, but it should be noted that consolidation is essentially a statistical rather than an accounting technique. In practice, company group relationships sometimes become very complicated indeed (e.g. when subsidiary companies themselves control the activities of other subsidiaries or when there are inter-company investments), and it will not be possible in this chapter to deal with the whole range of possible problems. We shall confine our attention to some of the more important tasks encountered in constructing consolidated balance sheets and income statements, distinguishing between wholly-owned and partly-owned subsidiaries. The two main tasks are:

(a) to eliminate from the consolidated balance sheet the amount represented by the investment of the holding company in its subsidiaries, making due allowance for the interests of any minority shareholders of the subsidiary companies; and

(b) to eliminate from the consolidated balance sheet, the consolidated profit and loss statements and other consolidated statements the effects of all other inter-company transactions.

It should be emphasized that inter-company transactions are recorded in the books of each company in the same way as transactions with entities outside the group, but a separate record of such transactions needs to be maintained for purposes of the subsequent consolidation of the accounting reports of the companies making up the group. The consolidations themselves, as has already been indicated, are statistical processes and do not involve any entries in the double-entry accounting records of any of the companies. Moreover, the consolidated statements of the group should not be regarded as replacing in any way the statutory accounting reports of the individual companies comprising the group. They are merely statistical supplements to the latter, which still record information that is of vital interest to creditors, minority shareholders and managements of the individual companies. As a corollary, it is important to remember that the consolidated statements are drawn up in such a way as to emphasize the group viewpoint, which is to say the viewpoint of the holding company, and that they therefore have little significance in relation to the minority shareholders, creditors, etc. of the individual subsidiary companies. [1]

Before a detailed examination of company consolidations is made, one or two other points may be noted. It is obviously necessary to adopt a uniform classification system within the group, and to synchronize the accounting periods of the different companies. If the accounting periods overlap, the holding company's balance date must be used for purposes of the consolidated statements and any inter-company transactions which cannot be eliminated, because they take place outside the current accounting period of one of the companies, must be recorded as 'inter-company balances not eliminated due to differences in balance dates'.

---

[1] Minority shareholders and creditors would be interested in the consolidated statements if cross-guarantees of indebtedness exist.

The problems encountered in consolidating the accounts of holding companies and their subsidiaries may be illustrated by a series of examples, beginning with a situation where a holding company has just taken over a subsidiary by acquiring all its shares, and introducing additional complications one by one. All examples in this chapter are based on the 'cost method of consolidation'. Under this method, the investment in the subsidiary is carried in the parent company's books at acquisition cost (adjusted for any dividends paid out of the subsidiary company's pre-acquisition profits), and on consolidation on the same or any subsequent date the parent's share of the shareholders' equity of the subsidiary *as at the date of acquisition* is eliminated by offsetting it against the cost of the investment. It will be noted that the first column in the worksheets that follow provides information on the subsidiary company's equity on the date of acquisition for this purpose.

1 Balance Sheet Consolidation at Date of Take-over—Purchase of 100 per cent Interest at Cost Equal to Book Value

Suppose that P Co. has paid $200 000 for all the shares in S Co. The abridged balance sheets of P Co. (after the take-over) and of S Co. are as follows:

	P Co.	S Co.
Shareholders' equity		
Paid-up capital	$350 000	$160 000
Reserves		10 000
Unappropriated profits	50 000	30 000
	$400 000	$200 000
Net assets		
Investment in S Co.	200 000	
Sundry net assets	200 000	200 000
	$400 000	$200 000

The consolidated worksheet, Table 12—1, shows the elimination of the investment asset in P Co.'s accounts and shareholders' equity in S Co.'s accounts in the eliminations columns, where total debits must equal total credits. The figures in the consolidated balance sheet are obtained by adding each row across, off-setting debits against credits where this is necessary. Since the amount paid for the shares is exactly equal to the recorded net assets or shareholders' equity of the subsidiary, the item 'investment in S Co.' in P Co.'s balance sheet is wholly eliminated along with the items of shareholders' equity in S Co.'s balance sheet. It will be seen that in this simple example the effect of the consolidation process is to expand the holding company's balance sheet by replacing the item 'investment in S Co.' by details of the assets and liabilities that are represented by this investment. The individual assets and liabilities of P Co. and S Co. are summed and presented in the consolidated balance sheet in classified form in the usual way. A simplified consolidated balance sheet is shown in Table 12—1A.

Table 12—1
Consolidation Worksheet

	S Co.'s Equity on Acquisition	At Date of Consolidation		Eliminations		Minority Interest (as at date of consolidation)	Consolidated Balance Sheet Items	Consolidated Profit and Loss Items
		P Co.	S Co.	Dr.	Cr.			
Paid-up capital	$(160 000)	$(350 000)	$(160 000)	$160 000a			$(350 000)	
Reserves	(10 000)	(50 000)	(10 000)	10 000a			(50 000)	
Unappropriated profits	(30 000)		(30 000)	30 000a				
Minority interest								
Shareholders' equity and minority interest	$(200 000)	$(400 000)	$(200 000)				$(400 000)	
Investment in S Co.		200 000			$(200 000)a			
Other net assets		200 000	200 000				400 000	
Total net assets		$400 000	$200 000	$200 000	$(200 000)		$400 000	

Notes: Credit items are shown in parentheses. Italicized letters next to amounts in eliminations columns identify debits with corresponding credits and are explained below:

a P Co. acquires 100% interest in S Co. at book value of its net assets. Balance sheet consolidation at date of acquisition.

Table 12—1A
Simplified Consolidated Balance Sheet at Date of Take-over

P Co. and its Subsidiary S Co.
Consolidated Balance Sheet as at 30 June 1984

Shareholders' equity		Assets	
Authorized and paid-up capital	$350 000	Sundry net assets	$400 000
Profit and loss appropriation	50 000		
	$400 000		$400 000

2 Balance Sheet Consolidation at Date of Take-over—Purchase of 90 per cent Interest at Price in Excess of Book Value

Suppose that P Co. has paid $220 000 for only 90 per cent of the shares in S Co. The abridged balance sheets of P Co. and S Co. after the take-over are as shown in the 'date of consolidation' columns in the consolidation worksheet, Table 12—2. In the worksheet the proportionate share (90 per cent) of S Co's shareholders' equity as at the date of acquisition is eliminated, and an equivalent amount is offset against the item 'investment in S Co.' in P Co.'s balance sheet.

It will be observed that 90 per cent of the book value of S Co., as represented by its net assets or shareholders' equity, is only $180 000, or $40 000 less than the price which P Co. has paid for the shares. This difference needs to be recorded separately in the consolidated balance sheet and it is customary to treat it as goodwill. It is implicitly assumed, in effect, that the holding company has been willing to pay an amount in excess of the book value for the shares because of some intangible benefit, such as the expectation of increased earning power arising out of the use of the subsidiary's established organization and reputation, that is conferred on the holding company through its ownership of the subsidiary's shares. If the price paid for the share is less than the recorded value of the net assets or shareholders' equity of the subsidiary company, the difference is recorded in the consolidated balance sheet as a 'reserve on consolidation'. Even in a system of historical record accounting, it is desirable to revalue the subsidiary company's assets and liabilities as at the date of the take-over in terms of their current values, in order to prevent the 'goodwill on consolidation' or 'reserve on consolidation' figures from merely reflecting differences between historical book values and current values. If the subsidiary employs a system of current value accounting, this result will of course be achieved automatically.

Some writers prefer the use of more explicit terminology, 'excess of purchase price of subsidiary over book value of its net assets' in place of 'goodwill on consolidation', and 'excess of book value of net assets of subsidiary over its purchase price' in place of 'reserve on consolidation'. It has also been suggested that a reserve on consolidation should not be recorded, but that the book values of the subsidiary company's assets should instead be written-down so that the surplus does not arise. Where the assets' book values reflect fair current values, as they should, this procedure cannot be justified.

When the subsidiary company is not wholly owned, it is necessary to account for the interests of the owners of the remaining shares in the subsidiary, known as the minority shareholders. Since they own 10 per cent of the shares, the minority shareholders are entitled to 10 per cent of the net assets or shareholders' equity of the subsidiary *as at the date of consolidation* (which in this example is the same as the

Table 12—2
Consolidation Worksheet

	S. Co.'s Equity on Acquisition	At Date of Consolidation P Co.	At Date of Consolidation S Co.	Eliminations Dr.	Eliminations Cr.	Minority Interest (as at date of consolidation)	Consolidated Balance Sheet Items	Consolidated Profit and Loss Items
Paid-up capital	$(160 000)	$(350 000)	$(160 000)	$144 000a		$(16 000)	$(350 000)	
Reserves	(10 000)	(50 000)	(10 000)	9 000a		(1 000)	(50 000)	
Unappropriated profits	(30 000)		(30 000)	27 000a		(3 000)	(20 000)	
Minority interest								
Shareholders' equity and minority interest	$(200 000)	$(400 000)	$(200 000)		(180 000)a	$(420 000)	$(420 000)	
Investment in S Co.		220 000					40 000	
Other net assets		180 000	200 000				380 000	
Total net assets		$400 000	$200 000	$180 000	$(180 000)		$420 000	

Notes: Credit items are shown in parentheses. Italicized letters next to amounts in eliminations columns identify debits with corresponding credits and are explained below:

a P Co. acquires 90% interest in S Co. at a premium above book value. Balance sheet consolidation at date of acquisition.

date of acquisition, but is not the case in (examples 4 and 5 that follow). The interests of the minority shareholders are shown in the 'minority interest (as at date of consolidation)' column of the worksheet, and the total extended into the 'consolidated balance sheet items' column.

A simplified consolidated balance sheet is presented in Table 12—2A.

Table 12—2A
Simplified Consolidated Balance Sheet at Date of Take-over

P Co. and its Subsidiary S Co.
Consolidated Balance Sheet as at 30 June 1984

Shareholders' equity		Assets	
Authorized and paid-up capital	$350 000	Sundry net assets	$380 000
Profit and loss appropriation	50 000		
	400 000	**Goodwill on consolidation**	40 000
Minority shareholders' interest			
in subsidiary	20 000		
	$420 000		$420 000

3 Balance Sheet Consolidation at Date of Take-over—Profits Earned Before Take-over Awaiting Distribution as Dividends

It should be noted that any profits earned by the subsidiary company before the take-over and awaiting distribution as dividends have the effect of reducing the recorded value of the holding company's investment in the subsidiary. If, for example, the liabilities of S Co. in the previous example include a provision for dividend of $6 000 which is to be paid at some date after the take-over, and the shares have been acquired by the holding company with the rights to all accumulated dividends ('*cum* dividend' is the sharemarket phrase used to describe such a transaction), it is clear that the purchase price paid for the shares includes an allowance for the dividend. When the dividend is subsequently received it needs to be recorded in the books of the holding company as follows (P Co.'s share is $5 400):

Bank		Dr.	$5 400	
Investment in S Co.		Cr.		$5 400

The dividend is treated, that is to say, not as income available for distribution by the holding company but as a capital receipt which partly offsets the initial cost of the shares. Because $5 400 of the initial $220 000 paid for the shares will ultimately be received back as dividends by the holding company, the net cost of the investment is only $214 600 and the goodwill figure, initially represented by the difference (between the original cost of the investment and the recorded value of the subsidiary's net assets) of $40 000, is reduced to $34 600. [2]

It is thus necessary to make allowance for the pre-acquisition profits awaiting distribution when the consolidated statement is being drawn up. Table 12—3 shows how this is done.

---

[2] The net assets of the subsidiary remain at $200 000 after the dividend is paid, since the effect of the payment is to reduce both assets (bank) and liabilities (provision for dividend) by $6 000.

Table 12—3
Consolidation Worksheet

	S Co.'s Equity on Acquisition	At Date of Consolidation P Co.	At Date of Consolidation S Co.	Eliminations Dr.	Eliminations Cr.	Minority Interest (as at date of consolidation)	Consolidated Balance Sheet Items	Consolidated Profit and Loss Items
Paid-up capital	$(160 000)	$(350 000)	$(160 000)	$144 000a		$(160 000)	$(350 000)	
Reserves	(10 000)	(50 000)	(10 000)	9 000a		(1 000)	(50 000)	
Unappropriated profits	(30 000)		(30 000)	27 000a		(3 000)	(20 000)	
Minority interest								
Shareholders' equity and minority interest	$(200 000)	$(400 000)	$(200 000)				$(420 000)	
Investment in S Co.		220 000			$180 000a (5 400)b		34 600	
Provision for dividend			(6 000)	5 400b		(600)	(600)	
Other net assets		180 000	206 000				386 000	
Total net assets		$400 000	$200 000	$185 400	$(185 400)		$420 000	

Notes: Credit items are shown in parentheses. Italicized letters next to amounts in eliminations columns identify debits with corresponding credits and are explained below:

a P Co. acquires 90% interest in S Co. at a premium above book value. Balance sheet consolidation at date of acquisition.

b Liabilities of S Co. include provision for dividend of $6 000, of which $5 400 relate to P Co. and $600 to the minority interest.

Any subsequent payment of dividends in future years by S Co. out of pre-acquisition profits or reserves will be recorded in the books of P Co. when the dividends are received, by debiting the bank account and crediting the investment in S Co. account. The balance of 'goodwill on consolidation' is not affected.[3]

A simplified consolidated balance sheet is presented in Table 12—3A.

Table 12—3A
Simplified Consolidated Balance Sheet at Date of Take-over

P Co. and its Subsidiary S Co.
Consolidated Balance Sheet as at 30 June 1984

Shareholders' equity		**Assets**	
Authorized and paid-up capital	$350 000	Sundry net assets	$386 000
Profit and loss appropriation	50 000		
	400 000	**Goodwill on consolidation**	34 600
Minority shareholders' interest			
in subsidiary	20 600		
	$420 600		$420 600

4 Balance Sheet and Profit and Loss Statement Consolidation One Year After Take-over—Inter-company Transactions

The abridged balance sheets and profit and loss statements of P Co. and S Co. one year after take-over are shown below. The dividend of $6 000 payable by S Co. out of pre-acquisition profits to P Co. (see previous example) has been paid, and the investment in S Co. account in P Co.'s books has been adjusted accordingly to $214 600 ($220 000 — $5 400).

Balance Sheets of P Co. and S Co. One Year After Take-Over

	P Co.	S Co.
Shareholders' equity		
Paid-up capital	$350 000	$160 000
Reserves	20 000	20 000
Unappropriated profits	54 000	40 000
	$424 000	$220 000
Net assets		
Investment in S Co.	214 600	
Loan to S Co.	30 000	
Loan from P Co.		(30 000)
Provision for tax	(30 000)	(33 000)
Provision for dividends payable	(15 000)	(20 000)
Dividends receivable	18 000	
Sundry net assets	206 400	303 000
	$424 000	$220 000

Note: Liabilities (to be deducted from assets) are shown in parentheses.

[3] Where a provision for dividends out of pre-acquisition profits has not been set up, S Co.'s pre-acquisition equity will be reduced by the amount of dividend paid out of pre-acquisition profits.

Profit and Loss Statements of P Co. and S Co. One Year After Take-over

	P Co.			S Co.
Sales		$115 000		$165 000
Less: Opening inventory	$10 000		$8 000	
Purchases	40 000		50 000	
	50 000		58 000	
Less: Closing inventory	15 000		12 000	
Cost of goods sold		35 000		46 000
Gross profit		80 000		119 000
Less: Expenses		33 000		36 000
Net profit		47 000		83 000
Dividends from S Co.:				
Received	9 000			
Receivable	18 000	27 000		
Net profit before tax		74 000		83 000
Estimated tax		30 000		33 000
Net profit after tax		44 000		50 000
Balance of unappropriated profits b/f		50 000		30 000
Profits available for appropriation		94 000		80 000
Dividends: Paid	5 000		10 000	
Payable	15 000		20 000	
Transfers to reserves	20 000	40 000	10 000	40 000
Balance of unappropriated profits c/f		$54 000		$40 000

It is necessary to explain the way in which the information contained in the two companies' financial statements is transcribed on to the second and third columns of the worksheet, Table 12—4. The balance sheets are duplicated in the upper section of the worksheet, and the profit and loss statements are reproduced in amended form in the lower section. As will be seen later, the consolidated profit and loss statement consists of two parts, the consolidated profit and loss statement proper and the consolidated profit and loss appropriation statement. The worksheet is similarly partitioned into two sub-sections by a broken horizontal line. The entries above the line contain the operating items of revenues (including revenues from entities outside the group), costs and expenses, and estimated tax. However, intermediate balancing items, such as cost of sales and gross profit, are excluded for simplicity and ease of computation. Certain inter-company transactions which will be fully eliminated by the consolidation procedures, e.g. dividends received or receivable by P Co. from S. Co., are excluded from this sub-section. The 'above the line' closing balance in each column represents net surplus[4] (excluding inter-company dividend receipts) after tax, and is a *debit* balance which maintains the equality of debits and credits in the column.

The entries below the line commence with the balance of net surplus brought down (a *credit*). This balance is apportioned to minority interest and holding company interest. Dividends paid and payable by P Co. and S Co. are then entered in the respective columns relating to each company. For convenience, the dividends paid

[4]The term 'net surplus' is used rather than 'net profit' because, in the column relating to P Co., dividend income from S Co. has not been included above the line.

Table 12—4
Consolidation Worksheet

	S Co.'s Equity on Acquisition	At Date of Consolidation — P Co.	At Date of Consolidation — S Co.	Eliminations Dr.	Eliminations Cr.	Minority Interest (as at date of consolidation)	Consolidated Balance Sheet Items	Consolidated Profit and Loss Items (From viewpoint of group operations)
Paid-up capital	$(160 000)	$(350 000)	$(160 000)	$144 000a		$(16 000)	$ (350 000)	
Reserves	(10 000)	(20 000)	(20 000)	9 000a		(2 000)	(29 000)	
Unappropriated profits	(30 000)	(54 000)	(40 000)	27 000a		(4 000)	(63 000)	
Minority interest							(22 000)	
Shareholders' equity and minority interest	$(200 000)	$(424 000)	$(220 000)				$(464 000)	
Investment in S Co.		214 600			$(180 000)a		34 600	
Loan to S Co.		30 000			(30 000)b			
Loan from P Co.			(30 000)	30 000b				
Provision for tax		(30 000)	(33 000)				(63 000)	
Provision for dividends payable		(15 000)	(20 000)	18 000d			(17 000)	
Dividends receivable		18 000			(18 000)d			
Other net assets		206 400	303 000				509 400	
Total net assets		$424 000	$220 000				$464 000	
Sales		(115 000)	(165 000)					$(270 000)
Opening inventory		10 000	8 000					18 000
Purchases		40 000	50 000	10 000c	(10 000)c			80 000
Closing inventory		(15 000)	(12 000)					(27 000)
Expenses		33 000	36 000					69 000
Estimated tax		30 000	33 000					63 000
Balance (after-tax surplus) c/d		17 000	50 000					67 000

				Eliminations	From viewpoint of holding company interest
Balance (after-tax surplus) b/d:					
Minority interest	(17 000)		(5 000)	(5 000)	⌐(62 000)
Holding company interest	5 000	(45 000)			5 000
P Co.: Dividends paid	15 000				15 000
Dividends payable	(9 000)	10 000		1 000	
S Co.: Dividends paid	(18 000)	20 000		2 000	
Dividends payable	20 000	10 000		1 000	29 000
Transfers to reserves					
Balance of unappropriated profits for year:					
Holding company interest	4 000	9 000		1 000	13 000⌐
Minority interest		1 000			
	$238 000		**$(238 000)**	**S(238 000)**	

Notes: Credit items are shown in parentheses. Italicized letters next to amounts in eliminations columns identify debits with corresponding credits and are explained below:

a P Co. acquired 90% interest in S Co. at a premium. Balance sheet and profit and loss statement consolidation one year later.

b Inter-company loan, $30 000.

c Sales by P Co. to S Co., $6 000; sales by S Co. to P Co., $4 000.

d P Co. provides for $18 000 dividends receivable from S Co.

(and payable) by S Co., and the corresponding dividends received (and receivable) by P Co. (proportional to P Co.'s interest in S Co.), are shown on the same row; thus elimination of these inter-company transactions is subsequently performed through a simple netting procedure. The remaining 'below the line' items are 'transfers to reserves' (a debit) and 'balance of unappropriated profits for year' (a debit). The balance of unappropriated profits for the year maintains the equality of debits and credits below the line. The transfers to reserves and the balance of unappropriated profits for the year explain the changes in the balance sheet items 'reserves' and 'unappropriated profits' respectively, at the top of the worksheet.

The 'above the line' items are employed in drawing up the consolidated profit and loss statement proper, which reflects the trading operations of the group as a whole. The 'below the line' items are employed in drawing up the consolidated profit and loss appropriation statement, which is presented from the viewpoint of the holding company interest, as will be readily seen in Table 12—4B on page 312.

For purposes of illustration, suppose that the following inter-company transactions had taken place during the year:

(a) P Co. made a long-term loan of $30 000 to S Co.

(b) Sales by P Co. to S Co. amounted to $6 000 and sales by S Co. to P Co. amounted to $4 000.

(c) Dividends paid during the year and dividends proposed at year-end were as follows:

	P Co.	S Co.
Dividends paid	$5 000	$10 000
Dividends payable	15 000	20 000

P Co. duly received its proportionate share of the dividends paid by S Co. and made a provision for the dividends receivable from S Co.

As noted above, all inter-company transactions must be eliminated in preparing the consolidated financial statements. In the balance sheet section, several inter-company transactions need to be eliminated. First, P Co.'s shares in the pre-acquisition equity funds of S Co. must be offset against the asset account, investment in S Co. If Table 12—4 is compared with Table 12—3, it will be seen that the book values of 'reserves', 'unappropriated profits' and 'minority interest' in the 'consolidated balance sheet items' column differ. These differences have resulted from the following changes in shareholders' equity:

	Apportioned to	
	Holding Company Interest	Minority Interest
Increase in shareholders' equity:		
Paid-up capital (no change)	—	—
Reserves: P Co., $20 000	$20 000	
S Co., $10 000	9 000	$1 000
Unappropriated profits: P Co., $4 000	4 000	
S Co., $10 000	9 000	1 000

Second, appropriate entries must be made in the eliminations columns which have the net effect of cancelling 'loan to S Co.' (in P Co.'s balance sheet) against 'loan from P Co.' (in S. Co.'s balance sheet). Third, appropriate entries in the eliminations columns are required to eliminate the item 'dividends receivable' (in P Co.'s balance sheet) of $18 000 against the 'provision for dividends payable' (in S Co.'s balance sheet). The outcome is the elimination altogether of 'provision for dividends receivable', while the 'provision for dividends payable' of the group is reduced by the equivalent amount. A simplified consolidated balance sheet is presented in Table 12—4A.

Table 12—4A
Simplified Consolidated Balance Sheet One Year After Take-over

P Co. and its Subsidiary S Co.
Consolidated Balance Sheet as at 30 June 1985

Shareholders' equity			Assets	
Authorized and paid-up capital		$350 000	Sundry net assets	$509 400
Reserves		29 000		
Profit and loss appropriation		63 000	**Goodwill on consolidation**	34 600
		442 000		
Minority shareholders' interest				
in subsidiary		22 000		
Current liabilities				
Provision for tax	$63 000			
Provision for dividends	17 000			
		80 000		
		$544 000		$544 000

In the profit and loss section, appropriate elimination entries above the line are made to reduce total sales by $10 000 ($6 000 + $4 000) and total purchases by the same amount. The balance of sales ($270 000) and purchases ($80 000) then represent transactions between the group and external parties.

Insofar as 'below the line' transactions are concerned, dividends received and receivable by P Co. from S Co. are effectively eliminated through the simple procedure of netting these revenue items of P Co. against dividends paid and dividends payable of S Co., respectively. The balances are extended into the 'minority interest' column, and explain how the minority interest in S Co.'s profit for the year has been appropriated. The minority shareholders' portion amounted to $5 000, of which $3 000 has been appropriated to dividends (paid and payable), $1 000 to reserves and $1 000 to unappropriated profits. The extensions into the last column of the worksheet are self-explanatory. For example, total transfers to reserves are $30 000, of which $1 000 has been apportioned to minority interest; thus the net balance attributable to the holding company interest is $29 000.

The consolidated profit and loss statement is presented in Table 12—4B. This statement consists of two parts. The first part is the profit and loss statement proper. This reflects the *trading operations of the group as a whole*, and is based on 'above the line' items in the worksheet. The second part is the profit and loss appropriation statement, which is presented from *the viewpoint of the holding company interest*, and is based on 'below the line' items in the worksheet.

Table 12—4B
Consolidated Profit and Loss Statement One Year After Take-over

P Co. and its Subsidiary S Co.
Consolidated Profit and Loss Statement for the Year Ended 30 June 1985

Sales		$270 000
Less: Cost of sales		
Opening inventory	$18 000	
Purchases	80 000	
	98 000	
Closing inventory	27 000	71 000
		199 000
Less: Expenses		69 000
Net profit before tax		130 000
Less: Estimated tax		63 000
Net profit after tax		67 000
Less: Minority interest in S Co.'s		
profit for the year		5 000
Profit attributable to holding company		62 000
Unappropriated profits b/f*		50 000
Profits available for appropriation		112 000
Less: Dividends paid and payable	20 000	
Transfer to reserves	29 000	49 000
Unappropriated profits c/f		$63 000

* This is the balance of unappropriated profits in the consolidated financial statements at the beginning of the year.

5 Balance Sheet and Profit and Loss Statement Consolidation One Year after Take-over—Treatment of Unrealized Profit Component in Closing Inventories

Only one additional complication is introduced in this last example. Assume that inter-company sales have taken place at prices which included a profit mark-up. Insofar as inventories purchased by one company from another within the group have subsequently been re-sold to outside parties, the correct profit or loss to the group effectively will have been recorded, and no adjustments are necessary. For example, suppose P Co. has recorded sales of $6 000 to S Co. of goods which cost P Co. $5 000. That is to say, P Co. has recorded a gross profit of $1 000 on sales to a company within the group. If these goods have been re-sold by S Co. for $7 500, from the group viewpoint both S Co.'s resulting profit of $1 500 and P Co.'s earlier profit of $1 000 will have been earned by sale to outside entities. The significant group profit figure with respect to the goods in question is the total profit of $2 500, represented by the revenue received from the final sales ($7 500) less the cost of the sales to the group ($5 000).

It will be readily appreciated that the prices charged in respect of inter-company transfers are a matter for determination by the holding company's board, and are therefore in the nature of notional charges. It follows that the apportionment of profits between the holding company and the subsidiary company is itself an arbitrary process. But for purposes of consolidation this does not matter, provided that the goods transferred between companies have been disposed of to outside parties during the same period. The total group profit can still be determined as part of the consolidation process merely by combining the holding company profit figure with that of the subsidiary. Under these circumstances, there can be no double-counting or mis-statement of group profit, since the holding company's profit is absorbed into the subsidiary company's costs, and is thereby taken into account in determining the subsidiary company's profit.

However, to the extent that not all the goods transferred from the holding company to the subsidiary have been sold by the latter company to outside parties, it is clear that the holding company has recorded an amount of profit that has not yet been realized by the group as a whole. It is then necessary to eliminate the profit pertaining to the unsold inventory from the consolidated financial statements.

Suppose that there is an unrealized profit component in the closing inventory of S Co. (relating to goods purchased from P Co.). Two sets of elimination entries are necessary to adjust the figures contained in the second and third columns of the worksheet (see Table 12—5). In the balance sheet section, the items 'unappropriated profits' and 'inventory' are reduced by appropriate entries in the eliminations columns. Similarly, in the profit and loss section above the line, the items 'closing inventory' and 'balance (after-tax surplus) c/d' are reduced by appropriate entries in the eliminations columns. (The elimination entries made below the line are merely balancing entries to reflect the reduction of net surplus shown above the line.)

The above adjustments suffice when the supplier in inter-company inventory transactions is the holding company or a wholly owned subsidiary. Now consider an unrealized profit component in the closing stocks of P Co. relating to goods supplied by S Co., a partly owned subsidiary. As before, in the profit and loss section the recorded value of closing inventory is reduced by the amount of the unrealized profit component and net surplus is correspondingly reduced, but the profit reduction is borne by the holding company interest and minority interest, in proportion to the ownership holdings in S Co., as shown:

| | Elimination of Unrealized Profit Component Apportioned to: | |
	Holding Company Interest	Minority Interest
Unrealized profit component in closing inventories of:		
S Co. (supplied by P Co.), $200	$200	
P Co. (supplied by S Co.), $400	360	$40
	$560	$40

The proportionate shares of the holding company and minority interest in the profit reduction, $560 and $40 respectively, must be reflected in the elimination entries against 'unappropriated profits' and 'minority interest' in the balance sheet section.[5]

[5] The adjustment to tax on account of the elimination of the unrealized profit component in inventories is not illustrated in the example.

Table 12—5
Consolidation Worksheet

	S Co.'s Equity on Acquisition	At Date of Consolidation P Co.	At Date of Consolidation S Co.	Eliminations Dr.	Eliminations Cr.	Minority Interest (as at date of consolidation)	Consolidated Balance Sheet Items	Consolidated Profit and Loss Items
Paid-up capital	$(160 000)	$(350 000)	$(160 000)	$144 000a		$(16 000)	$(350 000)	
Reserves	(10 000)	(20 000)	(20 000)	9 000a		(2 000)	(29 000)	
Unappropriated profits	(30 000)	(54 000)	(40 000)	27 000a		(4 000)	(62 440)	
				560e				
Minority interest				40e		40	(21 960)	
Shareholders' equity and minority interest	$(200 000)	$(424 000)	$(220 000)				$(463 400)	
Investment in S Co.		214 600			$(180 000)a			
Loan to S Co.		30 000			(30 000)b		34 600	
Loan from P Co.			(30 000)	30 000b				
Provision for tax		(30 000)	(33 000)				(63 000)	
Provision for dividends payable		(15 000)	(20 000)				(17 000)	
Dividends receivable		18 000		18 000d	(18 000)d			
Inventory		15 000	12 000		(600)e		26 400	
Other net assets		191 400	291 000				482 400	
Total net assets	$(200 000)	$424 000	$220 000				$463 400	
Sales		(115 000)	(165 000)	10 000c				$(270 000)
Opening inventory		10 000	8 000					18 000
Purchases		40 000	50 000		(10 000)c			80 000
Closing inventory		(15 000)	(12 000)	600e				(26 400)
Expenses		33 000	36 000					69 000
Estimated tax		30 000	33 000					63 000
Balance (after-tax surplus) c/d		17 000	50 000		(600)e			66 400

From viewpoint of group operations

				From viewpoint of holding company interest	
Balance (after-tax surplus) b/d:					
Minority interest		(5 000)		(4 960)	
Holding company interest	(17 000)	(45 000)			(61 440)
P Co.: Dividends paid	5 000	10 000			5 000
Dividends payable	15 000	20 000			15 000
S Co.: Dividends paid	(9 000)	10 000		1 000	
Dividends payable	(18 000)			2 000	
Transfers to reserves	20 000			1 000	29 000
Balance of unappropriated profits for year:					
Holding company interest	4 000	9 000	560	(560)	12 440
Minority interest		1 000	40	(40)	960
			$239 800	$(239 800)		

Notes: Credit items are shown in parentheses. Italicized letters next to amounts in eliminations columns identify debits with corresponding credits and are explained below:

a P Co. acquired 90% interest in S Co. at a premium. Balance sheet and profit and loss statement consolidation one year later.

b Inter-company loan, $30 000.

c Sales by P Co. to S Co., $6 000; sales by S Co. to P Co., $4 000.

d P Co. provides for $18 000 dividends receivable from S Co.

e Unrealized profit component in closing inventory of: S Co., $200; P Co., $400.

Since it has been assumed in the example that P Co. acquired S Co. one year ago, opening inventories do not reflect any inter-company profits. However, in subsequent years any inter-company profits on opening inventories need to be adjusted on consolidation. The elimination entries are made in the profit and loss section above the line: 'opening inventory' is reduced by the amount of unrealized profit and 'balance (after-tax surplus) c/d' increased by the same amount, apportioning to the holding company interest and minority interest where necessary. These are the basic adjusting entries. Balancing adjusting entries reflecting the increase in net surplus must of course be made below the line, but no eliminations are necessary in the balance sheet section. (In the consolidated profit and loss appropriation statement, the increase in net profit exactly offsets the decrease in 'unappropriated profits b/f' from the preceding year on account of the adjustment to closing inventory made in that year.)

The consolidated balance sheet and consolidated profit and loss statement in respect of Example 5 are shown in Tables 12—5A and 12—5B. For purposes of illustration some individual assets and liabilities are displayed in Table 12—5A.

Table 12—5A
Consolidated Balance Sheet One Year After Take-over

P Co. and its Subsidiary S Co.
Consolidated Balance Sheet as at 30 June 1985

Shareholders' equity			Non-current assets		
Authorized and paid-up			Building at cost	$600 000	
capital—			*Less*: Provision for		
P Co.: 350 000			depreciation	150 000	
$1 shares		$350 000			
Revenue reserves—					$450 000
General reserve	$29 000				
Profit and loss					
appropriation	62 440				
		91 440	**Current assets**		
			Inventory	26 400	
		441 440	Trade debtors	63 900	
			Bank	8 500	
Minority shareholders'					98 800
interest in subsidiary		21 960			
			Goodwill on		
Current liabilities			**consolidation**		34 600
Provision for tax	63 000				
Provision for dividends	17 000				
Trade creditors	40 000				
		120 000			
		$583 400			$583 400

Table 12—5B
Consolidated Profit and Loss Statement One Year After Take-over

P Co. and its Subsidiary S Co.
Consolidated Profit and Loss Statement for the Year Ended 30 June 1985

Sales		$270 000
Less: Cost of sales		
Opening inventory	$18 000	
Purchases	80 000	
	98 000	
Closing inventory	26 400	71 600
		198 400
Less: Expenses		69 000
		129 400
Net profit before tax		
Less: Estimated tax		63 000
Net profit after tax		66 400
Less: Minority interest in S Co.'s		
profit for the year		4 960
Profit attributable to holding company		61 440
Unappropriated profits b/f*		50 000
Profit available for appropriation		111 440
Less: Dividends paid	5 000	
Dividends payable	15 000	
Transfer to reserves	29 000	49 000
Unappropriated profits c/f		$ 62 440

* This is the balance of unappropriated profits in the consolidated financial statements at the beginning of the year.

The consolidation of group accounts may become considerably more complicated in practice, but the foregoing illustrations are sufficient to indicate the general principles of consolidation. It is emphasized that the consolidation technique may be applied to different kinds of accounting systems (e.g. government accounts and social or national economic accounts as well as business enterprise accounts); and that different kinds of accounting statements (e.g. funds statements) may be consolidated by procedures that are essentially similar to those illustrated above in respect of the balance sheet and the profit and loss statement.

Appendix

Two special issues in accounting for company combinations are now briefly discussed. Like so many other accounting issues they are, to a large extent, a product of historical record accounting. The first issue is sometimes referred to as 'purchase v. pooling of interests', and is concerned with the application of different accounting methods to a business combination depending on whether the combination is treated as an acquisition or a merger. The second problem relates to accounting for the earnings and book value of an investment in which a company holds a significant, but not a controlling, interest in the equity of another company.

Purchase v. Pooling of Interests

Basically a purchase represents the take-over or acquisition of one company by another company, while a pooling of interests represents a merger by means of an exchange of shares between two or more companies for the purpose of combining their resources in a single business entity. Under the purchase method of combination, the assets acquired are usually written up to their current values (as recommended earlier in this chapter), and in the consolidated balance sheet the pre-acquisition equity of the purchased company is written off against the cost of acquisition. As has been seen, this often results in the creation of 'goodwill on consolidation'. On the other hand, in a pooling of interests the assets of the merging companies are not usually revalued. Also, a summation of the income statements of the individual merging companies is presented in the income statement of the group, while a summation of the net assets and shareholders' equities of the individual companies is presented in the balance sheet of the group (i.e. the equities of one or more parties to the merger are not eliminated).

Example: Suppose that X Co. combines with Y Co., and that X Co. (which will 'house' the new entity from the combination) issues 160 000 $1 shares at the market price of $1.50 for the purpose of a one-to-one share exchange. The abridged balance sheets of X Co. and Y Co. before and after the combination, the consolidated balance sheet under the purchase method and the balance sheet of the group under the alternative pooling method, are shown:

	Before Combination		After Combination		Balance Sheet of Group Under	
	X Co.	Y Co.	X Co.	Y Co.	Purchase	Pooling
	($'000)	($'000)	($'000)	($'000)	($'000)	($'000)
Shareholders' equity						
Paid-up capital—$1 shares	200	160	360	160	360	360
Share premium reserve			80		80	
Other reserves		10		10		10
Unappropriated profits	50	30	50	30	50	80
	250	200	490	200	490	450
Net assets						
Investment in Y Co.			240		40*	
Sundry net assets	250	200	250	200	450	450
	250	200	490	200	490	450

* Goodwill on consolidation

The different accounting methods that are applied to a business combination, depending on whether the combination is a purchase or a pooling of interests, can be traced to accounting practice in the U.S.A., but such methods are now also applied in a number of other countries (e.g. Australia). In theory, whether a combination represents a purchase or a pooling depends on the circumstances of the combination rather than on contractual or legal considerations (and certainly not on whether certain benefits of a financial nature are expected to accrue from the method of accounting for the combination). The essence of a purchase is that one company clearly has bought out the interests of another company, whereas under pooling there is a continuity of interests of the merging companies. Continuity of interests is usually taken to mean the continuity of ownership, management and business operations of the individual predecessor companies. But the criteria for distinguishing between purchase and pooling remain obscure, e.g. some accountants believe that continuity of management is not important in pooling. Accountants are also divided on whether the relative size of the companies is an important factor, although it is difficult to see how a mouse can pool interests with an elephant.

There are several reasons for concern about the purchase v. pooling approach in accounting for business combination. First, there is a lack of definitive guidelines to distinguish between a purchase and a pooling. Thus companies have considerable discretion as to how a combination is reported. Second, there is no consistent approach to valuation. Companies should be required to revalue their assets for reporting purposes when a significant event, such as a purchase or a pooling, takes place. Under current accounting practice the assets of the acquired company are usually revalued under the purchase method, while the assets of the acquiring company are not revalued. Under the pooling method, the assets of all merging companies are usually not revalued, although it can be argued that revaluation should be necessary to ensure what is called 'fair-value' pooling. Both accounting methods suffer from the defects of historical record accounting for disclosure purposes.

The lack of clear guidelines and the differences in valuation methods in turn have led to financial manipulations and an abuse of the pooling method of accounting. It is believed that some company acquisitions have been accounted for and reported as a pooling of interests because of certain so-called financial advantages, such as the ability of the group to pay dividends out of pre-merger revenue reserves and unappropriated profits, which must be capitalized under the purchase method. Also, the purchase method often leads to the recording of goodwill, which may need to be amortized in future periods. Those controlling the merging companies fear that, under the purchase method, goodwill amortization and larger depreciation charges (on account of asset revaluations) will result in lower reported profits in future years, while future rates of return will be affected adversely both by lower profits and higher asset book values.

In a current value accounting system, the alleged defects of the purchase method resulting from asset revaluations are no longer present. But the availability or non-availability of pre-combination reserves and profits for distribution is likely to remain a critical and controversial issue.

Associated Companies and Equity Accounting

There is another form of company combination, which occurs when one company (the investor company) holds between 20 and 50 per cent of the participating share capital of, and exerts significant influence over, another company (known as an *associated company*). In an historical record accounting framework, the investor company records its share investment in its books at cost of acquisition, and treats dividends from the associated company as income, as and when the dividends are received. When significant amounts of profits are retained for reinvestment by the associated company, the recorded cost of the investment in the investor company's books becomes increasingly out of line with the true worth of the investment, either in terms of its market value or the share of the investor in the resources currently deployed by the associated company.

Equity accounting is a method of accounting for long-term investment by one company in another company (or companies), where the holdings are significant but are not large enough to constitute a parent-subsidiary relationship. Under equity accounting, the investor company discloses its proportionate share of the associated company's annual net profit (or loss) as investment income in its consolidated [6] (or so-called equity) profit and loss statement, and discloses the acquisition cost *plus* its proportionate share of the associated company's post-acquisition profits (or losses) *less* dividends received as the investment asset value in its consolidated or equity balance sheet.

There are several complications. For example, where the investor company is not able to dispose of the investment or where the associated company is exploiting a wasting asset, the reported value of the investment under equity accounting is likely to overstate the investment's true worth. But in many situations the investment will be reported at a more realistic value under equity accounting than under strict historical record accounting.

This reporting problem is largely resolved under a current value accounting system. For example, the investment may be reported at its market value if the shares are listed, or at the appropriate proportion of the current value of the net assets employed by the associated company.

Discussion Questions

1 What is a holding company? What are the advantages and disadvantages of the holding company form of organization, relative to those of semi-autonomous branches, as a means of decentralizing administrative control?

2 In consolidating the financial statements of company groups, what problems arise which do not exist for divisionalized single firms?

3 Under what circumstances would you expect to see the following items in the consolidated financial statements of a company group? Briefly consider their accounting significance:
   (a) goodwill;
   (b) minority interest; and
   (c) inventories in transit.

4 Deakin Ltd, a manufacturing wholly-owned subsidiary of Parkes Wholesalers Ltd, sells most of its output to the latter company at normal prices. It also supplies a number of other wholesale companies, charging comparable prices. Examine the accounting measurement problem which arises in relation to the group's consolidated financial statements, when inventories received by the holding company from its subsidiary have not been sold at the time of consolidation.

5 Do you consider that the consolidated financial statements of a company group provide all the information needed to assess the performance of the group? Discuss.

---

[6] If the investor company is also a holding company.

6 Why is it important to distinguish between a purchase of one company by another and a merger of two or more companies in order to combine their resources in a single economic entity?

7 Explain what is meant by 'equity accounting'.

Exercises

1 Holding Co. Ltd purchases all of the shares in Subsidiary Co. Ltd for $60 000. The balance sheets of the two companies at the date of acquisition are as follows:

	Holding Co.	Subsidiary Co.
Fully paid-up $1 shares	$150 000	$36 000
General reserve	30 000	18 000
Profit and loss appropriation	15 000	6 000
Current liabilities	30 000	30 000
	$225 000	$90 000
Shares in Subsidiary Ltd (at cost)	60 000	
Fixed assets	120 000	42 000
Current assets	45 000	48 000
	$225 000	$90 000

You are required to prepare a consolidated balance sheet for Holding Co. Ltd and Subsidiary Co. Ltd as at date of acquisition. Show worksheet.

2 Gigantic Co. Ltd purchases 75 per cent of the issued shares of Miniature Co. Ltd for $32 000. The balance sheets of the two companies at the date of purchase are:

	Gigantic Co.	Miniature Co.
Authorized and paid-up capital	$150 000	$24 000
Profit and loss appropriation	30 000	12 000
Accounts payable	30 000	10 000
Long-term liabilities	25 000	10 000
	$235 000	$56 000
Shares in Miniature Co. Ltd	32 000	
Plant and machinery	84 000	18 000
Accounts receivable	48 000	20 000
Inventories	28 000	13 000
Bank	43 000	5 000
	$235 000	$56 000

You are required to prepare a consolidated balance sheet as at the date of purchase. Show worksheet.

3 Alpha Ltd owns 60 per cent of Omega Ltd. The two companies' income statements for the year ended 30 June 1985, are as follows:

	Alpha Ltd.		Omega Ltd	
Sales		$16 000		$6 400
Inventory, 1 July 1984	$3 520		$640	
Purchases	12 000		5 280	
	15 520		5 920	
Inventory, 30 June 1985	3 840		960	
Cost of goods sold		11 680		4 960
Gross profit		4 320		1 440
Expenses		2 240		480
Net profit		$2 080		$ 960

You are given the following additional information:

(a) Sales by Omega Ltd to Alpha Ltd during the year amounted to $2 000.

(b) The opening inventory of Alpha Ltd includes goods bought from Omega Ltd for $1 000. The cost of these goods to Omega Ltd was $750.

(c) The closing inventory of Alpha Ltd includes goods bought from Omega Ltd for $1 900. The cost of these goods to Omega Ltd was $1 250.

Prepare a consolidated profit and loss statement. Show worksheet.

4 Barracuda Ltd acquired 80 per cent of Wobbegong Ltd for $66 000 on 1 January 1985. The shareholders' equity of Wobbegong Ltd at the time of acquisition was:

Authorized and paid-up capital	$50 000
Profit and loss appropriation	27 500
General reserve	10 000
	$87 500

The balance sheets of the two companies as at 31 December 1985 recorded the following information:

	Barracuda Ltd		Wobbegong Ltd	
Authorized and paid-up capital		$500 000		$50 000
Profit and loss appropriation		71 500		20 000
General reserve		42 500		22 500
Proposed dividend		50 000		10 000
Accounts payable		166 000		33 750
Estimated tax liability		40 000		17 500
		$870 000		$153 750
Bank		50 000		20 000
Accounts receivable		208 500		28 750
Inventories		170 000		22 500
Shares in Wobbegong Ltd		66 000		
Fixed assets	$500 000		$100 000	
Less: Accumulated depreciation	124 500	375 500	17 500	82 500
		$870 000		$153 750

The closing inventories of Barracuda Ltd included goods purchased from Wobbegong Ltd for $20 000, which had cost Wobbegong Ltd $15 000, and the closing inventories of Wobbegong Ltd included goods purchased from Barracuda Ltd for $10 000, which had cost Barracuda Ltd $8 000.

Prepare a consolidated balance sheet as at 31 December 1985, with a supporting worksheet.

5 On 30 June 1984 Mako Co. Ltd. acquired 90 000 fully paid shares of $1 each in Remora Co. Ltd for $120 000. At the date of acquisition the balance sheet of Remora Co. Ltd was as follows:

Balance Sheet as at 30 June 1984

Shareholders' equity		**Current assets**	
Authorized and paid-up capital		Bank	$15 000
(120 000 shares of $1 each)	$120 000	Accounts receivable	60 000
General reserve	30 000	Inventories	27 000
Unappropriated profits	22 500		102 000
	172 500		
Current liabilities		**Fixed assets**	$140 000
Accounts payable	$30 000	*Less*: Accumulated	
Proposed final dividend	12 000	depreciation	20 000 120 000
Estimated tax liability	7 500 49 500		
	$222 000		$222 000

On 1 October 1984, the proposed final dividend was paid by Remora Co. Ltd. On 30 June 1985, the balance sheets of the two companies were as follows:

Balance Sheets as at 30 June 1985

	Mako Co.	Remora Co.
Authorized and paid-up capital	$300 000	$120 000
General reserve	60 000	42 000
Unappropriated profits	45 000	28 500
Mako Co. Ltd—Loan		15 000
Accounts payable	45 000	19 500
Proposed final dividend	30 000	12 000
Estimated tax liability	24 000	9 000
	$504 000	$246 000
Bank	29 000	22 000
Accounts receivable	85 000	74 000
Inventories	84 000	30 000
Investment in Remora Co. Ltd	111 000	
Remora Co. Ltd—Loan	15 000	
Fixed Assets	$180 000	$150 000
Less: Accumulated depreciation	18 000 162 000	30 000 120 000
Goodwill	18 000	
	$504 000	$246 000

The closing inventory of Remora Co. Ltd includes $18 000 for goods supplied by Mako Co. Ltd on the basis of cost plus 20 per cent.

You are required to prepare a consolidated balance sheet as at 30 June 1985. Show worksheet.

13 Devolution of Control—Departments and Branches

The growing size and complexity of business organizations and governments in the modern world have led to the development of numerous devices designed to decentralize executive control and decision making. This chapter will be concerned with the accounting implications of two such devices—departmentalization and the establishment of separate branches. These two forms of devolution involve the breaking down of the legal entity into a number of separate managerial and accounting divisions. On the other hand, the subject matter of Chapter 12—the holding company device—involves the combination of a number of distinct legal entities into a single managerial group, the activities of which are co-ordinated in the interests of the group (or the holding company which controls the group), rather than in the interests of the separate entities which comprise the group. All three devices, however, have this in common—they are intended to decentralize managerial decision making and, by making each subordinate manager responsible for his performance in a clearly defined area, to facilitate the control of top management.

Departmental Accounts

When a business (or other entity) is divided into different departments, it is necessary to account separately for the activities of each department in order that its efficiency or profitability may be measured. This involves the maintenance of a separate record of the transactions attributable to each department. Such a record may be built up in the ledger in one of two ways:

(a) by using columnar ledger accounts, with a separate column for each department; or

(b) by adopting the control account technique described in Chapter 2, with control accounts recording total transactions and subsidiary ledgers recording the transactions attributable to each department.

The different techniques may be illustrated by reference to the hypothetical transactions carried out during a period by a retail trading business organized into three operating departments, A, B and C:

| | Department | | |
	A	B	C
Sales (at selling price)	$200	$250	$150
Sales (at cost)	120	150	120
Purchases	100	175	75
Opening inventories	60	50	65
Closing inventories	40	75	20
Wages	40	50	20

1 Columnar Ledgers

Where the number of departments is not too large, it is possible to introduce separate analysis columns, one for each department, into the appropriate ledger accounts. Apart from this innovation and a corresponding analysis in the journals, the usual recording and summarizing procedures are employed:

Departmental Columnar Ledger

Inventory

	Department A	B	C	Total Dr.		Department A	B	C	Total Cr.
Balance b/d	$60	$50	$65	$175	Cost of sales	$120	$150	$120	$390
Purchases	100	175	75	350	Balance c/d	40	75	20	135
	$160	$225	$140	$525		$160	$225	$140	$525
Balance b/d	$40	$75	$20	$135					

Sales

	Department A	B	C	Total Dr.		Department A	B	C	Total Cr.
Trading account	$200	$250	$150	$600	Debtors, etc.	$200	$250	$150	$600

Purchases

	Department A	B	C	Total Dr.		Department A	B	C	Total Cr.
Creditors, etc.	$100	$175	$75	$350	Inventory	$100	$175	$75	$350

Wages

	Department A	B	C	Total Dr.		Department A	B	C	Total Cr.
Bank	$40	$50	$20	$110	Profit and loss account	$40	$50	$20	$110

Cost of Sales

	Department A	B	C	Total Dr.		Department A	B	C	Total Cr.
Inventory	$120	$150	$120	$390	Trading account	$120	$150	$120	$390

Trading

	Department			Total Dr.		Department			Total Cr.
	A	B	C			A	B	C	
Cost of sales	$120	$150	$120	$390	Sales	$200	$250	$150	$600
Profit and loss account (gross profit)	80	100	30	210					
	$200	$250	$150	$600		$200	$250	$150	$600

Departmental Profit and Loss

	Department			Total Dr.		Department			Total Cr.
	A	B	C			A	B	C	
Wages	$40	$50	$20	$110	Trading account (gross profit)	$80	$100	$30	$210
General profit and loss account (departmental profits)	40	50	10	100					
	$80	$100	$30	$210		$80	$100	$30	$210

Other expenses not directly attributable to the departments (usually known as indirect or overhead expenses) are not analysed on a departmental basis, but are matched in total against the total of the departmental profits in the usual way.

2   Departmental Control Accounts

The number of columns that can be fitted into a ledger sheet is limited, and when the number of departments is very large (e.g. in the case of a large retail department store) it may just not be possible to operate a columnar accounting system. An alternative procedure that may be employed under these circumstances is the control account technique that was described in Chapter 2. Applied to departmental accounting, this involves the design and maintenance of journals in such a way as to permit the recording of all transactions of the business in total in the general ledger, leaving the detailed transactions affecting each department to be recorded in separate subsidiary ledgers which are maintained for each class of transaction. In the following system of accounts (which records the same data that were used to illustrate columnar accounting), the accounts in the general ledger are all control accounts backed by separate subsidiary ledgers. The balance in each control account at any time must correspond to the sum of the balances in the corresponding subsidiary ledger, which records all the detailed accounting information relating to individual departments that is needed for managerial purposes.

Departmental Control Accounts
General Ledger

Inventory Control

Balance b/d	$175	Cost of sales	$390
Purchases	350	Balance c/d	135
	$525		$525
Balance b/d	$135		

Sales Control

Trading account	$600	Debtors, etc.	$600

Purchases Control

Creditors, etc.	$350	Inventory	$350

Wages Control

Bank	$110	Departmental profit and loss account	$110

Cost of Sales Control

Inventory	$390	Trading account	$390

Trading Control

Cost of sales	$390	Sales	$600
Departmental profit and loss (gross profit)	210		
	$600		$600

Departmental Profit and Loss Control

Wages	$110	Trading account (gross profit)	$210
General profit and loss account (departmental profits)	100		
	$210		$210

Inventory Ledger

Inventory—Department A

Balance b/d	$60	Cost of sales	$120
Purchases	100	Balance c/d	40
	$160		$160
Balance b/d	$40		

Inventory—Department B

Balance b/d	$50	Cost of sales	$150
Purchases	175	Balance c/d	75
	$225		$225
Balance b/d	$75		

Inventory—Department C

Balance b/d	$65	Cost of sales	$120
Purchases	75	Balance c/d	20
	$140		$140
Balance b/d	$20		

Sales Ledger

Sales—Department A

Trading account	$200	Debtors, etc.	$200

Sales—Department B

Trading account	$250	Debtors, etc.	$250

Sales—Department C

Trading account	$150	Debtors, etc.	$150

Purchases Ledger

Purchases—Department A

Creditors, etc.	$100	Inventory	$100

Purchases—Department B

Creditors, etc.	$175	Inventory	$175

Purchases—Department C

Creditors, etc.	$75	Inventory	$75

Wages Ledger

Wages—Department A

Bank	$40	Departmental profit and loss account	$40

Wages—Department B

Bank	$50	Departmental profit and loss account	$50

Wages—Department C

Bank	$20	Departmental profit and loss account	$20

Cost of Sales Ledger

Cost of Sales—Department A

Inventory	$120	Trading account	$120

Cost of Sales—Department B

Inventory	$150	Trading account	$150

Cost of Sales—Department C

Inventory	$120	Trading account	$120

Trading Ledger

Trading—Department A

Cost of sales	$120	Sales	$200
Departmental profit and loss (gross profit)	80		
	$200		$200

Trading—Department B

Cost of sales	$150	Sales	$250
Departmental profit and loss (gross profit)	100		
	$250		$250

Trading—Department C

Cost of sales	$120	Sales	$150
Departmental profit and loss (gross profit)	30		
	$150		$150

Department Profit and Loss Ledger

Profit and Loss—Department A

Wages	$40	Trading account (gross profit)	$80
Departmental profit	40		
	$80		$80

Profit and Loss—Department B

Wages	$50	Trading account (gross profit)	$100
Departmental profit	50		
	$100		$100

Profit and Loss—Department C

Wages	$20	Trading account (gross profit)	$30
Departmental profit	10		
	$30		$30

The departmental inventory accounts in the subsidiary inventory ledger are themselves in the nature of sub-control accounts controlling the departmental perpetual inventory stock cards in the manner described in Chapter 3.

The trading account ledger and the departmental profit and loss account ledger record the summarized results of each department, which may be conveniently brought together in the form of the departmental profit and loss statement illustrated in Table 13—1.

Table 13—1
Departmental Profit and Loss Statement ... Ending ...

	Department A	Department B	Department C	Total
Sales	$200	$250	$150	$600
Less: Cost of sales	120	150	120	390
Gross profit	80	100	30	210
Less: Wages	40	50	20	110
Departmental profit	$40	$50	$10	$100

Application of Departmental Accounting

The foregoing example has been concerned only with departmentalization of revenue statement transactions, but the techniques that have been illustrated may easily be extended to cover balance sheet transactions. The main significance of different methods of departmental accounting lies in their applicability to various kinds of operating conditions and managerial organization. Thus, a system of departmental control accounts is usually more appropriate than columnar ledgers when the number of departments is very large. Where the departments are autonomous, it is usually desirable to have a separate accounting system for each department and this involves the use of branch accounting procedures that will be described in the following section. It should be emphasized that there is no hard and fast dividing line between departmental and branch accounts.

Indirect or Overhead Expenses in Departmental Accounting

It is often dangerous to carry the departmental analysis of transactions beyond the stage where the transactions can be clearly and directly associated with the activities of particular departments. Expenses which cannot be directly attributed to particular departments or other cost units are usually known as indirect or overhead expenses; general office expenses are overhead expenses in this sense. Arbitrary apportionment of general office overhead can interfere with the usefulness of accounting in its task of providing information for managerial control and policy-making purposes. If, in the illustrative example, a general office overhead of $60 was to be allocated to departments in accordance with their respective sales revenues (a not uncommon practice), departmental results would be recorded as in Table 13—2.

Table 13—2
Misleading Overhead Expense Allocations to Departments

	Department A	Department B	Department C		Total
Sales	$200	$250	$150		$600
Less: Cost of sales	120	150	120		390
Gross profit on trading	80	100	30		210
Less: Wages	$40	$50	$20	$110	
Share of general office overhead	20	25	15	60	
	60	75	35		170
Assumed departmental profit (loss)	$20	$25	($5)		$40

There are two reasons why such results would be misleading. In the first place, they would have the effect of charging departmental managers with expenses over which they have no control, and recorded departmental profits could in consequence vary indeterminately and in a way that would be inconsistent with the change in total profits of the enterprise. Suppose, for example, that in the following accounting period the manager of Department A were to succeed in lifting his department's sales to $250, the corresponding figure for cost of sales and wages being $150 and $55, respectively. The additional $50 earned as revenue would be partly offset by the additional cost of sales ($30) and wages ($15), so that the increase in departmental profit would be $5. This would also quite clearly be the figure by which the total profits of the enterprise had increased as a result of the improvement in Department A's trade. If, however, the general office overhead was allocated to departments along the lines indicated above, there is no certainty that the Department A manager would receive credit for his action. Whether or not his department recorded an increased profit would depend, not only on his own department's performance, but also on that of other departments and, indeed, on the performance of the general office itself. If, say, the sales of Department B (or C) were to fall by $50 with the general office overhead remaining constant, or if the latter were to increase by $5 with the sales of the other departments remaining constant, Department A would be burdened with an additional charge of $5 for the general office overhead. This would have the effect of eliminating the extra profit which the Department A manager had earned by his own efforts. Under these circumstances the departmental manager could hardly be held responsible for the performance of his department, and there is a consequential loss of control by top management.

The second reason why an arbitrary allocation of indirect expenses tends to be misleading is associated with the policy-making function of management. If general office overhead was allocated in the manner illustrated in Table 13—2, Department C would record a loss of $5 on the period's operations. If management were not aware of the significance of the overhead expense allocation that had been made, it might decide that Department C is unprofitable and close it down. It is evident, however, that if all other factors were to remain unchanged this would not increase the total profits of the enterprise, and would actually have the effect of reducing them from $40 to $30 (the reduction of $10 equals the amount by which Department C's revenue exceeds the expenses directly incurred by that department):

Gross profits earned by Departments A and B		$180
Less: Wages incurred by Departments A and B	$90	
General office overhead	60	
		150
Total profit		$30

The inclusion of general office overhead in the calculation of departmental profit would obscure the fact that Department C is being asked to make a contribution to total overhead (and profits) of $15 and is in fact making a contribution of $10. It would not pay to close down Department C if, as a direct consequence of this action, the total profits of the enterprise were to be increased (as they would be, for example, if the continued operation of Department C prevents some other more favourable profit opportunity from being exploited, or if general office overhead could be reduced by more than $10 as a result of the elimination of Department C).

A correctly presented departmental profit and loss statement, which shows the *departmental surplus* of each department and does not allocate indirect expenses to departments, is given in Table 13—3.

Table 13—3
Departmental Profit and Loss Statement

	Department A	Department B	Department C	Total
Sales	$200	$250	$150	$600
Less: Cost of sales	120	150	120	390
Gross profit on trading	80	100	30	210
Less: Direct expenses	40	50	20	110
Departmental surplus	$40	$50	$10	100
Less: General office expenses				60
Total profit				$40

There is a danger in carrying departmentalization of accounts too far. In general, only revenues, costs and expenses over which departmental managers have direct control should be analysed on a departmental basis. This policy may seem to be unduly restrictive in relation to some expenses, such as rentals and other occupancy expenses, which it might appear could reasonably be apportioned on some logical basis that has regard to the benefits accruing from the expense (e.g. in the case of occupancy expense, floor space occupied by each department). Frequently, however, such expenses may be converted into expenses that can be directly charged to individual departments; thus rates for given areas of floor space can be established by general management (in accordance with the total occupancy expenses of the enterprise), and departmental managers can be given the opportunity of indicating the amount of space they want at those rates. If the space allocated differs from the area sought, however, occupancy expenses cease to be controlled by the departmental manager and apportionment to departments can have the misleading results that have been discussed.

Branch Accounts

It has already been suggested that there is no clear dividing line between departmental accounts and branch accounts. The main distinction between departments and branches is a geographical one—branches are usually situated some distance from each other and from their head office, whereas departments are usually concentrated together in a single building or locality.

It does not follow, however, that different accounting methods are needed for the two types of organization, and in practice the departmental accounting techniques that have been described in the preceding section may be adapted for use in a branch undertaking. They are particularly likely to be relevant to the problem of branch accounting when the branches are subject to a good deal of direction and control by the head office, and where it is desired to maintain all the branch accounting records in the head office books. Under these circumstances, it is merely necessary to see that the head office books contain such separate accounts (or separate columns in accounts) for each branch as are necessary to derive branch profit and loss figures and to maintain a record of branch assets and liabilities. Transfers of assets, such as cash and inventories, between head office and branches are recorded by means of appropriate entries in the respective head office and branch asset accounts. Other transactions may be recorded by one or a combination of the techniques described in the previous section. The main problem in branch accounting is likely to be the collection and transmission of transaction data from the branches, as a first step in the establishment of the accounting record.

When a branch is not only physically separated from its head office but is allowed to operate as an autonomous managerial unit, it is likely that both the branch and the head office will maintain separate accounting systems. Such systems, while they may incorporate familiar techniques such as control accounts and consolidations, are essentially different from other systems that have been illustrated and it is these that will be distinguished by the term branch accounting.

The essential feature of branch accounting, then, is that separate ledgers are maintained for each of the branches and for the head office. The head office ledger is linked with each branch ledger by means of a current account, which in this context is somewhat analogous to a control account. Thus all transactions between the head office and a particular branch are recorded both in the branch current account in the head office ledger, and in the head office current account in the branch ledger. The balance of the former account represents, at any point of time, the net investment in the branch; while in the branch books the balance of the head office current account represents the funds that have been made available by head office. From the point of view of the branch, the head office current account takes the place of the capital account of a non-branch organization. If allowance is made for timing (transactions may be recorded at different dates in the two sets of books), it is apparent that the head office current account in the branch ledger is essentially a mirror image of the branch current account in the head office ledger. The branch accounting technique may be illustrated by reference to a simple example.

Example: Suppose that a retail trading business consisting of a head office and a single branch is established on 1 January 1985, with a capital of $5 000. On the same day, $1 500 cash is remitted to the branch and used to finance branch operations. The branch spends $1 000, and the head office $1 200, on shop fittings and other fixed capital assets, and during the year the following transactions occur (for the sake of simplicity it is assumed that all the transactions with outside parties are cash transactions):

	Head Office	Branch
Purchases of trading inventories	$2 000	$1 500
Goods sent to branch	600	
Goods received by branch		550
Sales (at selling price)	1 750	2 950
Sales (at cost)	1 220	1 850
Expenses	250	500
Cash remitted to (and received by) head office	1 000	1 000
Closing inventories	180	200
Depreciation on fixed capital assets (10% p.a. on cost)	120	100

In the Head Office Books

In the head office ledger the record of these transactions takes the following form:

Head Office Ledger

Proprietorship Capital

		Bank	$5 000

Bank

Proprietorship capital	$5 000	Branch current account	$1 500
Sales	1 750	Fixed capital assets	1 200
Branch current account	1 000	Purchases	2 000
		Expenses	250
		Balance c/d	2 800
	$7 750		$7 750
Balance b/d	$2 800		

Inventory

Purchases	$2 000	Goods sent to branch	$600
		Cost of sales	1 220
		Balance c/d	180
	$2 000		$2 000
Balance b/d	$180		

Branch Current Account

Bank	$1 500	Bank	$1 000
Goods sent to branch	600	Balance c/d	1 600
General profit and loss account	500		
	$2 600		$2 600
Balance b/d	$1 600		

Fixed Capital Assets

Bank	$1 200		

Provision for Depreciation on Fixed Capital Assets

	Depreciation on fixed capital assets	$120

Sales

Trading account	$1 750	Bank	$1 750

Goods Sent to Branch

Inventory	$600	Branch current account	$600

Purchases

Bank	$2 000	Inventory	$2 000

Expenses

Bank	$250	Head office profit and loss account	$250

Depreciation on Fixed Capital Assets

Provision for depreciation on fixed capital assets	$120	Head office profit and loss account	$120

Cost of Sales

Inventory	$1 220	Trading account	$1 220

Trading

Cost of sales	$1 220	Sales	$1 750
Head office profit and loss account (head office gross profit)	530		
	$1 750		$1 750

Head Office Profit and Loss

Expenses	$250	Trading account (gross profit)	$530
Depreciation on fixed capital assets	120		
General profit and loss account (head office profit)	160		
	$530		$530

General Profit and Loss

Balance c/d	$660	Branch current account (branch profit)	$500
		Head office profit and loss account (head office profit)	160
	$660		$660
		Balance b/d	$660

It will be observed that the branch current account is:

(a) debited with cash and other assets sent to the branch, and credited with cash and other assets returned from the branch; and

(b) debited with the profit earned by the branch on its operations for the year (the amount of which, as will shortly be observed, is calculated in the branch ledger).

The profit earned by the branch, to the extent that it is not withdrawn by the head office in the form of cash remittances, is matched by a build-up of branch assets, and represents additional investment by the head office in the branch (or, from the branch viewpoint, additional funds made available by head office). At the end of the year the net investment in the branch, as shown by the balance of the branch current account, is $1 600. This figure reflects the following transactions:

Investment in branch	
Cash remittances to branch	$1 500
Goods sent to branch	600
Profit on branch operations	500
	2 600
Less: **Disinvestment**	
Cash remittances from branch	1 000
Net investment in branch	$1 600

Corresponding to the debit entry in the branch current account is a credit entry recording the branch profit of $500 in the general profit and loss account. Normal accounting procedures are used to record head office trading transactions and to calculate the profit resulting therefrom, and the balance of head office profit is transferred to the general profit and loss account, which in practice also records indirect or overhead expenses incurred for the benefit of the whole organization and therefore not directly attributable to either of the component parts.

In the Books of the Branch

In the branch ledger, the head office current account, serving as a kind of capital account, records the funds made available to the branch by means of:

(a) credit entries in respect of cash and other assets supplied by the head office, and debit entries in respect of cash and other assets sent back to head office; and

(b) a credit entry in respect of the profit earned by the branch, which has the effect of increasing the financial obligation of the branch to the head office. Other transactions are recorded in the usual way:

Branch Ledger

Head Office Current Account

Bank	$1 000	Bank	$1 500
Balance c/d	1 550	Goods received from head office	550
		Profit and loss account (branch profit)	500
	$2 550		$2 550
		Balance b/d	$1 550

Bank

Head office current account	$1 500	Fixed capital assets	$1 000
Sales	2 950	Purchases	1 500
		Expenses	500
		Head office current account	1 000
		Balance c/d	450
	$4 450		$4 450
Balance b/d	$450		

Inventory

Purchases	$1 500	Cost of sales	$1 850
Goods received from head office	550	Balance c/d	200
	$2 050		$2 050
Balance b/d	$200		

Fixed Capital Assets

Bank	$1 000	

Provision for Depreciation on Fixed Capital Assets

	Depreciation on fixed capital assets	$100

Sales

Trading account	$2 950	Bank	$2 950

Purchases

Bank	$1 500	Inventory	$1 500

Goods Received from Head Office

Head office current account	$550	Inventory	$550

Expenses

Bank	$500	Profit and loss account	$500

Depreciation on Fixed Capital Assets

Provision for depreciation on fixed capital assets	$100	Profit and loss account	$100

Cost of Sales

Inventory	$1 850	Trading account	$1 850

Trading

Cost of sales	$1 850	Sales	$2 950
Profit and loss account			
(gross profit)	1 100		
	$2 950		$2 950

Profit and Loss

Expenses	$500	Trading account (gross profit)	$1 100
Depreciation on fixed capital assets	100		
Head office current account			
(branch profit)	500		
	$1 100		$1 100

It will be observed that the balance in the head office current account in the branch ledger is $1 550, compared with a balance of $1 600 in the branch current account in the head office ledger. The difference is due to the fact that goods to the value of $50 sent to the branch by head office have not yet been received by the branch, i.e. they are still in transit at the end of the accounting period. This means that, from the head office viewpoint, investment in the branch is $50 greater than head office has been given credit for in the branch books. The difference is accounted for when the two sets of results are brought together to form consolidated accounting reports in the manner that will now be illustrated.

Consolidation of Branch Accounts

Because the head office and branch ledgers are maintained independently of each other, the double-entry accounting records do not automatically produce aggregate profit and loss or balance sheet figures for the whole organization. In the head office ledger the various assets (and liabilities, if any) of the branch are reflected by only one figure, the balance of the branch current account, and the net branch profit is the only profit and loss item brought into the head office books. In order to obtain aggregate figures it is necessary to make use of the consolidation technique described in Chapter 12. The information contained in the head office and branch profit and loss accounts, and the balances of the asset and other accounts which remain open in the two ledgers after the preparation of the profit and loss accounts, may be recorded and consolidated as in Table 13—4.

When the balance of the head office current account in the branch ledger is offset against the balance of the branch current account in the head office ledger, a balance of $50 is left in the latter account. This is recorded as inventory in transit in the consolidated statement.

Accounting reports may now be drawn up on the basis of the information contained in the consolidation columns of the worksheet (see Table 13—5).

Different methods of accounting for branches are sometimes employed, involving the incorporation of the whole of the branch trial balance in the head office ledger, or the maintenance of all branch fixed asset accounts in the head office ledger. These

Table 13—4
Consolidation Worksheet—Branch Accounts

	Head Office Dr.	Head Office Cr.	Branch Dr.	Branch Cr.	Eliminations Dr.	Eliminations Cr.	Consolidation Dr.	Consolidation Cr.
Profit and loss statement								
Sales		$1 750		$2 950				$4 700
Cost of sales	$1 220		$1 850				$3 070	
Gross profit c/d	530		1 100				1 630	
	$1 750	$1 750	$2 950	$2 950			$4 700	$4 700
Gross profit b/d		530		1 100				1 630
Expenses	250		500				750	
Depreciation	120		100				220	
Net profit	160		500				660	
	$530	$530	$1 100	$1 100			$1 630	$1 630
Balance sheet								
Proprietorship capital		5 000						5 000
General profit and loss account		660						660
Bank	2 800		450				3 250	
Inventory	180		200				380	
Branch current account	1 600					$1 550	50*	
Fixed capital assets	1 200		1 000				2 200	
Provision for depreciation on fixed capital assets		120		100				220
Head office current account				1 550	$1 550			
	$5 780	$5 780	$1 650	$1 650	$1 550	$1 550	$5 880	$5 880

* Inventory in transit in consolidated statement.

produce the same results as the method used in the foregoing illustration, but they are considerably more complicated to operate and tend to defeat the purpose of granting local managerial autonomy to the branch.

Table 13—5
Consolidated Accounting Reports—Branch Accounts

... Trading Company—Head Office and Branch Consolidated Profit and Loss Statement for Year Ended ...

Sales		$4 700
Less: Cost of sales		3 070
Gross profit		1 630
Less: Expenses	$750	
Depreciation	220	
		970
Net profit		$660

... Trading Company—Head Office and Branch Consolidated Balance Sheet as at ...

Assets		
Bank		$3 250
Inventory (in store)		380
Inventory (in transit)		50
Fixed capital assets	$2 200	
Less: Provision for depreciation	220	
		1 980
Proprietorship equity		
Capital	5 000	
Profit and loss account	660	
		$5 660

Foreign Branches or Subsidiaries—Currency Translation

Branches that are established in foreign countries are likely to have a large degree of independence in their operations, maintain independent accounting systems and publish their own financial statements. In these respects they are akin to subsidiary companies. For consolidation purposes it is necessary to translate the figures in the branch profit and loss statement and the balance sheet into the currency used by the head office. Where there has been a change (or changes) in the exchange rates ruling at two successive balance dates, there will be a 'gain or loss on currency translation' in the financial statements of the branch after translation. This difference may be treated as an operating item (abnormal item, if large) or an extraordinary item (if there has been a 'currency realignment', i.e. a major movement in the exchange rate) in the consolidated profit and loss statement.[1] The size of the gain or loss will depend in part on the currency translation method selected. Four alternative translation methods are displayed in Figure 13—A, which greatly oversimplifies the complex variety of translation methods encountered in practice. There is little consensus among accountants on the appropriate currency translation method to employ.

[1]   See Chapter 11 for the definition of abnormal items and extraordinary items according to professional accounting standards in Australia.

Figure 13—A
Four Alternative Currency Translation Methods

	Translation Rate Criterion	Historic Rate as at Date of Transaction	Current (i.e. Closing) Rate	Current (i.e. Closing) or Current Average-of-Year Rate	Acceptance by Professional Bodies
Historical method (1)	Current/non-current				American Institute of Certified Public Accountants
Current assets and liabilities			✓		Institute of Chartered Accountants in England and Wales
Non-current assets and liabilities		✓			
Either All revenue items		✓			
Or Depreciation		✓			
Other revenue items				✓	
Historical method (2)	Monetary/non-monetary				National Association of Accountants (U.S.A.)
Monetary assets and liabilities			✓		
Non-monetary assets and liabilities		✓			
Either All revenue items		✓			
Or Depreciation		✓			
Other revenue items				✓	
'Temporal' method	Temporal characteristics of measurement				Financial Accounting Standards Board *Statement No. 8.* (U.S.A.)
Money, receivables and payables			✓		
Assets and liabilities measured at current prices			✓		
Assets and liabilities measured at historical cost		✓			
Revenue items measured at current prices				✓	
Revenue items measured at historical cost		✓			
Closing-rate method	End-of-period rate				Australian Society of Accountants
Balance sheet items			✓		Institute of Chartered Accountants in Australia
Revenue items			✓	✓	Institute of Chartered Accountants in England and Wales etc.

In historical method (1), current assets and liabilities are translated at the current rate as at the date of the balance sheet, while non-current assets and liabilities are translated at the historic rate as at the time the asset was acquired or the liability incurred. Historical method (2) is basically similar, except that it substitutes a monetary/non-monetary classification criterion for the current/non-current classification criterion of the first method. In both of the historical methods, the profit and loss items may be translated at their historic rates. Where there have not been any significant fluctuations in the exchange rate in the year, an alternative treatment is often used for convenience. This involves translating the depreciation expense only at the historic rate in effect at the time the fixed asset was acquired, and translating all other revenue items at the single current, or average-of-year, rate.

The so-called 'temporal' method may be considered a logical extension of the monetary/non-monetary method. Translation is defined as a measurement scale adjustment process analogous to general price-level restatement (described in Chapter 18). Translation is treated as the conversion of financial statements expressed in one measurement scale (i.e. the foreign currency) into statements expressed in a different measurement scale (i.e. the domestic currency). It is not proposed to examine the arguments underlying this approach. A serious deficiency which it shares with the historical methods is illustrated below.

A disadvantage of the methods which employ historic exchange rates (i.e. the two historical methods and the temporal method) is that the translation process may transform a profit in the branch account into a loss (or vice-versa), as in the following simple example:

	Foreign Currency Units	Conversion Factor	Head Office Currency Units
Sales	1 000	1 : 1	1 000
Less: Cost of sales	(600)	1 : 1	(600)
Depreciation	(400)	2 : 1	(200)
Other expenses	(150)	1 : 1	(150)
Profit (loss)	(150)		50

Note: Debit items are shown in parentheses

The closing-rate method translates all items in the balance sheet and profit and loss statement at the single current rate in effect at the date of the balance sheet. Although the closing-rate method represents a departure from strict historical record accounting, it is a widely adopted method in Australia and the U.K., and its use in these countries is likely to become mandatory. It is simple, and free of the disadvantages from employing historic exchange rates explained above. Further, since a single conversion factor is applied to all items, relations between magnitudes in the financial statements (i.e. financial ratios) have the same values before and after translation.

However, one may question the usefulness of translating the financial statements of foreign branches or subsidiaries into the currency used by the head office at all. The main reason given for currency translation is that it is necessary for consolidation purposes. But often the foreign branch or subsidiary operates under very different political, economic and legal environments from those of the head office, and possibly different accounting and reporting standards as well. In addition there may well be restrictions on the transfer of funds between the two countries. Under these conditions it is doubtful whether consolidation of the two sets of financial statements produces meaningful results.

In order to evaluate the profitability and financial condition of the foreign branch, management may look at a number of key ratios (see Chapter 7) based on the financial statements and other information relating to the branch. The shareholders of the parent company also will be interested in the success or otherwise of its foreign-based operations. A useful indicator of performance is the rate of return achieved by the branch, which must be evaluated against the expected return from that particular foreign investment. An order of magnitude of branch operations in terms of the domestic currency may be obtained by translating branch sales and net assets at the end-of-period exchange rate, but other indexes which do not require currency translation may also be relevant, such as sales in physical units (this assumes homogeneity of units sold) and number of employees. The overall rate of return of the head office and the branch taken together can then be obtained, if desired, as a weighted average of the head office rate of return and the branch rate of return, where the weights represent the relative size, in terms of, say, sales in physical units, of the head office and the branch.

Discussion Questions

1 (a) What are the main purposes for which departmental accounts are prepared?

(b) Distinguish between different kinds of departmental accounting systems in relation to their applicability to different kinds of business organization.

2 In assessing the performance of departmental managers, to what extent is allocated head office overhead relevant? Discuss.

3 'For accounting purposes, it is not necessary to distinguish between departmental and branch forms of organization.' Contrast the conditions under which so-called departmental and branch accounting systems may be effectively employed in a divisionalized business.

4 What is the purpose of consolidation in branch accounting?
What are the main problems encountered in relation to consolidation of divisional accounting reports?

5 How is a firm's investment in a branch determined in a branch accounting system? Illustrate your answer by reference to the main kinds of transactions which take place between the head office and branch.

6 Critically examine the valuation assumptions underlying conventional methods of converting foreign branch balance sheets for consolidation purposes.

Exercises

1 Adam Smith, trading as Mitre Four Stores, conducts a local hardware business in four departments—Plumbers' Supplies, Builders' Supplies, General and Gardening. Trading figures for the 12 months ended 30 June 1985 were as follows:

	1 Plumbers' Supplies	2 Builders' Supplies	3 General	4 Gardening
Opening inventory	$15 270	$14 630	$8 170	$5 670
Purchases	48 750	66 870	22 500	16 700
Sales	70 700	105 600	35 750	25 600
Cost of goods sold	45 370	71 940	20 470	15 810
Closing inventory	18 650	9 560	10 200	6 560
Wages	9 750	17 850	4 780	5 600
Other expenses	1 500	2 120	1 150	1 050

You are required to record the above transactions in a system of columnar ledger accounts and prepare an income statement for the business as a whole for the period.

2 Record the transactions listed in Exercise 1, above, in a system of departmental control accounts.

3 The Vogue Fashion Shop operates three departments—Sports Clothes, Evening Clothes and Accessories. You are required to record the summarized transactions listed below in a system of columnar ledger accounts:

	Sports Clothes	Evening Clothes	Accesories
Sales	$16 000	$28 000	$12 000
Purchases	11 000	20 000	8 000
Opening inventory	2 200	5 200	1 200
Closing inventory	2 000	3 600	1 100
Wages	2 500	3 400	1 200
Office expenses	1 700	1 900	500

4 (a) I. Shore carries on a retail business, which has four departments, A,B,C and D. From the information set out below, prepare a departmental income statement for the year ended 31 December 1985. Show departmental surpluses and net profits. Discuss the usefulness of these revenue measures.

	Dept. A	Dept. B	Dept. C	Dept. D
Opening inventory	$8 000	$16 000	$40 000	$36 000
Purchases	16 000	40 000	40 000	48 000
Sales	30 000	50 000	70 000	50 000
Closing inventory	10 000	26 000	32 000	52 000
Departmental salaries and wages	7 000	8 000	9 000	12 000

Insurance of $1 440 is to be allocated to the departments in proportion to the closing inventories. Rent of $8 000 and lighting and heating of $700 are to be allocated in proportion to floor space: A, 10 per cent; B, 20 per cent; C, 30 per cent; and D, 40 per cent.

(b) State the advantages and disadvantages of allocating indirect expenses to departments.

5 A. Penny, proprietor of Pennywise Trading Co., operates a wholesale business with three departments, A,B and C. The income statement given below has been prepared to show the results of trading for the year ended 30 June 1985.

Income Statement for the Year Ended 30 June 1985

	Dept. A		Dept. B		Dept. C	
Sales		$84 000		$72 000		$60 000
Less: Cost of sales		34 460		35 150		27 660
Gross profit		49 540		36 850		32 340
Less: Expenses						
Direct departmental expenses	$15 140		$12 220		$20 140	
Occupancy expenses	5 750		3 450		4 600	
Office expenses	10 500		9 000		7 500	
General expenses	6 300	37 690	5 400	30 070	4 500	36 740
Net profit (loss)		$11 850		$6 780		($4 400)

Occupancy expenses have been apportioned to departments on the basis of floor space and the allocation of area to departments cannot be improved. Office expenses have been apportioned according to department sales. If Department C was closed there would be an approximate annual saving in office expenses of $4 500.

A. Penny is considering two possible courses of action:

    (a) to continue existing operations; or

    (b) to close Department C and let the area occupied by this department to other firms for an annual rental of $2 000.

Show by means of projected income statements which course of action would be more profitable.

6 Norman and Lindsay Art Products consists of a head office in Sydney and a branch in Melbourne. Assets at the branch on 1 July 1985 were:

Fixtures and fittings	$9 000
Inventory	19 000
Accounts receivable	4 900
Cash at bank	7 500

During the year ended 30 June, 1986, the following transactions were recorded by the branch:

Cash sales	$170 000
Credit sales	50 000
Returns from customers	1 500
Cash received from customers	44 000
Goods received from head office	123 500
Goods returned to head office	850
Cash remitted to (and received by) head office	147 750
Cash purchases	4 200
Cash expenses	58 700
Inventory on hand at end of period	17 500

Depreciation of 10 per cent is to be provided on fixtures and fittings.

Show how these transactions would be recorded in the branch ledger and the branch current account in the head office ledger.

7 The Superdeal Trading Co. has established an overseas branch in Hong Kong. The following is a trial balance of its overseas branch for the year ended 30 June 1985 in Hong Kong dollars.

Head office account, 1 July 1984		$35 000
Accounts receivable	$17 570	
Accounts payable		4 500
Fixtures and fittings	5 700	
Inventory, 1 July 1984	5 400	
Purchases	20 200	
Sales		36 780
Wages and salaries	5 530	
Insurance	430	
Cash at bank	4 600	
Remittances to head office	16 850	
	$76 280	$76 280

The inventory at 30 June 1985 is valued at HK$6 780. The closing rate of exchange is: $1 (Australian) = $5.25 (Hong Kong). In the books of the head office in Sydney, the overseas branch account had a balance on 1 July 1984 of $7 120 and remittances from branch to head office for the year totalled $3 020 (in Australian dollars).

You are required to prepare the trading and profit and loss accounts of the branch in the books of the head office, using the closing-rate method of translation.

14 Public Authorities

The Conventional Basis of Accounting for Public Authorities

Accounting for a government or public authority poses special problems. The financial objectives of public authorities are usually different from those of business enterprises. Governments are concerned with methods of financing the collective services they provide, and do not seek to make profits. In democratic countries they are subject to various legal and political restraints, designed to make the governments accountable to elected parliaments in respect of their financial activities and to give the parliaments ultimate power to control those activities.

At the beginning of each financial year a government commonly has to submit to parliament for approval its financial plan (or budget) outlining its expenditure estimates for the year and the ways and means by which it is proposed to finance the expenditure. If parliament approves the plan it appropriates funds for the purposes requested by the government, and the latter's subsequent activities must be confined within the limits of those appropriations. At the end of the year unexpended appropriations lapse, and the government must seek fresh parliamentary approval for further expenditure.

The different financial objectives of governments and their need to account to parliaments have combined to differentiate their accounting procedures from those used in business accounting in a number of important respects. Only in their business undertakings do governments usually adopt commercial accounting procedures.

Fund Classification

The first point of difference between government accounting and business accounting is one of classification. The finance which parliament makes available to the government is usually classified in accordance with the sources from which it is derived, and the government's economic transactions are then all grouped on the basis of these different sources of funds. Three main sources of funds are usually distinguished. The main working fund, which is financed by taxation, fees and other current receipts, is called the consolidated revenue fund. A second fund, which is financed by borrowing, is called the loan fund; and the third, which depends partly on appropriations made by parliament for specific purposes and partly on receipts which the government handles in a trustee capacity, is called the trust fund.

Superimposed on the fund basis of classification is a departmental division, so that the government's transactions are also classified in terms of administrative responsibility. As noted below, the classification process may be carried further by means of functional, economic or program groupings, but such groupings until recently have been given a minor role in government accounting. Traditionally, government accounting has been concerned with recording the nature of government transactions rather than their purpose, and with the recording of inputs into programs and activities rather than their outputs.

It should be emphasized, perhaps, that recording transactions on the basis of funds is more than a method of classification; it involves the use of a different system of accounting from the one that has so far been described in this book. Not only is the government as a whole allotted separate funds for which it has to account to parliament; within the executive branch of government each department is allotted funds which it must spend in accordance with the appropriations which parliament has approved. These funds are significantly different from the proprietorship funds of a business enterprise. The latter are in the nature of permanent capital funds which are used to finance the purchase of operating assets and provide working capital, and which are automatically replenished as a result of the operations of the business and used again. The funds which parliament makes available to the government are in the nature of temporary, self-liquidating funds, which the government is required to disburse within a set period in accordance with the stated purposes approved by parliament. Only the trading activities of government involve the establishment of capital funds that are analogous to the proprietorship funds of business enterprises.

The use of the fund basis of accounting by governments not only implies a lack of continuity in the transactions being recorded, but also imparts in practice a certain lack of comprehensiveness or unity to the accounting structure. The accounting unit becomes, in effect, not the government as a whole but the particular section of government which can be identified as coming within the ambit of a fund. The fund assumes the role of the accounting entity. It will be seen below that the use of a single cash account can exert a unifying influence over the government's accounts, and the application of consolidation techniques can integrate the accounts of the different funds and permit the presentation of a comprehensive statement covering the whole of the government's financial activities. Traditionally, however, the government's accounts have been maintained in a fragmentary form.

Cash Basis of Accounting

The lack of continuity and lack of comprehensiveness, to which reference has just been made, constitute important differences between the assumptions underlying government accounting and those on which business accounting procedures are based. There is, however, an even more important difference between the two systems, and this stems partly from the divergence in the fund concepts which each employs and partly from the absence of a profit measurement objective in government accounting. This difference lies in the conventional practice whereby governments record only those transactions involving cash. Transactions not involving cash, e.g. the purchase of goods on credit, are not recorded in government accounts, which do not take cognizance of the receipt of the goods until such time as a cash settlement is made. In terms of concepts that will now be familiar to the reader, government accounts merely record cash receipts and outlays, not revenue receivable and costs incurred.

The adoption of a cash basis of accounting does not preclude the use of double-entry procedures, but it does have several other consequences which further differentiate government accounting from business accounting. In the first place, the only assets recorded within the double-entry framework of a system of governmental cash accounts are cash and other assets which may best be described as near-cash, i.e. liquid investments held as substitutes for cash. It follows that the accumulated funds of government do not take acccount of other assets. Likewise, the only liabilities recorded are those which arise as a direct result of cash borrowing by the government, i.e. the cash loans which the government has received and which constitute the public debt.

In recording the government's cash receipts and payments, until recently no attempt has been made to distinguish between cost and revenue flows on the one hand and capital transactions on the other. Indeed such a distinction, implying as it does that transactions extending beyond the current accounting period need to be distinguished from those taking place within the period, is irrelevant for accounting purposes because of the assumption of non-continuity which, as has been seen, underlies fund accounting. Since expenditure on fixed capital assets does not result in the creation of asset accounts, it follows that depreciation is not recorded in the accounts. These factors, coupled with the absence of any record of changes in inventories and amounts receivable by, or payable to, the government, naturally limit the usefulness of the double-entry record as a measure of the government's financial activities. The cash basis of accounting also poses difficulties in integrating the accounts of business undertakings (maintained on a commercial basis) in the central government's accounts; and in marshalling accounting data for use in controlling the efficiency of government operations and formulating the government's economic policy. However, it will be seen that new forms of classification along functional and economic lines are now being introduced by many governments with a view to overcoming or alleviating these limitations.

An Illustration

The foregoing description of conventional practice may be illustrated and expanded by reference to a hypothetical example. The example, while it is directed to the particular problem of government accounting, illustrates the technique of accounting on a cash basis which has applications outside the government sphere (e.g. in relation to trusts) and which may be contrasted with the 'accrual' basis of accounting normally adopted by business enterprises.

Suppose that a government which maintains its accounts on a cash basis in three separate funds—consolidated revenue fund, loan fund and trust fund—commences the financial year 1985 with the following balances:

	Dr.	Cr.
Loan fund		
Accumulated expenditure from loan fund	$4 950	
Cash balances	50	
Public debt		$5 000
	$5 000	$5 000
Trust fund		
Cash balances	100	
Investments	400	
Trust fund		500
	$500	$500

During the year it engages in the following transactions:

Consolidated revenue fund. Tax collections amount to $1 200 and receipts from business undertakings are $500. Payments are made by departments for administrative purposes ($800), by business undertakings ($400), on cash social service benefits, i.e. pensions, hospital benefits, etc. ($200), and on interest payable on the public debt ($200). The surplus or deficit on the fund's operations for the year is to be transferred to the trust fund, which may be regarded for this purpose as a kind of equalization account analogous to the appropriation account of a partnership or company. One of the individual trust funds that is usually established by governments is a public debt redemption or sinking fund, and a consolidated revenue surplus may be transferred to the credit of that fund and used for purposes of debt redemption. Alternatively, the consolidated revenue fund surplus or deficit may be transferred to the loan fund and used directly for debt redemption (if a surplus) or financed by borrowing (if a deficit). In the example, it is assumed that the former course is followed.

Loan fund. Proceeds from the issue of new securities amount to $800, of which the sum of $200 is used to redeem existing securities. The further redemption of securities is made possible by the transfer of $100 from the trust fund (the public debt redemption fund). Works expenditure financed from the loan fund amounts to $625.

Trust fund. In addition to the consolidated revenue surplus or deficit and the debt redemption transfer to the loan fund, the trust fund receives interest on investments ($20), purchases new investments ($50) and spends $50 on approved trust fund purposes.

These transactions are recorded in the ledgers of the three funds as shown below. First, consolidated revenue fund transactions will be recorded in the following accounts:

Consolidated Revenue Fund Ledger

Cash

Taxation	$1 200	Departmental expenditure	$800
Business undertakings—receipts	500	Business undertakings—payments	400
		Cash social service payments	200
		Public debt interest	200
		Transfer to trust fund	100
	$1 700		$1 700

Taxation

Revenue and expenditure account	$1 200	Cash receipts	$1 200

Business Undertakings

Cash payments	$400	Cash receipts	$500
Revenue and expenditure account —surplus	100		
	$500		$500

Departmental Expenditure

Cash payments	$800	Revenue and expenditure account	$800

Cash Social Service Payments

Cash payments	$200	Revenue and expenditure account	$200

Public Debt Interest

Cash payments	$200	Revenue and expenditure account	$200

Trust Fund

Cash payments	$100	Revenue and expenditure account —consolidated revenue fund surplus	$100

Revenue and Expenditure

Departmental expenditure	$800	Taxation	$1 200
Cash social service payments	200	Business undertakings—surplus	100
Public debt interest paid	200		
Surplus (transferred to trust fund)	100		
	$1 300		$1 300

It will be observed that the double entry is complete within the consolidated revenue fund ledger. The balances of the accounts created as a result of the various cash receipts and payments are transferred to the revenue and expenditure account, which fulfils the same function in the system as the profit and loss account in a business enterprise. Only the net cash results of business undertakings need to be transferred to the summary account, and the overall surplus in the revenue and expenditure account is disposed of by means of a cash transfer to the trust fund. As a result of this action, all the resources that have been accumulated by the consolidated revenue fund during the year have been disbursed and, since no assets or liabilities remain, the ledger accounts are all closed.

The loan fund ledger will take the following form:

Loan Fund Ledger

Cash

Balance b/d	$50	Public debt—redemption	$300
Public debt—proceeds of new issues	800	Loan fund expenditure on goods and services (works)	625
Transfer from trust fund	100	Balance c/d	25
	$950		$950
Balance b/d	$25		

Loan Fund Expenditure

Balance b/d	$4 950	Transfer from trust fund	$100
Cash payments	625	Balance c/d	5 475
	$5 575		$5 575
Balance b/d	$5 475		

Trust Fund

Loan fund expenditure	$100	Cash receipts	$100

Public Debt

Cash payments—redemption	$300	Balance b/d	$5 000
Balance c/d	5 500	Cash receipts—borrowing	800
	$5 800		$5 800
		Balance b/d	$5 500

The loan fund ledger records changes in public indebtedness resulting from new borrowing and debt redemption. The loan fund expenditure account is, in effect, a balancing account which records the total amount spent from the loan fund; in practice it may be sub-divided into several accounts indicating the purposes of the expenditure, e.g. war, works and services and consolidated revenue deficit finance. The effect of the cash transfer from the public debt redemption fund in the trust fund is to provide the loan fund with cash resources which are used to redeem securities and thereby reduce the public debt. The balance of the trust fund account in the loan fund ledger (which is credited with the amount of the cash transfer) is transferred to the loan fund expenditure account, thereby reducing the balance of the latter account. This recognizes, in effect, that an expenditure of $100, which was previously recorded as having been financed from the loan fund, is now regarded as having been financed from the trust fund. The public debt at the end of the period, $5 500, is then represented by $25 cash and $5 475 accumulated expenditure from the loan fund. Because the loan fund records only changes in assets and liabilities, no revenue and expenditure account is needed.

The trust fund ledger will record transactions as follows:

Trust Fund Ledger

Cash

Balance b/d	$100	Investments	$50
Transfer from consolidated		Transfer to loan fund	100
revenue fund	100	Other trust fund payments	50
Interest on investments	20	Balance c/d	20
	$220		$220
Balance b/d	$20		

Consolidated Revenue Fund

Revenue and expenditure account	$100	Cash receipts	$100

Interest on Investments

Revenue and expenditure account	$20	Cash receipts	$20

Investments

Balance b/d	$400	Balance c/d	$450
Cash payments	50		
	$450		$450
Balance b/d	$450		

Loan Fund

Cash payments	$100	Revenue and expenditure account	$100

Other Trust Fund Payments

Cash payments	50	Revenue and expenditure account	$50

Revenue and Expenditure

Transfer to loan fund	$100	Consolidated revenue surplus	$100
Other trust fund payments	50	Interest	20
		Deficit (transferred to accumulated trust fund)	30
	$150		$150

Trust Fund

Revenue and expenditure deficit	$30	Balance b/d	$500
Balance c/d	470		
	$500		$500
		Balance b/d	$470

In the trust fund ledger, the accumulated balance of the trust fund (representing the financial obligations of the government to those on behalf of whom it is acting as trustee) is matched at any time by assets in the form of cash and investments. Apart from the transaction relating to the purchase of investments (which is debited to the asset account, investments), cash receipts and payments (including transfers to or from other funds) are credited or debited to accounts which may subsequently be closed by transferring their balances to a revenue and expenditure account (which thus corresponds to the revenue and expenditure account in the consolidated revenue fund ledger). The revenue deficit is transferred to the debit of the trust fund account, the balance of which at the close of the period is again equal to the sum of the assets, cash ($20) and investments ($450).

In practice, as has already been indicated, a number of separate trust funds is likely to be required. Each trust is a separate accounting entity and, strictly speaking, should be represented by its own system of accounts. For the same reason it is somewhat artificial to construct, as has been done, a single trust fund revenue and expenditure account. If, however, the government is to be placed in a position to measure the overall economic effect of its financial operations, some such summary of trust fund activities must be regarded as essential. More emphasis may be placed on the activities of the individual trust funds, without disintegrating the accounting structure, by using the control account technique described in Chapter 2 and recording the transactions of the individual trust funds in a subsidiary trust fund ledger.

Integration of Fund Accounts

In the foregoing example, it has been assumed that the government maintains three separate double entry systems of accounting, one for each fund. In practice some integration of these accounting systems is usually achieved by passing all cash transactions, irrespective of the fund they affect, through a single bank account, known as the public account. All government receipts are paid into this account and all payments (having been duly authorized by a representative of parliament, such as the auditor-general, as falling within the parliamentary appropriations) are made therefrom. Separate appropriation ledgers are kept outside the double-entry system to maintain a running record of expenditure against appropriations.

Where there is only one cash account, it is possible to construct a simplified double-entry framework consisting of accounts for cash, for each of the three main funds (consolidated revenue, loan and trust funds) and for any other assets and liabilities which it is desired to record in the system (investments and public debt in the above example). Consolidated revenue receipts such as taxation are then debited to cash and credited to the consolidated revenue fund account; proceeds of loans are debited to cash and credited to the loan fund account; and so on. To obtain a break-down of the transactions affecting each fund, it is necessary to make use of the control account technique whereby each of the fund accounts in the double-entry system becomes a summary account controlling a subsidiary ledger, in which are recorded the fund's transactions in detail.

As a means of providing information useful to government in maintaining efficient control over its operations and formulating policy, this kind of integration is by no means adequate. New developments are now taking place in government budgeting, accounting and auditing with a view to ensuring that budgetary accounts are better suited to the task of providing information needed for purposes of controlling efficiency in government activities and facilitating public sector decision making.

Limitations of Conventional Methods of Government Accounting

The limitations of conventional methods of government accounting stem from their almost exclusive concern with the problem of establishing the accountability of the executive government to parliament, i.e. ensuring that parliament maintains effective control over funds raised and spent. Whilst government accounting has and must continue to have an important role to play in attesting to the integrity of the executive government's financial activities and the regularity of its transactions, a simple record of cash transactions does not provide the information needed to improve the government's performance with respect to managerial efficiency, cost effectiveness, program evaluation and review, or economic management. The processes of government accounting have been described as being hardly superior in technique and usefulness to those of a simple cash book.

In the first place, the conventional system of government accounting has proved quite inadequate and unsuitable as a means of accounting for public authority business undertakings. On the one hand, the incorporation of the accounts of trading activities in the budgetary framework of cash accounts has destroyed the logic and simplicity of government accounting as a system for reporting on parliamentary appropriations and the stewardship of the executive government; on the other, the cash accounts have failed to provide the information needed to manage, or to evaluate the performance of those responsible for managing, the business activities in question.

Secondly, by emphasizing the nature of the inputs into government activities rather than the purpose of those activities, conventional methods of government accounting have failed to provide a rational basis for priority determination and review as essential elements of the budgetary process. Associated with this has been a third defect, namely the tendency for government budgets to be regarded merely as cash appropriations rather than as predetermined plans of performance, and for the accounting system to ignore the essential link between the costs of providing public goods and services and the benefits which flow from those goods and services. Government accounts have thus failed to provide the information needed for systematic program evaluation and review.

A fourth deficiency in government accounting has been its preoccupation with the short term, in that the record of transactions has usually been restricted to a single year, unexpended appropriations have lapsed at the end of the year and information about long-term plans, records and reports has not been incorporated into the conventional budgetary framework even where it exists.

Fifthly, the budgetary accounts have traditionally failed to provide information relevant to resource allocation, distribution and stabilization aspects of economic policy formulation. This means that there has been no distinction between resource-using and transfer activities, between recurrent and capital transactions, or between different kinds of financing transactions; so that it has been difficult to assess the fiscal and monetary impact of budgetary transactions on the economy.

Finally, there has been such a fragmentation of government accounting records and financial statements, even for a single unit of government, as to make it impossible to obtain a comprehensive overview of the activities of that government. This problem arises partly because of the fund basis of accounting (a particular problem has been the multiplicity of trust funds used by most governments), and partly because of the failure of governments to integrate the activities of many of their business undertakings into their summary financial statements. Usually no attempt has been made to present consolidated financial statements which record the transactions of trust funds along with those of consolidated revenue and loan funds, and which incorporate the results of those business activities which are carried on outside the framework of budget appropriations by independent public corporations.

Reforms in Government Accounting

During recent years, several important developments have been taking place which are having the effect of blunting these criticisms of government accounting and helping to improve its effectiveness as a managerial tool and a data base for purposes of economic policy decisions. These developments, which in no way weaken the effectiveness of government accounting in relation to its accountability function, include:

(a) the separation of the business activities of governments from the activities of general government, and the adoption of accrual accounting and other business accounting methods by the public enterprises so distinguished;

(b) the adoption of a system of functional classification in accounting for the transactions of general government;

(c) the delineation of programs and activities in such a way as to fix responsibility for performance and, by emphasizing the purpose of government expenditures and the relationship between inputs and outputs, to enable costs to be related to accomplishments;

(d) the extension of the time scale of government budgeting and accounting, so that transactions are not necessarily treated as having significance only for a single budget year and government activities are increasingly subjected to systematic forward planning;

(e) the introduction of an economic classification of transactions that is consistent with the national accounting classification for the public sector as a whole; and

(f) the consolidation of government accounts in such a way as to provide a comprehensive record of all public sector activities.

Public Enterprise Accounting

It is becoming increasingly recognized that, whatever the arguments for accounting for the administrative and spending activities of general government on a cash basis, all trading activities of public authorities need to be recorded, reported and evaluated by reference to accounts maintained in accordance with business accounting principles, i.e. on an accrual basis. Where trading enterprises remain in the so-called budget sub-sector and are therefore required to bring their cash receipts and payments into the fund/cash appropriation accounts of general government (as in the case of most Australian railway authorities), the adoption of commercial accounting necessitates the maintenance of a dual system.

Some of the more unsatisfactory features of these arrangements may be overcome by incorporating the net results of the trading operations of each government enterprise, along with net advances appropriated to the enterprise for capital purposes, in the accounts and financial statements of the central government as balancing cash transfers. The enterprise will then use its commercial accounts for managerial purposes and as a basis for financial reporting to the executive government and to parliament, in the same way as a business in the private sector.

The unnecessary waste and duplication involved in maintaining dual accounting records may be wholly avoided, and the accountability and managerial purposes of government accounting satisfactorily achieved, by removing government-operated enterprises from the budget sub-sector and incorporating them as statutory corporations or commissions, each of which then maintains its own accrual accounting system independently of the central government. There has been a long history of such public corporations in Australia, and recently the responsibility for the Australian Post Office was transferred from a public service department within the budget sub-sector to two statutory bodies—the Australian Postal Commission and the Australian Telecommunications Commission. The direct accounting links between such public enterprises and the budgetary accounts of the central government are then limited to transactions between the parties concerned in the form of advances, repayments of advances, interest, rent, dividends and taxes. To the extent that such bodies are required to make payments of company tax and dividends to the central government (as, for example, the Australian National Airlines Commission must do), their business and accounting activities are strictly analogous to those of companies in the private sector, except that their capital funds are provided by a government, usually in the form of advances, rather than by the issue of shares through the mechanism of the capital market.

Functional Classification

The Australian (Commonwealth) Government has recently adopted a functional classification of its budget sub-sector outlays with a view to indicating, in an aggregative or summary form, the extent to which financial resources are being devoted to the different objectives of government, and facilitating assessments of the effectiveness of outlays in meeting those objectives. The Australian functional classification is based on national accounting concepts and conventions which have been established in the United Nations publication, *A System of National Accounts*, and which also form the basis of the economic classification discussed below. The Australian Bureau of Statistics publishes what it calls a purpose classification of the outlays of other public authorities in the Australian public sector (the Commonwealth non-budget sub-sector, State authorities and local authorities); this is essentially the same as the classification adopted by the Commonwealth for its own budgetary purposes.

The adoption of the standard functional classification for a government's budgetary accounts means that its financial statements record transactions between the budget sub-sector and all other sectors of the economy. This has the effect of consolidating all transactions within the budget sub-sector, while eliminating by consolidation any transactions between the consolidated revenue fund, the loan fund and the trust fund. The fund classification thereby effectively disappears in the process of deriving the functional classification. As already observed, the activities of public enterprises operating outside the budget sub-sector are recorded only to the extent that they have an impact on the budget sub-sector.

Figure 14—A illustrates the functional grouping which was adopted by the Australian Government for purposes of its 1977-78 Budget.

Figure 14—A
Functional Classification of Australian Government Budget Outlays

1. Defence
2. Education
3. Health
4. Social security and welfare
5. Housing
6. Urban and regional development not elsewhere classified (nec) and the environment
7. Culture and recreation
8. Economic services—
    A. Transport and communication
    B. Water supply and electricity
    C. Industry assistance and development
    D. Labour and employment
    E. Other economic services
9. General public services—
    A. Legislative services
    B. Law, order and public safety
    C. Foreign affairs and overseas aid
    D. General and scientific research nec
    E. Administrative services
10. Not allocated to function—
    A. Payments to or for the States and local government authorities nec and natural disaster relief
    B. Public debt interest

Source: 1977-78 Budget Paper No. 1, *Budget Speech 1977-78*, Australian Government Publishing Service, Canberra, 1977, p. 39.

Planning-Programming-Budgeting Systems

The functional classification of government outlays has relevance to the processes of resource allocation, the determination of expenditure priorities and the evaluation of government performance in a broad sense, but because of its aggregative nature it has only limited significance with respect to the problems of achieving efficiency, effective policy formulation and responsibility for performance in government.

There have therefore been developed (initially in the U.S.A.) systems of budgeting, decision making and accounting known as planning-programming-budgeting systems (PPBS), the main purposes of which are to identify the objectives of specific programs and activities planned within the main functional groupings and, by relating the costs of programs and activities to their accomplishments, to indicate the extent to which those objectives are achieved. The term planning-programming-budgeting has come to be used to describe both the accounting and other data sources used for decision-making purposes and the decision processes themselves.

As originally conceived, the PPBS approach thus identified a number of distinct but inter-related phases in the budgeting, decision making and accounting cycle. First, program goals were to be specified, along with budgetary or other constraints affecting the choice of goals and the alternative means which were available for achieving the goals.

Secondly, the budgeting, appropriation and accounting system was to be structured in such a way as to facilitate decision making in the pursuit of the goals. This involved relating information about cost inputs associated with each program to the intended accomplishments or outputs of the program. This in turn required a classification of government revenues and expenditures along program lines, the development of measures or indicators of output or performance, and the extension of the time span of the planning and budgeting process so that the long-term impact of decisions would be recognized and taken into account.

The third phase of PPBS involved the establishment of decision criteria and the use of methods of analysis intended to choose the most effective means of achieving program goals. The most important of these analytical devices have come to be described as cost-benefit analysis (if the problem is one of maximizing net benefits, where both costs and accomplishments are variables) and cost-effectiveness analysis (if the problem is one of maximizing accomplishments from given resource inputs, or minimizing cost inputs in achieving given program goals). These techniques are very similar to the capital budgeting and other present value techniques used to facilitate decision making in the private sector (see Chapter 29), the main difference being the difficulty of measuring outputs or quantifying the benefits of public expenditures.

The final element in PPBS was concerned with management control and involved the evaluation of past performance. This implied a periodic review of costs actually incurred and results achieved in each program relative to budgeted or planned levels of cost and performance, and it was envisaged that for this purpose a program classification would be incorporated in the accounting system.

Although the PPBS approach was thus intended to provide a comprehensive and integrated system of parliamentary appropriations, accounting, financial reporting and management control by the executive government, there has been some retreat from this ambitious aim in the U.S.A. It now seems likely that governments in other countries, including Australia, will come to use PPBS mainly as a managerial and decision-making tool rather than as an inherent element in their budgetary appropriation and accounting systems. However, the PPBS approach has already had a significant effect on auditing arrangements in some countries. In the U.S.A., the Comptroller-General now has a tripartite role; in addition to his traditional concern with accountability, involving an audit of financial regularity and compliance with laws and regulations, he is now also responsible for reporting on efficiency and for undertaking program evaluations. In Australia, the Commonwealth and some States are moving towards an extension of the Auditor-General's role to embrace efficiency audits as well as accountability audits, but it seems likely that responsibility for program evaluations will be vested in an agency of the executive government.

Forward Planning

The use of forward planning techniques has been linked with the development of PPBS. Indeed, as has already been observed, forward budget estimates may be regarded as an essential element of PPBS. Although the introduction of forward planning has implications for the organization of a government's accounting system, its purpose is to improve the processes of resource allocation, financial co-ordination and control by both the legislative and executive branches of government.

The approach to forward planning which has been adopted by the U.K. Government involves the inclusion of rolling estimates of expenditure, covering the immediate past year, the current and the two following years for which the Government has already taken decisions (with the third of these years as the main focus year in which decisions are reviewed), and two further years representing merely projections of existing policies. Forward projections are likewise made in respect of receipts on the basis of projections of existing policies. The Australian Government is engaged in developing a system of forward estimates.

Economic Classification

In order to facilitate economic policy formulation and indicate the impact of government activities on the economy, government financial statements are now being presented in a form which classifies transactions in accordance with their economic significance.

Although economic classifications are based on data recorded in government accounts and financial statements, they are usually in the nature of statistical tabulations rather than accounting statements. The Australian Bureau of Statistics compiles annual economic classifications for all Australian public authorities. Like the functional classifications which are also published by the Bureau (see above), the economic classifications are based on the structure recommended in the U.N. publication *A System of National Accounts*. The Australian Government has also recently begun to publish an economic classification of budget outlays (or what it calls a classification in 'national accounts form') in a form which is consistent with the one used by the Australian Bureau of Statistics for public authorities generally.

The three main groups of transactions distinguished by the economic classification are: (a) transactions relating to the production or consumption of goods and services, i.e. activities involving real resources; (b) transfer payments; and (c) financing transactions. Superimposed on this tripartite classification is a further distinction between recurrent and capital transactions, and a sectoral classification (which distinguishes the other sectors of the economy involved in particular transactions).

The economic classification of outlays which has been used in recent Australian Government Budget Papers is illustrated in Figure 14—B.

Figure 14—B
Classification of Australian Government Budget Outlays in National Accounts Form

Net expenditure on goods and services—
  Current expenditure
  Capital expenditure

Transfer payments—
  Cash benefits to persons
  Grants to or for States and local government authorities—
    for current purposes
    for capital purposes
  Interest paid
  Transfers overseas
  Subsidies
  Grants for private capital purposes
  Purchases of existing assets

Net advances—
  to States
  to Commonwealth Government authorities
  to other sectors

Source: 1977-78 Budget Paper No. 1, *Budget Speech 1977-78*, Australian Government Publishing Service, Canberra, 1977, p. 172.

Receipts, Budget Balance and Financing Transactions

The Australian Government's receipts are now also consolidated to eliminate inter-fund transactions, the main classes of receipts being:
  Taxation revenue (by type of tax)
  Interest, land rent, royalties and dividends
  Surplus of public enterprises
  Sales of existing assets

The difference between total outlays and total receipts represents the overall budget deficit or surplus, which is offset by financing transactions involving the following:
  Net overseas borrowing (or lending)
  Domestic borrowings less redemptions
  Residual financing —
    Use of cash balances
    Borrowing from the Reserve Bank

Strictly, advances less repayments should be recorded in the financing section of the budget as offsets to borrowing (instead of among government outlays in the expenditure section). This would have the effect of reducing the size of a deficit and net financing transactions.

Consolidation of Government Accounts

It will be evident from the foregoing discussion of public enterprise accounts, functional classification and economic classification that significant progress is being made by some governments in the direction of consolidating their financial statements, so as to eliminate inter-fund transactions and integrate the results of their business undertakings to provide a comprehensive record of all financial activities.

The Australian Government's annual budget now takes the form of a consolidated cash budget, which meets accountability requirements whilst simultaneously providing a comprehensive record of government activities classified separately according to purpose and economic significance. Following a recommendation from a Presidential Commission on Budget Concepts in 1967, the U.S. Federal Government also adopted a unified and comprehensive budget intended to enhance understanding of the budget and to make it more useful for purposes of decision making, public policy determination and financial planning. [1] The unified budget includes revenue and loan transactions in respect of the programs of all Federal Government agencies and incorporates the net results of public enterprises. As noted below, action has been taken recently to develop a more ambitious set of consolidated financial statements for the U.S. Government, based on a comprehensive system of accrual accounting.

Meanwhile, the work of executive governments in presenting consolidated budgets and financial statements has been considerably extended by government statistical agencies, which in some countries have begun to publish consolidated statistical tabulations based on the U.N. System of National Accounts, to which reference has been made above.

The Australian Bureau of Statistics publishes two annual bulletins—*Public Authority Finance*: *Federal Authorities* and *Public Authority Finance*: *State and Local Authorities*—which together provide a complete record of all public sector activity in Australia. These bulletins provide a record of transactions by the following institutional sub-sectors: (a) level of government (Commonwealth, State and local); and (b) individual States. A Commonwealth budget document (*National Accounting Estimates of Receipts and Outlays of Australian Government Authorities*) and another Australian Bureau of Statistics publication (*Public Authority Finance*: *Public Authority Estimates*) record, for the Commonwealth and for State and local authorities respectively, the transactions of the budget and non-budget sub-sectors, depending on whether or not the transactions are subject to parliamentary approval. So far separate tabulations for general government and public enterprises are made only for purposes of, and in the detail required for, the *Australian National Accounts*, also published by the Australian Bureau of Statistics.

The following principles have been adopted by the Australian Bureau of Statistics in developing the detailed financial statistics for the several sub-sectors, which generally incorporate a cross-classification according to the functional and economic categories distinguished above:
(a) all public authorities are included;
(b) transactions of all funds and authorities are included;
(c) tables are presented on a consolidated basis;
(d) a uniform system of classification is applied to all authorities; and
(e) the statistics reflect the institutional structures of government as far as possible.

Accrual Accounting?

Perhaps the major issue in government accounting which still needs to be resolved is whether or not the accounts of general government (as opposed to those of public enterprises) should be converted to an accrual basis.

---

[1] The Commission incidently supported the use of PPBS in budget preparation and review, the adoption of an accrual basis of accounting and the provision of forward estimates.

The U.S. Government has been moving in the direction of accrual accounting since 1949, and in 1969 the President gave instructions that all Federal departments and agencies should convert their accounts to an accrual basis. This process is still continuing; during recent years an Advisory Committee on Federal Consolidated Financial Statements has been appointed to assist the Treasury with this task. The Committee has prepared two sets of prototype statements to encourage discussion of the issues and problems involved. The statements comprise the following:

(a) a consolidated statement of financial position (balance sheet), which records:

   (i)   assets, classified into cash and monetary reserve assets, receivables, inventories, property and equipment (and accumulated depreciation thereon), and deferred charges and other assets;

  (ii)   liabilities, classified into accounts payable, unearned revenue, borrowings from the public, accrued pensions, loss reserves, and other liabilities; and

 (iii) the accumulated fiscal deficit;

(b) a consolidated statement of operations, which records:

   (i)   revenues, classified into taxes and earnings from public enterprises;

  (ii)   expenses classified by function and cross-classified by object and agency; and

 (iii) the current period fiscal deficit.

One of the major, stated purposes of the Committee's work has been to bring government accounting standards into line with those of the private sector. To this end, it proposes eventually to adopt a current value basis of valuation[2] and to include among the government's assets the continental shelf and all public domain lands. The prototype statements already record liabilities in respect of accrued pensions and allow for the effect of tax benefits on revenues, and it seems to be intended eventually to include as assets the government's powers to tax and to create money.

The conceptual basis of this approach depends on the premise that government accounting standards need to conform to those of the private sector. However, the purposes of government accounting are quite different from those of business accounting.

General government is involved in providing free services and making cash transfers, and for the most part it finances these transactions through compulsory cash levies in the form of taxation. In no sense can these activities be described as market transactions which need to be recorded on an accrual basis as part of a process of matching revenues and expenditure for the purpose of measuring income. General government is not interested in measures of income which reflect arbitrary cost allocations such as depreciation, or in measures of assets and liabilities which reflect speculative valuation procedures unrelated to any decisions that need to be made by government. Accountability and national economic policy objectives can be adequately and, indeed, more satisfactorily met by suitably classified information about cash flows; decisions about taxing, borrowing and spending are all decisions which involve cash flows and not revenue and cost flows in a business accounting sense. While information about assets and liabilities is needed by general government for management purposes, this information can be provided in supplementary financial statements without any need to establish artificial and arbitrary financial values for such items as defence establishments and equipment, public domain land, taxing rights and pension liabilities.

---

[2] Values in the prototype statements are based on historical costs, but there is a supplemental schedule in which the financial statements are restated for general price-level changes (i.e. on a current purchasing power basis).

Not only does the valuation of existing assets and liabilities pose enormous data problems, but any attempt to derive capitalized values of future hypothetical flows of receipts and payments, such as tax and pension payments, must be regarded as pure speculation. To the extent that such future flows may reasonably be viewed as current transfers which take place at the time the payments are made, their capitalization in the Government's statement of financial position cannot be justified on grounds of either logic or necessity.

Insofar as general government is concerned, the case for accrual accounting is at best not proven, and the conversion of the budgetary accounts to an accrual basis would require a wasteful use of resources for no real purpose.

References

Jay, W.R.C. and Mathews, R.L., (eds.), *Government Accounting in Australia—A Book of Readings*, Cheshire, Melbourne, 1969.

Report of the President's Commission on Budget Concepts, U.S. Government Printing Office, Washington, 1967.

United Nations, *A System of National Accounts*, United Nations, New York, 1968.

Discussion Questions

1 Contrast the financial objectives, accounting systems and periodic financial statements of public authorities and business enterprises.

2 Why do public authorities normally adopt a cash basis of accounting when business enterprises find it necessary to use accrual accounting procedures?

3 Describe and evaluate the fund system of government accounting. Is such a system necessary for purposes of parliamentary control over expenditures?

4 It has been argued that a theory of accounting based on the fund as the accounting unit has certain advantages over theories of accounting which emphasize the interests of the proprietor or of the organizational entity. What form might these arguments take and to what extent do you consider they are justified in relation to business enterprise accounting?

5 'Government accounting systems are about as sophisticated as the accounting procedures involved in keeping a petty cash book.' Discuss.

6 A government has been operating a monopoly enterprise whose receipts and payments have been recorded in the consolidated revenue fund on a cash basis. Capital expenditure, including expenditure on the replacement of fixed assets, has been charged to the loan fund. Interest and sinking fund contributions on the debt so incurred have been included in the payments of the enterprise recorded in the consolidated revenue fund. Charges by the enterprise have been set so as to cover, approximately, the total payments recorded in the consolidated revenue fund.

The government decides that, in future, charges by the enterprise will be set so as to cover, approximately, the 'true costs' of the enterprise. Any capital required from general government funds will henceforth be provided from the consolidated revenue fund.

Advise the government as to the composition of 'true costs', how they should be estimated, and what transactions, if any, should be recorded in the consolidated revenue fund.

7 'Four major reforms seem to be necessary to overcome the deficiencies of conventional methods of government accounting. First, government budgets need to be prepared and presented as predetermined plans of performance and not merely as cash appropriations. Second, departments engaged in trading activities need to be separated from purely administrative departments and their accounts maintained on a commercial basis. Third, it is necessary for the accounts to have regard to the economic significance of government activities; in particular, a distinction between current and capital transactions is necessary. Fourth, the various financial statements presented by a particular government need to be consolidated.'

Explain what is meant by each of these suggested reforms. To what extent do you consider that the propositions are valid?

8 Examine the problems involved in designing an accounting system for a non-profit organization such as (a) an independent school; and (b) a hospital.

9 Contrast the accrual and cash systems of accounting from the point of view of purposes, recording procedures and the kinds of decisions for which they provide relevant information.

10 Discuss the problem of classifying sectors and transactions for purposes of government accounting.

11 Contrast functional, program and economic classification in relation to their significance for government accounting.

12 Discuss the contribution which PPBS can make to informed decision making in the public sector. Consider its application to (a) defence, and (b) education, by discussing problems of identifying and measuring costs and outputs in each area.

13 Examine the relationship between the accounts of public enterprises and those of central governments, with special reference to the problem of accounting for depreciation, debt redemption and interest charges, and operating surpluses.

14 'If standards of government accounting and financial reporting are to meet those of the private sector, the government accounting system must be converted from a cash to an accrual basis.' Discuss.

15 Consider the application of a PPBS approach to a university's budgeting and accounting system, with special reference to program classification and planning decisions.

Exercises

1 Record the transactions listed in Chapter 3, Exercise 10, in a double-entry cash accounting system and prepare a summary receipts and expenditure statement and balance sheet at the end of the fourth week. Explain the differences between these results and those obtained in answering Exercise 10 in Chapter 3.

2 The government of Pacifica maintains its accounts on a cash basis in three separate funds—consolidated revenue fund, loan fund and trust fund. Transactions during 1985 were recorded in financial statements as follows:

Consolidated Revenue Fund ($'000)

Tax collections	43 350
Revenue from land sales	1 980
Receipts from business undertakings	17 440
Fines	530
Total receipts	63 300
Administrative expenditure	29 330
Business undertakings' expenditure	13 100
Social service benefits	11 980
Interest on national debt	4 730
Capital works and services	1 130
Surplus to trust fund	3 030
Total expenditure	63 300

Loan Fund ($'000)

Opening balances—Bank	50	
Accumulated expenditure	46 370	
		46 420
Proceeds of public loan raisings		15 400
Transfer from national debt sinking fund		2 170
Debt redemption		10 200
Expenditure on capital works and services		12 300

Trust Fund ($'000)

Opening balances—Bank	70	
Investments	13 450	
		13 520
Consolidated revenue fund surplus		3 030
Transfer to loan fund for debt redemption		2 170
Interest receipts		840
Purchase of investments		420
Other trust fund expenditure		1 300

Show how the transactions would have been recorded in each fund's double-entry cash accounting system.

3 What do you consider would be the implications of the adoption of a PPBS approach to the analysis of a country's defence expenditures, having regard particularly to: (a) strategic planning and the formulation of defence goals; (b) the classification of expenditures along program lines; (c) the size of the total defence budget and its allocation among different purposes; and (d) the evaluation of defence performance through measures intended to relate costs to accomplishments?

What additional information would be required to develop a defence strategy under such an approach? How would the adoption of program budgets affect the traditional accountability requirement, whereby formal parliamentary approval is required for defence expenditures proposed by the executive government? To what extent would a change in the format of the defence budget have national security implications? What implications would the PPBS approach have for organization of defence forces?

Present your answer in the form of a report to the government on defence organization for the purpose of strategic planning.

4 From the data given in the most recent official national income accounting estimates, construct tables giving a cross-classification of the expenditure of the public sector as a whole and of each of its major sub-sectors, by functional and economic categories. Make estimates on the basis of best available information if the official estimates are incomplete for the purpose.

What use may be made of these tables?

5 Construct a pro-forma budget for the education function of a central government which is designed to meet both accountability requirements and the objectives of planning-programming-budgeting-systems.

6 Contrast the functional and economic classifications of government expenditures in the U.N. System of National Accounts and in the most recent budget papers of your national government. Evaluate the differences with special reference to the purposes of government accounting.

7 The following figures relate to a government transport authority which maintains its accounts and presents its reports on a cash basis:

	$ million
Revenue	29.6
Operating expenditure—	
Salaries and payments in the nature of salaries	17.6
Stores and materials	5.7
Administrative expenses	3.3
	26.6
Cash surplus	3.0

If it were decided to record the transactions of the authority in such a way as to derive a measure of profit or loss, what additional information would be needed, and on what basis should the items concerned be calculated?

8 The following table gives a comparison for the year 1985 between the revenue and expenses of a national railway authority recorded on a cash basis in the government's consolidated revenue fund and those recorded on an accrual basis in the annual report of the Commissioner. What is the significance of the differences shown? Do you regard the expenses shown in the annual report as a good estimate of the true costs of operating the railways?

Revenue and Expenditure, Commonwealth Railways, 1985

	Consolidated Revenue Fund $'000	Annual Report $'000
Revenue	24 962	25 371
Expenditure—		
Working and administrative expenses	19 751	19 681
Interest*	—	—
Deferred charges written off †	—	529
Provision for depreciation‡	—	3 211
Superannuation liability §	—	712
Furlough liability	—	227
Contribution to Railway Accident and Insurance Fund	248	254
Total	19 999	24 614
Cash surplus or operating profit ‖	4 963	757

* No interest is paid to Treasury or included in advances from Treasury. Advances from Treasury totalled $128.4 million at 31 December 1985, an increase of $7.9 million during the year.

† The cost of track rehabilitation in 1983 and 1984, about $4 million, was capitalized and is to be written off as an expense over a period of years.

‡ Assume that the provision for depreciation represents straight-line depreciation over the estimated life of the asset based on historical cost.

§ Superannuation liability is not paid to Treasury in cash but is added to the cash advance from Treasury to give the advance shown in the annual report.

‖ Accumulated operating losses at 31 December 1985 are shown in the annual report as $13.2 million.

9 The following table compares, for the year 1985, the results of the Antipodean Post Office as recorded in the annual report of the Post Office and in the government's consolidated revenue fund. What is the significance of the differences? Comment also on the differences between Postal Services and Telecommunications.

Antipodean Post Office 1985 ($ million)

	Annual Report			Consolidated Revenue Fund
	Postal Services	Telecommunications	Total	
Earnings	138.2	364.5	502.7	486.7
Expenditure—				
Operating and general	103.2	92.6	195.8	
Maintenance of plant and equipment	3.9	83.6	87.5	
Carriage of mails	33.1	—	33.1	
Sub-total	140.2	176.2	316.4	338.9
Superannuation	6.7	10.6	17.3	12.5
Furlough	2.4	3.8	6.2	3.5
Depreciation	3.0	91.1	94.1	—
Interest	6.1	72.3	78.4	—
Total expenditure	158.4	354.0	512.4	354.9
Profit or surplus (loss or deficit)	(20.2)	10.5	(9.7)	131.8

15 National Economic Accounts

The principles and methods developed in earlier chapters may be readily adapted to the problem of accounting for the transactions of the national economy. National economic accounting is a comparatively new field of enquiry which has developed out of statistical studies in national income and wealth. It is concerned with recording, classifying and analysing the nation's economic activities in terms of their economic significance. Just as a business accounting system formally records and summarizes the transactions of an individual business, so a national accounting system is designed to record and summarize the economic transactions of the whole community. Just as business accounts are used as a basis for planning and controlling the activities of the business and making policy decisions within the enterprise, so national accounts are intended to provide information as a basis for planning and controlling the activities of the economy in general and for formulating national economic policy. The purpose of national accounting, in short, is to increase knowledge of the economic system and to use this knowledge to make the system function more effectively. In particular, it is possible to gain information from the national accounts that may be used to guide policy in four major problem areas:

(a) making decisions which influence economic welfare through their effect on the size and the distribution of the national income;
(b) making decisions which influence resource allocation or efficiency;
(c) choosing the rate and direction of the nation's economic growth; and
(d) making decisions which influence economic stability through their effect on prices, employment and the balance of payments.

In the historical development of studies in national income and wealth, there have been two important changes in emphasis. For many years, such studies concentrated almost wholly on questions associated with the size and distribution of income and wealth, whereas recently considerably more emphasis has been given to the task of providing information directed towards maintaining economic stability and achieving efficient use of resources. The second switch in emphasis has been associated with a new method of presenting the data, with an integrated accounting form of presentation replacing the use of unrelated statistical tables. Behind this formal variation lies an important change in the purpose of national accounting, which is no longer concerned only with building up unrelated aggregates of national income and wealth. National accounting today concentrates attention on significant income, expenditure and financial flows and relationships between different economic groups in the community, and the use of an accounting framework to record these flows and relationships serves to emphasize the mutual interdependence of the different groups and of the transactions in which they engage.

The most convenient and reliable source of national accounting data is the information that is presented in the final accounting reports which individual accounting entities prepare for their own purposes. In this chapter it will be shown how the accounting reports of business enterprises, governments and other entities may be adapted to provide the information which is needed for purposes of national economic accounting. This means analysing, in terms of its economic significance, the information contained in the accounts of individual entities and aggregating the reports of similar entities.

Just as accounting for an individual entity may be regarded as a system of classification, so may national accounting. But because the purposes of the two systems are different, their schemes of classification also differ. The analysis of accounting data in terms of economic significance therefore involves the construction of a new classification framework. It is necessary to classify the transacting entities and the transactions in which they engage, in accordance with the policy-making purposes which the national accounts are designed to serve. This involves consideration of the problems of classifying: (a) national accounting entities or sectors; and (b) the economic activities which are undertaken by the different entities. Three major systems of national accounting will be distinguished, known respectively as national income and expenditure accounts, flow-of-funds accounts and national balance sheets. Each of these national accounting systems requires its own detailed classification framework, but for the time being the differences between the various systems will be ignored to enable concentration on the relevance of private accounting data to the national economic accounts in general. Since the different systems of national accounts need to be integrated as far as possible into a single social accounting system, it is in any case desirable that they should all be based on a common economic classification.

National Accounting Sectors

The classification of accounting entities for national accounting purposes is concerned with the problem of distinguishing different economic groups, i.e. groups such as producers, consumers and governments which engage in different kinds of economic activity. These groups are usually described as sectors of the economy and the following sectors may be distinguished:
(a) business enterprises, which may be further classified into:
    (i) enterprises engaged in the production or sale of goods and non-financial services, usually called productive enterprises or trading enterprises, and
    (ii) banks and other financial enterprises;
(b) consumers, persons or households;
(c) public authorities, which may be further classified into:
    (i) public authorities engaged in general government, often described simply as governments, and
    (ii) public authority business undertakings, sometimes referred to as public enterprises;
(d) the rest of the world or the overseas sector.

Business enterprises include companies, unincorporated businesses, farms, professions and private persons in their capacity as landlords or house-owners. If government business undertakings are not treated as a separate sector, they may be grouped with business enterprises.

The activities of trading enterprises and financial enterprises are so different in their economic significance that it is usually convenient to treat them as separate sectors. Trading enterprises may then be defined as enterprises which produce or sell goods or non-financial services. The trading enterprise sector thus comprises all those organizations which engage in productive activities of a non-financial kind, including primary producers, manufacturing enterprises, wholesale and retail traders, service organizations and house-owners. Financial enterprises play a different role in the economy; they are essentially concerned with the provision of finance to other sectors. Their activities are concerned with borrowing and lending as distinct from buying and selling, although viewed in another light they may be said to be sellers of financial services. The financial enterprise sector includes banks, life assurance companies, provident funds, investment trusts and other institutions whose functions are purely financial in character.

Consumers engage in a different kind of activity from business enterprises, namely the final consumption of goods and services. The consumer sector includes all persons (in their household or personal as distinct from their business capacity) as well as those non-profit-making organizations which may be said to consume goods and services collectively, e.g. clubs. Governments also provide for collective consumption as one of their functions, but their activities loom so large in the national economy that they need to be treated as a separate sector.

Public authorities or governments have a multi-purpose role, since they engage in numerous productive activities as well as redistributing income, providing for the collective consumption needs of the community and regulating the activities of all other sectors. The public authority sector includes all the agencies of government— federal, state and local. Government business enterprises are often treated as separate sub-sectors of the trading enterprise and financial enterprise sectors.

The remaining sector which needs to be distinguished for national accounting purposes is the rest of the world or the overseas sector. To the extent that domestic sectors engage in transactions with overseas entities (e.g. through exports and imports of goods and services), it is necessary to recognize these overseas entities as a separate economic group.

Later it will be seen that the foregoing sectors are further subdivided for certain purposes. For example, the financial enterprise sector is broken down into a large number of separate sectors for purposes of flow-of-funds accounts and national balance sheets.

The U.N. System of National Accounts adopts a sector classification which is somewhat different from that described above. Although the U.N. grouping is more elaborate in some respects, it is unsatisfactory in that it combines the activities of consumers and unincorporated business enterprises in the one sector (households). The following is the U.N. classification:

(a) non-financial enterprises, corporate and quasi-corporate —
   (i) private,
   (ii) public;
(b) financial enterprises —
   (i)   central bank,
   (ii) other monetary institutions,
   (iii) insurance companies and pension funds,
   (iv) other financial institutions;
(c) general government —
   (i)   central government,
   (ii) state and local government,
   (iii) social security funds,
(d) private non-profit institutions serving households; and
(e) households, including private non-financial unincorporated enterprises.

The Australian national accounts classification is based on the U.N. system and contains the following four sectors:

(a) corporate trading enterprises (including public trading enterprises);
(b) financial enterprises;
(c) households (including unincorporated enterprises); and
(d) general government.

In the Australian system non profit organizations serving households (other than those included in financial enterprises) are included in the household sector.

Major Classes of Economic Activity

It is possible to distinguish the following major classes of economic activity, and all national accounting systems are concerned with recording transactions that fall in one or more of these classes:
(a) production (or the creation of income);
(b) the distribution of income;
(c) the disposal of income (or the allocation of income between consumption and saving);
(d) capital formation; and
(e) borrowing and lending.

Transactions relating to the production, distribution and disposal of income constitute current transactions, while capital formation, borrowing and lending represent capital transactions. Irrespective of the national accounting system which is employed, it is usually convenient to record each kind of economic activity in a separate account which may be called an activity account. In a fully integrated system of social accounts, one may expect to find a separate account for each sector in respect of each kind of activity in which the sector engages. If a sector participates in the full range of economic activity, it is represented by a production account, an income distribution account, an income disposal account, a capital formation account and a financial capital transactions account. Briefly, the production account records the contribution made by the sector to the national output; the income distribution account shows how incomes derived from productive activities are distributed as well as recording transfers of income from or to other sectors; the income disposal account shows how incomes are allocated between consumption and saving; the capital formation account records investment by the sector in inventories and fixed capital assets, and shows net borrowing or net lending to other sectors as a residual item; and the financial capital transactions account records the composition of the sector's borrowing and lending activities.

The capital formation account and the financial capital transactions account, like the three accounts concerned with current transactions, record flows as distinct from stocks of assets and funds. If it is desired to emphasize stocks rather than flows (as is the case when attention is focused on national balance sheets), the capital formation and financial capital transaction accounts may be replaced in the national accounting system by a series of accounts recording assets and financial obligations in total. Data relating to asset and fund flows may then be derived by analysing changes in these asset and equity accounts in the manner illustrated in Chapter 5 in relation to the preparation of a funds statement for an individual enterprise.

The data contained in the everyday accounting reports of the different entities may be adapted to form the basis of the national economic activity accounts. This will now be considered in relation to each of the major sectors.

The Economic Activity Accounts of Trading Enterprises

Trading enterprises normally engage in all the economic activities which have been distinguished above, so that it is necessary to establish separate accounts for the sector in respect of production, income distribution, income disposal, capital formation and financial capital transactions. The activity accounts for a trading enterprise are illustrated in Figure 15—A.

Figure 15—A
The Economic Activity Accounts of a Trading Enterprise

Production

Purchases of intermediate goods and services	$x	Sales of goods and services	$x
Gross product c/d	x	Additions to inventories	x
	$x		$x

Income Distribution

Depreciation allowances	$x	Gross product b/d	$x
Indirect taxes	x		
Net product at factor cost c/d	x		
	$x		$x
Factor payments—		Net product at factor cost b/d	x
Wages and salaries	x		
Surplus (interest and earned income) c/d	x		
	$x		$x
Transfer payments—		Surplus b/d	x
Interest	x	Transfer incomes	x
Direct taxes	x		
Dividends	x		
Other transfers	x		
Disposable income c/d	x		
	$x		$x

Income Disposal

Saving c/d	$x	Disposable income b/d	$x

Capital Formation

Investment in inventories	$x	Saving b/d	$x
Fixed capital investment	x	Depreciation allowances	x
Purchases of second-hand fixed assets	x	Sales of second-hand fixed assets	x
Capital transfers	x	Capital transfers	x
Net lending c/d	x	(Net borrowing c/d)	x
	$x		$x

Financial Capital Transactions

(Net borrowing b/d)	$x	Net lending b/d	$x
Increases in financial assets	x	Increases in financial liabilities and proprietorship equity	x
	$x		$x

The data for the production and income distribution accounts may be derived substantially from the profit and loss statements of the individual enterprises which compose the sector. The production account of an individual enterprise, which needs to show the contribution that the enterprise makes to the national product, should record the gross output of the enterprise (representing sales plus additions to processed inventories) on the credit side, and inputs (representing purchases of current goods and services from other enterprises less additions to inventories resulting from those purchases) on the debit side. For accounting purposes, however, it is convenient to record all additions to inventories (i.e. increases in both processed and unprocessed inventories) as one item on the credit side of the production account (see Figure 15—A). When this is done the aggregate entries in respect of sales and additions to inventories do not necessarily represent the value of the enterprise's output.

Purchases of current goods and services are usually described as intermediate products in the national accounts, because they are subject to further processing or subsequent resale by the purchasing enterprise. By contrast, final products are goods and services sold to final purchasers (e.g. consumers) or added to wealth (e.g. as inventories or fixed capital assets) during the accounting period. Intermediate purchases include all costs and expenses in the accountant's sense other than wages and salaries, depreciation and interest. They thus include, in addition to purchases of trading goods and materials, such things as advertising expenses, freight charges, power and occupancy expenses. The balance of the production account is called the value of production added by the enterprise or, because it indicates the contribution made by the enterprise to the national product, gross product. The term gross product is used because so far no allowance has been made for the using up of fixed capital assets in producing the output.

When the production accounts of all trading enterprises are consolidated, sales of current goods and services by enterprises to other enterprises (which appear as intermediate purchases in the production accounts of other enterprises) are eliminated, leaving only final products to be recorded as credit entries. Sales of capital assets to other enterprises are not eliminated because, as will be seen, the corresponding debit entries appear in the capital formation account and not in the production account. In effect, they represent final and not intermediate products. The consolidated production account of the trading enterprise sector thus records sales of current goods and services to other sectors, all sales of capital goods and additions to inventories on the credit side, and purchases of intermediate products from other sectors on the debit side, with gross product as the balancing item which is carried down to the income distribution account. This item is sometimes called gross product at market prices and is contrasted with net product at market prices (equal to gross product less depreciation allowances) and net product at factor cost (equal to net product at market prices less indirect taxes).

The income distribution account of an individual enterprise records on the credit side the gross product of the enterprise plus any income transfers received from other entities, and on the debit side depreciation charges and indirect taxes (which represent the amounts that must be deducted from gross product to derive a measure of net product at factor cost), payments to factors of production, income transfers to other entities and the enterprise's disposable income, which as the balancing item in the account is carried down to the income disposal account (see Figure 15—A). Payments to factors of production comprise two items: (a) wages and salaries; and

(b) surplus. Surplus is calculated before charging interest and thus includes both interest payable on borrowed funds and income earned by the owners of the enterprise. Interest payments are then treated as transfers of surplus in the same way as dividends and other income withdrawals.

Conventionally the surplus of an unincorporated business is recorded as being fully distributed to persons (earned income that is retained for use within the business is then recorded as fresh capital raising in the financial capital transactions account). The surplus of a company is recorded in two parts: (a) surplus distributed to other entities by way of interest, dividends and direct taxes; and (b) undistributed income which by definition equals disposable income. When the income distribution accounts of individual enterprises are consolidated to form an income distribution account for the trading enterprise sector, interest and dividends distributed to other enterprises are eliminated in the usual way, leaving only distributions to other sectors to be recorded.

Since a trading enterprise cannot engage in final consumption of goods and services, the whole of its disposable income represents saving. There are thus only two entries in the income disposal account of a trading enterprise, disposable income on the credit side and saving on the debit side. The latter item is carried down to the capital formation account, which also records depreciation allowances on the credit side (this is the matching entry for the charge recorded in the income distribution account), and additions to inventories (this matches the entry in the production account) and fixed capital investment on the debit side. Apart from capital transfers and transactions involving second-hand assets, this leaves only a net borrowing or net lending item to be carried down to the enterprise's financial capital transactions account, which records in detail changes in financial assets and liabilities (see Figure 15—A). For national accounting purposes, capital contributions by proprietors are regarded as borrowing from persons, and are recorded in the financial capital transactions account.

The consolidation of the income disposal accounts, capital formation accounts and financial capital transactions accounts of individual enterprises to form sector activity accounts results in the usual elimination of transactions between enterprises.

The data recorded in the income disposal, capital formation and financial capital transactions accounts of an individual enterprise may all be derived from the funds statement which, as seen in Chapter 5, is one of the basic accounting reports which the business needs for its own purposes.

An inspection of Figure 15—A reveals that most of the items which need to be recorded in the national economic accounts of the trading enterprise sector may be identified in the accounting reports prepared by individual enterprises. The major difference between the two accounting records stems from differences in classification. For national accounting purposes it is necessary:

(a) to classify costs, expenses and income allocations among:
    (i)   purchases of intermediate goods and services,
    (ii) capital consumption (i.e. depreciation) allowances,
    (iii) payments to factors of production,
    (iv) transfers of surplus;
(b) to differentiate between saving, capital formation and financial capital transactions; and
(c) to classify transactions according to sectors. Transactions which affect only one sector can be transposed into the national accounts without difficulty, but where

transactions affect several sectors (e.g. sales) the breakdown required for national accounting purposes may need to be derived from statistical sources or by analysing the accounts of other sectors which, as will be seen, record the matching entries in the integrated social accounting system.

It remains to consider the question of valuation. If the accounting reports of individual enterprises are to be consolidated to form sector activity accounts, it is necessary to ensure not only that consistent bases of classification are used, but also that consistent valuation procedures are employed within the sector. This means that the effect of any financial valuation adjustments, such as result from the application of a policy of conservatism (see Chapter 6), must be eliminated from the individual accounting reports before they are consolidated. It also means that the effect of the accountant's historical record and monetary assumptions must be eliminated by recording all transactions in terms of their current values.

If historical cost figures (e.g. in respect of depreciation and inventory values) were to be carried into the national economic accounts without adjustment, the accounts would lack a consistent basis of valuation and their usefulness for economic policy purposes would be impaired. Most items in Figure 15—A relate to transactions of the current period and thus reflect current values, but care must be taken to ensure that additions to inventories, depreciation allowances, the earned income component of surplus, and disposable income are all valued in terms of current prices. If the current valuation adjustments described in Chapter 19 are made by individual enterprises for their own accounting purposes, depreciation and inventories are converted to current values and the required measure of current value income is derived. The ordinary business accounts then automatically provide the data needed to record transactions in the national accounts in terms of current values. If the valuation adjustments are not made explicitly in the accounts of individual enterprises, equivalent statistical calculations need to be made to repair the deficiency.

The Economic Activity Accounts of Banks and Other Financial Enterprises

Financial enterprises differ from other business enterprises in that they deal in money claims rather than goods or services. Although their profit and loss statements and balance sheets bear a formal resemblance to those of trading enterprises, there are important differences in substance between the two sets of accounting reports. Interest receipts and payments (or premiums and claims) replace sales revenue and purchases of goods and services as the main items in the profit and loss statements of financial enterprises, while financial assets and liabilities tend to dominate their balance sheets. These differences, which of course reflect important differences in economic function, make it necessary to treat financial enterprises as a separate sector in the national economic accounts. For many national accounting purposes, however, it is not sufficient merely to separate financial enterprises from other business enterprises; it is necessary to distinguish between classes of financial enterprises themselves. In this section we shall confine our attention to banks. Other financial intermediaries have some of the characteristics of banks, but give rise to special problems which cannot be explored in this book.

In constructing the economic activity accounts of banks, the major problems concern the valuation of output and gross product, and the treatment of interest.

The charges made by banks and other financial enterprises typically do not fully cover the costs of the services they provide; rather the enterprises seek to cover their costs and to derive their profits from differences between their interest receipts and payments (or premium income and claims). In the case of trading enterprises, it was suggested that all interest receipts and payments should be treated as transfers. However, to the extent that the interest receipts and payments of financial enterprises are treated as transfers, there is a problem of deriving measures of the value of their output and of their gross (and net) product.

Insofar as banks are concerned, the problem may be resolved by resorting to indirect methods of valuation (a similar approach may be adopted for other financial enterprises). On the assumption that banks provide services to the community which, to the extent they are not charged for directly, represent final output, it is possible to value these services on the basis of cost plus bank profit. Cost for this purpose is interpreted as the sum of purchases of goods and services from other sectors, wages and salaries paid by banks, indirect taxes, and depreciation allowances on bank premises and equipment.

The production account of a bank will then record, as the value of the bank's output, both actual and imputed charges for its services, the imputed charges being the difference between the total value of services as defined above and the fees, commissions and other charges which it imposes directly on its customers. On the debit side, the production account will record purchases of goods and services from other enterprises and its gross product, defined as the difference between the value of its output and the purchases from other enterprises.

This procedure has the effect of valuing the gross product of banks (defined as the value of output less the cost of intermediate goods and services) as the equivalent of costs and earned income. Gross product is carried down to the income distribution account, where deductions are made for depreciation allowances and indirect taxes so as to derive a measure of net product, which by definition is equal to the sum of wages and salaries plus profit (or earned income). Imputed bank charges are deducted from interest receivable in the income distribution account, so as to derive a net figure for interest receivable which may be regarded as an income transfer (see Figure 15—B).

The imputed charges for bank services are treated as imputed purchases of intermediate goods and services insofar as other enterprises and governments are concerned, and as imputed final consumers' expenditure insofar as consumers are concerned. To achieve these results, offsetting deductions must be made against interest payable in the income distribution accounts of the entities concerned.

Entries in the other activity accounts of a bank are similar to those for a trading enterprise, except that the financial capital transactions assume special importance for a bank and, as will be noted below, need to be classified in more detail. The economic activity accounts of a bank are illustrated in Figure 15—B.

Figure 15—B
The Economic Activity Accounts of a Bank

Production

Purchases of intermediate goods and services	$x	Charges for bank services— Actual	$x
Gross product c/d	x	Imputed	x
	$x		$x

Income Distribution

Depreciation allowances	$x	Gross product b/d		$x
Indirect taxes	x			
Net product at factor cost c/d	x			
	$x			$x
Factor payments—		Net product b/d		x
Wages and salaries	x			
Earned income c/d	x			
	$x			$x
Transfers—		Earned income b/d		x
Interest payable	$x	Transfers—		
Direct taxes	x	Interest receivable	$x	
Dividends	x x	*Less*. Imputed charges	x x	
Disposable income c/d	x			
	$x			$x

Income Disposal

Saving c/d	$x	Disposable income b/d	$x
	$x		$x

Capital Formation

Fixed capital investment	$x	Saving b/d	$x
Purchases of second-hand fixed assets	x	Depreciation allowances	x
Capital transfers	x	Sales of second-hand fixed assets	x
Net lending c/d	x	Capital transfers	x
		(Net borrowing c/d)	x
	$x		$x

Financial Capital Transactions

(Net borrowing b/d)	$x	Net lending b/d	$x
Increases in financial assets	x	Increases in financial liabilities	
		and proprietorship equity	x
	$x		$x

The Economic Activity Accounts of Consumers

Consumers or households do not usually maintain formal accounting records, so that it is necessary to construct their economic activity accounts from statistical sources or from the double-entry accounts of other sectors which engage in transactions with consumers.

By definition, consumers do not undertake productive activity and therefore do not require a production account. The ownership of houses by consumers is treated as a trading activity. This means that purchases of new houses are recorded in the capital formation account of trading enterprises along with other capital investment, while the matching entry to record sales appears in the trading enterprise production account in the usual way. Savings made by persons to finance new houses are recorded in financial capital transactions accounts as lending by consumers to trading enterprises.

Revenue derived from renting houses to other persons is credited to the trading enterprise production account and debited to the income disposal account of consumers. Maintenance costs and depreciation allowances are recorded in the production account and income distribution account of trading enterprises in the usual way, and the surplus is transferred to consumers along with other income of unincorporated businesses. Where houses are occupied by their owners, it is customary to impute values to the above transactions in order that the national product may reflect the services rendered by owner-occupied houses as well as the services of rented houses.

Figure 15—C illustrates the economic activity accounts of a consumer. The income distribution account records sources of personal income (wages and salaries, interest, dividends and income withdrawals, income transfers such as cash social service benefits) and transfer payments including personal income taxes. The balance of the income distribution account, representing undistributed or disposable income, is carried down to the disposal account, which shows how disposable income is allocated among consumers' expenditure and saving.

Apart from expenditure on houses discussed above (and sometimes expenditure on durable consumer goods, such as motor cars), all expenditure by persons on goods and services is recorded as final consumers' expenditure. According to the treatment in Figure 15—C, consumers cannot engage in capital formation, so that the residual saving item in the income disposal account (usually known as personal saving) *plus* or *minus* net capital transfers *equals* net lending to other sectors.

Net lending is carried down from the capital formation account to the financial capital transactions account, which records lending and borrowing transactions in detail.

Figure 15—C
The Economic Activity Accounts of a Consumer

Income Distribution

Personal income taxes	$x	Wages and salaries	$x
Other transfer payments	x	Income derived from surpluses	
Disposable income c/d	x	of business enterprises	x
		Cash social service benefits	x
		Other transfer incomes	x
	$x		$x

Income Disposal

Consumers' expenditure	$x	Disposable income b/d	$x
Saving c/d	x		
	$x		$x

Capital Formation

Capital transfers	$x	Saving b/d	$x
Net lending c/d	x	Capital transfers	x
	$x		$x

Financial Capital Transactions

Increases in financial assets	$x	Net lending b/d	$x
		Increases in financial liabilities	x
	$x		$x

The Economic Activity Accounts of Public Authorities

It is a comparatively simple matter to construct economic activity accounts for a government from financial statements prepared on the basis of the economic classification described in Chapter 14. (For the time being, it will be assumed that government business undertakings are treated as separate sectors, and that their activity accounts correspond to those of the relevant business enterprise sectors.) It has been seen that the main requirements for national accounting are the classification of transactions (a) by sectors and (b) in accordance with their economic significance. The production account in Figure 15—D is designed to measure the

Figure 15—D
The Economic Activity Accounts of a Government

Production

Purchases of intermediate goods and services from other sectors	$x	Value of government output— Fees for administrative services	$x
Gross product c/d	x	Collective consumption	x
		Fixed capital investment	x
			$x
	$x		$x

Income Distribution

Net product c/d	$x	Gross product b/d	$x
	$x		$x
Wages and salaries	$x	Net product b/d	$x
Transfer payments—		Transfer incomes—	
Interest	x	Direct taxes	x
Subsidies	x	Indirect taxes	x
Cash social service payments	x	Surplus of business undertakings	x
Disposable income c/d	x		
	$x		$x

Income Disposal

Government expenditure on goods and services (collective consumption)	$x	Disposable income b/d	$x
Saving c/d	x		
	$x		$x

Capital Formation

Fixed capital investment	$x	Saving b/d	$x
Purchases of second-hand fixed assets	x	Sales of second-hand fixed assets	x
Capital transfers	x	Capital transfers	x
Net lending c/d	x	(Net borrowing c/d)	x
	$x		$x

Financial Capital Transactions

(Net borrowing b/d)	$x	Net lending b/d	$x
Increases in financial assets	x	Increases in financial liabilities	x
	$x		$x

contribution made by the government to the national product, and therefore needs to record purchases of intermediate goods and services from other sectors on the debit side and the value of government output on the credit side. Because governments do not make any direct charges for many of the services they provide, the same kind of difficulty in valuing government output is met as was previously experienced in valuing financial enterprise output. For national accounting purposes, government output is conventionally valued at cost, which in turn is equal to purchases of goods and services plus wages and salaries paid to civil servants. The gross product which is carried down to the income distribution account is thus equal by definition to wages and salaries and, in the absence of depreciation, the net contribution of governments to the national product is also taken to be equal to wages and salaries.

Apart from any fees which other sectors are required to pay for administrative services, the value of government output reflects expenditure undertaken by the government collectively on behalf of the community. Expenditure on current goods and services is recorded as final expenditure (collective consumption) in the income disposal account, and the matching entry for fixed capital expenditure appears in the capital formation account.

The income distribution account records, as transfer incomes or payments, the trading surpluses or deficits of business undertakings, calculated before charging interest. The difference between transfer incomes and transfer payments in the income distribution account represents the undistributed or disposable income of the government, which is carried down to the income disposal account, and the difference between disposable income and collective consumption represents government saving.

The capital formation account records the usual saving and investment items, with net lending or net borrowing as a residual item which is carried down to the financial capital transactions account. The financial capital transactions account records the details of government's lending and borrowing transactions in the usual way.

Given a consistent classification framework along the lines of Figure 15—D, the budgetary accounts of federal, state and local governments may be consolidated to form the national economic accounts of the government sector.

The Overseas Sector and the Balance of Payments

The economic activity accounts of the overseas (or rest of the world) sector may be derived from the domestic economy's balance of payments. Since, however, the economic activity accounts of the overseas sector record transactions with the domestic economy from the point of view of overseas entities, they represent in effect a mirror image of the domestic economy's balance of payments. Although overseas entities engage in productive activity in their own countries, they do not add anything to the output of the domestic economy. No production account is therefore required for the overseas sector.

The income distribution account records incomes received by overseas entities from local entities (in the form of interest, dividends, etc.) on the credit side, and incomes paid by overseas entities to local entities on the debit side. The balance, representing the disposable income of the overseas sector, is carried down to the income disposal account, which also records the proceeds of sales of goods and services to local entities (i.e. imports and other payments for goods and services of the domestic economy) on the credit side, and purchases of goods and services from local entities (i.e. exports and other receipts for goods and services of the domestic economy) on the debit side. Net expenditure by the overseas sector on goods and services (export proceeds of the domestic economy *minus* its import payments) represents final expenditure which absorbs national production in the same way as consumption expenditure, investment expenditure, etc. The balance of the income disposal account, which represents saving by the overseas sector, is carried down to the capital formation account, which also records capital transfers and residual net lending by the overseas sector to the domestic economy. The financial capital transactions account of the overseas sector records lending and borrowing transactions between overseas and local entities in detail.

Disposable income of the overseas sector, net expenditure by the overseas sector on goods and services, overseas saving and net lending by the overseas sector may all be positive or negative, depending on the magnitudes of the transactions recorded in the accounts. The income distribution and income disposal accounts (when reversed to reflect the interests of the domestic economy) together constitute what is referred to as the domestic economy's balance of international payments on current account, and overseas saving is known in balance of payments parlance as the deficit on current account. The capital formation and financial capital transactions accounts reflect the balance of international payments on capital account.

Figure 15—E illustrates the economic activity accounts of the overseas sector.

Figure 15—E
The Economic Activity Accounts of the Overseas Sector

Income Distribution

Incomes paid by overseas entities to domestic entities	$x	Incomes received by overseas entities from domestic entities	$x
Disposable income c/d	x		
	$x		$x

Income Disposal

Purchases of goods and services from domestic entities (exports of the domestic economy)	$x	Disposable income b/d	$x
		Sales of goods and services to the domestic economy (imports of the domestic economy)	
Saving c/d	x		x
	$x		$x

Capital Formation

Capital transfers by overseas sector	$x	Overseas saving b/d	$x
Net lending c/d	x	Capital transfers to overseas sector	x
	$x		$x

Financial Capital Transactions

Increases in financial assets of overseas sector	$x	Net lending by overseas sector b/d	$x
		Increases in financial liabilities of overseas sector	x
	$x		$x

It has now been seen how the accounts of different entities may be adapted to record the major forms of economic activity. In the next section, the task of combining sector activity accounts into different kinds of national accounting systems for the whole economy will be considered.

National Accounting Systems

In the rest of this chapter, three different kinds of national accounting systems—national income and expenditure accounts, flow-of-funds accounts and national balance sheets will be examined. No attention will be given to a fourth major system of national accounts, known as input-output analysis, which is used to derive inter-industry technological relationships and which may be regarded as an alternative method of recording income and expenditure flows.

It has been seen that economic transactions need to be classified rather differently for national accounting purposes than is customary for the more specific purposes of individual entities. If allowance is made for this fact, there is a real sense in which national income and expenditure accounts may be regarded as an aggregation of the revenue and expenditure or profit and loss statements of the individual entities which make up the economy; national flow-of-funds accounts may be regarded as an aggregation of individual funds statements; and national balance sheets may be regarded as an aggregation of individual balance sheets or statements of financial position.

National Income and Expenditure Accounts

The oldest and best-developed system of national accounting is represented by the national income and expenditure accounts which express, in accounting form, the fundamental economic relationships for a closed economy implicit in the following identities:
(a) consumption + investment = national product;
(b) national product = national income;
(c) national income = consumption + saving;
   from which it follows that
(d) saving = investment.

In particular, the national income and expenditure accounts show how the nation's output is produced, distributed and consumed or added to wealth. Although they may be used to throw light on other aspects of national economic policy, the national income and expenditure accounts are designed especially to emphasize economic relationships of significance in connection with the task of maintaining stability and balanced growth in the economy. National income accounting has thus come to be closely identified with government fiscal policy; and in some countries, including Australia, the annual national income and expenditure accounts are presented as key budget papers. In the following discussion, attention will be confined to the recording of historical accounting data, but the national income accounting framework may be used for planning purposes by economic policy-makers to ensure that their budget policies are internally consistent, having regard to the assumptions and estimates of economic relationships and behaviour which they make in formulating the policies. It follows from what has been said that the national income accounts are concerned primarily with the recording of flows of goods and services, and are not intended to throw much light on changes in financial relationships either within or between groups. This point may be illustrated by comparing the double-entry system used in national income accounting with the double-entry system used by an individual entity.

For example, consider the way in which each system records a simple economic transaction, say the credit sale of goods worth $100 by a trading business to a consumer. Such a transaction may be interpreted as involving two flows—a flow of goods from the business to the consumer, and a financial flow (reflecting a change in indebtedness) from the consumer to the business. The double-entry accounts of each individual entity record both flows from the viewpoint of that particular entity. The business enterprise may thus be expected to record the transaction by means of a credit entry in the sale of goods account and a debit entry in the trade debtors account. At the same time it can be envisaged (at least notionally) that the transaction is recorded in the books of the consumer by means of a debit entry in the purchase of goods account and a credit entry in the trade creditors account:

(a) Books of Trading Enterprise

Sale of Goods		Trade debtors	
	Trade debtors $100	Sale of goods $100	

(b) Books of Consumer

Purchase of Goods		Trade Creditors	
Trade creditors $100			Purchase of goods $100

Each individual system of accounts thus records one side of the flow of goods and one side of the financial flow.

By contrast, national income accounting usually ignores financial flows and records only movements in goods and services. Although the national income accounts are based on double entry, transactions are interpreted from the viewpoint of the economy in general and not from the viewpoint of individual entities or groups. The above transaction is thus recorded as a flow of goods from a trading enterprise to a consumer, and the double entry is achieved by combining the credit entry in the books of the business (the sale of goods) with the debit entry in the books of the consumer (the purchase of goods):

National Income Accounts

Trading Enterprises		Consumers	
	Sales to consumers $100	Purchases from trading enterprises $100	

The financial flow is not recorded, since for purposes of national income accounting the means of financing individual transactions is immaterial. Only net changes in indebtedness during a period are recorded, and it will be seen that these are residual or balancing items in the accounts of the different sectors.

Because the national income accounting system is concerned primarily with the recording of flows of goods and services, it requires a sector classification which distinguishes between the major groups participating in exchanges of goods and services, and a classification of transactions which emphasizes flows of goods and services as distinct from financial flows. The usual sector classification adopted in the national income and expenditure accounts follows that described above, with separate sectors in respect of trading enterprises, financial enterprises, consumers, governments and overseas. Since financial transactions are not recorded, the activity accounts required for each sector are restricted to the production account, the income distribution account, the income disposal account and the capital formation account.

The national income accounting system may be illustrated by means of a series of models, beginning with a simple two-sector model recording only current transactions and subsequently adding sectors and transactions to make the models more realistic.

National Income Model 1—Current Transactions for Two Sectors

Suppose that there are only two sectors in the economy, trading enterprises and consumers, and that the only transactions to be recorded in a particular year are current transactions involving: (a) the purchase of goods ($1 000) from trading enterprises by consumers; and (b) the payment of wages ($900) and distribution of profits by way of dividends ($100) by trading enterprises to consumers.

If no distinction is made between the different transactions according to their economic significance, the income and expenditure flows may be recorded in an integrated double-entry system consisting of two accounts only, one for trading enterprises and one for consumers:

Trading Enterprises

Wages	$900	Sales to consumers	$1 000
Profits (distributed as dividends)	100		
	$1 000		$1 000

Consumers

Purchases	$1 000	Wages	$900
		Dividends	100
	$1 000		$1 000

Since, however, the economic activities of each sector are of particular interest, a more useful system of double-entry accounts may be constructed by recording the transactions in sector activity accounts of the kind described earlier:

National Income and Expenditure Accounts—Current Transactions in Two Sectors
Trading Enterprises Production

Gross product c/d	$1 000	Sales to consumers	$1 000

Trading Enterprises Income Distribution

Factor payments—		Gross product b/d	$1 000
Wages	$900		
Surplus c/d	100		
	$1 000		$1 000
Transfer payments—			
Dividends	$100	Surplus b/d	$100

Consumers Income Distribution

Disposable income c/d	$1 000	Wages	$900
		Dividends	100
	$1 000		$1 000

Consumers Income Disposal

Purchases of goods from trading enterprises	$1 000	Disposable income b/d	$1 000

This also is a fully integrated system of double-entry accounts. By recording the transactions in this way, measures of two important concepts, gross product and disposable income, are obtained. It will be recalled that the gross product of a sector is represented by the residual balance of its production account and indicates the contribution which the sector makes to national production. The gross product of trading enterprises is equal in this simple case to sales to consumers. The disposable income of a sector is represented by the residual balance of the sector's income distribution account, and is thus equal to the excess of income receivable over income payable, i.e. undistributed income.

Given an integrated system of activity accounts of this kind, important aggregate data in respect of the economy in general may be derived by consolidating the activity accounts of the different sectors to obtain a consolidated national production account, a consolidated national income distribution account, etc. The usual consolidation techniques described in Chapter 12 may be employed to eliminate inter-sector transactions recorded on the debit side of an activity account of one sector and on the credit side of the same activity account of another sector. In our simple model, the consolidated accounts take the following form:

Consolidated National Income and Expenditure Accounts—Current Transactions in Two Sectors

Consolidated Production

Gross product of trading enterprises	$1 000	Sales to consumers	$1 000

Consolidated Income Distribution

Disposable income of consumers	$1 000	Gross product of trading enterprises	$1 000

Consolidated Income Disposal

Consumers' expenditure	$1 000	Disposable income of consumers	$1 000

The consolidated production account records on the left-hand side the gross products of the productive sectors which make up the total value of production of the economy for the year (gross domestic product at market prices), and on the right-hand side the total value of the final expenditures which absorb the production (gross national expenditure at market prices). The consolidated income distribution account shows how the gross national product is distributed (in this simple example it is distributed wholly to consumers), and the consolidated income disposal account shows how it is finally spent or saved (in this case it is spent wholly on goods and services for current consumption).

It will be seen that the three consolidated activity accounts dealing with current transactions reflect three different ways of looking at national production, which may be described as the production viewpoint, the income viewpoint and the expenditure viewpoint respectively. Because policy-makers are especially interested in the income-creating effects of national production, the practice is frequently adopted of compiling a summary national income and expenditure account, which differs from the consolidated production account in that incomes created (factor incomes and surplus items) are substituted for the gross products of the productive sectors on the left-hand side, while the right-hand side is expressed in the form of final expenditures instead of revenues from sales. The resulting income aggregate, described as gross national income, is identically equal to gross national expenditure:

Summary National Income and Expenditure

Income		Expenditure	
Wages	$900	Consumers' expenditure	$1 000
Trading enterprises' surplus	100		
Gross national income at market prices	$1 000	Gross national expenditure at market prices	$1 000

National Income Model 2 — Capital Transactions Added

The next step is to introduce capital transactions into the two-sector system. In the national income accounts, interest is centred on saving and capital formation, but there is also a need to record each sector's net borrowing or net lending. It has been seen that capital formation may take two forms, investment in inventories and investment in fixed capital assets, and that as fixed capital assets are used up in the course of production it is necessary to set aside portion of the value of production as depreciation allowances, which thus constitute a special kind of saving. By deducting depreciation allowances from gross domestic product at market prices, it is possible to measure net domestic product at market prices. If it is assumed that the depreciation allowances accurately measure the consumption or using up of the capital assets, a distinction can be made between gross investment and net investment, the latter being defined as gross investment *minus* depreciation allowances.

Saving takes place when a sector does not distribute or spend the whole of its available income. The saving of a sector may thus be defined as the disposable income of the sector *minus* its final expenditure on goods and services, and is represented by the residual balance of the sector's income disposal account. This saving is carried down to the capital formation account and there used to finance capital formation directly (as in the case of trading enterprises), or indirectly (as in the case of consumers, who lend their savings to trading enterprises or other sectors which engage in investment activity).

When saving and investment transactions are introduced into the system, it is necessary to provide a separate capital formation account for each sector. However, the national income accounts do not include sector financial capital transactions accounts. The net lending (or net borrowing) item in each sector's capital formation account is reflected in a matching net borrowing (or net lending) item in the capital formation account of another sector.

To illustrate the effect of capital transactions on the system, assume that the gross product of trading enterprises takes the form of goods and services sold to consumers, $750, and sales of fixed capital assets, $250; that, after providing for depreciation of

$50, the gross product is allocated between wages ($700) and surplus ($250); that $200 of the trading enterprise surplus is distributed through dividends and profit withdrawals, leaving $50 as trading enterprise undistributed or disposable income (because it is assumed that profits of unincorporated businesses are wholly withdrawn by their owners, the disposable income of trading enterprises represents undistributed company profits); and that consumers lend their savings to trading enterprises. These transactions are recorded in the double-entry activity accounts of the two sectors as illustrated:

National Income and Expenditure Accounts—Two Sectors with Capital Transactions

Trading Enterprises Production

Gross product c/d	$1 000	Sales to consumers	$750
		Sales of fixed capital assets	250
	$1 000		$1 000

Trading Enterprises Income Distribution

Depreciation allowances	$50	Gross product b/d	$1 000
Net product c/d	950		
	$1 000		$1 000
Factor payments—		Net product b/d	950
Wages	700		
Surplus c/d	250		
	$950		$950
Transfer payments—		Surplus b/d	250
Dividends and withdrawals	200		
Disposable income c/d	50		
	$250		$250

Trading Enterprises Disposal

Saving c/d	$50	Disposable income b/d	$50

Trading Enterprises Capital Formation

Fixed capital investment	$250	Saving b/d	$50
		Depreciation allowances	50
		Borrowing from consumers	150
	$250		$250

Consumers Income Distribution

Disposable income c/d	$900	Wages	$700
		Dividends and withdrawals	200
	$900		$900

Consumers Income Disposal

Purchases of goods and services	$750	Disposable income b/d	$900
Saving c/d	150		
	$900		$900

Consumers Capital Formation

Lending to trading enterprises	$150	Saving b/d	$150

Consolidated activity accounts may now be constructed as follows:

Consolidated National Income and Expenditure Accounts—Two Sectors with Capital Transactions

Consolidated Production

Gross product of trading enterprises	$1 000	Sales to consumers	$750
		Sales of fixed capital assets	250
	$1 000		$1 000

Consolidated Income Distribution

Depreciation allowances	$50	Gross product of trading enterprises	$1 000
Disposable income of trading enterprises	50		
Disposable income of consumers	900		
	$1 000		$1 000

Consolidated Income Disposal

Trading enterprises' saving	$50	Disposable income of trading enterprises	$50
Consumers' expenditure	750	Disposable income of consumers	900
Consumers' saving	150		
	$950		$950

Consolidated Capital Formation

Fixed capital investment	$250	Consumers' saving	$150
		Depreciation allowances	50
		Trading enterprises' saving	50
	$250		$250

The summary national income and expenditure account may again be compiled by substituting incomes created for the gross product which is recorded on the left-hand side of the consolidated production account, and expressing the right-hand side in the form of final expenditures. The expenditures which make up gross national expenditure are automatically expressed in terms of selling prices, while the income earned by factors of production (net national income at factor cost) is net of depreciation. Accordingly, depreciation must be added to factor incomes in order to arrive at gross national income and thereby make the two sides of the summary account balance:

Summary National Income and Expenditure

Income		Expenditure	
Wages	$700	Consumers' expenditure	$750
Trading enterprises' surplus	250	Fixed capital investment	250
Net national income at factor cost	950		
Depreciation allowances	50		
Gross national income	$1 000	Gross national expenditure	$1 000

National Income Model 3 — Government Sector Added

It is now necessary to consider how the economic activities of governments are fitted into the national income accounting framework. It has been seen that governments engage in productive activities by buying goods and services from other sectors and employing public servants, with a view to providing for the collective wants of the community. Governments are also concerned with other transactions of a kind that so far have been considered only incidentally in this section, viz. transfer transactions as opposed to exchange transactions.

To an important degree, the activities of governments are financed by means of taxation, which may be regarded as one form of transfer. Indirect taxes imposed on particular forms of expenditure are included in the selling prices of the goods and services concerned, and the proceeds transferred to governments by the enterprises making the sales. Direct taxes imposed on income or wealth are paid directly to governments by the entities on whom they are imposed. Other transfer transactions of governments include interest payable on the national debt and cash social service benefits, such as old-age pensions and child endowment payments.

It will be recalled that, because of the nature of government services, there is a problem in valuing government output and measuring the contribution which governments make to national product. Conventionally, government output is valued at cost, with the result that, in the absence of depreciation allowances, the gross product of governments is equal to wages and salaries paid to public servants.

Suppose that trading enterprises sell goods and services to consumers ($650), to governments ($100) and to other trading enterprises in the form of fixed capital assets ($250); that after providing for depreciation ($50) and paying indirect taxes ($50) and direct taxes on companies ($50), their gross product is allocated among wages ($700), dividends and withdrawals ($100) and undistributed company income ($50). Suppose further that governments, in addition to buying the aforementioned goods and services from trading enterprises, pay the wages of public servants ($100), interest on the national debt ($20) and cash social service benefits ($50); that they receive, in addition to the taxes paid by trading enterprises, direct taxes from persons ($150); and that they spend $50 on public works. Consumers may be assumed to lend their savings to the other two sectors to the extent that it is necessary to achieve balance in the capital formation accounts. These transactions may be recorded in a fully integrated set of double-entry activity accounts as follows:

National Income and Expenditure Accounts—Three Sectors
Trading Enterprises Production

Gross product c/d	$1 000	Sales to consumers	$650
		Sales to governments	100
		Sales of fixed capital assets	250
	$1 000		$1 000

Trading Enterprises Income Distribution

Depreciation allowances	$50	Gross product b/d	$1 000
Indirect taxes	50		
Net product at factor cost c/d	900		
	$1 000		$1 000
Factor payments—		Net product at factor cost b/d	900
Wages	700		
Surplus c/d	200		
	$900		$900
Transfer payments—		Surplus b/d	200
Direct taxes on companies	50		
Dividends and withdrawals	100		
Disposable income c/d	50		
	$200		$200

Trading Enterprises Income Disposal

Saving c/d	$50	Disposable income b/d	$50

Trading Enterprises Capital Formation

Fixed capital investment	$250	Saving b/d	$50
		Depreciation allowances	50
		Borrowing from consumers	150
	$250		$250

Governments Production

Purchases from trading		Value of output—	
enterprises	$100	Collective consumption	$150
Gross product c/d	100	Fixed capital assets	50
	$200		$200

Governments Income Distribution

Net product c/d	$100	Gross product b/d	$100
Wages	$100	Net product b/d	$100
Transfer payments—		Transfer incomes—	
Interest	20	Indirect taxes	50
Cash social services benefits	50	Direct taxes on companies	50
Disposable income c/d	180	Direct taxes on persons	150
	$250		$250

Governments Income Disposal

Government expenditure on		Disposable income b/d	$180
current goods and services			
(collective consumption)	$150		
Saving c/d	30		
	$180		$180

Governments Capital Formation

Fixed capital investment	$50	Saving b/d	$30
		Borrowing from consumers	20
	$50		$50

Consumers Income Distribution

Direct taxes	$150	Wages from trading enterprises	$700
Disposable income c/d	820	Wages from governments	100
		Dividends and withdrawals	100
		Interest from governments	20
		Cash social service benefits	50
	$970		$970

Consumers Income Disposal

Purchases of goods and services	$650	Disposable income b/d	$820
Saving c/d	170		
	$820		$820

Consumers Capital Formation

Lending to trading enterprises	$150	Saving b/d	$170
Lending to governments	20		
	$170		$170

Consolidation of the sector activity accounts results in the following set of national activity accounts:

Consolidated National Income and Expenditure Accounts—Three Sectors
Consolidated Production

Gross product of trading enterprises	$1 000	Sales by trading enterprises to consumers	$650
Gross product of governments	100	Sales by trading enterprises of fixed capital assets	250
		Government output for collective consumption	150
		Government output of fixed capital assets	50
	$1 100		$1 100

Consolidated Income Distribution

Depreciation allowances—		Gross product of trading enterprises	$1 000
Trading enterprises	$50	Gross product of governments	100
Disposable income of trading enterprises	50		
Disposable income of governments	180		
Disposable income of consumers	820		
	$1 100		$1 100

Consolidated Income Disposal

Government expenditure on current goods and services	$150	Disposable income of trading enterprises	$50
Consumers' expenditure	650	Disposable income of governments	180
Trading enterprises' saving	50	Disposable income of consumers	820
Governments' saving	30		
Consumers' saving	170		
	$1 050		$1 050

Consolidated Capital Formation

Trading enterprises' fixed capital investment	$250	Depreciation allowances— Trading enterprises	$50
Governments' fixed capital investment	50	Trading enterprises' saving	50
		Governments' saving	30
		Consumers' saving	170
	$300		$300

Gross domestic product is again represented by the gross products of the various sectors as recorded on the left-hand side of the consolidated production account:

Gross product of trading enterprises	$1 000
Gross product of governments	100
Gross domestic product	$1 100

The introduction of indirect taxes into the system makes it necessary to distinguish between net product (or income) at factor cost, and net product (or income) at market prices, the relationship between the various concepts of national product (or income) being expressed as follows:

Wage incomes from trading enterprises	$700	
Surplus of trading enterprises	200	
Wage incomes from governments	100	
Net domestic product (or net national income) at factor cost		$1 000
Add: Indirect taxes		50
Net domestic product (or net national income) at market prices		1 050
Add: Depreciation allowances of trading enterprises		50
Gross domestic product (or gross national income) at market prices		$1 100

Gross national expenditure is automatically expressed in terms of market prices. The summary national income and expenditure account may again be constructed by substituting the above income data for items recorded on the left-hand side of the consolidated production account, and by expressing the items on the right-hand side of the consolidated production account as final expenditures. The introduction of the government sector results in: (a) a distinction between current expenditure on goods and services undertaken directly by consumers and current expenditure by governments in the form of collective consumption; and (b) a distinction between capital formation by trading enterprises and capital formation by governments. The aggregate of capital formation by the non-government sectors (fixed capital investment before providing for depreciation *plus* investment in inventories) is usually described as gross private investment, and the aggregate of capital formation by governments (fixed capital investment before providing for depreciation *plus* investment in inventories) may be called gross government investment:

Summary National Income and Expenditure

Income		Expenditure	
Wages	$800	Consumers' expenditure	$650
Trading enterprise surplus	200	Government expenditure on collective consumption	150
		Gross private investment	250
Net national income at factor cost	1 000	Gross government investment	50
Indirect taxes	50		
Net national income at market prices	1 050		
Depreciation allowances	50		
Gross national income at market prices	$1 100	Gross national expenditure at market prices	$1 100

Before the national income accounting system can be regarded as complete, it needs to be extended further by including at least two other sectors (financial enterprises and the overseas sector). The problems associated with these sectors have already been discussed and it is a simple matter to integrate their activity accounts into the double-entry framework which has been illustrated in the above models. When the overseas sector is introduced into the system, it is necessary to distinguish between concepts of gross domestic product at market prices and gross national product at market prices. Gross domestic product at market prices has been defined above as the sum of the gross products of the productive sectors (trading enterprises, governments and financial enterprises). This is in accordance with standard international terminology, which defines gross national product at market prices as the market value of the production attributable to the normal residents of the economy (as opposed to factors of production located in the economy). The international terminology thus treats gross national product as the gross products of the domestic sectors minus the disposable income of the overseas sector (the latter being equivalent to the income earned by overseas factors of production located in domestic economy *minus* the income earned by locally-owned factors of production located overseas).

Because of the lack of data, the system of national income accounts that has been described in this section often needs to be condensed in practice. The Australian system of national income and expenditure accounts, which is based on the U.N. System of National Accounts, consists of consolidated or summary accounts as follows:

(a) a summary domestic production account, which is in effect a consolidated production account for the economy;

(b) a summary national income and outlay account, which shows how the national income is distributed among factors of production in the form of wages, surplus items, etc.;

(c) a summary national capital account, which is in effect a consolidated capital formation account for the economy; and

(d) an overseas transactions account, which records transactions with the rest of the world.

The national income and outlay account and the national capital account are then both disaggregated into four separate accounts for each of the domestic sectors— corporate trading enterprises (including public trading enterprises), financial enterprises, households (including unincorporated enterprises) and general government.

The U.N. System of National Accounts suggests that depreciation (which is called consumption of fixed capital) and inventories should be the subject of valuation adjustments (of the kind described in Chapter 19), in order that all transactions recorded in the national income accounts for any year should be valued in terms of the average current prices ruling in that year. In the Australian National Accounts a so-called stock valuation adjustment is made but no valuation adjustment is made in respect of depreciation.

The U.N. System of National Accounts also proposes the presentation of national income and expenditure estimates in constant prices, and the Australian National Accounts provide estimates of gross domestic product, gross national expenditure and some of their main components in terms of constant prices. Although specific price indexes are applied to the different components for the purpose of deriving estimates at constant prices, the general effect of adjusting current price data to constant prices is similar to the results which are achieved under the relative price change approach. The latter is described in Chapter 21 as one of the measurement and valuation systems used by business enterprises, but it should be noted that current prices in national accounting systems are usually interpreted to mean current replacement costs and not market selling values.

The use of the international system helps to ensure uniformity in international comparisons, but for the purposes of detailed economic analysis in a particular country it is not nearly as useful as the expanded system of integrated activity accounts that has been described in this chapter.

Flow-of-funds Accounts

Flow-of-funds accounts represent a different kind of national accounting system from national income and expenditure accounts, being designed to throw light on financial flows (which are largely ignored in national income accounting) as well as the flows of goods and services (sometimes called non-financial flows) which are recorded in the national income accounts. Flow-of-funds accounts in particular are intended to measure changes in the financial structure of the economy and in the financial relationships between different groups, and incidentally to illustrate the inter-dependence of financial and non-financial flows. The flow-of-funds accounts show, in relation to significant sectors of the economy, how funds have been derived (through the earning of revenue or the incurring of financial obligations) and used (through the incurring of costs or the creation of assets). Flow-of-funds analysis is particularly important because of the information it provides as a basis for monetary policy, but it also throws light on the financial effects of fiscal and other aspects of economic policy.

The difference between flow-of-funds accounting and national income accounting may be illustrated by reference to the recording of a simple transaction, such as the credit sale of goods worth $100 by a trading enterprise to a consumer. It has been seen that such a transaction is recorded in the accounts of the individual participating entities by means of two entries in each set of books:

(a) **Books of Trading Enterprise**

Sale of Goods		Trade Debtors	
	Trade debtors $100	Sale of goods $100	

(b) **Books of Consumer**

Purchase of Goods		Trade Creditors	
Trade· creditors $100			Purchase of goods $100

On page 383 it was shown that, for purposes of national income accounting, this transaction is recorded by ignoring the change in indebtedness between the parties to the transaction and concentrating on the flow of goods. This means, in effect, combining the credit entry in the accounts of the trading enterprise with the debit entry in the accounts of the consumer:

National Income Accounts

Trading Enterprises		Consumers	
	Sales to consumers $100	Purchases from trading enterprises $100	

Flow-of-funds accounts, on the other hand, record both financial flows (reflecting changes in indebtedness) and flows of goods and services. This means that each transaction is recorded *four* times in the flow-of-funds system, reflecting the debit and credit entries in the books of both parties to the transaction. The above transaction may be accounted for in the following way:

Flow-of-funds Accounts

	Trading Enterprises		Consumers	
	Dr.	Cr.	Dr.	Cr.
Non-financial flow Sales and purchases of goods		$100	$100	
Financial flow Change in financial claims (trade credit)	$100			$100

If 'Uses of Funds' and 'Sources of Funds' are substituted for the abbreviations 'Dr.' and 'Cr.', in effect two flow-of-funds statements (or sources and uses tables, as they are sometimes called) have been constructed. It will be observed that the four entries result not only in lateral balance (with equal debits and credits in each half of the transaction) but also in vertical balance (with equal debits and credits in each sector).

Not all transactions involve the transfer of goods and services. Some transactions, such as the repayment of a debt, are wholly financial. If the debt incurred by the consumer as a result of the foregoing transaction is subsequently repaid, the books of the consumer record a debit entry in the creditors' account and a credit entry in the cash account, while the books of the trading enterprise record a debit entry in the cash account and a credit entry in the debtors' account. All four entries are recorded as financial flows in the flow-of-funds accounts:

	Trading Enterprises		Consumers	
	Dr.	Cr.	Dr.	Cr.
Non-financial flows				
—				
Financial flows				
Change in cash balances	$100 .			$100
Change in financial claims		$100	$100	

Transactions such as barter, which do not involve any financial flows at all, are not recorded in the flow-of-funds accounts. Likewise transactions such as depreciation, which are internal to a particular accounting unit, are usually not recorded in the integrated system of accounts, although they may be recorded by way of memoranda. The only transactions which are recorded in conventional flow-of-funds systems are those which (a) involve two economic units and (b) involve financial flows.

For an individual sector, a flow-of-funds account can be drawn up that is somewhat similar in form to the funds statement which forms one of the accounting reports of a business enterprise (see Figure 15—F).

Figure 15—F
Flow-of-funds Account for the Trading Enterprise Sector

Sources of Funds

(a) **Non-financial**
   Revenue from sale of goods and services
   Proceeds from sale of fixed assets
(b) **Financial**
   Increases in financial obligations _____
      Total sources $ _____

Uses of Funds

(a) **Non-financial**
   Purchases of goods and services
   Capital expenditure on fixed assets
   Wages and salaries
   Dividends
   Taxes
(b) **Financial**
   Increases in financial assets (cash, debtors, securities, etc.) _____
      Total uses $ _____

For the whole economy, the individual sector flow-of-funds accounts are combined in such a way as to describe flows between sectors as well as the sources and uses of funds of an individual sector. For this purpose, it is convenient to set out the flow-of-funds accounts in the form of Figure 15—G. The sectors and transactions are merely intended to be illustrative, and an indication is given of the way in which a hypothetical transaction, the sale of goods and services by trading enterprises to consumers for cash, is recorded in the system.

It will be seen that only transactions involving movements in cash or changes in indebtedness are recorded as financial transactions. The payment of taxes thus reflects a non-financial flow (in addition to the financial flow associated with the movement in cash), even though goods and services are not directly involved. The method of recording transactions which is used in flow-of-funds accounting and the special emphasis placed on the financing aspect result in a different classification of

Figure 15—G
Hypothetical Flow-of-funds Accounts for an Economy

Sector / Transactions	Trading Enterprises		Banks		Other Financial Institutions		Governments		Consumers		Overseas		Totals	
	U.	S.	U.	S.	U.	S.	U.	S.	U.	S.	U.	S.	U.	S.
Non-financial														
Sales and purchases of trading goods and services		x							x					
Sales and purchases of fixed assets														
Wages and salaries														
Dividends														
Taxes														
... : ...														
... : ...														
Financial														
Cash and bank deposits	x									x				
Bank advances														
Government securities														
Shares and debentures														
Mortgages														
Trade credit														
... : ...														
... : ...														
Totals														

Note : The sale of goods and services by trading enterprises to consumers for cash is reflected by entries (x) in these cells.

U. = uses of funds; S. = sources of funds.

sectors and transactions from that adopted for national income accounting purposes. The detailed recording of financial transactions is matched by a much finer sector classification, with the financial enterprises sector in particular being broken down into a number of different sectors, e.g. central bank, trading banks, savings banks, life assurance companies and hire-purchase companies.

Because the conventional flow-of-funds accounting system does not record transactions internal to a sector, it does not measure incomes produced by different sectors or differentiate between the different forms of economic activity, such as production, consumption and investment, which as has been seen are recorded in separate activity accounts for each sector in the national income accounting system. The exclusion of internal book entries from the flow-of-funds accounts also means that accounting profits and losses are not measured in the system, and that the revenue and expenditure flows which are recorded do not always coincide with accounting revenues and costs. The full cost of acquiring fixed capital assets is recorded as a non-financial use of funds at the time the transaction takes place, and the proceeds from the sale of fixed assets appear as a non-financial source of funds. It does not follow, as might appear at first sight, that the flow-of-funds accounts are drawn up on a purely cash basis. Whether a transaction is recorded on a cash or an accrual basis depends rather on its effect on inter-sector financial relationships. Business transactions, such as the sale of goods, are recorded on an accrual basis because the financial position of the business changes as soon as the title to the goods is transferred, whether or not cash is received immediately in payment for the goods. The receipt of taxes, on the other hand, is usually recorded in the flow-of-funds accounts on a cash basis, because the government maintains only cash accounts and its recorded financial position does not change until cash is actually received. This difference in recording procedures is likely to cause difficulties if the two parties to a transaction do not record it at the same time, as may happen when the accounts of one party are maintained on a cash basis and the other employs an accrual system of accounting.

It has been seen that in national income accounting most intra-sector transactions are eliminated by consolidating the accounts of individual entities within the sectors. In flow-of-funds accounting, on the other hand, not all the sector accounts are consolidated. The accounts of individual trading enterprises, for example, are merely combined when they are aggregated, with the result that the flow-of-funds accounts for the trading enterprise sector include transactions between businesses as well as transactions with other sectors. Usually the only sectors whose accounts are consolidated (i.e. whose intra-sector transactions are eliminated) are the government, banking and overseas sectors. This is done in order to measure the net impact of the activities of each of these sectors on the rest of the economy.

An Illustration of a Flow-of-funds Accounting System

If it is assumed that transactions are classified in accordance with Figure 15—G, and that the economy consists of four sectors (trading enterprises, banks, central government and consumers), the technique of flow-of-funds accounting and the construction of an integrated system of flow-of-funds accounts can be illustrated by reference to the following types of hypothetical transactions:

(a) the payment of wages and salaries by trading enterprises and the government;

(b) the sale of goods and services to and by trading enterprises;

(c) the sale of goods and services by trading enterprises to the central government and consumers;

(d) the payment of taxes by trading enterprises and consumers;

(e) the sale of securities by the government to banks; and

(f) the sale of houses or property by trading enterprises.

(a) *Payment of Wages and Salaries*

Suppose that wages and salaries are paid by trading enterprises ($600) and the government ($25). Each of these transactions consists of a non-financial flow of labour services and a financial flow reflecting the movement in financial assets (cash or bank deposits), and may be recorded as follows:

Sector Transactions	Banks		Trading Enterprises		Central Government		Consumers	
	U.	S.	U.	S.	U.	S.	U.	S.
Non-financial Wages and salaries			$600		$25			$625
Financial Cash and bank deposits				$600		$25	$625	

(b) *Sale of Goods and Services to and by Trading Enterprises*

Suppose that trading enterprises buy $500 worth of goods and services from each other, consisting of trading goods and services ($400) and fixed capital assets ($100); that some of the purchases of trading goods and services enter cost of sales ($340) and some represent additions to inventories ($60); and that the buyers pay $300 in cash (increasing their bank overdrafts by $150 in order to do so) and receive credit for the remainder. This series of transactions may be interpreted as a number of non-financial flows (resulting from the purchase and sale of goods and services) accompanied by financial flows (involving movements in cash and changes in indebtedness). If all the cash received by the supplying firms is deposited in their bank accounts, the rise in bank advances resulting from the increased overdrafts of the purchasing firms is matched by either an equivalent increase in the bank deposits of the supplying firms or a reduction in *their* overdrafts. If the supplying firms increase their holdings of cash, on the other hand, this implies a fall in bank cash and the net rise in bank advances exceeds the net rise in bank deposits by the amount of this cash outflow. On the assumption that the supplying firms do not use the proceeds to reduce overdrafts, the transaction may be recorded in the banks' flow-of-funds accounts as a debit entry in respect of bank advances ($150) and a credit entry in respect of cash and deposits ($150). The sales of the supplying firms ($500) are matched by increases in their cash and deposits ($300), and debtors ($200), while the purchasing firms finance the transactions by running down their cash and deposits ($150), increasing their bank overdrafts ($150) and increasing their trade credit obligations ($200):

Sector Transactions	Banks		Trading Enterprises		Central Government		Consumers	
	U.	S.	U.	S.	U.	S.	U.	S.
Non-financial								
Sales and purchases								
of trading goods								
and services—								
Sales				$400				
Purchases entering								
cost of sales			$340					
Purchases added								
to inventories			60					
Sales and purchases								
of fixed assets—								
New assets			100	100				
Financial								
Cash and bank								
deposits		$150	300	150				
Bank advances	$150			150				
Trade credit			200	200				

(c) Sale of Goods and Services by Trading Enterprises to Government and Consumers

Suppose that the central government buys trading goods and services worth $50 from trading enterprises (paying in cash) and that consumers buy goods and services worth $550 from trading enterprises, paying $470 in cash and receiving the remainder on credit. These are straightforward transactions involving both non-financial and financial flows which may be recorded as follows:

Sector Transactions	Banks		Trading Enterprises		Central Government		Consumers	
	U.	S.	U.	S.	U.	S.	U.	S.
Non-financial								
Sales and purchases								
of trading goods								
and services				$600	$50		$550	
Financial								
Cash and bank								
deposits			$520			$50		$470
Trade credit			80					80

(d) Payment of Taxes

The payment of income taxes by trading enterprises ($50) and consumers ($25) also needs to be recorded as a non-financial flow (reflecting the taxes levied), matched by a corresponding financial flow (the movement in cash):

Transactions \ Sector	Banks U.	Banks S.	Trading Enterprises U.	Trading Enterprises S.	Central Government U.	Central Government S.	Consumers U.	Consumers S.
Non-financial Taxes			$50			$75	$25	
Financial Cash and bank deposits				$50	$75			$25

(e) Sale of Securities by the Central Government to Banks

Suppose that the government issues securities which it sells to banks ($65). Both aspects of this transaction are financial. The national debt increases and the government's command over bank deposits rises by a corresponding amount, while from the banks' point of view the increase in financial assets is matched by an increase in deposit liabilities:

Transactions \ Sector	Banks U.	Banks S.	Trading Enterprises U.	Trading Enterprises S.	Central Government U.	Central Government S.	Consumers U.	Consumers S.
Financial Cash and bank deposits			$65		$65			
Government securities	$65					$65		

(f) Sale of Houses or Land by Trading Enterprises

If house-ownership is treated as a trading activity in flow-of-funds accounting (as is usual in national income accounting), the sale of new houses by trading enterprises to persons may be recorded in the same way as other sales of fixed assets. If, however, one wishes to ascertain the effect of house-ownership on the financial relationship between households and firms (a likely aim in view of the emphasis which flow-of-funds accounting places on financial relationships between different groups), there are advantages in placing house-owners in the consumer sector or in treating them as a separate sector altogether. If house-owners are regarded as consumers and they buy new houses ($50) and land ($30) from trading enterprises, paying $10 cash and borrowing on mortgage from banks to finance the balance, the transactions may be recorded as non-financial flows (the transfer of ownership) matched by financial flows (the changes in cash and indebtedness). As in (b) above, it is assumed that the advances made by banks are accompanied either by increased deposits (if the trading enterprises deposit the proceeds derived from the sale of the houses) or by cash outflows:

Sector Transactions	Banks U.	S.	Trading Enterprises U.	S.	Central Government U.	S.	Consumers U.	S.
Non-financial								
Sales and purchases of fixed assets—								
New assets				$50			$50	
Land transfers				30			30	
Financial								
Cash and bank deposits		$70	$80					$10
Mortgages	$70							70

Summary Flow-of-funds Statements

If it is assumed that there are no other transactions, the foregoing entries may be aggregated into summary flow-of-funds statements, one for each sector, as illustrated in Table 15—1. It has already been observed that the accounts of banks, governments and the overseas sector are consolidated (netted) to form the summary statements, while the accounts of the other sectors are combined (aggregated). Where debit and credit entries both exist in respect of a particular type of transaction (e.g. cash and bank deposits of consumers), the question arises whether both flows or only the net

Table 15—1
Summary Flow-of-funds Statements for a Four-sector Economy

Sector Transactions	Banks U.	S.	Trading Enterprises U.	S.	Central Government U.	S.	Consumers U.	S.
Non-financial								
Sales and purchases of trading goods and services—								
Sales				$1 000				
Purchases consumed or absorbed in cost of sales			$340		$50		$550	
Purchases added to inventories			60					
Sales and purchases of fixed assets—								
New assets			100	150			50	
Land transfers				30			30	
Wages and salaries			600		25			$625
Taxes			50			$75	25	
Financial								
Cash and bank deposits		$285	900	800	140	75	625	505
Bank advances	$150			150				
Government securities	65					65		
Mortgages	70							70
Trade credit			280	200				80
Totals	$285	$285	$2 330	$2 330	$215	$215	$1 280	$1 280

change should be recorded in the summary statement. This depends on the information which it is desired to obtain, but a good working rule is to record gross flows when in doubt. These can be easily netted but gross flows cannot be calculated from net figures.

In Australia, flow-of-funds accounts (so-called financial flow accounts) are published annually by the Reserve Bank of Australia. These differ in some respects from the accounts recommended in the U.N. System of National Accounts. Essentially the Australian accounts represent an elaboration, for nine major sectors, of the transactions which are included in two of the economic activity accounts—the capital formation account and the financial capital transactions account—which have been distinguished earlier in this chapter.

The major sectors in the Australian system are the Reserve Bank, other banks, life offices and pension funds, other financial groups, Australian Government, State and local governments, corporate trading enterprises (excluding public enterprises), households (including unincorporated enterprises), and rest of world.

In the Australian flow-of-funds accounts, the balancing item in each sector's capital formation and saving account—net lending or net borrowing—is carried down to a financial account, which records the detailed changes in financial assets and liabilities which in the aggregate make up the so-called financial surplus (equal to net lending) or financial deficit (equal to net borrowing).

The financial account records 14 classes under the heading 'Acquisition of financial assets' and 14 classes under the heading 'Incurrence of liabilities'; individual entries may be either positive or negative. The financial asset classes are as follows:

> bank deposits, notes and coin;
> savings bank deposits;
> advances of trading banks;
> other advances;
> Australian Government securities;
> local and semi-governmental securities;
> shares in co-operatives, etc.;
> ordinary and preference shares;
> debentures, notes and deposits;
> net contributions to life insurance, etc.;
> interest on life and superannuation funds;
> trade credit: debtors;
> asset formation abroad; and
> other claims.

The same 14 liability classes are distinguished, except that 'Trade credit: creditors' replaces 'Trade credit: debtors', and 'Liabilities incurred abroad' replaces 'Asset formation abroad'.

National Balance Sheets and National Wealth Statements

Whereas flow-of-funds accounts are concerned with movements in the assets and financial obligations of economic sectors or groups over time, national balance sheets record assets and financial obligations of the different sectors at particular points of time. They therefore provide information about financial relationships between sectors and about the financial structure of individual sectors. Because they throw light on such things as liquidity and the relative importance of physical assets and different classes of financial claims, national balance sheets have a useful role to play in the formulation of monetary and fiscal policy. When supplemented by national income data, they make it possible to measure capital-output relationships and thereby facilitate the analysis of economic growth.

The classification of sectors for purposes of national balance sheet analysis is naturally similar to that used in flow-of-funds accounting, and the classification of assets involves the same kind of division, between non-financial assets (fixed capital assets and stocks) and financial assets, which underlies the flow-of-funds accounts. Non-financial assets are sometimes called tangible assets in national balance sheet analysis and are sub-divided into non-reproducible assets (land and other natural resources) and reproducible assets (other fixed capital assets and inventories). If this basis of classification is used financial assets are called intangible assets. All items on the funds side of the national balance sheet are, of course, in the nature of financial claims.

The balance sheet of a sector may be constructed by aggregating the balance sheets of the individual entities which compose the sector. Whether the aggregation process takes the form of a consolidation or a combination of the individual balance sheets again depends on the purposes of the analysis, but it is usually desirable to present the sector balance sheets of banks, central governments and the overseas sector on a consolidated basis in order to measure their net relationship with other sectors. The balance sheets of other sectors may be compiled by combining the balance sheets of the individual entities of the sectors.

In order to construct the national balance sheet, the sector balance sheets are combined and not consolidated, so that inter-sector financial claims are not eliminated. In constructing what is called the national wealth statement, on the other hand, the sector balance sheets are consolidated and inter-sector financial claims are eliminated. The national wealth statement thus records three major components of national wealth, viz. fixed assets, inventories and net foreign claims (which may be negative if the assets of the overseas sector exceed its financial obligations). In calculating net foreign claims, allowance needs to be made for the foreign ownership of domestic physical assets. When paid-up equity (i.e. ordinary) shares are owned by foreign shareholders, it is necessary to allocate a pro-rated portion of the accumulated capital (i.e. reserves) of the companies concerned.

It follows from what has been said that the sector balance sheets must distinguish between domestic and foreign financial claims. Ideally, all financial claims in sector balance sheets should be classified by sectors. Table 15—2 shows how a national balance sheet and national wealth statement may be compiled by combining and consolidating respectively the hypothetical sector balance sheets of five sectors. It is assumed that the overseas sector owns $\frac{25}{300}$ of the equity capital of trading enterprises and is entitled to that proportion of the accumulated capital of $420, or

$$\frac{25}{300} \times \$420 = \$35.$$

Table 15—2
Constructing a National Balance Sheet and National Wealth Statement in a Five-sector Economy

Balance Sheet Item	Sector Balance Sheets										National Balance Sheet		National Wealth Statement	
	Trading Enterprises		Financial Enterprises		Governments		Consumers		Overseas					
	Assets	Equities	Assets	Equities	Assets	Equities	Assets	Equities	Assets	Equities	Assets	Equities	Assets	Equities
Non-financial assets														
Land	$100		$10		$50		$50		$10		$220		$220	
Buildings	185		30		100		120		25		460		460	
Other fixed assets	190		10		65		20		25		310		310	
Inventories	105		—		10		—		5		120		120	
Financial claims														
Cash and bank deposits	60			$240	35		140		5		240	$240		
Trade credit	165	$75				$10		$85	5		170	170		
Government securities	35		90			170	30		15		170	170		
Tax liabilities		40		10	100			40		$10	100	100		
Bank advances		65	105			15		20		5	105	105		
Mortgages	10	15	95					90			105	105		
Debentures		40		20			55		5		60	60		
Preference capital		15		10			25				25	25		
Equity capital—Contributed	50	300		20			245		25		320	320		
Accumulated	70	420		40			355		35		460	460		
Net claims of overseas sector										140		140		$140
Net wealth of domestic sectors	—		—			165		805				970		970
Totals	$970	$970	$340	$340	$360	$360	$1 040	$1 040	$155	$155	$2 865	$2 865	$1 110	$1 110

The net wealth of the economy is represented by the residual wealth of the domestic sectors claiming final ownership (i.e. governments and consumers), the net claims of the overseas sector being treated as a deduction from the total assets of the economy. The net wealth of the government sector may, of course, be negative in circumstances where governments have accumulated a heavy debt on unproductive expenditure or wars. On the basis of Table 15—2, a national wealth statement may be prepared in a form which emphasizes the major components of national wealth (see Table 15—3).

Table 15—3
National Wealth Statement for an Economy as at 31 December 1985

Non-financial assets		
Land		$220
Buildings		460
Other fixed assets		310
Inventories		120
		1 110
Less: **Net foreign claims**		
Foreign ownership of non-financial assets	$65	
Foreign ownership of financial assets	90	
	155	
Less: Foreign liabilities to the domestic economy	15	140
Net wealth of consumers	805	
Net wealth of governments	165	
National wealth		$970

The major problems in constructing national balance sheets and wealth statements are concerned with collection of data and valuation rather than definition and classification. As far as possible the sector and national balance sheets should be compiled by aggregating the balance sheets of individual entities. However, an obvious difficulty arises in respect of governments and consumers, who traditionally do not maintain formal accounting records of assets or, in the case of consumers at least, financial obligations.

The valuation problem is essentially one of expressing balance sheet items in terms of current or market values. Historical accounting figures provide a satisfactory means of valuing short-term financial claims, but assets and claims for which an active market exists (e.g. land and securities) need to be recorded on the basis of their current market values, while the current values of other assets subject to price changes need to be estimated in accordance with procedures described in Chapter 19 of this book. A final difficulty is to ensure that the valuation procedures adopted in preparing national balance sheets are consistent with those used in other systems of national accounting. This is one aspect of a general problem, which will now be considered, of integrating the different systems of national economic accounts into a single accounting framework.

No official national balance sheets or national wealth statements have been published in Australia, but the Reserve Bank's financial flow accounts are supplemented by some sector balance sheets for the main financial sectors.

Business Enterprise Accounts in Relation to National Accounting Systems

The satisfactory integration of the different national economic accounts requires action:

(a) to ensure that the data presented in the various systems are derived as far as possible from the same basic sources; and

(b) to develop an accounting framework which is capable of bringing the different systems together without sacrificing any of their essential characteristics or functions in the process.

Insofar as the first of these problems is concerned, attention will be concentrated on the relationship between the national economic accounts and business enterprise accounts.

In practice, the information which forms the basis of the various national accounting systems is derived from a multitude of often quite unrelated sources, so that the resulting estimates frequently contain statistical errors and lack mutual consistency. If a fully integrated structure of accounts is to be achieved, differences between the various systems ought to be confined to differences in concept, classification and coverage (reflecting their respective purposes) and should not contain discrepancies resulting from differences in statistical source material. The same basic data, that is to say, should be used in all the constituent systems of national accounts which make up the unified whole.

Insofar as business enterprises are concerned, this means making use of the accounting reports which firms prepare for their own internal purposes. The relationship between business enterprise accounting and national economic accounting may be illustrated by showing how the information contained in the hypothetical reports of a business enterprise can be adapted to serve the requirements of each of the national accounting systems. The accounting reports used in the following example are those of a trading company that does not engage in any manufacturing activity, and it is assumed that the values recorded in the reports do not require any adjustment for national accounting purposes.

The Accounting Reports of Business Enterprises

Table 15—4 illustrates the form in which accounting reports are usually presented to shareholders and the management of a company (with the detailed accounting classification omitted). The profit and loss statement proper records revenue and cost flows during the period and the derivation of profit; the appropriation statement shows how the profit is distributed; the balance sheet provides details of the firm's assets and equities at the end of the period; while the funds statement records movements in assets and financial obligations during the period. For purposes of subsequent analysis, Table 15—4 also includes the balance sheet of the company at the beginning of the year (the presentation of comparative figures is in any case a desirable practice). The number which appears in brackets after each line in the table is included to assist the reader and facilitate discussion.

Table 15—4
Accounting Reports of a Business Enterprise

(a) Profit and Loss Statement for Year

Sales (1)		$20 000
Less: Cost of sales (2)		
Opening inventory (3)	$5 000	
Purchases (4)	12 000	
	17 000	
Less: Closing inventory (5)	6 000	
		11 000
Gross profit (6)		9 000
Less: Expenses (7)		
Advertising (8)	800	
Wages and salaries (9)	2 000	
Payroll taxes (10)	500	
Depreciation of fixed assets (11)	1 200	
Interest on debentures (12)	500	
		5 000
Net profit (13)		$4 000

(b) Appropriation Statement for Year

Balance at beginning (14)		$1 000
Net profit (13)		4 000
		5 000
Less: Direct company taxes (15)	$1 000	
Dividends (16)	2 000	
		3 000
Balance at end (17)		$2 000

(c) Balance Sheet

At beginning of year			At end of year		
Assets			**Assets**		
Cash (18)		$500	Cash (27)		$1 000
Trade debtors (19)		2 500	Trade debtors (28)		4 000
Inventories (3)		5 000	Inventories (5)		6 000
Fixed assets			Fixed assets		
(at cost) (20)	$10 000		(at cost) (29)	$11 000	
Less: Provision			*Less*: Provision for		
for depreciation (21)	2 000		depreciation (30)	3 200	
		8 000			7 800
		$16 000			$18 800
Financial obligations			**Financial obligations**		
Trade creditors (22)		4 000	Trade creditors (31)		4 800
Debentures (23)		5 000	Debentures (32)		5 000
Shareholders'			Shareholders'		
equity (24)—			equity (33)—		
Contributed (25)	$6 000		Contributed (34)	$7 000	
Accumulated (26)	1 000		Accumulated (35)	2 000	
		7 000			9 000
		$16 000			$18 800

(d) Funds Statement for Year

Sources of funds	
Revenue from sales (1)	$20 000
New capital raised (34 — 25)	1 000
Increase in liabilities—Trade creditors (31 — 22)	800
Total funds available	$21 800
Uses of funds	
Costs and expenses incurred through external transactions (4 + 7 — 11)	15 800
Direct taxes (15)	1 000
Dividends (16)	2 000
Purchases of fixed assets (29 — 20)	1 000
Increases in financial assets (27 + 28) — (18 + 19)	2 000
Total funds applied	$21 800

National Income and Expenditure Accounts

It has been seen that the national income accounts are concerned primarily with the recording of economic activities involving the production of goods and services, the distribution of incomes, the allocation of incomes between consumption and saving, and the forms and financing of capital formation. Table 15—5 shows how the data recorded in Table 15—4 may be fitted into a framework of activity accounts designed to provide this information.

The classification of transactions according to economic significance instead of managerial function involves a substantial rearrangement of the data contained in the business accounting reports. In effect, it is necessary to break down the value of the enterprise's output (equal in the example to its sales) into two parts—the product created by the business (its gross product or value added) and the inputs of intermediate goods and services which are incorporated in its output. Since the additions to inventories represent unprocessed goods, they need to be deducted from purchases in order to calculate the net inputs of the business to be deducted from its output in calculating gross product. The gross product may thus be calculated as follows:

Value of output (sales)		$20 000
Less: Inputs of intermediate goods and services—		
Purchases of goods	$12 000	
Less: Additions to inventories	1 000	
	11 000	
Advertising	800	11 800
Gross product		$8 200

Part of the gross product is absorbed by depreciation allowances and indirect taxes, and the remainder is allocated to factors of production (wages and salaries, and surplus). For reasons that have already been discussed, interest payments are treated as transfers of surplus in national income accounting and not as costs.

The company's undistributed or disposable income represents the saving it makes available, along with depreciation allowances, to finance its capital formation. Although the capital formation account is generally similar to the business funds statement, certain differences in classification may be noted. In particular, the capital formation account emphasizes investment in inventories or fixed capital assets on the one hand, and savings used to finance investment on the other. Net lending to (or net borrowing from) other entities is in effect a residual item in this account, and for national income accounting purposes the raising of new share capital has much the same significance as other borrowing from the consumer sector. The number in brackets after each item in Table 15—5 refers to the source of the entry in Table 15—4.

Table 15—5
National Income and Expenditure Accounts of a Business Enterprise

Production

Purchases of intermediate goods and services—		Sales to consumers (1)	$20 000
Goods (4)	$12 000	Additions to inventories (5 — 3)	1 000
Advertising (8)	800		
Gross product c/d	8 200		
	$21 000		$21 000

Income Distribution

Depreciation allowances (11)	$1 200	Gross product b/d	$8 200
Indirect taxes (10)	500		
Net product at factor cost c/d	6 500		
	$8 200		$8 200
Factor payments—		Net product at factor cost b/d	6 500
Wages and salaries (9)	2 000		
Surplus c/d	4 500		
	$6 500		$6 500
Transfer payments—		Surplus b/d	4 500
Interest (12)	500		
Direct taxes (15)	1 000		
Dividends (16)	2 000		
Disposable income c/d (17 — 14)	1 000		
	$4 500		$4 500

Income Disposal

Saving c/d	$1 000	Disposable income b/d (17 — 14)	$1 000

Capital Formation

Investment in inventories (5 — 3)	$1 000	Saving b/d	$1 000
Fixed capital investment (29 — 20)	1 000	Depreciation allowances (11)	1 200
Net lending to (+) or borrowing from (—) other entities [(27 + 28) — (18 + 19)] — (34 — 25) — (31 — 22)	200		
	$2 200		$2 200

Flow-of-funds Accounts

It has been seen that flow-of-funds accounts record in detail external non-financial and financial flows, but usually do not record internal book entries such as depreciation. They therefore omit reference to accounting profits and losses, since these are not significant in relation to movements of funds among sectors.

In Table 15—6 the information recorded in Table 15—4 is reclassified and presented in the form of a conventional flow-of-funds account. Apart from the important distinction between non-financial and financial transactions, the main difference between Table 15—6 and the business funds statement included in Table 15—4 lies in the greater detail recorded in the flow-of-funds account. The numbers in brackets again refer to items in Table 15—4.

Table 15—6
The Flow-of-Funds Account of a Business Enterprise

Sources of Funds		
(i) **Non-financial**		
Sales revenue (1)		$20 000
(ii) **Financial**		
New capital issues (34 — 25)	$1 000	
Increase in trade liabilities (31 — 22)	800	1 800
Total		$21 800
Uses of Funds		
(i) **Non-financial**		
Purchases of goods and services—		
Purchases of goods entering		
cost of sales [4 — (5 — 3)]		11 000
Advertising (8)		800
Purchases resulting in additions to inventories (5 — 3)		1 000
Wages and salaries (9)		2 000
Interest (12)		500
Indirect taxes (10)		500
Direct taxes (15)		1 000
Dividends (16)		2 000
Fixed capital expenditure (29 — 20)		1 000
		19 800
(ii) **Financial**		
Increase in cash (27 — 18)	500	
Increase in trade debtors (28 — 19)	1 500	2 000
Total		$21 800

National Balance Sheets

In the analysis of business balance sheets for purposes of national accounting, it has been seen that it is necessary to distinguish between physical (or tangible) assets and financial assets, and to classify financial claims by sectors. In Table 15—7, the information contained in the end-of-year balance sheet in Table 15—4 is reclassified and presented in a form that is appropriate to the construction of a national balance sheet. It is assumed that the financial claims (both assets and equities) are wholly domestic. The figures in brackets again provide a cross reference to items in Table 15—4.

Table 15—7
The National Balance Sheet Statement of a Business Enterprise

Financial Obligations			Assets		
Domestic—			**Physical assets—**		
Trade			Fixed assets (29 — 30)	$7 800	
creditors (31)	$4 800		Inventories (5)	6 000	
Debentures (32)	5 000				$13 800
Shareholders' equity—			**Financial assets—**		
Contributed			**Domestic**		
(34)	$7 000		Cash (27)	1 000	
Accumulated			Trade debtors (28)	4 000	
(35)	2 000				
		9 000		5 000	
		$18 800	**Foreign**	—	
Foreign		—			5 000
		$18 800			$18 800

Although there are certain difficulties associated with sector classification and valuation, it is clear that the ordinary accounting reports of business enterprises provide most of the information required to build up a record of business transactions in the various national accounting systems. There are obvious advantages in having, for all systems, a common source of data which extends right back to the original accounting records. Given a consistent and sufficiently detailed classification framework in the accounts of individual entities, the economic accounting problem resolves itself into the task of collecting the data from individual entities (e.g. by enlarging the scope of income tax returns) and classifying and tabulating the data in accordance with the needs of each national accounting system. Although a formidable amount of cross-classification is required, the availability of electronic accounting equipment means that the tabulation process can easily be reduced to a rapidly performed, routine operation.

Towards a Unified Framework of National Economic Accounts

There remains the task of integrating the different systems into a single framework of national economic accounts. The careful reader will have observed that the national income and flow-of-funds accounts may be integrated merely by merging the full set of activity accounts for each sector.

It has been seen that the national income system is based on four activity accounts for each sector (production account, income distribution account, income disposal account and capital formation account). These four accounts record only non-financial flows, with the exception of the net lending or net borrowing item which appears as a balancing item in the capital formation account of each sector and which has its matching entry (to complete the double-entry record) in the capital formation account of another sector. If each of these net lending or net borrowing items, instead of being offset by entries in the accounts of other sectors, is carried down to a fifth activity account, established for the purpose of analysing financial flows (the financial capital transactions account), this in effect records both non-financial and financial flows within a single system of double-entry accounts.

Table 15—8 shows how the data given in Table 15—4 may be recorded in such a system, assuming four sectors. For purposes of the illustration, assume that the accounting reports of trading enterprises are combined rather than consolidated, so that transactions between trading enterprises (e.g. purchases of intermediate goods and services) are recorded as debit and credit entries in the same accounts. The reference numbers used to illustrate the double-entry are again taken from Table 15—4. Where the original reports do not automatically indicate the other sector involved in any transaction, a particular sector is assumed (thus it is supposed that interest on debentures is paid to financial enterprises). Since the accounts are incomplete, they have not been closed.

By expanding the classification of transactions and sectors, the system illustrated in Table 15—8 may thus be used to record both non-financial and financial flows. If the possibility of differences in sector classification and definition is ignored, the integrated system may be seen to differ from the national income system principally in that it incorporates the analysis of financial flows into the double-entry framework, while it differs from the conventional flow-of-funds system in that it records internal flows as well as the external transactions to which the latter system is restricted.

At this stage, the question naturally arises as to whether national balance sheets may be fitted into the scheme of integration. It is a relatively simple matter to incorporate national balance sheet data into the system, by substituting the total values of assets and equities at the end of the period for changes in values during the period (i.e. by substituting end-of-period stocks of assets and equities for periodic flows). This involves transforming the capital formation account and the financial capital transactions account for each sector into a series of accounts recording the assets and financial obligations of the sector. Table 15—9 shows how this may be done for the trading enterprise sector using the data recorded in Table 15—8 and combining different groups of assets and financial obligations into columnar ledger accounts (with a separate column for each class of asset or financial obligation). If this procedure is adopted, the complete system of national economic accounts consists of six accounts for each sector, of which three (production, income distribution and income disposal) record current revenue and expenditure flows, and three (physical assets, financial assets and financial obligations) record the assets and equities of the sector. The system is fully integrated, the double entry in respect of each transaction being achieved by a matching entry either in another account of the same sector or in an account of another sector. The recorded increases in contributed and accumulated shareholders' equity in the financial obligations account are thus matched by an increase in the financial assets of consumers and by the saving item in the trading enterprise income disposal account respectively.

From the balances of the accounts for assets and financial obligations as recorded in Table 15—9, it is possible to construct a national balance sheet in the form of Table 15—7. The flow-of-funds accounts in respect of capital transactions may, of course, be constructed merely by analysing the changes that have occurred in assets and financial obligations during the year.

The system that has been described is obviously over-simplified; in practice refinements in classification and definition must necessarily be made and valuation conflicts must be resolved. However, it is clear that there exists a conceptual framework of double-entry accounts within which national income and expenditure accounts, flow-of-funds accounts and national balance sheets all form constituent

Table 15—8
An Integrated National Income and Flow-of-funds Accounting System in a Four-sector Economy

Trading Enterprises

Production

Purchases from trading enterprises (4 + 8)	$12 800	Sales to trading enterprises (4 + 8)	$12 800
Gross product c/d	8 200	Sales to consumers (1)	20 000
		Sales of fixed assets (29 — 20)	1 000
		Additions to inventories (5 — 3)	1 000

Income Distribution

Depreciation allowances (11)	$1 200	Gross product b/d	$8 200
Indirect taxes (10)	500		
Wages and salaries (9)	2 000		
Interest (12)	500		
Direct taxes (15)	1 000		
Dividends (16)	2 000		
Disposable income c/d	1 000		

Income Disposal

Saving c/d	$1 000	Disposable income b/d	$1 000

Capital Formation

Fixed capital investment (29 — 20)	$1 000	Depreciation allowances (11)	$1 200
Additions to inventories (5 — 3)	1 000	Saving b/d	1 000
Net lending c/d	200		

Financial Capital Transactions

Increase in cash (27 — 18)	$500	Net lending b/d	$200
Increase in debtors (28 — 19)	1 500	Increase in creditors (31 — 22)	800
Increase in debtors (31 — 22)	800	Increase in ordinary share capital (34 — 25)	1 000

Financial Enterprises

Production

Income Distribution

Interest (12)	$500

Income Disposal

Capital Formation

Financial Capital Transactions

Reduction in cash (27 — 18)	$500

Governments

Production

Income Distribution

Indirect taxes (10)	$500
Direct taxes (15)	1 000

Income Disposal

Capital Formation

Financial Capital Transactions

Consumers

Income Distribution

Wages and salaries (9)	$2 000
Dividends (16)	2 000

Income Disposal

Purchases from trading enterprises (1) $20 000

Capital Formation

Financial Capital Transactions

Increase in ordinary share capital (34 − 25)	$1 000
Increase in creditors (28 − 19)	$1 500

Table 15—9

The Integration of Assets and Financial Obligations with the National Economic Accounts

Trading Enterprise Sector

Production

Purchases from trading enterprises (4 + 8)	$12 800	Sales to trading enterprises (4 + 8)	$12 8
Gross product c/d	8 200	Sales to consumers (1)	20 0
		Sales of fixed assets (29—20)	1 0
		Additions to inventories (5—3)	1 0

Income Distribution

Depreciation allowances (11)	$1 200	Gross product b/d	$8 2
Indirect taxes (10)	500		
Wages and salaries (9)	2 000		
Interest (12)	500		
Direct taxes (15)	1 000		
Dividends (16)	2 000		
Disposable income c/d	1 000		

Income Disposal

Saving c/d	$1 000	Disposable income b/d	$1 0

Physical Assets

	Inventories	Property	Other Fixed Capital Assets		Inventories	Property	Other Fixed Capital Assets
Balance b/d	$5 000	$3 000	$5 000	Sales	—	—	—
Additions	1 000	—	1 000	Depreciation allowances	—	$200	$1 0
				Balance c/d	$6 000	2 800	5 0
	$6 000	$3 000	$6 000		$6 000	$3 000	$6 0
Balance b/d	$6 000	$2 800	$5 000				

Financial Assets

	Cash	Trade Debtors	Government Securities		Cash	Trade Debtors	Government Securities
Balance b/d	$500	$2 500	—	Reductions during year	—	—	—
Increases during year	500	1 500	—	Balance c/d	$1 000	$4 000	—
	$1 000	$4 000	—		$1 000	$4 000	—
Balance b/d	$1 000	$4 000	—				

Financial Obligations

	Trade Creditors	Deben- tures	Shareholders' Equity Contri- buted	Shareholders' Equity Accumu- lated		Trade Creditors	Deben- tures	Shareholders' Equity Contri- buted	Shareholders' Equity Accum- late
Reductions during year	—	—	—	—	Balance b/d	$4 000	$5 000	$6 000	$1 00
Balance c/d	$4 800	$5 000	$7 000	$2 000	Increases during year	800	—	1 000	1 00
	$4 800	$5 000	$7 000	$2 000		$4 800	$5 000	$7 000	$2 00
					Balance b/d	$4 800	$5 000	$7 000	$2 00

parts of an integrated national accounting system. In its essential characteristics, the framework of national economic accounts that has been described in this chapter may thus be seen to be remarkably similar to the business enterprise accounting system which has been examined in earlier chapters. Nothing could illustrate more clearly the universality of the accounting approach.

References

Australian Bureau of Statistics, *Australian National Accounts*: *National Income and Expenditure* (annual series), Australian Bureau of Statistics, Canberra.
Reserve Bank of Australia, *Statistical Bulletin*: *Financial Flow Accounts Supplement* (annual series), Reserve Bank of Australia, Sydney.
United Nations, *A System of National Accounts*, United Nations, New York, 1968.

Discussion Questions

1 Discuss the relationships between gross domestic product, gross national product and gross national expenditure.

2 Explain the treatment of interest in the economic activity accounts of a bank, by reference to differences in the services provided by banks and trading enterprises.

3 Explain the differences between:
    (a) final and intermediate goods and services;
    (b) gross and net product;
    (c) gross product at market prices and gross product at factor cost;
    (d) disposable income and saving.

4 Discuss the significance of the following in relation to the economic activity accounts of a national income accounting system:
    (a) intermediate goods and services;
    (b) transfer payments of financial enterprises;
    (c) saving by consumers;
    (d) gross product of governments;
    (e) disposable income of trading enterprises.

5 Write explanatory notes on the following concepts used in national income accounting:
    (a) value of output of the government sector;
    (b) gross product of financial enterprises;
    (c) net borrowing by the overseas sector;
    (d) disposable income of consumers;
    (e) net product at factor cost of trading enterprises;
    (f) gross domestic product at market prices;
    (g) gross national expenditure at market prices.

6 Consider the possible role of a national income accounting system in economic forecasting.

7 Contrast national income and flow-of-funds accounting systems from the point of view of: (a) purpose; (b) types of transactions recorded; and (c) sector classifications. Would it be possible to integrate the two systems in a single double-entry framework?

8 To what extent can the purposes of national income and flow-of-funds accounting be served by the same set of economic activity accounts? Consider with reference to both sectors and transactions.

9 Discuss the possible uses of the national balance sheet.

10 To what extent do the financial statements of business enterprises provide data relevant to different kinds of national accounting systems?

11 Consider the case for establishing separate sector accounts for (a) private non-profit institutions and (b) public enterprises in a national income accounting system.

12 Discuss the problem of valuation in relation to national income accounting systems, with special reference to (a) price changes and (b) the need to impute values for some transactions.

Exercises

1 (a) Record the following transactions in a four-account system of sector accounts for a closed economy with no financial enterprises:

Transactions	$million
Net interest on government debt paid to persons	50
Dividends and withdrawals	120
Depreciation allowances	80
Sales by businesses — to persons	780
— to governments	130
Fixed capital investment (by businesses)	290
Increase in business inventories	50
Indirect taxes	70
Income taxes paid — by persons	130
— by companies	50
Wages and salaries paid — by businesses	630
— by governments	180
Cash social service payments	70
Borrowing by governments — from businesses	40
— from persons	140

(b) From the accounts presented in accordance with (a) above, construct:
(i)   consolidated accounts for the whole economy; and
(ii) a summary national income and expenditure account.

2 The following economic transactions took place in Ruritania in 1985:

Sales of current goods and services by trading enterprises to—	
Governments	$1 000
Financial enterprises	100
Persons	2 500
Sales of capital equipment by trading enterprises to other enterprises	300
Indirect taxes paid by trading enterprises	245
Interest received by financial enterprises from—	
Trading enterprises	200
Governments	230
Cash social service payments by governments to persons	225
Additions to trading enterprise inventories	150
Direct taxes paid by—	
Trading enterprises	180
Financial enterprises	10
Persons	2 200
Government expenditure on public works	680
Wages and salaries paid by—	
Trading enterprises	2 000
Financial enterprises	110
Governments	1 280
Depreciation allowances charged by trading enterprises	90
Dividends and profit withdrawals paid to persons by—	
Trading enterprises	1 140
Financial enterprises	20
Interest paid by financial enterprises to persons	160
Imputed charges for financial enterprise services—	
Trading enterprises	130
Governments	140

You are required:

(a) to record the transactions in a four-sector system of activity accounts in such a way as to measure the following concepts for each sector:

(i) gross product;

(ii) disposable income;

(iii) saving;

(iv) net borrowing or net lending;

(b) to construct a consolidated production account for Ruritania in such a way as to record the components of the following aggregates:

(i) gross domestic product;

(ii) gross national expenditure.

3 Construct a chart of accounts which classifies public expenditures by reference to (a) transacting entities, (b) the economic significance of expenditures, and (c) the purpose of expenditures.

4 By reference to the most recent budget papers of your national government, construct a set of economic activity accounts for the government as follows and record transactions to the extent that the data permit: production account; income distribution account; income disposal account; and capital formation account.

Comment on any deficiencies in the data.

5 On the basis of the information in the most recent official national income accounting estimates, prepare a set of activity accounts (production, income distribution, income disposal and capital formation accounts) for trading enterprises, financial enterprises, households, public authorities and overseas, and consolidated accounts for the whole economy. Any gaps in the official estimates may be estimated on the basis of the best information available.

Evaluate the accounting structure of the official estimates with special reference to the derivation of measures of major sector and national production, income and expenditure concepts.

6 Prepare sector balance sheets, sector wealth statements, a national balance sheet and a national wealth statement (all as at 30 June) for South Pacific, a country with only two sectors, persons and companies. The following valuations may be used for national balance sheet purposes:

	Assets $million	Financial Obligations $million
Persons' sector		
Physical assets	100	
Shares	?	
Loans to persons	10	
Loans from companies		120
Loans from persons		10
Companies' sector		
Physical assets	200	
Loans to companies	20	
Loans to persons	120	
Loans from companies		20
Shares—all held by persons		?

All the shares are ordinary shares and the following valuation information is available about these shares:

	$ million
Par value	130
Issue price	190
Price paid by present holders	280
Market value on 30 June 1985	300

Part III

Accounting Measurement and Valuation

Introduction to Part III: Accounting Measurement and Valuation

It has been suggested in the literature that accounting valuation systems can be evaluated at three different levels—structural, semantic and behavioural. The different criteria are related in the manner shown in the following chart:

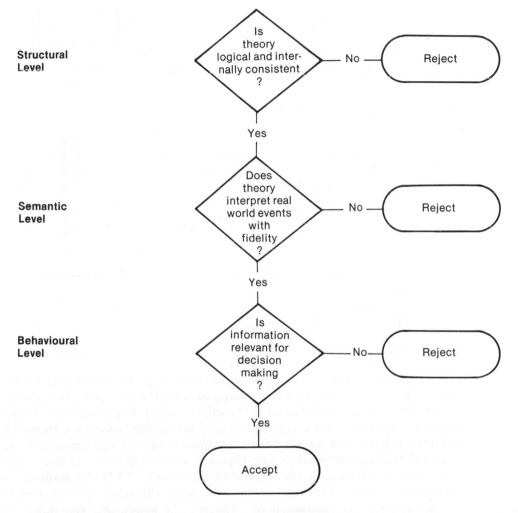

At the structural level, a theoretical system is required to be logically rigorous and internally consistent. At the semantic level, the system output must provide a true interpretation of the real world. At the behavioural level, the information must be relevant for decision making, one aspect of which involves prediction of real world events (such as a share price). Some writers believe that a theory must be validated at all three levels before it should be accepted, but there is controversy on the relevance of accounting information for predictive purposes. Accounting data may be used to provide input (among inputs from other information sources) into a prediction model, but the results are a reflection of a joint effect—the predictive ability of accounting and other information inputs *and* the use of a particular prediction model. Critics have pointed out that accounting data by themselves have no predictive ability.

Further, it may not be possible to evaluate predictive ability, because the costs to users of prediction errors are not known.

Theory validation at the semantic level is of particular interest, as illustrated in the following diagram:

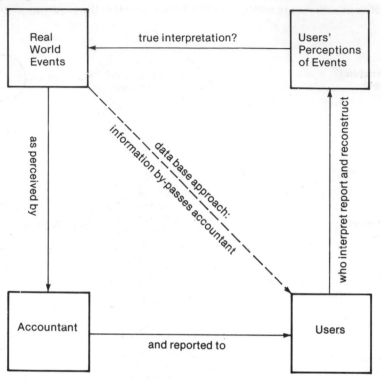

Critics, who hold diverse views in other matters (e.g. Hendriksen and Thomas on the one hand and Chambers on the other), consider the perception and reporting of real world events a crucial accounting function, which is ill-performed. For example, because allocation is not a real world event, accounting reports are biased by any arbitrary cost and revenue allocations contained in them. Some accountants see the eventual development of a data-base approach in which users would directly tap the information contained in the company's data bank. Thus the transmission of information to users would by-pass the accountant altogether, as illustrated by the broken arrow in the diagram above. However, the notion that accounting reports should exactly describe real world events soon runs into difficulty. Some important concepts of interest to users, such as net wealth and income, cannot be equated to real world events.

The problem is this: If the function of an accounting theory and the system based on it is to tell the story as it is, how do accountants explain the proliferation of rival accounting theories, and their inability after so many years of controversy and debate to achieve any agreement? An explanation may be found in Sterling's analysis of the verification process in auditing. Auditing is concerned with verifying the accuracy of the *inputs* into the accounting system and their manipulation. Auditing is not concerned with the system's final *outputs*, because by their very nature these are not independently verifiable. For example, it is not possible independently to verify an artificial construct, such as a measure of net income, by observing its counterpart in the real world. Similarly, it is not possible to validate an accounting theory in the same way as a theory of astronomy, which may be confirmed or rejected by direct observation of the objects or events and the relationships that the theory purports to describe.

We have attempted to provide in the following chapters an adequate exposure to the main accounting valuation systems that compete to displace historical record accounting. We believe that, judged by important criteria which we discuss, there are particular advantages in one such model—the current distributable income/operating capital maintenance approach discussed in Chapter 19. However, as Rosenfield has pointed out, the current purchasing power and the current value accounting proposals are complementary responses to independent questions, not competing responses to a single question. The two proposals are not mutually exclusive, as is clear from the following diagram:

Measurement Standard \ Measured Attribute	Historical Cost	Current Value
Money units (nominal dollar accounting)	x^u_1	x^u_2
Purchasing power units (stabilized dollar accounting)	x^a_1	x^a_2

Note: x_1 and x_2 are the respective historical cost and current value measures. Superscript u denotes measures are unadjusted, and superscript a denotes measures are adjusted, for changes in the general price level respectively.

In Chapter 17, we discuss the relative strengths and weaknesses of historical record accounting (x^u_1). In subsequent chapters, we deal with alternative responses to accounting measurement and valuation—current purchasing power accounting (x^a_1) in Chapter 18, current value accounting (x^u_2) in Chapters 19 and 20, and relative price change accounting (x^a_2) in Chapter 21. The income measure in each particular accounting system is related to an associated capital maintenance concept. Thus historical cost income implies that capital is maintained in dollar units; purchasing power adjusted accounting income implies that capital is maintained in terms of general purchasing power units; current value income implies that capital is maintained in terms of some notion of operating capacity; income in a system employing market resale prices implies that capital is maintained in terms of adaptive capacity; and so on.

The professional accounting bodies have adopted the term 'current cost accounting' as the generic term for current value accounting, thereby recognizing the fact that current value systems usually place primary emphasis on current costs as the valuation basis. It should be pointed out that the adoption of an alternative system based on current values, of the kind discussed in Chapter 19, Chapter 20 or Chapter 21, need not involve an immediate and universal transformation of the accounts. There are advantages in a gradual process of change in which cost-based data are replaced gradually and in successive stages by current value data. For example, current value reporting may be confined initially to a limited number of asset classes, such as share investments, and gradually expanded over a period of time to embrace additional assets, such as land, vehicles and inventories. It is also plausible that a flexible arrangement may be adopted involving, for example, the use of market prices (say, for share investments), as well as specific price indexes (as for some fixed assets) and the use of current entry (i.e. replacement costs) as well as exit values (i.e. market selling prices or net realizable values).

We have not dealt with all proposals for reform in the literature; this would be a herculean task. In particular, the proposal that *all* relevant values be reported has some merit, but the problems of cost and timeliness, and of information overload leading to communication break-down and inability to interpret the results, need to be considered in evaluating this approach.

A further issue relates to the central role of the income statement in present reporting practice. It may be held that the income figure is only a surrogate for the more fundamental wealth measure. The replacement of the income statement by a funds flow or cash flow statement is seen by some writers to be a significant development in the reform of the accounting reporting framework. An important advantage of funds or cash flow statements is that they can be specially designed to avoid the arbitrary allocations that plague the income statement. We believe, however, that the profitability concept is firmly entrenched in the minds of businessmen and the public. The income or profit figure is a measure of the firm's success in the market place, imperfect though the measure may be, and the funds statement is not intended to perform this function.[1]

References

Hendriksen, E.S., *Accounting Theory*, Irwin, Homewood, Ill., 1977, Chapter 1.

Rosenfield, P., 'The Confusion Between General Price-Level Restatement and Current Value Accounting', *Journal of Accountancy*, October 1972, pp. 63-8.

Sterling, R.R., 'On Theory Construction and Verification', *Accounting Review*, July 1970, pp. 444-57.

[1] In financial accounting (and in law) the term 'firm' refers to an unincorporated business enterprise. In the economics and accounting theory literature, the term is often used to refer to all forms of business enterprise, including sole traders, partnerships and companies.

16 Economic Income and Discounted Cash Flows

It is possible to conceive of values being derived for accounting purposes in accordance with expectations of future events rather than by reference to the prices of past transactions. Assets may thus be regarded as bundles of future services and valued by capitalizing the net receipts expected to be yielded by those services in future periods. Values derived by capitalizing expected future receipts and payments are known as present values.

The process of capitalization involves the discounting of expected future cash flows by means of an appropriate interest rate. In this way, all expected future cash flows are recorded in terms of their equivalent present values. The discounting operation reflects the fact that the benefits (or costs) of services received (or supplied) today are worth more than the benefits (or costs) of the same services at some future time. This is because of time preference and, possibly, uncertainty. Discounting for time preference recognizes the time value of money, which results partly from the preference which most people have for present consumption over future consumption, and partly from the fact that $100 received today can usually be invested to return more than $100 in, say, one year's time. Discounting for uncertainty reflects the possibility that expectations may not be realized. Alternatively, uncertainty may be allowed for by applying a probability factor to the expected future cash flows, leaving the discount rate to reflect only time preference.

In a present value accounting system, wealth (or net worth) would then be defined as the discounted present value of expected future cash flows, and income would be defined as the difference between wealth at the beginning and wealth at the end of the period, after adjusting for any contributions from owners or distributions to owners in the period. This definition of income corresponds to what is sometimes called economic income *ex post*. Economists are not agreed on an economic income concept, and it will be seen below that economic income *ex post* differs from economic income *ex ante*, as advocated by Hicks.[1]

No accounting writer has yet advocated the adoption of an accounting system in which all elements of net worth and income are based on expectations of future flows. Because of the uncertainty surrounding future events and the subjectivity of estimates relating to such events, such estimates would fall far short of levels of reliability, objectivity, hardness and comparability (across firms) that are acceptable for external reporting purposes. But it may be argued that considerations of uncertainty and subjectivity are matters of implementation. Many accountants believe that the Hicksian income concept provides theoretical support for the accounting notion of capital maintenance. Further, Hicksian income is said to be an ideal income concept, which provides a benchmark for choosing between competing accounting valuation systems. These propositions may be challenged.

[1] Hicks's concept is probably the best known and most widely accepted economic income concept.

Economic Income

Economists generally define income in terms of two components: consumption plus net increases in wealth (net saving). Hicks believes that the purpose of calculating income is to reveal how much an individual can consume without impoverishing himself. According to Hicks, the central meaning of income may thus be expressed as follows:

> A man's income is the maximum value which he can consume during a [period] and still expect to be as well off at the end of the [period] as he was at the beginning. [2]

The above definition of income *ex ante* is seemingly simple, but this is deceptive. Well-offness is a matter of the individual's personal preferences and expectations. The notion of well-offness, when based on a comparison between subjective states of expectation at two points of time, is ambiguous and lacks operational meaning.

Hicks therefore proposes the following three approximations to the central meaning of income, in order to avoid using a concept of well-offness in the analysis:

(1) Income is the maximum amount the individual can spend this period, and still expect to maintain intact the capital value of prospective receipts (in money terms).

(2) Income is the maximum amount the individual can spend this period, and still expect to be able to spend the same amount in each ensuing period.

(3) Income is the maximum amount the individual can spend this period, and still expect to be able to spend the same amount *in real terms* in each ensuing period.

In the case of Income No. 1 the future is assumed to be constant, and both income and capital are maintained intact. Indeed, income is simply the interest on the opening capital. This limiting assumption of an unchanging future is relaxed in the case of Income No. 2, when interest rates are expected to be subject to change, and further relaxed in Income No. 3, when prices are expected to be subject to change.

Of the three approximations, Income No. 3 is closest to the central meaning, but there are some intractable problems. The basic difficulty lies in the difference between expenditure and consumption with respect to durable consumer goods. [3] Income is consumption plus saving, not expenditure plus saving, and expenditure on durable goods will equal consumption of durable goods in any particular period only by chance. To compound the difficulty, it is not possible to observe and measure *ex post* the consumption of durable goods (an example of the allocation problem). Therefore one cannot know whether consumption matches expenditure in the period.

Hicks believes that it is not possible to formulate a practical definition that conforms to the central meaning of the income concept in economic theory. While a rough calculation based on an approximation to the income concept may be made in order to provide an indication of income available for prudent consumption, the concept itself is not well defined and is a poor tool for economic analysis.

Economic Income and Capital Maintenance

Critics have pointed out that Hicks's capital, as defined in Income No. 1, is merely the capitalized value of an expected receipts stream. It is not a separate source, such as a

---

[2] Hicks's definition refers to 'a week'. For generality, 'week' may be replaced by 'period'.

[3] A durable consumer good is a consumer good whose life in terms of expected service provision extends beyond one period, e.g. a motor car or a refrigerator.

stock of physical goods. If this criticism is justified, then the Hicksian income concept has no relevance to accountants. But Hicks also bases part of his analysis on income from property, such as securities, land and buildings. The following discussion is based on this more realistic assumption.

Because of the implicit limiting assumption in Income No. 1 that the future is constant, this income concept is not a good approximation to the central meaning of income. Now suppose that this assumption is relaxed; for example consider an investment of $100 which is expected to yield 10 per cent in the first period and 20 per cent in the second and all subsequent periods. If income is defined as the maximum amount which can be consumed after maintaining the money capital intact, and if it is assumed that consumption takes place at the end of the period, the stream of consumption will be:[4]

$$\$10, 20, 20, 20, \ldots$$

However, this is not consistent with Hicks's definition, for under these circumstances the individual will not be as well-off at the end of the first period as he was at the beginning; he will be better-off. To be as well-off, he must consume $18.33 at the end of the first period, i.e. he must reduce his money capital by $8.33, to give the following stream of consumption (corresponding to Income No. 2):

$$\$18.33, 18.33, 18.33, 18.33, \ldots$$

Next, the assumption that the future is constant is relaxed further by introducing price changes. Suppose that the price level at the end of the third period is expected to increase by 10 per cent and remain stable thereafter. The stream of consumption in real terms is:

$$\$18.33, 18.33, 16.67, 16.67, \ldots$$

Under these circumstances, the individual will not be as well-off at the end of the first (or second) period as he was at the beginning; he will be worse-off. To be as well-off, he must save $1.19 at the end of the first period and $1.43 (equivalent to the saving in the first period plus interest on the saving) at the end of the second period, to give the following constant stream of consumption in real terms (corresponding to Income No. 3):

$$\$17.14, 17.14, 17.14, 17.14, \ldots$$

It is evident that Hicksian income focuses on the maintenance of the flow rather than the capital stock.

A Company's Economic Income

In order to provide a benchmark for evaluating different accounting valuation systems, enterprise economic income has been defined as follows: income is the amount a company can distribute to its shareholders without impairing its net worth. In operational terms, a company's income *ex post* is the difference between its net worth (defined as the present value of expected future net receipts) at the beginning of the period and its net worth at the end of the period, plus net cash flows received in the

---

[4] For ease of exposition and to come to closer grips with the central meaning of income, one may abstract from the problem of durable consumer goods. For the individual who rents instead of buys durable consumer goods (his car, his television set, etc.), his expenditure equals his consumption in the period.

period.[5] A company's economic income *ex post* includes windfall gains and losses, comprising unexpected cash flows in the period and changes in expectations at the end of the period (compared with expectations held at the beginning of the period). Income measured in this way is no longer a constant stream, partly on account of relaxations of the limiting assumption that the future is constant, and partly on account of windfall gains and losses.[6]

The *ex post* concept of a company's economic income as defined above is similar in some respects to Hicks's income concept. However, the *ex post* concept focuses on the maintenance of the capital stock rather than that of the income stream, as shown in the following illustration. It will be seen that under this concept the assumption of an unchanging future implies the maintenance of both the company's capital and its income stream. When this assumption is relaxed, the company's capital is maintained while its income stream is not.

An Illustration

Case 1: Assume an unchanging future and an interest rate of 10 per cent per annum. A company commences business with a capital of $300, which it can invest on an annual basis at 10 per cent. Thus its cash flows will be $30 per year. Alternatively, it can use its funds to acquire an asset with a three-year life and the following pattern of

	Year 1 Beginning	Year 1 End	Year 2 Beginning	Year 2 End	Year 3 Beginning	Year 3 End
Expected net receipts from asset for the year		$130		$120		$110
Present value of future net receipts from asset	$300	200	$200	100	$100	—
Temporary investment at beginning of year	—		100		200	
Receipts at end of year—						
From asset		130		120		110
From temporary investment		—		110		220
Capital position	$300	$330	$300	$330	$300	$330
Economic income—						
From asset		30		20		10
From temporary investment		—		10		20
		30		30		30
Cash available for investment at end of year		$100		$200		$300

[5] An equivalent measure of a company's economic income is the difference between the net worth of its equity (defined as the present value of expected future cash distributions to shareholders) at the beginning of the period and the net worth of its equity at the end of the period, after adjusting for any distributions to, or contributions from, shareholders during the period.

[6] Similarly, definitions of income *ex post*, i.e. income including windfall gains or losses, can be formulated for individual income.

expected net receipts, which have a net present value of $300 at 10 per cent per annum. Assume that expectations are realized and that any cash surplus is reinvested in a temporary investment at 10 per cent. The company's economic income is calculated below. It will be seen that both capital and the income stream are maintained.

Case 2: Suppose that the unchanging future assumption is relaxed in the following manner: the expected interest rate is 10 per cent in Year 1 and 20 per cent in subsequent years. As in Case 1, the company can invest its funds on an annual basis at the going interest rates, to earn the following cash flows: $30, $60, $60 ... Alternatively, it can acquire an asset with a three-year life and net cash receipts (discounted at 10 per cent in the first year and 20 per cent in subsequent years) with a present value of $300. Assume that expectations are realized and that any cash surplus is reinvested in a temporary investment at the relevant interest rate in the particular year. The company's economic income is calculated below. But it should be noted that while capital is maintained, income is not. This is not consistent with the Hicksian approach, which focuses on maintenance of the income stream.

	Year 1		Year 2		Year 3	
	Beginning	End	Beginning	End	Beginning	End
Expected net receipts from asset for the year		$130		$120		$144
Present value of future net receipts from asset	$300	200	$200	120	$120	—
Temporary investment at beginning of year	—		100		180	
Receipts at end of year—						
From asset		130		120		144
From temporary investment		—		120		216
Capital position	$300	$330	$300	$360	$300	$360
Economic income—						
From asset		30		40		24
From temporary investment		—		20		36
		30		60		60
Cash available for investment at end of year		$100		$180		$300

Economic Income is Not an Ideal Standard

It has been noted earlier that economic income falls short of acceptable levels for most of the qualitative criteria governing external reporting. Because a company's economic income relates to expectations about *future* flows, it also is inconsistent with important accounting reporting objectives. In particular, it does not directly relate the income figure to the economic activities and events associated with the period, and hence it does not provide information useful for evaluating performance in the period. We conclude that economic income is not an ideal standard by which accounting income measurement may be judged. The appeal by some accounting writers to Hicksian income is all the more surprising, in view of its inconsistency with the accountant's objective of maintaining capital and Hicks's doubts about the intelligibility and usefulness of the concept.

It is not necessary to appeal to economic income to provide a rationale for adopting a capital maintenance concept in corporate income measurement and reporting. Capital maintenance seems to us to be an eminently sensible notion in accounting, and can be justified by reference to basic accounting objectives, such as the stewardship function and the protection of creditors.

It is not intended to imply that present value computations are conceptually invalid or that they lack any practical significance. For example, the present value of the equity in a company whose future net cash flows are expected to be relatively large will be greater than that of other companies, which have similar current earnings and which face similar market risks but for which expectations about future net cash flows are lower. The reflection of the present value in the company's share price in turn provides a valuable guide to investment decisions in the market place.[7] But the increase in the present value of the equity is certainly not income in any accounting sense.

Discounted Cash Flows and Accounting

Discounted Cash Flows and Decision Making

The reasons for rejecting present values as the substantive base for an accounting system are now clear. But the present value concept has economic significance in many decision contexts. It was mentioned earlier that discounted values of expected cash flows are reflected in the share price, which in turn influences resource allocation in the market place. The role of present values in resource allocation in this case is an indirect one. A more explicit example is capital budgeting, which is an important aspect of resource allocation within the firm. Capital budgeting is discussed in more detail in Chapter 29. A brief example is given below in order to illustrate the principle in present value calculations.

Suppose that a person is proposing to exploit a two-year timber lease by purchasing equipment costing $1 125. His operations are expected to yield net returns of $500 at the end of each year, and a further $750 will be realized at the end of the second year when the venture will be wound up. Suppose also that the rate of return, i, required to be earned on such a venture is 25 per cent per annum.

There are two methods of evaluating the proposal which typically give the same result for accept-reject decisions. Both methods discount the expected net future benefits by means of an appropriate interest rate in order to derive their equivalent present values.

---

[7]Although it is the present value of wealth rather than economic income that is important for investment decisions.

Net Present Value Method

In general terms, the net present value of the venture, V, at time $t=0$, is given by the formula:

$$V_0 = B_0 + \frac{B_1}{1+i} + \frac{B_2}{(1+i)^2} + \ldots + \frac{B_n}{(1+i)^n}$$

where $B_0, \ldots, B_n$ are the expected cash flows at $t = 0, \ldots, n$ respectively.

$$V_0 = -1\,125 + \frac{500}{1.25} + \frac{1\,250}{(1.25)^2}$$

$$= -1\,125 + 400 + 800$$

$$= \$75$$

It will be noted that while the present value of the cost of the capital outlays associated with the venture (in the example, B_0) is a negative amount, the net present value for the venture as a whole is positive. On the basis of the expected costs and benefits and the required rate of return, therefore, the venture may be judged to be profitable enough to warrant proceeding with, subject to the proviso that this would not prevent participation by the firm in more lucrative alternative forms of activity.

Internal Rate of Return Method

It is possible to evaluate activities such as the timber venture in another way, by calculating the rate of return which equates the present value of the initial outlays undertaken for purposes of the venture with the present value of the future net benefits expected to flow from it. This approach involves a variation of the present value formula as follows:

$$C_0 = \frac{B_1}{(1+r)} + \frac{B_2}{(1+r)^2} + \ldots + \frac{B_n}{(1+r)^n}$$

where C is the initial cash outlay undertaken in connection with the activity, $B_1, \ldots,$ B_n are the net proceeds in periods $1, \ldots, n$ respectively, and r is the rate of return to be calculated. In the venture example,

$$1\,125 = \frac{500}{(1+r)} + \frac{1\,250}{(1+r)^2}$$

from which it may be calculated that $r = 0.30$, or 30 per cent, approximately.

Given the expectations about costs and benefits, a rate of return can be calculated in this way and compared with the required rate of return in order to determine whether the activity is worth undertaking. This internal rate of return, as it is called, is higher in the example than the required earning rate (25 per cent). It is therefore sufficient to justify acceptance of the activity, again provided that there are no more profitable alternatives available to the firm which would be ruled out if the activity were proceeded with. Under both the net present value and internal rate of return approaches, it will be seen that profitability is subjectively determined by reference to expectations about the costs and returns associated with the activity.

The Present Value Approach to Depreciation

Some writers in the past have used the present value approach as a means of clarifying the concept of depreciation. Depreciation can be thought of as a reduction in the value of a fixed capital asset, arising out of a change in the expected future earning power of the asset (rather than as an allocation of the original cost of the asset as under historical record accounting). In measuring this concept of depreciation, it is necessary to estimate the net cash receipts in future periods which the asset is expected to yield over the remainder of its working life. Depreciation between any two points of time can be measured simply by the difference between the discounted values of the future net receipts at those points of time. Deciding on the appropriate rate of interest for purposes of calculating discounted values at different points of time is itself a difficult problem, but one possibility is to take the internal rate which makes the present value of the expected stream of net receipts, at the time when the asset is originally purchased, exactly equal to its cost.

In general terms, if an asset is expected to produce net receipts of B per annum for n years, its present value equals: [8]

$$\frac{B}{r}\left[1 - \left(\frac{1}{1+r}\right)^n\right]$$

where r is the discounting rate as calculated above. After one year, it will only be expected to produce net receipts of B per annum for $(n-1)$ years, and its present value at that point of time will be:

$$\frac{B}{r}\left[1 - \left(\frac{1}{1+r}\right)^{n-1}\right]$$

Its depreciation during the year thus equals:

$$\frac{B}{r}\left[1 - \left(\frac{1}{1+r}\right)^n\right] - \frac{B}{r}\left[1 - \left(\frac{1}{1+r}\right)^{n-1}\right]$$

$$= \frac{B}{(1+r)^n}$$

This method of calculating depreciation charges can result in constant (i.e. straight-line), or reducing, or even increasing depreciation charges over the asset's life, depending on the estimates made during its life with respect to the stream of future net receipts and the rate used for discounting purposes. Thus if the initial cost of an asset with a life of three years is $300, and it is estimated at the end of Year 1 that the discounted value of its future net receipts is $200, at the end of Year 2 that it is $100, and at the end of Year 3 that it is $0 (i.e. scrap value is nil), the depreciation charge corresponds to the straight-line figure of $100 per annum. This is the result that occurs if the estimated net receipts and the discounting rate (the internal rate of return is 10 per cent per annum for all three examples below) are as follows, and if expectations not only remains unchanged throughout the asset's life but are exactly confirmed by events:

---

[8] Its present value is the sum of the geometric series: $\dfrac{B}{1+r}, \dfrac{B}{(1+r)^2}, \dots, \dfrac{B}{(1+r)^n}$

	Beginning of Year 1	End of Year 1	End of Year 2	End of Year 3
	$	$	$	$
Estimated net receipts	—	130	120	110
Present value of future net receipts at 10% p.a.	(118.2 + 99.2 + 82.6) = 300	(109.1 + 90.9) = 200	(100) = 100	0
Depreciation		(300 − 200) = 100	(200 − 100) = 100	(100 − 0) = 100

It will be observed that a constant depreciation charge (corresponding to a straight-line allocation) implies a gradually diminishing periodic return in terms of undiscounted net receipts. This is a consequence of the fact that the net receipts figure in respect of a particular period is discounted less heavily as that period approaches closer to the time at which the discounting calculation is made. A pattern of gradually diminishing periodic net receipts may arise in practice as a result, say, of the need for increasing maintenance expenses in the later years of the asset's life.

In general terms, straight-line depreciation requires that the undiscounted net receipts decline linearly as follows:

$$\frac{C}{n}(1 + rn), \; \frac{C}{n}\left[1 + r(n - 1)\right], \; \frac{C}{n}\left[1 + r(n - 2)\right], \; ..., \; \frac{C}{n}(1 + r)$$

where C is the original cost of the asset, n the life of the asset in years and r the internal rate of return used for discounting purposes.

If the estimated periodic net receipts diminish more rapidly than this, calculations of depreciation on the basis of present value comparisons can result in reducing depreciation charges, as the following illustration shows:

	Beginning of Year 1	End of Year 1	End of Year 2	End of Year 3
	$	$	$	$
Estimated net receipts	—	165	121	66.6
Present value of future net receipts at 10% p.a.	(150 + 100 + 50) = 300	(100 + 55) = 165	(60.5) = 60.5	0
Depreciation		(300 − 165) = 135	(165 − 60.5) = 104.5	(60.5 − 0) = 60.5

The periodic depreciation charges calculated on the present value method can even increase, as in the following example when the estimated net receipts per period rise during the asset's life. Such a pattern of net receipts might occur in the early years of an asset's life when gradually reducing developmental or selling expenses have to be incurred in order to open up a market for the asset's product. However, it is unlikely that the net receipts will continue to increase throughout the asset's life until the asset is ready for scrapping, and for this reason the example is rather unreal. [9]

[9] Constant net receipts may be more realistic. If receipts are constant, depreciation compounds at the rate of r per cent per annum.

	Beginning of Year 1	End of Year 1	End of Year 2	End of Year 3
	$	$	$	$
Estimated net receipts	—	110	121	133.1
Present value of future net receipts at 10% p.a.	(100 + 100 + 100) = 300	(110 + 110) = 220	(121) = 121	0
Depreciation		(300 − 220) = 80	(220 − 121) = 99	(121 − 0) = 121

This method of calculating depreciation is clearly based on a different approach from that underlying the cost-allocation techniques used in historical record accounting. However, as has been seen, the same kinds of depreciation patterns can result from the two approaches. Even though they are firmly wedded to the idea of depreciation as a cost allocation procedure, accountants usually have no clear idea why they choose one method of allocation rather than another. Even if they adhere to the historical record approach, they might therefore profitably make use of the present value of future net receipts concept to help them decide how to allocate an asset's cost over the periods of its working life. To the extent that the present value method is used to help cost allocation, moreover, the residual balance sheet value of the asset at any point of time is likely to approximate more closely its value based on future earning power.

Criticisms of the Present Value Approach to Depreciation

Thomas has criticized the present value approach to depreciation, on the ground that it involves a number of arbitrary allocation procedures:

(a) the allocation of a joint revenue stream to individual inputs cannot be justified; and

(b) the use of an average interest rate to determine intermediate values cannot be justified.

Thomas argues that an individual asset is not employed in isolation, but always jointly with other assets in the firm. The net receipts of the firm form a joint revenue stream, and because of asset interaction it is not possible to allocate this joint stream to individual input factors, except on an arbitrary basis.

This problem may conceivably be overcome by aggregating associated assets for purposes of calculating depreciation charges and assessing depreciation in relation to the aggregation of assets. A ship, a blast furnace, a factory assembly-line or even a supermarket's fixtures and plant may thus be depreciated in this way. The main problem which is likely to arise under this approach is that of differential working lives of the individual asset components. This may be resolved by treating the aggregation of assets as a perpetual inventory, the value of which is diminished by annual depreciation charges and increased by the cost of major additions and net replacements. [10]

---

[10] Provided the cost of minor replacements is spread relatively evenly over time, it may be treated analogously to the cost of repairs and maintenance expenditures and charged directly as an expense of the period in which the outlays occur.

Now suppose that the allocation problem can be ignored and the net receipts associated with an asset's use can be determined. Thomas then argues that the use of the internal rate of return in discounting future net receipts to obtain asset values at different stages of the asset's life is arbitrary. The internal rate of return is some weighted average rate over the asset's life. Thomas suggests that its use cannot be defended theoretically, because there is a large number of interest rates and rate combinations which equate the present values of receipts with outlays, as shown for a three-period case:

$$C_0 = \frac{B_1}{(1+r)} + \frac{B_2}{(1+r)^2} + \frac{B_3}{(1+r)^3}, \text{ or}$$

$$C_0 = \frac{B_1}{(1+a_1)} + \frac{B_2}{(1+a_1)(1+a_2)} + \frac{B_3}{(1+a_1)(1+a_2)(1+a_3)}, \text{ etc.}$$

where r is the (average) internal rate of return, and a_1, a_2 and a_3 are assumed rates associated with the individual periods one, two and three respectively. While the average rate r is uniquely determined, the assumed individual period rates, a's, are not. In the above three-period example the rates for any two of the periods may be selected arbitrarily. Generally, for n periods there are $n-1$ degrees of freedom. Further, the period rates are themselves averages of component sub-period rates, and Thomas asserts that the use of any particular period rate also cannot be justified. In the present value approach, there is an infinitely large number of interest rate combinations, and hence an infinitely large number of depreciation patterns.

It is important to point out that, to the extent that the foregoing criticisms are valid, they do not in any case relate to the use of the present value approach in capital budgeting. In capital budgeting the relevant flows are incremental flows, i.e. changes in future net receipts arising from the adoption of an asset or project. These incremental flows include the contributions of existing assets which are expected to interact with the new asset, but there is no attempt to allocate the interaction effect to individual assets. Further, the use of the internal rate of return does not vitiate the analysis in capital budgeting, which is concerned with a one-off evaluation of future cash flows over the whole life of the asset. Thomas's criticism is concerned with the use of the internal rate of return, which is an average rate over the whole life of the asset, to evaluate future cash flows at *intermediate stages* of that life. It is argued that the use of an average discount rate may be appropriate for capital budgeting, but not for calculating present value depreciation.

Discounted Cash Flows and Liability Valuation

The present value concept has a further application in accounting, with respect to liability valuation. In the historical record accounting system, liabilities which carry interest are stated at their face value; examples are long-term liabilities, such as debentures, and some short-term liabilities, such as inter-company loans. Implicitly the future cash flows have been discounted at the historical interest rate associated with the loan, i.e. at its internal rate of return. Suppose a debenture with face value of $100 and interest coupon of 10 per cent per annum is issued at par and is redeemable at the end of three years. Its face value is simply the present value of future flows discounted at the promised coupon rate, as shown:

$$\$100 = \frac{\$10}{1.1} + \frac{\$10}{(1.1)^2} + \frac{\$110}{(1.1)^3}$$

Valuing liabilities at the contractual amounts is consistent with historical record accounting, but reporting liabilities in the balance sheet at amounts which reflect different historical rates may be criticized. Such information lacks comparability and relevance to user needs.

It is interesting to note that the market value of the debenture at any point of time will be roughly equal to the present value of the future cash receipts accruing to the debenture holder, discounted at the *market* rate of interest appropriate for loans of that particular risk class. Suppose that soon after the issue the market rate rises to 12 per cent. The debenture market price is then determined as follows:

$$\$95.20 \approx \frac{\$10}{1.12} + \frac{\$10}{(1.12)^2} + \frac{\$110}{(1.12)^3}$$

Under historical record accounting, the debenture is reported at its face value of $100. However, there is a strong case for reporting the liability at its market price in a current value accounting system. [11]

Present Value and Accumulated Value

The net present value method is particularly useful for valuing future cash flows where the magnitudes are relatively certain and the rate of interest is fixed. Some special cases of future cash flows are annuities and perpetuities. An annuity is a series of equal receipts or payments made at regular time intervals over a pre-determined period, such as instalment payments or the repayments on a bank loan. A perpetuity is an annuity in which the periodic receipts or payments continue forever, e.g. certain British Government bonds known as 'Consols'.

The reader is referred to the Appendix to this chapter for a discussion of the basic compound interest procedures which underlie the derivation of the 'accumulated value' and 'present value' of single amounts, annuities and perpetuities. It will be apparent that the discounting rate of interest is the link between the expected future receipts (or payments) and the value of the asset (or liability) itself.

Conclusion

Present value accounting may be evaluated by reference to the criteria of relevance, objectivity, hardness, reliability and comparability which were specified in Chapter 6. It is clear that present value accounting represents a different kind of information system from historical record accounting, and that the information which it provides has much more relevance for purposes of many economic decisions which owners, managers and others have to make. The role of discounted present values in evaluating investment decisions will be considered in more detail in Chapter 29.

Present value accounting must also be given high marks in respect of the comparability criterion, since the act of converting all data to equivalent present values ensures comparability both over time and as between different accounting entities. But if present value accounting scores well in relation to relevance and comparability, by definition it fails to provide objective and hard data. Present value data are based on expectations about future events and, because expectations are necessarily subjective and the future is necessarily uncertain, present value data fail to

[11] Advocates of current value accounting often confine their recommendations to asset valuations, and ignore liabilities.

meet the objectivity, hardness and reliability criteria. The role of present value accounting must therefore generally be restricted to the provision of information for purposes of internal decision making. The present value approach is of limited usefulness for purposes of external reporting.

Appendix

Introduction to Financial Mathematics

For purposes of this book, there are four basic compound interest problems which need to be considered, namely:

(a) the calculation of the accumulated value, S, of a single amount of principal, P, invested at a rate of interest, i, per period compounded for n periods and payable at the end of the nth period;

(b) the calculation of the present value, P, of a single amount, S, payable at the end of the nth period and discounted at a rate of compound interest, i, per period for n periods;

(c) the calculation of the accumulated value of an annuity of n payments of equal amounts, immediately after the last payment, when interest is compounded at a rate, i, per period on the dates when the payments are made; and

(d) the calculation of the present value of an annuity of n payments of equal amounts, one period before the first payment, when discounted at a rate of compound interest, i, per period on the dates when the payments are made.

Accumulated Value of a Single Amount

If a principal sum, P, can be invested at a rate of interest, i, per period for one period, it will accumulate to $(P + iP)$ at the end of that period, iP representing the amount of interest earned. An amount of \$100 invested at 10 per cent per annum for one year will thus accumulate to $\$100 + (0.10 \times \$100) = \$110$ at the end of the year. $(P + iP)$ can be restated as $P(1 + i)$, and if this is re-invested for a second period it will itself earn interest, $iP(1 + i)$, in the second period so that the accumulated value, S, at the end of that period will be:

$$S = P(1 + i) + iP(1 + i)$$
$$= P(1 + i)(1 + i)$$
$$= P(1 + i)^2$$

More generally, S can be derived by multiplying the principal P by $(1 + i)$ for each period in which interest is compounded, so that in the case of n periods:

$$S = P(1 + i)^n$$

This is the general compound interest formula for calculating the accumulated value of a single amount. Given P, i and n, it is then possible to calculate S by using the formula. Where n is large, this could involve extensive arithmetical calculations; several simple methods of deriving solutions have therefore been devised. These include the use of logarithms, binomial expansion and compound interest tables.

Example: Calculate the amount to which $100 will accumulate in 10 years at a rate of interest compounded annually at 5 per cent per annum.

(a) Using logarithms, $S = P(1 + i)^n$

$$= 100(1 + 0.05)^{10}$$

thus $\log\ S = \log 100 + 10 \log 1.05$

From logarithmic tables, it is found that

$$\log S = 2.000000 + (10 \times 0.0211893)$$
$$= 2.211893$$

thus $S = 162.89$ approximately.

(b) Binomial expansion involves using the formula:

$$(1 + i)^n = 1 + \frac{i(n)}{1} + \frac{i^2(n)(n-1)}{1 \times 2} + \frac{i^3(n)(n-1)(n-2)}{1 \times 2 \times 3} + \ldots$$

Provided i and n are not very large, only three or four terms of the expansion need to be calculated to get reasonable accuracy. In the example,

$$(1 + i)^n = 1 + \frac{0.05(10)}{1} + \frac{(0.05)^2 \times 10 \times 9}{2} + \frac{(0.05)^3 \times 10 \times 9 \times 8}{6}$$

$$+ \frac{(0.05)^4 \times 10 \times 9 \times 8 \times 7}{24}$$

$$= 1 + 0.5 + 0.1125 + 0.015 + 0.0013$$
$$= 1.6288.$$

The inclusion of a fifth term would give greater accuracy beyond the fourth decimal place, if this is considered necessary. The value of the accumulation factor $(1 + i)^n$, 1.6288, must now be multiplied by the amount of the principal $100 to derive the accumulated value, which is therefore $162.88.

(c) Using compound interest tables, the value of the accumulation factor $(1 + i)^n$ may be obtained by inspection from the tables, which conventionally record the number of compounding periods on one axis and rates of interest on the other:

Compound Interest Tables $(1 + i)^n$

n	1%	2%	3%	4%	5%	6%	...
1							
2							
3							
4							
5							
6							
7							
8							
9				1.42331	1.55133	1.68948	
10				1.48024	*1.62889*	1.79085	
11				1.53945	1.71034	1.89830	
12							
.							
.							
.							

The accumulated value may be calculated as $100 x 1.62889 = $162.89.

Extension of Tables

Where the compound interest tables are limited to lower values of n than needed for a calculation, the law of exponents $x^{a+b} = x^a x^b$ may be used to extend them. Thus if $n = 100$, and the tables only give values of n up to 50, $S = P(1 + i)^{100}$ may be solved as $S = P(1 + i)^{50} (1 + i)^{50}$.

Further, if the tables record the required value for n but do not contain the required rate of interest, it is possible to obtain an approximate value for the accumulation factor $(1 + i)^n$ by interpolation. If, for example, we wish to derive the accumulation factor when $n = 10$ and $i = 4\frac{1}{2}\%$, using the information in the above table we can say that the value of $(1 + 0.045)^{10}$ should be approximately half-way between 1.48024 and 1.62889, or 1.55456. This is not quite correct; the real value is 1.55296. The error arises because it has been incorrectly assumed that values in the table increase proportionately, but for practical purposes the interpolated result may be a close enough approximation.

Frequency of Compounding

Although the rate of interest is usually given as a nominal annual rate, the compounding may take place more frequently than annually. Under these circumstances, it is necessary to distinguish between the interest rate per period, i, the nominal annual rate, j, and the number of compounding periods per year, m. The rate, i, still needs to be used in calculating the accumulated value, and will be derived as $i = \dfrac{j}{m}$. The general compound interest formula then becomes:

$$S = P \left(1 + \frac{j}{m}\right)^n$$

where n is the number of years multiplied by m. If the yearly rate is 8 per cent compounded twice a year, $i = \dfrac{0.08}{2} = 0.04$. That is to say, the interest rate compounded half-yearly is 4 per cent. The notation conventionally used to describe the nominal rate and the number of compounding periods is $j_2 = 0.08$, where j is 8 per cent and m is 2. The effective annual rate of interest, r, may then be calculated from

$$(1 + r) = \left(1 + \frac{j}{m}\right)^m.$$

$$(1 + r) = (1 + 0.04)^2$$
$$= 1.0816$$
thus $\quad r = 8.16\%.$

This exceeds the nominal rate, j, because of the compounding that has taken place during the year; but $i = 4$ per cent is exactly equivalent to $r = 8.16$ per cent, where $m = 2$.

Equivalent Rates

The rates j, i and r are said to be equivalent whenever they yield the same amounts of compound interest at the end of the year; in the above example $j_2 = 8$ per cent, $i = 4$ per cent and $r = 8.16$ per cent are therefore all equivalent.

Equivalent interest rates are of some significance, because for ease of calculation it is frequently useful to replace one interest rate by another equivalent one. Equivalence may be used to demonstrate the method of handling what are known as fractional periods.

Fractional Periods

Where, for example, it is necessary to calculate the value of $1 000 accumulated for $2\frac{1}{2}$ years at compound interest j_1 = 5 per cent, it is possible to convert the fractional period of time, $2\frac{1}{2}$ years, into 5 whole periods of 6 months, and to substitute an equivalent rate of interest, to be compounded half-yearly, for j_1 = 5 per cent.

Let i be the half-yearly rate of interest which is equivalent to j_1 = 5 per cent. Then:

$$(1 + i)^2 = 1.05$$
$$\text{and} \quad 1 + i = (1.05)^{\frac{1}{2}}$$

The problem may thus be expressed as:

$$S = 1\ 000[(1.05)^{\frac{1}{2}}]^5$$
$$= 1\ 000(1.05)^{2\frac{1}{2}}$$

But this is identical to the result which would have been obtained if we had merely substituted i = 0.05 and n = $2\frac{1}{2}$ in the basic compound interest formula $S = P(1 + i)^n$, so that it follows that the basic compound interest formula holds for fractional periods. Using logarithms or compound interest tables, if these are available for fractional values of n, S may be calculated as follows:

$$S = 1\ 000(1.05)^{2\frac{1}{2}}$$
$$= 1\ 000(1.05)^2(1.05)^{\frac{1}{2}}$$
$$= 1\ 000(1.1025)\ (1.0247)$$
$$= \$1\ 129.73$$

Alternatively, an approximate solution to the problem of fractional periods may be obtained by interpolation or by combining a compound interest calculation with a simple interest calculation. Thus, in the above example, the problem may be expressed as:

$$S = 1\ 000(1.05)^2[1 + (0.05 \times \tfrac{1}{2})]$$
$$= 1\ 000(1.1025)\ (1.025)$$
$$= \$1\ 130.06$$

Solving for 'i' and 'n'

Since $S = P(1 + i)^n$, provided that values are given for any three of the variables S, P, i and n, it is possible to derive the fourth. Using the data in the above compound interest table, for example, it may be deduced that, if S = \$189.830, P = \$100 and n = 11, then i is 6 per cent. Conversely, if P = \$200, S = \$284.662 and i = 4 per cent, then n is 9.

Present Value of a Single Amount

It also follows that, if $S = P(1 + i)^n$,

$$\text{then} \quad P = \frac{S}{(1 + i)^n}$$

P is the present value of the sum which, if invested at a rate of interest, i, per compounding period for n periods, will amount to S at the end of the nth period. If S, i and n are given, it is then possible to calculate P by applying a discount factor $\dfrac{1}{(1 + i)^n}$ to S. It will be seen that the discount factor $\dfrac{1}{(1 + i)^n}$ is the reciprocal of the accumulation factor $(1 + i)^n$ used in the preceding section, and it follows that similar methods of evaluation may be employed in calculating present values as were used in calculating accumulated values. The equation $P = \dfrac{S}{(1 + i)^n}$ is usually written $P = S(1 + i)^{-n}$, and present value tables may be used to derive the value of the discount factor $v^n = (1 + i)^{-n}$ which is to be applied to the future sum S.

Example: Calculate the present value of $10\ 000 due in five years where $j_4 = 12$ per cent. Since i is given as 0.03 and n as 20, it is merely necessary to look up present value tables $v^n = (1 + i)^{-n}$ for $i = 3$ per cent and $n = 20$. It will be found that the value of the discount factor v^n is 0.55368, which applied to the future sum of $10\ 000 gives a present value $P = \$5\ 536.80$.

Accumulated Value of an Annuity

An annuity is a series of equal periodic payments made at regular intervals. In this appendix, attention is confined to ordinary annuities, in which payments are made at the ends of periods, and simple annuities, in which payment intervals and interest compounding periods coincide. The accumulated value of an annuity of n payments of $1 immediately after the last payment, when interest is compounded at a rate, i, per period on the dates when the payments are made, is equal to the series $1 + (1 + i) + (1 + i)^2 \dots (1 + i)^{n-1}$, where 1 is the value of the last payment on which no interest has been accumulated, $(1 + i)$ is the value of the second last payment which has accumulated interest for one period, and so on until $(1 + i)^{n-1}$ is the value of the first payment, which has accumulated interest in every period except the first. The notation $s_{\overline{n}/i}$ is used to denote the accumulated value of an annuity of n $1 payments at rate of interest i per payment interval. It follows that:

$$s_{\overline{n}/i} = 1 + (1 + i) + (1 + i)^2 \dots (1 + i)^{n-1} \tag{1}$$

Multiplying both sides of the equation (1) by $(1 + i)$,

$$s_{\overline{n}/i}(1 + i) = (1 + i) + (1 + i)^2 + (1 + i)^3 \dots (1 + i)^n \tag{2}$$

Subtracting (1) from (2),

$$s_{\overline{n}/i}(1 + i) - s_{\overline{n}/i} = -1 + (1 + i)^n \tag{3}$$

$$s_{\overline{n}/i}(1 + i - 1) = (1 + i)^n - 1$$

$$\text{therefore} \qquad s_{\overline{n}/i} = \frac{(1 + i)^n - 1}{i} \tag{4}$$

which is the general formula used to derive the accumulated value of an annuity of $1. If R is the periodic payment and S is the accumulated value of the annuity,

$$S = Rs_{\overline{n}|i} \tag{5}$$

Example: Find the accumulated value of a series of 10 payments of $100 made at the end of each year into a savings account which earns interest at 6 per cent per annum compounded annually at the time the payment is made. This involves inspecting the annuity tables for $s_{\overline{n}|i} = s_{\overline{10}|.06} = 13.18079$. This represents the accumulated value of an annuity of $1 per period, so that the value of the total annuity in this instance is:

$$S = Rs_{\overline{n}|i} = \$100 \times 13.18079$$
$$= \$1\,318.08$$

Present Value of an Annuity

Given S, the accumulated value of an annuity, its present value A can be calculated as:

$$A = S(1 + i)^{-n} \tag{6}$$

Substituting from equations (4) and (5) above, it follows that:

$$A = R\frac{(1 + i)^n - 1}{i} \times (1 + i)^{-n}$$

$$= R\left[\frac{1 - (1 + i)^{-n}}{i}\right] \tag{7}$$

If the notation, $a_{\overline{n}|i}$ is used for the discount factor $\dfrac{1 - (1 + i)^{-n}}{i}$, the general formula for the present value A of an annuity is then given by:

$$A = Ra_{\overline{n}|i} \tag{8}$$

Example: Find the present value of a series of 10 annual payments of $20 one year before the first payment, when interest is at the rate of $j_1 = 5$ per cent. Using the formula:

$$A = 20a_{\overline{10}|.05}$$

one may proceed to derive the value of $a_{\overline{10}|.05}$ from the tables giving present values of annuities $a_{\overline{n}|i} = \dfrac{1 - (1 + i)^{-n}}{i}$. Since this is 7.72173,

$$A = \$20 \times 7.72173$$
$$= \$154.43.$$

Reciprocals of $s_{\overline{n}|i}$ and $a_{\overline{n}|i}$

Tables are also usually supplied for the reciprocals of $s_{\overline{n}|i}$, because it is often necessary to solve for $R = S\dfrac{1}{s_{\overline{n}|i}}$, where S, n and i are known. R is known as the periodic sinking fund payment which must be made at the end of each period in order to accumulate, at rate of interest i, the amount of S at the end of the nth period. Sinking funds are established for many purposes, including for example the repayment of debts.

The reciprocal of $a_{\overline{n}|i}$ is also of some significance, since for purposes of debt amortization it may be necessary to solve for $R = A\dfrac{1}{a_{\overline{n}|i}}$. In this case, R is the periodic amortization payment which must be made at the end of each of n periods, in order both to meet interest charges at rate, i, and to repay the principal, A, by the end of the nth period. Each payment will represent in part interest on the outstanding principal at the end of the previous period and the balance of the payment will represent repayment of principal. Separate tables are not necessary for $\dfrac{1}{s_{\overline{n}|i}}$ and $\dfrac{1}{a_{\overline{n}|i}}$, because it can be shown that $\dfrac{1}{s_{\overline{n}|i}} + i = \dfrac{1}{a_{\overline{n}|i}}$, i.e. it is simply necessary to add the interest rate, i, to the reciprocal of $s_{\overline{n}|i}$ in order to derive the reciprocal of $a_{\overline{n}|i}$.

Thus, since
$$R = S\frac{1}{s_{\overline{n}|i}}$$

and
$$R = A\frac{1}{a_{\overline{n}|i}}$$

and
$$S = A(1 + i)^n$$

it follows that
$$s_{\overline{n}|i} = a_{\overline{n}|i}\,(1 + i)^n$$

But
$$s_{\overline{n}|i} = \frac{(1 + i)^n - 1}{i}$$

Therefore
$$1 + is_{\overline{n}|i} = (1 + i)^n$$

and
$$s_{\overline{n}|i} = a_{\overline{n}|i}\,(1 + is_{\overline{n}|i})$$

and
$$\frac{1}{a_{\overline{n}|i}} = \frac{1 + is_{\overline{n}|i}}{s_{\overline{n}|i}}$$

$$= \frac{1}{s_{\overline{n}|i}} + i.$$

Perpetuities

A perpetuity is an annuity in which the periodic payments continue forever. By definition a perpetuity can have no accumulated value, but it does have a present value. In the case of an ordinary simple annuity, in which the interest payment is made at the end of each interest period, the present value can be calculated as $A = \frac{R}{i}$, since the amount of the periodic payment R is determined by the rate of interest, i, applied to the amount originally invested A (i.e. $Ai = R$). Alternatively, the present value of a perpetuity may be obtained by inserting an infinite value for n in the general present value formula:

$$A = R\left[\frac{1 - (1 + i)^{-n}}{i}\right]$$

As n becomes infinite the term $(1 + i)^{-n}$ approaches 0, so that the equation reduces to:

$$A = \frac{R}{i}$$

Example: Find the present value of an asset, say, a loan instrument, which is expected to yield net cash receipts worth $100 per year in perpetuity. A capitalization rate of 10 per cent per annum is considered appropriate.

$$A = \frac{\$100}{0.1}$$

$$= \$1\,000$$

Where i is the market interest rate, A would represent the market price of the perpetuity. This is, of course, merely another way of saying that a 10 per cent per annum rate of return, yielded in perpetuity by an asset valued at $1 000, is equivalent to a return of $100 per annum.

References

Hicks, J.R., *Value and Capital*, Clarendon Press, Oxford, 1946, Chapter 14.
Thomas, A.L., *The Allocation Problem in Financial Accounting Theory*, Studies in Accounting Research No. 3, American Accounting Association, 1969.

Additional Reading

Hendriksen, E.S., *Accounting Theory*, Irwin, Homewood, Ill., 1977, pp. 144-52.

Compound Interest Table

Amount of 1: viz., $(1 + i)^n$

n	1%	2%	3%	4%	5%	6%	10%	n
1	1.01000	1.02000	1.03000	1.04000	1.05000	1.06000	1.10000	1
2	1.02010	1.04040	1.06090	1.08160	1.10250	1.12360	1.21000	2
3	1.03030	1.06121	1.09273	1.12486	1.15763	1.19102	1.33100	3
4	1.04060	1.08243	1.12551	1.16986	1.21551	1.26248	1.46410	4
5	1.05101	1.10408	1.15927	1.21665	1.27628	1.33823	1.61051	5
6	1.06152	1.12616	1.19405	1.26532	1.34010	1.41852	1.77156	6
7	1.07214	1.14869	1.22987	1.31593	1.40710	1.50363	1.94872	7
8	1.08286	1.17166	1.26677	1.36857	1.47746	1.59385	2.14359	8
9	1.09369	1.19509	1.30477	1.42331	1.55133	1.68948	2.35795	9
10	1.10462	1.21899	1.34392	1.48024	1.62889	1.79085	2.59374	10
11	1.11567	1.24337	1.38423	1.53945	1.71034	1.89830	2.85312	11
12	1.12683	1.26824	1.42576	1.60103	1.79586	2.01220	3.13843	12
13	1.13809	1.29361	1.46853	1.66507	1.88565	2.13293	3.45227	13
14	1.14947	1.31948	1.51259	1.73168	1.97993	2.26090	3.79750	14
15	1.16097	1.34587	1.55797	1.80094	2.07893	2.39656	4.17725	15
16	1.17258	1.37279	1.60471	1.87298	2.18287	2.54035	4.59497	16
17	1.18430	1.40024	1.65285	1.94790	2.29202	2.69277	5.05447	17
18	1.19615	1.42825	1.70243	2.02582	2.40662	2.85434	5.55992	18
19	1.20811	1.45681	1.75351	2.10685	2.52695	3.02560	6.11591	19
20	1.22019	1.48595	1.80611	2.19112	2.65330	3.20714	6.72750	20
25	1.28243	1.64061	2.09378	2.66584	3.38635	4.29187	10.83471	25
30	1.34785	1.81136	2.42726	3.24340	4.32194	5.74349	17.44940	30
35	1.41660	1.99989	2.81386	3.94609	5.51602	7.68609	28.10244	35
40	1.48886	2.20804	3.26204	4.80102	7.03999	10.28572	45.25926	40
45	1.56481	2.43785	3.78160	5.84118	8.98501	13.76461	72.89048	45
50	1.64463	2.69159	4.38391	7.10668	11.46740	18.42015	117.39085	50

Compound Interest Table

Present Value of 1: viz., $(1 + i)^{-n}$

n	1%	2%	3%	4%	5%	6%	10%	n
1	0.99010	0.98039	0.97087	0.96154	0.95238	0.94340	0.90909	1
2	0.98030	0.96117	0.94260	0.92456	0.90703	0.89000	0.82645	2
3	0.97059	0.94232	0.91514	0.88900	0.86384	0.83962	0.75131	3
4	0.96098	0.92385	0.88849	0.85480	0.82270	0.79209	0.68301	4
5	0.95147	0.90573	0.86261	0.82193	0.78353	0.74726	0.62092	5
6	0.94205	0.88797	0.83748	0.79031	0.74622	0.70496	0.56447	6
7	0.93272	0.87056	0.81309	0.75992	0.71068	0.66506	0.51316	7
8	0.92348	0.85349	0.78941	0.73069	0.67684	0.62741	0.46651	8
9	0.91434	0.83676	0.76642	0.70259	0.64461	0.59190	0.42410	9
10	0.90529	0.82035	0.74409	0.67556	0.61391	0.55839	0.38554	10
11	0.89632	0.80426	0.72242	0.64958	0.58468	0.52679	0.35049	11
12	0.88745	0.78849	0.70138	0.62460	0.55684	0.49697	0.31863	12
13	0.87866	0.77303	0.68095	0.60057	0.53032	0.46884	0.28966	13
14	0.86996	0.75788	0.66112	0.57748	0.50507	0.44230	0.26333	14
15	0.86135	0.74301	0.64186	0.55526	0.48102	0.41727	0.23939	15
16	0.85282	0.72845	0.62317	0.53391	0.45811	0.39365	0.21763	16
17	0.84438	0.71416	0.60502	0.51337	0.43630	0.37136	0.19784	17
18	0.83602	0.70016	0.58739	0.49363	0.41552	0.35034	0.17986	18
19	0.82774	0.68643	0.57029	0.47464	0.39573	0.33051	0.16351	19
20	0.81954	0.67297	0.55368	0.45639	0.37689	0.31180	0.14864	20
25	0.77977	0.60953	0.47761	0.37512	0.29530	0.23300	0.09230	25
30	0.74192	0.55207	0.41199	0.30832	0.23138	0.17411	0.05731	30
35	0.70591	0.50003	0.35538	0.25342	0.18129	0.13011	0.03558	35
40	0.67165	0.45289	0.30656	0.20829	0.14205	0.09722	0.02210	40
45	0.63905	0.41020	0.26444	0.17120	0.11130	0.07265	0.01372	45
50	0.60804	0.37153	0.22811	0.14071	0.08720	0.05429	0.00852	50

Compound Interest Table

Amount of 1 per Period: viz., $s_{\overline{n/i}}$

n	1%	2%	3%	4%	5%	6%	10%	n
1	1.00000	1.00000	1.00000	1.00000	1.00000	1.00000	1.00000	1
2	2.01000	2.02000	2.03000	2.04000	2.05000	2.06000	2.10000	2
3	3.03010	3.06040	3.09090	3.12160	3.15250	3.18360	3.31000	3
4	4.06040	4.12161	4.18363	4.24646	4.31013	4.37462	4.64100	4
5	5.10101	5.20404	5.30914	5.41632	5.52563	5.63709	6.10510	5
6	6.15202	6.30812	6.46841	6.63298	6.80191	6.97532	7.71561	6
7	7.21354	7.43428	7.66246	7.89829	8.14201	8.39384	9.48717	7
8	8.28567	8.58297	8.89234	9.21423	9.54911	9.89747	11.43589	8
9	9.36853	9.75463	10.15911	10.58280	11.02656	11.49132	13.57948	9
10	10.46221	10.94972	11.46388	12.00611	12.57789	13.18079	15.93742	10
11	11.56683	12.16872	12.80780	13.48635	14.20679	14.97164	18.53117	11
12	12.68250	13.41209	14.19203	15.02581	15.91713	16.86994	21.38428	12
13	13.80933	14.68033	15.61779	16.62684	17.71298	18.88214	24.52271	13
14	14.94742	15.97394	17.08632	18.29191	19.59863	21.01507	27.97498	14
15	16.09690	17.29342	18.59891	20.02359	21.57856	23.27597	31.77248	15
16	17.25786	18.63929	20.15688	21.82453	23.65749	25.67253	35.94973	16
17	18.43044	20.01207	21.76159	23.69751	25.84037	28.21288	40.54470	17
18	19.61475	21.41231	23.41444	25.64541	28.13238	30.90565	45.59917	18
19	20.81090	22.84056	25.11687	27.67123	30.53900	33.75999	51.15909	19
20	22.01900	24.29737	26.87037	29.77808	33.06595	36.78559	57.27500	20
25	28.24320	32.03030	36.45926	41.64591	47.72710	54.86451	98.34706	25
30	34.78489	40.56808	47.57542	56.08494	66.43885	79.05819	164.49402	30
35	41.66028	49.99448	60.46208	73.65222	90.32031	111.43478	271.02437	35
40	48.88637	60.40198	75.40126	95.02552	120.79977	154.76197	442.59256	40
45	56.48107	71.89271	92.71986	121.02939	159.70016	212.74351	718.90484	45
50	64.46318	84.57940	112.79687	152.66708	209.34800	290.33590	1163.90853	50

Compound Interest Table

Present Value of 1 per Period: viz., $a_{\overline{n/i}}$

n	1%	2%	3%	4%	5%	6%	10%	n
1	0.99010	0.98039	0.97087	0.96154	0.95238	0.94340	0.90909	1
2	1.97040	1.94156	1.91347	1.88609	1.85941	1.83339	1.73554	2
3	2.94099	2.88388	2.82861	2.77509	2.72325	2.67301	2.48685	3
4	3.90197	3.80773	3.71710	3.62990	3.54595	3.46511	3.16987	4
5	4.85343	4.71346	4.57971	4.45182	4.32948	4.21236	3.79079	5
6	5.79548	5.60143	5.41719	5.24214	5.07569	4.91732	4.35526	6
7	6.72819	6.47199	6.23028	6.00205	5.78637	5.58238	4.86842	7
8	7.65168	7.32548	7.01969	6.73274	6.46321	6.20979	5.33493	8
9	8.56602	8.16224	7.78611	7.43533	7.10782	6.80169	5.75902	9
10	9.47130	8.98259	8.53020	8.11090	7.72173	7.36009	6.14457	10
11	10.36763	9.78685	9.25262	8.76048	8.30641	7.88687	6.49506	11
12	11.25508	10.57534	9.95400	9.38507	8.86325	8.38384	6.81369	12
13	12.13374	11.34837	10.63496	9.98565	9.39357	8.85268	7.10336	13
14	13.00370	12.10625	11.29607	10.56312	9.89864	9.29498	7.36669	14
15	13.86505	12.84926	11.93794	11.11839	10.37966	9.71225	7.60608	15
16	14.71787	13.57771	12.56110	11.65230	10.83777	10.10590	7.82371	16
17	15.56225	14.29187	13.16612	12.16567	11.27407	10.47726	8.02155	17
18	16.39827	14.99203	13.75351	12.65930	11.68959	10.82760	8.20141	18
19	17.22601	15.67846	14.32380	13.13394	12.08532	11.15812	8.36492	19
20	18.04555	16.35143	14.87747	13.59033	12.46221	11.46992	8.51356	20
25	22.02316	19.52346	17.41315	15.62208	14.09394	12.78336	9.07704	25
30	25.80771	22.39646	19.60044	17.29203	15.37245	13.76483	9.42691	30
35	29.40858	24.99862	21.48722	18.66461	16.37419	14.49825	9.64416	35
40	32.83469	27.35548	23.11477	19.79277	17.15909	15.04630	9.77905	40
45	36.09451	29.49016	24.51871	20.72004	17.77407	15.45583	9.86281	45
50	39.19612	31.42361	25.72976	21.48218	18.25593	15.76186	9.91481	50

Compound Interest Table

Periodical Payment that 1 will purchase: viz., $\dfrac{1}{a\overline{n/i}}$.   Note that $\dfrac{1}{s\overline{n/i}} = \dfrac{1}{a\overline{n/i}} - i$.

n	1%	2%	3%	4%	5%	6%	10%	n
1	1.01000	1.02000	1.03000	1.04000	1.05000	1.06000	1.10000	1
2	0.50751	0.51505	0.52261	0.53020	0.53780	0.54544	0.57619	2
3	0.34002	0.34675	0.35353	0.36035	0.36721	0.37411	0.40211	3
4	0.25628	0.26262	0.26903	0.27549	0.28201	0.28859	0.31547	4
5	0.20604	0.21216	0.21835	0.22463	0.23097	0.23740	0.26380	5
6	0.17255	0.17853	0.18460	0.19076	0.19702	0.20336	0.22961	6
7	0.14863	0.15451	0.16051	0.16661	0.17282	0.17914	0.20541	7
8	0.13069	0.13651	0.14246	0.14853	0.15472	0.16104	0.18744	8
9	0.11674	0.12251	0.12843	0.13449	0.14069	0.14702	0.17364	9
10	0.10558	0.11133	0.11723	0.12329	0.12950	0.13587	0.16275	10
11	0.09645	0.10218	0.10808	0.11415	0.12039	0.12679	0.15396	11
12	0.08885	0.09456	0.10046	0.10655	0.11282	0.11928	0.14676	12
13	0.08241	0.08812	0.09403	0.10014	0.10646	0.11296	0.14078	13
14	0.07690	0.08260	0.08853	0.09467	0.10102	0.10758	0.13575	14
15	0.07212	0.07782	0.08377	0.08994	0.09634	0.10296	0.13147	15
16	0.06794	0.07365	0.07961	0.08582	0.09227	0.09895	0.12782	16
17	0.06426	0.06997	0.07595	0.08220	0.08870	0.09544	0.12466	17
18	0.06098	0.06670	0.07271	0.07899	0.08555	0.09236	0.12193	18
19	0.05805	0.06378	0.06981	0.07614	0.08274	0.08962	0.11955	19
20	0.05541	0.06116	0.06722	0.07358	0.08024	0.08718	0.11746	20
25	0.04541	0.05122	0.05743	0.06401	0.07095	0.07823	0.11017	25
30	0.03875	0.04465	0.05102	0.05783	0.06505	0.07265	0.10608	30
35	0.03400	0.04000	0.04654	0.05358	0.06107	0.06897	0.10369	35
40	0.03046	0.03656	0.04326	0.05052	0.05828	0.06646	0.10226	40
45	0.02770	0.03391	0.04078	0.04826	0.05626	0.06470	0.10139	45
50	0.02551	0.03182	0.03886	0.04655	0.05478	0.06344	0.10086	50

Discussion Questions

1 Explain the concept of economic income.

2 Examine the relationship between economic income and capital maintenance.

3 Can economic income be used as a benchmark for evaluating different accounting valuation systems?

4 Examine the concept of discounted present value as a criterion in business decisions.

5 Present values have been rejected as the substantive base for an accounting system. Why?

6 Explain the following terms in relation to the concept of present value:
   (a) time preference;
   (b) uncertainty; and
   (c) rate of return.

7 Evaluate the role of present value accounting in relation to (a) decision making, and (b) external reporting.

8 Explain the present value approach to depreciation.

9 On what grounds has Thomas criticized the present value approach to depreciation?

10 Under what circumstances would you expect the present value of liabilities to be equal to their nominal value?

Exercises

1 Calculate the accumulated value after five years of $1 250 invested at 8 per cent per annum compounded half-yearly. What is the effective annual rate of interest?

2 If $j_2 = 10$ per cent, what is the accumulated value of $2 000 invested for 10 years?

3 What is the present value of $10 000 due in eight years, where $j_4 = 8$ per cent?

4 Calculate the accumulated value after 30 years of $1 000 invested at 8 per cent per annum compounded quarterly.

5 What is the value of $5 000 accumulated for four and a half years at compound interest $j_1 = 6$ per cent?

6 Miss Smith took out a life assurance policy when she reached 21 years of age, requiring a payment of $200 premium on that and each successive birthday until age 35. Immediately after making the final payment on her 35th birthday, she received the maturity value of the policy and bonuses, a total of $4 000. What was the effective rate of interest yielded by the policy?

7 A man buys a property for $40 000, making a cash payment of $10 000 and obtaining a mortgage loan for the remainder, repayable by equal annual instalments over 10 years to include repayment of principal and interest at 10 per cent per annum compounded annually. What will be the annual payment? What will be the amount owing on the property after five years?

8 A firm can buy an asset for $20 000. It would expect the asset to yield net returns of $5 000 per annum for five years before being disposed of for $6 000 at the end of the five years. If the firm's required rate of return is 10 per cent, and it is assumed that the net returns accrue at the end of each year, should it purchase the asset?

9 A company has made a loan of $8 000 to one of its distributors, at 8 per cent per annum compounded quarterly.

(a) If the loan were to be repaid by equal quarterly instalments over a period of 15 years, the first payment to be made at the end of the first quarter, show how you would calculate the amount of the quarterly payments which the distributor should make.

(b) To provide an incentive for prompt payment, the company will accept 60 equal instalments of $225 on the due dates in full settlement of the loan. Calculate how much of the loan will be outstanding just after the distributor has made his twelfth payment.

10 A finance company advertises 'Borrow $100 for a total cost of $5. You repay the loan in seven easy monthly instalments of $15 each, the first one due one month after the loan.' What gross rate of interest compounded monthly does the finance company earn?

11 A shipping company wishes to replace one of its ships in four years' time, and due to the increased cost of shipbuilding it is estimated that it will need to accumulate a further $2 000 000 by the purchase date. If it can invest funds at 8 per cent per annum compounded half-yearly, what equal amount must it set aside at the end of each of the next four years to accumulate the $2 000 000? (Ignore taxation.)

12 An asset is expected to yield net receipts of $3 000 per annum for five years. Its cost is the present value of those receipts discounted at 10 per cent per annum. What depreciation should be charged each year during the asset's life on the basis of the discounted present value method?

13 A manager is considering the purchase of an asset which will yield net cash flows as follows at the end of each of the next four years:

Year 1	$2 000
2	3 000
3	2 000
4	4 000
	$11 000

(a) What is the maximum amount that can be paid for the asset, if the required rate of return is 10 per cent?

(b) If this amount is paid for the asset, what will be the depreciation expense in each year as calculated in accordance with the discounted values of the net cash flows?

17 Accounting Valuation Systems 1— Historical Record Accounting

Historical record accounting is the valuation system which has provided a framework for explaining the accounting process in Part I, and its application to various accounting entities in Part II. It is also known as the historical cost accounting system. The term 'historical record accounting' is ambiguous and unsatisfactory, as it is largely identified with current generally accepted accounting practices. Because of the permissiveness in prevailing accounting practices, it is often asserted that historical record accounting produces uninterpretable information. But if a stable general level of prices (i.e. there is no definite trend of inflation or deflation) is assumed, it is feasible to provide an entirely logical interpretation of the system.

As noted above, the term 'historical record' does not adequately describe the conventional accounting system. In terms of its essential characteristics, it could be better labelled an 'invested cost', 'invested funds' or 'fund accountability' system. In this system, costs of all resources committed to an entity are accounted for; i.e. they are locked into a double-entry framework with a record of the sources. All movements of resources must therefore be tracked. The profit and loss statement becomes a focal point in relating revenues and expired costs. In this framework, a balance sheet is a static statement indicating the sources and disposition of funds at a point of time. Apart from the underlying stewardship function, information is provided to assist in assessing the return on funds actually invested (as distinct from a return on the value of the assets employed).

Basically the historical record system accounts for invested funds—their sources, investment and movements. The special emphasis in the system on profitability and financial position obscured for a time the necessity for the balance sheet and profit and loss statement to be accompanied by a statement of fund flows, whereby a firm's important financing and investment activities during a reporting period could be shown along with profits earned and end of period balances.

Maintenance of an entity's original money capital, a concept which originated during the 19th century, is one of the basic characteristics of the historical record accounting system as we know it today. Chronologically, the original rationale for maintaining the money capital of the entity intact was to afford protection to creditors of limited liability companies, who had no recourse to the owners of those companies which became insolvent. Subsequently, as the schism between ownership and management of corporate enterprises widened, the protection of the owner's investment in the business, i.e. the notion of stewardship, became the dominant objective of historical record accounting. Of course, these objectives are not always achieved, partly because of defects in the system such as the valuation of assets at amounts that reflect price levels of past periods, and partly because of the complexities of and rapid changes in modern business conditions. Nonetheless, the system continued to work well in the long periods of stable prices before the turn of the 20th century.

Uses of Historical Record Accounting

Accountability and Stewardship

Part of the dispute over historical record accounting concerns the identification of accounting objectives and the emphasis to be given to certain qualitative characteristics of accounting information. Ijiri has rigorously defended historical record accounting in terms of certain external reporting objectives which he regards as dominant. His views are given below. He regards 'accounting [as] a system designed to facilitate the smooth functioning of *accountability* relationships among interested parties'. The accountability relationship requires the accountor (i.e. management) to keep records and prepare reports for the benefit of the accountee (i.e. owners). These records and reports have two main functions: accountability and the measurement of the economic performance of the accountor. Accountability is regarded as the central objective of accounting. The most important function in accountability is stewardship, which requires a full accounting to the accountee of past transactions and their effects. Ijiri argues that the historical record system ensures the keeping of records which trace the cause and effect relationships of past transactions and the firm's current state of affairs. Because the detailed recording of all past economic activities of the entity in a causal increment-decrement recording network is a basic requirement of historical record accounting, it fulfils the accountability function better than alternative valuation systems.

Performance Evaluation

A performance measure can be used to indicate whether certain economic objectives have been achieved. However, the fact that an accountor (i.e. a manager) is reporting on himself can be troublesome if he uses data which can be manipulated to show himself unfairly to best advantage. The distinctive value of historical cost information here is its relative hardness. A hard measure is one which is rigid and resistant to bias when the measurer is motivated to manipulate the measure in one direction or the other. Under existing institutional arrangements, hard information is necessary to counter competitive pressures which may otherwise encourage bias in external reporting by management. There is scope for bias with historical cost, but it is less than the bias which is likely under alternative accounting systems. Of course, the requirement for the provision of hard information does not exclude supplementary disclosure of soft data, where it is useful to do so. The provision of hard data which are less open to dispute is also important in accounting for social and organizational equity, i.e. in resolving the conflicting group interests of management, owners, creditors, workers, consumers, government and society.

Relevance for Decision Making

While it is not the function of external reports to provide information for the manager's decision making, it is pertinent to ask whether historical cost figures are relevant for decision making in general, whether by managers or owners. Ijiri argues that historical cost could be relevant in some decisions. First, in evaluating and selecting decision rules now, the decision maker needs to analyse the relative success of different past decision rules. Since an historical cost outcome is a consequence of a past decision rule, the historical cost figure is relevant in evaluating that rule, and hence in evaluating and selecting current decision rules as well. Second, historical cost is often relevant to the decision maker with a satisficing objective (as opposed to a maximizing one). [1] Under conditions of uncertainty, satisficing, involving for example the achievement of a satisfactory rate of return on invested cost, becomes the relevant goal. Suppose an investor buys 100 shares in a company with the intention of selling the shares at a profit. If he is a maximizer, the acquisition cost is a sunk cost, irrelevant for future decision making. But under uncertainty he is more likely to be a satisficer, e.g. his objective may be to achieve a return of 20 per cent on his investment. Thus it is argued that historical costs are relevant costs for decision making in a satisficing situation under uncertainty.

While the relevance of historical costs for decision making may be debatable, historical record accounting clearly has undisputed advantages for stewardship reporting and, it is argued, performance evaluation as well, because of its objectivity and hardness. But data hardness has significance only if the accounting processes are not subject to abuse, as hardness otherwise is not retained in the system output. Thus the case for retaining the historical record accounting system is dependent on abolishing the present state of permissiveness in accounting practices, and on strengthening the authority and power of auditors for the exercise of true independence in achieving fair and substantive disclosure.

Historical Cost in a Period of Stable Prices

Historical record accounting has the following advantages in a period of stable prices. The profit for the year is an indicator of the firm's profitability and viability as an economic unit, and total assets disclosed in the balance sheet give an indication of the nature and order of magnitude of the firm's investment base. Thus rates of return are comparable over time as well as between companies. The operation of the system is consistent with a policy of retaining adequate funds for the replacement of facilities used up in producing revenue, and the measure of profit provides a prudent guide to the amount that owners may consume without impairing capital.

Limitations of Historical Record Accounting

It is necessary to distinguish three sets of criticisms of historical record accounting. The first group focuses on the instability of the measuring standard (i.e. the dollar) employed by the accountant, and in particular on the impact of inflation on the businessman and his accounts. The second group of criticisms centres on the relevance of historical record accounting reports for decision making in periods of rapid changes in the relative prices of specific items recorded in the reports, partly on account of accelerated technological innovation in the 20th century.

Thirdly, some criticisms relate to the diversity and permissiveness of accounting practices, the need for increased disclosure and the need to keep the process of accounting measurement separate from financial or other aspects of business policy. We have commented, earlier in this chapter, on the need to abolish the present state of permissiveness in the principles and rules governing accounting practice. One aspect of the need for increased disclosure is the separation of accounting measure-

[1] The satisficer is a decision maker who is seeking a 'satisfactory' solution rather than an optimal solution.

ment from business policy, e.g. by showing the effects on profit measurement and inventory valuation of the application of the cost or market rule. As to disclosure generally, there is considerable unexploited potential for innovative reporting already available in the system, e.g. segmented reporting (i.e. reporting by major product lines); commitment reporting (i.e. recognizing resources already contracted for, even though the contract has not been fulfilled, such as leases and contracts for future deliveries); and the early disclosure of pertinent new information, including more frequent interim reports. It is only fair to note that these criticisms are not directed specifically at historical record accounting, but are relevant to other accounting valuation systems as well.

Historical Record Accounting and General Price Level Changes

Price Level Error in the Accounts

Changes in the general price level introduce a price level error into financial statements. The businessman's accounts are influenced in two ways, which have been called the money effect and the historic cost effect. The money effect is easily understood. When prices rise, the person who holds money assets and the person whose income is a fixed money stream both suffer a loss of real purchasing power. Similarly, a firm which holds money assets (such as cash or accounts receivable) will lose from the fall in the purchasing power of those items. Conversely, a firm which holds money liabilities (e.g. accounts payable or debentures) will gain. The money effect makes it possible to hedge against inflation by holding an appropriate mix of money and non-money assets and liabilities, and indeed to profit by switching to a more highly geared (or levered) capital structure.

The historic cost effect is not as obvious as the money effect. In a period of rising prices the historical record profit figure is likely to be higher than a measure of profit in current dollars. The reason is that currently earned revenues (expressed in current dollars) are matched with expenses, particularly cost of goods sold and depreciation, which are expressed in dollars of past periods. For the same reason, historical record asset values are likely to be lower than measures expressed in current dollars. These differences make it difficult to interpret accounting data, either for the purpose of evaluating the performance of an individual firm or for the purpose of comparing the results of different firms.

The Additivity Problem

There is a fundamental criticism of historical record accounting which is related to the historic cost effect. A price level change is equivalent to a change in the purchasing power of the dollar. As a measurement standard, the 1965 dollar and the 1975 dollar (like the Australian dollar and the U.S. dollar) represent different measurement scales, in the sense that they possess different purchasing power or command over goods and services. Thus two amounts expressed in dollars of different years, i.e. 'dated historical dollars', are no more comparable than if they have been expressed in Australian and U.S. dollars respectively. Essentially, such amounts are not additive, i.e. it is theoretically incorrect to perform any arithmetic operations (of addition, subtraction, multiplication or division) using amounts expressed in different measurement scales.

Empirical Studies and Other Evidence

A number of case studies has been undertaken in the U.S.A., the U.K. and other countries to determine the quantitative effects of price level changes on income and other financial statements. Their results indicate that both long-term and short-term price movements have a significant impact on accounting figures. One of the earliest and best known studies was by Sweeney, the exponent of general price level accounting, who applied its techniques to measure, in dollars of a constant purchasing power, the corporate incomes of three enterprises in the years 1929-31. Other price level studies commented on below were undertaken by Jones and Rosenfield in the U.S.A. and Baxter, Cutler and Westwick in the U.K.

Jones restated the accounts of nine steel companies (comprising over 80 per cent of output and employment in the U.S. steel industry) for the years 1941-47 in terms of 1935-39 dollars. He found that although the audited accounts showed that earnings exceeded dividends by a substantial margin each year, adjusted statements in 1935-39 dollars showed that dividends were not covered by earnings in any year between 1941 and 1947 inclusive. The companies' statements recorded accumulated retained earnings of $540 million and an increase in working capital of 51 per cent in the seven-year period; the adjusted statements showed that dividends, interest and taxes *paid out of capital* amounted to over $400 million and a 'real' increase in the working capital of only 2 per cent over the seven years. Jones showed that a reported profit in 1946 of $200 million was equivalent to an adjusted profit of $123 million in 1946 dollars and an adjusted loss of $88 million in 1935-39 dollars.

Jones's findings generally agreed with those in Baxter's study of British steel companies for the period 1939-57. Baxter found that between 1939 and 1947, when the general price level index rose at an average of 8 per cent per annum, adjusted profits in current pounds were lower than reported profits by about 12 per cent at the beginning of the period, 40 per cent in mid-period, and as much as 80 per cent at the end of the period. Adjusted profits in current pounds were insufficient to cover the payment of taxes and dividends in all years. Baxter's findings differed in the latter period of the study, 1949-57, when the general index rose by about 4 per cent per annum. Adjusted profits in current pounds were lower than reported profits by about 13 per cent throughout, but a surplus always remained after taxes and dividends.

Rosenfield's report on a relatively small field test of general price level accounting, in which 18 U.S. companies took part, is of special interest. By contrast with most other studies of this kind the inflation rate, which averaged about 2 per cent per annum in the decade prior to the test period 1966 and 1967, was exceptionally low. [2] The companies represented a wide range of industries and most were quoted on stock exchanges, although a few were relatively small. Adjusted net income in current dollars for most companies was somewhat higher than historical-dollar income, partly as a result of purchasing power gains on monetary items, but adjusted rates of return on owners' equity were lower than historical rates of return by one to three percentage points for most companies. The results suggest that adjusted earnings and rates of return are not substantially different from the corresponding historical figures in periods of low inflation rates, but the sample of companies is too small to warrant any valid generalizations.

[2] The rate of inflation was 2.7 and 3.0 per cent in 1966 and 1967, respectively.

Cutler and Westwick adjusted the earnings of 137 large British companies for the effects of inflation on their accounts in 1971-72. The companies were selected to represent a wide range of industries, and together they comprised about 75 per cent of the market value of U.K. equities quoted on the London Stock Exchange. The study shows that in current pounds the adjusted profits of companies in manufacturing industries were generally from 20 to 70 per cent lower than reported profits and, in particular, that in the electrical and shipping industries reported profits on average were converted into losses after adjustment. On the other hand, the adjusted profits of companies in service industries, such as breweries, hotels and insurance, were higher than reported profits. Dividends paid by over 30 manufacturing companies were not covered by adjusted earnings; eight of the 30 had adjusted losses (i.e. earnings were negative after adjustment).

Historical Record Accounting and Changes in Specific Prices

Lack of Relevance for Decision Making

Many accountants believe that although the effect of inflation on accounts (i.e. the price level error) is serious, it is not the focal problem for accounting reform. The main purpose of the accounting system is seen to be the provision of information relevant for decision making. While controversy exists about the identities of financial statement users, their objectives, and their data needs for decision making, most accountants agree that historical cost data represent bygone or sunk costs with at best limited relevance for decision making. On the other hand, it is believed that current market prices are relevant for a broad range of management decisions as well as for important objectives of users of accounting information outside the firm.

This question of relevance may be readily extended to historical cost figures adjusted for changes in the general price level. The general price index is a weighted average of the prices of specific goods and services in its regimen, i.e. a market basket of goods and services especially defined for the purpose for which the general price index is constructed. But current prices of the specific goods and services employed by the firm, in particular its fixed assets and inventories, may change at different rates from or even in the opposite direction to a general price level change. If, as is argued, current market prices are what decision makers need, then past costs adjusted for inflation simply will not fit the bill.

Empirical Studies and Other Evidence

There has been a number of empirical studies on the effect of specific price changes of factor inputs on profitability. Mathews and Grant conducted a study of the corporate sector and of industrial sub-sectors in Australia for the period of 1945-46 to 1952-53; adjustments to the accounts were made for changes in the replacement costs of inventories and non-current assets. Their study showed that realized savings (i.e. profits *less* taxes and dividends) were less than anticipated (or planned) savings in that period of rising prices, and that for some industries and firms current savings were negative, with deleterious effects on business liquidity, stability and growth.

Table 17—1 shows the effect of stating cost of sales and depreciation at current replacement costs on the savings *ex post* of Australian companies in recent years.

Table 17—1
Retained Profits of Australian Non-Finance Companies, 1970-77

Year Ended 30 June:	1970	1971	1972	1973	1974	1975	1976	1977
Retained profits after tax and dividends—								
(1) Reported historical cost figures ($ million)	1 046	1 038	1 174	1 421	2 018	1 946	2 604	3 049
(2) Adjusted for cost of sales and depreciation at current prices ($ million)	633	438	275	434	413	−961	−964	−316
(2) as a percentage of (1)	61%	42%	23%	31%	20%	*	*	*

* Tax and dividends in these years represent payments out of capital.

Source: Derived from Australian Bureau of Statistics, *National Income and Expenditure*, 1976-77 and the Institute of Applied Economic and Social Research. *The Australian Economic Review*, 3'75 and 4'77. The figures are for non-government, non-financial corporate trading enterprises.

Since 1976, 1 000 of the largest non-financial companies in the U.S.A. have been required by the Securities and Exchange Commission to disclose, in financial statements filed with the Commission, replacement cost information relating to cost of sales, depreciation, inventories and fixed assets. These show that income adjusted for cost of sales and depreciation is generally lower than historical cost profits. The picture for certain capital-intensive industries and companies is particularly gloomy. In the case of some companies, e.g. Bethlehem Steel and Alcan, replacement cost calculations indicate that current operations do not achieve a desired return on invested capital, and the maintenance of existing productive capacity may not be justified.

Conclusion

The case for urgent reform of historical record accounting rests on the following evidence. First, both the general price level and most specific prices are rising, and these trends are likely to persist. As a result historical cost based financial statements become distorted. Second, the distortions in accounting reports have harmful consequences.

The general price level in Western countries was relatively steady in the 19th century, but since 1900 there has been a tendency for the general price level to rise, so that each successive business cycle has tended to peak at a higher level than its predecessor. Inflation has accelerated in recent years. For example, over the five-year period 1967-71 the Consumer Price Index in the U.K. rose by about 30 per cent and in Australia by only 15 per cent. But by the mid-1970s inflation rates in both countries had climbed well beyond 10 per cent per annum and had become a matter of grave economic and social concern. The inflation rate in the U.S.A. had also increased to about 10 per cent per annum by the mid-1970s.

Empirical studies such as those undertaken by Jones, Baxter, and Mathews and Grant show that in past periods, when both the general price level and specific prices were rising, reported profits for many firms and industries far exceeded profits measured in current dollar or current value terms. Distributions by way of tax and dividends were often made inadvertently out of real capital, resulting in negative savings in the period. Negative savings mean, of course, an erosion of invested capital in terms of its command over real resources. It is clearly evident that historical cost information has proved inadequate and misleading with respect to important interrelated decisions based on the reported profit figure, in particular dividend and tax payouts and the level of corporate savings.

Although essentially an historical record, the income statement is often used to assist in the formulation of future expectations. Management seeks to maximize returns from alternative courses of action, and its decisions are often based on the results of past performance. Investors seek to obtain the best returns available from investment funds at their disposal, and again the search is based on past performance measures. Admittedly, management and investors make use of non-accounting information as well, but accounting information is often an important element of the total information set employed by decision makers. Many accountants charge that historical record accounting provides information which is irrelevant for decision making, and see this as its most serious defect. Historical record information may even be misleading and not merely irrelevant. Thus in periods of inflation rates of return may be gravely distorted; in terms of current price levels, reported profits are overstated while net assets, i.e. the resources forming the investment base, are understated.

Taxation considerations are also important. Corporate income tax represents a very large transfer of funds between individual firms and the government. It is desirable that the tax burden be shared as fairly as possible. While equity, in this as in all things, involves value judgments, some of the effects of reported profits on the incidence of tax may be noted. In inflationary times, the historical cost accounting system introduces a tax bias in favour of less capital intensive firms (and industries), recently established firms, and other firms which have purchased fixed assets at relatively high prices. Such firms have relatively high deductible expenses which reduce their tax payments; thus a labour intensive firm has a high wage bill, and a new firm records high depreciation charges on its plant. It is unlikely that these tax consequences reflect the intention of the elected legislature; further, they are unlikely to promote an efficient allocation of scarce resources in the economy.

The Commonwealth Committee of Inquiry into Inflation and Taxation (the Mathews Committee) noted that one of the principal effects of inflation was its tendency to change the effective tax base of companies and other enterprises. The Committee argued that if, in a time of inflation, a firm's historical record profit is fully distributed through taxation and dividends, one or more of the following requirements must be met if the firm is to remain financially viable:

(a) the firm must continuously increase its profit mark-up, selling prices and rate of return on its historical cost investment;

(b) it must continuously increase it indebtedness;

(c) it must continuously raise fresh capital; or

(d) it must continuously reduce the volume of its operating assets, and hence reduce the scale of its operations and its future profitability.

The Committee believed that in a period of slowly rising prices a firm can adapt by using one or more of these options, but that when the rate of inflation passes a critical level the firm will need, if its historical record profit is fully paid out in tax and dividends, either to increase its indebtedness to the point of financial collapse or reduce the scale of its operations to the point of liquidation. The Committee therefore recommended a change in taxing, accounting and pricing policies, so that these would no longer be related to historical record accounting data.

Some writers have also asserted that distortions in accounting profit are significant causative factors in trade cycles. It is believed that the overstatement of income in times of inflation encourages an optimistic outlook, while its understatement in periods of falling prices adds to the general pessimistic gloom, with resultant effects on the level of employment, incomes and prices.

References

Cutler, R.S. and Westwick, C.A., 'The Impact of Inflation Accounting on the Stock Market', *Accountancy*, March 1973, pp. 15-24.

Ijiri, Y., *Theory of Accounting Measurement*, Studies in Accounting Research No. 10, American Accounting Association, 1975, Chapter 3.

Inflation and Taxation, Report of Committee of Inquiry into Inflation and Taxation, Australian Government Publishing Service, Canberra, 1975 (referred to as the Mathews Report).

Jones, R.C., 'Effect of Inflation on Capital and Profits: The Record of Nine Steel Companies', *Journal of Accountancy*, January 1949, pp. 9-27.

Mathews, R.L. and Grant, J. McB., *Inflation and Company Finance*, Law Book Co., Sydney, 1958.

Rosenfield, P., 'Accounting for Inflation — A Field Test', *Journal of Accountancy*, June 1969, pp. 45-50.

Additional Reading

Barton, A.D., *The Anatomy of Accounting*, University of Queensland Press, St. Lucia, Qld, 1977, Chapter 19.

Baxter, W.T., *Accounting Values and Inflation*, McGraw-Hill, London, 1975.

Discussion Questions

1 What do you consider to be the strengths and weaknesses of historical record accounting?

2 Do you consider that the term 'historical record' adequately describes the conventional accounting system?

3 'The process of profit measurement in an historical record accounting system provides a measure of periodic surplus which is unsuitable as a basis for distribution policy.' Discuss.

4 Professor Ijiri's views on financial accounting theory differ from those of many other writers. Evaluate his defence of the historical record accounting system.

5 In the case against historical record accounting 'it is necessary to distinguish three sets of criticisms'. Discuss.

6 Explain the price level error introduced into the financial statements as a result of changes in the general price level.

7 Explain the effects of inflation on accounting profits and evaluate the alleged merits of the general purchasing power solution to the inflation problem.

8 Discuss the alleged effects of employing historical cost accounting procedures in periods of changing price levels on the incidence of taxes borne by companies and on the volatility of trade cycle fluctuations.

9 One of the conventions underlying the accounting process is the assumption that in general a revaluation of assets above cost should not be recognized in the accounts until a process known as 'realization' has taken place. Assume you are trying to explain the accountant's concept of realization and its application to the problems faced by the accountant to an economist (who feels that the accountant should deal in 'values' and not in 'costs') and make the best case for it that you can. You are expected to anticipate the arguments he will make and to answer them in your defence.

18 Accounting Valuation Systems 2—Current Purchasing Power Accounting

The condition of inflation is characterized by a rise in the general level of prices, i.e. a fall in the purchasing power of money. As was observed in Chapter 17, historical record accounting, which adheres to the original cost convention, implicitly assumes that the monetary unit (e.g. the dollar) commands equivalent purchasing power as between one accounting period and another. Under conditions of a changing price level, however, this assumption is invalid, with the result that financial reports prepared on an historical record basis provide irrelevant or misleading information.

Current purchasing power (CPP) accounting has been developed in an attempt to overcome some of the deficiencies inherent in historical record accounting under conditions of changing price levels. CPP accounting is concerned with the adjustment of historical cost data so as to convert the varying purchasing power potential of the dollars of past years, e.g. as reflected in the acquisition costs of inventories and fixed assets purchased in those years, into the equivalent purchasing power of current year dollars. By this means a 'common dollar' equivalent is derived, without which a useful and meaningful comparison of inter-period financial statements is not possible. The principle in CPP accounting is to convert dollars of an older vintage to their present-day purchasing power equivalents.

Although it would be feasible to incorporate price-level changes *directly* in the accounting records, the approach generally adopted is to adhere to normal historical record accounting and to prepare historical record financial statements, but also to provide supplementary financial statements in which all items are restated in terms of dollars of constant purchasing power.

General Price Level Adjustment Procedures

Balance Sheet

The usual technique of CPP adjustment in the balance sheet involves the restatement of all *non-monetary items* in terms of common dollars. The adjustment to common dollars will reflect the proportionate change in the general price level between the time of the original record and the date of the balance sheet. Non-monetary items consist of all those items other than cash, claims to cash, receivables and payables. Non-monetary items therefore include land and buildings, plant and equipment, inventories and the like.

Monetary items (sometimes described as 'financial items') are those items which have a fixed monetary exchange value that is not affected by a price level change, e.g. cash, bank balances, debtors, other accounts receivable, and liabilities generally. The dollar amounts recorded for these items automatically relate to current dollars. Thus cash on hand commands only the current purchasing power of the face value of the currency; while receivables and payables will, at the time of settlement, automatically be paid out in current dollars. There is no legal requirement that a greater or lesser number of dollars must be tendered to compensate for a changing price level.

But although monetary items are not subject to adjustment in the financial statements, these items are significant in another way. This is because the holding of monetary assets under conditions of inflation must result in a loss of purchasing power during the period concerned. Conversely, the holding of liabilities during a period will result in a gain of purchasing power. It will be seen that these losses and gains on monetary items are calculated and accounted for in the adjusted income statement.

Symbolically, the adjustment procedures in the balance sheet may be illustrated by assuming three groups of items, which will be represented by the symbols M, N and R. M denotes the measure of net monetary assets or financial claims (financial assets minus liabilities), N denotes the measure of non-monetary assets such as fixed capital assets and inventories, while R denotes the measure of proprietor's residual equity. The proportionate change in the general price level between t_0 and t_1 is expressed by p ($p = \dfrac{p_1 - p_0}{p_0}$).

At time t_0, the balance sheet of the firm may be expressed as follows:

$$M + N = R \tag{1}$$

where M, N and R all represent measures valued in accordance with the assumptions underlying historical record accounting.

If the firm engages in no transactions between times t_0 and t_1, but if the general price level rises by p, a general price level adjustment may be made at time t_1 by multiplying each item in the time t_0 balance sheet by $(1 + p)$:

$$M(1 + p) + N(1 + p) = R(1 + p) \tag{2}$$

But since the legal significance of M has not been affected by the price level change, it is more meaningful to express equation (2) in a different form by, in effect, transposing the purchasing power gain or loss, Mp, from one side of the equation to the other:

$$M + N(1 + p) = R(1 + p) - Mp \tag{3}$$

Mp measures the firm's purchasing power gain (if the price change is negative) or loss (if the price change is positive) on the net monetary assets. There is no change in the purchasing power of non-monetary assets, the adjusted value of which records a purchasing power at time t_1 which is equivalent to that at time t_0. As already indicated, the purchasing power loss, Mp, may be deducted from price level adjusted profit in the income statement.

Income Statement

The adjustment procedures become more complicated when the income statement is introduced into the analysis, but again the intention is to restate all items appearing in the income statement in terms of the price level prevailing at the end of the period. The following simple example illustrates the adjustment procedures in relation to both income statement and balance sheet.

Example: Suppose that a new firm commenced the year 1985 with net monetary assets of $20 and non-monetary assets of $80, and that during the year it earned profits of $11 (calculated in accordance with historical record assumptions) which were reflected in increased net monetary assets. Assume that non-monetary assets at the end of the year remained unchanged at $80.

At the beginning of the year the balance sheet situation would be represented thus:

M	$20
N	80
R	$100

Also suppose that:

(a) the general price level increased from a base of 100 at the beginning of the year to 120 at the end of the year;

(b) the average price level for the year, for purposes of income statement adjustment, was 110; and

(c) at the end of the year the proprietor withdrew an amount equal to the adjusted profit.

On the basis of this information, general price level adjustments would be made in financial statements at the end of the year in the manner illustrated in Table 18—1. The adjustment procedures are intended to record all items in the historical financial statements in terms of the price level prevailing at the end of the year.

Table 18—1
General Price Level Adjustments
Income Statement for 1985

	Historical Basis	Adjustment	Adjusted Basis
Net profit	11	$11 \times \dfrac{120}{110}$	12
Purchasing-power loss (Mp)	—	$-\left[\left(20 \times \dfrac{20}{100}\right) + \left(11 \times \dfrac{10}{110}\right)\right]$	−5
Adjusted profit	—		7
Proprietorship withdrawals	−7	$-7 \times \dfrac{120}{120}$	−7
Retained profits	$4		$—

Balance Sheet at End 1985

	Historical Basis		Adjustment	Adjusted Basis
M		24	—	24
N		80	$80 \times \dfrac{120}{100}$	96
R—Capital	100		$100 \times \dfrac{120}{100}$	120
Retained profits	4	104	—	— 120

In the income statement, on the assumption that net profit was expressed in average prices for the year (an assumption which, as will be seen in a more detailed example later, needs to be varied in practice) an adjustment factor of $\dfrac{120}{110}$, representing the ratio of end-year to average prices, needs to be applied to the historical net profit of $11, giving an adjusted profit of $12. The calculation of the purchasing power loss is complicated by the fact that, in addition to the reduction in the purchasing power of net monetary assets existing at the beginning of the year (20 per cent of $20 = $4), a further loss was incurred on the build-up of monetary assets which occurred during the year as a result of the $11 profit earned. If it is assumed that the increase in net monetary assets was originally valued at average prices of the period, the purchasing power loss which resulted from holding them until the end of the period was equal to $11 x $\left(\dfrac{120 - 110}{110}\right)$ = $1. Thus the total purchasing power loss was $5 and the adjusted profit (which was withdrawn by the proprietor) was $7. No restatement of proprietorship withdrawals is necessary because they did not take place until the end of the year.

In the year-end balance sheet, no adjustment of net monetary assets is necessary. Non-monetary assets need to be restated in terms of the end-year price level, which has increased by 20 per cent since the beginning of the year. Proprietorship equity must also be adjusted in accordance with the price increase during the year; the purchasing power loss does not directly affect the restatement of proprietorship equity because it has been charged against net profit in the adjusted income statement. There is no figure for retained profits in the adjusted balance sheet, because adjusted profits have been fully distributed.

The assumption that only adjusted profit was withdrawn by the proprietor is consistent with the rationale of the general price level approach, since it results in the generalized purchasing power of proprietorship equity being maintained during the period; increased holdings of net monetary assets have compensated for the fall in the purchasing power of money, and the firm holds the same quantity of non-monetary assets at the end of the period as it did at the beginning.

Adjustment Problems

The foregoing simple example has ignored a number of adjustment problems which are likely to arise when the technique is used in practice. In order to compare beginning and end net worth in a set of articulated financial statements, the book values of all items in the opening balance sheet must be restated in terms of end-of-period dollars. There is a difference in the treatment of monetary and non-monetary items. Non-monetary items such as inventories and fixed assets need to be adjusted by reference to their dates of acquisition.[1] Monetary assets (liabilities) in the opening balance sheet are adjusted by reference to the change in the price level that has taken place between the beginning of the period and the end of the period, in order to reflect the purchasing power loss (gain) in the period (see Table 18—2).

With respect to the closing balance sheet, non-monetary items (such as inventories and fixed assets) are revalued in end-of-period dollars, in the same way as these items have been adjusted in the opening balance sheet; the adjustment factors will reflect price changes since dates of acquisition. Monetary items in the closing balance sheet are already stated in end-of-period dollars and no adjustments are necessary.

The calculation of the total purchasing power loss or gain in the period, which is a component of adjusted net profit, is complicated by the fact that it is necessary to adjust not only monetary assets and liabilities in existence at the beginning of the period, but also changes in those items which result from the transactions of the

---

[1] The compilation of an age schedule of fixed assets will be needed for this purpose; this will also permit the calculation of adjusted depreciation in the income statement in the manner described later.

period. In a period of rising price levels, purchasing power losses will therefore be incurred both on opening monetary assets and on increases in net monetary assets resulting from sales or other external transactions; purchasing power gains will be recorded in respect of opening liabilities, purchases, expenses or other items which, because they involved external transactions, had the effect of reducing net monetary assets during the period.

In the income statement, it is necessary to differentiate between transactions which occur regularly throughout the income period, such as sales revenue and purchases, and items such as depreciation and opening inventory absorption which relate to transactions (such as purchases of assets) that occurred at particular points of time. Transactions which are evenly spread throughout the period may reasonably be adjusted by reference to the average price level of the period, but the adjusted values of the other items need to be related to dates of acquisition of the assets in question, or to the dates on which the transactions occurred. In the case of depreciation, this means that each kind of asset needs to be classified by age, and separate depreciation adjustments must be made for each age group. In revaluing opening and closing inventories for the purpose of calculating the adjustment for cost of sales, adjustments must be made by reference to changes in the respective price levels since the time of acquisition. Significant items for which the averaging assumption is not valid, e.g. interest or taxation payments made annually, must be adjusted separately.

It has been observed that general price level accounting involves the restatement of income statement and balance sheet items in terms of the price level prevailing at the end of the accounting period. Where it is desired to present comparative financial statements for a number of accounting periods, each must be revalued in terms of the price level at the end of the last accounting period. Provided adjustments for each earlier period have already been made, this will merely involve a further adjustment to each statement by means of a ratio, $\frac{p_n}{p_m}$, where p_n is the price level at the end of the last period and p_m is the price level used for purposes of the original adjustment.

A comprehensive example, which illustrates the adjustment techniques that have been discussed, follows. Two simplifying assumptions will be made in the example, namely, that there was an even flow of transactions throughout the year and that there were no purchases of fixed assets. Businesses which are subject to seasonal or irregular fluctuations in their transactions will need to adopt more sophisticated adjustment procedures.

An Illustration

X Trading Co. commenced business on 1 January 1983. Financial statements prepared in accordance with historical record accounting assumptions, relating to the company's third year of operations, are given in the first column of Table 18—2. The adjustment factors appropriate for restating the individual items in the statements to the year-end price level and the adjusted financial statements are shown in the second and third columns respectively.

The following information relates to the general price index employed in restating the accounts:

	General Price Index
At 1 January 1985	120
At 31 December 1985	140
Average-1985 transactions	132
At date of purchase of:	
Equipment	100
Opening inventories	117
Closing inventories	138

It is assumed that income tax of 50 per cent on the historical record accounting profit is paid on the last day of the financial year. The illustration shows that an apparent surplus after tax and dividends (if any) could represent payments out of capital, after the accounts have been adjusted for changes in the general price level.

The net purchasing power loss of \$308 shown in the income statement is calculated as follows:

Losses on—		
Opening monetary assets	$2\,200 \times \frac{20}{120}$	− 367
Sales	$12\,000 \times \frac{8}{132}$	− 727
Gains on—		
Opening liabilities	$1\,000 \times \frac{20}{120}$	+ 167
Purchases	$9\,300 \times \frac{8}{132}$	+ 564
Expenses	$900 \times \frac{8}{132}$	+ 55
Tax	$1\,000 \times \frac{0}{140}$	—
Net purchasing power loss		− \$308

The Case for CPP Accounting

It will be seen that CPP accounting constitutes a restatement of historical record financial statements in terms of a common measurement scale. Provided that the conversion process and its underlying assumptions are accepted as valid, therefore, the adjusted accounts will have the same utility and relevance during a period of changing price levels as do historical record accounts in a period of stable prices. Proponents of CPP contend that, in the absence of price level adjusted figures, it is impossible to ascertain whether, and to what extent, capital is being maintained in terms of general purchasing power. Because the maintenance of capital underlies income determination (and ultimately enterprise survival), it is asserted that historical record data must be adjusted to ensure that this objective is achieved.

It must be emphasized that CPP accounting is concerned solely with a restatement of historical costs. It does not address itself to the problem of valuation changes associated with changes in the prices of the specific resources and obligations of the

Table 18—2
Restatement of X Trading Co. Financial Statements to Current Dollars as at 31 December 1985

	Historical Dollars	Adjustment Factor	Current Dollars as at 31 December 1985
Balance sheet as at 1 January 1985			
Monetary assets*	2 200	140/120	2 567
Inventories	2 000	140/117	2 393
	4 200		4 960
Equipment	7 000	140/100	9 800
Less: Provision for depreciation	2 800	140/100	3 920
	4 200		5 880
Total assets	8 400		10 840
Liabilities	1 000	140/120	1 167
Proprietorship equity	$7 400		$9 673†
Income statement for year ended 31 December 1985			
Sales	12 000	140/132	12 727
Opening inventory	2 000	140/117	2 393
Purchases	9 300	140/132	9 864
	11 300		12 257
Closing inventory	3 600	140/138	3 652
	7 700		8 605
Gross profit	4 300		4 122
Depreciation on equipment	1 400	140/100	1 960
Other expenses	900	140/132	955
Purchasing power loss	—		308
	2 300		3 223
Net profit before tax	2 000		899
Less: Tax at 50%	1 000		1 000
Net profit (loss) after tax	$1 000		$(101)Dr.
Balance sheet as at 31 December 1985			
Monetary assets*	3 000		3 000
Inventories	3 600	140/138	3 652
	6 600		6 652
Equipment	7 000	140/100	9 800
Less: Provision for depreciation	4 200	140/100	5 880
	2 800		3 920
Total assets	9 400		10 572
Liabilities	1 000		1 000
Proprietorship equity	$8 400		$9 572†

* Monetary assets comprise cash and debtors.
† Adjusted proprietorship equity is a balance sheet residual. The adjusted income statement is a link between adjusted proprietorship equity at the beginning and end of the period.

enterprise. It appears that the validity and usefulness of CPP accounting are dependent on a number of propositions and assumptions. Certain issues are of special relevance: the need for a uniform measurement standard; the choice of a suitable general price index to reflect changes in the value of money; and the significance of maintaining capital in terms of general purchasing power, when the firm is concerned with the specific goods and services it employs and not with goods and services in general.

Accounting as a Measurement System

From a theoretical viewpoint, there is a strong justification for deflating accounting data by means of a general price index in periods of changing price levels. Accounting is concerned with measurement and accounting processes must conform consistently to measurement rules, the most fundamental of which in this context is additivity. The necessary conditions for additivity are, first, that the properties of objects being measured are identical for all objects, [2] and, second, that the measurement standard is uniform for all measurements. CPP accounting is an attempt to fulfil the second condition for additivity within the existing historical cost framework. In inflationary times the dollar is a poor measurement standard and amounts expressed in dollar terms are not additive; the measurement standard employed does not have a stable dimension over time.

The need for accounting processes to conform consistently to measurement rules applies to other accounting valuation systems as well as to historical record accounting. A CPP system based on general price level adjustments to historical cost may be rejected for reasons given in a subsequent section, but general price level adjustments may also be made in a current value system, as discussed in Chapter 21.

Adoption of a Suitable General Price Index

Price indexes may be general or specific. General price indexes are intended to reflect, as closely as possible, movements of prices in general throughout the economy. Specific indexes, on the other hand, are designed to represent price movements in the goods or services of a defined class or in a specific industry. For the purposes of CPP accounting, one is concerned only with general price indexes.

Like all price indexes, a general price index is an average based on a sample. It is computed by combining in a summary figure the specific prices of the individual goods and services comprised in the sample. Critics have pointed out the limitations of a general price index. In particular, the regimen of goods and services on which the index is based may lack generality, e.g. a consumer price index may be based on the expenditures of a particular group, such as urban wage-earner households. Inherent limitations are also imposed by the method of weighting. If weights are fixed by reference to the pattern of expenditures at one point of time, changes in prices as measured by the index will not be representative of price changes affecting the sample group to the extent that its expenditure patterns change over time. More generally, because specific prices do not move together, any general index will be unrepresentative of individual price movements.

---

[2] For example, one can add the heights of bookcases in one's study in order to calculate their average height, but the heights of some bookcases and the widths of others are not additive.

Criticisms of the use of a general index, on grounds such as these, appear to rest on a misconception. A general price index is intended to reflect changes in the general price level and is not merely a statistical summary or average of the secondary price levels in the economy. Conceptually, the notion of the general price level has economic significance because it is the reciprocal of the purchasing power of the dollar over goods and services in general. Ideally, changes in the purchasing power of the dollar are reflected in corresponding inverse changes in the price index.

A general price index used for purposes of CPP accounting should meet certain essential tests. Its construction should be undertaken by an independent, expert and impartial body such as a Bureau of Statistics, because the implementation of price level accounting will have implications for the distribution of the tax burden between different companies, for the resolution of competing claims of shareholders, creditors, workers, etc. and for the allocation of resources. The publication of the index should be timely; it is desirable that an index be published on a monthly basis; firms will otherwise be restricted in their choice of financial year. Furthermore, an index published at frequent intervals enhances the use of averaging procedures in adjusting the accounts. It is evident that an overriding requirement of the index is that its movements should reflect closely changes in the value of the dollar, and for this reason the adoption of a broadly based index is preferable.

A number of general price indexes is available in Australia. The consumer price index is a fixed weight index based on the expenditures of a sample of urban wage-earner households. It is published quarterly and is available about three weeks after the end of each quarter. The weights are changed approximately every five years. It is the most commonly adopted general price index, and is widely used in Australia for purposes of actual or contemplated adjustments to wages, personal income tax indexation, justification of price increases and related matters.

Other general price indexes include retail, wholesale, import and export price indexes. The so-called comprehensive indexes are sometimes recommended, e.g. the Gross Domestic Product Implicit Deflator, which reflects all goods and services produced in the economy, and the Private Final Consumption Expenditure Deflator, which reflects consumer expenditure generally. Because such indexes are calculated by dividing the relevant aggregates expressed in current prices by the same aggregates expressed in constant prices, changes in the pattern of production or expenditure are reflected in the index along with changes in prices.[3] That is to say, such indexes are based on changing weights. Although wider in coverage, deflator indexes necessarily reflect any deficiencies in the current price and constant price aggregates on which they are based. Because an implicit deflator is a function of both price changes and expenditure patterns in the economy, it does not measure directly changes in the value of money, which is the purpose underlying price level adjustments of the accounts.

Much of the controversy over the choice of a general price index may not be very significant in practice, because there is evidence of a close correlation in the inflation rates revealed by different general price indexes. If CPP accounting was to be implemented, the adoption of an appropriate index might well be circumscribed by the availability of broadly based indexes that are both neutral (in the sense that they are constructed by an independent agency) and reported on a timely basis.

---

[3] The GDP Implicit Deflator in period t is: $\dfrac{t \text{ period GDP at } t \text{ period prices}}{t \text{ period GDP at base period prices}}$

GIPPI and Capital Maintenance

A special case is sometimes made for the use of a general investment purchasing power index (GIPPI). Such an index is intended to reflect changes in the purchasing power of the dollar as it relates to the firm's investment inputs. Its use is consistent with a special capital maintenance concept, involving maintenance of the general investment purchasing power of the firm and more generally of the real capital endowment invested in commerce and industry.

From the viewpoint of preventing the erosion of industrial capital by rising prices, the use of GIPPI has a certain affinity with the objectives of current value accounting. It may be observed, however, that the GIPPI method seeks to maintain invested capital as general investment purchasing power potential—a view of capital maintenance that emphasizes flexibility and responsiveness to changes in the business environment. The method does not provide for the maintenance of the productive capacity of the individual firm in terms of its specific assets.

Limitations of CPP Accounting

Equity as Hypothetical Wealth

In Table 18—1 it was seen that the general price level approach results in an adjusted profit concept such that, if adjusted profits are to be fully withdrawn by the proprietor of the firm, his proprietorship capital will be maintained intact, in the sense that it will still command the same generalized purchasing power after the profit distribution as it did at the commencement of the period. In effect, income is treated as the difference between two hypothetical measures of wealth, namely the generalized purchasing power of proprietorship equity at the beginning and at the end of the income period.

It is difficult to see how any significant meaning can be ascribed to the individual balance sheet figures which appear in price level adjusted financial statements. When a firm first commences business there may be some justification for regarding its funds as representing generalized purchasing power. At that time its undeployed assets, which may be exclusively cash or other liquid assets, may be regarded as having an infinite range of alternative uses and may therefore be represented as generalized purchasing power. But once the firm's funds are invested in specific assets and it begins to engage in specialized kinds of operating activity, these conditions no longer hold. The fact that most operating assets are, to a large extent, specific to the firm means that they cannot even notionally be regarded as representing generalized purchasing power. Even the funds which flow into the business as a result of its operating activity cannot be regarded as constituting generalized purchasing power, because most of these funds are immediately reinvested in operating assets which are related to the particular kinds of economic activity which the firm undertakes.

Most writers assume that a major objective of CPP accounting is the maintenance of the general purchasing power of capital. The above criticism addresses this issue. However, if we regard CPP adjustments as simply providing a measurement scale correction, the criticism loses its force.

Lack of Relevance for Decision Making

As prices affecting the firm's actual transactions change, the historical cost figures which record cost of goods sold, depreciation, inventories, fixed assets and investments come to reflect neither their current value in use to the firm nor their current value in exchange. The historical values cease to be relevant to the firm for most purposes of operating and investment policy. The application of a general price index to historical record data merely perpetuates the problem.

Suppose, for example, that a machine with an expected service life of two years and an expected scrap value of nil is purchased for $100 at time t_0 and that an identical machine is purchased for $200 at time t_1. Suppose also that, although there is no further change in the price of machines, the general price level (which stood at 100 at t_0) increases from 150 at t_1 to 200 at t_2. Assuming straight-line depreciation, the application of general price level adjustments will require depreciation of the first machine, in respect of the period ending at t_2, to be recorded at $100 in terms of t_2 prices, while depreciation on the second machine in the same period will be recorded at $133 in terms of t_2 prices. The date of purchase of the machine affects the adjusted cost figure in the same arbitrary way as it affects the historical cost figure, and it is necessary to ask what sensible meaning can be given to accounting data which record different amounts of depreciation in respect of two identical machines. Historical cost figures cannot be converted to a uniform basis of valuation merely by applying a general price index.

The same point may be made by reference to two identical blocks of land,[4] purchased on different dates, t_0 and t_1, for different prices, $1\,000 and $1\,800. At time t_2, identical blocks may be bought or sold in the market for $3\,000. If the general price level has increased from 100 at t_0 to 150 at t_1, and 200 at t_2, a general price level adjusted balance sheet at t_2 would record the two blocks at different values as follows:

1st block	$1\,000 \times \dfrac{200}{100}$	$2 000
2nd block	$1\,800 \times \dfrac{200}{150}$	$2 400

However, a balance sheet that places different values on identical blocks of land, which can be used to earn equal amounts of revenue or which can be sold for the same amounts in the market, clearly lacks relevance to the purposes for which accounting information is required, just as unadjusted historical record data lack relevance. The relevant value for purposes of deciding on its use or sale is the same for each block, and at t_2 is given by its current market value of $3\,000.

Conclusion

Proponents of the general price level approach argue that the adjusted financial statements provide information relevant to the decisions of owners (in formulating distribution policy) and management (in maintaining capital at its *real historical value*). At the same time, it is claimed, the adjusted statements contain data which

---

[4] The blocks are assumed to be identical in the sense that they have identical values in use or exchange.

are statistically more reliable and more consistent for purposes of inter-temporal or inter-firm comparisons, because they have been expressed in terms of a uniform instead of a fluctuating monetary unit. The use of index numbers prepared by independent government agencies is regarded as sufficient to ensure objectivity and hardness, and to permit easy verification of the adjusted statements. The criteria of relevance, objectivity, hardness, reliability and comparability are therefore all said to be met by the adoption of the general price level approach.

It may reasonably be accepted that general price level adjustments can be made objectively. But it has been shown that, because they are based on historical data, price level adjusted financial statements do not provide information which has a consistent or unambiguous meaning to those who need to use the information for purposes of making economic decisions.

There is also an important sense in which reliability is not achieved, namely that of fidelity or correspondence with actual events and conditions. Now general price level changes may reasonably be regarded as actual events, but the significance of general price level adjustments in relation to the individual firm is at best conjectural and in most cases must be regarded as hypothetical, as has been explained above.

However, the main objection to the general price level approach is based on its lack of relevance for many of the purposes for which accounting data are required. In particular, adjusted historical data represent bygone or sunk costs that are of little consequence for decision making. However, as has been noted earlier, general price level adjustments are also possible in a current value system. Such adjustments correct for distortion in the measurement standard, while it will be seen that a current value system itself has relevance for many forms of decision making.

Finally, if inflation adjusted financial statements contain informational content for investors, their publication should result in price adjustments on the share market. Morris tested the market reaction to inflation adjusted earnings of British companies in the study published by Cutler and Westwick (see Chapter 17), which received widespread publicity at the time. [5] Test results indicate the market took no notice of the adjusted earnings figures and suggest either that the data are irrelevant or that the market has already made its own assessment of the effects of inflation on company profits and impounded these into share prices.

Appendix

A Note on the Gain on Long-term Debt

The view that purchasing power losses and gains on all monetary assets and liabilities are part of net income is gaining increasing acceptance by writers on CPP accounting. This has particular significance for highly geared firms, which stand to benefit in inflationary times from the diminished real burden of existing debt. It is of some concern to borrowers that this form of purchasing power gain may be subject to company income tax as a component of reported income in a CPP system.

From the viewpoints of both external reporting and taxation, the prevailing emphasis on operating income after interest stems from a 'proprietorship' concept of

---

[5] It is assumed that the market impounds publicly available information into the share price in an instantaneous and unbiased manner.

the business enterprise. From an 'entity' viewpoint, which reflects modern business conditions more realistically, both shareholders and long-term creditors are regarded as suppliers of capital funds, on the reasonable ground that long-term debts are recycled or otherwise replaced by equity funds. Thus Jones has argued that while purchasing power gains and losses on net short-term monetary assets must be recognized to obtain a reasonable picture of operating results, the purchasing power gains and losses on long-term debt represent shifts in the *real* equities of various classes of permanent investors and should therefore not be included in the income of the entity itself.

This approach is consistent with the capital maintenance objective associated with the use of GIPPI. The real resources invested in the private sector encompass the total operating assets under the control of the individual corporate units and not only those operating assets financed by equity funds. Given a social objective of at least maintaining the investment capacity in productive resources in the private sector, there seems no convincing reason why the operating profit of the individual enterprise and the associated tax liability should be dependent on the firm's capitalization structure. A corollary of this view is that no deductible loss arises on long-term loan investment.

References

Jones, R.C., *Price Level Changes and Financial Statements — Case Studies of Four Companies,* American Accounting Association, 1955.

Ma, R. and Miller, M.C., 'Inflation and the Current Value Illusion', *Accounting and Business Research*, Autumn 1976, pp. 250-63.

Morris, R.C., 'Evidence of the Impact of Inflation Accounting on Share Prices', *Accounting and Business Research*, Spring 1975, pp. 82-90.

Additional Reading

Barton, A.D., *The Anatomy of Accounting*, University of Queensland Press, St. Lucia, Qld., 1977, Chapter 22.

Baxter, W.T., *Accounting Values and Inflation*, McGraw-Hill, London, 1975.

Hendriksen, E.S., *Accounting Theory*, Irwin, Homewood, Ill., 1977, Chapter 7.

Discussion Questions

1 Contrast historical record accounting and CPP accounting with particular reference to valuation assumptions, concepts of income and capital employed, recording procedures and financial statements.

2 Distinguish purchasing power gains and losses from price level adjusted operating profits and losses.

3 Do you consider that, in a CPP accounting system, a purchasing power gain or loss arising from the holding of net monetary assets should be taken into account in measuring income? What other action might be taken?

4 Summarize the effects of holding monetary items in:
(a) periods of rising prices, and
(b) periods of falling prices.

5 Distinguish between general and specific price indexes. Discuss their relevance from a manager's viewpoint.

6 Discuss the problem of finding suitable general price (or purchasing power) indexes for use in a CPP accounting system. What does such an index purport to measure?

7 In what sense may it be said that the concept of general price level adjusted income succeeds in maintaining capital intact? Discuss.

8 Examine the view that CPP accounting facilitates inter-temporal comparisons of accounting data, by providing a measuring rod that is comparable to that provided by international exchange rates in respect of international transactions.

9 What do you consider to be the case against adopting a CPP accounting system?

10 To what extent do you consider that the general price level approach to accounting measurement meets information requirements of relevance, reliability, objectivity, hardness, comparability and consistency?

Exercises

1 A firm invested $10 000 in interest-bearing deposits at the Australian Bank on 1 January 1985, earning 9 per cent per annum interest for a 12-month term. Assuming that the general price level increased by 5 per cent during the year 1985, what income in real terms do you consider has been earned by the firm during the year?

2 A firm's plant and machinery register records the following information at 31 December, 1985:

Asset	Date of Acquisition	Cost	Annual Straight-line Depreciation
Machine A	1 January 1980	$10 000	$1 000
Machine B	1 January 1983	15 000	3 000
Building	1 January 1979	40 000	1 000
Land	1 January 1979	5 000	—
Fittings	1 January 1981	5 000	200

Information on the general price level index on relevant dates is given below:

1 January 1979	100
1 January 1980	90
1 January 1981	110
1 January 1983	140
31 December 1985	150

Calculate general price level adjusted depreciation and balance sheet data in respect of the assets.

3 A firm commenced the year with monetary assets of $10 000, inventories which cost $45 000 and liabilities of $15 000. During the year it sold the inventories for $90 000, replaced them with new inventories costing $60 000, and paid expenses of $30 000. Proprietorship withdrawals at the end of the year amounted to $15 000.

It may be assumed that:

(a) there was no change in monetary assets;

(b) liabilities increased to the extent necessary to finance the firm's activities;

(c) purchases, expenses and sales occurred regularly throughout the year; and

(d) the general price level increased from 100 at the beginning of the year to 140 at the end of the year, and that the year average was 120.

You are required to prepare: (i) historical record financial statements; and (ii) general price level adjusted financial statements for the firm in terms of end-year prices. Show workings.

4 The following historical record data relate to a firm which commenced operations at t_0. Trading activities and the incurring of expenses took place evenly throughout each year, but profit withdrawals took place at the end of each year. Assume that opening and closing inventories in the second year were purchased at average $t_0 - t_1$ and $t_1 - t_2$ price levels, respectively.

You are required to prepare general price level adjusted comparative financial statements in terms of t_2 prices. If adjusted income were to be fully distributed each year, what effect would this have on the firm's financial position?

Balance Sheets

	t_0		t_1		t_2
Bank	$10 000		$10 000		$20 000
Debtors	—		20 000		20 000
Inventories	40 000		50 000		60 000
Total assets	$50 000		$80 000		$100 000
Creditors	—		15 000		15 000
Proprietors' equity—					
Capital	$50 000		$50 000		$50 000
Retained profits	—	50 000	15 000	65 000	35 000	85 000
Total equities	$50 000		$80 000		$100 000

Income Statements

	$t_0 - t_1$	$t_1 - t_2$
Sales	$100 000	$120 000
Cost of sales	50 000	60 000
Gross profit	50 000	60 000
Expenses	20 000	20 000
Net profit	30 000	40 000
Profit withdrawals	15 000	20 000
Retained profits	$15 000	$20 000

Price Index

t_0	100
average $t_0 - t_1$	110
t_1	120
average $t_1 - t_2$	125
t_2	130

5 Models Inc. Ltd started operations at the beginning of 1983 with a paid-up capital of $80 000 and physical assets of $100 000. On 31 December 1985 the following information was available:

Balance Sheet as at 31 December 1984

Fully paid-up capital	$80 000	Monetary assets		$25 000
Retained earnings	15 000	Fixed assets	$100 000	
Monetary liabilities	10 000	*Less*: Accumulated		
		depreciation	20 000	80 000
	$105 000			$105 000

Income Statement for Year Ended 31 December 1985

Sales (cash)		$45 000
Less: Operating expenses—		
Depreciation	$10 000	
Miscellaneous expenses (cash)	22 500	32 500
Net profit		$12 500

The company depreciates its non-monetary assets at 10 per cent per annum on a straight-line basis. All revenues and expenses (other than depreciation) are on a cash basis and tend to occur evenly throughout the year.

The following information relates to the general price index:

Year	Annual Average	Year-end Average
1983	100	100
1984	108	110
1985	115	120

You are required to:

(a) restate the 1984 balance sheet in 1985 prices in order to derive the adjusted retained earnings at the beginning of 1985;

(b) determine the net purchasing power gain or loss for the year ended 31 December 1985;

(c) restate the income statement for year ended 31 December 1985 in current dollars; and

(d) prepare the balance sheet as at 31 December 1985 in current dollars.

19 Accounting Valuation Systems 3— Current Value Accounting (A)

Many accountants believe that a major objective of financial statements is to provide information relevant for decision making, and that current values are more useful for this purpose than historical costs or historical costs adjusted by a general price index. The problem of relevance for decision making is an empirical issue. The necessity for firms to disclose current value data, given that users of financial statements have access to other sources of information, has sometimes been questioned. The usefulness of current value accounting reports is discussed later in this chapter.

Several current value accounting systems have been proposed and are listed in Figure 19—A. In a current value accounting system a firm's net worth may be defined as the value of its assets less its liabilities, stated in prices prevailing at the time the calculation is made (e.g. at balance date). For purposes of this chapter the term current value will be used to describe any measure of value derived by reference to the current price of an asset, whether that price is determined by reference to the cost of replacing the asset, its realizable or market selling value, or some combination of the two. The term 'current cost accounting' is widely used as a synonym for current value accounting but is unnecessarily restrictive as a description of the current value approach. Current cost accounting is strictly a special case of current value accounting.

Figure 19—A
Current Value Accounting Systems

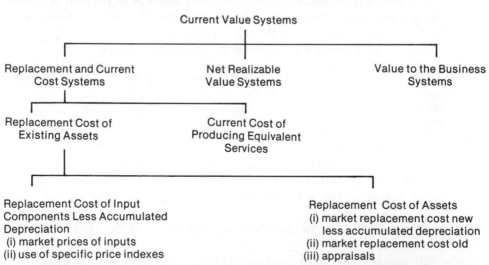

In Figure 19—A, three types of current value systems have been distinguished, depending on whether current value is related to replacement cost (an entry value), net realizable or market selling value (an exit value), or value to the business (which may be some combination of replacement cost and net realizable value). Replacement cost systems may incorporate valuations based on either the replacement cost of existing assets or the current cost of assets producing equivalent services. The former is often described as a replacement cost system and the latter as a current cost system.

As explained in the Introduction to Part III, the measurement standard used in valuation systems or sub-systems may be either money units or purchasing power units. The relative price change approach, in which a general price level adjustment is superimposed on a current value system, can be adopted as readily in a replacement or current cost system as in a net realizable value system, by employing similar adjustment techniques.

The concern of this chapter is with an approach to current value accounting which has particular merit (as will be explained below) and which is designated as 'the current distributable income/operating capital maintenance approach'. Chapter 20 presents an alternative approach (which is strictly a replacement cost of input components sub-system), which is designated as 'the business profit/financial capital maintenance approach'. Chapter 20 also discusses some proposed guidelines for selecting between entry and exit values in an eclectic approach to current value accounting. Chapter 21 deals with the relative price change accounting systems, in particular Chambers's model which is based on current cash equivalent (or net realizable value) measures.

Current Distributable Income/Operating Capital Maintenance Approach

Concepts of Income and Net Worth

In essence a system of current value accounting based on the current distributable income/operating capital maintenance approach differs from historical record accounting in the following way. Historical record accounting is usually restricted to recording actual transactions with other entities and certain activities internal to the firm (such as manufacturing operations). Current value accounting also recognizes external events in the form of price changes which affect the current value of external transactions, internal operations and the net worth of the accounting entity.

Current distributable income is measured as the difference between revenues and expenses, both expressed in terms of current prices of the accounting period. The current value concept of income is both a flow concept and a transactions concept. Because it is measured as the difference between revenues and expenses (both expressed in terms of current prices of the period), it is related to transactions which actually take place during the period.

Current distributable income, like any other income concept, represents an increase in net worth. Although it is tempting to define current distributable income as the change in an entity's net worth during the year, this can lead to error. Net worth is also affected by proprietorship capital contributions and withdrawals, gains and losses on disposal of fixed assets, and gains and losses on revaluation of individual assets. All these are treated as capital adjustments or restatements of capital, rather than as components of income, under the current distributable income approach.

The *current value of net worth* at any point of time is represented by the non-monetary assets of the business (in their existing form but revalued to reflect their current worth to the enterprise), together with its net monetary assets (the current values of which are their face values). Like the current distributable income concept, current net worth reflects the actual deployment of enterprise assets. There is, of course, nothing to prevent a firm from redeploying its assets (and in practice it will be doing this continuously), but at any point of time its net worth is measured by reference to the current prices of its assets as currently deployed.

The *operating capital maintenance* concept implies that the operating capacity of the firm, i.e. its ability to generate future income, is maintained. Capital is maintained in the sense that there is an appropriation of profit to reserves to the extent that is necessary to finance the higher cost of holding and using non-monetary assets. Financial or monetary assets and liabilities remain unchanged; there is therefore no appropriation of profit to reserves on account of holding monetary assets and liabilities in the system described in this chapter. Some writers have argued that provision should also be made, when prices rise, for an increase in the holding of net monetary assets in order to service a given volume of transactions. Other writers have argued that current valuation adjustments should be supplemented by purchasing power adjustments (of the kind described in Chapter 18) on monetary assets and liabilities, net purchasing-power gains being treated as distributable income and proprietorship equity being reduced accordingly. Gynther has proposed a variant of the current distributable income/operating capital maintenance approach, whereby the capital to be maintained includes a firm's long-term liabilities as well as its proprietorship equity, while purchasing-power adjustments are restricted to monetary assets and short-term liabilities.

Although there is no question that the holding of monetary assets and liabilities during a period of inflation gives rise to purchasing-power losses and gains, such losses and gains are not brought into income in a pure current value system. Proposals for the adaptation of the current distributable income approach to take account of purchasing-power losses or gains on monetary items are considered in Chapter 22.

Asset Valuation Adjustments

Symbolically, the adjustment of accounting data to record current values may be illustrated by reference to the simplified balance sheet relationship used in Chapter 18:

$$M + N = R \tag{1}$$

where M, N and R denote the measures of net monetary assets, non-monetary assets and net worth (or residual equity), respectively, all at t_0.

If there are no income-earning activities during the period t_0 to t_1, but if the current value of N increases by q (where q is a proportionate price change, $\frac{q_1 - q_0}{q_0}$, as the result, say, of an increase in the current purchase price of the assets represented by N), the balance sheet at t_1 will take the following form:

$$M + N(1 + q) = R + Nq \tag{2}$$

A separate valuation adjustment needs to be made for each kind of non-monetary asset, so that strictly $N(1 + q)$ should be expanded into $\sum_{i=1}^{n} N_i (1 + q_i)$ and Nq should become $\sum_{i=1}^{n} N_i q_i$, but in the present exposition attention will be confined to a single class of non-monetary asset, N. The valuation adjustment may be made as soon as the external event (i.e. the price change) occurs, but again for simplicity it will be assumed that the adjustment is recorded at the end of the accounting period.

The increase in asset values resulting from the valuation adjustment is matched by an equivalent increase in residual equity. Although it would be possible to record current value adjustments in supplementary financial statements, there are advantages in incorporating the adjustments in the double-entry records. This may be done, quite simply, by means of a journal entry debiting the asset account (or an asset adjustment account) and crediting an accumulated capital account called an asset revaluation reserve account. The balance of the asset revaluation reserve account will thus be recorded in the balance sheet as a component part of net worth or residual equity. This has the effect of recognizing an increase in the current value of residual equity resulting from the increased value of the firm's holding of assets.

Income Valuation Adjustments

So far income arising from trading or operating activities has been ignored, but this must now be introduced into the analysis. If the non-monetary assets, which it may be assumed for the sake of simplicity are trading inventories, are sold during the period t_0 to t_1, it is necessary to record a current value adjustment at the time the inventories are absorbed into cost. The inventories may be thought of conceptually as being absorbed into cost as they are turned over or sold.

It will be recalled that, under historical record accounting, profit is measured as:

$$Y_h = S_h - C_h \tag{3}$$

where Y_h denotes accounting profit, S_h sales revenue and C_h costs and expenses, all expressed in terms of historical record values. Under current value accounting, the concept of current distributable income is measured by:

$$Y_c = S_c - C_c \tag{4}$$

where Y_c denotes current distributable income, S_c sales revenue and C_c costs and expenses all expressed in terms of current prices of the period.

Now $S_h = S_c$, because sales revenue is automatically expressed in current prices in the historical record system, but C_h differs from C_c by the amount of the current value adjustment. For measurement purposes, it would therefore be possible to derive current income as the arithmetical difference between accounting profit and the valuation adjustment on assets absorbed into cost, which may be called the income valuation adjustment Q_y:

Since
and
it follows that
$$C_c = C_h + Q_y$$
$$S_c = S_h$$
$$Y_c = S_h - (C_h + Q_y)$$
$$= Y_h - Q_y \tag{5}$$

Rearranging equation (5),
$$Y_h = Y_c + Q_y \tag{6}$$

Y_c is the income derived from trading operations, measured consistently by recording all revenues and expenses in terms of current prices, while Q_y is the valuation adjustment which has been recorded on assets absorbed into cost for the purpose of earning revenue.

The accounting entries to record the income valuation adjustment comprise a debit to an income valuation adjustment account, the balance of which will be offset against the balance of accounting profit to derive the measure of current distributable income, and a credit to an income revaluation reserve.

Relationship between Asset Valuation Adjustments and Income Valuation Adjustments

When income arising from trading or operating activities is introduced into the analysis, the valuation adjustment, Nq, in equation (2) has two components — Q_y, an income valuation adjustment which reflects the price change up to the time the assets are absorbed into cost for the purpose of earning revenue, and Q_a, an asset valuation adjustment which reflects the price change on the assets held at the end of the period which has occurred since those assets were acquired: [1]

$$M + N(1 + q) = R + Nq \tag{2}$$

Since
$$Nq = Q_y + Q_a \tag{7}$$

it follows that
$$M + N(1 + q) = R + Q_y + Q_a \tag{8}$$

The equation $Nq = Q_y + Q_a$ holds irrespective of the number of times the assets turn over during the income period. Thus if a firm commences the period with trading inventories worth $100 (in terms of both historical and current values), if they are sold during the period for $140 and replaced at a cost of $110, and if the cost of replacing them at the end of the period is $130, the total valuation adjustment Nq is $30, which may be subdivided into an income valuation adjustment of $10 and an asset valuation adjustment of $20. Accounting profit of $40 consists of an operating component, which we have called current distributable income, of $30, and the income valuation adjustment of $10.

If the inventories are turned over twice during the period, if their selling prices are $140 and $150 respectively and the costs of replacing them at the times of sale are $110 and $125, and if the current replacement cost at the end of the period is $130, the following calculations show that the total valuation adjustment is still $30, while the income valuation adjustment becomes $25 and the asset valuation adjustment is $5:

Income Statement

	First Sale	Second Sale	Income Statement for Period
Sales	$140	$150	$290
Historical cost of sales	100	110	210
Accounting profit	40	40	80
Income valuation adjustment	10	15	25
Current distributable income	$30	$25	$55

In effect, the asset revaluation necessary just before each sale is converted into an income valuation adjustment by the act of sale, leaving the final asset valuation adjustment to reflect only the price change which has occurred since the inventories were last replaced, as shown:

[1] In a sense, the income valuation adjustment Q_y may be said to be 'realized' and the asset valuation adjustment Q_a may be said to be still 'unrealized'.

	Just Before First Sale	Just Before Second Sale	End of Period
Inventories (at historical cost)	$100	$110	$125
Asset valuation adjustment	10	15	5
Inventories (at current value)	$110	$125	$130

If the current income of $55 is distributed to the proprietor at the end of the period, the balance sheet at the end of the period will take the following form:

Balance Sheet

Inventories (at historical cost)	$125
Asset valuation adjustment	5
Inventories (at current value)	$130
Proprietor's capital	100
Income revaluation reserve	25
Asset revaluation reserve	5
Proprietorship equity	$130

Significance of Valuation Adjustments

The distinction between the income valuation adjustment (and income revaluation reserve) and the asset valuation adjustment (and asset revaluation reserve) is of some significance because they relate to different stages in the income cycle. Although the asset valuation adjustment reflects an 'unrealized' price change (on assets held at the end of the period), while the income valuation adjustment represents a 'realized' price change (on assets that have been absorbed into cost), they are both locked into the current value of the assets, say inventories, held at the end of the period, and can only be released by running down the physical quantity of inventories held. It is for this reason that it is normally necessary to treat both adjustments as transfers to reserves, thereby augmenting proprietorship equity by the amounts necessary to finance the holding of the assets at their increased prices, an approach that is consistent with the operating capital maintenance concept discussed earlier.

Valuation Adjustments in Respect of Inventories

Cost of Sales (Income) Valuation Adjustment

In computing current distributable income, the theoretically correct approach is to calculate the current cost of sales each time a selling transaction takes place. But if the number of selling transactions is large, as must be expected in a normal business, fresh information about current costs will need to be obtained each time a sale is made. Where many lines are being handled, this will obviously be a formidable task, especially in a manufacturing business where the cost of sales depends on manufacturing costs and not simply on the purchase prices of the goods sold.

If it can be assumed that sales, purchases and the accumulation (or running down) of inventories take place evenly throughout the period, it is possible to employ an approximate method to adjust the historical cost of sales figure. The cost of sales valuation adjustment is represented by the sum of the valuation adjustments for opening and closing inventories in terms of the *average* current cost (which may be computed as the weighted average purchase price in the period).

Example: Suppose inventories worth $100 (in terms of both historical cost and current value) at the start of the year are turned over twice during the year, being replaced by the same quantities of inventories each time. The total sales revenue in the year is $290. Replacement costs on the two occasions are $110 and $125 respectively, and the year-end replacement cost is $130. The average current cost of sales may be computed as $\dfrac{\$110 + \$125}{2}$ or $117.50, and the cost of sales adjustment is calculated as follows:[2]

Opening inventory adjustment	$17.50 ($117.50 — $100)
Closing inventory adjustment	7.50 ($125 — $117.50)
Cost of sales adjustment	$25.00

The opening inventory adjustment is positive in a time of rising prices, because the inventories need to be absorbed into cost at the average current cost (which is higher than their historical cost). The closing inventory adjustment is also positive, because although the current value of closing inventories, in terms of average prices of the period, is lower than their historical cost, this negative difference needs to be deducted from the historical cost of sales to arrive at the current cost.

The following procedure may thus be used in calculating the income valuation adjustment necessary to revalue cost of sales in current prices, and hence to derive a measure of current income by reference to the accounting profit figure:

Income Statement for Year Ended 31 December 1985

Sales revenue		$290
Cost of sales—		
Opening inventory	$100	
Purchases	235	
	335	
Less: Closing inventory	125	210
Accounting profit		80
Less: Cost of sales valuation adjustment—		
Opening inventory adjustment	17.50	
Closing inventory adjustment	7.50	
		25
Current distributable income		$55

In the example, the physical quantities of opening and closing inventory are assumed to be the same, but the above procedure may also be employed to compute the cost of sales at current prices when the opening and closing inventories differ. With respect to both opening and closing inventories, the adjustment is simply the difference between the historical record book value of the inventory and its average current cost, i.e. the respective number of units times the average purchase price per unit.

[2] An alternative average current cost of sales figure may be computed by including the opening and closing values, i.e. $\dfrac{\$100 + \$110 + \$125 + \$130}{4}$ or $116.25. It is emphasized that all average measures represent approximations to the true cost of sales.

The corresponding credit entry of $25 is made in the cost of sales revaluation reserve account. This reserve account is shown in the balance sheet in the following section.

Inventory (Asset) Valuation Adjustment

The asset valuation adjustment calculation for inventory is straightforward. This is given by the difference between the historical record book value of the closing inventory and its current cost at the end of the period. Entries in the inventory valuation adjustment account have the effect of adjusting inventory values for balance sheet purposes. At the end of the period, the debit balance on this account is raised or lowered to reflect the current value of the closing inventory. The other part of the double entry is made in the inventory revaluation reserve account.

In the foregoing example, the inventory valuation adjustment at the end of the period amounts to $5 (replacement cost of closing inventory, $130, less the book value of closing inventory, $125). Assuming that sales and purchases have been on credit terms and no payments have been made to the proprietors, the balance sheet will record the following historical record and current value data:

Balance Sheet as at 31 December 1985

Assets		
Debtors		$290
Inventories—		
Historical cost	$125	
Add: Valuation adjustment	5	
Current value	——	130
		420
Less: **Liabilities**—creditors		235
Proprietorship equity		
Contributed capital	100	
Retained profits	55	
Cost of sales revaluation reserve	25	
Inventory revaluation reserve	5	
	——	
Current value of proprietorship equity		$185

In this way, information is provided in the balance sheet about both the historical value and the current value of inventories and proprietorship equity.

Valuation Adjustments in Respect of Depreciation and Fixed Assets

Depreciation Valuation Adjustment

It has been seen that historical record depreciation represents an allocation of the original money cost of a fixed asset, which is charged against revenue during a particular accounting period in order to measure the historical cost of the services which the asset has yielded in producing revenue during that period. Current value depreciation, by contrast, may be defined as an allocation of the current value of an equivalent new asset, which is charged against revenue during a period and is intended to measure the current cost of utilizing the asset's services in producing revenue during that period. The relationship between historical record depreciation and current value depreciation may therefore be expressed as follows:

$$\begin{array}{c}\text{Current value} \\ \text{depreciation}\end{array} = \begin{array}{c}\text{Historical record} \\ \text{depreciation}\end{array} \text{ x } \begin{array}{c}\text{Average current value of asset} \\ \hline \text{Historical cost of asset}\end{array}$$

In calculating current value depreciation, the average current value of the asset during the year is used. If an asset is used only during part of an accounting period, it is the average current value during that time which is relevant.

Example: Consider a simplistic example which focuses on the valuation adjustment problem in respect of a fixed asset. Suppose that a new firm has only one asset, a machine with an estimated 10-year life purchased for $100. The following financial statements have been prepared on historical record assumptions (using straight-line depreciation) at the end of the firm's first year of operations:

Income Statement for the Year Ended 31 December 1985

Net revenue before charging depreciation	$160
Less: Depreciation on machine	10
Accounting profit	$150

Balance Sheet as at 31 December 1985

Bank		$160
Machine (at cost)	$100	
Less: Accumulated depreciation	10	90
Proprietorship equity—		
Contributed capital	100	
Retained profits	150	$250

Suppose also that the current value of a new machine, as given by the current cost of replacing it, is $120 at 31 December 1985. The average current value for the year may be estimated at $\dfrac{\$100 + \$120}{2} = \$110$ and the depreciation valuation adjustment may be calculated as follows:

$$\begin{array}{rcl}\begin{array}{c}\text{Depreciation valuation} \\ \text{adjustment}\end{array} & = & \begin{array}{c}\text{Current value} \\ \text{depreciation}\end{array} - \begin{array}{c}\text{Historical record} \\ \text{depreciation}\end{array} \\[2ex] & = & \left(\$10 \text{ x } \dfrac{110}{100}\right) - \$10 \\[2ex] & = & \$1\end{array}$$

Current distributable income may now be derived as follows:

Accounting profit	$150
Less: Depreciation valuation adjustment	1
Current distributable income	$149

The amount of the depreciation valuation adjustment will reduce the retained profits available for distribution from $150 to $149.

Fixed Asset Valuation Adjustment

In adjusting the value of fixed assets, year-end current values are used. Calculating this adjustment is complicated by the existence of the accumulated provision for depreciation for each asset. The valuation adjustment for a fixed asset is the difference between its written-down historical record value and the current value equivalent of this written-down value at the end of the period. The current value of a new asset may be used as a starting point to arrive at the written-down value.

A fixed asset not subject to depreciation, e.g. land, is revalued by simply taking the difference between historical cost and current value.

Using the data in the previous example, the fixed asset valuation adjustment at the end of 1985 may be calculated as follows. As with the inventory valuation adjustment account, the debit balance in the fixed asset valuation adjustment account at the end of the period is raised or lowered to reflect the current value of the fixed asset less accumulated depreciation. A corresponding entry is made in the fixed asset re-valuation reserve account, so as to adjust proprietorship equity in line with the revaluation.

$$
\begin{aligned}
\text{Fixed asset valuation} \ &= \ \text{Depreciated current value of asset} \\
\text{adjustment} \ &\qquad - \text{Depreciated historical value of asset} \\
&= \left(\$90 \ \times \ \frac{120}{100} \right) - \$90 \\
&= \quad \$18
\end{aligned}
$$

The balance sheet at that time will record the following historical record and current value data:

Balance Sheet at 31 December 1985

Assets		
Bank		$160
Machine—		
Historical cost	$100	
Less: Accumulated depreciation	10	
	90	
Add: Valuation adjustment	18	
Current value		108
Proprietorship equity		
Contributed capital	100	
Retained profits	149	
Depreciation revaluation reserve	1	
Fixed asset revaluation reserve	18	
		$268

If the current distributable income of $149 is to be fully distributed to the proprietors of the business, the bank balance will fall to $11. It will be observed that the bank balance which has accumulated as a result of the depreciation charge and depreciation valuation adjustment, $11, and the depreciated current value of the machine, $108, together do not add up to the current value of a new machine at the end of 1985 ($120). There may be a shortfall of this nature in a period of rising prices for an individual asset. The depreciation valuation adjustment is related to the *average* current value of the fixed asset (and not its year-end value), while no further allowance is made for so-called 'back-log' depreciation, i.e. the deficiency in a particular year's depreciation charge which arises when the price of the asset continues to increase in subsequent years.

How, then, can it be said that the current value approach succeeds in maintaining the value of proprietorship equity in terms of its command over operating assets? If the current value of the machine increases further in 1986, how will the depreciation allowances recorded in terms of 1985 values be sufficient to finance operating assets at their higher, 1986, values?

The answer to these questions lies in an assumption, which is usually not unrealistic in practice, that is made about the re-investment of funds retained in the business as a result of the depreciation allowances recorded during the year. It is assumed that these funds are invested in operating assets rather than being held as idle bank balances. This requirement will be met if the firm has a balanced stock of operating assets, which participate in a regular and continuous cycle of purchase, use and re-placement. If the firm has three equivalent machines, each of which needs to be replaced in turn every three years, current value depreciation on the three machines taken together will in fact be sufficient to finance the replacement of the machine needing to be replaced in any year. Under these circumstances, the problem of backlog depreciation does not arise. However, it needs to be emphasized that in current value accounting, as in historical record accounting, there is no presumption that existing assets are always replaced in their original form. Nevertheless, the re-investment assumption implies that the value of proprietorship equity is maintained in terms of its command over the operating assets which are actually held from time to time.

The Recording of Valuation Adjustments and Their Significance

It has been suggested that the income and asset valuation adjustments should be made in the double-entry records at the end of each accounting period, in order that they, and the financial statements which are derived from them, may provide information about both historical and current values. The provision of multi-valued data is recommended because of the different purposes which historical record data and current value data may need to serve.

The accounting entries which are necessary to record the valuation adjustments take the following form (it is assumed that prices or current values are rising):

Valuation adjustments to inventories—

(a) Income valuation adjustment account   Dr. ⎱ Revaluation of inventories
       Cost of sales revaluation reserve account   Cr. ⎰ absorbed into cost of sales

(b) Inventory valuation adjustment account   Dr. ⎱ Revaluation of closing
       Inventory revaluation reserve account   Cr. ⎰ inventories

Valuation adjustments to fixed assets—

(a) Income valuation adjustment account (IVAA)   Dr. ⎱ Revaluation of depreciation
       Depreciation revaluation reserve account (DRRA)   Cr. ⎰

(b) Fixed asset valuation adjustment account (FAVAA)   Dr. ⎱ Revaluation of fixed assets
       Fixed asset revaluation reserve account (FARRA)   Cr. ⎰ at end of period

---

Example: Suppose a fixed asset with an estimated 10-year life is purchased at t_0 for $100, and straight-line depreciation is appropriate. Current valuation adjustments in the first three years of its operation are shown below. The depreciation valuation adjustment is based on the average current cost for the year, and the fixed asset valuation adjustment on the year-end current cost.

	Year 1	Year 2	Year 3
	$	$	$
Average current cost	110	125	135
Depreciation valuation adjustment—	11 − 10	12.50 − 10	13.50 − 10
Debit IVAA, credit DRRA	1	2.50	3.50
Year-end current cost	120	130	150
Fixed asset valuation adjustment	$\left(90 \times \frac{120}{100}\right) - 90$	$\left(80 \times \frac{130}{100}\right) - 80$	$\left(70 \times \frac{150}{100}\right) - 70$
Equals: Fixed asset revaluation reserve	18	24	35
Annual addition to fixed asset revaluation reserve—			
Debit FAVAA, credit FARRA	18	6	11

Adjustments to profit for cost of sales and depreciation are recorded as debit entries in the income valuation adjustment account. Historical record accounting profit may be transferred from the profit and loss account in the ledger to the credit side of the income valuation adjustment account, the balance of which will then represent current distributable income. As has been seen, this may be regarded as the distributable surplus of the enterprise for the period. Current distributable income may be transferred to the proprietor's current account in the case of a sole proprietorship or to the appropriation account in the case of a partnership or company. The income valuation adjustment account is thus closed at the end of each period.

The revaluation reserves which have been created as a result of the two income valuation adjustments constitute part of proprietorship equity. They represent retention of profits, which have been reserved or held within the business to allow for the increased values of assets absorbed into cost. The income valuation adjustments should not be regarded as a discretionary measure, but are an essential accounting procedure based on the objective measurement of differences between historical and current values. The cost of sales and depreciation revaluation reserves are not normally distributable to proprietors of the enterprise. (They will, however, be drawn upon during periods of falling prices in order to make positive valuation adjustments to accounting profit.)

In contrast to income valuation adjustments, which represent income appropriations, the asset valuation adjustments are capital adjustments which restate assets and proprietorship equity in current values. The balances in the inventory and fixed asset valuation adjustment accounts are affected not only by subsequent price changes but also by variations in the quantities of assets held; if the level of inventories or net fixed assets falls, the balances in the adjustment accounts must also be reduced. The income and asset revaluation reserves which have been established in respect of the assets in question may then be treated as general reserves.

Example: If the machine in the foregoing example were to be disposed of at the end of Year 3 at its then current value of $105, the following entries would record the sale and the transfer of the revaluation reserves to a general reserve account:

Year 3				
Dec. 31	Bank	Dr.	$105	
	Provision for depreciation on machine	Dr.	30	
	Machine	Cr.		$100
	FAVAA	Cr.		35
	Sale of machine at end of Year 3			
Dec. 31	DRRA	Dr.	7	
	FARRA	Dr.	35	
	General reserve account	Cr.		42
	Transfer of revaluation reserves to general reserve on sale of machine			

If the machine is disposed of at a price above (below) its depreciated current value of $105, a profit (loss) on sale is recorded.

The existing balance on FARRA reduces while that on DRRA accumulates as the asset continues in use, reflecting a siphoning-off relationship between the two revaluation reserves. This is clearly seen in the example below where the asset price has risen and then remained stable at the higher price level.

Example: Suppose the machine in the foregoing example continues in use until the end of its 10-year life, its current cost (new) remains at $150 from the end of Year 3 onwards, and the residual value at the end of the period is zero. The following ledger accounts illustrate the siphoning-off relationship between FARRA and DRRA and the closing-off of the two accounts FAVAA and FARRA at the end of the asset's life. (For convenience, balances on accounts are not brought down at the end of each year.)

Machine			
Cash	$100		

Depreciation			
Year 1 Acc. depn.	$10	Year 1 P & L	$10
Year 2 Acc. depn.	$10	Year 2 P & L	$10
.	.	.	.
.	.	.	.
Year 10 Acc. depn.	$10	Year 10 P & L	$10

Accumulated Depreciation		
	Year 1 Depn.	$10
	Year 2 Depn.	10
	.	.
	.	.
	Year 10 Depn.	10
		$100

FAVAA			
Year 1 FARRA	$18	Year 4 FARRA	$5
Year 2 FARRA	6	Year 5 FARRA	5
Year 3 FARRA	11	.	.
		.	.
		Year 10 FARRA	5
	$35		$35

IVAA			
Year 1 DRRA	$1.00	Year 1 P & L	$1.00
Year 2 DRRA	$2.50	Year 2 P & L	$2.50
Year 3 DRRA	$3.50	Year 3 P & L	$3.50
Year 4 DRRA	$5.00	Year 4 P & L	$5.00
Year 5 DRRA	$5.00	Year 5 P & L	$5.00
.	.	.	.
.	.	.	.
Year 10 DRRA	$5.00	Year 10 P & L	$5.00

FARRA			
Year 4 FAVAA	$5	Year 1 FAVAA	18
Year 5 FAVAA	5	Year 2 FAVAA	6
.	.	Year 3 FAVAA	11
.	.		
Year 10 FAVAA	5		
	$35		$35

DRRA		
	Year 1 IVAA	$1.00
	Year 2 IVAA	2.50
	Year 3 IVAA	3.50
	Year 4 IVAA	5.00
	Year 5 IVAA	5.00
	.	.
	.	.
	Year 10 IVAA	5.00
		$42.00

An Illustration

The current value system described in this chapter may be illustrated by reference to the X Trading Co. example in Table 18—2. The financial statements relating to the third year of the company's operations, prepared in accordance with historical record accounting assumptions, are reproduced below. Assume that 1985 is the first year in which current value accounting is implemented.

Balance Sheet as at 31 December 1985

Monetary assets		$3 000
Inventories		3 600
		6 600
Equipment	$7 000	
Less: Accumulated depreciation	4 200	2 800
Total assets		9 400
Liabilities		1 000
Proprietorship equity		$8 400

Income Statement for Year Ended 31 December 1985

Sales		$12 000
Less: Cost of sales—		
Opening inventory	$2 000	
Purchases	9 300	
	11 300	
Closing inventory	3 600	7 700
Gross profit		4 300
Less: Depreciation on equipment	1 400	
Other expenses	900	2 300
Net profit before tax		2 000
Less: Tax at 50%		1 000
Net profit after tax		$1 000

Assume that the contributed capital is $7 000 and that income tax of 50 per cent on the historical record accounting profit is paid on the last day of the financial year. Additional information on the average historical cost of inventories is as follows:

	Number of Units	At Cost	Average Cost per Unit
Opening inventories	2 000	$2 000	$1.00
Purchases	6 200	9 300	1.50
Closing inventories	1 800	3 600	2.00

The current value of the closing inventories is $2.20 per unit. The current value (new) of the equipment is estimated to be $15 000 at 30 June (suppose that this represents the average current value for the year), while at 31 December it is $20 000.

The financial statements reproduced in Tables 19—1 and 19—2 illustrate the dual measurement system and the effect of the current value adjustments in 1985.

Table 19—1
Current Distributable Income/Operating Capital Maintenance Approach

X Trading Co.
Balance Sheet as at 31 December 1985

Assets			
Cash and debtors			00 000
Inventories—			
Cost		$3 600	
Add: Valuation adjustment		360	
Current value			3 960
Fixed capital asset—			
Cost		7 000	
Less: Provision for depreciation		4 200	
		2 800	
Add: Valuation adjustment		5 200	
Depreciated current value			8 000
			14 960
Less: **Liabilities**			1 000
Proprietorship equity			
Contributed capital		7 000	
Retained earnings (opening)	$400		
Less: Current loss for year after tax	(2 500)	(2 100)	
		4 900	
Income revaluation reserves—			
Cost of sales	1 900		
Depreciation	1 600	3 500	
Asset revaluation reserves—			
Inventory	360		
Fixed asset	5 200	5 560	
Current value of proprietorship equity			$13 960

Table 19—2
Current Distributable Income/Operating Capital Maintenance Approach

X Trading Co.
Income Statement for Year Ended 31 December 1985

Sales		$12 000
Less: Cost of sales		
Opening inventories	$2 000	
Purchases	9 300	
	11 300	
Less: Closing inventories	3 600	
		7 700
Gross accounting profit		4 300
Less: Expenses		
Depreciation	1 400	
Other expenses	900	
		2 300
Net accounting profit		2 000
Less: Cost of sales adjustment	1 900	
Depreciation adjustment	1 600	
		3 500
Current loss (Dr.)		(1 500)
Less: Tax based on accounting profit		1 000
Current loss after tax (Dr.)		$(2 500)

The above illustration shows how, because of increases in the current values of inventories and fixed assets, an historical cost profit may represent an operating loss in current value terms, while tax and dividend payments will lead to a further erosion of the firm's operating capacity. It is interesting to note that the current loss after tax is considerably larger than the corresponding deficit in the CPP accounting illustration in Chapter 18. This is because the price increases affecting inventories and the fixed asset far exceed the rise in the general price level. In this situation, adjustments for the change in the general price level will not enable the firm's operating capacity to be maintained.

Evaluation of the Current Distributable Income/Operating Capital Maintenance Approach to Current Value Accounting

Usefulness from Viewpoint of the Firm

The current distributable income/operating capital maintenance approach to current value accounting has two major related objectives. The first is to derive the figure of distributable income for the period, which serves both as a measure of management performance and a measure of distributable surplus. The second objective is related to the operating capital maintenance concept. It is to provide for the recovery of invested capital used up in the income-earning activities of the firm, by charging revenues with cost of sales and depreciation at the current prices (instead of the historical costs) of inventories and fixed assets, respectively. To a large extent the case for implementing such a system of current value accounting depends on the ability of the new system to remedy the defects in the existing accounting system, and thus provide more useful information for decision making.

Current value financial statements avoid the limitations of historical record statements which result from the mixing up of prices of different periods and the failure to preserve the value of the enterprise's capital in terms of its command over operating assets. Because the current value concepts of income and wealth reflect conditions obtaining in the present rather than in the irrelevant past, there is a presumption that they will usually be more relevant to the purposes for which accounting information is required than concepts which have regard to historical costs (as discussed in Chapter 17) or to hypothetical notions of generalized purchasing power (as discussed in Chapter 18).

It is difficult to understand how accountants have managed for so long to deny information about current values to users of financial statements. A current value balance sheet provides valuable information on the total resources deployed by the firm in its operations. As has been seen in Chapter 7, it is necessary to relate current distributable income to the current value of assets employed in order to evaluate managerial efficiency and ascertain whether the firm is achieving a satisfactory rate of return. The relationship between accounting profit and resources employed in an historical record accounting system gives a dangerously optimistic indication of a firm's earning power when prices are rising, because accounting profit exceeds income available for distribution while the historical value of assets employed is less than their current value.

The ratio of current distributable income to the current value of assets is affected by numerous factors, but the maintenance of a satisfactory rate of return in current value terms requires *revenues* as well as costs and expenses to be related to the current value of assets. In other words, the prices charged by a business for its products must be related to current asset values if the firm's earning power is to be maintained at a satisfactory level. Current value accounting thus not only provides a measure of distributable surplus and helps to focus attention on concepts of cost which are relevant for managerial purposes; it also has significance with respect to the firm's pricing policy.

The system of current value accounting which has been described thus earns high marks with respect to the relevance criterion, and may also be seen to meet the consistency requirement in its two senses of uniformity of valuation procedures and consistency of meaning to the users of accounting data. It is sometimes asserted that current value data are less objective and less reliable than information prepared in accordance with historical record assumptions, but this assertion needs careful examination. Information about current replacement costs or market selling values can often be derived from observable, measurable and verifiable sources, e.g. in the market place, or by reference to actual price lists or appropriate specific price indexes.

Finally, the adoption of a current value approach may be expected to simplify accounting procedures and to make the resulting information more meaningful, by reducing the need for arbitrary valuation rules (e.g. in relation to inventories) and limiting valuation assumptions (e.g. in respect of a realization criterion which fails to recognize the existence of value changes in assets held at the end of the accounting period).

Usefulness from Viewpoint of the Economy

It is also necessary to consider the implications of the current distributable income/operating capital maintenance approach in relation to the problem of effectively managing the economy. On the one hand, it has been argued that the adoption of this system of current value accounting is less likely than historical cost accounting to give rise to optimistic expectations about profitability when prices are rising or to pessimistic expectations when prices are falling, with the result that firms are less likely to engage in destabilizing investment activity. More important as a stabilizing factor, however, is likely to be the greater business saving which is generated by a combination of accounting, dividend distribution and taxation policies based on a current value concept of income.

On the other hand, the effect of combining current value accounting with replacement cost pricing will be to raise prices further during periods of inflation, thereby seemingly intensifying inflationary pressures. But the higher prices will normally cut back consumption expenditures to the extent necessary to support the continued deployment of business resources. Provided the increased revenues are saved by businesses (by remaining insulated in revaluation reserves), pressures on demand will be reduced in the same way as when an increase in indirect taxation is not accompanied by an increase in government spending. The increase in prices must therefore be interpreted as a consequence and response to inflation, and not as a cause.

Since one of the principal purposes of current value accounting is to derive a measure of income which may be distributed whilst maintaining operating capital and hence financial stability, it follows that both dividend and tax distributions need to be related to current distributable income and not to accounting profit. The use of current distributable income as the tax base is especially necessary in a period of rapid inflation, such as that recently experienced in Australia and other Western countries. As noted in Chapter 17, if the rate of inflation passes a critical level the use of accounting profit as the tax base may eventually have the effect of making firms increase their indebtedness to the point of financial collapse, or reduce the scale of their operations to the point of liquidation. The financial instability that results from excessive dividend and tax distribution, inadequate company saving and excessive borrowing in a period of rapidly rising prices thus threatens the equilibrium of the whole economic system.

Criticisms of Current Value Accounting

Current value accounting has also been criticized on the ground that it presupposes continued replacement of the assets held by a firm and discourages redeployment of resources when circumstances justify changes in the nature of a firm's economic activities. It has thus been argued that, to the extent that current value accounting, pricing and taxing policies insulate firms from the effects of specific price changes affecting their operations, they are discouraged from adapting to the changing requirements of the economy. This argument is based on an assumption that firms subject to rapid increases in current values are somehow less efficient than those subject to less rapid increases, and that it is inequitable and inefficient for the consumer (through higher prices) and the government and other taxpayers (through lower taxes) to subsidize this inefficiency.

These arguments seem to be based on misconceptions about the reason for current value adjustments and what it is that they are designed to achieve. In the first place, the fact that one industry faces higher replacement prices than another, in respect of the assets which it uses to generate income, tells us nothing about the relative efficiency of the two industries. The relative prices reflect conditions in the supplying industries and not in the industries acquiring the assets. This is not to deny that, if the latter industries are to operate efficiently, they must be ready to adapt when relative costs change. It may reasonably be argued, for example, that greater efficiency will be achieved if industries using oil as a source of power switch to other fuels when the price of oil rises relative to other fuels.

However, the use of the kind of system of current value accounting, pricing and taxing[3] which has been proposed in this chapter will not prevent such substitutions from taking place. Indeed, the higher selling prices which may be associated with an increase in replacement costs will induce a response from consumers and indicate whether or not they are prepared to pay the higher prices. If they are so prepared, the current value adjustments are necessary to ensure that the industry is able to continue supplying them. If the consumers are not prepared to pay the higher prices, the industry will need to switch to other sources of supply or to other products. The efficient allocation of resources thus depends on responses by firms to the interaction of the forces of supply and demand, and not merely on their responses to changes in the prices charged by suppliers. There can be no presumption that efficiency requires the elimination of all relative price changes.

Despite the advantages of the current value approach, it seems likely that for some years to come historical cost financial statements will continue to be a basic part of the external reporting framework. For this reason, and because the historical record accounting system can be adapted so easily to the task of providing current value data, the dual measurement system described in this chapter seems most likely to meet the multifarious requirements of an effective accounting information system.

The following chapter discusses an alternative approach to current value accounting — the business profit/financial capital maintenance approach — in which the valuation adjustments described in this chapter are treated as holding gains which are available as distributable income for the period. Also examined are some complex and controversial issues in current value accounting, including the establishment of valuation rules to enable appropriate current values to be selected and the related problem of determining the current costs of producing equivalent services.

References

Inflation and Taxation, Report of Committee of Inquiry into Inflation and Taxation, Australian Government Publishing Service, Canberra, 1975 (referred to as the Mathews Report).

Additional Reading

Barton, A.D., *The Anatomy of Accounting*, University of Queensland Press, St. Lucia, Qld, 1977, Chapter 23.

Gynther, R.S., *Accounting for Price-Level Changes: Theory and Procedures,* Pergamon Press, Oxford, 1966.

---

[3] See Chapter 22 for a brief discussion of taxation policies.

Discussion Questions

1 Explain what is meant by the term 'current value accounting'.

2 Income is usually defined by reference to some notion of maintaining capital intact. Contrast the different interpretations of capital which have been postulated in this context.

3 Briefly discuss the problems which result from the use of historical record accounting assumptions and procedures during a period of inflation, and indicate the action you would take to deal with the problems.

4 What is the significance of (a) income valuation, and (b) asset valuation adjustments in relation to the measurement of income and funds employed in a current value accounting system?

5 You are the accountant in a large manufacturing company which has a considerable proportion of its funds invested in inventories and fixed assets. The directors are worried by the financial problems involved in replacing the inventories and fixed assets at rapidly rising prices, and ask you whether you can recommend accounting procedures which will provide them with the information they need for purposes of formulating financial, pricing and production policies. What would be your advice?

6 What is the significance of the realization assumption in relation to current value accounting?

7 To what extent and under what conditions does current-cost depreciation provide funds sufficient for the replacement of assets?

8 'The current value approach succeeds in maintaining the value of proprietorship equity in terms of its command over operating assets.' Evaluate this statement.

9 In a system of accounting which has regard to current values, what criteria would you suggest for determining the current values of inventories and fixed assets?

10 Evaluate current value accounting with respect to the managerial uses of accounting data.

11 Evaluate the usefulness of current value accounting from the wider viewpoint of the economy.

12 Discuss some of the criticisms levelled at current value accounting.

Exercises

1 Given the following information, how would you prepare financial statements designed to measure surplus and funds employed in both historical record and current value terms?

	Historical Cost	Current Value
For year ended 30 June		
Sales		$25 000
Opening inventories	$2 500	3 000*
Closing inventories	3 750	3 500*
Purchases	15 000	15 000
Depreciation on fixed assets	500	625
Other expenses	750	750
Balances as at 30 June		
Bank	250	250
Accounts receivable	11 000	11 000
Inventories	3 750	3 875
Fixed assets (net of depreciation)	2 500	3 250
Accounts payable·	2 500	2 500

* Current value at 31 December.

2 You are the accountant of a large manufacturing company. At 30 June 1985, finished inventories are recorded in the books of the company at cost, $150 000, but because of a trade recession it is expected that they can be sold for no more than $140 000. At the same time, plant owned by the company is recorded at cost, $250 000, with accumulated depreciation provisions of $100 000 (before depreciation is charged in the current period). The current replacement cost of the plant, which has not changed during the last year, is estimated to be $400 000, and because of changes in the pattern of production there is expected to be no further difficulty in operating the plant profitably.

The directors of the company ask you to make provision for the anticipated loss on inventories when preparing accounting reports for the year ended 30 June 1985. They also instruct you to provide for depreciation on plant on the basis of current replacement cost, using the same rate as before (20 per cent per annum on cost). In discussing the matter with them it is confirmed that they have no desire to distort the income measurement process or to conceal their action from shareholders.

What action would you take to meet their wishes? Give reasons.

3 At 1 July 1984 the V.I.P. Co. commenced business with $1 000 in the bank, inventories which cost $5 000, and plant and equipment which had just been bought for $10 000. During the year total sales were recorded at $45 000, cost of sales was $30 000, depreciation of $1 000 was written off and other expenses totalled $5 000. At 30 June 1985, although the same quantity of inventories was held, their recorded cost had risen to $6 000 and it would currently cost $6 250 to replace them. The current replacement value of plant and equipment had increased by 5 per cent during the latter half of 1984 and by 30 June 1985 was 10 per cent above the original cost.

Prepare financial statements incorporating both historical record and current value data.

4 By means of algebraic models, demonstrate the relationship between asset valuation adjustments and income valuation adjustments in a current value accounting system.

5 The Getrich Development Corporation has borrowed $5 000 000 from Building Credit Ltd, a finance company, in order to build a shopping arcade in a rapidly expanding suburban area on the outskirts of Parramatta. The sole owner of Getrich Development Corporation, Mr B. Cassidy, had paid $100 000 for the land when he acquired it in 1970. Although the consumer price index has only doubled since 1970, the value of the land was appraised by an independent valuer at $4 500 000. Assuming that the buildings in the shopping arcade have just been completed at a cost of $5 800 000 — Mr Cassidy having provided $800 000 as a new capital contribution to the Getrich Development Corporation — what form should the balance sheet take if it is to provide information which is relevant to the interests of the proprietor and the finance company? Do these interests diverge? To what extent does the information presented in the balance sheet meet the tests of relevance, objectivity, hardness, reliability and comparability?

6 The latest income statement for the Redwood Co. Ltd (in historical dollars) is as follows:

Income Statement for Year Ended 30 June 1985

Sales		$310 000
Cost of goods sold—		
Opening inventory	$40 000	
Purchases	225 000	
	265 000	
Less: Closing inventory	47 500	217 500
Gross profit		92 500
Less: Operating expenses—		
Selling	15 000	
Administration	12 500	
Depreciation	7 500	35 000
Income before tax		57 500
Less: Income tax		25 000
Net income after tax		$32 500

Prices in general rose by 25 per cent over the period. The average current costs of the opening and closing inventories were $50 000 and $65 000, respectively. Fixed assets, which were purchased on 1 July 1983, cost $75 00 and were being depreciated on a straight-line basis at the rate of 10 per cent per annum. The replacement cost (new) of these fixed assets was $100 000 at 30 June 1984 and $125 000 at 30 June 1985.

You are required to prepare an income statement incorporating both historical record and current value data.

20 Accounting Valuation Systems 3—Current Value Accounting (B)

Business Profit/Financial Capital Maintenance Approach

An alternative current value system, the business profit approach, has been proposed by Edwards and Bell. The business profit approach, like the current distributable income approach (discussed in Chapter 19), represents an extension of the historical cost framework, in that only minor changes to existing accounting procedures are necessary. Under this approach, the net worth of an enterprise is the difference between the current value of its assets and that of its liabilities, while the income for the period, which Edwards and Bell call *business profit*, is the difference between the net worth at the beginning and end of the period (after adjustments for any withdrawals or contributions of new capital by proprietors in the period).

Although the current distributable income and business profit approaches both represent current value accounting systems, there is a marked difference in the capital maintenance concepts associated with these approaches. The business profit approach treats valuation adjustments as holding gains and losses which are included in income for the period rather than in proprietorship equity. Thus it may be said to espouse a *financial capital maintenance concept*, akin to that adopted in historical record accounting. In the business profit approach, realizable holding gains or cost savings are recognized in the period in which they arise; thus the pattern of reported profits differs from that in historical record accounting. However, the total reported profit over the lifetime of an entity is the same under both methods (since all realizable cost savings eventually become realized). Because the business profit approach is concerned with the maintenance of financial capital, income for the period may include amounts that are required to maintain the firm's operating capacity.

As defined by Edwards and Bell, business profit comprises two components, which they call current operating profit and realizable cost savings. *Current operating profit* is defined as the excess of sales revenue in the period over the current cost of goods sold. *Current cost* relates specifically to the current costs of component factor inputs (such as materials, labour and manufacturing expense) embodied in assets. Current operating profit is thus equivalent to the current value concept of current distributable income which was distinguished in the preceding chapter, provided the measures of current cost used by Edwards and Bell are equivalent to the current values used in calculating current distributable income.

Realizable cost savings are defined as increases in the current costs of assets during the period, comprising both realized and unrealized holding gains of the period. There is no counterpart of realizable cost savings in the current distributable income approach to current value accounting, but a reconciliation of the two approaches will be given below.

Cost savings may be realized or unrealized. *Unrealized cost savings* are transformed into *realized cost savings* when assets are sold in the normal course of business or used in production. Similarly, because current operating profit is the excess of sales revenue over current cost, realized cost savings represent the excess of current cost over historical cost associated with transactions affecting the income statement.

Realized cost savings are thus equivalent in amount to income valuation adjustments under the current distributable income approach (subject to the qualification stated earlier), and the act of sale or production converts unrealized cost savings into realized cost savings in the same way as it converts asset valuation adjustments into income valuation adjustments.

Edwards and Bell develop a subsidiary profit concept which they call *realized profit*. Realized profit has three components: current operating profit, realized cost savings and realized capital gains. Realized capital gains (or losses) arise from the irregular sale of fixed assets and for convenience may be ignored in the present discussion. Realized profit is equal in amount to accounting profit, but unlike the latter clearly distinguishes between current operating profit and realized cost savings resulting from the holding of assets sold or used in production during the period.

Reconciliation of the Two Approaches to Current Value Accounting

A reconciliation of realizable cost savings in the business profit approach with the income and asset valuation adjustments in the current distributable income approach is given below. Realizable cost savings may be defined as follows:

$$\text{Realizable cost savings in period } t = \text{Realized cost savings of period } t$$
$$+ \text{ unrealized cost savings which accrue in period } t$$
$$= Q_y + (Q_a^{te} - Q_a^{tb})$$

where Q_y denotes the income valuation adjustment in t, and Q_a^{te} and Q_a^{tb} denote the asset valuation adjustments at the end and the beginning of period t, respectively. $(Q_a^{te} - Q_a^{tb})$ is in fact equal to the accumulated asset revaluation reserves at the end of period t minus the accumulated asset revaluation reserves at the beginning of period t.

The different income measures may be compared as follows:

$$\text{Current distributable income} = Y_c$$
$$\text{Realized profit (or accounting profit)} = Y_c + Q_y$$
$$\text{Business profit} = Y_c + Q_y + (Q_a^{te} - Q_a^{tb})$$

where Y_c is the excess of sales revenue over costs at current prices.

Example: The example in Chapter 19 will be used, where a fixed asset was purchased for $100 and has an expected life of 10 years (see page 489). Average and year-end current cost data are given in the table below.

Realizable cost savings in Year 1 are computed as follows. Assume that the proportion of the original stock of machinery at the beginning of the year (1.0) is held over the first half of the year while the price rises from $100 to $110, and the proportion available at the end of the year (0.9) is held over the second half of the year while the price rises from $110 to $120. This is effectively the same assumption which was made in Chapter 19 in calculating the income and asset valuation adjustments. Thus realizable cost savings are 1.0 ($110 − $100) + 0.9 ($120 − $110) or $19. The amounts accruing in Years 2 and 3 are calculated in a similar way.

	Year 1	Year 2	Year 3
	$	$	$
Average current cost	110	125	135
Year-end current cost	120	130	150
Current distributable income approach—			
Depreciation revaluation reserve (annual credits)	1	2.50	3.50
Fixed asset revaluation reserve (annual credits)	18	6.00	11.00
Business profit approach— Realizable cost savings	$(1.0)\,10 + (0.9)\,10 = 19$	$(0.9)\,5 + (0.8)\,5 = 8.50$	$(0.8)\,5 + (0.7)\,15 = 14.50$

The above example indicates that the annual credits to the depreciation revaluation reserve and the fixed asset revaluation reserve and the total credit to the two revaluation reserves in the current distributable income approach are equivalent to realized cost savings, unrealized cost savings and the realizable cost savings credited to income at the end of the year respectively in the business profit approach.

An Illustration

The business profit approach may be illustrated by reference to the X Trading Co. example in Table 18—2, which was also used to illustrate the current distributable income approach in Chapter 19. The financial statements relating to the third year of the company's operations, prepared in accordance with historical record accounting assumptions, are reproduced below. Assume that 1985 is the first year in which current value accounting is implemented.

Balance Sheet as at 31 December 1985

Monetary assets		$3 000
Inventories		3 600
		6 600
Equipment	$7 000	
Less: Accumulated depreciation	4 200	2 800
		9 400
Total assets		
Liabilities		1 000
Proprietorship equity		$8 400

Income Statement for Year Ended 31 December 1985

Sales		$12 000
Less: Cost of sales—		
Opening inventory	$2 000	
Purchases	9 300	
	11 300	
Closing inventory	3 600	7 700
Gross profit		4 300
Less: Depreciation on equipment	1 400	
Other expenses	900	2 300
Net profit before tax		2 000
Less: Tax at 50%		1 000
Net profit after tax		$1 000

Assume that the contributed capital is $7 000 and that income tax of 50 per cent on the historical record accounting profit is paid on the last day of the financial year. Additional information on the average historical cost of inventories is as follows:

	Number of Units	At Cost	Average Cost per Unit
Opening inventories	2 000	$2 000	$1.00
Purchases	6 200	9 300	1.50
Closing inventories	1 800	3 600	2.00

In order to compute realizable cost savings in 1985, additional information on the current value of assets held at the beginning of the year is required (whereas in the current distributable income approach it is only necessary to know the average and year-end current values). Suppose that the current cost of opening inventory is $1.00 per unit, i.e. the same as its historical acquisition cost, average current cost in the year is $1.50, i.e. the same as average cost of purchases, and the year-end current cost is $2.20 per unit.

The realizable cost savings on inventory in 1985 are calculated as follows:

On opening inventories—2 000 units x ($1.50 − $1.00)	=	$1 000
On closing inventories—1 800 units x ($2.20 − $1.50)	=	1 260
		$2 260

Since the current cost of the opening inventory has been assumed to be the same as its historical cost, realizable cost savings for the year are equal to the sum of the credits to the cost of sales revaluation reserve ($1 900) and the inventory revaluation reserve ($360), as calculated under the current distributable income approach. Let us digress and consider the situation had the current cost of opening inventory been, say $1.10. Realizable cost savings then would be $2 060. In the current distributable income approach, the inventory revaluation reserve account would have a credit balance of $200 (2 000 x $0.10) at the beginning of the year, and the credit to this account at year-end would be $160 ($360 − $200). The total credits in 1985 would have been $2 060 ($1 900 + $160), the same amount as realizable cost savings under the business profit system.

Suppose also that the current cost (new) of the fixed asset at the beginning of 1985 is $12 000, and that the corresponding average and year-end values are $15 000 and $20 000, respectively.

The realizable cost savings on the fixed asset in 1985 are as follows:

On opening 'stock' of fixed asset—$\frac{3}{5}$ ($15 000 − $12 000)	=	$1 800
On closing 'stock' of fixed asset—$\frac{2}{5}$ ($20 000 − $15 000)	=	2 000
		$3 800

Realizable cost savings on the fixed asset which have accrued as at the beginning of 1985 are $\frac{3}{5}$ ($12 000 − $7 000) or $3 000.

The amounts of realized and unrealized surplus[1] in the balance sheet at the end of 1985 are calculated as follows:

[1] Surplus is used here as a generic term to include retained profits, operating profit for the year and cost savings.

	Total Surplus	Realized Surplus	Unrealized Surplus
At end of 1984—			
Retained earnings	$400	$400	
Realizable cost savings on fixed asset	3 000		$3 000
	$3 400	$400	$3 000
Profit and loss items in 1985—			
Current operating loss (Dr.)	(1 500)	(1 500)	
Realizable cost savings in the year:			
On inventories	2 260	1 900*	360
On fixed asset	3 800	1 600*	2 200
Tax for the year (Dr.)	(1 000)	(1 000)	
	$3 560	$1 000	$2 560
At end of 1985	$6 960	$1 400	$5 560

* Cost savings realized in the period are equivalent to transfers to income revaluation reserves in the current distributable income approach.

The financial statements in this system are illustrated in Tables 20—1, 20—2 and 20—2A.

Table 20—1
Business Profit/Financial Capital Maintenance Approach

X Trading Co.
Balance Sheet as at 31 December 1985

Assets		
Cash and debtors		$3 000
Inventory—		
Cost	$3 600	
Add: Valuation adjustment	360	
Current value		3 960
Fixed capital asset—		
Cost	7 000	
Less: Provision for depreciation	4 200	
	2 800	
Add: Valuation adjustment	5 200	
Depreciated current value		8 000
		14 960
Less: **Liabilities**		1 000
Proprietorship equity		
Contributed capital	7 000	
Realized surplus	1 400	
Unrealized surplus	5 560	
		$13 960

Table 20—2
Business Profit/Financial Capital Maintenance Approach

X Trading Co.
Income Statement for Year Ended 31 December 1985

Sales		$12 000
Less: Cost of sales	$9 600	
Depreciation	3 000	
Other expenses	900	
		13 500
Current operating loss (Dr.)		(1 500)
Realizable cost savings—		
On inventories	2 260	
On fixed asset	3 800	
Total cost savings arising during the year		6 060
Business profit		4 560
Less: Tax based on accounting profit		1 000
Business profit after tax		$3 560

Table 20—2A
Business Profit/Financial Capital Maintenance Approach

X Trading Co.
Supplementary Statement of Realized Profit for Year Ended 31 December 1985

Current operating loss (Dr.)		$(1 500)
Realized cost savings—		
On inventories	$1 900	
On fixed asset	1 600	
		3 500
Realized profit before tax		2 000
Less: Tax based on accounting profit		1 000
Realized profit after tax		$1 000

Note: Realized profit is the same as historical record accounting profit, but current operating profit (loss), realized capital gains and realized cost savings are reported separately in the realized profit statement.

Alternative Current Value Financial Statements Compared

The difference between profits calculated under the current distributable income/operating capital maintenance approach and the business profit/financial capital maintenance approach is analysed in Table 20—3. Note again that the cost of sales and depreciation adjustments in the former approach are equivalent to the realized cost savings in the latter.

Table 20—4 compares the balance sheet under the two alternative current value accounting systems. The opposing views on capital maintenance are highlighted. The capital maintenance reserves in the current distributable income/operating capital maintenance approach are treated as retained earnings (which, it must be emphasized, are regarded as distributable) in the business profit/financial capital maintenance approach.

Table 20—3
Current Distributable Income and Business Profit Compared

Current Distributable Income/ Operating Capital Maintenance		Business Profit/ Financial Capital Maintenance	
Net accounting profit before tax	$2 000	Net accounting profit before tax	$2 000
Less: Cost of sales valuation		*Less*: Realised cost savings	
adjustment	(1 900)	inventories	(1 900)
Depreciation valuation		Realised cost savings—	
adjustment	(1 600)	fixed asset	(1 600)
Current operating loss	(1 500)	Current operating loss	(1 500)
		Realizable cost savings*—	
		On inventories	2 260
		On fixed asset	3 800
		Business profit	4 560
Less: Tax based on accounting profit	1 000	*Less*: Tax based on accounting profit	1 000
Current loss after tax	$(2 500)	Business profit after tax	$3 560

* Some of the realizable cost savings have already been realized.

Table 20—4
Alternative Current Cost Balance Sheets Compared

Current Distributable Income/ Operating Capital Maintenance		Business Profit/ Financial Capital Maintenance	
Net assets at historical cost	$9 400	Net assets at historical cost	$9 400
Add: Valuation adjustments	5 560	*Add*: Valuation adjustments	5 560
Net assets at current value	14 960	Net assets at current value	14 960
Less: Current liabilities	1 000	*Less*: Current liabilities	1 000
	$13 960		$13 960
Contributed capital	7 000	Contributed capital	7 000
Retained earnings	(2 100)	Retained earnings—	
Capital maintenance adjustments—		Realized surplus	1 400
Income revaluation reserve	3 500	Unrealized surplus	5 560
Asset revaluation reserve	5 560		
	$13 960		$13 960

Evaluation of the Business Profit Approach

The fundamental criticism of the business profit approach is that it reports cost savings as income, although the distribution of such amounts could seriously threaten the financial viability of the firm. Consider, for example, the effect on X Trading Co. in the foregoing example of distributing the realizable cost savings. Either assets would have to be substantially reduced and the scale of the firm's activities reduced, or liabilities or contributed capital would need to be increased. In a sense the approach overstates the income figure in inflationary times even more seriously than does historical record accounting, since some unrealized cost savings are a component of business profit. Most supporters of this approach probably concede that only the operating profit component of business profit is distributable, but it is difficult to justify the classification of an income measure into distributable and non-distributable categories. By definition, if any amount is non-distributable, it is not income.

Are Cost Savings Income?

Whether cost savings should be treated as income available for distribution or as non-distributable valuation adjustments to proprietorship equity depends on the purposes for which the assets are held. If a firm has been established expressly for buying inventories in anticipation of a price rise, and is to be wound up when the speculative gains are realized, the gains obviously qualify as income which may be distributed as soon as realization occurs. But although firms engaged in continuing trading operations may sometimes participate in speculative activities, one would normally expect them at least to maintain their holdings of assets in quantitative terms (although the pattern of asset holding will presumably be changing continuously). To the extent that non-monetary assets continue to be held, cost savings resulting from price changes are locked in and can only be distributed as income by running down the quantity of net monetary assets.

In Chapter 19 it was shown that, if the current value of a firm's non-monetary assets, N, increases by q during the period t_0 to t_1, then in the absence of trading operations the balance sheet equation at t_1 will take the following form:

$$M + N(1 + q) = R + Nq$$

It is clear from this that if Nq were to be fully distributed as income, either non-monetary assets would need to be cut back to N, which at their higher prices would imply holding a smaller quantity of assets, or there would need to be a reduction in net monetary assets, M. This argument applies with equal force to realizable cost savings. If realizable cost savings were fully distributed each year, this is equivalent to treating Nq as distributable income. The financial position of the firm would be weakened and it would be necessary for it to raise fresh capital or to reduce the scale of its operating activities. For this reason, it is recommended that Nq normally be treated not as income but as an addition to revaluation reserves. This increases residual equity by the amount necessary to finance the holding of non-monetary assets at their increased current values. It follows that the value of proprietorship equity is maintained in terms of its command over operating assets (whilst net monetary assets remain unchanged).

Determination of Current Values

So far it has been assumed that current values are capable of easy and unambiguous interpretation and identification. It will be seen that this is an oversimplification of the true position. Critics of current value accounting have pointed out that some of the basic assumptions underlying specific replacement cost or net realizable value systems lack general relevance for all asset valuation situations. Asset replacement costs or net realizable values are not relevant information for reporting purposes for all firms at all times. For example, the current distributable income/operating capital maintenance approach is based on a valuation philosophy which limits distributable income to an amount that will not impair the maintenance of the firm's operating capital and hence the continuity of its production process. The concept of net worth or proprietorship equity in this system reflects the actual deployment of enterprise assets. There is, of course, nothing to prevent a firm from redeploying its assets (and in practice it will be doing this continuously), but at any point of time the proprietorship equity is measured by reference to the current prices of its assets as currently deployed. Since the system objective is to maintain the value of proprietor-ship equity in terms of its command over *operating assets*, the appropriate asset valuation base in normal circumstances is replacement cost. However, owing to changes in technology or demand factors, the replacement cost of an asset or machine complex may cease to be recoverable from revenues generated by its use. Under these circumstances, it is appropriate to measure the asset or machine complex at its market selling value.

For these reasons some writers have advocated the adoption of an eclectic approach to asset valuation. An eclectic approach does not refer to the presentation of multiple-valuation accounting reports, i.e. the publication of different sets of financial statements in response to different user needs. [2] The eclectic approach makes use of different valuation bases in the accounting system and reports the values considered most appropriate to the needs of users. The unique signals which are generated by the replacement cost system and the net realizable value system respectively require separate identification and interpretation in an eclectic system. [3] But the separate identification of such information signals may often not be possible because of asset interactions and the highly aggregated nature of accounting reports. The adoption of an eclectic approach involves an information loss, but this may not be serious if, as is generally believed, most assets are valued at their replacement cost on the basis of the valuation criteria used under this system. There are more fundamental defects in the concept, as will be explained in the following sections.

Three methods for determining what are the appropriate current values are discussed below. The most widely known and accepted method is the so-called value to the business method. Unfortunately, this approach has certain serious conceptual difficulties which have not been resolved.

1 The Edwards and Bell Method

The business profit system of Edwards and Bell is a replacement cost system which normally employs the current cost [4] of existing assets as its valuation base. The reason given by these authors for adopting a replacement cost approach to asset valuation is interesting and important. They argue that if current operating profit (i.e. the operating profit component of business profit, as described earlier) exceeds interest on the current cost of the firm's net assets at the beginning of the period, this denotes that the current revenue generated is sufficient to cover the current cost of the factors of production. Thus the production process of the firm is worth continuing. On the other hand, if *realizable profit*, which is defined as the profit concept associated with the use of net resale values as the valuation base, exceeds interest on the net realizable value of the firm's net assets at the beginning of the period, the decision to continue operations during the period rather than selling out at the beginning of the period has been justified. Thus current operating profit provides an indication of the

---

[2] This proposal has merit, but problems of cost, timeliness and information overload impose constraints on the extent to which multiple-valuation reports can be presented.

[3] The replacement cost system is said to evaluate the firm as a going concern, while a net realizable value system is said to evaluate the firm's adaptive capacity.

[4] The term 'current cost' has a special meaning in the Edwards and Bell System, as explained earlier. It refers to the current cost of input components, i.e. labour, materials, etc. used to produce the asset.

firm's long-run profitability and evaluates the firm as a going concern,[5] while the realizable profit figure indicates only whether the firm is profitable in the short run. For most firms, a long-run profit concept provides more useful information on the efficiency and economic viability of their operations; hence the replacement cost basis of valuation is preferred. But if the current operating profit of the firm (or of a segment such as a department or division) fails to meet the required return on net assets, the abandonment of the firm (or of the assets concerned) is indicated. The firm (or its segment) has now a limited life, and the realizable profit concept and the net realizable value basis of valuation become more relevant to performance measurement. The assets will continue to be employed only for as long as the realizable profit is satisfactory.

The above analysis is similar to that in a project disinvestment situation. The limitation of the analysis is that it relates only to a profit centre, such as a project, department or division. The method is difficult to apply to the valuation of individual assets. The problem in current value accounting, of formulating a principle which can help to identify assets in the business that should be valued at their net realizable values rather than replacement costs, the normal valuation base, is a particularly vexatious one.

2 Value to the Business

Value to the business (VB), *value to the owner or deprival value accounting* is a concept that originated from the writings of Bonbright. Bonbright's definition of value to the owner is as follows: 'The value of a property to its owner is identical in amount with the adverse value of the entire loss, direct and indirect, that the owner might expect to suffer if he were to be deprived of the property.' Bonbright was concerned with the interests of litigants who have been deprived of their property and the assessment of their loss. The estimated value of the loss may be represented by a number of alternatives, such as the property's market selling price, its replacement cost, replacement cost plus the incidental costs from temporary deprival before replacement can be effected, or some capitalized measure of income forgone. The choice of the correct measure among the alternatives will depend on the conditions in which the loss is assumed to have occurred.

Bonbright's interpretations are eminently sensible given the objective of his analysis, which is concerned with the recompense for an actual loss, but they do not provide sufficiently precise or objective guidelines for asset valuation in accounting. Wright has adapted Bonbright's ideas in such a way as to overcome this objection, by developing a relatively concise definition of asset value which he calls *opportunity value*. The opportunity value of an asset is 'the cost, loss or sacrifice which the firm would have to incur if it did not already own that asset'. Opportunity value is 'measured by the minimum or unavoidable financial loss which disappearance of the article would cause to the firm'.

The application of the VB concept to the valuation of inventories and fixed assets is discussed below.

---

[5] It is interesting to note that Edwards and Bell employ the current operating profit concept (which is equivalent to current distributable income) and not business profit in their analysis.

Valuation to the Business of Inventories

A modern day version of the 'lower of cost or market' rule in valuing inventory may be formulated as the 'lower of replacement cost and net realizable value' rule. The reformulated rule reflects the VB approach to inventory valuation, rather than the philosophy of conservatism in historical record accounting. If the replacement cost of an inventory item is higher than its net realizable value, the item will not be replaced if it is lost, hence the opportunity value of the item to the firm is net realizable value, i.e. the measure of a lost sale. On the other hand, if its resale value is higher than its replacement cost, a lost item will be replaced, so that the opportunity value to the firm is the replacement cost. While this new rule correctly interprets the VB concept, it is somewhat simplistic in its application.

A more sophisticated approach to the measurement of opportunity value has been suggested by Wright:

(a) for profitable items the opportunity value is—
   (i) replacement cost if sales are limited by demand,
   (ii) net realizable value if sales are limited by supply; and

(b) for unprofitable or discounted items the opportunity value is net realizable value.

We conclude that inventory measurement rules consistent with Wright's opportunity value concept can be formulated and justified by the same line of reasoning which has been used to derive the lower of replacement cost and net realizable value rule.

Valuation to the Business of Fixed Assets

What is the Replacement Cost of a Fixed Asset?

Replacement cost asset valuation rules have been classified in Figure 19—A in Chapter 19 as: (a) the replacement cost of existing assets; and (b) the current cost of producing equivalent services.

Value to the business systems interpret replacement cost as the current cost of equivalent services. This concept is fraught with measurement problems. First, because of asset interaction effects, it is difficult to measure the services of an asset or define concisely what is meant by equivalent services. If a conveyor belt can be replaced by three fork-lift trucks, can their services be said to be equivalent? And should the conveyor belt be valued by reference to the three fork-lift trucks? Second, the operational requirements of a machine complex may be violated if all individual units in the complex are simultaneously replaced by their most efficient substitutes (or perhaps even if one or more of the individual units is replaced). As Canning has commented: 'it must be emphatically asserted that adequately to consider possible future substitutions is as difficult and expensive a task as re-designing of all plant and fixed equipment—obviously not a task to be undertaken annually and obviously not a task for accountants'.

The difficulty in employing the current cost of equivalent services concept can be avoided by defining replacement cost in some other way.

Asset Valuation and the Decision Matrix

Wright has not extended the methodology he uses for inventory valuation to the valuation of fixed assets, although this analysis has been undertaken by other writers. In the United Kingdom, the Sandilands Report on Inflation Accounting has recommended the adoption of a VB approach to the valuation of fixed assets:

Assets should be shown at their 'value to the business'. In the majority of cases this will be their written down current replacement cost (or current purchase price) but may in some cases be their net realizable value or 'economic value'.

The Sandilands Report analyses the opportunity value of a fixed asset as a function of the interrelationships between three variables: replacement cost, net realizable value and the present value of expected net receipts from the asset. There are six possible relationships; these are displayed in Table 20—5. The table shows that only three of the six possible relationships between replacement cost (RC), net realizable value (NRV) and the present value of expected net receipts from using the asset in the business (PV) conform to the notion of VB of fixed assets in use (the objective of the exercise). Two other cases are concerned with the measurement of VB of assets in trade, and one case to scrap value.

Table 20—5
Value to the Business as a Function of the Relationship Between Replacement Cost, Net Realizable Value and Present Value in Fixed Asset Measurement

Case	Interrelationship between RC, NRV, PV	VB
Asset in use:		
1	PV > RC > NRV	RC
2	PV > NRV > RC	RC
3	RC > PV > NRV	PV†
Asset in trade:		
4	NRV > PV > RC	RC
5	NRV > RC > PV	RC
Asset divestiture:		
6	RC > NRV > PV	NRV

Note: PV† is defined differently from PV, as explained in the text.

It will be seen that Table 20—5 is concerned with establishing a measure of VB on the basis of a decision rule which is intended to determine whether an asset will continue to be used, sold and replaced, or scrapped. The decision rule is defined as follows: In Cases 1 and 2 the asset should be held for use, and replaced at the end of its life or if it is lost. In Case 3 the asset should be held for use, but it should not be replaced. In Cases 4 and 5, the asset should be bought for resale, and in Case 6 the asset should be sold and not replaced.

The presence of PV in the structural relationships displayed in Table 20—5 does not invalidate the analysis in a decision context, and the decision rule is consistent with defining and measuring PV as the discounted value of a differential or incremental flow. The use of PV makes it possible to differentiate between Cases 2, 4 and 5, and thereby help management decide whether to use or trade (i.e. sell and replace) the asset. Similarly, the rule differentiates between Cases 1, 3 and 6 and gives management the information needed to decide whether to use or divest itself of the asset.[6]

The application of the above decision rule has some odd consequences for asset measurement. Management's expectations of future flows from current operations are a function of economic conditions. Even if a stable relationship exists between market entry and exit prices, the adoption of the VB concept can introduce

[6] Our analysis contradicts some of the conclusions of the Sandilands Report, e.g. the statement that 'in cases where net realizable value is the correct measure of the value of an asset to a business, no intention to sell the asset is implied'.

considerable variability in the valuation base underlying asset measurement when business optimism fluctuates, with consequential effects on the dependent income figure. In particular, it can be hypothesized by reference to Table 20—5 that certain assets previously classified as Case 1 could be translated into Case 3 in a period of economic recession, and in a subsequent period could revert to Case 1. But there is a more fundamental issue than the 'yo-yo' effect described above.

The accountant's problem is posed by Case 3. There is no evidence to indicate that this situation, which represents the typical locked-in asset, is relatively infrequent. Indeed, we suspect that Case 3 may represent a variety of fixed assets in use in many industries, whenever economic conditions become unfavourable. This is an empirical question that needs to be investigated. Writers have noted that the VB in Case 3 has as its limiting magnitudes replacement cost (the upper bound) and resale price (the lower bound). It is possible that the stretch between the two limits is relatively large. Nonetheless, we examine below the proposal that a market price or an average market price (e.g. some average of replacement cost and net realizable value) may serve as a surrogate for the indeterminate measure of value to the business in Case 3.

The Use of Surrogates

A simple definition of the principal-surrogate relationship is provided by Ijiri. Things or phenomena that are used to represent other things or phenomena are called 'surrogates', and the things or phenomena that are represented by surrogates are called 'principals'. Principals are things one is primarily concerned with, whereas surrogates are things one is concerned with only insofar as one can determine the principals from them. In most instances the representation is more or less imperfect. Some writers have held that the weaknesses in reporting present value measures lie in the uncertainty of future flows and the subjectivity of estimates. The use of a surrogate or surrogates to represent a difficult-to-measure principal has been justified as a convenient method of dealing with such problems.

However, while measurement problems (of uncertainty, subjectivity, etc.) are important, they are not germane to the main issue. For external reporting purposes, the appropriate present value measure in Case 3 is one given by the unique cash flow (PV†) associated with the asset, and not the differential flow (PV) which captures the entire synergistic effects from employing the asset jointly with other assets (including human resources) in the firm.[7] If a present value measure based on the differential flow is used in reporting the asset's value, it will give an upward bias. The extent of the bias is not known but is likely to be serious, and the danger of double counting is present where there is more than one locked-in asset. Second, it is not possible to identify or even conceive of the unique cash flows generated by individual assets. The problem is one of allocation of the joint revenue stream to input units, and is intractable at the individual asset level, even if *ex ante* certainty is assumed. The problem of reporting an asset in present value terms can be resolved if an asset is redefined such that allocation of the firm's revenue flows to individual input units is avoided. Thomas writes: 'It is hard to see how such compression could stop short of having almost all unexpired non-monetary economic goods reflected in a single figure on the balance sheet, and almost all expirations of such goods reflected in a single expense figure on the income statement'. It is improbable that such aggregated reporting would be acceptable, or useful, to readers of financial statements.

---

[7] Synergistic effects arise from asset interactions. The use of an asset in combination with other assets often affects favourably the productivity of the other assets as well as its own productivity.

The main issue is that the present value of an individual asset for external reporting purposes is not defined. If a principal can be abstractly defined, but not necessarily operationally defined, at least theoretically a surrogate can be defined. But if the principal cannot be defined even abstractly, it is logically impossible to conceive of a surrogate and the search for proxy measures is a meaningless quest.

Below, some alternative proposals for fixed asset valuation under the VB approach are examined.

The Essentiality Criterion

In June 1975, the Institute of Chartered Accountants in Australia and the Australian Society of Accountants published a Preliminary Exposure Draft, *A Method of 'Current Value Accounting'*. This proposed the exclusion of present values as a general valuation basis for use in financial statements, and suggested that an essentiality criterion should be adopted to discriminate between the use of replacement cost and net realizable value. The essentiality criterion was abandoned subsequently by the profession, but it is subjected to critical analysis below because it could reappear in the literature one day, in the same or some amended form. [8] The criterion was described as follows:

> Given continuity of the entity, the selection of the appropriate measure of current value for non-monetary assets would have to be based on the distinction between what is essential and what is not essential to the continuance of operations. If any asset or component of an asset is essential to the continuance of operations, it is worth to the entity no more than it would cost to replace the operating capability which it provides. If it is not essential to operations, it is worth no more than its net realizable value.

The use of the essentiality criterion in the Exposure Draft can be criticized on several grounds. First, given the assumption of enterprise continuity, it does not follow that *particular* operations of the enterprise are also viable. The continuity of a specific operation (which the Exposure Draft takes for granted) is a function of economic factors and is a decision choice in a decision context, similar to that displayed in the second column of Table 20—5, which subsumes present value considerations. Second, in respect of a specific operation, the relevant factors to be considered in assessing the viability of that operation are the services generated by assets, not the assets themselves. Furthermore, it is difficult to conceive of any specific asset being essential, given the ability to lease assets, the use of sub-contracting and the scope for resource substitutions in most continuing operations. Referring to an earlier example, we may question whether a conveyor belt is essential if its services can be replaced by hired fork-lift trucks.

Further, while the Draft does not provide a definition of essentiality, it does refer explicitly to an asset or component of an asset in this context. There is only one feasible interpretation: an asset is essential if replacement is intended, and if it is essential it should. be measured at replacement cost. The essentiality criterion is superfluous; it has been demonstrated above that few assets are essential in themselves for enterprise continuity. The relevant guideline is in fact a *replacement intention* criterion, but this cannot be encompassed in the framework of the Draft. A decision on asset replacement can be made only by reference to the choice criteria set

---

[8] The New Zealand *Report of the Committee of Inquiry into Inflation Accounting* (known as the Richardson Report), published in 1976, also made use of the essentiality criterion for asset valuation. See Chapter 22.

out in Table 20—5, which inform management's replacement intentions. We conclude that the exclusion of present value calculations and the adoption of an essentiality criterion in its stead in an eclectic asset measurement system leads to a logical impasse, and does not provide an operational guideline for asset valuation in accounting.

3 An Alternative Approach to Determining Current Values

A weakness of the proposals for fixed asset valuation in the Sandilands Report is that certain assets are valued at their present value, whereas a weakness in the essentiality criterion concept lies in its exclusion of present value altogether. An alternative approach to the problem of determining current values is now offered.

Management will equate the current worth of the fixed asset to the business with the present value of its incremental net receipts, and will presumably have regard to this concept of present value in deciding on the use which it proposes to make of the asset. Because present value is a subjective concept, however, it is not suitable for use in a system of objectively determined current values. The question thus becomes one of deciding which of the two current value concepts, current replacement cost or net realizable value, represents the best approximation to the current worth of the assets to the firm, and hence of the cost of using or selling them. The answer to this question will depend essentially on whether the continued operation of fixed capital assets is more profitable to the business than their sale in the market.

Under conditions of normal operation, in the absence of changes in technology or demand affecting products or production processes, it may be assumed that the present value of an asset exceeds its current replacement cost. Under these circumstances, the firm will continue to use and replace the asset, and it is appropriate to use current replacement cost as the measure of its current value.

If current replacement cost exceeds present value, however, it must be assumed that the asset will not be replaced when it is sold or wears out. Under these circumstances, current replacement cost no longer provides a satisfactory measure of current value and it is necessary to value the asset by reference to net realizable value of the asset. If present value, while less than current replacement cost, exceeds market selling value, the firm will continue to use the asset until its service potential has expired, but will then not replace it. If present value is less than net realizable value, on the other hand, it will be necessary for the firm to sell the asset immediately and again it will not replace it. In each case, net realizable value is the appropriate measure of current value.

To summarize, current replacement cost provides a measure of current value when present value exceeds current replacement cost, while net realizable value becomes the appropriate measure of current value when current replacement cost exceeds present value.

If, for example, the present value of an asset is estimated at $100 and its current replacement cost is $80, its current value is $80 irrespective of its net realizable value. If, however, the current replacement cost of the asset is $120, and its present value remains at $100, its net realizable value becomes the relevant measure of current value. Although the subjective concept of present value enters into the valuation criterion, the choice which is made between current replacement cost and net realizable value may be objectively verified after the valuation date, by confirming that assets valued at net realizable value were not in fact replaced.

References

Bonbright, J.C., *Valuation of Property*, McGraw-Hill, New York, 1937, (reprinted) Michie, Charlotteville, 1965.

Canning, J.B., *The Economics of Accountancy*, Ronald Press, New York, 1929.

Conceptual Framework for Financial Accounting and Reporting: Elements of Financial Statements and Their Measurement, Financial Accounting Standards Board Discussion Memorandum, 1976, paras. 283-316.

Ijiri, Y., *The Foundations of Accounting Measurement, A Mathematical, Economic and Behavioral Inquiry*, Prentice-Hall, Englewood Cliffs, N.J., 1967.

Inflation Accounting, Report of the Inflation Accounting Committee, H.M.S.O., London, 1975 (referred to as the Sandilands Report).

Institute of Chartered Accountants in Australia and Australian Society of Accountants, *A Method of 'Current Value Accounting'*, Preliminary Exposure Draft, June 1975.

Ma, R., 'Value to the Owner Revisited', *Abacus*, December 1976, pp. 159-65.

Thomas, A.L., *The Allocation Problem in Financial Accounting Theory*, Studies in Accounting Research No. 3, American Accounting Association, 1969.

Additional Reading

Chambers, R.J., 'Value to the Owner', *Abacus*, June 1971, pp. 62-72.

Edwards, E.O. and Bell, P.W., *The Theory and Measurement of Business Income*, University of California Press, Berkeley and Los Angeles, 1961.

Wright, F.K., 'A Theory of Inventory Valuation', *Abacus*, December 1965, pp. 150-5.

Discussion Questions

1 Explain the following terms employed by Edwards and Bell in their business profit approach: current operating profit, current cost, realizable cost savings, unrealized and realized cost savings, business profit and realized profit.

2 Examine the relationship between realizable cost savings and realized cost savings in the Edwards and Bell approach to profit measurement.

3 Edwards and Bell developed a subsidiary profit concept of realized profit. Explain what they mean by this concept, and how it differs from accounting profit.

4 The current distributable income and business profit approaches both represent current value accounting systems. Explain the differences in the concepts underlying these two approaches.

5 Under what circumstances would cost savings be treated as income available for distribution or as non-distributable valuation adjustments to proprietorship equity?

6 Critically examine the eclectic approach to asset valuation.

7 What arguments are employed by Edwards and Bell to justify the use of a replacement cost accounting system? Under what circumstances do they advocate that a firm's assets be valued at their exit values?

8 Explain the concept of value to the business, and how this concept can be applied to the valuation of inventories.

9 Critically examine the alternative proposals for fixed asset valuation under the value to the business approach.

10 Discuss the benefits and limitations in reporting current values in financial statements to investors.

Exercises

1 The Adonis Co. Ltd purchased a fixed asset at the beginning of 1983 for $20 000. The expected economic life of the asset is 10 years and depreciation is on a straight-line basis. On 1 January 1983 the price index stood at 100 and had risen to 110 by December 1983 and 125 by the end of 1984. On 31 December 1985 the price index stood at 140. At this stage the company decided to change from historical cost to a current value accounting system. Show how this asset and accumulated depreciation would appear in the balance sheet on 31 December 1985 under current value accounting.

2 Assume that the data are as given in the previous exercise. What is the effect of the depreciation expense on the net profit for the year under (a) the accounting profit concept, (b) the realized profit concept, and (c) the business profit concept?

3 The financial statements of the Mozart Piano Co. Ltd prepared in accordance with the historical record accounting system are set out below:

Balance Sheet as at 31 December 1985

Monetary assets		$75 000
Inventories		125 000
Land		40 000
Plant and equipment (purchased 1 Jan. 1984)	$150 000	
Less: Accumulated depreciation	37 500	112 500
		$352 500
Current liabilities		57 500
Long-term liabilities		120 000
Proprietorship equity	125 000	
Retained earnings	50 000	175 000
		$352 500

Income Statement for Year Ended 31 December 1985

Sales		$1 000 000
Less: Cost of sales—		
Opening inventory	$110 000	
Purchases	690 000	
	800 000	
Closing inventory	125 000	675 000
Gross profit		325 000
Depreciation on plant and equipment	18 750	
Wages	125 000	
Other expenses	50 000	193 750
Net profit before tax		131 250
Less: Tax at 50%		65 625
Net profit after tax		65 625
Less: Dividends paid		15 625
Retained earnings		$50 000

You are given the following additional information on the historical cost of inventories:

	Number of Units	At Historical Cost	Average Cost per Unit
Opening inventory	50	$110 000	$2 200
Purchases	300	690 000	2 300
Closing inventory	50	125 000	2 500

The current cost of opening inventory is the same as its historical acquisition cost of $2 200 per unit, the average current cost for the year is $2 300 per unit, and the year-end current cost is $2 700 per unit. The current cost (new) of plant and equipment at the beginning of 1985 is $160 000, and its average and year-end values are $170 000 and $200 000 respectively. Assume that the current value of the land is $40 000.

You are required to present current value financial statements using the business profit/financial capital maintenance approach.

4 Assume the same data as those given in the previous exercise. You are required to present current value financial statements using the current distributable income/ operating capital maintenance approach.

21 Accounting Valuation Systems 4—Relative Price Change Accounting

Relative Price Change Accounting

In order to overcome some of the limitations which are inherent in the general price level approach, some writers have developed a valuation model which combines some of the features of current purchasing power accounting with the current value system. This is described as the relative price change approach to accounting valuation.

The approach starts from the position that no income can be regarded as having been earned in a period unless the generalized purchasing power of the firm's proprietorship equity at the beginning of the period is preserved. In times of rising price levels, therefore, a negative adjustment needs to be made to income representing the proportionate increase in the general price level during the period applied to proprietorship equity at the beginning of the period. But increases in the specific prices of non-monetary assets during the period are also taken into account in measuring income. The gains (or losses) which accrue to the firm from the holding of non-monetary assets, because the assets are worth more (or less) at the end of the period than at the beginning, are added to income as separate items which are usually described as holding gains (or losses). (For this purpose, it should be noted, the definition of non-monetary assets needs to be extended to include marketable investments.) The basic income which is adjusted in these ways is itself determined on a current value basis, by measuring revenues, costs and expenses in terms of their current values.

Symbolically, therefore, the income concept underlying this approach may be expressed as follows:

$$\text{Income} = S - C - Rp + Nq \tag{1}$$

where S denotes sales revenue, C denotes costs and expenses expressed in terms of current values, R is proprietorship equity at the beginning of the income period, N denotes the measure of non-monetary assets, and p and q are the proportionate increases in the general price level and the specific prices of non-monetary assets, respectively.

Given that $R = N + M$, where M denotes the measure of net monetary assets (i.e. monetary assets less liabilities), and that $Rp = Np + Mp$, it follows that equation (1) can be restated as follows:

$$\text{Income} = S - C + N(q - p) - Mp \tag{2}$$

This is the concept of income which is adopted in the relative price change approach. In addition to the current value component of income represented by $(S - C)$, it includes a holding gain on non-monetary assets and the already familiar purchasing power loss on net monetary assets. The holding gain on non-monetary assets is calculated by applying the differential price change, as between the specific prices of the non-monetary assets and the general price level, to the value of non-monetary assets. If the initial value of an investment is $1 000, its current value at the end of the period is $1 200, and the general price level has increased by 10 per cent during the period, $N(q - p) = \$1\,000\,(0.20 - 0.10) = \$100$.

In effect, it is assumed that, although a gain of $200 in terms of current prices was achieved by holding the investment throughout the period, $100 of this was a fictitious gain to the extent that the purchasing power of money fell during the period. Only the balance of $100 is regarded as a substantive increase in the value of the investment which may be added to income.

The relative price change concept of income, like the general price level (or current purchasing power) concept, is thus measured by reference to the difference between two hypothetical measures of wealth, namely the generalized purchasing power of measures of proprietorship equity at the beginning and end of the income period. But whereas the general price level concept ignores the effect of specific price changes affecting non-monetary assets, the relative price change concept of income includes the gain or loss resulting from changes in specific prices relative to changes in the general price level.

If income as defined were to be fully distributed during the period, the relative price change approach would result in proprietorship equity being maintained in terms of its generalized purchasing power. If the balance sheet at time t_0 is given by $R = M + N$, and if income from trading operations is ignored, at t_1 the balance sheet before distribution of any income may be expressed as follows:

$$M + N(1 + q) = R(1 + p) + N(q - p) - Mp \tag{3}$$

But if $N(q - p) - Mp$ is treated as income (as proponents of the relative price change approach suggest) and fully distributed, holdings of assets must change by an amount equal to $N(q - p) - Mp$. The effect of this on the balance sheet may be shown as follows:

$$M + N(1 + q) - N(q - p) + Mp = R(1 + p) \tag{4}$$

If $N(q - p)$ exceeds Mp, i.e. if Nq exceeds Rp, this means that residual equity no longer commands the same quantity of assets at the end of the period as it did at the beginning. The same quantity of non-monetary assets, N, at their new prices, $(1 + q)$, can only be held by running down net monetary assets by an amount equal to $N(q - p) - Mp$.

This may be illustrated by a simple numerical example, in which income from trading income is ignored and it is assumed that at time t_0 $M = \$100$, $N = \$300$ and $R = \$400$, and that during the period to t_1 price increases occur at rates $p = 0.10$ and $q = 0.20$.

At t_0	$M + N = R$	(5)
	$\$100 + \$300 = \$400$	
At t_1	$M + N(1 + q) = R(1 + p) + N(q - p) - Mp$	(3)
	$\$100 + \$360 = \$440 + \$30 - \$10$	

If $N(q - p) - Mp$ is treated as income and distributed, the original quantity of non-monetary assets can only be held at their new value, $360, by running down net monetary assets, i.e.

$$\$80 + \$360 = \$440$$

The attempt to preserve the generalized purchasing power of residual equity has thus resulted not in a strengthening but in a weakening of the firm's financial position during the period t_0 to t_1. This is a fundamental weakness of the relative price change approach to income measurement. Any definition of income which tries to allow for the differential effects of general and specific price changes will run up against this difficulty, which can only be avoided by treating $N(q - p) - Mp$ as a restatement of capital rather than as distributable income.

Relationship between Current Value and General Price Level Adjustments in Relative Price Change Accounting

Provided all items in financial statements have been adjusted to a current value basis, general price level adjustments can be made by means of simple statistical deflation procedures.

Suppose again that a firm's balance sheet at t_0 may be represented symbolically by the following equation:

$$t_0: \qquad\qquad M + N = R \qquad\qquad (5)$$

Following a period in which there have been no income transactions, now suppose that non-monetary assets have been revalued by a factor $(1 + q)$ in response to an increase in the current value of the assets. The firm's current value balance sheet at t_1 may then be represented in terms of t_1 prices as follows:

$$t_1 \text{ (at } t_1 \text{ prices):} \qquad M + N(1 + q) = R + Nq \qquad\qquad (6)$$

If the general price level has increased at a rate p during the same period, the t_1 balance sheet may be deflated and expressed in terms of the general price level prevailing at t_0 by means of the following adjustment procedure:

$$t_1 \text{ (at } t_0 \text{ prices):} \qquad \frac{M}{1 + p} + \frac{N(1 + q)}{1 + p} = \frac{R + Nq}{1 + p} \qquad\qquad (7)$$

The equation (7) balance sheet, representing as it does the firm's financial position at t_1 expressed in terms of t_0 prices, may then be compared with the equation (5) balance sheet, in which the financial position at t_0 is expressed in the same t_0 prices. Alternatively the equation (5) balance sheet, provided it consistently records current values at t_0, may be expressed in terms of t_1 prices and thus made comparable to the equation (6) balance sheet:

$$t_0 \text{ (at } t_1 \text{ prices):} \qquad M(1 + p) + N(1 + p) = R(1 + p) \qquad\qquad (8)$$

In this way, financial statements for a series of years may be expressed in terms of a constant price level, and it may be seen whether the purchasing power of residual equity is being maintained.

It can be shown that, if the rate of increase in the general price level, p, is exactly equal to the rate of increase, q, in the current value of N, the deflation of the current value balance sheet records the same reduction in residual equity (resulting from a purchasing power loss on net monetary assets) as results from the general price level approach described in Chapter 18. This is because equation (7) then becomes:

$$t_1 \text{ (at } t_0 \text{ prices):} \qquad \frac{M}{1 + p} + N = \frac{R + Nq}{1 + p} \qquad\qquad (9)$$

Subtracting equation (5) from equation (9), the change in residual equity between t_0 and t_1 is $\dfrac{R + Nq}{1 + p} - R$ and equals:

$$(\frac{M}{1 + p} + N) - (M + N)$$

$$= \frac{M}{1 + p} - M$$

$$= \frac{-Mp}{1 + p}$$

Now $\frac{Mp}{1 + p}$ in t_0 prices equals Mp in t_1 prices. This is the same purchasing power loss which is recorded under current purchasing power accounting. But because prices p and q do *not* change at uniform rates in practice, it is necessary to convert each financial statement to current value terms before any sensible meaning can be attached to constant price level data. It should also be emphasized that the deflation procedures which have been illustrated are statistical rather than accounting operations, and are subject to all the limitations of statistical deflation procedures.

It is easily shown that applying constant price level adjustments to current value balance sheet data is equivalent to the relative price change approach. On the basis of equations (5) and (7), which record respectively the financial position of the firm at t_0 and t_1 in terms of t_0 prices, the change in residual equity between t_0 and t_1 may be expressed as follows by subtracting equation (5) from equation (7):

$$\frac{R + Nq}{1 + p} - R = \frac{M}{1 + p} + \frac{N(1 + q)}{1 + p} - (M + N)$$

$$= \frac{M}{1 + p} - M + \frac{N(1 + q)}{1 + p} - N$$

$$= -\frac{Mp}{1 + p} + \frac{N(1 + q) - N(1 + p)}{1 + p}$$

$$= -\frac{Mp}{1 + p} + \frac{N(q - p)}{1 + p} \tag{10}$$

Now $\frac{-Mp}{1 + p} + \frac{N(q - p)}{1 + p}$ in t_0 prices equals $N(q - p) - Mp$ in t_1 prices. This is the change in residual equity which results from relative price change accounting.

Evaluation of Relative Price Change Accounting

The relative price change accounting system possesses many of the advantages of a current value system, the most important of which is that the system output has relevance for decision making. The assets in the relative price change accounting balance sheet and the income figure in the income statement are stated in current values, making it possible to derive the rate of return on investment in current value terms. This is a measure of particular relevance to investors, since it enhances the comparability of the performance of different firms.

Although income is measured under the relative price change approach by reference to differential price changes which take account of current values, the capital maintenance concept adopted under this approach is concerned only with maintaining the generalized purchasing power of proprietorship equity. It is thus the same capital maintenance concept as that used in current purchasing power accounting and is subject to all the weaknesses of that system.

Where the current values used in the relative price change system are the current values discussed in Chapter 19, its income concept may be said to be directed in one sense towards the maintenance of the generalized purchasing power of the firm's operating capital. On the other hand, if the system employs net realizable values (as in Chambers's model described in the following section), then the income concept is directed in this narrow sense towards the maintenance of the firm's adaptive capacity. However, the relative price change system is essentially oriented towards maintaining the generalized purchasing power of the proprietorship equity, and if income derived by reference to relative price changes is fully distributed, neither operating capital nor adaptive capacity is wholly maintained when the current values of the firm's assets increase at a faster rate than the general price level. As noted earlier, the major shortcoming of relative price change accounting is thus its failure to provide a satisfactory measure of distributable income. Advocates of the relative price change approach treat as income an amount represented by $N(q - p) - Mp$, the distribution of which may seriously weaken the financial viability of the firm. We have recommended that this amount be regarded as a valuation adjustment of proprietorship equity and not as income.

A special valuation system within the relative price change accounting framework is discussed below. As explained in Chapters 19 and 20, asset values in current value systems are based on market prices. These market prices may be represented by entry or buying values (i.e. current replacement costs) or by exit or selling values (i.e. net realizable values, comprising sales less selling costs such as discounts and salesmen's commissions) or both. The best known exit value system is Chambers's continuously contemporary accounting model, which also incorporates a method of accounting for relative price changes.

Continuously Contemporary Accounting

Chambers's *continuously contemporary accounting* (CoCoA) model is a relative price change system which makes use of market resale prices for the firm's assets. In principle, current resale prices are recorded in the accounts continuously, as price movements take place in the market. As it is not practicable to record continuously both market prices and the general price level change, Chambers resorts to what he calls a 'black box' strategy. The recording of the general price level change is held in abeyance until the end of the period, when opening proprietorship equity is adjusted by reference to the change in the general price level during the period. If there has been an increase in the general price level, the amount of the capital maintenance adjustment is debited to profit and loss and credited to the opening proprietorship equity balances (capital, reserves and retained earnings) proportionately.

Symbolically the adjustment processes may be illustrated by reference to the simplified balance sheet at t_0:

$$M + N = R \tag{5}$$

Assume that there are no income-earning activities during the period t_0 to t_1, but that the general price level increases by p (where $p = \dfrac{p_1 - p_0}{p_0}$) and the market selling price of the non-monetary assets increases by s (where $s = \dfrac{s_1 - s_0}{s_0}$). The increase in net worth for the period t_0 to t_1 may be derived as follows. First, an adjustment is made for the general price level change, so that the balance sheet at t_1 takes the following form:

$$M(1 + p) + N(1 + p) = R(1 + p)$$
$$M + N(1 + p) = R(1 + p) - Mp \tag{11}$$

An adjustment also needs to be made to the balance sheet at t_1 to reflect the change in the selling price of the non-monetary assets, i.e. to restate N as $N(1 + s)$. Since the non-monetary assets in equation (11) are already stated at $N(1 + p)$, the net adjustment factor is simply $(s - p)$:

$$M + N[(1 + p) + (s - p)] = R(1 + p) - Mp + N(s - p)$$
$$M + N(1 + s) = R(1 + p) - Mp + N(s - p) \tag{12}$$

To obtain the increase in net worth for the period, equation (5) is subtracted from equation (12) and rearranged as follows:

$$Ns - Rp = N(s - p) - Mp \tag{13}$$

Income thus includes (in addition to current profit resulting from operations) the net effect of changes in the general price level and in the selling prices of the specific non-monetary assets held by the firm. The right-hand side of equation (13) represents the purchasing power loss in a period of inflation from holding monetary assets, $-Mp$, and the real holding gain on non-monetary assets, $N(s - p)$. On the left-hand side, Ns represents adjustments for selling price variations that take place during the period, while Rp represents the general purchasing power adjustment of the opening equity. Rp is the consequence of a measurement scale transformation, to ensure that income is measured by reference to the maintenance of capital in terms of the end-of-period scale.

It will be seen that the CoCoA model is identical in form to the general case of the relative price change system. Since $N(s - p) - Mp$ is treated as income, the same criticism that has been made earlier applies, i.e. that distribution of this amount can lead to a weakening of the firm's financial position. However, the capital maintenance concept in the CoCoA model does not relate to the firm's operating capital but to its adaptive capacity.

Assumptions Underlying CoCoA

A large number of assumptions, consistent with certain received doctrines in the behavioural sciences, economics, accounting and other related disciplines, form the foundations of Chambers's theory of continuously contemporary accounting. Some of the more important assumptions are:

(a) A person or a group in an organization operates as a system which maintains continuous decision making processes, in order to adapt to changes in itself and in its environment.

(b) A person's behaviour is rational, i.e. he seeks the optimal choice from competing alternatives.

(c) A person's behaviour is, however, subject to his own limited capacity, costs of obtaining information, as well as the relative scarcity of resources under that person's control.

(d) Information about present and past events must be (i) objectively verifiable, and (ii) neutral (i.e. free from personal bias), to constitute accounting information useful for decision making. Information must be protected from manipulation by accountants and others providing the information. On this ground Chambers excludes from the domain of accounting measurement data oriented to the future, such as forecasts.

(e) The firm is a going concern. This does not necessarily imply that the size and pattern of its current production process must remain unchanging.

Chambers's theory of accounting may be classified as *scientific*, rather than normative, in the sense that the author claims it is based on observation of real world events, the most significant of which in the context of accounting theory development is adaptation. Adaptation, according to Chambers, is the dominant mode of economic behaviour, of persons and of firms. Persons and firms adapt continuously to changes, of which some of the most important are those in the market place. Adaptive behaviour is a function of a person's rationality, i.e. desire to optimize, on the one hand, and his limited capacity and resources on the other.

The key features of Chambers's theory are:

(a) Knowledge of one's present financial position is essential for evaluating past actions and making decisions about the future.

(b) The accounting system accumulates and supplies knowledge about present financial position to persons and firms.

(c) Knowledge of present financial position is only part of the data input necessary for making an informed choice. In addition, the decision maker must take into account other available market information as well as his own personal expectations and attitude toward risks.

Computation of Financial Position and Income under CoCoA

Financial Position and Current Cash Equivalents

Chambers argues that the domain of accounting is limited to the measurement of past and present events (future expectations are not events that can be measured for external reporting purposes). Financial position, then, may relate to a present or a past state, and it is defined as the capacity of an entity at any time (present or past) to engage in indirect exchanges in the market. This capacity is determined by the measure of net wealth or, equivalently, the net assets of the entity. An asset is any severable means owned by the entity, and its net assets are represented by its total assets less its liabilities. The relevant measure for assets and liabilities is their current cash equivalent (CCE), which for assets is the same as net realizable value and for liabilities is equal to face value.

There are several assumptions underlying the measurement of CCEs of assets. A perfect market is not necessary, but an actively trading market in the firm's assets must be assumed. Where the market price of an asset traded in the market place is used to determine the CCE of an asset held by the firm, there must be a near-exact identity between the two assets if arbitrary allocations are to be avoided. Chambers has made it clear that ideal conditions will not be met in practice and that approximations to CCE measures may be necessary.

The following assets may be measured at zero CCE, where there are no identical assets in the market place: (a) specialized plant and equipment; and (b) specialized work in process.

Net Income Measures and CCEs[1]

If it is assumed that there are no capital contributions or withdrawals, the net income measure in Chambers's system is the difference between the sum of the CCEs of assets minus liabilities at the beginning and at the end of the period, after adjustment for any change in the measurement scale on account of a general price level movement in the period. In theory at least, the asset accounts should be adjusted for market price variations on a continuous basis (hence the name given to the system, 'continuously contemporary accounting'). In practice, adjustments may be made at the end of the period only. Depreciation is not recognized as a separate expense item in a CoCoA income statement. It is simply part of the price variation adjustment relating to a depreciable asset.

Where the asset accounts (in particular inventory accounts) are adjusted to CCE measures at the end of the period only, the net income for the period is the sum of the following components:

(a) transaction surpluses, defined as the excess of revenues over outlays in the period, represented by actual amounts receivable (or received) and amounts payable (or paid);

(b) changes in the CCE measures of assets between the beginning and end of the period (these comprise both price and quantity variations in assets during the period); and

(c) the capital maintenance adjustment, which is an adjustment to the opening amount of net assets (or proprietorship equity) to reflect a general price change over the period. This adjustment is a measurement scale transformation.

Under the alternative procedure, asset accounts (in particular inventory accounts) are adjusted continuously or, more realistically, whenever inventories are bought or sold and at the end of the period. Under this procedure, transaction surpluses do not arise, because sales revenue is equal to the CCEs of inventories at the time a sale takes place plus selling expenses associated with the sale. Price variation adjustments are recorded on inventories sold as the difference between the CCE and book values of the inventories at the time they are sold. Price variation adjustments are recorded on inventories purchased as the difference between the CCE and purchase prices at the time of purchase. Price variation adjustments are recorded on inventories held at the end of the year as the difference between CCEs and book values at that time. Price variation adjustments on fixed assets sold, purchased and held are recorded in the same way. Income will then be measured (in a period of rising prices) by:

(a) the net upward price variations, *less*

(b) wage or other expenses (other than selling expenses and manufacturing expenses absorbed into inventories), *less*

(c) the capital maintenance adjustment.

The difference between the two methods lies in the frequency of updating asset accounts to CCE measures, and is a matter of convenience rather than principle. The net income figure and the statement of financial position are the same under both methods, as illustrated in the following simple example.

Example: At the beginning of the year, a firm held inventories, purchased in the previous year for $95, which had a CCE of $100. The inventories were sold for

---

[1] Net income in the CoCoA system may be computed in a number of ways. The methods presented in this section reflect the authors' preferences. For an alternative method, see Chambers, *Accounting for Inflation*. Exposure Draft, 1975.

cash during the year for $130 and replaced immediately at a cash cost of $120. Cash selling expenses were $5. By the end of the year, the CCE of the inventories had increased to $140. During the year the general price level index rose from 100 to 115.

Method 1 — Recording CCE measures at the end of the period only: Under this approach, the inventory account is not maintained continuously; it records only opening and closing inventories at their CCE measures, the offsetting entries being to the income account. This approach is thus analogous to the physical inventory method of maintaining inventories in a conventional accounting system. It is also not necessary to establish a separate price variation adjustment account, and in fact the amounts of price variation adjustments are not calculated directly under this method, but are simply the sum of the transaction surplus and the change in CCE measures after allowing for quantity changes. The CoCoA measure of income may be calculated as follows:

Sales		$130
Less: Purchases	$120	
Selling expenses	5	125
Transaction surplus		5
Add: Increase in CCE measure of inventories—		
CCE of inventories at end of period	140	
CCE of inventories at beginning of period	100	40
		45
Less: Capital maintenance adjustment		15
Net income		$30

The CoCoA statements of financial position at the beginning and end of the year may be represented thus:

	Beginning of Year		End of Year	
Cash		—		$5
Inventories at CCE		$100		140
Total assets		$100		$145
Proprietorship equity—				
Contributed capital	100		100	
Add: Capital maintenance reserve	—		15	
		100		115
Retained income		—		30
Total proprietorship equity		$100		$145

The relationship between the CoCoA income measure and proprietorship equity may be illustrated as follows. CoCoA income is measured as the increase over the period in the CCE of assets minus liabilities ($145 − $100 = $45) after allowing for capital contributions or withdrawals (nil), *less* the capital maintenance adjustment to the opening equity (a scale transformation, $15), i.e. $45 − $15 or $30.

Method 2 — Continuously updating CCE measures: Under this approach an inventory account and a price variation adjustment account are maintained continuously in a manner which is analogous to a perpetual inventory system of recording inventories. It will be seen that the price variations on sales and purchases are recorded at the time of the sales and purchases, and that a separate price variation adjustment is also made on inventories held at the end of the period:

Inventory

Balance b/d	$100	CCE of goods sold	$125
Price variation adjustment on goods sold	25	Balance c/d	140
Purchases	120		
Price variation adjustment on purchases	5		
Price variation adjustment on balance c/d	15		
	$265		$265
Balance b/d	$140		

Price Variation Adjustment—Inventory

Profit and loss account	$45	Inventory account—	
		Price variation adjustment on goods sold	$25
		Price variation adjustment on purchases	5
		Price variation adjustment on closing inventory	15
	$45		$45

Since the inventories are updated to their CCE measures whenever transactions take place, there is no transaction surplus. The sales account will record sales, selling expenses and the CCE of goods sold, which by definition will have the effect of closing the account:

Sales

Inventory account— CCE of goods sold	$125	Cash (or accounts receivable)	$130
Cash (or accounts payable)— Selling expenses	5		
	$130		$130

The CoCoA measure of income may then be calculated as follows:

Price variation adjustments—		
On goods sold	$25	
On purchases	5	
On closing inventory	15	$45
Less: Capital maintenance adjustment		15
Net income		$30

The CoCoA statements of financial position at the beginning and end of the period are the same as in Method 1.

Adapting Historical Record Measures to CoCoA

It is also useful to note that net income under the CoCoA approach may be derived from the historical cost profit figure. It should be noted, however, that the price variation adjustments are not the same as those calculated under Method 2 above. This is because the adjustments reflect the difference between (a) the adjustment necessary to bring the historical cost of closing inventories up to their CCE measure at the end of the period and (b) the adjustment necessary to bring the historical cost of opening inventories up to their CCE measure at the beginning of the period; i.e. the price variation adjustments are to historical cost data used in deriving the measure of net accounting profit. In practice a further adjustment will be necessary for depreciation.

Sales		$130
Less: Cost of sales—		
Opening inventory	$95	
Purchases	120	
	215	
Less: Closing inventory	120	95
Gross profit		35
Selling expenses		5
Net accounting profit		30
Add: Price variation adjustments—		
Closing inventory ($140 — $120)	20	
Less: Opening inventory ($100 — $95)	5	15
		45
Less: Capital maintenance adjustment		15
Net CoCoA income		$30

A more comprehensive illustration follows.

An Illustration

The CoCoA approach may be illustrated by reference to the X Trading Co. example in Table 18—2, which has also been used to illustrate the current value systems in Chapters 19 and 20. The financial statements relating to the third year of the company's operations, prepared in accordance with historical record accounting assumptions, follow:

Balance Sheets as at 31 December 1984 and 31 December 1985

	31 December 1984		31 December 1985	
Monetary assets		$2 200		$3 000
Inventories		2 000		3 600
		4 200		6 600
Equipment	$7 000		$7 000	
Less: Accumulated depreciation	2 800	4 200	4 200	2 800
Total assets		8 400		9 400
Liabilities		1 000		1 000
Proprietorship equity		$7 400		$8 400

Income Statement for Year Ended 31 December 1985

Sales		$12 000
Less: Cost of sales—		
Opening inventory	$2 000	
Purchases	9 300	
	11 300	
Closing inventory	3 600	7 700
Gross profit		4 300
Less: Depreciation on equipment	1 400	
Other expenses	900	2 300
Net profit before tax		2 000
Less: Tax at 50%		1 000
Net profit after tax		$1 000

The following transactions in 1985 are recorded at their actual amounts: sales, $12 000; and out-of-pocket expenses, $900. An amount of $1 000, in respect of the income tax on the historical record accounting profit, is paid on the last day of the financial year. Assume that the contributed capital is $7 000 and that 1985 is the first year in which the CoCoA system is implemented. Assume also that the general price index was 100 in 1983 (when the company commenced trading) and was 110, 120 and 140 at the end of 1983, 1984 and 1985, respectively.

Additional information relating to the CCEs of inventories and equipment at the end of 1984 and 1985 follows:

	31 December 1984	31 December 1985
Inventories	$2 500	$4 200
Equipment	5 280	4 300

Method 1 — Recording CCE measures at the end of the period only: The transaction surplus of $1 800 records revenues receivable and received ($12 000) net of purchases ($9 300) and out-of-pocket expenses ($900). The change in CCE measures of inventories is calculated as the difference between closing inventories ($4 200) and opening inventories ($2 500), while the change in CCE measures of equipment is also measured as the difference between the closing and opening CCE measures of equipment ($4 300 − $5 280 = − $980).

The capital maintenance adjustment in 1983 is $\frac{110 - 100}{100}$ ($7 000) or $700, and in 1984 is $\frac{120 - 110}{110}$ ($7 000 + $700) or $700. Thus the capital maintenance reserve in the CoCoA statement of financial position at 31 December 1984 in Table 21—2 is $1 400. The retained earnings figure of $580 at 31 December 1984 is a residual amount.

The capital maintenance adjustment on contributed capital in 1985 is:

$$\frac{140 - 120}{120} \text{ (\$7 000 + \$1 400) or \$1 400,}$$

while the capital maintenance adjustment on retained earnings is $\frac{140 - 120}{120}$ ($580) or $97, making a total capital maintenance adjustment of $1 497.

The financial statements of X Trading Co. are given in Tables 21—1 and 21—2.

Table 21—1
Continuously Contemporary Accounting System

X Trading Co.
Income Statement for Year Ended 31 December 1985

Sales		$12 000
Less: Purchases	$9 300	
Out-of-pocket expenses	900	
		10 200
Transaction surplus		1 800
Add: **Change in CCE measures—**		
On inventories	1 700	
On equipment including depreciation	− 980	720
		2 520
Less: **Capital maintenance adjustments—**		
On retained earnings	97	
On contributed capital	1 400	
		1 497
		1 023
Less: Tax based on accounting profit		1 000
Net income		$23

Table 21—2
Continuously Contemporary Accounting System

X Trading Co.
Financial Position as at 31 December 1984 and 31 December 1985

	31 December 1984		31 December 1985	
Monetary assets		$2 200		$3 000
Inventories		2 500		4 200
Equipment		5 280		4 300
Assets		9 980		11 500
Less: **Liabilities**		1 000		1 000
Ordinary share capital	$7 000		$7 000	
Retained earnings	580		603	
Capital maintenance reserve	1 400		2 897	
Proprietorship equity		$8 980		$10 500

As shown in an earlier example, CoCoA income is measured as the increase over the period in the CCE of assets minus liabilities ($10 500 − $8 980 = $1 520) after allowing for capital contributions or withdrawals (nil) *less* the capital maintenance adjustment on the opening equity (a scale transformation, $1 497), i.e. $1 520 − $1 497 or $23.

Method 2 — Continuously updating CCE measures: The inventory account and the price variation adjustment account—inventory are shown below. Insufficient data are given to record price variation adjustments in detail, but in the absence of selling expenses the CCE value of goods sold is equal to their selling price, and the total amount of price variation adjustments may be calculated as a residual figure.

Inventory

Balance b/d	$2 500	CCE of goods sold	$12 000
Purchases	9 300	Balance c/d	4 200
Price variation adjustments	4 400		
	$16 200		$16 200
Balance b/d	$4 200		

Price Variation Adjustment—Inventory

Profit and loss account	$4 400	Inventory	$4 400

The CoCoA measure of income is calculated under this method as follows:

Price variation adjustments—		
On inventories	$4 400	
On equipment, including depreciation	−980	$3 420
Less: Out-of-pocket expenses		900
		2 520
Less: **Capital maintenance adjustments—**		
On retained earnings	97	
On contributed capital	1 400	1 497
		1 023
Less: Tax based on accounting profit		1 000
Net income		$23

Methods 1 and 2 Evaluated

In practice, the choice between Methods 1 and 2 will depend on the availability of data and the sophistication of the recording processes which are adopted. Method 2 is theoretically superior, but Method 1 will usually be easier to apply. The procedure under Method 1 of revaluing assets only at the end of the period is inconsistent with the philosophy of CoCoA, which implies that the books of account are continuously updated.

A Comparison of CoCoA Income and Current Distributable Income

In Chapter 19 it was shown how the current value measure of income, called current distributable income, is derived as an extension of the historical record accounting framework. Although CoCoA income is not calculated in this manner, it has been seen in an earlier simplified example that it can be similarly derived. A comparison of the two income measures is given in Table 21—3.

Supporters of CoCoA believe that the statement of the firm's financial position under this system reveals the firm's adaptive capacity and has a special relevance for decision makers (which will be explained below). But it is difficult to see any special merit in the CoCoA income measure. On the other hand, as noted in Chapter 19, current distributable income is useful as a measure of management performance and as a measure of distributable surplus. That is, current distributable income discloses the return on the firm's capital resources measured at current prices, and also the amount that may be distributed to owners without impairing the firm's operating capacity. A case can be made for reporting a combination of a current distributable

Table 21—3
Current Distributable Income and CoCoA Income Compared

Current Distributable Income			CoCoA Income	
Net accounting profit before tax		$2 000	Net accounting profit before tax	$2 000
Less: Cost of sales valuation			*Add*: Price variation adjustments—	
adjustment	$1 900		Inventories*	100
Depreciation valuation			Equipment*	420
adjustment	1 600	3 500		
Current operating loss		(1 500)		2 520
			Less: Capital maintenance	
			adjustment†	1 497
				1 023
Less: Tax based on accounting			*Less*: Tax based on accounting	
profit		1 000	profit	1 000
Current loss after tax		$(2 500)	CoCoA profit after tax	$23

* The price variation adjustments on inventories and equipment are calculated as follows:

(a) Closing inventory ($4 200 − $3 600)	$600
Less: Opening inventory ($2 500 − $2 000)	500
	$100
(b) Equipment at year-end ($4 300 − $2 800)	1 500
Less: Equipment at year-beginning ($5 280 − $4 200)	1 080
	$420

† The capital maintenance adjustment figure can be derived as a residual in the CoCoA balance sheet.

income statement and a CoCoA statement of financial position. This notion has interesting possibilities, but its exploration is beyond the scope of this book.

Some accountants believe that historical cost data are more objective and harder than current value data (whether entry or exit values). Table 21—3 indicates that historical cost data can be retained as part of the reporting framework in a hybrid current value-CoCoA system.

Uses of CoCoA

Relevance for Decision Making

It has been argued that the most important criterion of a good accounting system is usefulness, and that the objective of accounting is to provide useful information, i.e. information which is relevant for decision making. It is largely on these grounds that Sterling has supported Chambers in the use of asset exit values in accounting valuation and reporting.[2] Sterling argues that accounting information must capture those elements that are common to all decisions. An economic decision implies a consideration of market alternatives and their consequences. Market alternatives depend upon the relationship between available funds and the required investment of new funds. The amount of available funds is given by the resale values of assets owned by the firm as well as its ability to raise loan or equity capital, while the required

[2] There are minor differences between Sterling's concept of current exit values and Chambers's concept of current cash equivalents.

investment is given by the purchase prices of assets not held by the firm, i.e. funds which will be absorbed by the proposed new projects.

Other factors in the decision are the consideration of consequences and pre-ferences. Consequences cannot be known, but they may be evaluated in terms of the future cash flows that are expected to accrue to alternative courses of action. Preferences reflect subjective utility functions, i.e. the attitudes of the decision maker to return and risk.

In the context of financial statements, the information that has general relevance for decision making relates to the resale values of assets owned by the firm, since it would be hardly appropriate to report in financial statements the purchase prices of assets not held. Other information relevant to decisions — the ability to raise capital, expected future cash flows and attitudes to risk — are either highly subjective and violate the accountant's objectivity criterion or are not quantifiable in money terms, or both.

The above argument on the relevance of asset exit values for decision making is consistent with Chambers's views. For example, a decision to substitute a new machine, B, for a machine, A, currently in use is a function of the following inequality. Choose B if:

$$[PV(A) - CCE(A)] < [PV(B) - P(B) - I]$$

where $CCE(A)$ = current cash equivalent of A,

$P(B)$ = purchase price of new machine B,

$PV(A), PV(B)$ = present value of (incremental) cash flows associated with employing A and B respectively (excluding $P(B)$ in the case of B), and

I = cost of additional borrowing where $P(B) > CCE(A)$.

It is readily evident that $CCE(A)$ is the only piece of information that can be reported objectively in financial statements, although expectations and present values have an important role in the decision context itself. Chambers stresses that CCEs represent necessary, but not sufficient, information relevant to all decisions.

CCEs as Measures of Net Worth, Liquidity and Risk

The relevance of reported measures in the exit value models of Chambers and Sterling to the information needs of managers has been demonstrated above. The relevance of exit values for creditors is readily evident, as the amount of collateral for their loans to the firm is given by the market selling prices of specifically pledged assets (for secured loans) and other assets (for all loans in general) held by the firm. The significant role of exit values in assessing the liquidity position of firms has already been discussed in Chapter 7.

Advocates of CoCoA thus believe that CCEs have general relevance for decision making. For example, the owners of a firm need to know the current market prices of its net assets when the firm is subject to a takeover bid. Takeover bids are made for a variety of reasons, one of which is asset stripping, i.e. the selling off of the assets of the company taken over. Asset stripping becomes a viable objective for the takeover bidder when the book values of a company's net assets are lower than resale values, and the share price is depressed. There is insufficient evidence to suggest that this is always an important motivation for company takeovers. But while asset resale values may or may not be the most critical consideration for the takeover bidder, such values are always relevant to the owners of the firm that is the subject of the bid. Asset resale values form the floor price below which it will benefit the owners to liquidate the firm themselves rather than accept the outside bid. As a second example, there is the reverse situation in which asset book values exceed asset resale values. The financial statements then can be dangerously misleading to owners and creditors alike, who may be induced to maintain or increase their investment in the company.

A characteristic of the CoCoA model is an uncompromising valuation rule, whereby assets must be valued at their market selling prices. As noted earlier, there are two classes of assets which may be valued at zero CCE: (a) durables without a market selling value, such as specialized plant and equipment or dies and moulds in the machine shop; and (b) specialized work in process. The acquisition or production of these assets has resulted in a reduction of the firm's adaptive capacity, which reflects a corresponding increase in risk should the firm come upon hard times. This particular dimension of risk in the firm's asset holdings is reflected in CCE measures.

Economic Significance of CoCoA Summary Measures

As noted in Chapter 18, measurement rules require that a constant measurement standard should be used and that a common property of objects should be measured. The capital maintenance adjustment in CoCoA and the uncompromising use of market selling prices satisfy these two conditions. Chambers claims that CoCoA does more than meet the additivity requirements. The sum of the CCEs of assets (including cash, the CCE of which is simply the face value of the amount) minus the CCEs of liabilities is an index of the firm's capacity to adapt, a magnitude which has an economic significance. On the other hand, it is asserted by Chambers that the sum of asset replacement costs and monetary assets is not a figure to which a well-defined economic meaning can be attached.

Consistency with Real World Events and the Allocation Problem

Transaction surpluses and price variation adjustments are CoCoA income components that represent real world events, while the capital maintenance adjustment represents a transformation of the measurement scale. Since the CoCoA income statement reflects only real world events,[3] it is claimed that it has a number of advantages, e.g. system outputs are objective and verifiable; they are also hard data in the sense that many market prices cannot be manipulated to serve sectional interests.

Thomas has noted that a particular merit of exit value income statements is their freedom from arbitrary allocations. The income statement is a factual statement representing either monetary flows or non-monetary asset price changes, whereas allocations by definition represent hypothetical flows and fictional assumptions that have no counterpart in real world events. Thomas argues that insofar as exit value income statements may appear odd to readers of financial statements, this may be attributable to an acceptance of conventional accounting allocations.

Limitations of CoCoA

A major objection to Chambers's system, other relative price change systems and the business profit approach of Edwards and Bell is their implication for operating

---

[3] For example there is no specific depreciation charge in the income statement, because depreciation represents an arbitrary allocation and is not an easily measurable real world event.

capital maintenance and the financial viability of the firm, arising from an income measurement method in which holding gains are treated as income. These matters have been discussed at some length in Chapters 19 and 20, and in an earlier section of the present chapter.

Not a Valuation Rule for All Seasons

Critics of CoCoA argue that the use of an arbitrary valuation rule means that the system lacks general applicability. In the first place, the valuation process is of little relevance to those firms which have a long-term commitment to their existing production processes. An Australian company, Hamersley, provides an illustration. This company has embarked on the production of metallized agglomerates, which involves a new and revolutionary process of treating iron ore. The plant has been established and the investment may well be irreversible, in which case adaptation is no longer a relevant objective. The counter-argument is that, even in the short run, no capital investment can be considered irreversible, provided another firm is prepared to acquire the plant and equipment. The Hamersley example has further connotations. Hamersley's main business is the mining of iron ore, and it is estimated that its mines can supply the world demand for ore for the next century or so. Hamersley's board and shareholders would undoubtedly find financial statements which report individual assets at their exit values irrelevant.

More generally, the use of a simple measure of market selling prices is not appropriate in circumstances where a firm continues to use particular assets. The general argument against single-valued accounting reports has been put earlier in the evaluation of current value accounting (see Chapter 20). Reporting the market resale prices of certain significant severable assets, such as land and buildings, is often relevant information for decision making. But there is not a strong case for reporting to management only the resale prices of all the firm's assets at the end of each financial year, when management is not contemplating the sale of all assets. The case for reporting such values to owners who take no part in the management of the firm is weaker still.

The Aggregation Problem

Several writers have pointed out that assets often command a price when sold in combination which is different from the sum of their prices when sold separately. This is the asset interaction problem, a typical example of which is the sale of a plot of land and the building thereon. Insofar as inventories are concerned, Chambers contends that the level of asset aggregation for the purpose of determining the CCEs should be consistent with the customary parcels, i.e. the way in which the firm sells the inventories in the ordinary course of business. The treatment for fixed assets should conform to the combinations in which the fixed assets are bought, sold or put out of use. The combination rule for inventories should work well, since this relates to a normal operation, but the parcelling of fixed assets is fraught with difficulties. These difficulties are compounded when assets can be combined horizontally (within asset classes) and vertically (across asset classes, i.e. by production units, such as motel units in a motel chain).

This is the aggregation problem in exit value accounting. A customary or probable parcel is not appropriate for fixed assets where there is no intention of sale. One possibility would be to use the combinations which lead to the highest figure for net worth, but the difficulty is that these combinations may embrace divisions or departments, or the entire firm itself, a distinct possibility where goodwill is present.[4] These issues are discussed by Thomas, who notes that the aggregation problem has not been resolved. Some writers believe the aggregation problem in current exit value accounting parallels the allocation problem (for which an eventual solution is unlikely to be found) in other accounting valuation systems.[5]

The Problem of Markets

If the CCEs of the firm's assets are to be readily measured, it is necessary that markets exist for the firm's assets. There are two aspects of the problem of markets which are of special importance. The first of these is concerned with identifying the market in which market selling value is to be determined, while the second is concerned with the fact that most markets are necessarily imperfect.

The measurement of income by reference to the CCEs of the firm's trading inventories poses a fundamental problem. If it is assumed (unrealistically) that there is only a single market for the firm's inventories, the application of the CoCoA approach to trading activities implies that income can only be earned by physically transforming or buying and holding inventories, and not by buying and selling inventories through the normal processes of distribution. If a firm were to sell inventories for $100, by definition it could earn no CoCoA income from the selling transaction, because the CCE of the goods sold would necessarily be $100. ·

It is obvious that the assumption of a single market must be replaced by an assumption of structured markets, because at many stages in the distribution process firms *do* buy the same commodity at one price and sell it for another. In effect, a wholesaler or retailer transforms a commodity by changing its location and by providing services which save potential purchasers from the need to organize their own purchasing activities at the wholesale or retail stage of distribution. In the system of structured markets which exists in the real world, a trading firm thus typically buys in one market and sells in another.

The question which must be answered under CoCoA accounting is, then, whether CCEs of inventories are to be determined by reference to a firm's buying market or its selling market. If CCEs are determined by reference to the selling price of the inventories in the firm's buying market, this will conform to the use of replacement value as the measure of CCE, a valuation rule that is inconsistent with the CoCoA philosophy. On the other hand, if CCEs are determined by reference to the firm's selling market, it follows logically that a trading (as opposed to a manufacturing) firm can never earn income from its *selling* activities. Rather it is implied that the firm derives income either from its *purchasing* activities, as the difference between the CCE of its inventory purchases (measured in the firm's selling market) and the cost of the inventory purchases in its buying market, or from its *holding* activities. Such a valuation rule is unrealistic, but supporters of CoCoA defend it on the ground that the basic objective of the system is to determine the firm's adaptive capacity in terms of the selling prices of its assets. The unrealistic nature of this valuation rule lies in its immoderate anticipation of profit. This may be mitigated to a small degree, if CCEs are related to the buyer's quote (rather than the seller's quote) in the selling market.

---

[4] Goodwill in the present context may be defined as the difference between the selling price of the firm as a going concern and the sum of the CCEs of its total net assets.

[5] The aggregation problem is also present, but in a less severe form, in current value accounting.

The second problem concerns market imperfections. A perfect market assumption is not necessary, but markets must exist in which there is regular trading in assets which are reasonable replicas of those owned by the firm. The assumption of active markets is not unreasonable, but may not hold in practice. For many fixed assets, second-hand markets may not exist or may be relatively thin, or the firm may have no knowledge of or access to these markets.

Where markets are thin, it may not be possible to monitor sporadic transactions. Thus CCEs may exist, but the information may prove costly or difficult to obtain.

Effect of Zero or Minimal CCEs on Income Measurement

Where specialized plant is to be written off, the loss is debited as a special price variation in the income statement. Where the amount of the loss is large, it will have an unduly adverse effect on the net income figure for the period. It is evident that considerable re-education of management as well as users of financial statements would need to be a necessary prelude to the introduction of a CoCoA system.

The valuation of partly processed goods at zero CCEs could make interpretation of the reported periodical profit figure even more difficult. New firms and expanding firms are likely to hold increasing amounts of work in process, while the reverse would apply to liquidating or contracting firms. For continuing firms, the problem may be lessened if the volume of work in process at the beginning of each accounting period is roughly equal to the volume at the end of the period. But this method of measuring work in process places in some managements' hands a tool for manipulating the reported periodical profit, which may be as damaging as devices currently available under the existing body of 'generally accepted accounting principles'.

Conclusion

Supporters of CoCoA claim that it provides more than a normative theory of accounting. It is a scientific theory based on observation of the real world. Sceptics query the dominant role of adaptation in the CoCoA system as an accurate description of how the economy functions. But a theory can lead to correct conclusions, even if its premises are in doubt. The difficulty is that it is not yet known how to test the conclusions of Chambers's theory, or indeed those of other systems.

Chambers has offered a revolutionary concept of measurement by reference to adaptive capacity. For comprehensiveness he has developed an internally consistent and logical measurement system, and has described methods of deriving CCEs as a means of obtaining objectively verifiable values for his system. Some of these methods are not free of seeming inconsistencies. While some aspects of CoCoA may be criticized, in particular its arbitrary valuation rule, the relative price change model which underlies Chambers's system has great analytical value.

References

Chambers, R.J., *Accounting, Evaluation and Economic Behavior*, Prentice-Hall, Englewood Cliffs, N.J., 1966.

Sterling, R.R., *Theory of the Measurement of Enterprise Income*, University Press of Kansas, Lawrence, Kans., 1970.

Thomas, A.L., *The Allocation Problem: Part Two;* Studies in Accounting Research No. 9, American Accounting Association, 1974, Chapter 7.

Additional Reading

Barton, A.D., *The Anatomy of Accounting*, University of Queensland Press, St Lucia, Qld, 1977, Chapters 23 and 24.

Chambers, R.J., *Accounting for Inflation*, Exposure Draft, University of Sydney, Sydney, 1975.

Chambers, R.J., 'Second Thoughts on Continuously Contemporary Accounting', *Abacus*, September 1970, pp. 39-55.

Sterling, R.R., 'Decision Oriented Financial Accounting', *Accounting and Business Research*, Summer 1972, pp. 198-208.

Wells, M.C., 'Costing for Activities', *Management Accounting*, May 1976, pp. 31-7.

Discussion Questions

1 What do you consider to be the strengths and weaknesses of a relative price change approach to income measurement?

2 Analyse the relationship between current value and general price level adjustments in the relative price change accounting model.

3 Compare the objectives and underlying assumptions of income concepts based on (a) market entry prices; (b) market exit prices; and (c) the value to the owner approach.

4 Outline the main underlying behavioural and economic assumptions of Chambers's theory and show how they lead to the formulation of the measurement rule for assets in his system. How does Chambers define an asset?

5 Examine the notion of additivity, with particular reference to the Chambers model.

6 It has been argued that the most important criterion of a good accounting system is usefulness and that the objective of accounting is to provide useful information relevant for decision making. Does CoCoA provide information which has relevance for decision making?

7 Examine and comment on the economic significance of CoCoA summary measures.

8 Critics of CoCoA argue that the use of an arbitrary valuation rule means that the system lacks general applicability. Do you agree with the critics?

9 Can the above criticism also be levied against current value and current cost systems? Discuss.

Exercises

1 By means of simple algebraic models show the relationship between current value and general price level adjustments in relative price change accounting.

2 On 1 July 1984 Mr Smith had monetary assets of $10 000 and non-monetary assets with a current value of $50 000. The corresponding figures on 1 July 1985 were $10 000 and $64 000, respectively. Assume that no transactions took place in the period and that the general price index rose from 104 to 110. What was Mr Smith's income under relative price change accounting? Relate your answer to equation (3) and equation (13) in the text.

3 The M.T. Co. Ltd had net assets with a current value of $70 000 on 31 December 1984. General price index numbers published quarterly on the last day of each quarter were as follows:

31 December 1984	105
31 March 1985	110
30 June 1985	112
30 September 1985	115
31 December 1985	120

(a) If the net assets of the company had a current value of $85 000 on 31 December 1985, what was its net income for the year under relative price change accounting?

(b) To arrive at the net income for the year is it necessary to make use of quarterly index numbers?

4 The balance of the opening inventory of the Punctured Tyre Co. was recorded in the inventory account at a CCE of $30 000. During the year goods with a CCE of $150 000 were purchased and the inventory account was debited with this amount. The purchase price was $147 000. Goods with a book value of $160 000 were sold during the year for $215 000, while selling expenses of $15 000 were incurred. The CCE measure of the closing inventory was $26 000. Calculate the total amount of the inventory price variation adjustment at the end of the year.

5 The financial statements of the Jaybee Trading Co., prepared in accordance with historical record accounting assumptions, are as follows:

Balance Sheets as at 31 December 1984 and 31 December 1985

	31 December 1984		31 December 1985	
Monetary assets		$11 500		$9 000
Inventories		5 000		8 000
Plant (at cost)	$10 000		$10 000	
Less: Accumulated depreciation	3 000	7 000	3 500	6 500
Freehold property		15 000		20 000
		$38 500		$43 500
Current liabilities		5 000		6 000
Proprietorship equity		33 500		37 500
		$38 500		$43 500

Income Statement for Year Ended 31 December 1985

Sales		$20 000
Less: Cost of sales—		
Opening inventory	$5 000	
Purchases	15 000	
	20 000	
Closing inventory	8 000	12 000
Gross profit		8 000
Less: Depreciation on plant	500	
Other expenses	1 500	2 000
Net profit before tax		6 000
Less: Tax at $33\frac{1}{3}\%$		2 000
Net profit after tax		$4 000

The company commenced trading on 1 January 1983 with a contributed capital of $28 000. On 1 January 1983 the general price index stood at 100. It rose to 105, 110 and 120 at the end of 1983, 1984 and 1985, respectively.

The CCEs of inventories and fixed assets are set out below:

	31 December 1984	31 December 1985
Inventories	$5 500	$9 000
Plant	8 000	7 000
Freehold property	16 000	25 000

You are required to prepare an income statement for the year ended 31 December 1985 and a statement of financial position as at 31 December 1984 and 31 December 1985 under the CoCoA system assuming:

(a) CCE measures are recorded at the end of the period only; and

(b) CCE measures are continuously updated.

22 Accounting Valuation Systems—Developments and Future Trends

It is possible that the next five years will witness wide-ranging and fundamental reforms in accounting practice, including the displacement of the historical record accounting system from its present dominant role in external reporting. The quickened pace of interest in accounting reform is evident from the official publications on current purchasing power (CPP) accounting and current value or current cost accounting (CCA) of the professional accounting bodies and committees of inquiry appointed by governments in recent years, as can be seen in Figure 22—A.

Figure 22—A
Official Publications on Inflation Accounting, 1973-77

Year of Publication	United Kingdom	United States	Australia	New Zealand
1973	Exposure Draft on CPP accounting			
1974	Provisional Standard on CPP accounting	Exposure Draft on CPP accounting	Exposure Draft on CPP accounting	
1975	Sandilands Report		Mathews Report Exposure Draft on CCA	Exposure Draft on CPP accounting
1976	Exposure Draft on CCA	Securities and Exchange Commission Replacement Cost Disclosure Requirements Conceptual Framework— Financial Accounting Standards Board Discussion Memorandum	Provisional Standard on CCA	Exposure Draft on CCA Richardson Report
1977	Hyde Report— Accounting Standards Committee Interim Recommendation			

Note: In Canada an exposure draft on CPP accounting was issued in 1975, and one on CCA in 1976.

There was a wide-ranging discussion of CPP accounting and CCA in the accounting literature during the 1950s and 1960s, but nearly forty years passed between the publication of Sweeney's *Stabilized Accounting* in 1936 and the promulgation of the first exposure draft on CPP accounting in 1973. The essential background to the interest of the accounting bodies and governments in adopting some form of inflation accounting was the dramatic change that was wrought in the world economy by a combination of rapid inflation and mounting recession in the 1970s; a phenomenon aptly ·described as stagflation. Taxing, accounting and pricing policies, which had traditionally evolved under conditions of relative economic stability, proved incapable of responding appropriately to a situation of rapid change. It was the principal message of the Mathews Report that, if changes were not made in accounting practices, business policies and taxing arrangements, and if rapid inflation continued, there would be an inexorable tendency to business failure.

The issue of an exposure draft on CPP accounting in 1973 by the professional bodies in the U.K. was followed by similar publications in the U.S.A. and Australia in 1974, and in N.Z. and Canada in 1975. Many accountants favoured the CPP proposals because general price level adjustments in supplementary financial statements do not represent a fundamental departure from the historical record accounting system. However, despite the merits of the latter system that are said to flow from its use of objective and hard data, the relevance of historical costs, whether indexed or not, for many user needs can be questioned. The exposure drafts on CPP accounting were subsequently superseded by exposure drafts on CCA, issued by professional accounting bodies in Australia in 1975, and in N.Z., Canada and the U.K. in 1976.[1] Further, government-appointed committees of inquiry in the U.K., Australia and N.Z. recommended in favour of adopting some form of CCA and against CPP accounting. Some of these developments are briefly explained below.

Recent Developments in Australia

The Australian Statement of Provisional Accounting Standards

The exposure draft on CPP accounting issued by the Australian Society of Accountants and the Institute of Chartered Accountants in Australia was closely modelled on the British document, but the profession never had much faith in CPP accounting and, oddly enough, said so in the draft. Within six months a new exposure draft advocating CCA was issued, followed by a statement of provisional accounting standards on CCA in October 1976. The professional bodies recommended that CCA financial statements be prepared voluntarily by companies whose accounting periods commenced on or after 1 July 1977, and indicated that it was intended that their adoption as the main financial statements would become mandatory in accounting periods on or after 1 July 1978.

The proposed CCA system represented a value to the business approach to asset valuation and income measurement. The exposure draft recommended that assets should be valued at current cost or net realizable value, depending on whether or not they were essential to on-going operations, but the notion of essentiality (which we criticized in Chapter 20) was modified in the statement of provisional standards. The latter statement recommended that non-monetary assets be measured at their

---

[1] As noted in the Introduction to Part III, the professional accounting bodies have adopted the term 'current cost accounting' as the general term for current value accounting, because of the primary emphasis on current costs as the valuation basis.

current cost (or depreciated current cost) or 'the recoverable amount', where it was not expected that current cost could be recovered through use or sale of the asset.[2] However, most assets would be valued at current cost or depreciated current cost. Current cost was to be interpreted by reference to the current cost of an asset of equivalent service potential (see Chapter 20 for a criticism of this approach).

All asset restatements were to be taken to a 'current cost adjustment account' (which was really an asset revaluation reserve), and a credit balance in this account was not to be regarded as income available for distribution. The profit of the accounting entity for the period was defined as the amount which could be distributed without impairing capital, i.e. the operating capability of the entity provided by its assets. Backlog depreciation was to be taken to the current cost adjustment account, on the ground that the adjustment formed part of the process of asset revaluation and was not an adjustment to current or past profits. Purchasing power gains and losses on monetary items were not to be recognized, but a firm decision on this issue was left open.

Generally, the recommendations were similar to the provisions of the current distributable income/operating capital maintenance approach to current value accounting, as described in Chapter 19.

There was considerable opposition by individual accountants and managements to the proposals. Additionally, there was disagreement on a number of conceptual issues, in particular the treatment of purchasing power gains and losses on monetary items. As a result, implementation of the provisional standard on CCA was deferred for a period of one year. Continuing opposition by some accountants and a large section of industry and commerce led to a revised program, which was announced by the Australian Society of Accountants and the Institute of Chartered Accountants in Australia in June 1978. Companies listed on the stock exchanges and public corporations were asked to publish voluntarily supplementary information on the current costs of fixed assets and inventories, and the current costs of depreciation and sales, for accounting periods beginning 1 July 1978. Information on gains and losses on monetary items and their method of calculation could be included. It was intended that this revised program would form a basis for the next development, the preparation of supplementary current cost financial statements. It will be seen that this revised program represents a retreat from the recommendations of the provisional standard issued in 1976, and this more cautious approach is consistent with the pace of current developments in the U.S.A. and the U.K.

In July 1978, the Australian Accounting Research Foundation published an Exposure Draft which had been prepared by the Current Cost Accounting Standards Committee on 'The Recognition of Gains and Losses on Holding Monetary Resources in the Context of Current Cost Accounting'. Unlike the proposals of the New Zealand Richardson Committee and the United Kingdom Hyde Committee (see below), the Australian Draft did not address itself to the gearing problem. It recommended that gains or losses on monetary items should be brought to account, by means of credits or debits in the profit and loss account with corresponding debits or credits in the current cost adjustment account, in respect of: '(a) monetary working capital; and (b)

---

[2] The recoverable amount was the net realizable value of assets held for sale and of non-depreciable assets. For depreciable assets, it was the amount of depreciation which would be covered by revenues after allowing for related expenses. It is doubtful if this notion can be made operational, because of the allocation problems involved.

long-term monetary assets (net of long-term borrowings where the assets form part of financing activities and it is established that they have been funded from such borrowings)'. Subject to the foregoing proviso, gains on long-term loan capital should not be recognized. It was proposed that the gains or losses be measured by reference to the rate of change during the period 'in those prices that affect the ability of the entity to service borrowers in terms of their purchasing power requirements'. For monetary working capital it was suggested that an appropriate measure would be the movement in the current cost of inventories for the period.

In July 1978, the Australian Society of Accountants and the Institute of Chartered Accountants also issued a CCA Working Guide, which was described as a manual for the use of those persons who have the responsibility for implementing CCA within business entities. The Working Guide contained four sections: dual basis accounting during interim period; fixed assets; inventories and cost of goods sold; and price indexes. The Guide did not cover the treatment of monetary items.

The Mathews Report

The moves by the professional accounting bodies in Australia to adopt a CCA system were strengthened by the report of a Commonwealth Government Committee of Inquiry into Inflation and Taxation (hereafter referred to as the Mathews Report), published in May 1975. The Mathews Report was concerned especially with taxation, although it emphasized the essential interdependence of accounting standards, business policies and taxation arrangements, and much of its analysis was directed to general questions of income measurement and capital maintenance. The Report was concerned with two principal effects of inflation, identified respectively as the tendency for rising money incomes to be associated with increasing rates of personal income tax, and the tendency for inflation to change the effective tax base of business enterprises. It was argued that when the rate of inflation passes a critical level, its effects on the taxation system change in kind as well as degree, so that it becomes difficult for the economic system to adapt in conventional ways. It was because this threshold of adaptation had long since been passed that substantial changes needed to be made in the bases of both personal and business taxation. With respect to personal income tax, the Report recommended a form of personal tax indexation to prevent effective *rates* of tax from rising merely because of inflation-induced increases in money incomes. The effects of inflation on business taxation, on the other hand, were seen to be concerned essentially with the tax *base* adopted for business enterprises, i.e. with the measure of income used for taxation purposes.

The Mathews Committee argued that, on the basis of existing accounting, pricing and taxing arrangements, a firm could only survive under conditions of rapid inflation by adopting one or more of the following policy options: continuously increasing its profit mark-up relative to costs, without simultaneously increasing its profit distribution; continuously increasing its indebtedness; or continuously raising fresh capital. If it could not do these things, it needed continuously to reduce the amounts of its profit distribution or reduce the scale of its operations, ultimately to the point of extinction. The Committee showed that, especially in a period of rapid inflation and depressed economic conditions, constraints operate to prevent firms from continuously increasing prices and profit margins, from continuously borrowing or raising fresh capital, or from continuously reducing its profit distributions.

This meant that if there was no diminution in the rate of inflation and if there were no changes in accounting practices, pricing policies and the basis of business taxation, the inevitable consequence would be business failure. The only hope of avoiding this cataclysmic situation lay in reducing the rate of inflation to a level where firms could adapt in one or more of the ways indicated; or in changing the basis of accounting measurement, pricing policy and business taxation. The Mathews Report was therefore directed to a consideration of how these changes might be effected.

After considering alternative proposals, including suggestions for modifying the historical record approach by means of devices such as the last-in-first-out method of inventory valuation, the Committee proposed the adoption of a modified concept of taxable income for all businesses, based on the current value concept of income. It was shown that, in order to adapt the existing concept of taxable income to such a current value concept, only two simple valuation adjustments were needed in the form of allowable deductions from assessable income. These were described as a cost of sales valuation adjustment and a depreciation valuation adjustment. The cost of sales valuation adjustment would be calculated approximately and simply as the difference between opening inventories valued at actual prices and opening inventories valued at the same prices as closing inventories. If inventory levels or prices fell, or if the ownership of a business changed hands, the cost of sales valuation adjustment would be positive, i.e. assessable income would be increased.

Insofar as depreciation was concerned, the Committee proposed a method of indexing depreciation allowances whereby replacement cost coefficients would be derived from a published index and applied to historical cost depreciation charges, classified by reference to the age structure of the assets being depreciated.

It is of interest to note that some of the recommendations in the Mathews Report were subsequently implemented by the Government. Personal tax indexation was introduced, more or less along the lines proposed by the Committee, on 1 July 1976. Also, a simplified and partial scheme of so-called trading stock valuation adjustments was introduced in respect of business incomes earned in 1976-77 and subsequent years.

Recent Developments in New Zealand

The N.Z. exposure draft on CPP accounting was issued in March 1975, and it was superseded by the exposure draft on current cost accounting (CCA) issued in August 1976. Of particular interest is the Report of the Committee of Inquiry into Inflation Accounting (hereafter referred to as the Richardson Report) published in December 1976. Like the Australian Statement on Provisional Accounting Standards and the Mathews Report, the Richardson Report also recommended the adoption of a form of CCA.

The Richardson Report

Under the Richardson recommendations, an *enterprise's* periodic profit was to be measured as the amount which was left after maintaining intact its operating capacity. This was described as its current cost operating profit, defined as the difference between its revenue and the current cost of the inputs used up or expended in generating the revenue. For the purpose of calculating current cost operating profit, cost of sales and depreciation would be valued by reference to the current cost of assets used or sold, the difference between historical cost and current cost being taken to a capital maintenance reserve. Depreciation would be measured by reference to the current cost of assets at the end of the accounting period.

The Richardson Committee proposed that assets should be valued on the basis of their value to the enterprise, which would be determined by reference to the notion of essentiality that had been formulated in the earlier Australian exposure draft on current value accounting (see our criticisms in Chapter 20). Asset valuation adjustments, like income valuation adjustments, would be carried to a capital maintenance reserve. Backlog depreciation would also be accounted for by means of an adjustment to the capital maintenance reserve. [3]

On monetary items, the Committee proposed that circulating monetary assets—those monetary assets needed to service an enterprise's normal operations—should be subject to a valuation adjustment. This was to be calculated initially by reference to changes in a general price index of inputs which was being developed by the Department of Statistics, and would be taken into account in calculating the current cost operating profit of the enterprise as well as being reflected in the capital maintenance reserve.

By contrast, no gains on liabilities were to be taken into the current operating profit of the enterprise. Instead the Committee made an important distinction between the current cost operating profit of the enterprise (the concept described above) and what it called profit attributable to the owners. The latter was to be calculated by deducting interest on borrowings from current cost operating profit, and by adding or deducting an amount representing the proportion of the change in the capital maintenance reserve which had been financed by total borrowings. In this way, the gain attributable to liabilities and the share of the loss on monetary assets which had previously been recorded would both be taken into the (distributable) profit attributable to the owners, and the capital maintenance reserve would be reduced to the extent necessary to restore the original relationship between owners' funds and borrowed funds.

The Committee envisaged that current cost concepts should also be used for pricing and taxation purposes. Its recommendations on taxation generally followed the recommendations on accounting and financial reporting; in particular, gains from the use of borrowed funds were to be taken into assessable income as an offset against the cost of sales, depreciation and circulating monetary asset adjustments. Taxable profit would then be profit attributable to the owners or historical cost profit, whichever was the lower. The Committee recommended that for taxation purposes the monetary asset adjustment should be limited to trade accounts receivable, and that there should be no clawback on the cost of sales adjustment.

The Treatment of Monetary Items

There is an internal consistency in either a pure current value system (in which all items are recorded in terms of current prices) or a relative price change system (which combines current value adjustments with general price level adjustments for all items). But there is no logic in a system which combines current value adjustments for

---

[3] The Richardson Report did not distinguish between income and asset revaluation reserves, or income and asset valuation adjustments. We believe that a conceptual distinction needs to be made between income and asset valuation adjustments. The logic of measuring current cost depreciation by reference to the average value of assets (instead of the end-of-period value, as suggested by the Committee), and of treating backlog depreciation as part of the asset revaluation process, will then become more obvious and more compelling.

non-monetary assets with general price level adjustments for only monetary assets and liabilities.

As noted in Chapter 19, however, some writers have argued that purchasing-power losses and gains on monetary assets and liabilities should be brought into the measurement of current distributable income. As the Richardson Committee emphasized, the owners of an enterprise do suffer losses or derive gains from holding monetary assets or liabilities under conditions of changing prices. Moreover, failure to recognize net gains on liabilities, while making valuation adjustments in respect of non-monetary assets, will result in a continuing reduction in the debt-equity ratio so long as inflation continues.

The Richardson Committee made a significant contribution to the income measurement problem in its proposed treatment of the vexed question of gains and losses on monetary items. The Committee's solution to the problem was to record the loss on circulating monetary assets as a current cost adjustment rather than as a general purchasing power loss, and to treat the net increase in the capital maintenance reserve as profit attributable to the owners to the extent that it was financed by liabilities.

The main reservations we have about the Richardson proposals concern the separation of cash, trade debtors and other monetary assets on the one hand from trade creditors, bank overdraft and other short-term liabilities on the other; and the proposed use of a general index to measure the loss on monetary assets. It would be more logical to offset short-term liabilities against monetary assets in order to derive a measure of net monetary assets, and to measure the loss on net monetary assets by reference to the current price changes of non-monetary assets (as given by the proportion of income valuation adjustments to the average current value of non-monetary assets). There would then be a lower loss on monetary assets than under the Richardson proposals, and the gain on liabilities would be limited to long-term liabilities.

Nonetheless, the distinction which the Committee made between current cost operating profit and profit attributable to the owners is most useful for purposes of analysis, and represents a major contribution by the Committee to the development of inflation accounting.

Recent Developments in the United Kingdom

The first exposure draft on CPP accounting in English-speaking countries was published by the professional accounting bodies in the U.K. in January 1973. It met with a mild but encouraging response from accountants and businessmen, and was followed by the issue of a provisional standard in May 1974. The U.K. Government was also concerned about the high rates of inflation and the movement towards accounting reform, and had responded by appointing in mid-1973 a Committee of Inquiry to consider inflation accounting and company accounts. The report of this Committee (hereafter referred to as the Sandilands Report), published in September 1975, spelt the death knell of the profession's CPP proposals (at least for the foreseeable future).

The Sandilands Report

The recommendations of the Sandilands Committee (which reported in June 1975) were remarkably similar to those of the Mathews Committee. Perhaps one reason for this was that the two Committees had been asked to report in similar circumstances of rampant inflation and developing malaise (in particular, a liquidity crisis) in the business sector, which made it impossible to maintain the long-standing illusion that accounting is not concerned with valuation.

The principal recommendations of the Sandilands Committee on financial accounting and reporting involved a change to a system described by the Committee as current cost accounting (CCA), in which valuation adjustments on inventories and fixed assets were to be distinguished from operating profit calculated by reference to current costs. The Committee suggested that current cost operating profit should be derived from historic cost profit, by making a cost of sales adjustment and a depreciation adjustment to bring historical costs into line with current costs. Assets should be recorded on the basis of their value to the business if it should be deprived of their use. This might be current replacement cost, so-called economic (or present) value or net realizable value. There should be no adjustments for monetary assets and liabilities.

The Committee recommended against alternative methods of accounting for inflation, such as the last-in-first-out method of inventory valuation or the current purchasing power method of accounting. The Committee envisaged that CCA would be adopted for purposes of taxation, pricing and other aspects of business policy, but believed that such a fundamental change in tax arrangements should not be introduced without a comprehensive review of the whole taxation system. The Committee also recommended that a steering group be established under the Accounting Standards Committee to develop a statement of standard accounting practice on CCA.

Criticisms of the Sandilands Committee recommendations have been made on various grounds. Its uncompromising rejection of general price level indexation particularly irked some academics and accountants. Another criticism concerned its failure to take account of purchasing power gains and losses on monetary items, but this was consistent with its underlying CCA philosophy. Judged by an objectively measurable and internally consistent current valuation model, the principal weaknesses in the Sandilands Report were its proposed use of economic or present value for the measurement of assets under some circumstances (which we criticized in Chapter 20) and the recommendation that depreciation should be calculated by reference to end-of-year values, which would have the effect of confusing the valuation adjustment required for purposes of income measurement with the asset valuation adjustment needed for purposes of the balance sheet.

The Exposure Draft on CCA

An Inflation Accounting Steering Group (Chairman: Mr D. Morpeth) was duly established by the U.K. professional bodies in accordance with the Sandilands recommendations, and its exposure draft on CCA (ED 18) was published in November 1976.

The exposure draft generally followed the Sandilands guidelines, the main innovations being:

(a) a requirement that the financial statements should 'include a statement, by way of note, setting out prominently the gain or loss for the period of account in the shareholders' net equity interest after allowance has been made for the change in the value of money during the period' (as measured by a general index of retail prices), and that a separate analysis should be provided of the gain or loss on holding monetary assets and liabilities during the period; and

(b) a requirement that the financial statements should include a new statement—the appropriation account—in which 'will be brought together the current cost profit, the revaluation surpluses, the amount which the directors consider should be retained within the business having regard to their assessment of its needs, and dividends'. (Although the draft adopted a permissive approach to transfers to or from revaluation reserves, guidelines for such transfers were provided in an appendix which did not form part of the standard.)

The British exposure draft thus incorporated a type of relative price change approach in the measurement of owners' equity.[4] ED 18 was criticized, among other things, for the complexity of its proposals. A special meeting of accountants in July 1977 rejected any mandatory system of current cost accounting, and by implication ED 18.

An Interim Recommendation by the Accounting Standards Committee

Following the rejection of ED 18 by the profession, the Accounting Standards Committee in November 1977 published new interim guidelines for inflation accounting and recommended that these be adopted by companies listed on the stock exchange with respect to financial statements ending on or after 31 December 1977. The interim proposals were prepared by a group under the chairmanship of Mr W. Hyde, and represented a modified (and more modest) approach to CCA. Initial responses from accountants and businessmen appeared to be favourable.

The Interim Recommendation revealed a philosophy characterized by simplicity, willingness to compromise and a low profile. First, the interim proposals constituted a recommendation rather than a mandate. Second, the historical cost financial statements were to remain the main financial reports and the CCA statements were to be supplementary reports for an indefinite trial period. Third, three adjustments were to be made to the historical cost financial statements in order to prepare CCA statements, as explained below:

(a) *Depreciation adjustment*. The Accounting Standards Committee first proposed that an adjustment should be made for the difference between depreciation based on historical cost and depreciation based on the current cost of fixed assets. A business could use its own established method of computing current cost depreciation. Otherwise, it was recommended that appropriate industry-specific or asset-specific indexes, as published by the government of the territory in which the fixed assets are located, should be employed.

(b) *Cost of sales adjustment*. It was suggested that a business could use its own established method of computing the current cost of sales. Otherwise, it was recommended that the appropriate index or indexes published by the government

---

[4] A similar approach (but one incorporating the purchasing power adjustment in the accounts) was recommended in a recent Canadian discussion paper, *Current Value Accounting*, published by the Canadian Institute of Chartered Accountants in August 1976, while the N.Z. exposure draft on CCA proposed that the effects on owners' equity of changes in general purchasing power should be shown in a separate statement.

of the territory in which the goods are traded should be employed. The averaging method of computing the current cost of sales should be used (see Chapter 19 for a description of an averaging method).

(c) *Gearing adjustment*. A major innovation in the Interim Recommendation involved the introduction of a so-called gearing adjustment. The Mathews Committee had noted that, to the extent that inventories and fixed assets are financed by liabilities rather than owners' equity, purchasing power gains could be regarded as a partial offset against cost of sales and depreciation valuation adjustments. As noted above, the Richardson Committee suggested that this problem could be dealt with by making a separate income adjustment for circulating monetary assets, and by taking account of interest and purchasing power gains on liabilities for the purpose of distinguishing between current cost operating profit and profit attributable to the owners. The Hyde Committee went further by proposing a gearing adjustment which would have the effect of overcoming the criticisms of the Richardson Report which we made earlier. A business could develop its own method of calculating a gearing adjustment. Otherwise, the following method was recommended.

Let MA = average total monetary assets (average of opening and end-year values),

L = average total liabilities plus preference share capital,

OE = average owners' equity, including asset revaluation reserves,

IVA = total income valuation adjustment (i.e. the cost of sales and depreciation valuation adjustments), and

z = percentage change in an appropriate index during the year.

(i) Where total liabilities exceed total monetary assets, an amount equal to $\dfrac{L - MA}{(L - MA) + OE} \times IVA$ should be credited as a gearing adjustment in the current cost income statement.

(ii) Where total monetary assets exceed total liabilities, an amount equal to $z(MA - L)$ should be charged as a gearing adjustment in the current cost income statement.

Where total liabilities exceed monetary assets, the gearing adjustment would thus have the effect of increasing the current operating profit, i.e. the income valuation adjustments in respect of cost of sales and depreciation would be restricted to the portion financed by owners' equity. On the other hand, where monetary assets exceed liabilities, the gearing adjustment would result in a smaller current operating profit, i.e. an additional amount would be set aside to maintain the operating capacity of the business. The adjustment would immediately have the effect of recognizing the erosion of the monetary assets of institutions such as banks, finance companies and insurance companies as a result of increases in the general price level.

Recent Developments in the United States

In line with its counterparts in other countries, the Financial Accounting Standards Board (FASB), a body in the U.S.A. concerned with the promulgation and development of accounting standards (replacing the old Accounting Principles Board), published an exposure draft on CPP accounting in December 1974. As in other countries, this statement was also soon overtaken by events.

Replacement Cost Disclosure Requirements of the Securities and Exchange Commission

On 24 March 1976, the Securities and Exchange Commission (SEC) issued a statement requiring most large companies (about 1 000 of the largest industrial companies in the U.S.A.) to disclose the following replacement cost data in financial statements ending on or after 25 December 1976:

(a) current replacement cost of closing inventories;

(b) current cost of sales, i.e. the replacement cost of goods at the time of sale;

(c) gross and depreciated replacement cost of productive capacity; and

(d) depreciation expense on a replacement cost basis.

Companies were also required to disclose the methods used in determining replacement cost data.

Many of the companies that complied with the SEC's requirements in the following year expressed grave concern about the misleading nature of the replacement cost data. Criticisms by the reporting companies included complaints that the disclosure rules were not well defined, so that some disclosures were meaningless while others lacked comparability as between different companies. Further, it was said that the use of replacement cost data led to distortions in the income statement; cost of sales and depreciation expense at replacement cost were higher than historical cost figures, but the replacement cost figures did not reflect operating economies which would have resulted from the use of more efficient assets had replacement taken place. Many managements said they were concerned with the subjectivity of the estimates they were required to make. The following statement by General Motors is an indication of a wide-spread dissatisfaction: [5]

> Although the replacement-cost data herein disclosed have, in the Corporation's view, been estimated in a reasonable manner, it is the opinion of management that these data are of no value because of the subjectivity necessarily involved in making these estimates, and because the concept is based on an unrealistic premise, i.e. the total replacement of all productive capacity at one time.
>
> Accordingly, these data must be viewed as simply the result of the mathematical calculations based on the guidelines established by the SEC.

These criticisms must be treated with reserve because for some purposes (e.g. capital raising) company managements have an interest in maintaining the historical record illusion with respect to income measurement and asset valuation. Nonetheless, there is a danger that the SEC might have unintentionally put back the clock with respect to the adoption of current value accounting in the U.S.A., by requiring companies to comply with replacement cost disclosure rules before a uniform current cost methodology has been formulated, indeed before a current value philosophy has won wide acceptance. The SEC has said it plans to conduct a major review of the entire program in 1978.

The Conceptual Framework Project of the Financial Accounting Standards Board

In December 1976, the FASB launched its conceptual framework project by publishing two documents, *Tentative Conclusions on Objectives of Financial*

---

[5] This should be contrasted with the position taken by Broken Hill Pty Co. Ltd, one of the largest companies in Australia, which voluntarily employs replacement cost depreciation in its accounts, because of the utility of this information for management decision making.

Statements of Business Enterprises (hereafter referred to as the Tentative Conclusions) and *Conceptual Framework for Financial Accounting and Reporting: Elements of Financial Statements and Their Measurement* (hereafter referred to as the Discussion Memorandum). A conceptual framework was defined as 'a *constitution*, a coherent system of interrelated objectives and fundamentals that can lead to consistent standards and that prescribes the nature, function and limits of financial accounting and financial statements. The objectives identify the goals and purposes of accounting. The fundamentals are the underlying concepts of accounting...' The project is an ambitious one; it is expected to chart future developments for financial accounting and reporting for many years. Specifically, the project is expected to lead to FASB pronouncements on the fundamental issues discussed below.

The Tentative Conclusions study was based on the *Report of the Study Group on the Objectives of Financial Statements* (also known as the Trueblood Report) published by the American Institute of Certified Public Accountants (AICPA) in October 1973. The Tentative Conclusions identified the users of financial statements as present and potential investors and creditors, and reaffirmed that the role of financial statements is to provide information useful to investors and creditors in making investment and credit decisions. Emphasis was laid on providing information to assess the prospects for cash flows to the business, on which the cash flows to investors and creditors depend. The Tentative Conclusions document provided a frame of reference for the conceptual framework project itself.

Unlike the Tentative Conclusions, the Discussion Memorandum contained no conclusions of the FASB, but rather was an analysis of issues, undertaken in three parts. In Part I, the nature of the elements of financial statements, i.e. assets, liabilities, revenues, expenses, etc. was explored. Three competing concepts of earnings were offered for discussion: the asset and liability view or capital maintenance view (i.e. earnings measured as a change in net resources); the revenue and expense view (i.e. the matching-accrual approach to income measurement); and the nonarticulation view in which different measurement systems may apply to the statement of financial position and the income statement, which are regarded as independent of each other and may not articulate. Part II dealt with the qualitative characteristics of financial information, i.e. qualitative criteria such as those discussed earlier in Chapter 6.

Part III was concerned with what attribute or attributes should be used in measuring assets and liabilities. Five attributes or valuation bases were suggested: (a) historical cost; (b) current cost; (c) current exit value in orderly liquidation; (d) expected exit value in due course of business; and (e) present value of expected cash flows. The Memorandum discussed the use of a particular attribute as an ideal and the use of surrogate measures when the ideal is not attainable. The view that different attributes may be appropriate depending on the nature or class of assets or liabilities to be measured was considered. As there had been an earlier discussion memorandum on CPP accounting, the unit of measurement was not given detailed consideration, but it was pointed out that each of the attributes could be measured in terms of dollars or purchasing power units.

Public hearings on the issues raised in the Discussion Memorandum were held in 1977 and more hearings were expected to follow. Further, some 25 to 30 companies were expected to participate in an experimental project conducted by the American Institute of Certified Public Accountants (AICPA), in which the companies would measure their performance by reference to each of several alternative accounting measurement models. [6]

Proposed Statement of Financial Accounting Concepts

As a result of the public hearings on the elements of financial statements contained in the Discussion Memorandum, the FASB issued an Exposure Draft, *Objectives of Financial Reporting and Elements of Financial Statements of Business Enterprises*, on 29 December 1977. This is the first in a series of Statements of Financial Accounting Concepts, which are intended to aid in the development of financial accounting and reporting standards, but are not intended to supersede any existing accounting standards and principles.

The recommendations of the Exposure Draft on objectives and elements of financial statements were to a large extent foreshadowed by the Tentative Conclusions study (which was itself based on the Trueblood Report). The Exposure Draft identified the users of financial statements as existing and potential investors and creditors, and specified that the basic goal of accounting is to meet their information needs for decision making. It was believed that investors and creditors need information useful in assessing cash flow prospects, i.e. the amounts, timing and uncertainty of cash flows accruing to them, which in turn are dependent on the amounts, timing and uncertainty of cash flows accruing to the firm itself. The focus of the analysis was on long-term cash flows, which reflect the firm's earning power. This earning power was believed to be a function of the firm's endowment and management of economic resources and obligations. The document thus argued that accounting's main function is to provide information about economic resources and obligations, and changes in them.

Although the Exposure Draft reflected the earlier thinking of the Tentative Conclusions study and the Trueblood Report, there were certain distinguishing features. The Exposure Draft placed an increased emphasis on *financial reporting*, and an implication of this could be the development of a dual reporting system. This development envisages that subjective, relatively soft and predictive purpose-oriented financial data may be disclosed in special financial reports, which are complementary to and outside the relatively objective financial statements. Some of these future oriented data are already provided, e.g. replacement cost data and forecasts. A further implication is that such data may fall within the auditor's ambit.

The Exposure Draft also placed emphasis on the fundamental roles of the relevance and reliability criteria. It stated that at least a minimum level of each of these qualities is essential if accounting information is to be useful to decision-makers. Unfortunately the document did not specify the trade-off between the two criteria. Insofar as an earlier study, *A Statement of Basic Accounting Theory*, published by the American Accounting Association in 1966 had emphasized relevance as the primary criterion, it may be said that the Exposure Draft had not broken any new ground (indeed it might have regressed in not recognizing the dominance of relevance) and that a conflict between it and other criteria could arise. On the other hand, the identification by an authoritative professional accounting body of relevance as one of the two most important qualities of accounting information was a significant step.

---

[6] Similar empirical programs are being conducted or planned in N.Z., Australia, the U.K. and other countries. The value of such research could be greatly increased by international co-operation.

The Exposure Draft did not deal with measurement problems, which presumably will be the subject matter of a subsequent document.

Status Reports, No. 63, March 1, 1978 and No. 64, April 13, 1978

The views of the FASB on the CCA controversy itself were expressed in two Status Reports issued in the first half of 1978. The FASB believed that 'a great deal of work must be done, including experimentation, before current value accounting could, if ever, replace the historical cost system, whether in general or in specific industries'. Moreover, if any major changes in measurement concepts and measurement methods were to be adopted, they would be introduced by way of supplementary disclosure. The FASB saw certain advantages in this approach; first, it would provide an opportunity to gain experience in preparing current cost financial statements under relatively flexible guidelines and, second, it would permit the larger companies to report in current cost terms in the initial development stages without implying that the basic financial statements of large and small companies should be based on different underlying concepts.

Statement on Accounting Theory and Theory Acceptance

The American Accounting Association (AAA) published *A Statement of Basic Accounting Theory* (ASOBAT) in 1966. ASOBAT, a forward looking and optimistic document, was intended to reflect accounting thought in the 1960s. The committee which produced ASOBAT argued that relevance was the most important of the four accounting standards [7] (the others being verifiability, freedom from bias and quantifiability), and on this ground concluded that current cost financial statements, adjusted for general price level changes, should be prepared, since it was believed that such statements would contain the most relevant accounting information for user needs.

No such staunch and confident spirit exists in the accounting thinking of the 1970s, as is evident in the *Statement on Accounting Theory and Theory Acceptance* (hereafter abbreviated to SATTA) published by the AAA in 1977. This document, too, was a synthesis of the accounting thought of its time, but otherwise differed drastically from its predecessor. The SATTA Committee found that there was no single universally accepted accounting theory, but discerned three basic approaches to accounting theory development, which the Committee called (a) classical models; (b) decision usefulness; and (c) information economics. The classical models comprised (i) the 'true income' approach, a normative deductive school in which many of the writers supported some form of current value accounting; and (ii) an inductive approach in which writers defended or rationalized existing accounting practice. The Committee discussed decision usefulness in terms of both decision models and decision users. With respect to the former they were particularly concerned with the relevance of cash flows as inputs to decision models. Decision users were analysed on an individual user basis and an aggregate market-level basis. Empirical research at the individual user level has been largely concerned with 'behavioural accounting research', i.e. with individual user behaviour and response to accounting disclosure. However, the Committee pointed out that this research lacks a sound theoretical and methodological base, and has been disappointing in its inability to produce positive

[7] The term 'standards' is synonymous with qualitative criteria.

results. In contrast, the aggregate market-level research has been successful in using well-grounded economic theory to develop empirically testable hypotheses about the informational content of accounting data. The results have helped considerably to enrich the knowledge of accounting.

The third approach, information economics, is perhaps the most recent approach to accounting theory development and has still to stand the test of time. Information is recognized as an economic good and hence accounting information too is an economic good. Thus the production of accounting information involves an economic choice based on a cost-benefit criterion. In particular, some writers claim that externally reported accounting information is a public good[8] and, moreover, that management can only provide accounting information to any single external user by making the information available to all users. This leads to the possibility of inefficient resource allocation, if the production of accounting information is left to the market. In turn, this raises the question whether the production should be regulated and, if so, in what manner.

The Committee also discerned a number of fundamental problem areas in accounting theory development. They comprise the general problem of relating theories to practice, the allocation problem, the roles of normative standards and cost-benefit considerations in accounting theories, the danger of the assumption that more disclosure is intrinsically desirable, and the implications of the theories and associated empirical research findings in finance (e.g. the work on the efficient market hypothesis and the capital asset pricing model). The Committee believed that these 'points of conflict ... collectively explain why no theoretical approach has achieved consensus acceptance'.

After all these years of debate and research, there is still no general agreement among accountants on the uses that are served by accounting data, the identity of the users and the nature of their decision processes, or the environment in which users and accountants operate. Even the Committee's observation and interpretation of the approaches that have been adopted to accounting theory formation, and its analysis of the contemporary points of conflict, are controversial and debatable. The Committee concluded that 'theory closure cannot be dictated' and further that 'all theory approaches are flawed when viewed from the perspective of some alternative approach'. What accounting so clearly lacks is a paradigm, i.e. a disciplinary matrix or central body of theory to which all (or nearly all) theorists and researchers sub-scribe, which in turn shapes their perceptions of the world and of the fundamental problems of their discipline. The major conclusion of the Committee was that 'until consensus paradigm acceptance occurs, the utility of accounting theories in aiding policy decisions is partial'. Accounting appears to be in a stage of transition, in which competing theories are evaluated and hotly debated, that necessarily precedes the emergence of a consensus paradigm. Unfortunately the process of achieving consensus is not well understood.

---

[8] Unlike most other economic goods, a public good is one whose consumption or use by one individual does not reduce the amount available for consumption or use by other individuals, once the good has been produced, e.g. television programs.

References

Inflation Accounting, Report of the Inflation Accounting Committee, H.M.S.O., London, 1975 (referred to as the Sandilands Report).

Inflation and Taxation, Report of Committee of Inquiry into Inflation and Taxation, Australian Government Publishing Service, Canberra, 1975 (referred to as the Mathews Report).

Proposed Statement of Standard Accounting Practice — ED 18: Current Cost Accounting, Accounting Standards Committee (U.K.), 1977.

Report of the Committee of Inquiry into Inflation Accounting, Government Printer, Wellington, 1976 (referred to as the Richardson Report).

Statement of Provisional Accounting Standards: Current Cost Accounting (DPS 1.1), The Institute of Chartered Accountants in Australia and Australian Society of Accountants, 1976.

Additional Reading

Burton, J.C., 'A Symposium on the Conceptual Framework', *Journal of Accountancy*, January 1978, pp. 53-8.

Conceptual Framework for Financial Accounting and Reporting: Elements of Financial Statements and Their Measurement, Financial Accounting Standards Board Discussion Memorandum, 1976.

Flynn, T.D., 'Why We Should Account for Inflation', *Harvard Business Review*, September-October 1977, pp. 145-57.

Mathews, R., 'The Shift to Current Values: The Mathews and Richardson Reports', *The Accountants' Journal*, April 1977, pp. 85-92.

Objectives of Financial Reporting and Elements of Financial Statements of Business Enterprises, Proposed Statement of Financial Accounting Concepts, Financial Accounting Standards Board, 1977.

Scope and Implications of the Conceptual Framework Project, Financial Accounting Standards Board, 1976.

Tentative Conclusions on Objectives of Financial Statements of Business Enterprises, Financial Accounting Standards Board, 1976.

Discussion Questions

1 Do you consider general price level accounting proposals a progressive or retrograde step in the present state of (a) accounting theory; and (b) accounting practice.

2 Over the past years there has been an acceleration of interest in accounting reform. Comment on recent developments in this area in Australia.

3 What was the main area of concern of the Mathews Report? Briefly describe the recommendations brought down by the Mathews Committe.

4 Compare and contrast the recommendations of the Mathews Report with the recommendations of the Richardson Report in N.Z.

5 Comment on the treatment of monetary items by the Richardson Committee.

6 Outline briefly the principal recommendations of the Sandilands Report. Do you agree with the criticisms levelled at its recommendations?

7 What innovations were made to the Sandilands recommendations by the Inflation Accounting Steering Group?

8 Following the rejection of ED 18 by the accounting profession in the U.K., the Accounting Standards Committee in November 1977 published new interim guidelines for inflation accounting. Comment on these interim recommendations.

9 Discuss the recent developments in the U.S.A. in accounting for inflation, with particular reference to:

(a) the replacement cost disclosure requirements of the SEC;
(b) the Conceptual Framework Project of the FASB; and
(c) the first Statement of Financial Accounting Concepts issued by the FASB.

10 In the year 2001, a Nobel Prize is to be awarded to the proponent of an accounting system which serves the objectives of accounting more adequately than other systems in the past. Describe the system you would submit to the Noble Prize Committee. What inherently insoluble problems still remain unanswered in your system? Discuss.

Part IV

Cost Accounting and Management Decision Making

Introduction to Part IV: Cost Accounting, Planning and Decision Making

Traditionally, accounting information is extracted from historical record data for the use of both internal and external parties. The internal users are the managers of the organization, and the external users include shareholders, investment analysts, customers, employees and government agencies. In the past, management has used accounting information mainly to evaluate and control the organization's performance, while external users have been interested in the profitability, dividend distribution and financial viability of the business as well as the credibility of the information itself. In effect, an historical data base accounting system is an information system designed to satisfy the traditional requirements of internal and external users.

In more recent years, management has placed greater emphasis on the relevance of the accounting system output for decision making. As a result, the role of the accounting information system has broadened and taken on new perspectives. From a management viewpoint, an effective accounting system is one which is oriented to the future and whose output fulfils the needs of complex management decision models.

However, as noted in Chapter 8, accounting information is only one of several essential inputs to management decision models. These models typically make use of information on production, marketing, personnel and the business environment, in addition to accounting and financial information. Thus the ideal information system is a unified structure containing several information sub-systems. Accounting may be a dominant sub-system in some organizations but may be less important in others. In Part IV, our focus will be on the development of an accounting information sub-system within a general frame of reference directed to management needs.[1]

Chapters 23 to 25 examine the role of historical record information for income measurement and product costing purposes and also as an input to the decision-making process, because feedback for the control of continuing operations depends on the recording and analysis of data relating to operations in past periods. The use of standard costs for control purposes is explained in Chapter 26.

Planning is perhaps the most important entrepreneurial function of top management. Successful planning is vital for the firm's future growth, often for survival itself. Chapter 27 is concerned with long-range planning; Chapter 28 with the formulation of short-term plans and budgets. Capital projects are the means by which management attempts to achieve the objectives of its long-range plans; capital budgeting problems are treated in Chapter 29. Finally, Chapter 30 deals with the role of an accounting information system in solving tactical business problems associated with the implementation of short-run plans.

Thus Part IV presents an overview of the role of an accounting sub-system in planning, control and decision making. While the coverage is not exhaustive, we have attempted to provide a balanced exposure to the fundamental problems that exist in the management accounting and cost accounting areas.

---

[1] Chapter 9 considered the development of an accounting information sub-system in a specialized frame of reference, i.e. computerized systems.

23 Cost Concepts

It is already clear from earlier chapters that cost is not a term to which one can attach an unambiguous or unequivocal meaning. There are many different concepts of cost in accounting, and the one which is relevant in any particular context depends very much on the purpose to be served by the cost calculation. In general, cost information is needed for three different purposes. The first is a financial accounting purpose, involving the measurement of costs as part of the process of income determination and asset valuation. The second is a cost accounting purpose, relating to planning and cost control. The third purpose in providing cost information is concerned with another managerial problem, that of formulating business policy and making operating decisions. [1]

With respect to the first and second of these purposes, different assumptions or objectives give rise to different methods of calculating costs. In measuring business income, for example, one is faced with the problems of deciding on satisfactory methods of calculating depreciation, valuing inventories and distinguishing costs from losses, as well as with wider problems associated with the treatment of overhead cost (see Chapter 25) and the accounting response to price changes. Likewise, in dealing with planning and the cost control problem, it is necessary to consider the effect on costs of changes in output, the extent to which different kinds of costs are controllable, and the significance of cost norms established for purposes of budgeting or standard costing (as will be explained in subsequent chapters).

The need to distinguish between relevant and irrelevant costs applies equally to the problems of formulating business policy and making business decisions, such as capital investment plans (Chapter 29) and certain production and pricing decisions (Chapter 30). In many decision contexts, the relevant costs may be non-accounting costs, i.e. costs that are not recorded in the accounting system (see Figure 23—A).

The cost classifications shown in Figure 23—A are grouped by the purpose which the cost concepts are believed to serve. This grouping is very tentative, e.g. all cost concepts have some degree of relevance for decision making. Figure 23—A highlights the dichotomization of accounting cost concepts (other than the cost element classification) into two opposed and mutually exclusive parts.

---

[1] Of course, some decision making is always involved in planning and control.

Figure 23—A
Cost Classifications

Broad Purpose of Classification	Cost Classification
Financial purpose—asset valuation and income measurement	Cost elements—material cost, labour cost and expense
	Direct and indirect costs
	Product and period costs
Cost accounting purpose—planning and control	Variable and fixed costs
	Controllable and non-controllable costs
Decision making: non-accounting costs	Opportunity costs
	Future costs
Decision making: accounting costs	Incremental and sunk costs
	Avoidable and non-avoidable costs

Cost Classifications for Income Measurement

Cost Elements

Manufacturing costs are classified for accounting purposes in order that the cost concepts which are relevant for managerial needs may be identified and measured. The primary classification which needs to be made is an extension of the natural basis of classification that was described in Chapter 2, and results in a division of manufacturing costs and expenses into three elements known as *material cost, labour cost* and *expense*. These three elements represent respectively the cost of raw materials used in manufacture, wages paid to factory employees, and all other expenses (such as rent, power, depreciation of machines) incurred by the factory.

Direct and Indirect Costs

A cost classification that relates to the traceability of costs to cost units is particularly useful for income measurement purposes (see the manufacturing statement illustrated in Table 24—1, in Chapter 24). The cost unit is the unit of activity the cost of which is being measured. There are several types of cost unit, such as a particular job or product or batch of products; or a particular manufacturing process; or a department. It will be seen in Chapter 24 that the cost unit is largely determined by the nature of the manufacturing activity in which the enterprise is engaged. Irrespective of the type of cost unit, however, costs are classified according to whether or not they can be identified directly with, and assigned to, the cost unit.

Costs that are directly associated with a particular unit of activity are called *direct costs*. Those costs that are incurred by the factory for the benefit of production in general, and which cannot be identified with individual units of activity, are known as *indirect costs*. The cost of labour applied to a particular product thus constitutes a direct cost, while the factory manager's salary is an example of an indirect cost. (Indirect costs also include those costs which it is inconvenient to trace to cost units, such as glue or nails in furniture manufacture.)

As a result of this division, the elements of material cost, labour cost and expense are all sub-divided into direct and indirect components. Most material and labour costs are direct, i.e. they can be seen to be absorbed by particular cost units. On the other hand, direct expense is not often encountered when the cost unit is relatively small; an example of a direct expense is the royalty paid on each unit of a product manufactured under licence. Direct materials, direct labour and direct expense are usually grouped together to form what are known as 'prime costs'.

Indirect materials (such as factory supplies), indirect labour and indirect expense are grouped together to form 'manufacturing overhead' (or 'manufacturing expense'). It is important to distinguish manufacturing overhead (which is incurred in manufacturing activities) from the selling and administrative overhead expenses commonly incurred by all business enterprises.

While the classification of direct and indirect costs is usually associated with the financial accounting purpose, it also has relevance in certain decision contexts. For example, where the cost unit is an entire product line, a department or a division, direct costs, i.e. costs traceable to the cost unit, provide a first approximation to the opportunity costs of maintaining the product line or the department, as explained in Chapter 13.

Further, in multiple product firms the products share the same plant facilities, and in some cases even material and labour costs cannot be traced to individual products. This is the case in a petroleum refinery or a meat processing plant. Where two or more products share non-separable material costs, they are usually described as 'joint products' and the common costs associated with their production are called 'joint costs'. Joint costs are a special case of indirect costs, and the joint cost problem in a decision context is examined in Chapter 30.

Product Costs and Period Costs

Another cost classification distinguishes between *product costs* and *period costs* in the valuation of manufactured inventories. Product costs are those factory costs which, in the form of factor costs of production, add value to raw materials and work in process, and constitute the value of the inventory at cost of manufacture. Period costs, on the other hand, are not traced to inventory in the inventory valuation process, but are simply written off against income for the period in the income statement. Two costing methods described below differ in their treatment of fixed manufacturing costs in this respect.

Absorption Costing versus Variable Costing Methods

The distinction between variable and fixed manufacturing costs is explained in greater detail in the next section. Briefly, variable manufacturing costs are factory costs that vary with the volume of output, while fixed manufacturing costs are factory costs that do not vary with the volume of output. Under conventional *full costing* or *absorption costing* procedures, all factory costs are treated as product costs. The alternative *variable costing* method[2] treats variable manufacturing costs as product costs, while fixed manufacturing costs are treated not as product costs but as period costs. The fixed manufacturing costs are regarded as being costs of providing the capacity to produce, and are written off in full against the income of the period.

---

[2] Also sometimes called 'direct costing'. Direct costing is a misnomer for this method, since the focus is on variable costs *versus* fixed costs.

Variable costing provides, as part of the normal accounting process, information that is relevant to some of the major short-run problems facing management in the fields of planning, decision making and control. It highlights the relationship between output, costs and profits and, other things equal, ensures that profits move in the same direction as sales and are unaffected by inventory changes. It avoids arbitrary and misleading allocations of fixed manufacturing overhead and emphasizes the impact of fixed costs on profits. Variable costing may, perhaps, be regarded as more directly relevant to management problems than to the financial accounting tasks of profit measurement and inventory valuation, and from the viewpoint of management it is clearly more significant for short-run than for long-run policy (in the long run all costs, including fixed manufacturing overhead, need to be covered). Variable cost analysis must be carried out if the managerial function is to be performed satisfactorily; perhaps the real issue is whether this analysis needs to be carried out within the double-entry framework, as is implied in the variable costing approach, or whether it can be left to be undertaken outside the accounts in accordance with ideas that will be further developed in Chapter 30.

Example: Suppose that the following information is given:

	Year 1	Year 2
Units produced	10 000	15 000
Units sold	10 000	10 000
Selling price (per unit)	$10	$10
Variable manufacturing costs (per unit)	$4	$4
Fixed manufacturing overhead	$60 000	$60 000
Fixed selling and administrative overhead	$10 000	$10 000

If an absorption costing system of accounting is employed, the revenue statements for the two years may be expected to take the form of Table 23—1 (the conventional form of presentation has been modified to facilitate comparison with revenue statements prepared on a variable costing basis).

Table 23—1
Effect of Inventory Changes on Absorption Costing Revenue Statements

	Year 1		Year 2	
Sales		$100 000		$100 000
Less: Cost of sales:				
Opening inventories	—		—	
Cost of goods manufactured—				
Variable	$40 000		$60 000	
Fixed	60 000		60 000	
	100 000		120 000	
Less: Closing inventories	—		40 000	
		100 000		80 000
Gross profit		—		20 000
Less: Fixed selling and administrative overhead		10 000		10 000
Net profit (or loss)		Loss $10 000		Profit $10 000

The increased volume of production in Year 2 results in a lower unit cost of production $\left(\dfrac{\$120\,000}{15\,000}\right.$ or \$8 per unit compared with $\dfrac{\$100\,000}{10\,000}$ or \$10 per unit in Year $\left.1\right)$. The cost of sales is thereby reduced to \$80 000 (10 000 units at \$8 per unit) in Year 2 and closing inventories in that year are recorded at \$40 000 (5 000 units at \$8 per unit). Looked at another way, the value of closing inventories in Year 2 is composed of \$20 000 of variable manufacturing costs (5 000 units at \$4 per unit) plus \$20 000 of fixed manufacturing overhead $\left(\dfrac{5\,000}{15\,000}\right.$ x \$60 000$\left.\right)$. It is this \$20 000 of fixed costs absorbed in closing inventories, and this alone, that is responsible for the difference in results between Year 1 and Year 2.

The question arises as to how this firm may be said to have made a profit of \$10 000 in Year 2, compared with a loss of \$10 000 in Year 1, when nothing has changed except the volume of production? Proponents of variable costing claim that results of this kind are misleading; and that more significant profit (and inventory value) figures may be derived by adopting the variable costing approach and preparing the revenue statements on the basis of Table 23—2.

Table 23—2
Effect of Inventory Changes on Variable Costing Revenue Statements

		Year 1		Year 2
Sales		\$100 000		\$100 000
Less: Variable cost of sales:				
Opening inventories	—		—	
Variable cost of goods manufactured	\$40 000		\$60 000	
	40 000		60 000	
Less: Closing inventories	—		20 000	
		40 000		40 000
Sales margin		60 000		60 000
Less: Fixed manufacturing overhead	60 000		60 000	
Fixed selling and administrative overhead	10 000		10 000	
		70 000		70 000
Net loss		\$10 000		\$10 000

Because all the fixed manufacturing overhead is charged against the revenue of Year 2, the same loss is recorded in that year as in Year 1. The closing inventory figure in Year 2 is equal to the variable cost of producing the 5 000 units of closing inventory.

It will be observed that, because there is no change in manufactured inventories during Year 1, the recorded loss of \$10 000 for that year is the same under variable costing as under absorption costing. In Year 2, on the other hand, the variable costing revenue statement records a loss of \$10 000 compared with the profit of \$10 000 that was recorded in the absorption costing revenue statement. The increase in inventory values in Year 2 is shown as \$20 000 under variable costing, and \$40 000 under absorption costing.

Absorption costing profit in a given period exceeds variable costing profit by an amount equal to:

$$\frac{\Delta I}{P} \quad \text{x} \quad \$F$$

where ΔI is the increase in the volume of inventories over the period, P is the volume of production over which manufacturing overhead is applied, and F is the amount of fixed manufacturing overhead. [3] If ΔI is positive (i.e. if production exceeds sales) absorption costing shows a greater profit than variable costing. If ΔI is negative (i.e. if sales exceed production) absorption costing shows a smaller profit than variable costing. If $\Delta I = 0$ (i.e. if sales and production are equal) there is no difference between profits derived under the two methods of costing.

Most firms employ the absorption costing method for external reporting of their manufacturing and other operations. The distinction is important to income measurement and reporting. The basic problem, as to whether fixed manufacturing costs are absorbed into inventory costs, is not easily resolved. In the following chapters it will be assumed that the absorption costing method is employed in valuing inventory.

Cost Classifications for Planning and Control

Variable and Fixed Costs

Variable costs are defined as costs which vary directly and necessarily with changes in the level of output. [4] They are also often assumed to vary more or less in proportion, so that average costs per unit of output remain relatively constant. Variable costs comprise prime costs and variable manufacturing overhead.

Fixed costs are those costs which are unaffected by changes in the level of production. Examples are factory rent and depreciation of machinery. [5] A fixed cost may be said to be 'fixed' only in relation to a given period of time and a given range of activity. Costs which are fixed in the short run when capacity is given may become variable in the longer run when capacity can be increased. The following types of costs are all treated as fixed costs—discretionary costs, step costs and standby costs. Discretionary costs are costs which are not related to the present level of activity and which can be changed at the discretion of management, e.g. research and development costs. Step costs are those which change at certain significant levels of activity. If, for example, one supervisor is needed for x number of workers, then x, $2x$, $3x$, etc. are significant 'steps' in the level of employment at which additional supervision costs will be incurred. Standby costs are costs that can only be changed in the medium to long run, e.g. land, buildings and plant.

---

[3] In practice there is a number of methods by which manufacturing overhead is applied to production (see Chapters 25 and 26), and the method used affects the magnitudes of P and F, and hence the spread between absorption costing profit and variable costing profit.

[4] This is the *usual* criterion. Some variable costs, e.g. sales commission, vary with the volume of sales.

[5] The depreciation example should be qualified. Some part of the depreciation is attributable to the effluxion of time, and some part (usually a relatively small part) is attributable to use and may be dependent on the volume of output.

Some costs and expenses are partly fixed and partly variable, e.g. electricity when charges are imposed on the basis of a two-part tariff, and machine repairs. Also, costs may be variable for some purposes and fixed for others. Generally, direct costs are variable, while manufacturing overhead may be either fixed or variable.

The relationship of the variable-fixed classification to other cost classifications may thus be expressed as follows:

Variable manufacturing costs:
(a) Prime costs:
    (i)   Direct materials
    (ii) Direct labour
    (iii) Direct expense
(b) Variable manufacturing overhead (indirect costs)
Fixed manufacturing costs:
    Fixed manufacturing overhead (indirect costs)

The surplus of sales over total variable costs (i.e. selling as well as manufacturing costs) is known as the *variable profit margin* or *contribution margin*.[6] Variable profit is a basic concept underlying cost-profit-volume analysis and is useful in planning and in some decision situations, such as in formulating short-term pricing policies (see Chapters 28 and 30). The problem for which the variable-fixed cost concept is relevant may be stated thus: how will costs behave with changes in the volume of production?

Controllable and Non-controllable Costs

The concept of *controllable costs* is used to establish responsibility for costs and performance at different management levels, and thus to facilitate the delegation of authority. Some costs are controllable at the factory-floor level, while other costs are controllable only at an executive-management level, perhaps on a discretionary basis, e.g. in the case of research and development expenditures. In the evaluation of efficiency, the only costs which should be taken into account are those which can be controlled by the person responsible for the department or activity under review. The other costs—the *non-controllable costs*—are irrelevant for purposes of fixing responsibility or assessing performance. Accounting techniques have been devised with a view to making the double-entry accounts throw more light on the costs which are relevant for purposes of cost control. Thus the standard costing techniques described in Chapter 26 make it possible to identify in the accounts the effect of changes in prices, wage rates, etc. that may not be controllable. It is necessary to abstract from irrelevant factors in assessing the efficiency of cost control. In evaluating performance, either in relation to past results or budget forecasts, attention must be restricted to controllable costs.

---

[6] Some writers employ the term 'contribution margin' to refer to sales *less* direct costs. This is confusing, and for this reason we have a preference for the term 'variable profit'.

Cost Classifications for Decision Making—Non-accounting Costs

While cost is often one of the most important variables in decision making, several factors should be borne in mind. First, as stated at the outset, the meaning of cost is ambiguous. For example, what is the cost of education at a tertiary institution? Should it include only the fees and other expenses, such as books, incurred by the student, or should it also include the income he forgoes by studying instead of seeking gainful employment and the amount of any subsidy paid by the government? Should it be considered from the viewpoint of society rather from that of the student, and therefore be measured in terms of the teaching and other resources which are used in providing the tertiary education? In either case there will be difficulties in quantifying the costs in dollar terms. This is partly because there is seldom precision in measuring costs under conditions of cost allocations and changing prices, and partly because the relevant costs in decision making are often non-accounting costs which are not recorded in the ledgers. The two most important non-accounting costs are opportunity costs and future costs.

Opportunity Costs

Opportunity cost is the value of the sacrifice or opportunity forgone. For example, if a young man can earn $10 000 a year in gainful employment, the *opportunity cost* to him of three years' study at a tertiary institution would appear to be $30 000. But this is only the dollar cost; what also should be counted as part of the opportunity cost is any satisfaction forgone from earning his own livelihood rather than undertaking the course of study. In business, the opportunity cost of a scarce resource may be defined simply as the earnings which may be derived from the best alternative use of the resource. For example, the opportunity cost of using funds for a particular purpose may be measured by reference to the highest interest which could be earned on those funds or by the highest return which could be obtained on alternative investments of similar risk. Similarly, the opportunity cost of processing partly-finished goods may be measured by reference to the proceeds from an immediate sale, which must be sacrificed in order to continue processing.

The opportunity cost concept may be illustrated by reference to a fixed asset committed to a specific use. It has been seen that, for financial accounting purposes, periodic depreciation is calculated by relating the net cost of the fixed asset concerned to its expected useful life. However, in deciding whether the asset should be used for one purpose rather than another, or whether it should be disposed of, this accounting charge is irrelevant. The cost which is relevant to the decision is the opportunity cost of the asset, and this depends on the alternatives which are being-considered. If the enterprise has no alternative use for the asset and is considering hiring or selling it, the opportunity cost of using it in a particular period is given by the higher of the rent forgone in using it rather than hiring it or the sacrifice involved in using it rather than selling it. The last-mentioned sacrifice is measured by the diminution in the asset's realizable value over the period, making appropriate allowance for any return forgone (on the notional sales proceeds at the beginning of the period). Should the asset have an alternative use within the enterprise, then the opportunity cost of its existing use is the *highest* of the three alternative earnings, i.e. the economic returns from hiring it, selling it or using it for another purpose within the business.

An asset which is quite specific to a particular use, i.e. one which has no alternative employment available to it either inside or outside the enterprise, clearly has no opportunity cost. An example of such an asset is a road to a desert mine, used solely for purposes of transporting ore or minerals to the extraction plant or market. The opportunity cost of using the road is zero, and this zero cost is the one which must be taken into account in making any decision relating to the use of the road, e.g. in deciding whether to replace the road by a railway line. The opportunity cost of using the motor trucks which carry the ore or minerals, on the other hand, is related to their disposal value.

The opportunity cost notion is often straightforward when applied to short-run business decisions, but it can become very complex in long-run situations such as corporate planning or capital budgeting. Not only do future estimates have to be made, but one has to conceive of future alternative courses of action that may be pre-empted by the commitment of a scarce resource to a particular use. While the opportunity cost approach refers to a non-accounting cost, it will be seen later that this approach is reflected in some of the accounting cost concepts which are used to guide business decisions.

Future Costs

For purposes of decision making, the most relevant costs are *future costs*, because decisions generally relate to the future. Current costs also have relevance for many decisions but, by and large, past costs are irrelevant for decisions.[7]

A past cost relates to the value of a sacrifice already made, such as the cost of a fixed asset purchased some time ago. Suppose a machine was purchased two years ago for $20 000, that accumulated depreciation is $5 000 and that it is now proposed to replace this asset by a more efficient machine. Is either the past cost of $20 000 or the net book amount of $15 000 of the old machine relevant to the decision that has to be made? The answer is clearly no (provided that institutional arrangements such as tax provisions governing the sale of fixed assets may be ignored), because these past costs cannot influence any future state.

Past costs are useful insofar as they can provide the data base for management to project its estimates of future costs relevant to a particular decision. This implicitly assumes that the past costs have predictive potential, i.e. that the conditions and relationships of past periods may be extended to govern future outcomes. If this assumption is unreasonable, it is safer for management to rely on careful guesswork for decision making than on irrelevant past cost data.

Examples of management's use of future costs may be found in a large number of areas, including cost control (Chapter 26), long-range planning (Chapter 27), budgeting (Chapter 28), evaluation of capital projects (Chapter 29) and business decisions in general (Chapter 30).

Cost Classifications for Decision Making—Accounting Costs

There are two accounting costs—incremental costs and avoidable costs—which correspond to non-accounting opportunity costs. In a sense, all three costs are based on the notion of differential cost, defined as the difference in total costs that results from choosing one course of action rather than another.

---

[7] But see the argument presented in Chapter 17 that past costs have some relevance for decision making.

Incremental and Sunk Costs

Incremental costs by definition relate to the additional costs of making a change, such as increasing the level of activity or adding a new product line. Incremental costs are sometimes regarded as synonymous with the economist's marginal costs, but a distinction should be drawn between the two concepts. Marginal costs are costs at the margin, i.e. the costs of a single additional unit of production, whereas incremental costs can be the costs of additional batches of production, the additional costs resulting from changes in the pattern of production, or indeed the additional costs of any change in policy. Marginal costs thus constitute a special case of incremental costs and their use in business decision making is restricted to areas where a single unit is of some significance. Incremental costs, like marginal costs, need to be considered in relation to a particular time interval, and for purposes of some decisions it is necessary to distinguish between long-run and short-run incremental costs.

Sunk costs comprise all those costs which remain the same irrespective of which alternative is chosen, and which are therefore not relevant to the decision in question. [8] The distinction between incremental and sunk costs depends on what alternatives are being considered. The incremental-sunk cost distinction is based on the notion of differential costs, and it is usually necessary to abstract from accounting allocations, such as depreciation or assigned manufacturing overhead, when incremental costs are estimated.

In many situations, incremental costs may be the same as variable costs. But it is important not to confuse one concept with the other (nor sunk costs with fixed costs). For example, suppose one has a choice of continuing to sell one million units of a product in Melbourne rather than in Sydney. The variable manufacturing costs are unlikely to be affected by the decision, hence they are sunk costs and can be ignored. On the other hand, certain non-manufacturing costs, such as transport and advertising, may be incremental costs for purposes of this decision.

Further, the incremental costs relating to a particular decision are often a function of the time span being considered. Costs which are sunk in the short run may be long-term incremental costs when fixed facilities come to the end of their useful lives. [9]

Since a business decision relates to a future action, the relevant incremental cost is a future cost, not a past historical cost. It must also be noted that costs are only one aspect of a business decision. The other aspect is the differential revenue that is associated with the decision, defined as the difference in total revenues that results from choosing one course of action rather than another. It is differential net profit that is the appropriate choice criterion when a business decision has implications for both costs and revenues.

Avoidable and Unavoidable Costs

Avoidable costs and *unavoidable costs* may be considered to be special types of incremental and sunk costs, respectively. While incremental costs are associated with an increase in activities, the concept of avoidable cost is relevant to a contraction of activities. Avoidable costs are costs that can be eliminated if activity is discontinued.

---

[8] Sunk costs are used by some writers in a more limited sense to refer only to past costs (money down the drain, as it were), e.g. fixed expenditures already incurred.

[9] From a different viewpoint these are long-term avoidable costs (see the following section).

Generally, it will be found that direct costs may often be avoided while allocated costs may not, as in the problem relating to the closure of a department in Chapter 13.

In applying this concept, it is important to consider the *net* results of the contemplated action. Apart from the issue of allocated costs which may not be avoidable, the closure of a department may have a direct effect on the revenues or costs of other departments. The removal of a product line may have an impact on the sales or costs of other products, and these estimates need to be incorporated into the data to be considered in relation to the overall problem. Similar considerations apply to decisions to reduce discretionary costs, such as research and development or certain advertising expenses.

Some applications of the cost concepts discussed in this chapter to decision making are illustrated in Chapter 30.

Additional Reading

Dean, J., *Managerial Economics*, Prentice-Hall, Englewood Cliffs, N.J., 1974, Chapter 5.

Solomons, D., 'Economic and Accounting Concepts of Cost and Value', in M. Backer (ed.), *Modern Accounting Theory*, Prentice-Hall, Englewood Cliffs, N.J., 1966, pp. 117-40.

Discussion Questions

1 Discuss the different purposes for which cost information is prepared by accountants.

2 'We need different costs for different purposes.' Explain.

3 Examine critically the following cost concepts:
   (a) direct and indirect costs;
   (b) product and period costs; and
   (c) variable and fixed costs.

4 Explain the pros and cons of adopting the absorption costing method of valuing inventory.

5 How does the variable-fixed cost classification aid management in planning and decision making?

6 What cost classification scheme would you recommend in order to establish the responsibility of individual managers for costs and performance?

7 Give examples of cost which, although important for decision making, are not reflected in the books of account. What problems do you envisage in measuring these cost items?

8 Under what circumstances will it be possible to identify opportunity cost for alternative decisions in the books of account? Explain, giving examples.

9 Explain the difference, if any, between the incremental-sunk and avoidable-unavoidable cost concepts.

Exercises

1 The Newcastle Steel Co. operates a plant which produces a single product, sheet steel. Operating and financial data for the years ended 31 December 1984 and 1985 are as follows:

	1984	1985
Units produced (tonnes)	20 000	25 000
Units sold (tonnes)	20 000	19 000
Selling price ($ per tonne)	100	100
Variable manufacturing costs ($ per tonne)	50	50
Fixed manufacturing overhead ($)	400 000	400 000
Fixed selling and administrative expenses ($)	300 000	300 000

(a) Prepare profit and loss statements for each of the two years: (i) assuming that an absorption costing system is in operation; and (ii) assuming that a variable costing system is in operation.

(b) Explain the reason for any differences in the results obtained. Which method do you think provides a better measure of periodic profit?

2 The following data refer to the operations of a manufacturing company, which produces a single product, for the years ended 31 December 1984 and 1985:

	1984	1985
Opening inventory (number of units)	nil	5 000
Units produced (number of units)	15 000	20 000
Units sold (number of units)	10 000	15 000
Selling price ($ per unit)	10.00	10.00
Variable manufacturing costs ($ per unit)	3.50	3.50
Fixed manufacturing overhead ($)	22 500	22 500
Fixed selling and administrative expenses ($)	30 000	30 000

(a) Prepare profit and loss statements for each of the two years: (i) assuming that an absorption costing system is in operation and that inventory issues are priced in accordance with the FIFO assumption; and (ii) assuming that a variable costing system is in operation.

(b) Explain the reasons for any differences in the results obtained.

24 Cost Accounting Systems

So far, our concern has been primarily with accounting for the trading activities of business enterprises — i.e. their buying and selling activities — with a view to deriving financial measures of periodic income and net worth. These aspects of accounting, which are sometimes described as financial accounting, have wide significance, but the resulting financial statements are of special interest to owners, investors and creditors who are directly interested in the financial activities of the enterprises. From the viewpoint of the managers of the business, however, the financial accounting statements are of limited usefulness. They may provide an indication of the efficiency with which the managers are doing their jobs, but the statements refer to external financial relationships which alone are not adequate for many managerial purposes of control and decision making.

In this and later chapters we turn, therefore, to an examination of the problems that arise in providing accounting information for management. In this field of management accounting, the task of providing financial information about external relationships remains, but there is an additional need to keep management supplied with cost and other information relating to events that take place within the enterprise.

This additional information is needed by management for two main purposes, *first* as a basis for planning and formulating enterprise policy and *second* as a means of exercising effective control over the activities of the enterprise and of achieving planned performance.

This chapter and the next are concerned with the problem of cost finding in an historical sense. Standard costs, which are widely used in manufacturing industry, are briefly explained in Chapter 26. Subsequent chapters deal with more general aspects of management planning and decision making.

The Cost Unit

For the purpose of inventory valuation and income measurement, there is a need to derive in the cost records information concerning the cost of individual units of activity. These units may be jobs or products or batches of production; or manufacturing processes; or departments. The choice of cost unit by a particular enterprise depends largely on the nature of the productive operations it carries out, but for cost accounting purposes a broad distinction can be made between two kinds of cost units — jobs or production orders on the one hand, and processes on the other. Corresponding to the distinction between jobs (or production orders) and processes, there are two methods of costing which may be employed — job (or production order) costing and process costing.

A production order is the authority to undertake the production of a specified quantity of goods. Job or production order costing techniques are employed whenever the bulk of material and labour costs can be identified closely with particular end-products or units of production, e.g. jobs carried out to customers' specifications, or batches of individual products. Each individual job is a cost unit.

On the other hand, in process costing the process itself becomes the cost unit (in relation to a particular period of time). For example, the manufacturing operations of an iron and steel mill comprise a number of processes (such as smelting, casting, semi-finishing and finishing), each of which may be used as a cost unit.

Job and process cost systems will be discussed in a later section of this chapter.

Integrated Cost Accounting Systems

It is necessary, if effective control is to be achieved over factory activities, to integrate the financial and cost records so that they all form part of the one double-entry system. The integrated or controlled cost accounting system makes use of the control account technique (described in Chapter 2), i.e. the cost records are controlled by accounts in the general or cost ledger. There are several different kinds of integrated cost systems, but basically they are all variations of a system in which control accounts in the ledger govern or control detailed records which are maintained in the factory office. Controlled cost accounts may thus be regarded as introducing the perpetual inventory method of inventory control (described in Chapter 3) into the cost accounting system. Two such systems are described as follows:

1 the general ledger control system, in which all control accounts are kept in the general ledger; and

2 the dual ledger control system, in which separate control accounts are kept in both the general ledger and the cost ledger.

1 General Ledger Control System

In the general ledger control system, three classes of control accounts in the general ledger record sequential steps in the manufacturing process. In the first class there are at least three control accounts, in which manufacturing costs and expenses incurred are recorded as debit entries and charges to production are recorded as credit entries. These accounts are the material inventory control account, the labour control account and the manufacturing overhead control account. The material inventory control account controls detailed material inventory records (on a perpetual inventory basis) which are maintained in the factory office. The labour control account controls various direct and indirect labour costs and serves as a clearing account. The manufacturing overhead control account controls various manu-facturing indirect expense accounts and is also in the form of a clearing account. (A clearing account is an account in which is accumulated a record of transactions of a similar kind, or relating to the same purpose or activity, pending their distribution to other accounts in the system.)

The second class typically comprises one account, the work in process control account, which records as debit entries the charges to production (i.e. the costs and expenses absorbed by jobs or processes in the course of production) and as credit entries the cost of finished work transferred from the factory to the warehouse. This account controls the detailed cost cards which record the progressive costs of unfinished individual jobs or processes.

The final account recording the flow of manufacturing costs is the finished goods inventory control account, which records the costs of finished production as debit entries and the cost of sales as a credit entry. The finished goods inventory control account controls detailed finished goods inventory records which are maintained in the finished goods store or warehouse.

An Illustration

ADC Manufacturing Co. incurred the following expenses in 1985:

Direct materials purchased	$12 000
Wages paid to direct labour force	24 000
Wages paid to indirect labour force	1 500
Factory rent	2 000
Power expense	3 000
Depreciation of machinery	1 000

Sales of $50 000 were recorded during the period. Opening and closing inventory values derived from the inventory control accounts and the supporting perpetual inventories are as follows:

	Opening Inventories	Closing Inventories
Material inventory control	$8 000	$7 000
Work in process control	6 000	3 000
Finished goods inventory control	10 000	12 500

The charges to production which are to be recorded in the general ledger are ascertained directly from the cost records on the basis of the material issues, labour costs and manufacturing overhead which are attributable to cost units. Assume that these charges amount to $12 800 for direct materials, $23 600 for direct labour, and $8 000 for manufacturing overhead. Any differences between direct material and labour costs charged to production and the direct material and labour costs which have to be accounted for must now be explained and recorded in the general ledger. Suppose that $200 under-absorbed material costs and $400 under-absorbed labour costs are represented by spoiled materials and idle time between jobs respectively, and that these are to be treated as additional items of manufacturing overhead.

The manufacturing overhead of $8 000 is 'applied' to production by means of pre-determined manufacturing overhead recovery rates, which will be discussed in Chapter 25. Under-absorbed or over-absorbed manufacturing overhead is not ascertained until the end of the accounting period; the explanation and treatment of these differences will be considered in Chapter 25. One possibility is to write the under-absorbed amount off as a loss in the trading account; this is illustrated in Table 24—2.[1]

The cost of finished production to be recorded in the general ledger is also calculated directly from the finished goods cards representing the output of completed jobs or processes; suppose that the cost of manufacture of finished goods in the period is $47 400. Cost of sales is thus $44 900.

On the basis of this information the general ledger may be expected to take the following form:

[1] The terms 'overhead applied to production' and 'overhead absorbed by production' are used synonymously. Similarly 'over- or under-applied overhead' and 'over- or under-absorbed overhead' have the same meaning.

General Ledger Control System
General Ledger

Material Inventory Control

Balance b/d (opening inventory)	$8 000	Work in process control (direct materials)	$12 800
Purchases	12 000	Manufacturing overhead control (spoiled materials)	200
		Balance c/d (closing inventory)	7 000
	$20 000		$20 000
Balance b/d (closing inventory)	$7 000		

Labour Control

Wages paid	$25 500	Work in process control (direct labour)	$23 600
		Manufacturing overhead control (indirect labour)	1 500
		Manufacturing overhead control (idle time)	400
	$25 500		$25 500

Manufacturing Overhead Control

Factory rent	$2 000	Work in process control (overhead applied)	$8 000
Power expense	3 000	Balance c/d (manufacturing overhead under-absorbed)	100
Depreciation of machinery	1 000		
Materials inventory control (spoiled materials)	200		
Labour control—			
Indirect labour	1 500		
Idle time	400		
	$8 100		$8 100
Balance b/d (manufacturing overhead under-absorbed)	$100		

Work in Process Control

Balance b/d (opening inventory)	$6 000	Finished goods inventory control	$47 400
Material inventory control	12 800	Balance c/d (closing inventory)	3 000
Labour control	23 600		
Manufacturing overhead control	8 000		
	$50 400		$50 400
Balance b/d (closing inventory)	$3 000		

Finished Goods Inventory Control

Balance b/d (opening inventory)	$10 000	Cost of sales	$44 900
Work in process control	47 400	Balance c/d (closing inventory)	12 500
	$57 400		$57 400
Balance b/d (closing inventory)	$12 500		

Cost of Sales

Finished goods inventory control	$44 900	Trading account	$44 900

Sales

Trading account	$50 000	Debtors, etc	$50 000

Trading

Cost of sales	$44 900	Sales	$50 000
Gross profit c/d	5 100		
	$50 000		$50 000
		Gross profit b/d	$5 100

A manufacturing statement and trading statement for internal management use may be prepared in the form of Tables 24—1 and 24—2, respectively.

Table 24—1
ABC Manufacturing Co.
Manufacturing Statement for Period Ended 31 December 1985

Work in process, opening inventory		$6 000
Costs incurred during the year—		
Direct materials	$12 800	
Direct labour	23 600	
Manufacturing overhead	8 000	
		44 400
		50 400
Less: Work in process, closing inventory		3 000
Total cost of finished goods manufactured		$47 400

Table 24—2
ABC Manufacturing Co.
Trading Statement for Period Ended 31 December 1985

Sales		$50 000
Less: Cost of sales—		
Opening inventory of finished goods	$10 000	
Cost of finished goods manufactured	47 400	
	57 400	
Less: Closing inventory of finished goods	12 500	
		44 900
Gross profit		5 100
Less: Manufacturing overhead under-absorbed		100
Adjusted gross profit		$5 000

The cost flows in the above example are illustrated in Figure 24—A.

Figure 24—A
Cost Flows in a General Ledger Control System

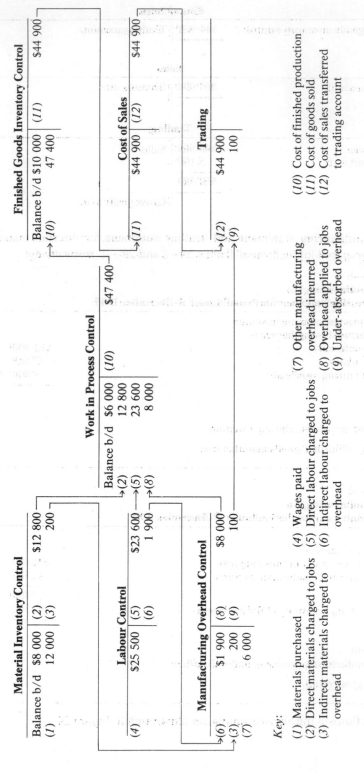

Material Inventory Control

Balance b/d	$8 000	(2)		$12 800
(1)	12 000	(3)		200

Labour Control

(4)	$25 500	(5)	$23 600
		(6)	1 900

Manufacturing Overhead Control

(6)	$1 900	(8)	$8 000
(3)	200	(9)	100
(7)	6 000		

Work in Process Control

Balance b/d	$6 000	(10)	$47 400
(2)	12 800		
(5)	23 600		
(8)	8 000		

Finished Goods Inventory Control

Balance b/d	$10 000	(11)	$44 900
(10)	47 400		

Cost of Sales

(11)	$44 900	(12)	$44 900

Trading

(12)	$44 900		
(9)	100		

Key:

(1) Materials purchased
(2) Direct materials charged to jobs
(3) Indirect materials charged to overhead
(4) Wages paid
(5) Direct labour charged to jobs
(6) Indirect labour charged to overhead
(7) Other manufacturing overhead incurred
(8) Overhead applied to jobs
(9) Under-absorbed overhead
(10) Cost of finished production
(11) Cost of goods sold
(12) Cost of sales transferred to trading account

2 Dual Ledger Control System

The dual ledger control system involves a similar kind of integration of financial and cost records. Two ledgers are maintained — the general ledger and the cost ledger. The general ledger in this system contains only one control account — known as the cost ledger control account — in which are recorded all transactions relating to manufacturing activity. In effect, the factory is regarded as a separate branch of the enterprise, so that the general ledger is analogous to the head office ledger in a branch accounting system. The cost ledger control account in the general ledger is debited with the costs incurred on behalf of the factory and credited with the cost of goods sold. After allowance has been made for any costs or expenses under-absorbed or over-absorbed in the cost records, the balance of the cost ledger control account in the general ledger at any time then represents the cost of raw material, work in process and finished goods inventories on hand.

Under this system the cost ledger itself becomes a complete system of double-entry accounts, some of which control subsidiary cost records in exactly the same way as in the general ledger control system. The cost ledger, and not the general ledger, thus contains the material inventory control, labour control, manufacturing overhead control, work in process control and finished goods inventory control accounts. The material inventory control account, the work in process control account and the finished goods inventory control account in the cost ledger are current asset accounts controlling and supported by the same kinds of subsidiary records which are involved in a general ledger control system. A general ledger control account in the cost ledger acts as a balancing account and thereby completes the double entry.

A brief explanation of how entries are recorded in the two ledgers follows. Transactions recording flows of resources to or from the factory are recorded in both ledgers. Thus material purchases of say, $12 000 will be recorded as follows:

Cost Journal

Material inventory control	Dr.	$12 000
General ledger control	Cr.	$12 000
Material purchases posted to cost ledger		

General Journal

Cost ledger control	Dr.	$12 000
Accounts payable*	Cr.	$12 000
Material purchases posted to general ledger		

* This account is not shown in the following illustration.

Internal factory operations or external transactions not affecting the factory are entered in one of the ledgers only, i.e. either the cost ledger or the general ledger. For example, materials issued to production are recorded only in the cost ledger (debit work in process control account, credit material inventory control account), while sales are recorded only in the general ledger (debit accounts receivable account, credit sales account).

An Illustration

The dual ledger control system may be illustrated by reference to the same data that have been used to explain the operation of the general ledger control system. In the dual ledger control system, the cost accountant sends a cost journal voucher to the financial accountant at the end of the accounting period, which becomes the basis of the following entries in the general journal:

General Journal

1985					
Dec. 31	Cost of goods sold		Dr.	$44 900	
	Manufacturing overhead under-absorbed		Dr.	100	
	Cost ledger control		Cr.		$45 000
	Cost of goods sold and under-absorbed manufacturing overhead credited to cost ledger control account				

It will be seen that the general ledger control account in the cost ledger is mirrored by the cost ledger control account in the general ledger. The opening and closing balances of the two accounts are represented by the following balances in the cost ledger:

	Opening Inventories	Closing Inventories
Material inventory	$8 000	$7 000
Work in process	6 000	3 000
Finished goods inventory	10 000	12 500
	$24 000	$22 500

Dual Ledger Control System
Cost Ledger

General Ledger Control

Finished goods inventory control (cost of goods sold)	$44 900	Balance b/d	$24 000
		Material inventory control	12 000
Manufacturing overhead control (under-absorbed manufacturing overhead)	100	Labour control	25 500
		Manufacturing overhead control—	
Balance c/d	22 500	Factory rent	2 000
		Power expense	3 000
		Depreciation of machinery	1 000
	$67 500		$67 500
		Balance b/d	$22 500

Material Inventory Control

Balance b/d (opening inventory)	$8 000	Work in process control (direct materials)	$12 800
General ledger control (purchases)	12 000	Manufacturing overhead control (spoiled materials)	200
		Balance c/d (closing inventory)	7 000
	$20 000		$20 000
Balance b/d	$7 000		

Labour Control

General ledger control (wages paid)	$25 500	Work in process control (direct labour)	$23 600
		Manufacturing overhead control (indirect labour)	1 500
		Manufacturing overhead control (idle time)	400
	$25 500		$25 500

Manufacturing Overhead Control

General ledger control—		Work in process control (overhead applied)	$8 000
Factory rent	$2 000	General ledger control	
Power expense	3 000	(manufacturing overhead	
Depreciation of machinery	1 000	under-absorbed)	100
Material inventory control (spoiled materials)	200		
Labour control—			
Indirect labour	1 500		
Idle time	400		
	$8 100		$8 100

Work in Process Control

Balance b/d (opening inventory)	$6 000	Finished goods inventory control	$47 400
Material inventory control	12 800	Balance c/d (closing inventory)	3 000
Labour control	23 600		
Manufacturing overhead control	8 000		
	$50 400		$50 400
Balance b/d (closing inventory)	$3 000		

Finished Goods Inventory Control

Balance b/d (opening inventory)	$10 000	General ledger control (cost of goods sold)	$44 900
Work in process control	47 400	Balance c/d (closing inventory)	12 500
	$57 400		$57 400
Balance b/d	$12 500		

General Ledger

Cost Ledger Control*

Balance b/d	$24 000	Cost of goods sold	$44 900
Material purchases	12 000	Manufacturing overhead	
Wages paid	25 500	under-absorbed in cost ledger	100
Factory rent	2 000	Balance c/d	22 500
Power expense	3 000		
Depreciation of machinery	1 000		
	$67 500		$67 500
Balance b/d	$22 500		

* The opening and closing balances are contras to the opening and closing balances in the general ledger control account in the cost ledger. The balances represent opening and closing inventories of raw materials, work in process and finished goods, respectively.

Cost of Goods Sold

Cost ledger control	$44 900	Trading account	$44 900

Manufacturing Overhead Under-absorbed

Cost ledger control	$100	Trading account	$100

Sales

Trading account	$50 000	Debtors, etc.	$50 000

Trading

Cost of goods sold	$44 900	Sales	$50 000
Gross profit c/d	5 100		
	$50 000		$50 000
Manufacturing overhead		Gross profit b/d	5 100
under-absorbed	100		
Profit and loss account			
(adjusted gross profit)	5 000		
	$5 100		$5 100

A description of the subsidiary cost records which are governed by the control accounts follows. While the subsidiary cost records are not part of the double-entry system of accounts, they are an essential part of the cost accounting system with respect to its functions of inventory valuation, income measurement and cost control.

Accounting for Job and Process Costs

Costs Classified by Departments

Irrespective of whether a job or process cost system is employed, it is usually necessary to departmentalize a factory in order to facilitate the tasks of cost accumulation and cost control. In a job cost system, costs may be classified by departments before any attempt is made to measure the costs of particular jobs or production orders; in a process cost system, the separate processes may themselves represent departments. The departmental structure of a particular factory will thus depend on such things as the nature of the production processes, the physical lay-out of the factory and the division of managerial responsibility.

Job Cost System

As noted earlier, job or production order costing techniques are employed whenever the bulk of material and labour costs can be identified closely with particular end-products or units of production, e.g. jobs carried out to customers' specifications or batches of individual products. In a job or production order costing system, the detailed cost record takes the form of a separate cost account, called a *job cost card*, for each job or production order. On this card the costs of the materials issued to the job or order, the labour employed thereon[2] and the share of manufacturing overhead charged to the job or order are recorded.

The characteristic feature of a job cost system is that each job is individually costed. However, for control purposes costs must be accumulated in cost centres. A cost centre is an area of responsibility for which costs are accumulated, usually a department. Thus the system must provide cost data which can be traced to jobs as well as to departments (see job card for Job 201 in the following illustration).

An Illustration

The example of ABC Manufacturing Co. will be extended below to illustrate the subsidiary cost records in a job cost system. Additional information relating to materials is as follows:

	Total Materials	Direct Materials Type M	Direct Materials Type N	Indirect Materials
Opening inventories	$8 000	$5 000	$2 000	$1 000
Purchases	12 000	7 000	5 000	
	$20 000	$12 000	$7 000	$1 000
Issues—Job 201 (Product X)	8 000	5 000	3 000	
202 (Product Y)	4 000	2 000	2 000	
203 (Product Y)	800	500	300	
Supplies	200			200
	$13 000	$7 500	$5 300	$200
Closing inventories	$7 000	$4 500	$1 700	$800

Information relating to individual jobs, which reflects entries in job cards, is given as follows:

	Total Jobs	201 (Product X)	202 (Product Y)	203 (Product Y)
Balance b/d	$6 000	$4 000	$2 000	—
Direct materials	12 800	8 000	4 000	$800
Direct labour	23 600	12 000	10 000	1 600
Manufacturing overhead	8 000	4 000	3 400	600
	50 400	28 000	19 400	3 000
Cost of completed jobs	47 400	28 000	19 400	—
Balance c/d	$3 000	—	—	$3 000

Assume that the opening balances in the finished goods ledger for products X and Y are $6 000 and $4 000 and the closing balances are $4 000 and $8 500, respectively. Thus cost of sales is $30 000 for X and $14 900 for Y.

Examples of the more important subsidiary records follow. They comprise stores ledger cards, a job cost card for Job 201, and finished goods ledger cards. For illustrative purposes, the job cost card will show expenditures incurred in two departments, A and B. Also it is assumed the opening balance on Job 201 comprises materials $2 000, labour $1 500 and overhead $500, all incurred in department A.

[2] These by definition constitute direct material and direct labour costs so far as the job or order is concerned.

Stores Ledger Card—Materials M

	Receipts	Issues	Balance
			$5 000
Purchases	$7 000		12 000
Issues—Job 201		$5 000	7 000
202		2 000	5 000
203		500	4 500

Stores Ledger Card—Materials N

	Receipts	Issues	Balance
			$2 000
Purchases	$5 000		7 000
Issues—Job 201		$3 000	4 000
202		2 000	2 000
203		300	1 700

Job Cost Card—Job 201

Product—X
Quantity—100 units

Job number—201
Date started ...
Date finished ...

	Total	Dept. A	Dept. B
Direct materials—			
Work in process b/d	$2 000	$2 000	—
Issued	8 000	6 000	$2 000
Direct labour—			
Work in process b/d	1 500	1 500	—
Charged	12 000	6 000	6 000
Manufacturing overhead—			
Work in process b/d	500	500	—
Applied	4 000	2 000	2 000
Cost of completed job	$28 000	$18 000	$10 000

Finished Goods Ledger Card—Product X

	Dr.	Cr.	Balance
			$6 000
Job 201	$28 000		34 000
Cost of sales		$30 000	4 000

Finished Goods Ledger Card—Product Y

	Dr.	Cr.	Balance
			$4 000
Job 202	$19 400		23 400
Cost of sales		$14 900	8 500

Process Cost System

A process is any manufacturing operation which transforms raw materials or partly-finished goods from one state to another. The process usually becomes the cost unit (in relation to a particular period of time) when it takes the form of a continuous operation, the end-product of which is not separable into a number of individual products; or when the bulk of material and labour costs can be traced to, or identified with, particular processes or operations rather than with the final output. The manufacturing operations of a textile mill, for example, may be broken down into a number of processes — scouring, spinning, dyeing, weaving, and so on — which may conveniently be used as cost units.

In a process cost system, the cost unit is often identical with the cost centre, i.e. the cost unit is the department itself. The characteristic features of process production are: (a) units of output are indistinguishable from one another within each department; (b) operations are uniform in nature in each department; and (c) production takes place in an ordered sequence from department to department.

In a process cost system, the detailed cost record takes the form of a separate cost account, called a *process cost card*, for each process for a given period of time. On this card are recorded the costs of materials issued to, and labour employed on, the process (the so-called direct costs of the process) and the manufacturing overhead charged to the process. A simple process cost card is illustrated in Figure 24—B.

Figure 24—B
Process Cost Card

Process A				Period March 1985
Date	Description of Cost Item	Direct Materials	Direct Labour	Manufacturing Overhead
	Total Costs	$18 950	$29 160	$8 190

Process cost accounting is similar to job cost accounting. In some respects it is a simpler system, e.g. it is very convenient for the cost unit to be also the cost centre. But process costing also presents some special problems, such as that of costing unfinished units at the end of the period.

Unit Costs — The Weighted Average Method

Historical process cost systems may adopt either the weighted average or FIFO assumption in computing unit costs. The weighted average method is the one commonly used. Closing work in process is expressed in equivalent full units, and unit costs are then computed by an averaging method, as shown in the following illustration.

An Illustration

A factory operates a process cost system with two departments. Materials are added at the beginning of the process in department A and at the end of the process in department B. For simplicity, it is assumed that the other two cost elements — labour and overhead — are added at a uniform or constant rate throughout the processing, so that they are present in the same proportions in unfinished units. The following information relates to the units processed in the month of March:

	Department A		Department B	
	Units	% completed*	Units	% completed*
Opening work in process (from previous month)	300	$33\frac{1}{3}\%$	300	30%
Units started	9 000	—	9 100	—
Units completed	9 100	100%	8 400	100%
Closing work in process c/d	200	50%	1 000	30%

* This refers to percentage completion with respect to each department's labour and overhead.

Assume that the costs brought forward in opening work in process and costs incurred in the current month in department A are as shown in the table:

Department A	Materials	Labour	Overhead
Units completed	9 100	9 100	9 100
Closing work in process	200	100	100
Equivalent units produced	9 300	9 200	9 200
Opening work in process	$580	$280	$90
Costs incurred in current month	18 950	29 160	8 190
	$19 530	$29 440	$8 280
Cost per equivalent unit	$2.10	$3.20	$0.90

The cost of a completed unit in department A is $6.20 ($2.10 + $3.20 + $0.90), so that the total cost of completed units transferred to department B is $56 420 (9 100 units at $6.20 each). The cost of a unit of closing work in process is $4.15 [$2.10 + $\frac{1}{2}$ ($3.20 + $0.90)], so that the total cost of closing work in process is $830 (200 units at $4.15 each).

The calculations for department B are more complex because of costs transferred from department A. The following illustration again assumes that the costs of opening work in process and the costs incurred in the current month are as shown in the table:

Department B	Transferred from Dept. A	Materials	Labour	Overhead
Units completed	8 400	8 400	8 400	8 400
Closing work in process	1 000	—	300	300
Equivalent units produced	9 400	8 400	8 700	8 700
Opening work in process	$1 672	—	$260	$100
Costs incurred in current month	56 420	$8 568	24 100	8 600
	$58 092	$8 568	$24 360	$8 700
Cost per equivalent unit	$6.18	$1.02	$2.80	$1.00

The cost of a completed unit in department B is $11.00 ($6.18 + $1.02 + $2.80 + $1.00), so that the total cost of completed units transferred to finished goods inventory is $92 400 (8 400 units at $11 each). The cost of a unit of closing work in process is $7.32 [$6.18 + $\frac{3}{10}$ ($2.80 + $1.00)], so that the total cost of closing work in process is $7 320 (1 000 units at $7.32 each).

The work in process accounts for the two departments are:

Work in Process—Department A

	Units	$		Units	$
Balance b/d	300	950	Transfer to Dept. B	9 100	56 420
Direct materials	9 000	18 950	Balance c/d	200	830
Direct labour		29 160			
Manufacturing overhead		8 190			
	9 300	$57 250		9 300	$57 250
Balance b/d	200	$830			

Work in Process—Department B

	Units	$		Units	$
Balance b/d	300	2 032	Transfer to finished		
Transfer from Dept. A	9 100	56 420	goods inventory	8 400	92 400
Direct materials		8 568	Balance c/d	1 000	7 320
Direct labour		24 100			
Manufacturing overhead		8 600			
	9 400	$99 720		9 400	$99 720
Balance b/d	1 000	$7 320			

Unit Costs — The FIFO Method

The FIFO method of computing unit costs is not widely used in historical cost systems, and therefore it will not be illustrated in this chapter. However, the FIFO assumption takes into account the opening work in process in computing equivalent units produced in the current period, and gives a more accurate analysis of the flow of units in each period (compared with the weighted average method which ignores opening work in process in computing equivalent units). Hence in a standard cost system the FIFO assumption is usually applied to the flow of units, in order to facilitate the analysis of variances between predetermined costs and actual costs in the period. (Standard costing is discussed in Chapter 26.)

The FIFO method assumes that units which are started first are finished first, as illustrated below by reference to department A in the previous example:

Department A	Materials	Labour	Overhead	Physical Flow*
Opening work in process	300	100	100	300($\frac{1}{3}$)
Units started				9 000
	300	100	100	9 300
Units completed in current month—				
From opening work in process	—	200	200	300($\frac{2}{3}$)
From units started	8 800	8 800	8 800	8 800
Closing work in process	200	100	100	200($\frac{1}{2}$)
Current month's production in equivalent units	9 000	9 100	9 100	9 300

* The fraction is parentheses denotes proportion of labour and overhead included in work in process.

The different forms which the framework of a cost accounting system may take have now been considered. The next chapter will be concerned with the collection and recording of cost data, and the maintenance of cost records with respect to materials, labour and manufacturing overhead.

Additional Reading

Horngren, C.T., *Cost Accounting — A Managerial Emphasis*, 4th ed., 1977, Prentice-Hall, Englewood Cliffs, N.J., Chapters 4 and 18.

Shillinglaw, S., *Managerial Cost Accounting*, 4th ed., 1977, Irwin, Homewood, Ill., Chapter 2.

Discussion Questions

1 It is said that financial statements are of limited usefulness to managers. What additional accounting information is needed by the manager of a manufacturing enterprise for planning, control and reporting purposes?

2 Compare and contrast job (or production order) costing and process costing systems with special reference to:
  (a) the conditions under which each system is likely to be adopted;
  (b) the derivation of cost data; and
  (c) the nature of the cost records.

3 Monolithic Constructions Ltd specializes in multi-storey office buildings which usually take two or three years to complete. Comment on the problems that may be encountered in:
  (a) designing a suitable accounting system for such a company; and
  (b) measuring periodic income and the book values of unfinished contracts.

4 Two types of integrated cost accounting systems, using control accounting techniques, have been suggested. Evaluate these systems with special reference to:
  (a) the conditions under which each system is likely to be used; and
  (b) the control techniques used in preparing cost data.

5 What steps would you take in planning an accounting system for a small production order factory? Indicate in particuiar how you would provide for the satisfactory integration of cost and financial records, assuming that an historical system of cost accounting is suitable for the enterprise in question.

6 What is the significance of equivalent performance calculations in a process cost system? Why is this not required in job costing?

Exercises

1 On the basis of the following information relating to 1985, calculate the cost of goods manufactured by Universal Foundry Ltd. Present your answer in the form of a manufacturing statement for the year.

	Opening	Closing
(a) Inventories:		
Raw materials	$2 000	$4 000
Work in process—		
Materials	1 100	1 200
Labour	600	700
Manufacturing overhead	700	800

(b) Purchases of materials, $7 000
(c) Wages paid, $5 500
(d) Manufacturing overhead incurred, $6 000

2 (a) By means of a diagram, illustrate the cost flow in a general ledger control system, in which the following accounts are included: raw materials; labour; manufacturing overhead; work in process; finished goods; cost of sales; and trading.

(b) In the case of the control accounts, indicate the nature of the subsidiary records which are controlled.

3 (a) Design a chart of accounts to illustrate the classification of general ledger accounts in an engineering workshop where:
(i)   work is carried out for individual customers on a job order basis;
(ii) an historical cost system is in operation; and
(iii) all cost and inventory records are controlled by a series of accounts in the general ledger.

(b) Set up general ledger accounts to show how the following transactions would be recorded in such a system:

(i) Materials purchased	$1 770
(ii) Materials issued to production—	
Direct	1 150
Indirect	200
(iii) Wages paid and charged to production—	
Direct	9 500
Indirect	710
(iv) Other manufacturing overhead	1 040
(v) Manufacturing overhead charged to production	1 900
(vi) Cost of jobs completed and transferred to customer—	
Material	1 120
Labour	8 500
Manufacturing overhead	1 700

4 The transactions for Pride Manufacturing Ltd in its first year of operations are summarized below:
   (a) Materials were purchased for $700 000.
   (b) Materials requisitioned were—
        direct materials, $460 000;
        indirect materials, $170 000.
   (c) Factory labour for the year amounted to $340 000. Income tax withheld amounted to $76 400, and the net amount paid to employees amounted to $263 600.
   (d) The classification of factory labour costs was as follows —
        direct labour, $194 000;
        indirect labour, $146 000.

(e) Manufacturing overhead was applied to production at 200 per cent of the direct labour cost.

(f) Manufacturing overhead costs (other than indirect materials and indirect labour) during the year amounted to $76 000. Depreciation of $28 000 is included in this amount.

(g) Orders costing $770 000 were completed during the year.

(h) Goods costing $430 000 were sold to customers on credit terms for $600 000.

You are required to enter the above transactions into appropriate ledger accounts and to calculate the closing balances on the inventory accounts.

5 The following data refer to the operations of Prompt Processing Ltd:

(a) On 1 January 1985, 6 000 units of opening inventory in stock were 40 per cent complete as to materials and 10 per cent complete as to conversion costs. The inventory was carried at a cost of $21 000 (materials, $14 000 and conversion costs $7 200).

(b) On 31 December 1985, 4 000 units of closing inventory in stock were 80 per cent complete as to materials and 40 per cent as to conversion costs.

(c) The company completed 80 000 units during the year 1985. Manufacturing costs incurred during 1985 were: materials, $485 200; and conversion costs, $890 400.

You are required:

(i) to calculate the equivalent production in 1985 with respect to materials and conversion costs; and

(ii) to determine the cost of closing work in process.

6 The manufacture of product X takes place in an ordered sequence of operations through departments A and B. All materials are issued in department A when production commences. Operating data for the month of January are as follows:

Department A—There was no opening work in process. During the month, 1 600 units were started and materials costing $16 000 were issued and charged to this account. The cost of operations during the month was $5 600. Department A completed 1 200 units and these were transferred to department B. Work in process in department A at 31 January was one-half completed with respect to labour and overhead costs incurred in department A.

Department B—There was no opening work in process. The output transferred from department A was duly received. Operating costs of $4 000 were incurred in department B in the month. 600 units were completed and transferred to finished goods. At the end of the month, 600 units were one-third completed with respect to labour and overhead costs incurred in department B.

Assume that there is no shrinkage or spoilage. You are required to calculate the production cost per equivalent unit, using the weighted average method.

25 Cost Accumulation: Materials, Labour and Manufacturing Overhead

This chapter examines the problems of accounting for materials, labour and manufacturing overhead. The methods that are discussed are consistent with the use of a general ledger control system, and are readily adaptable to other integrated cost accounting systems. In general, the methods are common to both job costing and process costing systems. Throughout, our concern will be primarily with the measurement of costs as part of the process of inventory valuation and income determination, and with cost control to the extent that this is applicable under historical cost systems. The use of the flexible budget for the control of manufacturing overhead costs will also be explained. It should be emphasized that adequate managerial control over different aspects of production is best obtained through the use of budgeted or standard costs, which will be explained in Chapter 26.

Accounting for Materials

The first requirement that needs to be met in accounting for materials is to exercise control over:
(a) ordering, receiving and paying for material purchases; and
(b) issuing materials to production.

Material Purchases

A series of authorities usually constitute the initial evidence records relating to a purchase transaction. These are:
(a) A *purchase requisition*, which is a request by the factory store (approved by a responsible officer) for the purchase of specified materials needed in production.
(b) A *purchase order*, which the purchasing officer prepares from the requisition and which he places with an outside supplier. The purchase order must include all necessary instructions regarding specifications, prices and quantities, delivery and invoicing.
(c) A *goods received report*, which the factory storeman makes out on receipt of the materials (after checking them against a copy of the purchase order to ensure that they conform to specifications and other requirements). A copy of the goods received report becomes the basis of an entry in the perpetual inventory stock records.

Copies of all three documents are sent to the accounts department, where they combine with the supplier's invoice to become an expenditure voucher. [1] This provides the evidence for an entry in the purchase journal, which will ultimately lead to a debit entry in the material inventory control account and a credit entry in the accounts payable account. The expenditure voucher in due course also becomes the authority for payment.

[1] A voucher is simply a document, or set of documents, which provides evidence of a monetary transaction, receipt of goods, etc.

Material Issues

A proper materials control system requires that materials be issued from the factory store only on the basis of a *materials requisition*, which is a request from a production or other operating department for materials to be used for a particular purpose. The materials requisition specifies the cost unit (i.e. the particular job or process account) or, in the case of indirect materials, the manufacturing overhead account which is to be charged with the materials. The requisition also contains a description of the materials and the price at which the issue is to be recorded. One copy of the materials requisition is used by the store in recording material issues in the perpetual inventory stock records; another becomes the basis of an entry on the job or process cost card or other cost record; and a third is used in preparing a periodical summary of materials requisitions, which is the evidence for an entry in the general ledger debiting the work in process control account (in respect of direct materials) or the manufacturing overhead control account (in respect of indirect materials) and crediting the material inventory control account.

The above forms and documents provide control over the acquisition and use of materials.

Cost Records

So far as the detailed cost records are concerned, the first requirement is to maintain perpetual inventory stock cards controlled by the material inventory control account in the general ledger. Receipts of materials are recorded from information contained in goods received reports, and issues are written up from the materials requisitions. In pricing out material issues, the same assumptions may be made as were discussed in Chapter 4 in relation to the task of calculating the cost of goods sold by a trading business, i.e. material issues may be valued on the basis of actual or identified cost, FIFO, average cost or LIFO assumptions. In the interest of uniformity, however, it is recommended that the FIFO assumption be used where actual or identified cost is inappropriate. Another possibility is to value materials on the basis of predetermined or standard costs.

In addition to the perpetual inventory stock cards, which are essentially part of the accounting system, bin cards are sometimes maintained in the store to record receipts, issues and the balance of each line of material inventory in terms of quantities only.

The final task relating to materials involves the recording of the issues on the cost cards of individual jobs or processes (or other cost units). It has been seen that the materials requisition is the source of information for these entries. The cost of finished work is derived in due course from the cost cards, and is recorded by means of debit entries on the finished goods inventory cards and in the finished goods inventory control account in the general ledger, where the corresponding credit entry is to the work in process control account.

The method of accounting for materials is illustrated in Figure 25—A.

Accounting for Labour

In accounting for labour, it is first necessary to determine the wages payable to each employee during each pay period (e.g. a week), to summarize this information on a

Figure 25—A
Accounting for Materials in an Integrated Cost System

Cost Records   **Financial Records**

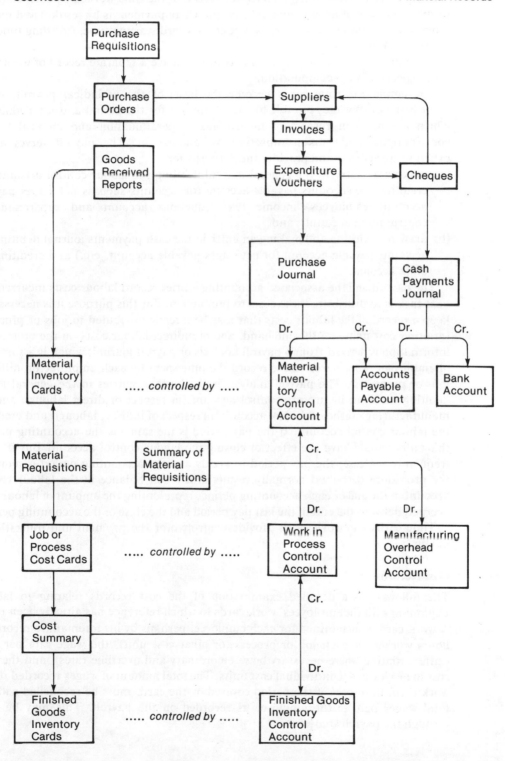

payroll, and to classify the payroll in order to distinguish between the direct and indirect labour force and permit analysis of labour costs by departments.

Wages payable are ascertained from a record of the time worked by each employee (or from a record of each employee's output where payment is by results) and for this purpose an employee's *time card* is needed to record starting time, finishing time and overtime. Where the worker is paid by results, a time card may be used for disciplinary purposes, but it is then necessary to have a separate record of work done for purposes of wage computation.

The employees' time cards become the basis of the periodical payroll, which records the gross wages payable to each employee for the period and the deductions which are made in respect of income tax, superannuation and medical benefit contributions, trade union subscriptions, and so on. The payroll serves as an expenditure voucher and provides the authority for:

(a) making an entry in the general journal debiting the labour control account and crediting the accounts payable account (or accounts such as net wages payable account, employees' income tax deductions account and superannuation contributions account); and

(b) drawing a cheque and making an entry in the cash payments journal debiting the accounts payable account (or net wages payable account, etc.) and crediting the bank account.

The payroll and the associated accounting entries record labour costs incurred; the next task is to distribute these costs to production. For this purpose it is necessary to keep a record of the labour costs that may be directly attributed to jobs or processes (or other cost units) on the one hand, and of indirect labour costs on the other. This information is derived from a payroll analysis or payroll journal, which is a summary of employees' *work cards* (these record the time spent by each employee on different jobs or processes). The payroll analysis is the basis of entries in the general ledger debiting the work in process control account (in respect of direct labour), and the manufacturing overhead control account (in respect of indirect labour), and crediting the labour control account. If the pay period is the same as the accounting period, this entry should have the effect of closing the labour control account. But if, as is frequently the case, the pay period is weekly and the accounting period is monthly, the procedure described normally results in a credit balance in the labour control account at the end of each accounting period, representing the amount of labour costs accrued between the end of the last pay period and the close of the accounting period.

Time cards and work cards provide controls over the payment and utilization of labour.

Cost Records

The following is a detailed examination of the cost records relating to labour, beginning with the employees' work cards to which reference has already been made. A work card is maintained for each employee, perhaps by his foreman, to record the hours worked on each job or process (or other cost unit), the wage rate per hour (differentiating where necessary between ordinary and overtime rates), and the total cost to be charged to individual cost units. The total amount of wages recorded on the work card, in respect of the period covered by the card, must be reconciled with the total wages paid to the employee as recorded on the payroll. This may be done through the payroll analysis.

The work cards become the basis of entries on the job or process cost cards. As with material costs, the direct labour costs of finished production are ascertained by summarizing information derived from the cost cards of finished cost units. These costs are debited to the finished goods inventory control account in the general ledger (and to the individual perpetual inventory records in respect of finished goods), the corresponding credit entry being to the work in process control account.

Separate cost cards are maintained in respect of so-called standing orders designed to cover different kinds of indirect labour costs incurred by the direct labour force. Each category of indirect labour, such as idle time during machinery repairs, lost time due to sickness, idle time due to insufficient orders, or labour cost of experimental work, is allotted a standing order number and charged with the relevant labour costs.

There may be some difficulty in deciding whether labour charges are direct or indirect. Overtime paid to the direct labour force may or may not be charged as direct labour, depending on the circumstances under which it is worked. If the factory has so many orders that it is necessary to work overtime on some jobs chosen at random, there is a case for charging all orders with direct labour at ordinary rates and for treating overtime payments as a separate item of manufacturing overhead. If, on the other hand, a particular order is treated as urgent at the customer's request, the whole of the labour costs attributable to that order, including overtime, may reasonably be charged to it.

Some labour related costs which at first sight may appear to be indirect costs, such as payroll tax and workers' compensation insurance in respect of direct labour, may be more usefully classified as direct because of their association with direct labour costs. The adjustments to direct labour costs to allow for such items may be made in the payroll analysis as well as on the work cards, thereby being reflected in the debit to the work in process control account in the general ledger as well as in the charges recorded on the job or process cost cards.

The charges to standing orders in respect of indirect labour eventually become the basis of debit entries in the manufacturing overhead control account.

The recording of the flow of labour costs is illustrated in Figure 25—B.

Accounting for Manufacturing Overhead

Accounting for manufacturing overhead serves a number of purposes: financial accounting, product costing and cost control. We shall examine first how manufacturing overhead costs are recorded, accumulated and distributed to production within an historical cost accounting system. The analysis of manufacturing overhead for control purposes is considered later.

Where the cost unit is a job or an output unit, overhead represents common costs which cannot be traced directly to the cost unit. Unlike material and labour costs, overhead cannot be controlled at the cost unit level, and can be controlled only at the departmental level. The analysis of manufacturing overhead for the control purpose is *not* part of the double-entry framework. Accounting for overhead thus has two separate and distinct functions. But it is desirable to adopt methods of recording and distributing overhead in the accounts that facilitate its subsequent analysis for control purposes, as will be explained below.

Figure 25—B
Accounting for Labour in an Integrated Cost System

Cost Records   **Financial Records**

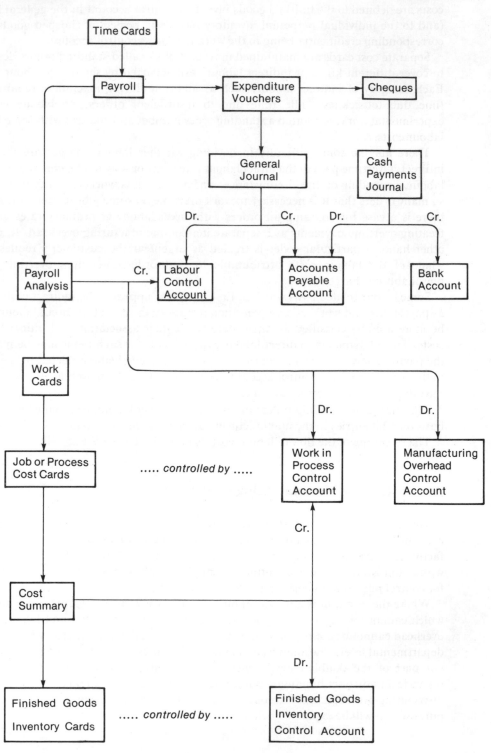

Accounting for Overhead—Product Costing

There are three major problems, and a number of smaller problems, involved in the conventional accounting treatment. Each of the major problems is associated with the measurement of a different aspect of manufacturing overhead: manufacturing overhead incurred budgeted manufacturing overhead and manufacturing overhead absorbed or applied.

1 Recording Actual Manufacturing Overhead Incurred

This is the financial accounting problem of ensuring that direct material and labour costs, and indirect overhead costs, are recorded separately. Since manufacturing overhead cannot be associated directly with cost units and, further, since expenses such as depreciation are not recorded continuously throughout the year, it is not possible to allocate actual manufacturing overhead incurred among production units.

2 Estimating Predetermined Overhead Recovery Rates

As it is not possible to charge actual overhead to cost units in the same way as direct material and direct labour costs, it is usual to predetermine overhead recovery rates as follows:
(a) estimate the manufacturing overhead that will be incurred in the ensuing period, i.e. the budgeted manufacturing overhead;
(b) estimate the level of activity (usually measured in terms of homogeneous units of output, or direct labour or machine hours) for the period; and
(c) use these two estimates to compute the predetermined overhead recovery rates that may be applied to the production which is actually carried out during the ensuing period.

3 Applying Predetermined Overhead Recovery Rates

This is essentially the cost accounting problem, whereby budgeted overhead is apportioned to actual production in the period by means of the predetermined overhead recovery rates. If the actual results turn out to be not in accordance with the estimates, the manufacturing overhead incurred will not be exactly absorbed by the work performed, as will be explained later.

Steps in Accounting for Manufacturing Overhead

To summarize, the following procedures are involved in accounting for manufacturing overhead:
(a) At the beginning of an accounting period, total manufacturing overhead and the level of activity for the ensuing period are estimated by means of a budget of manufacturing overhead and a production budget, respectively.[2]
(b) Predetermined overhead recovery rates are estimated by relating the budgeted overhead to the budgeted level of activity.
(c) The predetermined overhead rates are applied to production carried out during the ensuing accounting period in order to charge it with its assumed share of manufacturing overhead. In the general ledger, the work in process control account is debited and the manufacturing overhead control account is credited.

---

[2] The preparation and significance of the production budget will be discussed in Chapter 28.

In the cost records, it is necessary to make charges, based on the predetermined rates, to individual job or process cost cards.

(d) In recording actual overhead incurred it is convenient to make a distinction between service departments and production departments. The former provide internal services (e.g. power or repair facilities) which are utilized by the production departments which are directly engaged in the manufacturing operations of the factory (and possibly by other service departments as well). All costs of operating a service department are accumulated in a service department expenses account (such as power expenses account or repair shop expenses account) and distributed at the end of the accounting period to the manufacturing overhead control account of the production departments, since overhead is applied to production through this account.

(e) At the end of the accounting period, when all incurred and absorbed overhead has been recorded, the balance of the manufacturing overhead control account represents manufacturing overhead under-absorbed (if a debit balance), or over-absorbed (if a credit balance). The analysis and treatment of this balance will be discussed later.

(f) For managerial control purposes, differences between incurred overhead and overhead applied to production are analysed by means of the flexible budget technique. This analysis is not part of the double-entry framework.

Estimating Predetermined Overhead Recovery Rates

There are several problems connected with estimating predetermined overhead rates: the concept of the factory's normal capacity; overhead allocation to departments; the classification of fixed and variable overhead; and the choice of the base for estimating and applying predetermined overhead rates.

Normal Capacity

The estimation of manufacturing overhead depends on the use of some concept of capacity, i.e. the capacity of the plant to produce over the accounting period in question, having regard to such factors as the size and utilization of the labour force available, the number of shifts and the pattern of production in general. Actual or annual capacity relates to the expected level of activity in any one year. Normal capacity, on the other hand, is a medium to long range concept, which relates to the expected level of activity over a period of years rather than to any particular year. Normal capacity may be defined as the capacity essential for efficient operation in the medium to long run. As this is also the criterion used in deciding on the installation and size of new plants, the concept is relevant in the context of competitive product pricing. Thus in most situations normal capacity is the appropriate measure to use in estimating overhead recovery rates.

Overhead Allocation to Departments

The first step in preparing the budget is to estimate the cost of each item of manufacturing overhead for the period under consideration, both in total and by departments. Indirect labour costs are thus estimated on the basis of such factors as employee establishments and expected changes in industrial awards. Repair costs may be estimated by reference to the general age and condition of machinery. Generally, many overhead costs can be traced directly to individual departments.

Otherwise an initial allocation of the estimated overhead is made to production and service departments on some appropriate but arbitrary basis.

The next step is to distribute service department overhead to production departments. The distribution may be made in a number of ways:

(a) *Direct method.* Each service department's overhead costs are allocated directly to production departments (i.e. no costs are allocated to other service departments).

(b) *Step method.* Where a service department provides services to other service departments, its overhead costs are allocated to the other service departments as well as to production departments. The logical order should be to allocate first the costs of that department which provides most services to other service departments, and so on. All overhead costs of service departments are eventually allocated to production departments by a series of steps.

(c) *Reciprocal services distribution method.* Where two or more service departments provide services to one another, the problem of redistributing the overhead costs between themselves (before the final allocation to production departments takes place) may be solved by using simultaneous equations or linear algebra analysis.

All costs of service departments are regarded as overhead costs. The distribution of the budgeted overhead of service departments to production departments is unavoidably arbitrary. Since all methods are arbitrary, one should use the simplest appropriate distribution method, which is often the direct method.

There are two important issues which need to be considered carefully at the budget stage, because they have implications for subsequent cost analysis and control. The first issue is the use of estimated rates for charging services to production departments. If the services of a service department (such as the power, maintenance or computing service department) can be charged out to production departments at an estimated rate (e.g. $x per kWh, $y per labour hour, or $z per unit of computing time), this will facilitate overhead cost analysis at a later stage. With respect to a production department, the difference between the budgeted allowance (estimated usage multiplied by an estimated rate) and the actual amount charged (actual usage multiplied by an estimated rate), represents under- or over-utilization of the service facilities by the production department, for which it may be held responsible. This procedure should leave spending variances [3] due to differences between budgeted and actual costs of service facilities in the service departments where they properly belong. Service department costs are best analysed by a comparison of the actual costs against flexible budget allowances at the actual level of production department usage. This means that flexible budgets should be prepared for service departments in the same way as for production departments.

The above method of charging out costs of services is one that is consistent with effective cost control. It is important that the rate employed for charging out services be based on an appropriate activity index, such as labour or machine hours, in the service department (i.e. there needs to be a cause and effect relationship between the index and the costs of providing the services). The principle is similar to that of selecting a measurement base for manufacturing overhead recovery rates, discussed in a following sub-section.

Example: A factory consists of two service departments, a power station and an engineering department, and two production departments, A and B. Suppose that A

[3] Spending variances are discussed in a later section of this chapter on pages 607-9.

and B have used 100 and 300 kWh of electricity, and 100 and 200 labour hours of the engineering department's facilities, respectively. The allocation of the service departments' costs to the production departments by the direct apportionment method and predetermined rates is as follows:

Service Department	Index of Activity	Predetermined Rate	Estimated Costs	Allocated to A	B
Power station	Kilowatt hours	$1 per kWh	$400	$100	$300
Engineering department	Labour hours	$2 per labour hour	600	200	400
			$1 000	$300	$700

Fixed and Variable Overhead Classification

The second issue which needs to be considered carefully at the budget stage, because of its implications for cost analysis and control, is the classification of each department's overhead into its fixed and variable components. In product costing, use is made of manufacturing overhead recovery rates for applying overhead to production. The estimation of these rates is based on a static *planning budget*, in which it is not necessary to classify overhead into fixed and variable. But this classification is a fundamental part of the *flexible budget* used for cost control. Hence it is desirable to separate all overhead items into their fixed and variable components in the initial stage of preparing the planning budget.

We shall discuss only briefly the problem of segregating the fixed and variable components of a particular item of estimated overhead. Some overhead items are obviously fixed (e.g. factory rent and supervision), and some obviously variable (e.g. supplies). In other cases the observations may be plotted on a graph in which the x axis represents volume of output or activity and the y axis represents total cost in past periods. It is frequently possible to confirm visually that a linear functional relationship between costs and volume is a reasonable assumption. The fixed and variable components in the overhead item then can be separated by means of linear regression analysis employing the least squares method.[4] A graph may be constructed for each item of overhead cost, and a regression line fitted to the data, as shown in Figure 25—C. The equation of the line is:[5]

$$\hat{y} = \hat{F} + \hat{V}x$$

where $\hat{y}$ is an estimate of total cost,[6] $\hat{F}$ is an estimate of the level of the fixed cost component, $\hat{V}$ is an estimate of variable cost per unit of x, and x is an index of the volume of activity. $\hat{F}$ is the y intercept and $\hat{V}$ the slope of the regression line. The correlation coefficient may be used to test the goodness of fit.

---

[4] Since the least squares method computations can be performed on small hand calculators, the use of crude methods, such as the 'high low' method (in which a straight line is fitted to the two most extreme observations), is inexcusable.

[5] The standard form is $\hat{y} = \hat{a} + \hat{b}x$, and the least squares normal equations for estimating a and b are:

$$\Sigma y - n\hat{a} - \hat{b}\Sigma x = 0$$
$$\text{and} \quad \Sigma xy - \hat{a}\Sigma x - \hat{b}\Sigma x^2 = 0$$

where n is the sample size.

[6] y is the actual value of total cost corresponding to a given value of x, while $\hat{y}$ is the value of total cost 'predicted' by the regression line.

Figure 25—C
The Analysis of Cost Behaviour

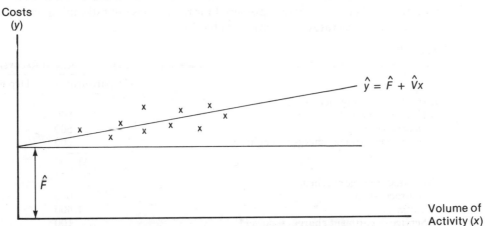

Table 25—1 on page 604 shows department A's fixed budget suitably classified into fixed and variable overhead components.

The Base for Estimating and Applying Overhead Rates

The purpose of calculating overhead recovery rates is to find a means of charging production in general, and individual jobs, products or processes in particular, with a fair share of manufacturing overhead incurred. This implies the need to find some base measure or index of activity in the production department to which manufacturing overhead may reasonably be related.

Physical output is theoretically a good base measure, since it is output that determines profits. A condition of its use is that the goods produced be reasonably homogeneous in character, as for example in some process industries. But in most cases the production of diverse products in the department or factory precludes the use of physical output units.

Therefore an index of input is commonly employed, such as direct material or labour costs, direct labour hours or machine hours. Generally, the use of direct labour hours is preferable to direct wages because overhead costs are largely a function of *time*. Many fixed costs, such as rent, are a function of time and, although variable overhead is related to the volume of output, volume itself is closely related to time. There is a further disadvantage in using direct wages where there are wage rate differentials. For example, a job can be performed by skilled labour in two hours at $12 an hour, or by relatively unskilled labour in five hours at $4 an hour. Total direct wages are $24 and $20 for skilled and unskilled labour respectively, yet it is reasonable to assume that overhead costs incurred in the second case would probably be higher.

With respect to a choice between direct labour hours and machine hours, certain overhead costs tend to be related to labour hours, others to machine hours. It is feasible, of course, for the overhead rate in one department (say, the machining department) to be based on estimated machine hours, and the rate in another department (say, the finishing department) to be based on estimated direct labour hours, depending on the capital or labour intensity of the production mode.

The Static Manufacturing Overhead Budget

Departmental budgets, in which manufacturing overhead is estimated at static planning levels of activity, are prepared for the purpose of estimating manufacturing overhead recovery rates, as shown in Table 25—1.

Table 25—1
Static Planning Manufacturing Overhead Budgets and Calculation of Overhead Recovery Rates

	Department A	Department B
Estimated fixed overhead—		
Indirect labour	800	200
Depreciation	500	1 400
Service department charges—engineering	200	400
	$1 500	$2 000
Estimated variable overhead—		
Indirect labour	1 000	200
Supplies	1 400	500
Service department charges—power*	100	300
	$2 500	$1 000
Estimated total overhead	$4 000	$3 000
Estimated direct labour hours (DLH)	5 000	—
Estimated machine hours	—	2 000
Predetermined overhead recovery rate	$0.80	$1.50
	(per DLH)	(per machine hour)

* Power costs are often treated as partly fixed and partly variable. They are classified as wholly variable in this table for convenience.

For economy of space, subsequent illustrations will be confined to department A. Suppose that actual overhead incurred and overhead applied to production in the period in that department are as follows:

Actual level of activity in period—DLH	6 000
Overhead applied to production at $0.80 per DLH	$4 800
Actual manufacturing overhead incurred	$4 700

There is a difference between overhead incurred and overhead applied of $100, which is a credit balance, i.e. manufacturing overhead has been over-absorbed by this amount. Manufacturing overhead under- or over-absorbed is often described as an overhead variance, and the accounting treatment of this variation is explained below.

Accounting Treatment of Variances

An overhead variance is usually transferred to the trading account as a separate expense or revenue item, when the amount is believed to arise from lack of control or variations in efficiency. In particular, a debit balance is dealt with in this way (see Figure 24—A) and idle capacity losses are regarded for this purpose as resulting from a particular kind of inefficiency.

If, however, the variance is believed to result from faulty budgeting or the adoption of erroneous overhead recovery rates (e.g. when the budgeted level differs from the actual level of activity), then the variance may be reallocated over the work in process control account, the cost of sales account and the finished goods inventory control

Figure 25—D
Accounting For Manufacturing Overhead in an Integrated Cost System

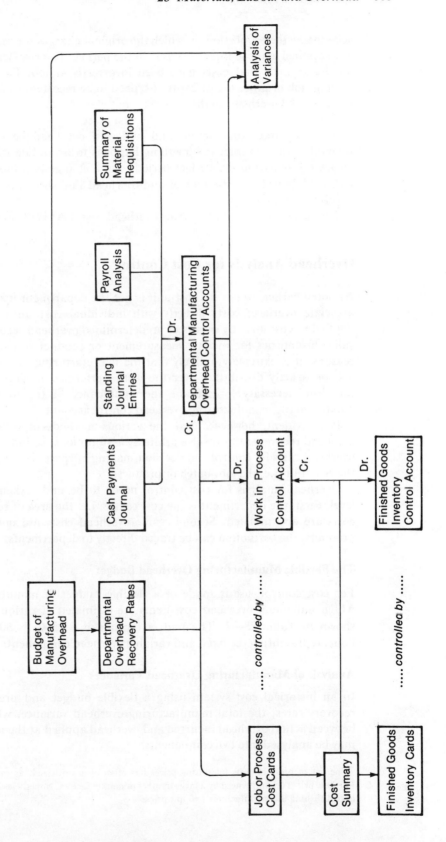

account, in the proportions in which the original charges for manufacturing overhead were applied to these three accounts in the period. The reallocations may be justified on the grounds that costs have been incorrectly stated. For purposes of product pricing, job or process cost cards also need to be recosted, so as to adjust the figures for absorbed overhead to the amounts that should have been recorded if the correct recovery rates had been adopted in the first place.

It is important that actual and budgeted overhead be compared at frequent intervals, e.g. monthly. If something happens to invalidate the budget or overhead recovery rate during the budget period (e.g. a change in industrial awards affecting indirect labour costs) the budget and overhead rate should be adjusted immediately to reflect the change.

The recording of manufacturing overhead cost flows is illustrated in Figure 25—D.

Overhead Analysis for Cost Control

As noted earlier, where the cost unit is not the department itself it is not possible to associate overhead costs directly with individual cost units. Instead overhead is applied to cost units by means of predetermined overhead recovery rates, in order to value inventories for income measurement or product pricing.[7] For a number of reasons, it is extremely unlikely that the manufacturing overhead actually incurred will be exactly distributed over the work performed during the period, and it is therefore necessary to examine the significance of the under- or over-absorbed balance in the manufacturing overhead control account.

It is evident, however, that the various methods of estimating and applying overhead recovery rates involve arbitrary assumptions, so that meaningful analysis of overhead costs for control and decision-making purposes is not possible at the level of the cost unit (i.e. the job, batch or product).

Overhead analysis for cost control needs to be undertaken at the departmental level. First, the department is the cost centre, i.e. the area of responsibility for which costs are accumulated. Second, while overhead costs are not traceable to jobs or products, the costs often can be traced directly to departments.

The Flexible Manufacturing Overhead Budget

For cost control, use is made of a flexible budget of manufacturing overhead, in which individual overhead cost items are estimated at various levels of activity, as shown in Table 25—2. The budget formula is $1 500 + $0.50 per direct labour hour, representing the fixed and variable overhead components respectively.

Analysis of Manufacturing Overhead Variances

In an historical cost system using a flexible budget and predetermined overhead recovery rates, the total manufacturing overhead variance, which is the difference between actual overhead incurred and overhead applied at the actual level of activity, may be analysed into two components:

---

[7] The use of product costs for setting prices has often been criticized, as many firms are price-takers. Further, prices are influenced by a large number of market factors. Nonetheless, product costs are relevant in establishing the manufacturer's supply prices.

Table 25—2
Department A—Flexible Budget of Manufacturing Overhead

Direct Labour Hours (DLH):	3 000	4 000	5 000	6 000	7 000
Estimated fixed overhead—					
Indirect labour	$800	$800	$800	$800	$800
Depreciation	500	500	500	500	500
Service department charges—Engineering	200	200	200	200	200
	$1 500	$1 500	$1 500	$1 500	$1 500
Estimated variable overhead—*					
Indirect labour	600	800	1 000	1 200	1 400
Supplies	840	1 120	1 400	1 680	1 960
Service department charges—Power	60	80	100	120	140
	$1 500	$2 000	$2 500	$3 000	$3 500
Estimated total overhead	$3 000	$3 500	$4 000	$4 500	$5 000

* For simplicity, strictly linear relationships between variable overhead costs and direct labour hours have been assumed.

(a) An *overhead spending variance*, which arises arithmetically as the difference between actual overhead incurred and the flexible budget amount determined for the actual level of activity. This variance is likely to arise from such causes as price differences on the purchase of goods and services of an overhead nature, or variations from the level of efficiency in the utilization of those goods and services which has been assumed in the calculation of the flexible budget formula.

(b) An *overhead volume variance*, which arises arithmetically as the difference between the flexible budget amount determined for the actual level of activity and the overhead applied at this level of activity (employing the predetermined overhead rate). The variance is attributable to the difference between the actual level of activity and the normal or planned level of activity used in determining the predetermined overhead recovery rate (e.g. in the case of department A, estimated direct labour hours). This variance, of course, applies only to fixed overhead, as by definition the variable overhead included in the flexible budget will be the same arithmetical amount as that applied to production for the period.

An overhead variance is said to be favourable if it is a credit balance, and unfavourable if a debit balance. The favourable overhead variance of $100 in department A may be analysed as shown in Figure 25—E, where it is assumed that actual overhead incurred comprises $1 600 for fixed costs and $3 100 for variable costs.

This example focuses on an important concept underlying the analysis of overhead variances. In meeting a financial accounting purpose, i.e. inventory valuation and income measurement, the accounts have thrown up a favourable overhead variance of $100. For purposes of 'responsibility accounting', whereby accounting information is associated with a responsibility function, it is necessary to separate this figure into controllable and non-controllable components. Thus total overhead variance is analysed into a favourable *volume variance* of $300, which is largely uncontrollable at the production level, and a controllable unfavourable *spending variance* of $200.

Figure 25—E
Analysis of Manufacturing Overhead Variances in an Historical Cost System

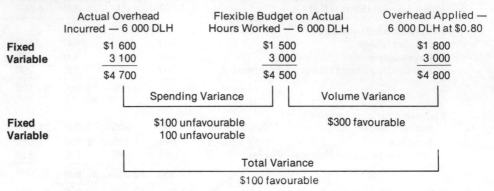

	Actual Overhead Incurred — 6 000 DLH	Flexible Budget on Actual Hours Worked — 6 000 DLH	Overhead Applied — 6 000 DLH at $0.80
Fixed	$1 600	$1 500	$1 800
Variable	3 100	3 000	3 000
	$4 700	$4 500	$4 800

	Spending Variance	Volume Variance
Fixed	$100 unfavourable	$300 favourable
Variable	100 unfavourable	

Total Variance
$100 favourable

The spending variance comprises an unfavourable fixed overhead variance of $100 and an unfavourable variable overhead variance of $100. Many fixed overhead costs are uncontrollable, e.g. depreciation, while most variable overhead costs are controllable at the departmental level. It is recommended that, instead of relying on conventional wisdom (since fixed and variable overhead are only loosely associated with uncontrollable and controllable items respectively), a comprehensive analysis be made of the spending variance for each individual overhead item, as shown in Table 25—3. It is assumed that the amounts of the individual expense items for actual overhead incurred are as shown in the first column.

Table 25—3
Department A—Analysis of Spending Variance

	Actual Overhead Incurred	Budget Adjusted to Actual Level of Activity—6 000 DLH	Spending Variance
Fixed overhead—			
Indirect labour	$850	$800	$50 U
Depreciation	500	500	—
Service department charges—Engineering	250	200	50 U
	$1 600	$1 500	$100 U
Variable overhead—			
Indirect labour	1 100	1 200	100 F
Supplies	1 850	1 680	170 U
Service department charges—Power	150	120	30 U
	$3 100	$3 000	$100 U
	$4 700	$4 500	$200 U

Note: F = favourable (a credit); U = unfavourable (a debit).

The spending variance derived from a flexible budget analysis represents the difference between actual overhead and budgeted overhead at the actual level of activity. The departmental head may reasonably be asked to explain large spending variations based on this kind of analysis, because the influence of changes in the level of activity has been allowed for.

It was recommended in an earlier section that production departments should be charged for their use of service facilities at an estimated rate, in order to facilitate cost control. It is seen in Table 25—3 that department A has been charged with excessive use of service facilities of both the engineering and power departments, relative to its entitlements in the flexible budget.

Problems in Variance Analysis

Variance analysis in the historical cost system has certain limitations, even where a flexible budget technique is employed.

The analysis does not address the question of whether the 6 000 direct labour hours incurred in department A are justified in terms of the volume of production achieved in the period. This requires a more detailed analysis of the kind which is provided in a standard cost system, as explained in the following chapter.

There is another seemingly intractable problem, which also applies to variance analysis in a standard cost accounting system. Suppose there is a relatively large number of service departments, which provide service facilities to one another as well as to production departments. An allocation of their costs to production departments by the direct method (which was earlier recommended because of its simplicity) then might not be meaningful. Some writers suggest that some other method, e.g. the step method or the reciprocal services distribution method, should be employed. Unfortunately the end result may be equally meaningless in terms of effective cost control. [8]

Under these circumstances, cost analysis can be based on the initial departmental budgets *before* any inter-department distributions of costs are made for the purpose of estimating overhead recovery rates. Service departments are treated as if they are production departments, and flexible budgets are prepared for service departments in the same way as for production departments. It has been said earlier that this is the best method of analysing and controlling service department costs. The present recommendation constitutes the *general case*, in which each department (whether production or service department) is responsible for *all* costs directly traceable to it in terms of flexible budget allowances at the actual level of activity in that department. [9] An analysis in monetary terms cannot cover the use of service facilities, and a complementary analysis in terms of physical usage needs to be undertaken to evaluate the usage of service facilities by each department. The analysis described above becomes cumbersome when there are more than a few service departments.

If a service department is large enough to be made autonomous, an alternative approach that would appeal to an aggressive management board is to treat the service department as a *profit centre*—i.e. the service department sells its services to other departments and is responsible for its revenue as well as its expenses. Under this approach, considerations relating to captive customers and sources of supply will need to be resolved. A further danger is that conflicts between departmental objectives may have adverse effects on the profitability or efficiency of the organization as a whole.

Where there is a large number of service departments which interact with one

---

[8] We are not suggesting that a little arbitrary allocation is valid, while a lot of it is not. Any allocation at all cannot be justified in theory. However, one may or may not feel confident in using figures for *cost control purposes*, depending on the extensiveness of the allocations by which the figures have been obtained.

[9] Direct materials and labour may be included in a comprehensive flexible budget control system.

another as well as with production departments, the problem of exercising effective cost control over overhead costs is complex and difficult.

The analysis of overhead variances can be justified only if it leads to better cost control. In some cases differences between actual and budgeted performance may be explained more effectively in terms of some physical index of activity rather than dollars, e.g. indirect labour hours rather than indirect labour costs. Analysis in terms of physical measurement units may be used to complement or replace analysis in dollar terms, where this would lead to more effective cost control.

Additional Reading

Horngren, C.T., *Cost Accounting—A Managerial Emphasis*, 4th edn., 1977, Prentice-Hall, Englewood Cliffs, N.J., Chapters 8 and 16.

Shillinglaw, S., *Managerial Cost Accounting*, 4th edn., 1977, Irwin, Homewood, Ill., Chapter 7.

Discussion Questions

1 Explain the steps that should be taken, in accounting for raw material inventories, to ensure effective control over ordering, purchasing, storing and issuing of raw materials.

2 Why is it necessary to establish manufacturing overhead absorption rates? How are they determined?

3 Explain which department of a manufacturing company should be held responsible for the following expenses:

(a) under- or over-utilized units of service, such as power or maintenance hours; and

(b) the difference between the budgeted and actual costs of service facilities.

How would you allocate service department expenses so that effective cost control can be exercised?

4 Consider the problem of unused plant capacity in relation to the absorption of fixed manufacturing overhead.

5 What factors are responsible for differences between manufacturing overhead incurred and manufacturing overhead charged to production? How may these differences be analysed in an historical cost accounting system?

6 Explain why the use of a flexible manufacturing overhead budget results in better cost control than the use of a static budget.

7 What are the limitations of a flexible manufacturing budget when used as a cost control tool in a manufacturing company?

Exercises

1 Prepare a diagram to illustrate the flow of information necessary to account for labour costs in a manufacturing enterprise operating under the following conditions:

(a) a system of historical job costs is in operation, and inventory and cost records are controlled by accounts in the general ledger;

(b) employees are paid on a weekly basis; and

(c) the accounting period is on a monthly basis, an analysis of monthly labour costs being carried out by means of a payroll journal.

Show clearly the relationship maintained between the cost and the financial records.

2 What would you recommend as a basis for allocating the following expenses to production departments in a manufacturing company: indirect labour; depreciation on plant; repairs to plant; occupancy expense; and power expense.

3 The following information refers to a manufacturing company for the coming year 1985:

(a) the company is divided into two production departments (A and B), and three service departments (occupancy, power and store);

(b) occupancy expenses are estimated to be $2 400 and it is proposed to allocate these expenses on the basis of the floor space occupied by the other departments, as follows: power, 500 m^2; store, 1 000 m^2; department A, 3 000 m^2; and department B, 1 500 m^2:

(c) estimated fuel costs are $3 500 and the power consumption of the two production departments is estimated as follows: department A, 300 kW; and department B, 200 kW;

(d) store expenses, estimated at $1 400, are to be evenly distributed between the two production departments; and

(e) departments A and B are expected to incur other manufacturing overhead expenses of $1 680 and $1 020, respectively.

You are required to:

(i)   prepare a manufacturing overhead budget;

(ii) evaluate the usefulness of the budget; and

(iii) discuss the limitations of the budget in controlling costs.

4 The Gold Coast Ltd produces a homogeneous product. Its budget is prepared for a normal activity level of 10 000 units per month. Budgeted costs and actual costs incurred in January 1985 are shown below:

Cost Items	Budgeted Costs	Actual Costs Incurred
Variable overhead—		
Indirect labour	$10 000	$9 500
Supplies	1 000	750
Power	1 000	1 000
Repairs	1 000	850
Other	2 000	1 700
Fixed overhead—		
Depreciation	5 000	5 000
Other	2 000	2 000
	$22 000	$20 800

You are required to:

(a) prepare a flexible budget for the activity levels of 8 000, 10 000 and 12 000 units per month;

(b) specify the formula for the relationship between costs and the volume of production;

(c) compare actual costs incurred with budgeted costs at the normal level of activity; and

(d) compare actual costs incurred with budgeted costs at the actual level of activity in January of 8 500 units. Explain which comparison is more useful for cost control.

5 In February the Gold Coast Ltd operated at a capacity of 9 000 units and actual overhead costs were as follows:

    fixed overhead incurred $7 500; and

    variable overhead incurred $13 000.

   You are required to:

(a) calculate the overhead absorption rate based on the normal activity level and budgeted costs, from the data supplied in Exercise 4; and

(b) analyse the overhead variances and explain what investigation you would carry out on the basis of your results.

6 Total overhead expenses of a manufacturing company at different levels of production are shown below. You are required to segregate the overhead costs into fixed and variable components.

Units Produced	Total Overhead Costs
1 020	$6 550
2 010	8 050
3 500	10 500
4 800	12 500
7 200	16 000
8 500	18 600
9 000	19 000

26 Standard Costs and Managerial Control

Standard cost systems have been devised as tools for planning costs and evaluating and controlling management performance. Standard costing involves the following steps: (a) setting predetermined targets or standards of performance for each cost element, (b) measuring actual performance, (c) comparing actual performance with standard performance, (d) reporting and analysing the differences or variances between actual and standard performance, and (f) recommending corrective action to management. These steps are basically similar to those used for budgetary control of manufacturing overhead, as discussed in the previous chapter.

Setting Standards

Standard costs are predetermined costs. These predetermined costs may be based on ideal standards or currently attainable standards.

Ideal standards imply absolute efficiency under perfect conditions, and are sometimes used in the hope of motivating performance. Because such efficiency is unattainable, they often have proved frustrating and have fallen short of the objective, but there are some special circumstances in which ideal standards may be employed. For example, in setting standard labour costs, it is necessary to specify the grade of labour for each operation. Suppose that the particular grade for an operation is not currently available. It may be desirable, nonetheless, to retain this grade in the specification, in order that the additional cost of substituting a different grade of labour is disclosed. The principle may also apply to a materials specification under some circumstances.

Generally, standards should reflect reasonable efficiency under expected actual operating conditions. Standards comprise physical or quantity targets, such as the amount of materials or the number of hours, as well as price standards. Quantity standards may be based on careful planning or engineering studies. For example, the number of standard hours to perform a particular operation may be based on methods time measurement and similar studies. It is also important for labour efficiency standards to reflect increasing efficiency as the worker gains experience on his task. This 'learning curve' effect applies both to individual and group performance, and is particularly important in complex, labour-intensive operations, such as those in electronic industries.

Price standards, on the other hand, reflect a prediction of future prices. However, tightly set price standards for materials and labour may promote efficiency in the purchasing and personnel departments, respectively.

The manufacturing overhead recovery rates in a standard cost system are based on total budgeted overhead for each production department and budgeted levels of activity in that department. They are the same as the predetermined overhead recovery rates in an historical cost accounting system, described in Chapter 25.

Material and Labour Variances

Causes of Variations from Standards

Variations between standard and actual costs may arise from a number of sources, although a general distinction may be made between variations that are due to price changes on the one hand and variations that are due to quantity or volume changes on the other. Thus, in the case of materials, variations known as 'material price variances' may result from fluctuations in the prices of materials, while 'material quantity variances' may be caused by changes in the efficiency with which materials are used.

Labour variations may likewise take two forms — 'labour rate variances' arising out of alterations in wage rates and 'labour efficiency, or labour time, variances' resulting from changes in the efficiency of labour, i.e. the time required to perform specified tasks. In countries where wage adjustments are decided by industrial tribunals, there may be a case for dispensing with 'labour rate variances' and adjusting standards whenever award rates are changed. However, even under these conditions over-award payments may exist, with the result that wage rate variations are not nearly so remote from the control of employers as may at first sight appear. In the system described in this chapter, the labour rate variance will be treated as one of the possible sources of difference between actual and standard costs.

Analysis of Material and Labour Variances

There are various methods of calculating and recording standard cost variances for direct materials and labour, most of which differ only in minor detail from one another. A simple system (usually called the Single or Comprehensive Plan) is summarized in Figure 26—A.

Figure 26—A
Material and Labour Variances

Type of Variance	Description of Variance	Computation
Material price variance (MPV)	Difference between SP and AP times AQ purchased	$(SP \times AQ) - (AP \times AQ)$ $= (SP - AP) AQ$
Material quantity variance (MQV)	Difference between SQ and AQ used times SP	$(SQ \times SP) - (AQ \times SP)$ $= (SQ - AQ) SP$
Labour rate variance (LRV)	Difference between SP and AP times actual hours worked (AQ)	$(SP \times AQ) - (AP \times AQ)$ $= (SP - AP) AQ$
Labour efficiency or labour time variance (LEV)	Difference between standard hours (SQ) and actual hours worked (AQ) times SP	$(SQ \times SP) - (AQ \times SP)$ $= (SQ - AQ) SP$

Note: AQ = actual quantity of materials or actual hours worked; SQ = standard quantity or standard hours; AP = actual price of materials or actual labour rate; and SP = standard price or standard rate.

An important principle in the Comprehensive Plan is that variances should be computed and recorded in the accounts at the earliest opportunity. Thus MPV is computed, and any difference between the actual price paid and the standard price is revealed, at the time when raw materials are purchased. The method emphasizes the cost control function, although there is a disadvantage in that MPV does not relate wholly to materials used on a particular job or cost unit. On the other hand, MQV is calculated on materials issued to production, so the two material variances, MPV and MQV, relate to different transactions.[1] From a cost control viewpoint, this is not an important consideration.

In the Comprehensive Plan, the direct material and labour variances are recorded as part of the double-entry framework. The three inventory accounts, i.e. material inventory control, work in process control and finished goods inventory control are all maintained at standard prices. The balance in the material inventory control account is represented by the actual quantities on hand at standard prices (AQ x SP), while the balances in the work in process control account and the finished goods inventory control account are represented by standard quantities on hand at standard prices (SQ x SP). Thus a variance does not arise when a transfer of goods from the work in process control account to the finished goods inventory control account is recorded.

The direct labour variances are computed on the same principles as the material variances, but unlike the latter the two labour variances arise simultaneously.

More complicated variance analysis may be performed where more than one type of material or labour is used in production. For example, the manufacture of chocolate requires a variety of materials, such as sugar, cocoa, flavouring and colouring materials. Instead of simply calculating total material variances, a detailed analysis relating to each raw material, as well as the proportions in which they are used (so-called material mix), can be made. However, the preparation of such a report will involve additional expense, which must be justified in terms of improved efficiency of operations.

An Illustration

The *standard cost card* for the production of a unit of product Z records the following information:

Materials:	20 kg at $10 each	200
Labour:	30 hours at $4 per hour	120
Overhead:	$0.80 per standard labour hour	24
		$344

Suppose that 300 kg of materials have been purchased at $10.50 per kg, and 220 kg have been issued for the production of 10 units of product Z. The payroll shows that 290 hours have been worked at $4.20 per hour, and an amount of $320 has been incurred on overhead costs in bringing the job to completion. The relevant ledger entries are as follows:

Material Inventory Control

Accounts payable	$3 000	Work in process control	$2 000
		Material quantity variance	200
		Balance c/d	800
	$3 000		$3 000
Balance b/d	$800		

---

[1] The material price variance relates to the job cost if materials are purchased for a specific job.

Material Price Variance

Accounts payable	$150

Material Quantity Variance

Material inventory control	$200

Labour Control

Cash	$1 218	Work in process control	$1 200
Labour efficiency variance	40	Labour rate variance	58
	$1 258		$1 258

Labour Rate Variance

Labour control	$58

Labour Efficiency Variance

	Labour control	$40

Manufacturing Overhead Control

Accounts payable	$320	Work in process control	$240
		Manufacturing overhead variance	80
	$320		$320

Manufacturing Overhead Variance

Manufacturing overhead control	$80

Work in Process Control

Material inventory control	$2 000	Finished goods inventory control	$3 440
Labour control	1 200		
Manufacturing overhead control	240		
	$3 440		$3 440

Finished Goods Inventory Control

Work in process control	$3 440

In the above example, the standard overhead absorption rate of $0.80 per standard direct labour hour is used for product costing, but is meaningless for cost control purposes. Unlike the direct material and labour variances, the unfavourable manufacturing overhead variance of $80 cannot be analysed meaningfully at the job or product level. For reasons explained in the previous chapter, overhead costs can be controlled only at the level of individual departments.

Overhead Analysis in a Standard Cost System

There is a number of methods of analysing manufacturing overhead variances in standard cost systems. Below is a simple explanation of overhead variance analysis in a standard cost system, which is an extension of the treatment of overhead variance analysis in the historical cost accounting system in Chapter 25. This is the so-called 'three-way variance analysis'.[2] The analysis is treated as a statistical exercise, although it may be incorporated into the double-entry framework. (For an illustration, see solution to Exercise 4 for this chapter in the *Student's Companion*.)

In a standard cost system using a flexible budget and predetermined overhead recovery rates, the total manufacturing overhead variance, which is the difference between actual overhead incurred and overhead applied at the standard level of activity, may be analysed into three components:

(a) An *overhead spending variance*, which arises arithmetically as the difference between actual overhead incurred and the flexible budget amount determined for the actual level of activity. This is the same variance as that analysed under the historical cost accounting system. The variable portion of the spending variance may be regarded as controllable at the foreman's level, whilst some of the fixed overhead may have been allocated to him from higher responsibility levels and may therefore be outside his control.

(b) An *overhead efficiency variance*, which arises arithmetically as the difference between the flexible budget amount determined for the actual level of activity and the flexible budget amount determined for the standard level of activity that is consistent with the output achieved. The historical cost analysis in Chapter 25 does not address the question of efficiency, which is a fundamental aspect of variance analysis in the standard cost system. The efficiency variance relates to the variable cost component of the predetermined overhead recovery rate, and is a function of the efficiency in the use of the input factor that serves as the selected base measure for that rate.

(c) An *overhead volume variance*, which arises arithmetically as the difference between the flexible budget amount determined for the standard level of activity and the overhead applied at that level of activity (employing the predetermined overhead recovery rate).[3]

The example of department A in the previous chapter will be used to illustrate overhead analysis in a standard cost system. To recapitulate, the overhead recovery rate is $0.80 per direct labour hour ($0.30 fixed, $0.50 variable), based on a flexible budget of $4 000 ($1 500 fixed, $2 500 variable) at a planned level of 5 000 direct labour hours. Department A incurred actual overhead of $4 700 ($1 600 fixed, $3 100 variable) as against a budgeted allowance of $4 500 ($1 500 fixed, $3 000 variable) for the 6 000 direct labour hours worked, giving rise to an unfavourable spending variance of $200. The overhead applied to production was $4 800 (6 000 direct labour hours at $0.80), giving rise to a favourable volume variance of $300. This analysis ignores the issue of the efficiency of the work performed in department A in the period, an omission that is remedied in the standard cost system.

---

[2] There is a two-way variance analysis, which does not make use of the flexible budget at the actual level of activity. There are also other more complicated versions.

[3] Note that this is not the same overhead volume variance as that in the historical cost accounting system.

Suppose that 5 400 standard labour hours have been worked in the period; this means that the 6 000 direct labour hours actually worked are equivalent to only 5 400 standard direct labour hours in terms of output achieved in the period. Using the flexible budget technique, the extended analysis that is now possible is illustrated in Figure 26—B.

Figure 26—B
Analysis of Manufacturing Overhead Variances in a Standard Cost System

	Actual Overhead Incurred 6 000 DLH	Flexible Budget on Actual Hours Worked 6 000 DLH	Flexible Budget on Standard Hours for Actual Output 5 400 DLH	Overhead Applied 5 400 DLH at $0.80
Fixed	$1 600	$1 500	$1 500	$1 629
Variable	3 100	3 000	2 700	2 700
	$4 700	$4 500	$4 200	$4 320

	Spending Variance	Efficiency Variance	Volume Variance
Fixed	$100 unfavourable	—	$120 favourable
Variable	100 unfavourable	$300 unfavourable	—

Total Variance
$380 unfavourable

The computation of the overhead variances is summarized as follows:

Actual overhead incurred	$4 700
Flexible budget for actual level of activity (6 000 DLH)	4 500
Unfavourable spending variance	$200
Flexible budget for actual level of activity (6 000 DLH)	4 500
Flexible budget for standard level of activity for output achieved (5 400 DLH)	4 200
Unfavourable efficiency variance	$300
Flexible budget for standard level of activity (5 400 DLH)	4 200
Overhead applied at standard level of activity (5 400 DLH)	4 320
Favourable volume variance	$120

To reiterate, manufacturing overhead variance is analysed at the departmental level, because the department is a cost centre and a responsibility centre. Many overhead costs can be traced directly to departments. But the accumulation of all overhead in production departments may contain a number of arbitrary allocations. Thus certain overhead items, such as factory office costs, cannot be traced directly and are allocated to departments; service department costs are allocated to production departments; and manufacturing overhead is apportioned arbitrarily into fixed and variable components. Further, the use of departmental overhead recovery rates to distribute overhead to production is also arbitrary in a number of respects. The use of arbitrary methods cannot be justified theoretically. But if the extent of arbitrary allocations is limited, overhead variance analysis may have a practical justification where it contributes to more effective cost control. If this is not achieved, alternative methods of accounting for manufacturing overhead should be considered. Some of these problems have been discussed in Chapter 25. If manufacturing overhead variance analysis cannot be justified on cost-benefit considerations, it should be abandoned altogether.

Some Control Aspects of Variance Analysis

When is a Variance Significant?

Few firms that operate standard cost systems employ scientific tests to determine whether a variance is significant, i.e. worth further investigation. Usually, some rule of thumb is used; e.g. a variance that deviates by more than 10 per cent from the standard is investigated, otherwise the difference is deemed insignificant. The danger is that a small variation which does not appear to be worth investigating may contain large unfavourable differences offset by large favourable ones. This danger is always present because many factors may impinge on, say, material usage or labour efficiency. The only safeguard is management vigilance and detailed checks at intervals, provided the benefits from such checks justify their cost.

Some writers have emphasized a different aspect of variance control—the use of statistical tools. Koehler, among others, has pointed out that certain variances, in particular labour and overhead efficiency, material usage and overhead volume variances, are affected by chance factors. It is uneconomical to investigate variances which may be attributable to chance rather than assignable causes. Thus control charts or similar statistical tools may be employed to monitor the process; so long as a variation seems to be chance or random, it is not investigated. When the variance is unlikely to have resulted from chance, if for example it lies outside a predetermined acceptance limit, investigation is warranted.

A decision model can be constructed to include the costs and benefits of investigating the variances. This is a sophisticated approach which may be difficult to implement in practice, because it is well-nigh impossible to specify the opportunity cost of investigating or not investigating a particular variance.

The issue of whether to investigate a particular variance is exceptionally complex, on account of the large number of assignable causes that may be present. Other unknowns are the recurrent nature of the cause, its controllability, the costs of the investigation and of corrective action, as well as the costs of not undertaking an investigation. Many accountants believe that this is a problem that only management experience and judgement can resolve. We believe there should be greater use of simple statistical control tools to fortify management experience and judgement in this area.

Responsibility for Variances

Cost control comprises a number of stages, such as setting standards, comparing actual performance with standards, investigating significant variances and taking corrective action. Generally, there is a number of options with respect to remedial action. For example, if the material price variance is unfavourable, one may consider using substitute materials, changing suppliers, buying in larger quantities to obtain bulk discounts, raising the selling price of the finished product, or doing nothing (i.e. accepting a lower profit margin). An unfavourable labour efficiency variance may lead one to consider establishing better working conditions, training schemes or incentive payment schemes. But first it is necessary to trace the cause of the labour inefficiency; e.g. idle time could be due to machine breakdown or waiting for materials. Suppose the cause is traced to inferior materials supplied to a particular job. The person normally responsible for labour efficiency is the departmental foreman, but in this instance the person responsible for remedial action is the purchasing officer.

A broad indication of the department or person normally associated with responsibility for a cost variance is given in Figure 26—C.

Figure 26—C
Responsibility for Cost Variances

Type of Variance	Department or Person Normally Responsible
Material price	Purchasing department
Material quantity	Foreman
Labour rate	Personnel department or foreman (where a worker works outside his classification)
Labour efficiency	Foreman
Overhead spending	Foreman (normally the variable part only is controllable by the foreman)
Overhead efficiency	Foreman (variance associated with labour efficiency if recovery rate based on DLH)
Overhead volume	Sales department or budget department

Note: Material quantity, labour efficiency, overhead spending and overhead efficiency variances refer to variances which arise at the departmental level.

The general principle is that a department head is responsible for those variances over which he has control. Thus the departmental foreman is responsible for material usage, but not for the material price. But for cost control to be effective, the analysis must establish the specific cause. An unfavourable labour efficiency variance may be due to inefficient labour utilization (responsibility: foreman), a new trainee (personnel department), or excessive set-up time because of a large number of short runs (sales department).

Most variances are controllable at the departmental level, hence it is important that the department which is the responsibility centre should also be the cost centre, i.e. all costs should be traced to the department. Certain variances which are considered uncontrollable, such as overhead volume, are in the long run controlled at higher levels of management.

Behavioural Implications of Budgeting and Standard Costs

The business budget, which is a quantified expression of the company's annual plan, is described in Chapter 28. The budget has a number of functions—planning, control, motivation and communication. For effective control, both budgets and standard costs are needed. Some firms employ budgeting and a standard cost system as means of motivating employees to greater productivity. Whether they are deliberately employed in this manner or not, the behavioural implications of the use of these control techniques must be recognized. The problem can be briefly stated: the short-run pressures of meeting predetermined targets often have counter effects with respect to long-run goals, because the imposed pressures may not be in the best interests of the firm.

Budgets and standards affect the motivation and behaviour of both managers and workers, but the pressure bears particularly on middle and lower management levels, i.e. sales managers, production managers, plant superintendents and foremen. Where the standards set are too tight this often leads to tension. Continuing inability to achieve a budgeted level of performance results in reduced morale and lower aspiration levels. On the other hand, if standards are too lax, the budgeted level of performance is easily achieved and the employees are not motivated to greater productivity.

Generally, most employees appear to regard the budget and the predetermined standards contained therein as a threat. Once a targeted level has been achieved, it is expected that it can be maintained in future periods. Further, senior management typically expects that the achieved targeted level can be improved, so that standards become progressively tighter.

Some writers have suggested that some form of participative budgeting is desirable, i.e. middle and lower level managers should participate in setting standards which will be employed in monitoring their own performance. Certain safeguards are necessary: first, participation must be real, i.e. there should be genuine give and take in the budgeting process; and second, the process should not be viewed as inability or unwillingness to take hard and unpopular decisions on the part of the budget committee or top management. But the connection between participative budgeting and productivity is indirect and, possibly, weak. Participative budgeting may lead to improved morale, provided employees view it as a team effort, and not resent a sharing of responsibility. Better morale could lead to increased production effort, but there is insufficient evidence to indicate that a strong positive relationship exists.

The budget itself is a means of communicating operational objectives to employees. A corollary of participative budgeting is that there should be feedback concerning his achievement to each participant. It is believed that the communication of successful performance increases a participant's aspiration level, while the communication of failure has the opposite effect. This sounds reasonable but, like other conventional wisdom, should be treated with some caution. However, it is generally true that an absence altogether of feedback will contribute to considerable frustration and lowering of morale.

Another recommendation aimed at relieving employee tension is that management should focus on favourable as well as unfavourable variances from standards. This implies the adoption of a reward and punishment system, but for control purposes unfavourable variances are likely to merit more urgent attention and investigation. It is also important to recognize a phenomenon called regression toward the mean.[4] A high level of achievement in one period, which may be rewarded, is likely to be followed by a less favourable achievement in the next period, while a poor performance in one period, which may entail punishment, is likely to be followed by an improved performance. Both results are an effect of regression toward the mean and do not indicate that punishment motivates more effectively than reward.

---

[4] The most often cited example is that the sons of relatively tall men tend to be shorter, and the sons of relatively short men tend to be taller, than their respective fathers.

As stated earlier, the main problem is that the pressures and tensions associated with the use of budgets and standards are likely to lead to a conflict of objectives within the firm. Budgets and standards focus on performance of divisions, departments and cost centres, often at the expense of the interests of the firm as a whole. Supervisors are motivated to give priority to the interests of those sections of the firm for which they are responsible. A similar type of conflict exists between short-run and long-run objectives. Supervisors may spend freely towards the end of a budget period in those cost areas in which there is a surplus of allocated funds, in order to forestall a downward revision of the allowance in the next period. On the other hand, undesirable economy often is exercised to keep within a tight budget, such as the postponement of repairs and maintenance or research and development expenditures. There are parallel examples in implementing a standard cost system; e.g. a foreman may select simple jobs to complete in preference to more urgent but difficult jobs, in order to enhance the labour efficiency record in the period. Unfortunately, all the above examples of a lack of goal congruence are frequently met with in practice.

Many conclusions about the behavioural implications of using budgets and standards rest on weak and insufficient evidence. Employees react differently, as individuals and as groups, to the pressures represented by budgets and standards. Further, management's leadership style, varying from considerate to autocratic, is an important factor. The problem is particularly complex and may not yield to systematic analysis. While definitive knowledge is lacking in this area, the accountant should be aware that the use of budgets and standards as control devices may have adverse consequences for the motivation and behaviour of employees, and that these may influence the attainment of corporate objectives, both in the short and the long run.

Disposition of Variances

Variances may be disposed of in several ways. First, variances determined at the end of each month or other short-run period should be carried forward as debit or credit balances, because some of the differences will balance out over the year.

Second, at the end of the year the accumulated variances may either be charged to cost of goods sold, written off against profit and loss or reallocated over the inventory accounts. If the variances represent avoidable losses, they should be written off. But if they have arisen because of unavoidable price changes or faulty budgeting, or both, then they represent true production costs. Under these circumstances, they should be reallocated over the inventory accounts in the manner explained with respect to overhead variances in the previous chapter.

Many accountants believe that standard costs represent true costs, and that variances represent inefficiencies which should be written off at the end of the period.[5] An income statement prepared in accordance with this view is as follows:

[5] We doubt that the notion of true costs is meaningful under all circumstances for two reasons. Some variances are unavoidable, as explained earlier. Further, there are different cost concepts for different purposes.

Sales—standard quantity at standard price		$1 000
Sales—actual quantity at standard price		900
Less: Cost of sales—		
Direct materials—standard*	$300	
Direct labour—standard*	200	
Manufacturing overhead—standard*	100	
		600
Standard gross profit		300
Variance adjustments—		
Material price	−20	
Material quantity	10	
Labour rate	−30	
Labour efficiency	15	
Overhead—spending	10	
efficiency	5	
volume	−5	−15
Accounting gross profit		$285

* Standard quantity at standard price of factor input relating to actual output sold.

Conclusion

There are several limitations and qualifications in the use of standard costs. First, budgeting and standard costing focus on control and efficiency. They do not ensure that the broad objectives of the enterprise are being achieved, e.g. that profits are being made or that research and development are adequate to ensure the firm's long-term survival. Maximum efficiency with respect to a given task is not a sufficient end in itself.

Second, the care and expense necessary in setting reliable standards, and the comparison of actual performance against standards, must be matched by the subsequent functions of variance analysis, the establishment of responsibility for the variances and the initiation of appropriate corrective action.

Third, it is useful to distinguish between favourable and unfavourable variances. A general principle is to minimize unfavourable variances, but this may need to be qualified in the context of overall organizational objectives. While favourable variances are, *prima facie*, attractive, a saving in a particular cost, e.g. material price, may be more than offset by cost increases in other areas, e.g. labour time. Favourable variances too should be investigated in order to establish the cause and extent, but investigation is usually not so urgent as with unfavourable variances.

Fourth, both management and the accountant must be aware that the use of budgets and standard costs for control purposes has consequences for the motivation and behaviour of employees, which in turn will affect productivity. Some of these behavioural implications may be beneficial and others harmful from the viewpoint of the attainment of corporate overall objectives.

A good standard cost system, if used imaginatively, is a powerful management tool for cost control and efficient production.

References

Bruns, Jr. W.J. and DeCoster, D.T., *Accounting and Its Behavioral Implications*, McGraw-Hill, New York, 1969.

Koehler, R.W., 'The Relevance of Probability Statistics to Accounting Variance Control', *Management Accounting*, October 1968, pp. 35-41.

National Association of Cost Accountants, 'The Analysis of Manufacturing Cost Variances', *Research Series No. 22, N.A.C.A. Bulletin*, August 1952. Reprinted in W.E. Thomas, Jr. (ed.), *Readings in Cost Accounting, Budgeting and Control*, South-Western Publishing Co., Chicago, 1960, pp. 546-81.

Additional Reading

Burke, W.L., Smyth, E.B. and Macmullen, J.S., *Accounting for Management*, 3rd ed., Law Book Co., Sydney (in press).

Horngren, C.T., *Cost Accounting—A Managerial Emphasis*, 4th ed., 1977, Prentice-Hall, Englewood Cliffs, N.J., Chapters 7 and 9.

Shillinglaw, S., *Managerial Cost Accounting*, 4th ed., 1977, Irwin, Homewood, Ill., Chapter 20.

Discussion Questions

1 Examine the view that standard costs impart a forward-looking slant to the accounting system. Does this introduce a subjective element into cost accounting systems?

2 What is the significance of variances in a standard cost system? What are the major cost variances which are likely to be recorded in the accounts of a manufacturing enterprise? What sources of information need to be drawn upon in measuring variances?

3 Consider the significance of standard costs in relation to managerial planning, control, decision making and financial reporting. Are standard cost data unequivocally relevant for all these purposes?

4 Explain the advantages of analysing the overhead variance into three components in a standard cost system.

5 You are required to make a recommendation to a large manufacturing company for the installation of a standard costing system. What features of such a system would you particularly draw attention to? What advice would you give the company about the cost of operating such a system, relative to the cost of its existing historical controlled cost system?

6 Explain why a department or officer may be held responsible for a particular cost variance. Illustrate your answer by reference to the different types of cost variances that can arise in a standard cost system.

7 Examine the criteria which may be used in deciding what action to take regarding the disposal of standard cost variances.

8 Discuss the problems that may be encountered in using a participative budgeting system for planning and performance evaluation.

9 Your company's management committee spends a good deal of time every month fussing over the report you prepare on the 50 individual costs the committee thinks most critical:

	Actual Cost	Standard Cost	Variance: Unfavourable (Favourable)
Cost A			
Cost B, etc.			

Though they had only talked about it in the past, at the most recent monthly meeting the committee called you in and asked you quite definitely hereafter to include a column to the right of the 'Variance' column, labelled 'Index of Significance'.

You are required to.

(a) List and discuss briefly the ways one might go about developing an 'Index of Significance' that would tell the committee which costs should receive first attention. Do not restrict yourself to 'established' ways, whatever they might be. Spread yourself a bit.

(b) Renumber your list to show the order in which you would recommend them. Worry somewhat about matters of utility and processing time. Throughout, avoid mathematical language.

Exercises

1 The direct labour cost incurred in a department for the past month was $70 000. The standard direct labour cost for the work performed was $66 000. What additional information is needed in order to analyse the $4 000 total variation?

2 Record the following information relating to material Q in the material control account, the work in process control account and appropriate variance accounts:

(a) purchased 30 000 units at 31c (standard price 30c);

(b) issued 8 400 units to production (standard quantity 8 000 units).

3 The following cost information refers to the operations of Sun Product Ltd in a recent period:

Wages paid for direct labour	$2 400
Cost of direct labour time actually worked (at standard rates)	2 160
Standard direct labour time (at standard rates)	2 070
Standard direct labour cost of finished production	1 890

You are required to:

(a) record these transactions in a system of standard cost accounts in such a way that variations from standards can be identified; and

(b) recommend the actions to be taken to dispose of the variations. Assume that the labour rate variance was due to an unexpected change in award rates, and that the labour time variance was due to inefficient control on the part of the foreman.

4 Record the following transactions, relating to the operations of a manufacturing business in January 1985, in a system of standard cost accounts, and prepare an operating statement for the period which shows both standard results and variations from standard. It may be assumed that there are no opening inventories.

	Standard	Actual
Materials purchased	$4 880	$4 800
Materials issued to production (at standard price)	3 080	3 100
Direct labour cost incurred	3 770	3 980
Direct labour cost charged to production (at standard rates)	3 700	3 770
Manufacturing overhead—		
Incurred		3 060
Absorbed	3 240	
Budgeted (adjusted to actual production)	3 000	
Budgeted (adjusted to standard allowance for actual production)	2 960	
Cost of completed work—		
Material	2 940	
Direct labour	3 600	
Manufacturing overhead	3 120	
Sales at selling price, $11 940		
Sales at standard price, $8 200		

5 Chemical Products Ltd produces a chemical compound using three ingredients. The standard quantities and costs of materials and labour incurred in producing one unit of the chemical compound are given below:

	Quantity (units)	Price per unit	Total Cost
Materials—			
A	50	$20	$1 000
B	100	15	1 500
C	200	10	2 000
			$4 500
Labour—			
Processing and packaging, 200 hours at $5 per hour			$1 000

During the month of January, the following materials and labour costs were incurred:

	Quantity (Units)	Price per Unit	Total Cost
Materials—			
A	55	$25	$1 375
B	110	16	1 760
C	190	9	1 710
			$4 845
Labour—220 hours at $5.30 per hour			$1 166

You are required to:

(a) compute the material price, material quantity, labour rate and labour efficiency variances; and

(b) explain any method you are familiar with by which the material price and quantity variances can be further analysed.

6 A factory's budgeted fixed overhead expenses are $10 000 and its variable overhead is $1.70 per direct labour hour. The overhead absorption rate is based on a normal activity level of 10 000 direct labour hours. The operating data and costs for the previous month are as follows:

actual hours worked, 8 900 hours;

standard hours allowed for output achieved, 9 000 hours;

actual fixed cost incurred, $11 000; and

actual variable cost incurred, $15 500.

You are required to analyse the difference between actual overhead incurred and overhead applied at the standard level of activity, into spending, efficiency and volume variances. How will you make use of this variance analysis for controlling costs?

27 Strategic and Long-range Tactical Planning

This chapter presents a classification of management plans and describes their inter-relationships with models and budgets. Management plans may be classified in a number of ways, e.g. into long-range and short-range plans. It is useful to distinguish between the strategic long-range plan, the tactical multi-period plan and the tactical annual plan, as illustrated in Figure 27—A.

The inverted pyramid in Figure 27—A emphasizes the crucial importance, the breadth of vision and the degree of innovation of the strategic long-range plan. Strategic plans relate to management's creative function in establishing new objectives or adapting existing ones. This is perhaps top management's most important function. Tactical planning, on the other hand, is a line or operating management function which is closely linked to the management control process, i.e. the efficient use of resources. While a strategic plan is innovative and relates to a specific new area of operations, tactical plans represent continuity and relate to projections of the whole set of current operations. Tactical plans must be consistent with the framework of the strategic plan. This link between the two types of management plans exists at several levels. First, the tactical plans must take as given the objectives formulated by top management in the strategic plan. Second, the annual and multi-period budgets in the tactical plans must be consistent with those aspects of the strategic plan which can be expressed in broad quantitative terms. Third, the capital budgets in the tactical plans must tie in with, and evolve from, the capital projects that underpin the strategic plan. Lastly, the corporate model, largely a tool of the tactical multi-period rolling plan, may be extended to certain less innovative types of strategic plan, which represent adaptations of existing goals. In this last situation, the dividing line between the strategic long-range plan and the tactical multi-period plan is not sharply defined, but may become somewhat hazy.

Figure 27—A also shows the inter-relationships between management plans, models and budgets. The strategic long-range plan is the output of a long-run decision model, as described in the following section. The variables in this decision model are typically qualitative, but the model may contain quantitative aspects, particularly where the strategic plan is adaptative rather than innovative. In this situation, corporate modelling may be employed in the planning process itself, considerably enhancing the usefulness and reliability of the latter. Normally, however, the corporate model reflects the objectives of the tactical multi-period plan. The strategic plan, tactical multi-period plan and corporate model are described in this chapter. The annual plan and annual budget are discussed in Chapter 28.

Strategic Planning

Strategic plans are essentially long-range plans. Drucker has defined certain features of strategic long-range planning. First, long-range planning is concerned with the future consequences of present decisions, i.e. with the decisions that are taken today. Second, planning is not the same as forecasting. Forecasting is a relatively precise process, e.g. a sales forecast may be the key figure in the development of a detailed operating budget. One can plan ten years or more into the future, but this plan is not

Figure 27—A
Relationship of Plans, Models and Budgets

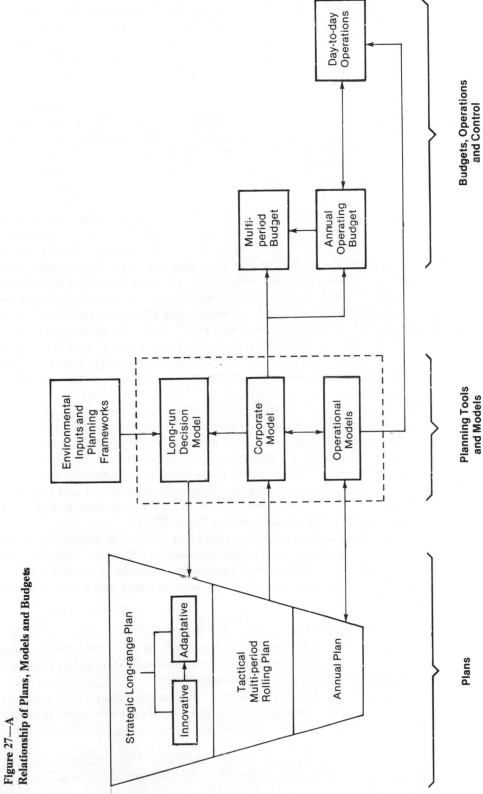

a forecast. However, certain parts of a long-range plan may be based on specific forecasts, e.g. future population growth. Third, strategic long-range planning is a vital, *entrepreneurial* top management function. Hence long-range planning is not the same thing as attempting to eliminate or reduce risk. The example of a company's long-range plan on this and the following page elucidates the points made above.

The strategic long-range plan is formulated by top management, often with the help of staff specialists. As will be seen shortly, a strategic plan is not prepared on a regular basis. Also, the time period covered by the plan is partly a function of the investment horizon (which in turn is partly dependent on business and industry risks), and it varies from plan to plan. The only general rules are that the period of the plan is likely to be longer than a year; it at least covers the time for which resources are being committed; and the greater the uncertainty of the environment, the shorter the time span is likely to be.

The most important steps in strategic planning are the formal generation of the company's long-range objectives and changes therein, and the identification of exceptional opportunities and threats in the environment in the light of the objectives. Some writers believe that a strategic plan typically comprises a series of so-called scenarios (or planning frameworks), which are based on a limited number of critical variables and leading assumptions about those variables. For example, a critical variable may be future economic growth in countries which are the company's trading partners, while the assumptions might cover a continuation of recent years' growth rates, and higher and lower (than the trend) growth rates. It is also believed that three or four scenarios are adequate to describe possible future environments, and in a sense these scenarios really constitute alternative plans that crystallize as the future unfolds.

It is possible to distinguish two types of strategic long-range plans. The first consists of plans which constitute the innovation of new goals and objectives, and which therefore represent *a change of direction* of the company's long-term goals. This type of plan is described below by reference to one of Australia's largest companies. The other type comprises plans which are adaptations of existing goals, representing capital commitments of considerable significance and impact *vis-à-vis* the company's existing operations, but which do not represent a major change of direction. This distinction is illustrated in Figure 27—B.

Normally strategic plans are always long-range plans. The strategic short-term plan is an aberration which may be adopted because of a temporary emergency, such as a strike or disruption of supplies of an essential raw material. Emergency measures are taken to modify the plan, but these measures are expected to be of a temporary nature.

Example: Broken Hill Proprietary Co. Ltd (BHP) was incorporated in 1885 to work a lead-silver-zinc mine at Broken Hill in New South Wales. From the viewpoint of an outside observer, it is possible to distinguish the formulation by its management of four strategic long-range plans since its inception.

(a) In the early 1900s the company decided to enter the iron and steel industry.
(b) In 1960 or earlier the company diversified into oil exploration and production.
(c) From about the mid-1960s the company diversified significantly into metals and minerals.
(d) In 1977 it planned to become a large exporter of coal with the acquisition of the share of a U.S. company, Peabody, in the Theiss-Peabody-Mitsui coal fields in Queensland.

Figure 27—B
Strategic Planning

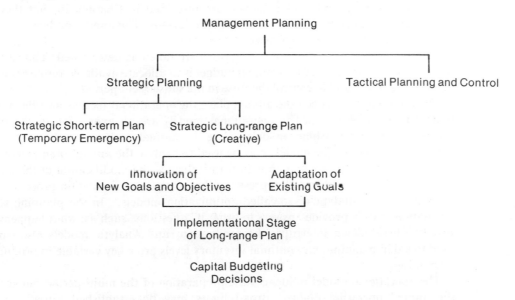

The above example of BHP and its innovative strategic long-range planning is illuminating. First, it appears that the opportunities for innovative strategic planning are, even in the case of one of Australia's largest companies, few and far between. For example, it was nearly 60 years before the iron and steel manufacturer expanded into the petroleum industry. Its diversification operations in this period, such as coal mining and shipping activities, represented examples of vertical integration that are more appropriately classified as adaptive, rather than innovative, strategic planning. Second, the implementational stage of a long-range plan can cover a protracted period, as the capital budgeting decisions intended to achieve the plan's long-run objectives come to fruition (see Chapter 29). For example, BHP's first steel-making plant did not come on stream until 1915, and its second steel plant was acquired in 1935. Also, while it formed a subsidiary to undertake oil exploration in the Bass Strait in 1961, it was not until 1964 that it entered into its successful partnership with Esso. Third, a feature of the innovative strategic plan is its intuitive nature and impreciseness. It seems that if BHP's management, as part of its strategic planning process, developed a series of alternative planning frameworks to represent possible future environments, the analysis could only have been a simple one. By its very nature, an innovative strategic plan cannot be captured in a computerized model or a set of mathematical equations. However, it may be possible to model successfully certain specific areas (in particular, those relating to adaptive planning) that are part of, or that impinge upon, the overall strategic plan.

Tactical Plans

Tactical plans relate to the projections into future periods of the whole of the firm's current operations. The important sub-classifications are the annual plan and the multi-period rolling plan. The annual plan, which typically is prepared in considederable detail, may be regarded as the first year of the multi-period plan, and the annual budget as the first year of the multi-period budget.

The annual plan and annual budget are discussed in Chapter 28, but they are briefly described below in the context of Figure 27—A. The annual budget is derived from, and may be said to be a quantitative expression of, the annual plan. Because the plan is short-range, all major operations are taken as determined. Thus a main purpose of the annual plan and annual budget is to allocate available resources in the most efficient way and to control their use in the subsequent period.

The relationship between the annual plan, the operational models and the annual budget is a complex one. The operational models are an expression of the firm's short-run objectives (some models relate to annual, others to daily or other short-term periods). The models may be used to analyse the annual plan or portions of the plan; their outputs may thus in turn influence the modification of the annual plan. Operational models may represent either analytic or simulation processes, but the majority are analytic or so-called optimization models.[1] In the planning stage, simulation models provide answers to 'what if' questions, such as: what happens if a machine break-down interrupts the production run? Analytic models also can be used to aid in planning, e.g. optimal inventory levels are a key variable in production scheduling.

The operational model influences the preparation of the multi-period budget and the annual operating budget. Broad limits may be established initially in the corporate model, e.g. it may be decided that inventories are not to exceed or fall short of specified levels. These broad limits are translated into precise figures by operational models. In turn the operational models' outputs are fed back into the corporate model for the preparation of the detailed budgets. In the implementational stage of the annual budget, operational models may be used for control purposes. For example, a computerized inventory model can monitor inventories automatically in terms of predetermined parameters, i.e. maximum and minimum inventory levels and reorder points. This is sometimes referred to as an automatic closed control system.

The Multi-period Tactical Plan

The multi-period tactical plan typically has a planned horizon of five years or so into the future. Unlike the strategic plan, the multi-period tactical plan needs to be formulated and reviewed on a regular basis, say once a year, when it is 'rolled' forward (hence it is sometimes referred to as a rolling plan). The appropriate life span for a multi-period tactical plan will be a function of management's ability to plan forward in the necessary detail, and of the necessity for the tactical plan to dovetail with the strategic plan. That is, the large uncertainties in the strategic plan may be a constraining factor on the life span of the detailed comprehensive tactical plan.

In a sense, all firms have a multi-period plan, i.e. someone in the firm will have formulated expectations of future developments and planned for the acquisition and disposition of resources to achieve them. The acquisition of resources and their management are important features of a multi-period tactical plan. The relevant

---

[1] A simulation approach provides information on the consequences associated with different alternatives, whereas an optimization approach provides the 'best solution' to a problem.

issues are whether this plan has been developed into a formal structure and whether there has been participation by other managers in the planning process. Otherwise consistency in objectives is unlikely to exist among top management or between managers at different levels.

There are certain well-defined steps in preparing a formal, structured, on-going tactical plan. The first step is to spell out the plan's broad objectives, such as future growth of sales or earnings per share. These objectives must be consistent with the objectives in the strategic plan. Then relevant aspects of the environment, such as political and economic factors and the firm's own strengths and weaknesses need to be taken into account. These three initial steps—establishing objectives, considering external environmental factors and taking into account the firm's own strengths and weaknesses *vis-à-vis* its competitors—must be considered simultaneously, since decisions to influence the environment or to strengthen certain aspects of the firm's operations in turn affect the establishment of objectives. The next steps are: first, to determine the alternatives that the firm can adopt to attain its objectives; second, to evaluate the alternatives; and third, to select the best alternative in accordance with appropriate choice criteria which reflect management's attitudes to return and risk. In other words, management formulates the appropriate policies to attain its broad objectives.

Certain assumptions may need to be specified in preparing a multi-period tactical plan, such as continuity in the production process, stable market conditions, or a target growth objective. However, management may deem it prudent to prepare a contingency plan to cover an unexpected emergency situation. Somewhat surprisingly, there is little evidence that companies engage in contingency planning.

A budget is a quantitative expression of a plan in financial terms. The output of most plans is expressed in financial terms, i.e. it comprises budgeted financial statements, including budgeted cash flow and funds statements. Non-financial measures, such as market share, growth rates and number of employees are, of course, important input components in all plans and budgets.

A corporate model often serves as the tool by which a tactical multi-period plan is transformed into a multi-period budget.

Corporate Models

A model can be defined as a simplified representation of reality (or hypothesized reality), and often it may be used to test the consequences of alternative states or actions. For example, the effects of wind conditions on an aircraft with a new design may be simulated by testing a model of the aircraft in a wind tunnel. A corporate model may be defined as a computer-based representation of a company. It relates to the company's multi-period tactical plan, and the output of a corporate model comprises aggregated budgeted financial statements and cash flows over a number of future periods, although the output sometimes includes physical, non-financial aggregates as well. It is typically a simulation model.

The advantages of a corporate model are attributable partly to formal planning itself and partly to the use of a computerized program. First, the formal planning process forces management to think explicitly about the company's objectives and the alternatives available to attain those objectives. Second, the existence and dissemination of a formal plan ensures goal consistency at all management levels. Third, management can experiment with the computer-based model by generating the different outcomes associated with alternative policies and thus enlist the aid of the computer to select the most desirable alternative. Fourth, a corporate model facilitates the use of simulation techniques, which can provide management with a probability profile of outcomes from a selected policy. Simulation analysis is often helpful for decision making under uncertainty. Management can obtain answers to 'what if' questions, such as: what if wage rates increase by 10 per cent or demand falls by 5 per cent per annum? Fifth, sensitivity analysis (whereby the model is used to determine the sensitivity of outputs to changes in assumptions about inputs) gives management an indication of the effects of variability of particular inputs on costs or profitability.[2]

Corporate planning models first came into use in the 1960s but it is only in the 1970s that their adoption has made any headway, and then mainly among large companies with sales of $100 million or more. This is surprising in view of the widespread use of computers and the obvious advantages of corporate models for tactical planning purposes. The explanation may lie in the failure of some of the early multi-million dollar projects in corporate modelling, because certain essential criteria for success were absent. The most important factors are management experience in formal corporate planning and forecasting techniques, and the support of top management in the development of the corporate model and in its subsequent use. To ensure top management support several requirements must be met. First, a 'top-down' approach needs to be employed in developing the model, i.e. the starting point must be a top-management statement of overall corporate objectives. Second, line or operating management in the operating divisions must participate effectively with planning specialists in developing the model, although some reliance on outside consulting help may also be necessary. Third, the model must be simple and free from technical jargon to ensure its continuing use at different management levels. The important principle is to start with the simplest model possible and to implement on a step by step basis. Care should be taken to educate management (including operating line management) in the use of the model at each step. One possible approach is to develop individual planning modules relating to distinct functional areas, such as production or sales, which are then linked to form the overall corporate model. Fourth, the model should be relevant to the company's specific needs. Obviously a tailored model will be most relevant, but its development cost may be high. Last, Grinyer and Wooller have pointed out the importance to the success of a corporate model of adequate documentation of the model at all stages of its development. Some interesting features are discussed below — the use of modelling systems and ready-made models, and the development of top-down and bottom-up approaches to corporate modelling.

There are two major tasks in developing a corporate model. First, it is necessary to formulate the mathematical relationships in the model and, second, it is necessary to prepare a set of instructions for the computer. As noted in Chapter 9, the latter step is commonly referred to as programming. Some companies develop their own corporate models, using a general purpose programming language such as Fortran or Cobol. Other companies, in constructing their corporate models, may make use of a modelling system, which is really a specialized language designed by an outside consultant. The advantage of modelling systems is that they reduce the programming

---

[2] See Chapter 28 for a detailed discussion of sensitivity analysis.

task and programming costs by providing a ready-made set of instructions for repetitive steps that are commonly encountered (e.g. instructions to report the financial statements, cash flows or accounting ratios). There is evidence of a growing popularity in the use of modelling systems.

Thus a model tailored to the company's specific needs may be constructed in one of two ways, i.e. by using a general purpose programming language or by using a modelling system. Alternatively, a company may buy a ready-made model from a computer manufacturer, whose output usually comprises financial statements, instead of developing its own model. These ready-made models are inexpensive, but are inflexible and cannot be modified easily. Grinyer and Wooller found that relatively few companies were using ready-made models in the U.K. in the early 1970s.

The top-down approach to corporate modelling conforms to the important principle of formulating broad corporate objectives as the first essential step in a long-term plan. This approach requires that a broad overall model be developed for the company as a total entity. More detailed plans relating to individual divisions, profit centres and cost centres are developed as separate modules which fit into the overall plan, as illustrated in Figure 27—C. The approach is particularly applicable to modelling by medium-sized companies, in which top management has a close relationship with and an intimate knowledge of all operating divisions in the company.

Figure 27—C
Top-down Approach to Corporate Modelling

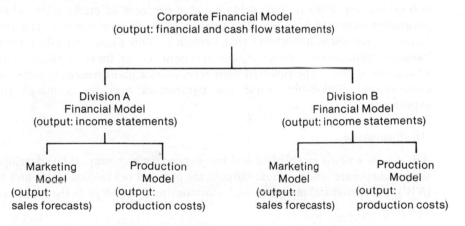

An alternative method often adopted by very large companies with *autonomous* divisions is the so-called 'bottom-up' approach. For example, financial models are developed at divisional levels and consolidated to form the overall corporate financial model. The corporate model shows the impact of divisional plans on overall corporate objectives, and thus it can be used as a tool in the negotiation process in which the divisional plans are modified and refined. *Prima facie*, the bottom-up approach appears to be inconsistent with the principle that formulation of the long-range plan is a function of top management rather than of divisional managers. But a reconciliation can be offered. In essence this principle relates only to strategic planning. In the more formal tactical planning situations in which corporate models are employed, there is some evidence that the bottom-up approach has been successful. In particular, large companies with autonomous divisions, where top management in less knowledgeable than the divisional managers concerning the opportunities and challenges in the different industries in which the divisions operate, often favour the bottom-up approach to corporate planning.

A corporate model may be extended under the following circumstances. The dividing line between a multi-period tactical plan and a strategic plan is sometimes not sharply defined. This may happen, for example, when the strategic plan represents an adaptation of existing goals, such as an expansion of current production, rather than an innovative change in the company's objectives. It is then often possible to extend the corporate model to evaluate the consequences of the strategic plan, and this is indeed one of the most important benefits the company can derive from its corporate model.

The corporate model seeks to capture the essence of the total company and its operations in a set of mathematical relationships. To represent reality adequately, the model may contain a large number of complex inter-relationships expressed in quantitative terms; thus several thousand equations may be present. However, these equations typically take a very limited number of basic forms, e.g. $y = a_1 x_1 + a_2 x_2$ or $y = be^x$.

The equations depict three kinds of relationships—accounting identities, definitional equations based on statistical estimates and behavioural relationships. Most of the equations are either identities or definitional. Some examples of accounting identities are: income *equals* sales *less* total costs; and net worth at the end of the period *equals* net worth at the beginning *plus* retained earnings. An example of a definitional equation is: bad debts equal x per cent of credit sales, where x is a parameter estimated from past data relating to the firm or industry. The behavioural equations represent hypotheses that explain certain cause and effect relationships based on management's observation and experience, as, for example, sales demand is a function of price. The function itself represents a management hypothesis about a cause-effect relationship, while the parameters may be estimated from past experience.

An Illustration

ABC Co. is a newly established and fast expanding company. It has developed a very simple corporate model, whose outputs are planned net income (NY), and net worth (NW). The structural mathematical relationships that comprise the model are set out as follows:

(A) Sales

$$R_t = \alpha R_{t-1} + \beta E_t \tag{A1}$$
$$S_t = S_{t-1} \times R_t \tag{A2}$$
$$M_t = M_{t-1} \times G_t \tag{A3}$$
$$s_t = M_t \times S_t \tag{A4}$$

(B) Revenue

$$P_t = P_{t-1} \times I_t^p \tag{B5}$$
$$TR_t = P_t s_t \tag{B6}$$

(C) Cost

$$UVC_t = UVC_{t-1} \times I_t^v \tag{C7}$$
$$TVC_t = UVC_t \times s_t \tag{C8}$$
$$FC_t = FC_{t-1} \times I_t^f \tag{C9}$$
$$A_t = \gamma TR_t \tag{C10}$$
$$TC_t = FC_t + TVC_t + A_t \tag{C11}$$

(D) Profit and Taxes

$$Y_t = TR_t - TC_t \tag{D12}$$
$$T_t = 0.4Y_t \tag{D13}$$
$$NY_t = Y_t - T_t \tag{D14}$$

(E) Net Worth

$$NW_{te} = NW_{tb} + NY_t \tag{E15}$$

where
R = industry sales growth factor
E = environmental factor, e.g. growth in GNP
S = industry sales in physical units
M = company's market share
G = company's market share growth factor
s = company sales in physical units
P = product price per unit
I^p = one *plus* annual rate of increase in product price
TR = company's total revenue
UVC = unit variable cost
I^v = one *plus* annual rate of increase in unit variable cost
TVC = total variable cost
FC = fixed cost excluding advertising
I^f = one *plus* annual rate of increase in fixed cost (excluding advertising)
A = advertising expense
TC = total cost
Y = income before tax
T = company income tax
NY = net income after tax
NW_{tb} = net worth at beginning of year t
NW_{te} = net worth at end of year t
t = future year, $t = 1, 2, ..., n$
α, β, γ = constants.

The outputs of the model, NY_t and NW_t, are a function of several factors: the exogenous (externally determined) independent variables, E_t, I_t^v and I_t^f, the endogenous (internally determined) policy variable G_t and the parameters α, β and γ (estimated from past data relating to the economy, industry or company). The variable, I_t^p, may be exogenous or endogenous, depending on whether the company is a price taker or price maker. For convenience, it is assumed that there are no dividend payments.

Certain information on current data and assumptions about price and cost increases are given as follows:

$R_{t-1} = 1.01, \quad \alpha = 1.005, \quad \beta = 0.05$

$S_{t-1} = 1\,000$ units, $\quad M_{t-1} = 0.10, \quad P_{t-1} = \$2$ per unit

$UVC_{t-1} = \$1$ per unit, $\quad FC_{t-1} = \$100, \quad \gamma = 0.035$

$NW_{tb} = \$50$

$I^P_t = 1.10$ p.a., $\quad I^v_t = 1.07$ p.a., $\quad I^f_t = 1.05$ p.a.

The following numerical values relating to E and G_t are assumed:

	1	2	3	4	5
E_t	0.10	0.11	0.10	0.10	0.10
G_t	1.03	1.02	1.01	1.00	1.00

For starting period t:

$$R_{t-1} = R^a_{t-1} \qquad \text{where } R^a_{t-1} = \frac{S^a_{t-1}}{S^a_{t-2}}$$

$$S_{t-1} = S^a_{t-1}$$

$$M_{t-1} = M^a_{t-1}$$

$$P_{t-1} = P^a_{t-1}$$

$$UVC_{t-1} = UVC^a_{t-1}$$

$$FC_{t-1} = FC^a_{t-1}$$

$$NW_{t-1} = NW^a_{t-1}$$

where superscript 'a' denotes actual observed values. For starting period t, lagged values of the above variables are their actual values, but for subsequent periods $t+1, t+2, ..., t+n$, estimated values are used in the model.

Table 27—1 shows how the model generates output relating to a number of future periods.

Table 27—1
ABC Co.
Operating Plans of Corporate Financial Model, Years 1—5

Operating Plans		1	2	3	4	5	Equation
Industry sales growth (*)	(R_t)	1.020	1.036	1.046	1.056	1.066	(A1)
Industry sales (million units)	(S_t)	1.020	1.056	1.104	1.165	1.241	(A2)
Market share (†)	(M_t)	0.103	0.105	0.106	0.106	0.106	(A3)
Company sales (thousand units)	(s_t)	105.06	110.88	117.02	123.49	131.54	(A4)
Unit selling price ($)	(P_t)	2.20	2.42	2.66	2.93	3.22	(B5)
Total revenue ($'000)	(TR_t)	231.13	268.32	311.27	361.82	423.55	(B6)
Unit variable cost ($)	(UVC_t)	1.07	1.14	1.22	1.31	1.40	(C7)
Total variable cost ($'000)	(TVC_t)	112.41	126.40	142.76	161.77	184.15	(C8)
Fixed cost ($'000)	(FC_t)	105.00	110.25	115.76	121.54	127.61	(C9)
Advertising cost ($'000)	(A_t)	8.08	9.39	10.89	12.66	14.82	(C10)
Total cost ($'000)	(TC_t)	225.49	246.04	269.41	295.97	326.58	(C11)
Income before tax ($'000)	(Y_t)	5.64	22.28	41.86	65.85	96.97	(D12)
Tax ($'000)	(T_t)	2.25	8.91	16.74	26.34	38.78	(D13)
Income after tax ($'000)	(NY_t)	3.39	13.37	25.12	39.51	58.19	(D14)
Net worth ($'000)	(NW_{te})	53.39	66.76	91.88	131.39	189.58	(E15)

*The numerical value of $1.005 S_{t-1}/S_{t-2} + 0.05E_t$

† A fractional number.

The output of the model, in the form of a summary budget and selected rates of growth and return (taken from Table 27—1), may be presented to management in the manner illustrated in Table 27—2.

Table 27—2
ABC Co.
Corporate Model Outcomes

	1	2	3	4	5
Summary budget					
Total revenue	$231 130	$268 320	$311 270	$361 820	$423 550
Total cost	225 490	246 040	269 410	295 970	326 580
Income before tax	5 640	22 280	41 860	65 850	96 970
Less: Tax	2 250	8 910	16 740	26 340	38 780
Net income after tax	3 390	13 370	25 120	39 510	58 190
Net worth	53 390	66 760	91 880	131 390	189 580
Rates of growth and return					
Sales growth (%)	—	16.1	16.0	16.2	17.1
After-tax earnings growth (%)	—	294.4	87.9	57.3	47.3
After-tax earnings as % of net worth	6.4	20.0	27.3	30.1	30.7

It is important that management should also be presented with a brief explanation of the figures representing the corporate model output and the underlying assumptions, e.g. along the following lines:

> It has been assumed that industry sales (in units) will expand by about 20 per cent over the next five years, and that our market share can be maintained at about 10.6 per cent of industry sales. It is assumed also that inflation will have the following effects: the unit selling price will increase at 10 per cent per annum and the corresponding annual rates for variable cost and fixed cost factors will be 7 per cent and 5 per cent, respectively. In order to maintain our share of the market, the advertising expense will be 3.5 per cent of total revenue in all years. It is expected that the after-tax rate of return of 30 per cent which is achieved in Year 4 in the above budget can be maintained in future periods, given normal trading conditions.

It is seen that the operation of the model represents a simulation technique, and does not provide an analytic optimal solution. The model lends itself readily to sensitivity analysis based on changes in the values of variables or parameters. Since the model outputs are more sensitive to some factors than to others, the results from sensitivity analysis provide important information, from the viewpoint of decision making as well as improving the model. The sensitivity of the model to environmental factors can be tested, e.g. by running the model for different values of β and E_t while holding all other input values constant.

The foregoing is only a simplistic example of a part (although an important part) of a full-scale corporate financial model. A corporate financial model typically will be required to generate additional information relating to the balance sheet; e.g. it will indicate growth in fixed investment such as land, buildings and machinery, provide information about debt-equity relationships, and generate fund flow and cash flow statements. The model may contain thousands of mathematical equations in order to capture the complex inter-relationships that describe a firm's dynamic operations in the real world.

Summary

Management plans can be classified in three groups: strategic long-range plans, tactical multi-period plans and tactical annual plans. Management plans, planning tools and models, and budgets are all inter-related. A budget may be defined as the quantitative expression of a plan and its preparation is based on the use of planning tools and models.

One of the most important of these planning tools and models is the corporate model. A corporate model is a computer-based representation of a company's operations by a set of mathematical equations. It typically provides answers to 'what if' questions, information that is needed for planning and decision making. A simplified version of a corporate model has been presented in this chapter to illustrate its usefulness and limitations.

References

Drucker, P.F., 'Long-Range Planning Means Risk-Taking', in D.W. Ewing (ed.), *Long-Range Planning for Management*, Harper and Row, New York, 1972, pp. 3-19.

Grinyer, P.H. and Wooller, J., *Corporate Models Today*, Institute of Chartered Accountants in England and Wales, London, 1975.

Additional Reading

Anthony, R.N. and Dearden, J., *Management Control Systems, Text and Cases*, Irwin, Homewood, Ill., 1976, Chapter 1.

Lorange, P. and Vancil, R.F., 'How to Design a Strategic Planning System', *Harvard Business Review*, September-October 1976, pp. 75-81.

Naylor, T.H., 'The Future of Corporate Planning Models', *Managerial Planning*, March-April, 1976, pp. 1-9.

Discussion Questions

1 Explain the relationships between plans, planning models and budgets. Figure 27—A may be used as a basis for your explanation.

2 Differentiate between the two types of strategic plans and explain the crucial elements in each.

3 What are tactical plans? Discuss the differences between a multi-period tactical plan and a strategic plan.

4 Discuss the procedures that should be followed in drawing up a multi-period tactical plan. Why should companies prepare more than one plan?

5 Explain what is meant by a 'corporate model', and the advantages associated with the use of a corporate model.

6 Distinguish between the two approaches — top-down and bottom-up — to corporate modelling, and explain the circumstances appropriate to each approach.

7 Regardless of the approach taken, what are the essential points that should be considered when developing a corporate model?

8 Discuss how the annual plan differs from the annual budget. What do they have in common?

Exercises

1 Subcontractors Co. produces assembly parts for the motor-car industry. You are given the following data for preparing profit projections for the next ten years:
(a) Actual sales in 1985 were 100 000 units.
(b) The production capacity in 1985 was 110 000 units.
(c) New machines for expansion will be available in future years with a normal capacity of 20 000 units per machine.
(d) Sales forecast — sales are expected to grow exponentially with a probability distribution as indicated below:

Growth per Year	Probability
5%	0.3
7%	0.6
10%	0.1

(e) The selling price in 1985 was $7 per unit and this is expected to increase exponentially at a rate of 7 per cent per annum.
(f) The cost of production in 1985 was $6 per unit. This is expected to increase in future years, as shown below:

Year	1	2	3	4	5	6	7	8	9	10
Rate	1%	3%	5%	7%	9%	10%	11%	12%	13%	14%

The rate of increase refers to the *base year 1985*. For example in the third year unit cost will be 5 per cent higher than the base year cost of $6.
(g) Expansion policy: it is planned to expand the plant capacity by 20 000 units in the 3rd year, 20 000 units in the 6th year and 20 000 units in the 9th year.
(h) Assume that production equals sales in all years.

Prepare a corporate model which can forecast profit for the next 10 years. Assume depreciation costs are included in the estimated unit production cost figures, and ignore administrative and selling expenses. You should present the corporate model outcomes in tabular form.

2 Assume the same data as in Exercise 1. The expansion policy, item (g), in that exercise, however, is replaced by the following policy:
(g) Expansion policy: guidelines to be followed in the next 10 years are:
(i)   A maximum of one machine, which has an annual capacity of 20 000 units, can be purchased in any one year.
(ii) An additional machine should be purchased only when the projected sales for a particular year exceed the existing plant capacity.

Prepare a corporate model which can forecast profit for the next 10 years. Assume depreciation costs are included in the estimated unit production cost figures, and ignore administrative and selling expenses. You should present the corporate model outcomes in tabular form.

28 Profit Planning and the Master Budget

From the accounting viewpoint, the chief significance of budgets lies in their use as instruments of managerial planning, and it is with the planning aspects of budgeting that this chapter is especially concerned. The distinction between planning and control is, of course, rather artificial; the two are so inter-related that it is difficult to say where one function ends and the other begins. There are, nevertheless, some advantages to be gained from undertaking a separate examination of the planning aspects of budgeting in order to see what the plans are designed to achieve.

Profit Planning

Break-even Analysis

The profit plan of an enterprise is frequently expressed in the form of a profit-graph or break-even chart, as illustrated in the following section. A simple form of break-even analysis is briefly explained below. If it is assumed that all units produced are sold in the period, the profit equation may be stated algebraically as follows:

$$\pi = px - vx - F$$

where
π = profit of the firm
x = number of units produced and sold
p = selling price per unit
v = variable cost per unit
F = total fixed cost

The level of output, x^*, at which total cost equals total revenue may be computed from the break-even equation as follows:

$$px^* - vx^* - F = 0$$

Re-arranging,

$$x^* = \frac{F}{p - v}$$

where $p - v$ is the variable profit margin per unit (sometimes called the contribution margin or the variable profit contribution). The level of sales at which the firm breaks even is simply x^* times the unit selling price:

$$px^* = \frac{F}{(p - v)/p}$$

where $(p - v)/p$ is the variable profit margin ratio.

Example: The Ontop Co. manufactures a specialized item for mountain climbers, which it sells for $8 per unit. Variable costs are 50 per cent of sales value and fixed costs are $200 000 per annum. The break-even points in units and in sales dollars are calculated as follows:

$$x^* = \frac{200\ 000}{8-4}$$
$$= 50\ 000 \text{ units}$$
$$px^* = \$400\ 000$$

If the company were to budget for a profit of \$100 000, the required sales, $x^\dagger$, would be calculated as follows:

$$x^\dagger = \frac{\pi + F}{p - v}$$
$$= \frac{100\ 000 + 200\ 000}{8 - 4}$$
$$= 75\ 000 \text{ units}$$
$$px^\dagger = \$600\ 000$$

Profit-planning and Profit-graph Analysis

The profit-graph is designed to illustrate the relationship between profits and sales volume or output. The graph describes the assumed behaviour of revenues and costs in relation to changes in the level of activity (an appropriate distinction being made between costs which are fixed and costs which vary with the volume of activity). In its usual form, the profit-graph assumes a linear relationship between total revenue and sales volume (i.e. constant selling prices per unit), and the total cost function is also assumed to be a linear one (with total fixed costs remaining constant and total variable costs increasing proportionately with output). This means that steadily decreasing losses are assumed to be made as output increases up to a certain level at which total costs equal total revenue, known as the break-even point. Thereafter profits are assumed to increase linearly as the volume of activity expands. The profit-graph relating to the Ontop Co. in the previous example is illustrated in Figure 28—A. For purposes of the following discussion, assume that the profit-graph refers to a single product or a constant product-mix, and that all units produced are sold in the period.

The significance of the profit-graph in relation to profit planning is obvious; it provides an indication of the sales volume which must be achieved in order to earn the budgeted level of profit, given selling prices, fixed costs and variable costs. The required sales volume may then be examined in the light of past trends and expected operating conditions with a view to deciding whether it is capable of attainment during the budget period. If the answer to this question is negative, either the planned level of profit must be revised or adjustments must be made in respect of some of the other factors affecting profit. In the latter event, the profit-graph may be used (varying the form of presentation where necessary) to illustrate the variations in profit, at different levels of activity, which result from changes in selling prices (Figure 28—B) or fixed·costs (Figure 28—C) or variable costs (Figure 28—D). The new break-even points are shown as break-even point (2) in the three respective figures. The variations in profit and the break-even point can also be obtained from the profit equation and the break-even equation. But the profit-graphs give a pictorial representation of the effects of the changed circumstances on profit over a wide range of output, in a way that is readily understood by management.

Figure 28—A
The Ontop Co.
Profit-graph (or Break-even Chart)

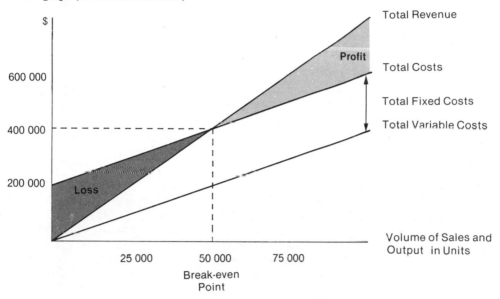

Figure 28—B
Effect on Profit of Change in Selling Price

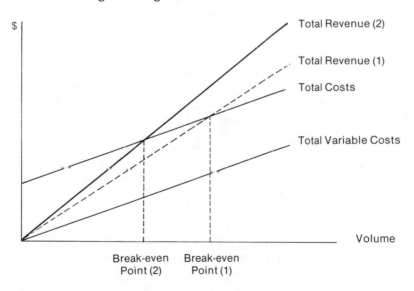

Figure 28—C
Effect on Profit of Change in Fixed Costs

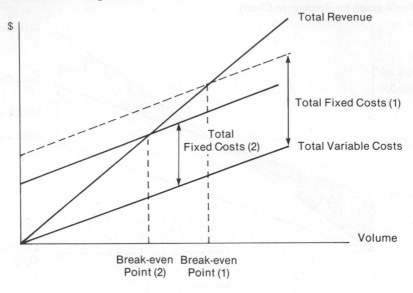

Figure 28—D
Effect on Profit of Change in Variable Costs

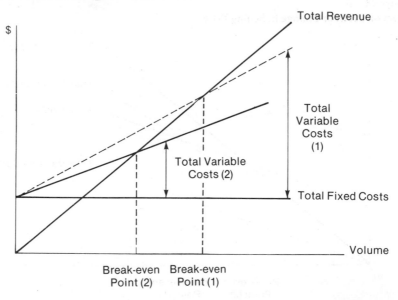

If it is considered that the required sales volume can be achieved, it becomes the basis of the budgeted level of activity, which is in turn one of the cornerstones in the construction of the master budget. In deciding whether the desired sales volume can be achieved, however, it is often necessary to take account of another limiting factor, such as production capacity, financial limitations, the supply of a critical raw material or even the existence of a suitably trained labour force. Such a factor then in effect becomes the key budget variable, sometimes known as the principal budget factor or the basic estimating factor. Profit planning cannot be regarded as a clear-cut operation; the emergence of a suitable plan is something of a trial-and-error process, involving a careful weighing-up of the different factors and constraints involved.

Profit-graph Assumptions

It has already been indicated that the usual form of profit-graph assumes linear cost and revenue functions. The assumptions underlying the profit-graph will now be examined in greater detail, with a view to making a judgement concerning the extent to which the assumed relationships accurately reflect the conditions of the real world. At the same time it is useful to contrast the profit-graph assumptions with traditional economic methods of analysing cost-output and revenue-output relationships.

The accounting treatment of these relationships, as expressed in the profit-graph, differs from the usual economic treatment in two ways. The first is merely a difference of presentation, resulting from the fact that the profit-graph records total costs and total revenues, whereas economic analysis tends to make use of average and marginal cost and revenue concepts. The second and more important difference is one of underlying assumptions. As has been seen, the profit-graph in its normal form assumes that there is a straight-line relationship between total costs and output. Translated into the economist's language of average and marginal costs, this implies that both average variable costs and marginal costs are constant. (Average total costs still fall as output expands, owing to the spreading of fixed costs over a greater volume.) Likewise, the profit-graph assumes a linear relationship between total revenue and output. This implies that average revenue (i.e. price) and marginal revenue are constant and equal, which is the kind of situation which is assumed under conditions of perfect competition.

Economists have traditionally regarded these assumptions as invalid under the usual conditions in which manufacturing and many other enterprises find themselves operating. In dealing with average variable costs, they suggest that, until a certain level of output is reached, the economies of increased scale may apply to variable costs as well as to fixed costs (owing, for example, to cheaper buying prices for large orders of materials, or more effective use of the labour force), so that average variable costs may fall for a time as output expands; but that after a certain point average variable costs start to increase (owing, for example, to limitations of plant capacity, the need to pay overtime rates for labour, or difficulties of controlling costs generally). According to economists, the average variable cost curve and the average total cost curve are thus generally U-shaped. In dealing with average revenue or price, economists traditionally suggest that there are very few markets for manufactured goods in the real world where perfect competition prevails, so that it is usually necessary for prices to be reduced in order to increase the volume of sales.

The accounting and economic treatments of cost-revenue-output relationships are contrasted in Figures 28—E and 28—F. It will be observed that economic analysis

Figure 28—E
Profit-graph Assumptions in Respect of Cost-Revenue-Output Relationships

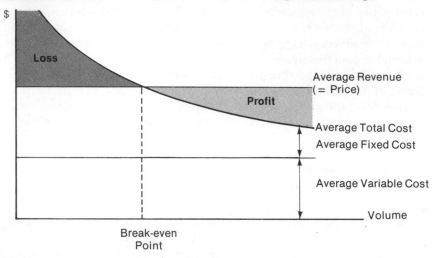

Figure 28—F
Conventional Economic Analysis of Cost-Revenue-Output Relationships

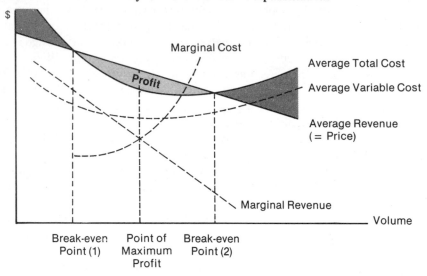

suggests that there are two break-even points, with a range of output in between at which production is profitable. As seen by economists the problem is not merely how to avoid a loss, but rather how to decide on a level of output, within the range of profitable production, that results in profits being maximized. The solution given by economists involves the use of the concepts of marginal cost and marginal revenue, and the most profitable output occurs where marginal cost equals marginal revenue (i.e. where the extra cost of producing an additional unit of output is equal to the extra revenue obtained from the sale of that unit).

What can be said about these differences in assumptions? In the first place, the purposes of the profit-graph are somewhat different from those of economic analysis, which is primarily intended to show how profits can be maximized. Although at first sight the profit-graph appears to describe cost and revenue behaviour over the whole range of output from zero to infinity, the production possibilities of any firm in practice are restricted to a fairly small range of output. Profit-graph analysis is essentially concerned with the task of relating costs and revenue to particular levels of output within this range for purposes of profit planning, but, as has been seen, it may also be used to indicate the effect on profits of shifts in the cost and revenue curves. Within the practicable range of production possibilities, there are grounds for believing that the profit-graph assumption of a linear cost function may be a reasonable approximation. As a result of empirical cost studies in a wide spread of industries, many economists now agree that average variable costs do tend to remain more or less constant over the relevant range of output, only rising in the short run as the limits of productive capacity are reached. Firms can of course take steps to ascertain their cost functions and thereby see whether the linearity assumption is justified.

The shape of the revenue function is also difficult to determine, and there seems to be a tendency for firms to take the prices of their products as given and to try to affect demand by other means, e.g. by increased selling expenses or product differentiation. This of course complicates the relationship between costs and revenue, but it suggests that it may not be unreasonable to adopt the profit-graph assumption that firms can bring about small changes in the volume of their sales without affecting selling prices.

The important thing is that management should be aware of the underlying assumptions of profit-graph analysis and of the limitations resulting from those assumptions, and be prepared to vary the assumptions where they can be shown to be unrealistic. Costs and revenues are functions of other variables besides the level of output and sales, e.g. size of plant, managerial efficiency or technological changes, and it needs to be clearly recognized that the procedure of relating profits to volume in a two-dimensional diagram over-simplifies the problem of profit planning. Nevertheless, profit-graph analysis does graphically illustrate some important functional relationships and is a convenient starting point.

The Annual Budget and the Product-mix Problem

Budgets for Cost Control and Planning

Both budgets and standards are applicable to planning, although budgeting has a broader role. Most budgets make use of standard costs in order to achieve effective managerial control over costs. Budgeting is, however, more than a technique for controlling costs. Budgeting in fact encompasses all aspects of the managerial function, so that budgets are just as relevant to the revenue-earning activities of business as to the cost side. Generally, budgeting is wider in scope than standard costing, and whereas the latter technique is usually restricted to manufacturing enterprises, budgeting can be used advantageously by all types of accounting entities. Indeed, the first steps to develop budgeting as a means of financial control were taken by governments.

The Budget Period

The first task in budgeting involves setting the goals for the budget period, and this in turn requires the predetermination of income on the one hand and the planning of financial resources on the other. Some consideration needs to be given to the choice of budget period. This may depend to some extent on the type of industry in which the enterprise is engaged. Thus firms whose products are subject to rapid obsolescence or fashion changes may be expected to favour a shorter budget period than those with a more stable product; while in industries subject to seasonal fluctuations the budget period must reflect the seasonal pattern of industrial activity. The type of budget itself influences the choice of budget period; capital expenditure thus needs to be planned on a long-term basis, whereas the preparation of cash budgets is virtually a day-to-day operation.

However, there are certain advantages in choosing the financial accounting period as the normal budget period. An important reason is that line or operating management makes use of an annual plan for profit planning as well as for control purposes. As noted in Chapter 27, this annual plan is often the first year of the tactical multi-period plan; the annual budget is the quantitative expression of this first-year plan.

Where longer-run budgets are being used for particular purposes, they may be broken down to make them fit the normal budget period. In any case it is necessary to break the budget period down into shorter periods of a week or a month—known as control periods—for purposes of budgetary control. This break-down, requiring as it does a careful study of seasonal patterns and trends in cost behaviour, profitability and financial relationships, is likely to prove a difficult task in practice, and care must be taken to avoid arbitrary allocations among control periods giving useless or even misleading estimates. Firms in industries subject to marked seasonal variations need to be especially careful in this regard.

Irrespective of the budget period, the original budget estimates need to be revised from time to time, by making appropriate adjustments both to the summary figures for the whole budget period and to the control period break-down.

The Budgeted Level of Activity

As has been shown above, the planned level of profit is related to a particular level of production, which becomes the budgeted level of activity and forms the basis of the detailed estimates in the individual profit and loss budgets. The budgeted level of activity has particular significance in relation to the manufacturing overhead budget and the problem of fixing overhead cost absorption rates, but is also a starting point in estimating other items affecting the profit and loss statement. It is important to remember that the estimates of costs and revenues are necessarily related to a particular volume of activity, so that adjustments need to be made to the budget figures if the actual level of activity turns out to be different from the budget estimate.

This implies, of course, that the budgets for sales revenue, direct material costs, direct labour costs, selling overhead and general administrative overhead, as well as for manufacturing overhead, all need to be prepared as flexible budgets. Some of these budgets (e.g. the direct material cost budget) may only record variable costs, while others (e.g. the selling overhead budget) may take the same form as the flexible budget of manufacturing overhead described above (with the exception that variable selling expenses need to be related to sales volume rather than production volume). In either case, however, effective budget control and the pin-pointing of managerial responsibility demand that the actual revenues earned or costs incurred be related to budget figures adjusted to the appropriate volume of activity.

The Product-mix Problem

The product-mix problem arises when the assumption of a single product firm or a constant product-mix is relaxed. When a number of product lines is produced and sold, profit planning and budgeting cannot proceed until after the optimal product combination has been established.

A number of situations can be distinguished in which the multi product firm faces one or more production constraints. Other things equal, where there is only one scarce input factor (e.g. direct labour hours), the firm should maximize production of the product which gives the largest variable profit per unit of the scarce factor.

Where a firm produces two products and there are several constraints, the optimal product-mix solution can be obtained by using a graphic linear programming approach. The situation of the firm with more than two products and multiple constraints is more complex. An algebraic solution can be obtained by using the so-called simplex linear programming technique. The simplex method has several advantages: it provides a generalized solution, and the computer can be programmed to give valuable information in addition to the optimal product-mix.

The Multi-product Single-constraint Case

The relative profitability of different products produced by a multi-product firm can be evaluated by reference to the variable profit concept. When the business is operating at full capacity, the decision as to which product line to expand should be based on each product's *variable profit contribution per unit of the limiting capacity factor*. This single production constraint could be time or factory space, often it is direct hours or hours available on a particular machine.

Example: A firm produces three products, X_1, X_2 and X_3, and there is a constraint on direct hours available. Suppose there is unlimited demand for all three products at the current selling prices (i.e. assume a perfect market). The particulars relating to the sales and manufacture of the three products are as follows:

	X_1	X_2	X_3
Selling price per unit	$10	$20	$30
Total manufacturing costs per unit	$8	$14	$18
Gross profit margin	$2	$6	$12
Gross profit margin ratio	20%	30%	40%
Total variable costs (mfg. and non-mfg.) per unit	$7	$10	$24
Variable profit margin	$3	$10	$6
Variable profit margin ratio	30%	50%	20%
Direct labour hours per unit	1 hour	5 hours	4 hours
Variable profit per hour	$3	$2	$1.50

If the production facilities can be committed to any combination of product lines, the most profitable line is X_1 which has the largest variable profit contribution per hour, and not X_2 (largest variable profit margin and variable profit margin ratio) or X_3 (largest gross profit margin ratio).

An example of a multi-product single-constraint case in which sales are limited by demand is illustrated on pages 657-8.

The Two-product Multi-constraint Case

A firm produces two products, X_1 and X_2, which require the use of production facilities in two departments, D_1 and D_2. The maximum hours of work that can be performed per day is 60 hours in D_1 and 32 hours in D_2. Details relating to the hours of processing time in each department and variable profit contributions per unit of X_1 and per unit of X_2 respectively are as follows:

Product	Processing Time (Hours)		Profit Contribution per Unit of Product
	D_1	D_2	
X_1	3	4	$20
X_2	6	2	$24

The objective function, Z, is usually specified in terms of the maximization of profits or the minimization of costs. In this case the objective function is to maximize the total variable profit contribution on units of X_1 (call these units x_1) and X_2 (call these units x_2). The maximization is subject to the constraint imposed by the maximum hours of work that can be performed in each department. The problem may be expressed as follows:

Maximize $\qquad\qquad Z = 20x_1 + 24x_2$
subject to $\qquad\qquad\qquad 3x_1 + 6x_2 \leqslant 60$
$\qquad\qquad\qquad\qquad 4x_1 + 2x_2 \leqslant 32$
$\qquad\qquad\qquad\qquad\quad x_1, x_2 \geqslant 0$

The graphical solution to this problem is given in Figure 28—G. The *set of feasible solutions* is represented by the shaded area, which is a convex polygon bounded by and thus common to both constraints. The slope of the objective function line

Figure 28—G
A Graphical Linear Programming Solution

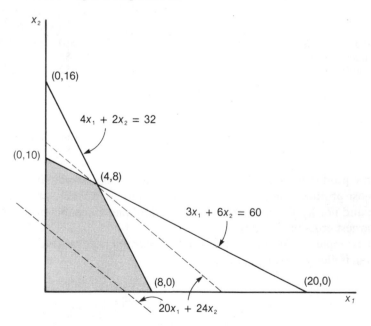

is $-\dfrac{20}{24}$, and may be represented by an infinite number of parallel straight lines (shown as broken lines in Figure 28—G). The optimal solution is obtained by moving the objective function line outwards from the origin until the line is only just touching the solution set. Figure 28—G shows that the optimal product mix is 4 units of X_1 and 8 units of X_2, representing a total variable profit contribution of $272.

Sensitivity Testing

Given the production constraints, the product mix of 4 units of X_1 and 8 units of X_2 maximizes profit when the variable profit contribution margins *per unit* of X_1 and X_2 (hereafter referred to as contribution margins of X_1 and X_2) are $20 and $24, respectively. If the contribution margin of X_1 decreases while that of X_2 is held constant (at $24), the objective function line in Figure 28—G will rotate in an anticlockwise direction until it is parallel to the constraint line $3x_1 + 6x_2 = 60$, at the lower bound to the contribution margin of X_1. All points on the constraint line between the ordered pairs of coordinates (0,10) and (4,8), both inclusive, now satisfy the optimal product mix solution. The new value of Z is $240, from which it follows that the lower bound to the value of X_1's contribution margin is $12.

Similarly, if the contribution margin of X_1 increases while that of X_2 is held constant, the objective function line will rotate in a clockwise direction until it is parallel to the constraint line $4x_1 + 2x_2 = 32$ at the upper bound to the contribution margin of X_1. All points on the constraint line between (4,8) and (8,0), both inclusive, constitute an optimal product mix. X_1's contribution margin is $48 and the new value of Z is $384.

A similar analysis may be performed with respect to the profit contribution margin of X_2. The lower and upper bounds to the objective function coefficients of x_1 and x_2 are summarized below:

	Lower Bound (l)	Original	Upper Bound (u)
X_1	$l/24 = 3/6$ $l = 12	$20	$u/24 = 4/2$ $u = 48
X_2	$l/20 = 2/4$ $l = 10	$24	$u/20 = 6/3$ $u = 40

The sensitivity analysis for a change in the profit contribution margin of X_1, while keeping the contribution margin of X_2 at the original level, has been explained above. Changes in the contribution margins of both products *simultaneously* will not alter the optimal solution mix, so long as the objective function has a slope between that of the two constraints. The limits are indicated by:

$$4/2 \geqslant C_1/C_2 \geqslant 3/6$$

where C_1 and C_2 are the coefficients of x_1 and x_2 respectively in the objective function, i.e. these are the contribution margins per unit of products X_1 and X_2, respectively.

The Multi-product Multi-constraint Case

Now suppose that a firm produces three products, X_1, X_2 and X_3, which yield different variable profit contributions per unit and use different quantities of materials, M_1, M_2 and M_3, which are available only in limited quantities. Details relating to the material requirements and variable profit contribution margins per unit of X_1, X_2 and X_3 are set out below:

Product	Material Requirements (kg)			Profit Contribution per Unit of Product
	M_1	M_2	M_3	
X_1	5	10	10	$100
X_2	5	8	5	$200
X_3	10	5	—	$50

The availability of materials M_1, M_2 and M_3 is limited to 1 000 kg, 2 000 kg and 500 kg, respectively. The problem may be expressed as:

$$
\begin{aligned}
\text{Maximize} \quad & 100x_1 + 200x_2 + 50x_3 \\
\text{subject to} \quad & 5x_1 + 5x_2 + 10x_3 + S_1 = 1\,000 \\
& 10x_1 + 8x_2 + 5x_3 + S_2 = 2\,000 \\
& 10x_1 + 5x_2 + S_3 = 500 \\
& x_1, x_2, x_3, S_1, S_2, S_3 \geqslant 0
\end{aligned}
$$

where x_1 = units of product X_1
x_2 = units of product X_2
x_3 = units of product X_3
S_1 = slack or unused kg of M_1
S_2 = slack or unused kg of M_2
S_3 = slack or unused kg of M_3

A summary of the simplex linear programming solution given by the computer is contained in Tables 28—1 to 28—4. Table 28—1 shows that the optimal product mix is 100 units of X_2 and 50 units of X_3, and the maximum value of the objective function is $22 500.

Table 28—1
Final Tableau

Solution Basis		x_1	x_2	x_3	S_1	S_2	S_3
x_2	100	2	1	0	0	0	0.2
x_3	50	−0.5	0	1	0.1	0	−0.1
S_2	950	−3.5	0	0	−0.5	1	−1.1
Z	22 500						

Note: Z = value of the objective function.

Table 28—2
Summary of Results

Variable	Status	Activity Level	Opportunity Cost
x_1	NB		275.00
x_2	B	100.00	—
x_3	B	50.00	
S_1	NB		5.00
S_2	B	950.00	—
S_3	NB		35.00

Maximum value of the objective function $= 22\ 500.00$

Note: B indicates that the variable appears in the final solution basis and NB indicates that the variable does not appear in the final solution basis.

Table 28—3
Optimality Range for Right-hand-side Constants Non-slack Resources Only

	Minimum	Original	Maximum
S_1	500.00	1 000.00	2 900.00
Z	20 000.00	22 500.00	32 000.00
S_3	0.00	500.00	1 000.00
Z	5 000.00	22 500.00	40 000.00

Table 28—4
Optimality Range for Objective Function Coefficients

	Minimum	Original	Maximum
C_2	62.50	200.00	INF
Z	8 750.00	22 500.00	INF
C_3	0.00	50.00	400.00
Z	20 000.00	22 500.00	40 000.00

Note: INF = infinity, i.e. the function has a maximum at infinity.

Interpretation of the Shadow Prices

Table 28—2 gives the value for M_1 and M_3 of their *opportunity costs*, also called *imputed costs*, *shadow prices* or *dual variables*. The shadow price of material M_1 is $5 and that of material M_3 is $35 per kg. In essence, the shadow prices reflect the allocation of the total profit from the optimal solution mix to these two non-slack resources, as shown:

Material	Quantity Available (kg)	Shadow Price per kg	Profit Contribution
M_1	1 000	$5	$5 000
M_3	500	35	17 500
Value of objective function as per solution			$22 500

These shadow prices may be used to evaluate the worth of acquiring additional resources. For example, if one additional kg of M_1 (M_3) can be acquired, the profit contribution will be increased by $5 ($35). Furthermore, since M_2 is in excess supply (unused capacity of 950 kg, as shown in the third column in Table 28—2), it has a shadow price of zero. Additional quantities of M_2 will not result in any increase in the value of the objective function but will merely increase the surplus.

A further fact to be elicited from Table 28—2 is that X_1 has a shadow price of $275, so that if one unit of X_1 was introduced into the product mix the profit contribution would decline from $22 500 by $275 to $22 225. This implies that X_1 should not be produced.

Table 28—3 indicates the ranges over which the shadow prices of M_1 and M_3 respectively are valid. For example, M_1 can be increased from 1 000 to 2 900 kg, an increase of 1 900 kg. Now, in terms of the above statement, each kg of M_1 is worth $5, so that the new profit contribution may be calculated as:

Existing profit contribution	$22 500
Incremental profit arising from 1 900 additional kg of M_1 at $5 per kg	9 500
New profit contribution	$32 000

The new product mix is determined as follows:

Product	Original Solution (units)	+	Change in Resource M_1	x	Substitution Factor as per Table 28—1	=	New Solution (units)	Profit per Unit	Total Profit Contribution
X_2	100	+	(1 900	x	0)	=	100	$200	$20 000
X_3	50	+	(1 900	x	0.1)	=	240	$ 50	12 000
									$32 000

Thus the shadow prices provide information about the worth of various resources to the firm and may be used to evaluate proposals to vary (upwards or downwards) the availability of those resources. Furthermore it is possible to compute the revised optimal product mix and value of the objective function arising from changes in resource availability, provided that such changes lie within the relevant range as given in Table 28—3.

Interpretation of the Sensitivity of the Objective Function Coefficients

Table 28—4 shows that the contribution margin X_2 (call this C_2), which is currently $200 per unit, can vary between $62.50 and infinity, with the contribution margins of X_1 and X_3 held at their original levels of $100 and $50 respectively, without altering the optimal product mix. The value of that product mix, of course, will change ($C_2 = \$62.50, Z = \$8\ 750; C_2 = INF, Z = INF$).

Now consider X_3. The contribution margin of X_3 (call this C_3), which is currently $50 per unit, can vary between $0 and $400, with the contribution margins of X_1 and X_2 held at their original levels of $100 and $200 respectively, without altering the optimal product mix. As before, the value of that product mix will change ($C_3 = \$0, Z = \$20\ 000; C_3 = \$400, Z = \$40\ 000$).

The Master Budget

The principles and methods underlying the preparation of the master budget are illustrated by reference to a firm with two products and a single production constraint. The Waratah Manufacturing Co. produces two products, X and Y, which are sold in a highly competitive market. Its balance sheet at the end of 1985 is as follows:

Shareholders' equity			Fixed assets		
Capital	$120 000		Plant and machinery		$115 000
Retained earnings	42 710		*Less*: Accumulated		
			depreciation		40 000
	$162 710				$75 000
Current liabilities			**Current assets**		
Accounts payable	5 000		Cash		4 000
Income tax payable	18 000		Accounts receivable	$24 000	
			Less: Bad debts		
	$23 000		provision	240	23 760
			Inventories—		
			Raw materials	8 000	
			Work in process	16 000	
			Finished goods	58 950	
					82 950
					$110 710
Total equities	$185 710		**Total assets**		$185 710

In preparing its comprehensive budget for the forthcoming year, 1986, information relating to the opening inventories and budgeted particulars of the two products, X and Y, are:

	X	Y
Opening inventory (units)	3 000	8 000
Budgeted closing inventory (units)	1 000	10 000
Budgeted selling price per unit	$20	$5
Budgeted variable profit per unit	$10	$3
Budgeted direct labour hours (DLH) required per unit	2 hours	$\frac{1}{5}$ hour
Variable profit per DLH	$5	$15
Sales constraints (units)	15 000	28 000

There is a production constraint of 26 000 direct labour hours. Let x and y denote sales in units of products X and Y, respectively. The production requirements, taking opening and closing inventories into account, are

for X: $$x + 1\ 000 - 3\ 000 = x - 2\ 000$$

and for Y: $$y + 10\ 000 - 8\ 000 = y + 2\ 000.$$

The production constraint of 26 000 direct labour hours may be represented by the following inequality:

$$2(x - 2\ 000) + \tfrac{1}{5}(y + 2\ 000) \leqslant 26\ 000$$
$$2x + \tfrac{1}{5}y \leqslant 29\ 600$$

The problem of determining the optimal sales mix may be expressed as follows:

Maximize $\quad\quad 10x + 3y$

subject to $\quad\quad 2x + \tfrac{1}{5}y \leqslant 29\ 600$
$$0 \leqslant x \leqslant 15\ 000$$
$$0 \leqslant y \leqslant 28\ 000$$

Where there is only one scarce resource, the rule to follow is straightforward—maximize sales in the product line which shows the largest variable profit *per unit of the limiting input factor,* in this case Y which has the higher variable profit per direct labour hour. Since sales of Y are limited by market demand and other factors to 28 000 units, $y = 28\ 000$ units, and it follows that $x = 12\ 000$ units. In line with budgeted closing inventory requirements, 30 000 units of Y will be produced and 10 000 units of X, as shown in the production budget in Table 28—5.

For convenience of presentation, the following budget statements of Waratah Manufacturing Company are presented by quarters:

Table	Budget Statement
28—5A	Sales and production budget
28—6	Direct material purchases budget
28—7	Direct labour budget
28—8	Manufacturing overhead budget
28—9	Cost of sales budget
28—10	Selling and administrative outlays budget
28—11	Budgeted income statement
28—12	Capital budget
28—13	Budgeted collections on accounts receivable
28—14	Budgeted disbursements on accounts payable
28—15	Cash budget
28—16	Budgeted balance sheet
28—17	Budgeted funds statement

Table 28—5
Monthly Budget of Sales and Production of Products X and Y for Year 1986

	Jan.	Feb.	Mar.	Apr.	May	June	July	Aug.	Sep.	Oct.	Nov.	Dec.	Year
Product X (units)													
Estimated sales	1 000	1 000	1 000	1 000	1 000	1 000	1 000	1 000	1 000	1 000	1 000	1 000	12 000
Budgeted closing inventory	2 833	2 666	2 500	2 333	2 166	2 000	1 833	1 666	1 500	1 333	1 166	1 000	1 000
	3 833	3 666	3 500	3 333	3 166	3 000	2 833	2 666	2 500	2 333	2 166	2 000	13 000
Less: Opening inventory	3 000	2 833	2 666	2 500	2 333	2 166	2 000	1 833	1 666	1 500	1 333	1 166	3 000
Budgeted production level	833	833	834	833	833	834	833	833	834	833	833	834	10 000
Product Y (units)													
Estimated sales	2 000	4 000	5 000	5 000	4 000	2 000	1 000	1 000	1 000	1 000	1 000	1 000	28 000
Budgeted closing inventory	8 500	7 000	4 500	2 000	500	1 000	2 500	4 000	5 500	7 000	8 500	10 000	10 000
	10 500	11 000	9 500	7 000	4 500	3 000	3 500	5 000	6 500	8 000	9 500	11 000	38 000
Less: Opening inventory	8 000	8 500	7 000	4 500	2 000	500	1 000	2 500	4 000	5 500	7 000	8 500	8 000
Budgeted production level	2 500	2 500	2 500	2 500	2 500	2 500	2 500	2 500	2 500	2 500	2 500	2 500	30 000

Notes: The sales of X are uniform throughout the year. The volume of opening inventory of X represents tied-up capital, hence the inventory is allowed to run down to a budgeted level of 1 000 units. Management's policy is to maintain a constant flow of production of both products X and Y.

The sales of Y are high in the first two quarters, peaking in March and April. The uniform production flow accounts for the fluctuations in inventory levels during the year.

There are alternative policies; e.g. management could plan for stabilized inventory levels, while permitting the level of production to fluctuate. Or management could prefer some trade-off between stable inventory and stable production levels.

Table 28—5A
Sales and Production Budget for Year 1986

	1st Qtr.	2nd Qtr.	3rd Qtr.	4th Qtr.	Year
Product X					
Estimated sales (units)	3 000	3 000	3 000	3 000	12 000
Estimated sales ($)	$60 000	$60 000	$60 000	$60 000	$240 000
Budgeted production in units	2 500	2 500	2 500	2 500	10 000
Product Y					
Estimated sales (units)	11 000	11 000	3 000	3 000	28 000
Estimated sales ($)	$55 000	$55 000	$15 000	$15 000	$140 000
Budgeted production in units	7 500	7 500	7 500	7 500	30 000

Table 28—6
Direct Material Purchases Budget for Year 1986

	1st Qtr.	2nd Qtr.	3rd Qtr.	4th Qtr.	Year
Material 1121 (kg)					
Used for manufacture of X	1 250	1 250	1 250	1 250	5 000
Used for manufacture of Y	1 500	1 500	1 500	1 500	6 000
Budgeted usage	2 750	2 750	2 750	2 750	11 000
Budgeted closing inventory	2 000	2 000	2 500	3 000	3 000
	4 750	4 750	5 250	5 750	14 000
Less: Opening inventory	2 000	2 000	2 000	2 500	2 000
Budgeted purchases	2 750	2 750	3 250	3 250	12 000
Cost of usage at $1.50 per kg	$4 125	$4 125	$4 125	$4 125	$16 500
Cost of purchases at $1.50 per kg	$4 125	$4 125	$4 875	$4 875	$18 000
Material 1122 (kg)					
Used for manufacture of X	7 500	7 500	7 500	7 500	30 000
Used for manufacture of Y	15 000	15 000	15 000	15 000	60 000
Budgeted usage	22 500	22 500	22 500	22 500	90 000
Budgeted closing inventory	12 000	14 000	17 000	20 000	20 000
	34 500	36 500	39 500	42 500	110 000
Less: Opening inventory	10 000	12 000	14 000	17 000	10 000
Budgeted purchases	24 500	24 500	25 500	25 500	100 000
Cost of usage at $0.50 per kg	$11 250	$11 250	$11 250	$11 250	$45 000
Cost of purchases at $0.50 per kg	$12 250	$12 250	$12 750	$12 750	$50 000
Budgeted total cost of material usage	$15 375	$15 375	$15 375	$15 375	$61 500
Budgeted total cost of material purchases	$16 375	$16 375	$17 625	$17 625	$68 000

Note: The total material cost of a unit of X is $2.25 ($0.75 of 1121 and $1.50 of 1122), and a unit of Y is $1.30 ($0.30 of 1121 and $1.00 of 1122).

Table 28—7
Direct Labour Budget for Year 1986

	1st Qtr.	2nd Qtr.	3rd Qtr.	4th Qtr.	Year
Budgeted direct labour hours in manufacture of X: 2 hours per unit (see Table 28—5A)	5 000	5 000	5 000	5 000	20 000
Y: $\frac{1}{5}$ hour per unit (see Table 28—5A)	1 500	1 500	1 500	1 500	6 000
	6 500	6 500	6 500	6 500	26 000
Budgeted direct labour cost at $2.00 per hour	$13 000	$13 000	$13 000	$13 000	$52 000

Note: The direct labour cost of a unit of X is $4.00 and a unit of Y is $0.40.

Table 28—8
Manufacturing Overhead Budget (Based on 26 000 DLH) for Year 1986

	1st Qtr.	2nd Qtr.	3rd Qtr.	4th Qtr.	Year
Budgeted variable overhead—					
Indirect labour	$3 000	$3 000	$3 000	3 000	$12 000
Electricity—power	2 500	2 500	2 500	2 500	10 000
Supplies	1 000	1 000	1 000	1 000	4 000
Budgeted total variable overhead	$6 500	$6 500	$6 500	$6 500	$26 000
Budgeted fixed overhead—					
Indirect labour	5 000	5 000	5 000	5 000	20 000
Electricity—lighting	2 500	2 500	2 500	2 500	10 000
Factory rates and insurance		5 500		5 500	11 000
Maintenance	2 000	2 000	2 000	2 000	8 000
	9 500	15 000	9 500	15 000	49 000
Depreciation	3 000	3 000	5 000	5 000	16 000
Budgeted total fixed overhead	$12 500	$18 000	$14 500	$20 000	$65 000
Budgeted total manufacturing overhead	$19 000	$24 500	$21 000	$26 500	$91 000

Note: The manufacturing overhead recovery rate is $91 000/26 000 direct labour hours or $3.50 per direct labour hour. Thus manufacturing overhead absorbed by a unit of X is $7.00 and by a unit of Y is $0.70.

Table 28—9
Cost of Sales Budget for Year 1986

Both Products X and Y	1st Qtr.	2nd Qtr.	3rd Qtr.	4th Qtr.	Year
Budgeted manufacturing costs					
Direct materials (Table 28—6)	$15 375	$15 375	$15 375	$15 375	$61 500
Direct labour costs (Table 28—7)	13 000	13 000	13 000	13 000	52 000
Manufacturing overhead ($3.50 per DLH — see Tables 28—7 and 28—8)*	22 750	22 750	22 750	22 750	91 000
	51 125	51 125	51 125	51 125	204 500
Opening work in process †	16 000	16 000	16 000	16 000	16 000
	67 125	67 125	67 125	67 125	220 500
Less: Closing work in process †	16 000	16 000	16 000	16 000	16 000
Cost of finished production	51 125	51 125	51 125	51 125	204 500
Opening inventory of finished goods ‡	58 950	43 925	28 900	33 075	58 950
	110 075	95 050	80 025	84 200	263 450
Less: Closing inventory of finished goods ‡	43 925	28 900	33 075	37 250	37 250
Budgeted cost of sales	$66 150	$66 150	$46 950	$46 950	$226 200

*The figures for manufacturing overhead in each quarter relate to overhead absorbed. (Alternatively, the manufacturing overhead budgeted for each quarter may be used.)
† The simplifying assumption is made that there are no changes in the inventory of work in process. The monthly or quarterly budgeted cost of sales figure is distorted by changes in work in process, unless such changes are taken into account in preparing the material usage, labour and manufacturing overhead budgets.
‡ The costs of opening and closing inventories of finished goods in each quarter are based on quantities given in Table 28—5 and the unit manufacturing costs of X ($13.25) and Y ($2.40) respectively, obtained from Tables 28—6, 28—7 and 28—8.

Table 28—10
Selling and Administrative Outlays Budget for Year 1986

	1st Qtr.	2nd Qtr.	3rd Qtr.	4th Qtr.	Year
Selling expenses—variable					
Commissions ($1.45 per unit of X sold)	$4 350	$4 350	$4 350	$4 350	$17 400
Deliveries—$0.10 per unit of X	300	300	300	300	1 200
$0.05 per unit of Y	550	550	150	150	1 400
Budgeted variable selling expenses	$5 200	$5 200	$4 800	$4 800	$20 000
Selling expenses—discretionary					
Advertising	5 000	5 000	5 000	5 000	20 000
Selling expenses—fixed					
Salaries	2 500	2 500	2 500	2 500	10 000
Budgeted total selling expenses	$12 700	$12 700	$12 300	$12 300	$50 000
Administrative expenses—					
Office salaries	5 000	5 000	5 000	5 000	20 000
Rent	4 000	4 000	4 000	4 000	16 000
Sundry expenses	3 000	3 000	3 000	3 000	12 000
Budgeted total administrative expenses	$12 000	$12 000	$12 000	$12 000	$48 000

Table 28—11
Budgeted Income Statement for Year 1986

	1st Qtr.	2nd Qtr.	3rd Qtr.	4th Qtr.	Year
Budgeted sales (Table 28—5A)—					
Y	$60 000	$60 000	$60 000	$60 000	$240 000
Y	55 000	55 000	15 000	15 000	140 000
Less: Estimated bad debts—					
1% of sales	(1 150)	(1 150)	(750)	(750)	(3 800)
	113 850	113 850	74 250	74 250	376 200
Less: Cost of sales (Table 28—9)	66 150	66 150	46 950	46 950	226 200
Gross profit	$47 700	$47 700	$27 300	$27 300	$150 000
Less: Selling expenses					
(Table 28—10)	12 700	12 700	12 300	12 300	50 000
Administrative expenses					
(Table 28—10)	12 000	12 000	12 000	12 000	48 000
	24 700	24 700	24 300	24 300	98 000
Net operating profit	23 000	23 000	3 000	3 000	52 000
Interest income (see subsequent					
Table 28—15)	200	600	1 000	200	2 000
Less: Loss on sale of plant					
(Table 28—12)	(1 000)				(1 000)
Net profit before tax	$22 200	$23 600	$4 000	$3 200	$53 000
Less: Income tax at 40%					(21 200)
Dividends					(12 000)
Budgeted undistributed profit for year					$19 800

Note: Figures in parentheses in the above table are used for convenience to indicate difference in sign.

Table 28—12
Capital Budget for Year 1986

	1st Qtr.	2nd Qtr.	3rd Qtr.	4th Qtr.	Year
Budgeted purchases of new					
machinery	$20 000	$30 000			$50 000
Less: Proceeds from sale of old plant	5 000				5 000
	15 000	30 000			45 000
Extension of factory premises			$10 000		10 000
Budgeted net capital expenditures	$15 000	$30 000	$10 000		$55 000

Note: There is a loss of $1 000 on the planned sale of old plant, which has a gross book value of $10 000 and depreciation provision of $4 000.

Table 28—13
Budgeted Collections on Accounts Receivable for Year 1986

Accounts Receivable	1st Qtr.	2nd Qtr.	3rd Qtr.	4th Qtr.	Year
Opening balance	$24 000	$45 000	$30 000	$25 000	$24 000
Budgeted sales (Table 28—5A)	115 000	115 000	75 000	75 000	380 000
	139 000	160 000	105 000	100 000	404 000
Less: Closing balance	45 000	30 000	25 000	25 000	25 000
Accounts due for collection	94 000	130 000	80 000	75 000	379 000
Less: Estimated uncollectibles (1%)	940	1 300	800	750	3 790
Budgeted collections	$93 060	$128 700	$79 200	$74 250	$375 210

Notes: All sales are payable in full in the following month. The opening balance in the first quarter is given in the opening balance sheet. The opening balances in subsequent quarters and closing balances are based on monthly sales given in Table 28—5.

Bad debt expense for the year is equal to $3 790 − $240 + $250 (bad debt provisions on opening and closing balances on accounts receivable, respectively) = $3 800.

Table 28—14
Budgeted Disbursements on Accounts Payable for Year 1986

Accounts Payable	1st Qtr.	2nd Qtr.	3rd Qtr.	4th Qtr.	Year
Opening balance	$5 000	$5 458	$5 458	$5 875	$5 000
Budgeted purchases (Table 28—6)	16 375	16 375	17 625	17 625	68 000
	21 375	21 833	23 083	23 500	73 000
Less: Closing balance	5 458	5 458	5 875	5 875	5 875
Budgeted disbursements	$15 917	$16 375	$17 208	$17 625	$67 125

Note: Purchases are paid for in full in the following month. The opening balance in the first quarter is given in the opening balance sheet. The opening balances in subsequent quarters and closing balances are estimated on the assumption that the amount owing at the end of a quarter is equal to the cost of one-third of that quarter's purchases, given in Table 28—6.

Table 28—15
Cash Budget for Year 1986

	1st Qtr.	2nd Qtr.	3rd Qtr.	4th Qtr.	Year
Budgeted receipts					
Opening cash balance	$4 000	$12 643	$36 368	$36 060	$4 000
Receipts from sales (Table 28—13)	93 060	128 700	79 200	74 250	375 210
Proceeds from sale of plant (Table 28—12)	5 000				5 000
Interest income*	200	600	1 000	200	2 000
	$102 260	$141 943	$116 568	$110 510	$386 210
Budgeted payments					
Payments for purchases (Table 28—14)	15 917	16 375	17 208	17 625	67 125
Wages (Table 28—7)	13 000	13 000	13 000	13 000	52 000
Manufacturing overhead outlays (Table 28—8) †	16 000	21 500	16 000	21 500	75 000
Selling outlays (Table 28—10)	12 700	12 700	12 300	12 300	50 000
Administrative outlays (Table 28—10)	12 000	12 000	12 000	12 000	48 000
Capital outlays (Table 28—12)	20 000	30 000	10 000		60 000
Income tax ‡				18 000	18 000
Dividends (Table 28—11)				12 000	12 000
Closing cash balance	12 643	36 368	36 060	4 085	4 085
	$102 260	$141 943	$116 568	$110 510	$386 210

* The interest income is derived from the temporary investment of surplus cash balances.
† Manufacturing overhead outlays refer to budgeted total manufacturing overhead excluding depreciation.
‡ Tax of $18 000 paid in the last quarter relates to tax owing at the beginning of the year (see opening balance sheet).

Table 28—16
Budgeted Closing Balance Sheet for Year 1986

Shareholders' equity			Fixed assets		
Capital		$120 000	Plant and machinery	$155 000	
Retained earnings—			*Less*: Accumulated		
Balance b/f	$42 710		depreciation	52 000	$103 000
Profit for year	19 800		Extension of factory		
		62 510	premises		10 000
		182 510			113 000
Current liabilities			**Current assets**		
Accounts payable	5 875		Cash		4 085
Income tax payable	21 200		Accounts receivable	25 000	
		27 075	*Less*: Bad debts provision	250	
					24 750
			Inventories—		
			Raw materials	14 500	
			Work in process	16 000	
			Finished goods	37 250	
					67 750
					96 585
Total equities		$209 585	**Total assets**		$209 585

Table 28—17
Budgeted Funds Statement for Year 1986

Budgeted applications of funds		
Costs incurred through external transactions—		
Purchases of raw materials (Table 28—6)	$68 000	
Direct wages (Table 28—7)	52 000	
Manufacturing overhead outlays (Table 28—8)	75 000	
Selling outlays (Table 28—10)	50 000	
Administrative outlays (Table 28—10)	48 000	
		$293 000
Appropriation of profits to income tax (Table 28—11)		21 200
Dividends (Table 28—11)		12 000
Purchases of plant and machinery (Table 28—12)		50 000
Extension of factory premises (Table 28—12)		10 000
Increase in cash holding*		85
Increase in accounts payable*		990
		$387 275
Budgeted sources of funds		
Revenue from sale of trading inventories (Table 28—11)	380 000	
Less: Estimated bad debts (Table 28—11)	3 800	
		376 200
Interest income (Table 28—11)		2 000
Proceeds from sale of plant (Table 28—12)		5 000
Increase in accounts payable*		875
Increase in income tax payable*		3 200
		$387 275

* Difference between book value of item in the opening balance sheet and the budgeted balance sheet in Table 28—16.

Additional Reading

Burke, W.L., Smyth, E.B., and Macmullen, J.S., *Accounting for Management*, 3rd edn., Law Book Co., Sydney (in press).

Dopuch, N., Birnberg, J.B., and Demski, J., *Cost Accounting: Accounting Data for Management's Decisions*, Harcourt Brace Jovanovich, New York, 1974, Chapter 10.

Discussion Questions

1 Compare and contrast budgets and standards, with special reference to their use as instruments of managerial control.

2 What is a profit-graph and what is its significance in relation to budgeting and profit planning?

3 Contrast accounting and economic assumptions about cost-output and cost-revenue relationships. What action might be taken by a firm to test these assumptions by reference to empirical data?

4 Examine the notion that budgeting is designed to facilitate decentralization of managerial responsibility whilst maintaining top management control.

5 What role do budgets play in relation to accounting information systems and business decisions? Briefly show how budgets may contribute to more effective resource allocation decisions within an enterprise.

6 What are the underlying assumptions of a profit-graph which limit its usefulness in computing the optimal product mix for a multi-product firm with multiple constraints? Explain how a linear programming algorithm can aid in analysing such problems, and the additional information you can derive from a linear programming solution.

7 Discuss the concept of normal capacity (or budgeted level of activity) and its relevance to managerial accounting and budgeting.

8 Discuss the significance of each of the following with respect to the problem of securing effective managerial control in a large departmental retail store:
  (a) budget control period;
  (b) budgeted level of activity;
  (c) cash budget;
  (d) budgeted income statement; and
  (e) performance report for a semi-autonomous department of the store.

9 You have recently been appointed accountant to a manufacturing enterprise which operates an historical controlled cost system, in which little use is made of budgets. As a first step towards the ultimate installation of a standard cost system, you propose to recommend that a comprehensive system of budgeting be operated. Write a report, for presentation to the board, discussing:
  (a) the advantages to be derived from the operation of a system of budgets;
  (b) the procedure that should be followed in the preparation of the budgets; and
  (c) the principal budgets and their uses.

10 Break-even analysis has been criticised by some economists because it assumes that the total cost and total revenue functions are linear for firms operating under conditions of imperfect competition. Evaluate these criticisms.

11 In the case of a firm operating in an uncertain environment, examine the justification for business budgeting and discuss the likely limits of its utility as a guide to action.

12 What circumstances would justify making changes in a business budget during its lifetime, and what criteria should guide management in making the changes?

13 Accounting systems, it has been said, are necessarily preoccupied with the present and the past. Planning by management is, by contrast, concerned with the future. How can accounting information systems be designed and operated to provide the information needed for planning purposes?

Exercises

1 (a) Retailers Ltd produces a household gadget which is in great demand. The production costs comprise fixed costs of $30 000 and a variable cost of $8 per unit. The sales price is $12 per unit. What is the break-even point (in terms of dollars of sales revenue)?
  (b) What would be the break-even point if fixed costs were increased to $40 000?

2 Given a price of $12 per unit, variable cost of $9 per unit, and fixed costs of $20 000, plot a break-even chart and complete the following sentences:

(a) The break-even point is $... of sales revenue.

(b) Variable costs are $... at the break-even point.

(c) The variable costs would be $... and the profit would be $... if sales were $240 000.

(d) If the selling price was reduced to $11 per unit, the new break-even point would be $... of sales revenue.

(e) Specify the assumptions which underlie your analysis in relation to the foregoing questions.

3 Mr Smith is an experienced cost accountant in an automobile company. He is sceptical of linear programming and he offers two arguments to support his claim.

(a) His company signed a contract in 1985 for the purchase of 20 000 units of component A at $20 per unit, and 5 000 units of component B at $2 per unit, which were intended for use in production in 1986. The above information on the respective purchase prices and amounts of the two components was used to prepare a cost-volume-profit linear programming model. The company's management was surprised when the linear programming solution indicated that the shadow price of component A was $0 per unit and that of component B was $20 per unit. It appeared to the management that the model outcomes were divorced from reality and that it would be risky to use them for decision making.

(b) In addition to the actual purchase prices and amounts of the two components, several engineering and accounting estimates were also used as inputs to the cost-volume-profit linear programming model. The company's management believed that these estimates were imprecise and doubted whether the model solutions based on such estimates were of any practical value.

You are required to:

(i) Explain why actual and shadow prices differed in (a) above? What inferences can you draw from the shadow prices of components A and B respectively? Explain whether the concept of shadow price is useful for decision making.

(ii) Explain what estimates Mr Smith is referring to in (b) above. Are these estimates usually imprecise? Do you agree that linear programming solutions based on estimations may not be of any practical value? If the estimates are known to be imprecise, are there any tests that you can make on the model solutions to confirm their practical usefulness?

4 A company produces two chemicals, X_1 and X_2. Three raw materials—M_1, M_2 and M_3—are used in the process. The particulars relating to the availability and the demand for raw materials are summarized below:

	M_1	M_2	M_3
	kg	kg	kg
Requirements per unit of—			
X_1	5	7	5
X_2	10	9	4
Quantities of available resources	300	315	200

Product X_1 has a profit contribution of $10.50 and product X_2 of $11.28. Both products can be produced in fractional amounts.

You are required to present a graphical linear programming solution for the optimal quantities of X_1 and X_2 that should be produced. Calculate the value of the objective function.

5 A linear programming computer solution of the problem in Exercise 4 is given below.

Table 1
Summary of Results

Variable	Status	Activity Level	Opportunity Cost
x_1	B	31.76	
x_2	B	10.29	
S_1	B	38.23	
S_2	NB		0.84
S_3	NB		0.91

Maximum value of the objective function = 449.65

Note: S_1, S_2 and S_3 represent slack variables for resources M_1, M_2 and M_3 respectively.

Table 2
Optimality Range for Right-hand-side Constants—Non-slack Resources Only

	Minimum	Original	Maximum
S_2	280.00	315.00	336.67
Z	420.00	449.65	468.00
S_3	174.00	200.00	225.00
Z	425.88	449.65	472.50

Table 3
Optimality Range for Objective Function Coefficients

	Minimum	Original	Maximum
C_1	8.77	10.50	14.10
Z	394.80	449.65	564.00
C_2	8.40	11.28	13.50
Z	420.00	449.65	472.50

You are required to:
(a) state the maximum amount you would be willing to pay for an additional kilogram of M_1, M_2 and M_3 respectively;
(b) determine the lower and upper bounds of the non-slack resources within which the opportunity costs of resources M_1, M_2 and M_3 remain valid;
(c) explain how the objective functions in Table 2 are computed; and
(d) explain how the objective functions in Table 3 are computed.

6 The following data refer to the operations of Choice Product Ltd:

(a) **Balance Sheet as at 31 December 1985**

Shareholders' equity—			
Capital			$100 000
Retained earnings			10 750
			110 750
Current liabilities—			
Accounts payable		$7 000	
Income tax payable		13 000	20 000
			$130 750
Plant		100 000	
Less: Accumulated depreciation		30 000	70 000
Current assets—			
Cash		5 000	
Accounts receivable		20 500	
Inventories—			
Raw materials	$7 000		
Work in process	12 000		
Finished goods	16 250	35 250	60 750
			$130 750

The following information and budgeted data relate to the forthcoming year 1986.

(b) Opening inventories and budgeted data relating to products X and Y are as follows:

	Product X	Product Y
Opening inventory (units)	500	7 000
Budgeted selling price per unit	$15	$4
Budgeted variable profit per unit	$6	$2
Budgeted direct labour hours required per unit (hours)	3	$\frac{1}{2}$
Budgeted variable profit per direct labour hour	$2	$4
Sales constraints (units)	10 000	15 000

(c) The budgeted closing inventory (in units) of each product at the end of the quarter is given by budgeted sales of the product in the following quarter.

(d) The factory direct labour hours available are 16 750 hours.

(e) The sales of X are uniform over the four quarters. The sales of Y are 6 000 units in the first quarter, and are then uniform over the remaining three quarters. The amounts and patterns of sales in the subsequent year (1987) are expected to be the same as in 1986.

(f) Products X and Y use the same raw material No. 5501. The production of unit X requires 4 kg and that of Y requires 1 kg of material. The material cost is $1 per kg.

(g) There are no changes in the inventory of work in process.

(h) The direct labour cost is $1 per hour.

(i) The budgeted variable costs of products X and Y are as follows:

	Per Unit of X	Per Unit of Y
Direct labour	3	0.50
Direct materials	4	1.00
Variable overhead	1	0.25
Variable selling expenses	1	0.25
	09	$2.00

Choice Product Ltd values its inventories at their budgeted variable manufacturing costs, i.e. opening and closing inventories of X are valued at $8 and Y at $1.75.

(j) The fixed manufacturing expense is estimated at $2 400 and the selling and administrative expense at $5 000. Indirect expenses are incurred uniformly over the year. The fixed manufacturing overhead includes depreciation expense of $4 000, and the selling and administrative expense includes depreciation expense of $1 000.

(k) The inventory of raw materials at the end of each quarter is an amount equal to the following quarter's requirements.

(l) The bad debt expense is estimated at 0.5 per cent of budgeted sales.

(m) Sales in a particular month are receivable in full in the following month. Assume that sales are evenly distributed within each quarter.

(n) All purchases are payable in full after a credit period of one and a half months.

(o) Tax of 40 per cent on the net profit and dividends of 30 per cent on profits after tax are payable in the last quarter of the year.

You are required to calculate the optimal sales-mix and production-mix in 1986 and prepare a master budget for 1986, including the following budgets:

(i)   sales and production budget;
(ii)   direct material purchase and usage budget;
(iii)   labour utilization budget;
(iv)   manufacturing overhead budget;
(v)   cost of sales budget;
(vi)   selling and administrative outlays budget;
(vii)   budgeted income statement for the year;
(viii)   cash budget;
(ix)   budgeted balance sheet at year-end; and
(x)   budgeted funds statement for the year.

29 Capital Budgeting

It was noted in Chapter 27 that the capital budgets in the annual and multi-period tactical plans must dovetail with the capital budgeting proposals that underpin the implementation of the strategic plan. Figure 29—A illustrates how a particular capital project in the strategic plan (hereafter referred to as a strategic capital project) would be reflected in the 1985 annual capital budget. The life of the project extends over the six-year period 1983 to 1988. The capital budget contains all capital projects undertaken in 1985, including projects in both the strategic and tactical plans.

Figure 29—A
Incorporation of a Six-year Life Strategic Capital Project in the 1985 Annual Capital Budget

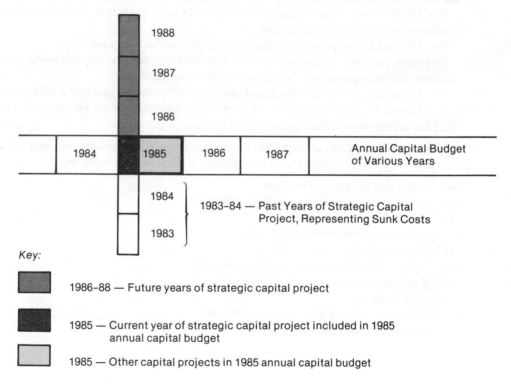

A similar relationship to that exhibited in Figure 29—A exists between capital projects associated with the implementation of the company's tactical rolling plan and its annual capital budget. There is one important difference between capital projects in the strategic plan and those in the tactical plan. The former, by virtue of their innovation, usually have more uncertain outcomes.

Significance and Problems of Capital Budgeting

A capital project may be defined as an investment of funds in the current and future periods in return for a stream of expected receipts in future periods. Given the objectives contained in the company's long-term plans, its capital projects represent the deployment of resources to attain its long-term objectives. Capital budgeting is the most crucial area in the whole field of managerial decision making, and the success or failure of a business primarily depends on the wisdom of the investment decisions made by its management.

Capital expenditures have special significance for a number of reasons. The expenditures tend to be large, but then so are expenditures on inventories. There are, however, two special features of capital expenditures: first, capital assets have a long life and their consequences extend far into the future; and, second, the markets for second-hand capital assets, in particular specialized equipment, are in many cases virtually non-existent. For these reasons, capital expenditure decisions are said to be irreversible, e.g. expenditures on an assembly line may commit the company to a given production mode for years to come.

Also, there are some complex measurement problems in capital expenditure analysis. The benefits, and usually some costs as well, lie in future periods, so that estimates of their magnitudes are subject to considerable uncertainty. Uncertainty may also attach to the problem of quantifying intangible benefits, e.g. the difficulty of evaluating the benefits of research expenditures or expenditures intended to promote staff morale (such as a sports ground). Costs and benefits also arise at different points in time, and it is necessary for purposes of comparison to introduce an interest or discount factor into the analysis. The discount factor usually employed is known as the cost of capital. While the cost of capital is one of the most important concepts in the theory of finance, there is still controversy on what it is or how it should be measured.

Lastly, there are often difficulties in determining what the suitable criteria are for a particular investment decision. Investment can take many forms—replacement, expansion, cost-reducing, quality improving, etc.—and the different forms may overlap to such an extent that it is difficult to sort out the underlying purposes of the investment and the data which are relevant in making the decisions. It needs to be emphasized, however, that the use of unadjusted financial accounting data, which have been assembled for purposes that are quite unrelated to the managerial problem of planning future operations, must inevitably lead to faulty investment decisions. The importance of employing the relevant cost and benefit concepts in capital project analysis will be discussed in a subsequent section.

The Administration of Capital Expenditures

There are several distinct stages in the administration of capital expenditures:
(a) the generation of project proposals;
(b) the analysis of proposals and selection between alternatives;
(c) the implementation of selected projects; and
(d) management control over the capital budgeting process, including interim audits of projects in progress and post-mortem audits of completed projects.

Generation of Project Proposals

While long-range plans are, by their very nature, formulated by top management, the responsibility for the implementation of these plans, including the generation of capital project proposals, is shared by all levels of management. The importance of generating new and viable project proposals cannot be over-emphasized; the growth of institutionalized research and development departments is evidence of the recognition of this managerial role.

Decision criteria are discussed in the following section. The decision-making process with respect to capital projects is always firmly placed under the control of top management. For example, in decentralized firms projects often are generated at divisional levels, but capital expenditures are approved by a highly centralized capital budgeting committee at top management level. This tight control serves two purposes. It enables top management to control the implementation of the company's long-range objectives and, secondly, it promotes goal congruence between the company and its divisions, and between the divisions themselves.

But there is a high opportunity cost in decision making by top management. In most organizations minor decisions, i.e. decisions involving predetermined small amounts, are delegated to successively lower management levels. All such decisions need to be regularly reviewed by the central budgeting committee. Managers have been known to circumvent constraints imposed on their authority to spend, by splitting up a large project into several small parts, each of which falls within the permitted amount.

There is a more fundamental problem. At many management levels there exist strong screening powers, whereby capital proposals generated at or below those levels may be delayed or rejected entirely by divisional and lower level managers. The reason is to safeguard the valuable time and effort of the central budgeting committee. But divisional screening decisions may be coloured by a divisional manager's personal utility function, i.e. his attitudes towards prestige, job safety and the annual bonus, which may not be consistent with overall corporate objectives. It is therefore important that these corporate objectives as well as the screening criteria be understood by all managers to whom this authority is delegated.

To conclude, it has been argued that the generation of new projects precedes, not only in the time sequence of events but also in economic significance, the decision making function itself, i.e. project evaluation and selection. It is not enough to have a good decision model, if the company is not able to generate appropriate capital project proposals in line with its objectives. The search for new investment opportunities is basic to the concept of strategic long-range planning. Some writers believe that more firms fail because they invest too little rather than too much, and too late rather than too early.

Management Control over Capital Expenditures

The implementation of a capital project is the responsibility of the operating departments. Accounting control is exercised over all capital expenditures to ensure that the outlays are within the limits approved by the central budgeting committee, and that payments for purchases, wages, etc. conform to established company policies and procedures. Accounting control over expenditures and the use of assets is effectively applied through the annual budget.

Comprehensive audits in which actual performance is checked against planned performance are often conducted at intermediate stages as well as at the completion of the project. Where performance has fallen far short of expectations, the interim audit may signal the need to abandon the project. The purpose of these audits is to provide continuous checks, not only on project implementation but also on the efficiency of project evaluation and decision making. There is nevertheless a danger in this method of control that has often proved difficult to overcome. The projects that are most likely to conform to plan are low-risk projects. Since return on investment is a function of risk, these low-risk projects also tend to be low-return projects. The introduction of a comprehensive audit control system, even where only post-mortem audits are conducted at the end of a project's life, has an unfortunate tendency to discourage the submission by lower managements of high-return projects for approval, where such projects are also associated (as they are likely to be) with high risks.

Relevant Costs and Benefits

A special sub-committee, the capital project evaluation sub-committee, is sometimes set up to examine capital expenditure proposals submitted to the central budgeting committee. The role of the evaluation sub-committee is to provide an independent check on estimates made by operating departments, first, to ensure that estimates relating to costs and benefits are realistic and, second, to ensure that they conform to appropriate concepts relevant to the decision. The estimates may need to be adjusted for unduly optimistic or pessimistic forecasts of particular variables, or otherwise brought into line with top management's overall risk perspective.

The relevant costs for project evaluation are differential or incremental costs. Full costs and arbitrarily allocated costs are not relevant. But certain fixed overhead costs may be incremental and should be included, e.g. where the introduction of a new product line requires an increase in factory supervision or head office overhead costs.

A special case concerns increased expenditures incurred for the purpose of a particular project's evaluation. The cost of evaluation is not a project cost, but is clearly unavoidable should the firm decide subsequently not to adopt the project, i.e. it is an example of a sunk cost that is not relevant to the analysis.

The measure of the cost should conform to the opportunity cost principle. For example, if the project will make use of certain by-products from another project, the appropriate cost is the sales value of the by-products forgone, and not their accounting cost or transfer price within the firm (unless the transfer price is equal to the sales value, or exceeds it under circumstances where there is an alternative use for the by-products within the firm and consequent higher opportunity cost). Another example of opportunity cost is the use of space in the factory for a new product line. The new project should be charged with the space, if and only if the space otherwise would be employed for another project, or could be leased out. For the purpose of the analysis, the cost of the space is not historical or replacement cost or some other allocated value, but is the value of the benefits forgone in the next best alternative use.

An important problem, for which there is no definitive solution, is how to account for opportunity costs that lie in the future but are relevant to the evaluation of a current project. For example, the use of excess space in the factory for a current purpose may pre-empt an alternative use of the space in two years' time. Although the space has no alternative use at present, its opportunity cost is not zero. Some writers have suggested that all projects be allocated with an arbitrarily determined figure in order to take account of such real, but hidden and unknowable, opportunity costs.

The difficulty of quantifying certain benefits of an intangible nature, such as improved staff morale, associated with a capital project has been mentioned earlier. Another problem is that the relevant concept of benefits is, like that of costs, also an incremental one. The relevant measure of revenues associated with a new product may be higher or lower than first suspected, depending on whether the sales of the new product are complementary or competitive with sales of existing products.[1]

Project Evaluation Criteria

Existing capital projects represent the outcome of investment decisions by which management expects to attain the company's long-range objectives. Investment decisions involve different time elements and risk considerations compared with other business decisions (such as those discussed in the following chapter). In evaluating new projects it is necessary to have regard to the timing and the amounts of future cash flows, and the uncertainty or risk attached to those flows. A discussion of project risk is deferred to the last section of this chapter. At this stage assume that the risks are homogeneous for all projects (existing and proposed) of the firm.

It is necessary to make explicit provision for what may be called the time value of the revenue and cost flows associated with each decision, i.e. to recognize that an immediate return (or sacrifice) of $1 is worth more than a return (or sacrifice) of the same amount at some future time. This may be done by introducing an appropriate discount factor, which reflects the time value and uncertainty of future cash flows, into the comparison of alternatives. In this way it is possible to reduce all investment proposals to an equivalent basis for purposes of comparison.

The expression of investment proposals in terms of their associated cash flows is easier to describe than it is to carry out in practice (since much of the basic information is unreliable and some of the estimates may be merely guesses). Estimates need to be made of the periodic cash outlays associated with each investment proposal and of the periodic cash receipts which the investment is expected to yield. The outlays and receipts associated with the investment in any one period are then combined to give net outlays or net receipts for the period, net outlays being regarded as negative cash flows and net receipts as positive cash flows. In this way, any investment project may be expressed in terms of the cash flows which are expected to result from it; if the investment takes the form of an initial cash outlay (when, say, plant is purchased) followed by a series of periodic net receipts (including the salvage value of the plant among the proceeds of the final period), the investment may be expressed as a negative cash flow followed by a series of positive cash flows. For discounting purposes, it is convenient to assume that the net receipts accrue at the end of each year, but this assumption may be varied if it significantly affects the results.

Suppose that investment in a vending machine, involving an initial outlay of $1 000, is expected to yield net receipts of $300 per annum (cash receipts *less* costs of

---

[1] Where the production of the new product leads to economy in the costs of other products, the new product's production costs should be adjusted accordingly for analysis purposes.

supplies, other cash operating expenses and taxation) during each of the following three years, and that at the end of this time it is anticipated that the machine can be sold for $400. This investment may be expressed as a series of expected cash flows as follows:

Year 0	Year 1	Year 2	Year 3
− $1 000	$300	$300	$700

The cash flow concept should not be confused with any income concept that has been discussed in this book. Discounting procedures cannot be applied consistently to the income flows accruing from alternative projects, because the time pattern of cash flows is likely to differ substantially from the time pattern of income flows. Some items which have to be taken into account in measuring income, in particular depreciation charges, do not involve cash and ought therefore to be excluded from the calculation. On the other hand, the initial cost of new plant, or the realizable value of existing plant at the time the decision is being made, is relevant to the calculation and needs to be brought in as a lump sum. Further, cash flows need to be recorded in such a way as to allow for tax. Tax payments are based on measures of income which take account of depreciation charges; to the extent that depreciation charges differ among alternative investment projects, tax outlays may also be expected to differ.

In the capital budgeting literature, it is generally assumed that the interests of the ordinary shareholders are paramount, and that these interests are best served if management pursues a policy of maximizing the market value of the firm. To evaluate a project's contribution to the firm's market value, some criterion of profitability or return on invested capital is necessary.

Crude Evaluation Techniques

Many different criteria are used for purposes of evaluating investment proposals, but some of these are relatively crude in their application and omit important variables such as cash flows or the discount factor from the analysis.

Accounting Rate of Return

A common method of evaluating investment proposals is to estimate a rate of return on the investment funds required by each project, by expressing expected average annual income as a percentage of the expected average book value of funds employed.[2] Suppose that the cost of an investment is $10 000 and that the income earned during its life (after depreciation) is expected to average $1 000 per annum. If it is assumed that there is no residual scrap value, the average book value of the investment is $\dfrac{\$10\ 000}{2}$ or $5 000, and average income is expressed as a percentage of this figure:

$$\frac{\$1\ 000}{\$5\ 000} \times 100 = 20 \text{ per cent}$$

This rate is compared with corresponding rates from alternative projects, or with minimum rates established by management for purposes of deciding whether or not a particular investment is profitable.

---

[2] Sometimes the return is calculated on the initial investment.

Superficially, this is attractive as a test of alternative investment proposals, since it uses the familiar concepts of income and capital. However, this method suffers from the serious limitation that it fails to give any weight to differences in the timing of the flows resulting from the investment, and this is sufficient to disqualify it as a satisfactory indicator of investment worth in circumstances where income fluctuates, or where the initial investment outlay is spread over a number of years. The accounting rate of return on funds employed may be a useful measure of past efficiency, but cannot be used satisfactorily to gauge future performance.

Payback

The widely used payback criterion merely takes account of the length of time required for the net receipts generated by the investment to equal the initial outlay. If an original outlay of $1 000 is expected to be followed by a stream of net cash receipts of $200 per annum for the first four years and $120 per annum for the next six years, the payback period is calculated at 5⅔ years.

Firms adopting this criterion usually tend to approve only those investment projects which have a payback period shorter than an arbitrary maximum, say four years, and where alternative projects are being compared they choose the one with the shorter payback period. The payback method omits too many relevant considerations to be useful as a *profitability* criterion in making investment decisions. It not only ignores differences in the timing of the cash flows resulting from different projects, but it also ignores some of the cash flows themselves (since cash flows occurring after the payback dead-line are omitted from consideration altogether).

However, payback may be useful under the following circumstances:
(a) the future is extremely uncertain, so that distant returns of longer-lived investments are not attractive; and
(b) the firm is in a severe capital rationing situation, and early recoupment of funds invested is desired.[3]

In a sense payback gives a measure of the rate at which the uncertainty attached to future cash flows will be resolved. Thus it is a rough and ready measure of *risk*. The use of payback may be justified as a screening device for risk, to be used in conjunction with a more sophisticated profitability or return criterion.

Greater flexibility in the use of the payback method can be obtained by a simple extension of the accept-reject rule, e.g. accept the project if the payback period is less than three years, reject it if the period is more than five years, and investigate further if the period lies between three and five years.

Methods of Evaluation which Involve Discounting of Cash Flows

In order to overcome the weaknesses of the foregoing methods of evaluation, it is necessary to express the cash flows resulting from each investment in terms of equivalent discounted values. Two methods of doing this have already been described in Chapter 16. The first is the present value method and the second is the internal rate of return method. Both methods make use of the concept of cost of capital in evaluating investment proposals.

---

[3] Capital rationing exists when for lack of funds the company cannot accept all projects promising positive net present values.

Cost of Capital

The cost of capital may be formally defined as that rate of return, k, which may be used by a company to evaluate projects and is such that the acceptance of a project, with an internal rate of return greater than k, will lead to an increase in the value of the company's shares. The cost of capital is also known as the 'minimum required rate of return' or the 'cut-off rate for capital expenditures', and is a crucial figure in the analysis of investment projects. Below is an example of how the cost of capital may be calculated. However the approach used implies a simplifying assumption that all projects (existing and proposed) in the company are of homogeneous risk (as would be the case where the company is considering a scale expansion of its existing activities). It should be emphasized that, if the assumption does not hold, the cost of capital measure as computed in the manner shown below is not applicable. In those cases the appropriate discount rate would be a market-determined rate which takes account of the non-diversifiable risks of the particular project, as will be explained in the last section of this chapter.

Given the above assumption, the cost of capital may be computed from the costs of the individual components of the company's capital structure, i.e. the different classes of equity and loan capital, weighted in accordance with the market capitalization of each class.

Example: XYZ Co. employs several classes of capital funds comprising ordinary shares, preference shares, debentures and unsecured notes. The costs of the preference shares, debentures and unsecured notes are given by their respective dividend and interest yields. The cost of ordinary equity capital (which includes the ordinary contributed capital, reserves and other retained earnings) may be derived by reference to the market-based rate of return (see Appendix to Chapter 7):

$$R(e)_t = \frac{P_t - P_{t-1} + D}{P_{t-1}}$$

where
$$\begin{array}{rcl}
R(e)_t & = & \text{return on ordinary equity in period } t \\
P_{t-1}, P_t & = & \text{share price at the beginning and end of the current} \\
 & & \text{period respectively} \\
D & = & \text{dividend paid in the period.}
\end{array}$$

Assume that the cost of ordinary equity based on appropriate past data is 10 per cent. This cost (as is also the case with the cost of preference shares) is the same before and after tax. However, because interest charges are tax-deductible, the cost of debt funds to the company is effectively reduced by the rate of tax (40 per cent). The weighted after-tax average cost of all classes of funds employed may then be computed in the manner shown in Table 29—1.

Table 29—1
XYZ Co.
Computation of Cost of Capital, 1985

	Market Capitalization ($ million)	Cost of Capital Before Tax (%)	Cost of Capital After Tax (%)	Annual Cost After Tax ($ million)
Ordinary shares	145.70	10.0	10.0	14.57
Preference shares	1.75	6.9	6.9	0.12
Debentures	11.53	6.9	4.1	0.47
Unsecured notes	13.53	7.2	4.3	0.58
	$172.51			$15.74

Thus the weighted after-tax average cost of capital is $\frac{15.74}{172.51}$ or 9.1 per cent.

Net Present Value (NPV) Method

The NPV method of evaluating investment proposals uses a cost of capital rate for discounting purposes, and involves the calculation of the present value of the cash flows—positive and negative—associated with each investment project. The net present value of a project must be positive to make the project worthwhile. Subject to other constraints (such as the supply of available funds), in using this criterion the company will continue to undertake additional investment so long as it yields a positive present value.

The acceptance rule may be represented thus:

$$\left[\sum_{t=1}^{n} b_t \, (1 + k)^{-t} - \sum_{t=0}^{n} c_t \, (1 + k)^{-t} \right] > 0$$

where b_t represents expected cash receipts from the project in period t, c_t represents expected cash outlays in period t, k is the appropriate cost of capital and n is the life span of the project. It is usually assumed that the initial outlay is incurred at the commencement of the first period (i.e. $t=0$), whereas all other cash flows occur at the end of the respective periods (e.g. $t = 1, 2, ...$, refers to the end of period one, period two, etc.).

Internal Rate of Return (IRR) Method

The IRR method involves the estimation of the rate of discount which equates the present value of the cash receipts which the investment is expected to yield with the present value of the cash outlays required for the project. The rate of return so derived is compared with the cost of capital, in order to determine whether a particular investment is worth undertaking. On this criterion, the company will undertake the new investment if its rate of return exceeds the appropriate cost of capital.

The internal rate of return, r, is computed from the following equation.[4] Acceptance of the project is indicated if $r > k$ where

$$\sum_{t=1}^{n} b_t(1 + r)^{-t} - \sum_{t=0}^{n} c_t(1 + r)^{-t} = 0$$

[4] See the Appendix to this chapter for a method of computing r.

The IRR calculation may yield an imaginary solution or multiple solutions for certain patterns of net cash flows. For conventional cash flow patterns, e.g. an initial outlay followed by net cash inflows only, these problems do not arise.

Comparison of NPV and IRR Methods

The two methods always give the same accept-or-reject decision for projects with a 'normal' stream of cash flows, i.e. an initial outlay followed by a series of positive net cash flows in subsequent periods. The reason is that if a project has a rate of return greater than the cost of capital, k, the present value of the project's cash receipts must be greater than the present value of its outlays, when both flows are discounted at k. However, the two methods may not provide the same project rankings. The ranking problem arises under either of two situations:

(a) the projects are mutually exclusive, e.g. a decision to build a motel or car park on an empty plot;
(b) capital rationing exists, whereby lack of funds prevents the company from accepting all projects promising positive net present values.

Suppose, for example, that a firm wishes to choose between two investment proposals that are expected to result in the following cash flows. The cost of capital is 10 per cent.

	Initial Cost	Net Cash Receipts in Year		
		Year 1	Year 2	Year 3
Project X	$1 000	$140	$140	$1 140
Project Y	1 000	438	438	438

The NPV and IRR of the two projects are:

	NPV	IRR
Project X	$99	14%
Project Y	$89	15%
Project preferred	X	Y

Since the rates of return of individual projects do not change, the IRR method provides an unchanging project ranking. On the other hand, where the cost of capital, k, is used to rank projects, there may be conflicting rankings depending on the value of k. Thus the project ranking for a particular value of k could be inconsistent with the ranking under the IRR method. Figure 29—B illustrates the present value profiles for two projects, A and B, and shows that an inconsistent ranking may arise when the present value profiles of projects intersect above the x-axis (rate-of-interest axis).

Figure 29—B
Present Value Profiles of Projects A and B

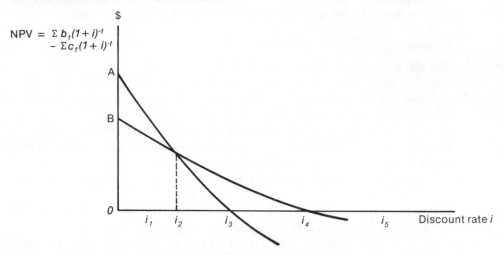

Under the IRR method (the sign > reads 'preferred to'):

$$B > A, \text{ since } i_4 \text{ is greater than } i_3$$

Under the NPV method:

$$A > B, \text{ for } k < i_2$$
$$B > A, \text{ for } k > i_2$$

$$k = i_2 \text{ is the point of indifference.}$$

Figure 29—B also shows that the two methods typically give the same accept-reject decision. (Consider the accept-reject decisions in respect of projects A and B under both methods for interest rates i_1 to i_5.)

Project Ranking under Capital Rationing

Most writers recommend that the NPV method be employed when it is necessary to rank projects, e.g. where investment proposals are mutually exclusive, since the objective is to maximize the net present value of the firm. The ranking problem posed by capital rationing, where lack of funds prevents the company from accepting all projects promising positive net present values, is more complex. [5] Where fractional investments can be accepted, projects may be ranked by the net present value index (NPVI), defined as the ratio of the net present value of net cash receipts to the initial cash outlay, i.e. $\sum_{t=1}^{n} (b_t - c_t) (1 + k)^{-t} / c_0$. Investments can be selected from the list of ranked projects, proceeding with the project with the highest NPVI, until the fixed amount of funds is exhausted. If this procedure is used, the net present value of the firm is maximized by accepting whole projects from the top of the list, down to the marginal project. It is likely that only a fractional part of the marginal

---

[5] A company can always raise additional funds provided it is prepared to pay the price. Capital rationing typically is self-imposed on the part of management and reflects its reluctance to raise additional funds (for whatever reason).

project can be accepted, depending on the funds remaining in the budget after allowing for the adoption of higher ranking projects.

However, in many capital rationing situations whole projects only can be accepted or the shortage of funds may extend over more than one period. Under these circumstances, an integer or dynamic programming algorithm can be used to select that subset of investment proposals which has the largest total net present value and satisfies all relevant constraints.

Ranking Projects with Unequal Lives

When it is necessary to choose between mutually exclusive projects, the project with the highest net present value should be adopted, since the objective is to maximize the net present value of the firm. This is a general rule which may be applied to selection between mutually exclusive projects with equal lives, or between mutually exclusive projects with differing lives where replacement considerations are not present, i.e. when the projects are one-off investment proposals. But in many situations the projects represent the provision of continuing services, so that replacement considerations are important.

Some writers have suggested the following method of ranking mutually exclusive projects which provide continuing services and have unequal lives. The net present values of the projects are converted into *equivalent annual benefits*, or the present values of projects' outlays (when revenues are the same for all projects) are converted into *equivalent annual charges*, which may then be compared. Suppose that a firm can purchase either machine A for $1 000 or machine B for $1 300. The two machines perform the same function,[6] but machine A has a life of five years with operating outlays of $400 per annum while machine B has a life of seven years with operating outlays of $350 per annum. Assume also that the scrap values of the machines at the end of their respective lives are nil, and the cost of capital is 20 per cent.

The present value of the cash outlays for machine A is $1\ 000 \ + \ \sum_{t=1}^{5} \dfrac{\$400}{(1.2)^t}$ or $2 196. The equivalent annual charge in respect of A is the five-year annuity with a present value of $2 196, i.e. $734. Similarly, the present value of the cash outlays for machine B is $1\ 300 + \sum_{t=1}^{7} \dfrac{\$350}{(1.2)^t}$ or $2 562, and the equivalent annual charge in respect of B is the seven-year annuity with a present value of $2 562, i.e. $711. This criterion indicates machine B is the superior project.

There is, however, a number of problems with this approach. In essence the analysis is the same as one in which the replacement of each machine, by an identical machine, to a common terminal life is assumed. In the present example, the common terminal life is 35 years and in many cases could be higher. Further, if at the time of the analysis one of the machines has been used for, say, three years, it is implicitly assumed that this machine at the end of its life will be replaced by another machine which has been used for three years, and that this pattern will be repeated to the end

[6] This is a simplifying assumption. A similar analysis can be undertaken for projects with different patterns of future cash receipts.

of the common terminal life. Generally, the use of equivalent annual benefits or equivalent annual charges in ranking projects with unequal lives suffers from the unrealistic replacement assumptions underlying the analysis.

Technological Forecasting and Project Evaluation

An evaluation method, which is of general application in capital budgeting and can be used in the special case of mutually exclusive projects with unequal lives, is explained below. The method takes into account technological forecasts and abandonment possibilities relating to each project.

Suppose that a firm can purchase either machine C which has a two-year life, or machine D which has a three-year life. Advancements in technology will make available machine X at the end of the first year, and machine Y at the end of the second year. Either machine can replace C or D, while Y can also replace X. Assume also that the lives of X and Y extend to two or more years.

Figures 29—C and 29—D give the net payoffs (shown in parentheses) for different replacement decisions. These payoffs are stated in terms of present values of expected cash flows (including expected abandonment values) in future periods, which are associated with different replacement assumptions. The rectangles in the figures indicate that a choice has to be made between alternative courses of action at a particular point of time; the circles in the figures represent events which are outside

Figure 29—C
Net Payoffs with a Two-year Investment Horizon

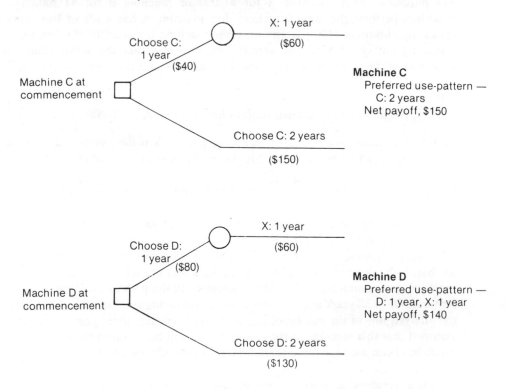

Figure 29—D
Net Payoffs with a Three-year Investment Horizon

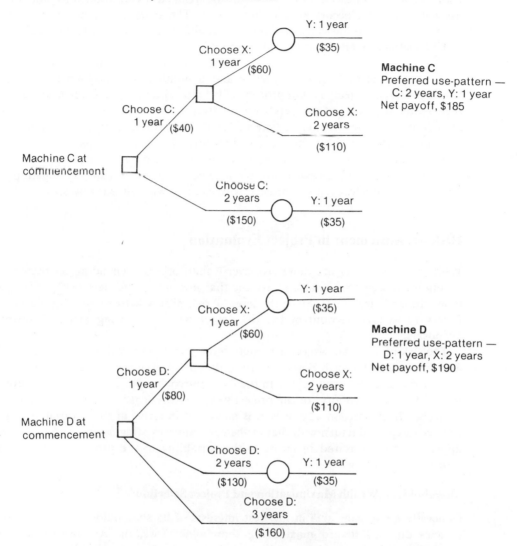

the control of the decision maker (given the investment horizon).[7] Asset lives and technological developments are assumed to be known with certainty. The net payoffs for a firm with an investment horizon of two years are illustrated in Figure 29—C and of three years in Figure 29—D.

The preferred use-pattern in a decision set is the one with the maximum net payoff associated with an initial course of action. If the firm has a two-year investment horizon and machine C is purchased at the outset, the maximum net payoff obtainable is $150; the corresponding net payoff for machine D is $140. Clearly machine C is the superior project. Similarly it can be seen that, where the firm has a three-year investment horizon, D is the superior project.

[7] 'Choose C: 1 year' refers to a decision to choose machine C and replace it at the end of one year. 'X: 1 year' refers to an event, i.e. the use of machine X for one year.

It has been assumed that asset lives and technological developments are known with certainty. These assumptions can be relaxed by introducing probabilities associated with the occurrences of these events. The analysis becomes more complex but in principle it is basically similar to that of the simplified cases discussed above.

The method of choosing between mutually exclusive projects explained in this section takes explicitly into account the time horizon of the firm's investment plan, the likelihood of technological change and a number of abandonment situations relating to each project. This approach is likely to capture and include in the analysis the greater flexibility of projects with relatively short lives and projects with high abandonment values in intermediate stages of their economic lives. Generally, it is a superior project evaluation method, and the use of probabilities associated with the occurrences of events under uncertainty can be incorporated in the analysis. The approach has general relevance for accept-reject decisions in capital budgeting, and for ranking mutually exclusive projects with equal or with differing lives.

Risk Measurement in Project Evaluation

While some investors are more risk averse than others, depending on their utility functions, it seems reasonable to assume that investors prefer less risk to more risk, other things being equal. Since the level of risk differs across capital projects, it is necessary to take account of the risk factor when evaluating capital investment proposals.

The risk of a capital project is related to the uncertainty with respect to the timing and amounts of the cash flows. Several different approaches to the measurement of project risk are discussed below. In the first approach a project's risk is measured in terms of the covariability[8] of the project's expected return [9] with that on the market portfolio. In the second approach it is measured in terms of the covariability of the project's expected return with that of the company's existing assets; and in the third approach it is measured in terms of the variability of the project's own expected return.

Shareholders' Wealth Maximization and Project Selection

Generally a company acts in the best interests of its shareholders when it pursues policies directed toward maximizing shareholders' wealth. An investment policy consistent with shareholder wealth maximization involves the selection of only those projects which will lead to an increase in the market value of a company's outstanding shares.

In modern finance theory it is assumed that shareholders hold well diversified portfolios, a good approximation of which may be given by the value-weighted market

---

[8] A covariance is a statistical measure of the degree of association between two series. The covariance is positive if the deviations of the two series from their expected values tend to have the same sign, and the covariance is negative if the deviations tend to have opposite signs.

[9] A return is a random variable, i.e. a variable subject to a probability distribution, and the expected return is the mean of that probability distribution. Asset returns may be defined in a number of ways. An appropriate measure of the return from an asset which is not traded, such as a capital project, is its internal rate of return, while that from an asset which is traded, such as a share, is its market-based rate of return (as explained in the Appendix to Chapter 7).

portfolio (a value-weighted combination of all assets traded on the market). Hence a shareholder will be concerned with the risk and return of his whole portfolio, rather than with the risks and returns of individual companies in the portfolio.

The expected return on the portfolio is merely a weighted average of the expected returns from all investments in the portfolio. The measure of risk is a little more complex. The variability of the portfolio's expected return is dependent not only on the variances of the expected returns from the constituent assets, but also on the pair-wise covariances of expected returns between assets in the portfolio. As the number of assets in a portfolio increases, the relative significance of the covariance between assets' returns also increases. In a large portfolio, the effect of a new asset's risk on the portfolio's risk is mainly determined by its covariance of expected return with that of the other assets held.

Modern finance theory postulates a linear relationship between expected return and risk on marketable assets, where risk is measured in terms of the covariance between the expected return on the asset and the expected return on the market portfolio.[10] Such a relationship is expressed in equation (1):

$$E(\tilde{R}_j) \ = \ R_f + \lambda \, \text{cov}(\tilde{R}_j, \tilde{R}_m) \tag{1}$$

where $E(\tilde{R}_j)$ = expected rate of return on asset j (the tilde - indicates that R_j is a random variable),

R_f = rate of return on risk-free assets,

λ = market price of risk (a positive constant equal to $\dfrac{E(\tilde{R}_m) - R_f}{\sigma_m^2}$, where $E(\tilde{R}_m)$ = expected rate of return on the market portfolio and σ_m^2 = variance of expected rate of return on the market portfolio), and

$\text{cov}(\tilde{R}_j, \tilde{R}_m)$ = covariance (a statistical measure of association) between the expected rate of return on asset j and the expected rate of return on the market portfolio.

A company which adopts a share price maximization objective will select only those projects for which the coordinates of expected rate of return and market covariance plot on or above the so-called 'security market line', which is defined by equation (1). Projects which plot below the security market line will be rejected, as their adoption would give an expected return less than that required by the market and therefore result in a fall in the market price of the company's shares.

Company's Existing Portfolio of Assets and Project Selection

An implicit extension of the above analysis is that attempts by companies to diversify are irrelevant to shareholders, because they can diversify on their own account by holding the appropriate portfolio.

However, management is more akin to undiversified shareholders, since managers normally are heavily committed (in terms of human capital) in the firm which

---

[10] Ideally it should be the value-weighted portfolio of all assets—marketable and non-marketable—but this approach is non-operational.

employs their services. As a result, management is motivated towards reducing the company's risk through the diversification of its projects, in order to ensure its survival (and hence the survival of the management team itself).

Because management has an interest in the expected return and risk of the portfolio of assets held by the company which is its employer, it will be concerned with the effects of a new project's adoption on that portfolio's return and risk. This can be inconsistent with shareholder wealth maximization, as the company's portfolio is unlikely to be fully diversified and management will be making risk-return investment decisions based on a relatively undiversified portfolio. Since the market does not pay for diversifiable risk, management would not always be acting in the interests of the shareholders. For example, suppose that a capital project plots below the security market line, but has an expected return that is negatively correlated with the expected return from the company's existing assets. The proposal may be attractive to management because of its favourable effect on the company's overall risk, although from a diversified shareholder's view its adoption is clearly not justified.

Although management has certain incentives to diversify, there are market forces in operation which tend to limit any divergences between the interests of shareholders and management. There is a competitive market for managers. A management that is not concerned with maximizing shareholders' wealth may soon find itself replaced. Also there is an active market for corporate control and firms whose value can be increased through more efficient management are likely to be the subject of takeover, thus increasing the probability that a management which is not perceptive of shareholders' interests will be replaced. Finally, there are monitoring and bonding activities,[11] which act as constraints on the possible divergence between the goals of shareholders and management.

Variability of Expected Return and Project Selection

In practice, capital project evaluation seldom takes formal cognizance of the importance of the covariance of a new proposal's expected return with that on the market portfolio or the company's existing asset holdings. Rather, project risk typically is defined as the variability of the expected return from the project and may be measured as the variance or standard deviation of the expected return. This approach may not be consistent with the wealth maximization objective. One of the best-known project risk analysis models using this approach is explained below.

Hertz's Risk Analysis Model

Hertz described a simulation method of risk analysis which has been employed in an American company for the purpose of evaluating capital investment proposals. As noted in Chapter 27, simulation is a technique which models an economic system in a set of mathematical equations, and manipulates the model to derive outcomes that represent those of the activities of the system. In Hertz's model, risk analysis refers to a process which recognizes that the outcome of a course of action, e.g. the rate of return on a project is dependent on the interaction of a large number of input variables, each of which has a range of possible values. Hertz's model, by taking

---

[11] Shareholders continuously monitor the performance of management through a variety of means, such as financial statements, the financial press and investment counsellors' reports. Management may bond itself to provide certain information, maintain a minimum debt-equity ratio, etc.

account of the probability of occurrence of each value in the range, derives a probability profile of rates of return associated with a capital project.

There are several key variables in computing the rate of return on an investment proposal. Hertz used an example in which he identified nine such input factors, comprising market size, selling prices, market growth rate, share of market, investment required, residual value of investment, operating costs, fixed costs and useful life of facilities. The conventional approach is to estimate the most probable value for each input factor and derive a single-valued rate of return.

Hertz's model rejects this conventional approach in favour of simulation analysis. The following steps are necessary in his model:

(a) The range of values for each input factor and the associated probabilities are estimated. This is the most difficult part of the analysis. For example, the sales manager is required to estimate a range of selling prices in the market and the associated probability for each price in the range.

(b) The computer is programmed to select at random from the distribution of values (appropriately weighted by their likelihood of occurrence) one particular value for each input variable in the model. Since some of the variables are inter-dependent, a constraint is introduced to govern the selection of values for certain dependent variables. Thus if product price determines the share of the market, the prior selection of a value of the product price is used to restrict the selection of a value for share of the market to that portion of the range that is consistent with the pre-selected product price figure.

(c) The model has a logic section which is programmed to calculate the required outcome, in this case the internal rate of return.

(d) The process described above is repeated again and again to obtain a continuous profile of rates of return, with the probability associated with each of these rates occurring.

Hertz gave an example in which the expected rate of return on a proposal was 25 per cent, using single expected input values. When the simulation approach was used, the expected return was only about 15 per cent. The following schedule of possible rates of return was obtained:

Rate of Return (%)	Probability of Achieving at least the Return Shown (%)
0	97
5	81
10	75
15	54
20	43
25	13
30	0

The project was disclosed to be less favourable than first thought. There was a 3 per cent chance of making a loss, only 13 per cent chance of achieving a return of 25 per cent and no chance of achieving 30 per cent.

The method lends itself readily to sensitivity analysis. The responsiveness of the solution to a particular input factor may thus be analysed by making defined changes in the input factor, while allowing the rest of the model to simulate randomly. For example, Hertz described how management was concerned with the imprecise estimates of market growth. Sensitivity analysis showed that variations in growth between 3 and 5 per cent per annum had little effect on rates of return.

There are other project risk analysis models in use, and in recent years models have become increasingly mathematical and complex. It is likely that, because of a rapidly changing and unpredictable future, the trend towards increasingly complex quantitative risk analysis models in capital budgeting will be reversed. In its stead there may evolve a relatively flexible dual system of risk analysis, in which simple quantitative models are complemented by a qualitative and more sophisticated approach, which incorporates unquantifiable but not less important risks into the analysis.

Some Conclusions

A considerable literature on project evaluation treats risk as synonymous with the variability (as measured by the variance or standard deviation) of the expected return from a project. Recent advances in knowledge of the working of the capital markets have shown such approaches to be invalid for firms which follow a market value maximization objective. Through diversification, an investor can eliminate from his portfolio those risks that are solely associated with individual securities, and his portfolio may be approximated by the market portfolio which contains only non-diversifiable market risks. It is only these non-diversifiable risks which the investor can expect the market to reward him for bearing, and hence they are relevant risks in evaluating projects. It follows that the appropriate risk measure to employ in capital budgeting is the covariance of the expected return from the project with that on the market portfolio.

Although an inherent weakness of conventional risk analysis models is that the concept of risk as the variability of the expected return from a project is inconsistent with shareholders' wealth maximization, the models do have some advantages. They can be used to generate some of the necessary information for measuring the covariability of the expected return from the project with that on the market portfolio. In particular, they can provide estimates of the project's expected rate of return and expected cash flows in each period of the project's economic life. Since capital projects are not traded on the market, these estimates may be regarded as surrogates of periodic market-based returns and used to compute covariability measures that are sufficiently reliable for decision making.[12] Initially the measures will be crude, but they can be refined and made operational as experience accumulates.

The important principle is that the appropriate risk concept for the value-maximizing firm, i.e. risk measured by the covariability of the expected return from the project with that on the market portfolio, be employed in the evaluation of project risk in capital budgeting.

---

[12] The risk of a capital project (say, a copper mine) can sometimes be represented by the market-based risk of an equivalent asset which is traded on the market (e.g. a copper mining company).

Appendix

Solving for the Internal Rate of Return (IRR)

Let r be the interest rate (expressed as a percentage) such that the net present value of the investment is zero:

$$f(r) = \sum_{t=1}^{n} \frac{b_t}{(1 + r)^t} - C_0$$

$$= 0$$

where C_0 is the initial outlay and b_t is the net cash inflow in period t, $t = 1, 2, ..., n$.

Where the net cash inflows are constant in each period ($b_1 = b_2 = ... = b_n$), the computation of r is straightforward.

$$\sum_{t=1}^{n} \frac{b}{(1 + r)^t} - C_0 = 0$$

$$\frac{C_0}{b} = \sum_{t=1}^{n} (1 + r)^{-t}$$

Example: The initial outlay of a project is $70 000, the expected life is four years and expected net cash receipts are $30 000 a year.

$$\frac{70\ 000}{30\ 000} = 2.3333$$

From compound interest tables, it is seen that the present value of $1 per period for four periods is 2.36 at $r = 25$ per cent. The internal rate of return for the project is thus approximately 25 per cent. An interpolation procedure may be employed when the value of r cannot be read directly from the tables. An illustration of interpolation is given in a following example.

Where the net cash inflows are not constant, there are several mathematical techniques that can be used to solve for the internal rate of return. The so-called bisection method for finding r will be explained below.

The function $f(r)$ may be illustrated as follows:

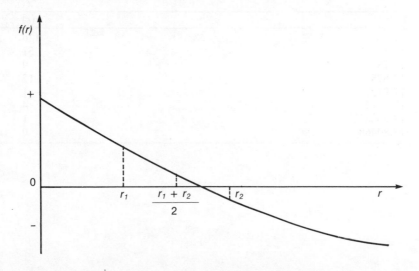

Identify an interval:

$$r_1 \leqslant r \leqslant r_2$$

such that $[f(r_1)][f(r_2)] < 0$. This implies that $f(r_1)$ and $f(r_2)$ have opposite signs.

Calculate the mid-point $\dfrac{r_1 + r_2}{2}$ and the function $f(\dfrac{r_1 + r_2}{2})$, and test as follows:

$$[f(r_1)]\left[f\left(\frac{r_1 + r_2}{2}\right)\right] = 0, \text{ then } \frac{r_1 + r_2}{2} \text{ is the IRR, since } f\left(\frac{r_1 + r_2}{2}\right) \text{ is zero}$$

$$> 0, \text{ IRR is on interval } \frac{r_1 + r_2}{2}, r_2$$

$$< 0, \text{ IRR is on interval } r_1, \frac{r_1 + r_2}{2}$$

Repeat this iterative procedure until the solution $f(r) = 0$ is achieved. An approximate solution through interpolation can be obtained once a relatively narrow interval has been identified.

Example: The initial outlay of a project is $10 000, the expected life is four years and expected net cash receipts are $5 000, $4 000, $3 000 and $2 000 in the respective years.

Let $r_1 = 16\%$ and $r_2 = 20\%$

$$[f(16\%)][f(20\%)] = (309)(-358)$$
$$< 0$$

Identify a new interval: $r_1 = 16\%$; $\dfrac{r_1 + r_2}{2} = 18\%$.

$$[f(16\%)][f(18\%)] = (309)(-34)$$
$$< 0$$

An iterative process identifies sequentially the following values of r, which are shown below together with their associated net present values:

r	$f(r)$
17	136
17.5	51
17.75	9
17.875	--12
17.8125	$-$ 1
17.78125	4
17.796875	1
17.8046875	0 (approximately)

The internal rate of return is 17.80 per cent (correct to two decimal places). It is interesting to note that one might have stopped after identifying the interval 16 per cent to 18 per cent, and obtained an approximate value of r through interpolation as follows:

$$16 + (\frac{309}{343} \times 2) = 17.8 \text{ per cent approximately.}$$

The interested reader is referred to J.M. Smith, *Scientific Analysis on the Pocket Calculator*, Wiley, New York, 1975, Chapter 9.

References

Fama, E.F. and Miller, M.H., *The Theory of Finance*, Holt, Rinehart and Winston, New York, 1972.

Additional Reading

Hertz, D.B., 'Risk Analysis in Capital Investment', *Harvard Business Review*, January-February 1964, pp. 95-106.
Higgins, R.C., *Financial Management — Theory and Applications*, Science Research Associates, Chicago, 1977, Part III.
Quirin, G.D., *The Capital Expenditure Decision*, Irwin, Homewood, Ill., 1967.
Van Horne, J.C., *Financial Management and Policy*, Prentice-Hall, Englewood Cliffs, N.J., 1977, Part II.

Discussion Questions

1 Why are capital investment decisions so important in relation to the long-run survival of a firm?

2 Discuss how investment in a capital project differs from other types of investment.

3 Explain the nature of the problems encountered in the generation of project proposals, and in evaluating estimates of the costs and benefits associated with these proposals.

4 Is the net present value method always superior to payback and accounting return methods in evaluating investment proposals?

5 Do you agree with the statement that the investment alternative yielding the highest internal rate of return is the most acceptable? Give reasons for your opinion.

6 Discuss the advantages and disadvantages of obtaining relatively large returns from an investment in its early years.

7 Compare and contrast the internal rate of return and net present value methods of evaluating investment proposals.

8 It is sometimes argued that the use of the internal rate of return criterion for evaluating investment decisions avoids the need to determine the firm's cost of capital. Do you agree?

9 Discuss the role of risk analysis in project evaluation. How does it differ from the conventional approach to project evaluation?

10 It is said that current methods of risk analysis are inconsistent with shareholders' wealth maximization. Evaluate this statement and its implications for capital project analysis.

Exercises

1 A project requires an initial investment of $37 000. The expected annual net cash inflows from the project over its life are as follows:

Year 1	$8 000
Year 2	12 000
Year 3	12 000
Year 4	8 000
Year 5	8 000
	$48 000

Evaluate the project on the basis of:
(a) the payback period;
(b) the accounting rate of return;
(c) the discounted net present value; and
(d) the internal rate of return.

It can be assumed that the investment has no salvage value at the end of five years and the appropriate discount rate is 10 per cent.

2 Eastern Canning Ltd is evaluating three alternative investments which are mutually exclusive. The project data are as follows:

	Net Amount Invested	Net Annual Return After Tax	Estimated Project Life
Project A	$350 000	$80 000	10 years
Project B	420 000	160 000	5 years
Project C	560 000	180 000	10 years

You are required to recommend the best project for investment. The appropriate discount rate is 20 per cent.

3 The market capitalization of the debt and equity components of Cloudview Products Ltd's capital structure and the costs of the preference shares, debentures and unsecured notes are as follows:

	Market Capitalization	Cost of Capital Before Tax
Debentures	$600 000	10%
Unsecured notes	200 000	12%
Preference shares	400 000	8%
Ordinary shares	800 000	

The cost of ordinary equity may be computed by reference to the following market-based data. The share price at the beginning of the period was $10 and the share price *ex div* at the end of the period was $11. The dividend paid in the period was $0.75.

You are required to calculate the weighted after-tax average cost of capital. Assume a tax rate of 40 per cent.

4 Investment Systems Ltd is considering two mutually exclusive projects. The appropriate discount rate is 10 per cent and the net cash flow patterns for the two projects are as follows:

	Project A	Project B
Initial investment outlays	$70 000	$70 000
Net cash inflows—		
Year 1	30 000	—
Year 2	30 000	15 000
Year 3	30 000	30 000
Year 4	30 000	100 000

You are required to:
(a) rank the two projects using the net present value method; and
(b) rank the projects using the internal rate of return method.
Are your rankings in (a) and (b) the same? Discuss.

5 Marine Sports Ltd is considering the manufacture of two alternative sports products. Product A requires an investment of $48 332 and has an expected net return of $10 000 per year. Product B requires an investment of $83 850 and has an expected net return of $20 000 per year. Both projects have an expected life of ten years.

You are required to:
(a) calculate the net present values of the projects (assume that the appropriate discount rate is 15 per cent); and
(b) calculate the internal rate of return on each project.
Which project would you select for investment? Discuss.

30 Differential Costs and Business Decisions

In a discussion of cost concepts, the simplifying assumption is often made that the best choice among alternatives is the one which maximizes profit. But other objectives, such as maximizing the firm's share of the market or improving customer goodwill, may also be important. A crucial function of cost analysis then is to disclose the opportunity cost to the firm of pursuing multiple objectives.

The solutions to many problems which involve cost considerations typically proceed as follows. First, management defines as precisely as possible the problem to be solved. Second, management defines the alternative solutions, some of which are not always evident. For example, suppose management is considering mechanizing the manual process used in the manufacture of a component. The obvious alternatives are purchase of the new machine or continuation of the existing manual process. Less evident alternatives that need to be considered include adaptations of the existing manual process, purchase of a different machine, and sub-contracting of the component's manufacture to an outside supplier. There is also a timing factor, as to when the change is to be implemented. Third, each alternative is expressed in quantitative terms. Finally, relevant aspects of the problem that cannot be expressed in quantitative terms are carefully evaluated before appropriate decision criteria are applied to arrive at a decision.

Costs have an important role in decision making. As noted in Chapter 23, the relevant costs for decision making are opportunity costs. The chief significance of the opportunity cost concept in the decision-making area is that it diverts attention from the recorded and often irrelevant costs of existing policies, and forces management to consider the costs (and benefits) of change. The cost of giving up one course of action in favour of an alternative may then be expressed in terms of the additional costs incurred as a result of the change. This re-introduces the notion of differential cost which has already been discussed in Chapter 23. Differential cost is measured by the added cost of any change of policy. The added cost of a change in policy may be negative, i.e. the effect of the change may be to reduce costs. As already noted, the corresponding accounting cost concepts are known as incremental-sunk cost and avoidable-unavoidable cost, respectively.

Differential cost analysis can assist in the determination of many management problems. However, where the range of alternatives is very large other procedures, e.g. mathematical programming techniques such as those illustrated in Chapter 28, are likely to prove more helpful. If the problem is one of minimizing production costs by combining input factors in the most economical way, for example, there are many combination possibilities and the minimum cost solution can be obtained more easily from linear programming than from differential cost analysis. Irrespective of the technique adopted, however, the principle employed in the analysis is given by the differential cost concept.

The use of differential costs in two management policy areas—production and pricing—is discussed below. The examples which follow are deliberately over-simplified and in actual situations non-quantifiable factors, such as employee or customer relations, may need to be taken into account. As far as possible, of course, all factors relevant to a decision need to be expressed in quantitative terms; if a factor cannot be so expressed it must be noted and used to supplement the quantitative data, in arriving at what must now be broad judgement as to what operating policy should be. For the sake of simplicity, most of the problems are discussed mainly in terms of short-run considerations, but it is emphasized that in practice long-run implications and possibilities must be borne in mind even when immediate or short-term policies are being decided. For example, important long-run factors affecting production policy are the effects on costs of changes in production facilities, and the effects on demand of competitors' actions and customers' reactions. In any case the net benefits of alternative courses of action must always be considered in relation to differences in funds or resources employed.

Differential Costs and Production Policy

The differential cost concept is relevant to many aspects of production or operating policy, and its use will be illustrated by reference to different kinds of business decisions which frequently have to be made:
(a) deciding whether to sell a product or process it further;
(b) deciding whether to make or buy a part used in manufacture:
(c) choosing the optimum level of output when the price is given; and
(d) deciding whether or not to cease operations when losses are being incurred.

Sale or Further Processing

If a single product is being manufactured, so that there is no joint cost problem, it is a simple matter to decide at any stage of the production process whether to sell or continue processing the product. It is merely necessary to compare the differential cost of further processing with the differential (or additional) revenue earned as a result of the further processing. So long as the differential revenue exceeds the differential cost, it pays to continue processing. In calculating differential cost and revenue, it is necessary to have regard to the profit opportunities forgone as a result of using the production facilities for purposes of further processing rather than for some alternative purpose, but apart from this complication the analysis is not likely to present any difficulties.

When joint costs are involved, the same kind of analysis may be undertaken, but it is not quite so easy to sort out the relevant from the irrelevant cost factors. Suppose that two products, A and B, are produced jointly at an annual joint cost of $50 000. The output of A is 20 000 kg, and this can be sold at $2 per kg. The output of B is 20 000 kg, and this can be either sold at $1 per kg or converted into 20 000 kg of product C by further processing costing $19 000. Product C can be sold at $2 per kg. The question is should the further processing be carried out?

One might be tempted to reach a decision by using conventional cost accounting methods to determine the cost of product C, and comparing this calculated cost with the revenue that can be derived from the sale of product C. In calculating the total cost of product C, one would need to take into account the cost of product B, which in turn would depend on the assumptions made in allocating the joint costs of production among products A and B. If, for example, the joint costs were to be allocated on an output basis, the calculated costs of product B, and hence of product C, would be different from the costs that would be derived if the allocation were made on the basis of market values. Conflicting answers would thus be given to the question whether the production of C is profitable (see Table 30—1).

Table 30—1
Unit Cost Methods of Deciding on Further Processing

	Joint Costs Allocated on Output Basis		Joint Costs Allocated on Market Value Basis
Cost of B $\frac{20\ 000}{40\ 000}$ x $50 000	$25 000	$\frac{20\ 000}{60\ 000}$ x $50 000	$16 667
Cost of further processing	19 000		19 000
Total cost of C	44 000		35 667
Sales value of C	40 000		40 000
Assumed profit or loss Loss	$4 000	Profit	$4 333

This kind of analysis is misleading. Neither solution correctly indicates the profitability of further processing, and both the joint costs and the costs allocated to product B are irrelevant from the point of view of the decision which has to be made. The only factors which are relevant in deciding whether further processing should take place are the added costs and revenues which are likely to result from the action. The profitability or otherwise of the further processing may be determined by comparing the differential cost and differential revenue as illustrated in Table 30—2.

Table 30—2
Differential Analysis Applied to the Problem of Further Processing (1)

	If No Further Processing	If Further Processing	Differential Revenue and Cost
Sales revenue			
A	$40 000	$40 000	
B	20 000	—	
C	—	40 000	
	$60 000	$80 000	+ $20 000
Costs			
Joint	50 000	50 000	
C	—	19 000	
	50 000	69 000	+ 19 000
Profit	$10 000	$11 000	+ $1 000

The net gain from further processing is thus $1 000, representing the differential revenue of $20 000 *minus* the differential cost of $19 000. It has been implicitly assumed that the production facilities needed for the further processing of product B cannot be used for other purposes if product B is sold. If this assumption is invalid, as is likely to be the case if the firm is working near full capacity and other profit opportunities exist, the differential cost and revenue calculations must take these alternative employment possibilities into account (and it may even be necessary to consider the differential costs and revenues that would result from expansion of the production facilities).

If, for example, 1 000 units of a new product D can be made at a cost of $5 000 and sold for $7 000 if product B is sold instead of being further processed, a different answer to the question is obtained (see Table 30—3).

Table 30—3
Differential Analysis Applied to the Problem of Further Processing (2)

	If No Further Processing	If Further Processing	Differential Revenue and Cost
Sales revenue			
A	$40 000	$40 000	
B	20 000	—	
C	—	40 000	
D	7 000	—	
	$67 000	$80 000	+ $13 000
Costs			
Joint	50 000	50 000	
C	—	19 000	
D	5 000	—	
	55 000	69 000	+ 14 000
Profit	$12 000	$11 000	— $1 000

Under these circumstances a net loss of $1 000, instead of a net profit of $1 000, may be expected to result from further processing. This illustrates the point that revenues *not* received as a result of a decision, and costs *not* incurred, are just as relevant to the decision as revenues which are received and costs which are incurred. The same answer to the question could have been obtained by considering the opportunity cost of further processing, i.e. the revenue and cost forgone by producing C rather than selling B and producing D (see Table 30—4).

Table 30—4
Opportunity Cost of Further Processing

Revenue from C	$40 000
Less: Costs of processing C	19 000
Net yield from C	21 000
Revenue forgone in producing C	
B	$20 000
D	7 000
	27 000
Less: Associated costs—	
D's production costs	5 000
Net revenue forgone	22 000
Net loss in producing C	$1 000

Make or Buy

A rather different problem of production policy arises when there is a possibility of having work done outside the enterprise as an alternative to carrying out the job internally. Once again the cost concept which is relevant in reaching a decision is that of differential cost. In this case, however, the differential cost is negative and may be interpreted as the cost that can be avoided by having the work done externally. Thus there is a new notion, avoidable cost, which is simply differential cost in another guise.

Suppose that a refrigerator manufacturer has been producing a shelf unit for use in his refrigerators at a cost of $2 per shelf unit, made up as follows:

Direct material	0.75
Direct labour	0.65
Manufacturing overhead—	
Variable	0.10
Fixed	0.50
Total unit cost	$2.00

The shelf unit can be purchased from a jobbing engineer for $1.75. Should the refrigerator manufacturer continue to make the part or buy it?

The answer to this question depends on what costs may be avoided by buying the part as opposed to making it, and this in turn depends to a large extent on the division between variable and fixed costs that has been noted. In the example, only the variable costs of $1.50 per unit (direct material, direct labour and variable overhead) can be avoided by buying the part outside—the fixed costs continue to be incurred whether the shelf unit is made internally or not. Subject to the proviso that more profitable opportunities do not exist for using the production facilities needed to make the shelf unit, it clearly pays to continue making it—the effective cost of $1.50 per unit is less than the outside purchase price of $1.75 per unit. If the factory is working below full capacity, it may be presumed that there are no production possibilities which are more profitable to the enterprise than the manufacture of the shelf unit.

However, if the factory is working at full capacity, the relevant cost of manufacture comprises the variable costs of $1.50 *plus* the opportunity cost, if any, of the fixed facilities (i.e. the earnings from the best alternative use). It is this relevant cost that needs to be compared with the outside purchase price.

A different analysis is necessary if additional fixed expenditures have to be incurred in order to manufacture the component part, e.g. if its manufacture is being considered for the first time, or additional units are needed and the factory is working to full capacity. The differential costs are those that are incremental to the production proposal, but the analysis depends on the assumptions about the fixed costs. Suppose that the incremental fixed costs are cash outlay costs, e.g. rent and equipment lease payments. Using the foregoing example, assume that incremental fixed costs for the relevant range of output are $1 000 per annum, while the variable costs are expected to be $1.50 per unit and the outside purchase price is $1.75 per unit. The decision to make or buy is a function of the modified break-even point, as shown:

$$x^* = \frac{F}{p^\dagger - v}$$
$$= \frac{1\ 000}{1.75 - 1.50}$$
$$= 4\ 000 \text{ units}$$

where x^* is the point of indifference in the make or buy decision, and $p\dagger$ is the outside purchase price. The manufacturer should purchase the component part if (additional) annual demand is less than 4 000 units, and he should manufacture if demand exceeds 4 000 units. A break-even chart, modified to illustrate the make or buy problem, is shown in Figure 30—A.

Figure 30—A
Modified Break-even Chart—Make or Buy

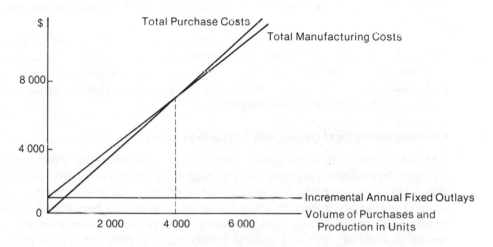

On the other hand, suppose that the firm has to purchase additional fixed equipment for manufacturing the components. This is a capital investment evaluation problem, and discounted cash flow analysis should be employed.

Example: Omega Co. proposes to manufacture a new line of product. The annual production cost estimates are as follows:

Wages	$42 000
Direct materials	37 000
Rent	2 500
Administration	4 000
Depreciation of plant (straight-line)	12 000

Further investigation discloses that wages and direct materials are incremental costs. Rent is an allocated expense that would be incurred whether the project is adopted or not, but $1 000 of the administrative expenses are avoidable if the project is not adopted. The manufacture of the product requires the purchase of plant costing $60 000 which has an economic life of five years. Sales are estimated at 10 000 units per year, but sales beyond five years are uncertain.

An outside supplier has offered to supply the product at $10 per unit. The company's cost of capital is 12 per cent, and the present value of an annuity of $1 per period for five periods at 12 per cent is $3.605.

Ignoring tax complications, the two alternative courses of action may be compared along the following lines. The incremental annual outlays associated with the manufacture of the product are:

Wages	$42 000
Direct materials	37 000
Administrative expenses	1 000
	$80 000

The present value of $80 000 per year for five years at 12 per cent is $80 000 (3.605) or $288 400. Thus the total cost of the investment, assuming a five-year investment horizon, is $288 400 + $60 000 (the purchase cost of the plant) or $348 400.

This figure should be compared with the present value of the cost of five years' purchases from an outside supplier, i.e. $100 000 (3.605) or $360 500. Abstracting from qualitative considerations, such as the effectiveness of product quality control and uncertainty of the cost estimates, the analysis shows that the make option is financially preferable to the buy alternative.

Choosing the Optimal Output with Selling Price Given

Although at first sight it may appear that a firm can maximize its profits (or minimize its losses) by choosing an output where average or unit cost is at a minimum, it can be shown that average or unit cost is irrelevant in deciding the level of production. The optimal output is achieved at the point where any further increase in production would result in differential costs increasing by a greater amount than differential revenues, while any reduction in output would result in differential costs falling by a lesser amount than differential revenues. If the economist's assumption that production can be varied in single-unit quantities is adopted, the differential costs and revenues of changes in production become marginal costs and revenues, and the optimal level of production is achieved where marginal costs and revenues are equal.

Suppose the unit selling price of a product is given by market conditions at $3, that costs vary with output in the manner shown and the following range of production possibilities exists:

Level of output and sales (units)	10 000	11 000	12 000	13 000
Variable manufacturing costs	$15 200	$17 000	$18 200	$19 800
Fixed manufacturing costs	10 000	10 000	10 000	10 000
Variable selling expenses	2 000	3 000	4 500	6 000
Fixed administrative expenses	6 000	6 000	6 000	6 000
Total costs	$33 200	$36 000	$38 700	$41 800
Average cost	$3.320	$3.273	$3.225	$3.216
Average variable cost	$1.720	$1.818	$1.892	$1.984

What is the most profitable level of output? The answer is not the level of production where average total costs are at a minimum (13 000 units), because it can be seen that if an output of 12 000 units is chosen instead of one of 13 000 units, costs are $3 100 lower while revenue falls by only $3 000; it is thus clearly more profitable to produce 12 000 units than 13 000 units. The most profitable output is likewise not achieved at the point where average variable costs are at a minimum (10 000 units) since by producing 11 000 units instead of 10 000 units revenue can be increased by $3 000 while costs are only $2 800 higher. The optimal level of output is achieved where the extra revenue of added production no longer exceeds the additional costs incurred as a result of that production. In deciding on the level of output, therefore, differential revenues resulting from changes in output need to be compared with differential costs (see Table 30—5).

Table 30—5
Differential Revenues and Costs Resulting from Changes in Output and Sales

	Changes in Output and Sales		
Units	10 000—11 000	11 000—12 000	12 000—13 000
Differential revenue—			
Total	$3 000	$3 000	$3 000
Unit	$3	$3	$3
Differential cost—			
Total	$2 800	$2 700	$3 100
Unit	$2.80	$2.70	$3.10
Net gain (or loss) from additional 1 000 units	+$200	+$300	−$100

It will be seen that the operating position can be improved by expanding output to 12 000 units but that any further increase in production beyond that point results in a worsening of the position. If, as assumed, production can only be varied in 1 000-unit quantities, the optimum level of output is thus 12 000 units. With the selling price given at $3, it can be seen that it pays to increase production and sales so long as the differential cost of added output does not rise above $3 per unit.

The same result could have been arrived at, of course, by comparing total revenue at each level of output and sales with total cost:

Output and sales (units)	10 000	11 000	12 000	13 000
Total revenue	$30 000	$33 000	$36 000	$39 000
Total costs	33 200	36 000	38 700	41 800
Loss	$3 200	$3 000	$2 700	$2 800

All the possible levels of output involve losses; the use of differential analysis has shown how the loss may be minimized. It may be questioned whether there is any point in carrying on production at all under these conditions. The answer again depends on the alternatives available. These include switching to other products and shutting down either permanently or temporarily. In considering each of these alternatives, differential analysis may need to be supplemented by other decision-making techniques.

Shut-down

Whether or not a permanent shut-down is warranted depends on such factors as expectations regarding future costs and revenues, and the amount that can be realized by selling the firm's assets. Revenues and costs not affected by the decision, e.g. depreciation on the original cost of fixed assets, are irrelevant and must be ignored. If it is believed that market prices will eventually increase to the point where operations will again be profitable in relation to the other alternatives available, liquidation or permanent shut-down will be decided against. In making this decision, it is necessary to compare the present realizable value of the firm's net assets with the cash flows (proceeds and outlays) that may be expected to result from policies of (a) continued operation with eventual replacement of plant, (b) continued operation with liquidation deferred until plant wears out, or (c) temporary shut-down. Because the cash flows resulting from the different alternatives take place in different time periods, they must be converted into equivalent present values by means of discounting techniques that have been discussed in Chapter 29. The concept of cash flows has also been examined, but it may be noted that the comparison is one of cash proceeds and outlays, and not accounting revenues and costs. Depreciation charges thus do not enter into the calculation at all, but the salvage value of assets disposed of is included among cash proceeds along with operating revenues.

If liquidation or permanent shut-down is ruled out as a possibility, and the choice is between temporary shut-down and continued operation, straight differential analysis may be used in making the decision. Under the conditions postulated in the above example, it is clear that it is worthwhile for the enterprise to keep on producing, even though book losses are being made This is because, in making a decision whether or not to close down temporarily, it is only the differential revenues and costs resulting from continued production (interpreted as the revenues that are sacrificed and the costs that are avoided by shutting-down), that are relevant. If it is assumed that avoidable costs in this instance correspond to variable costs, [1] shutting-down temporarily is clearly disadvantageous; by reducing production from 12 000 units to nothing, periodic costs are reduced by $22 700 but revenue falls by $36 000.

Differential Costs and Pricing Policy

Differential analysis is just as relevant in making price decisions as it is in formulating production policy. Just as preoccupation with conventionally-determined average or unit costs has often led to incorrect production policy decisions, so have accountants and businessmen tended to make use of unit costs as a basis for pricing policy. Empirical studies have shown that a procedure which is widely used by business in determining selling prices is to add a margin, intended to cover overhead and provide a profit, to average direct costs. [2] Average direct costs are usually assumed to correspond to average variable costs and to remain constant over the range of production which is open to the firm. The margin which is added to average direct costs is sometimes a percentage and sometimes an absolute amount. In fixing this margin the firm commonly has regard to some concept of normal or expected output, which will result in average indirect and hence average total costs being such that the desired level of profit will be achieved. After a selling price has been determined in this way, it is normally not varied unless average direct costs change. Changes in the level of output usually do not affect the price charged, and it is left to demand factors to determine the quantity sold at the price that has been fixed.

This method of price determination, which economists have described as the full cost principle, differs in important respects from the classical economic view which sees marginal analysis as the key to price behaviour. The marginal theory starts from

---

[1] This assumption may not be valid in practice, since some so-called variable costs may need to be incurred in order to maintain the nucleus of a work force, while certain so-called fixed costs may be avoidable even in the short run.

[2] An alternative procedure is to add a margin to average factory cost (including allocated manufacturing overhead).

the assumption that the businessman wishes to maximize his profits, and shows that this involves fixing a price, and a level of production and sales, where the cost of the final unit of output is equal to the revenue derived from the sale of that unit. Under conditions of perfect competition, price (and hence marginal revenue) is constant and must be taken as given, output being adjusted to the point where marginal cost equals price (and marginal revenue). Where competition is not perfect, it is assumed that prices need to be reduced in order to expand output and sales; and that the price of the product is determined by the position of the demand schedule at the level of output and sales that equates marginal cost and marginal revenue (see Figure 28—F in Chapter 28).

Several empirical studies have shown that the businessman does not know very much about the nature of the demand schedule for his product, and hence about marginal revenue at different levels of output and sales. Some economists have been influenced by such studies into substituting the full cost principle for the marginal theory as a rationale of price behaviour. Paradoxically, while this has been happening there has been a growing awareness on the part of accountants and businessmen of the importance of marginal (or, more generally, differential) analysis in making pricing decisions. The difference between the full cost and marginal approaches to pricing policy may be explained in terms of different assumptions in respect of the businessman's behaviour. The full cost principle implies some concept of normal or satisfactory profit as the businessman's goal, whereas marginal analysis assumes that he is concerned with maximizing his profits.[3]

At first sight, it might appear that the full cost basis of pricing ignores competitors' prices and the influence of demand, except insofar as the latter is considered to respond passively to the decisions taken. This is not necessarily the case, since the behaviour of competitors and the state of demand may be reflected in the size of the margin which is added to the cost base. As soon as this point is conceded, however, one is forced back to the position that some objective criterion, such as the marginal principle provides, is needed in order to determine the size of the indirect cost and profit margin. The importance of marginal analysis is underlined when the fact is recognized that pricing decisions, like most other business decisions, are concerned not with the formulation of policy in a vacuum, but rather with adapting or directing policy to relatively small changes from existing situations. In considering these changes, the businessman must inevitably take into account their expected effects on costs and revenues, and if he acts rationally he will conform to the marginal principle as far as he is able.

In looking at problems of price policy, therefore, it is necessary to have regard to demand factors as well as cost factors, and a distinction between different pricing situations may be made according to whether prices are predominantly demand-determined or cost-determined. Where the demand for a firm's product is highly price-elastic, i.e. highly responsive to price charges, the firm has little flexibility in its pricing policy and it may be described as a 'price-taker'. The problem under these circumstances is not to fix prices but to decide on the output that is to be produced at the given price. (This is the question which was considered on page 702.) Where the demand for a firm's product is not highly price-elastic, the firm can take the initiative in determining the price it will charge for the product and it may be described as a

---

[3] It has been suggested that in the long run the two assumptions may amount to the same thing, if normal profits are determined with a view to maximizing long-run profits.

'price-maker'. The problem in this case is one of choosing the optimum price under given cost and demand conditions. The quantity sold (and produced) at this price depends on demand factors about which little may be known, but the pricing decision is facilitated by the existence of definite limits to the price which can be charged. The lower limit is fixed by the differential cost notion of avoidable cost—the cost that may be avoided by not producing at all—and in the very short run when the firm is working below capacity this usually corresponds closely to average variable cost. The upper limit is fixed by the prices that are currently being charged by competitors (or which may be charged by potential competitors). The lower pricing limit is necessarily an emergency or short-run concept. In formulating price and production policy, the firm must have regard to longer-run factors such as changes in costs resulting from possible innovations in production techniques or the expansion of production facilities, and changes in demand for the firm's products resulting from the response of customers and competitors to the prices charged. Often the lower pricing limit will not be adopted for fear of the ill effects of competitor reaction. To the extent that differential or marginal analysis is used for purposes of pricing policy, it is thus usually necessary to have regard to long-run differential (or marginal) costs and revenues with a view to maximizing long-run rather than short-run profits.

It will be apparent that a firm's ability to be a price-maker rather than a price-taker largely depends on the kind of market in which it sells its products. In open market situations, such as exist in respect of many raw materials and other primary commodities, prices have to be taken as given. In most manufacturing industries, however, there is sufficient product differentiation, advertising, etc. to break up the market and make it possible for cost factors to come into their own in the pricing process. Irrespective of whether prices are demand-determined or cost-determined, however, it is important to remember that the concept of cost which is relevant in determining policy is current replacement cost and not historical cost. Even where prices are demand-determined, production policy must be decided by reference to cost and only current replacement cost provides an adequate measure of the sacrifice involved at different levels of output. In other words, in deciding the quantities that he is prepared to supply at different prices, the producer must have regard to current replacement cost, irrespective of whether he is a price-taker or price-maker.

In the light of this general discussion on pricing policy, three specific problems, which serve to illustrate some of the generalizations that have been made, will now be examined:

(a) deciding whether to accept a special order at a special price;
(b) determining the optimum price under given cost and demand conditions; and
(c) deciding on the price to be charged in respect of goods transferred from one department or division of a business to another (or services performed by one department for another).

Special Orders

The differential cost concept in relation to pricing policy may be usefully illustrated by reference to the problem of the special order at the special price. Suppose that a firm makes a certain kind of garden tool and sells it in its local city, Jonesville, for $1.25 each. The unit cost of the tool is $1.10, comprising:

Direct material cost	$0.30
Direct labour cost	0.40
Manufacturing overhead	0.40
Unit cost	$1.10

The manufacturing overhead rate is fixed at 100 per cent of direct labour cost, based on budget figures of $5 000 for fixed overhead, $5 000 for variable overhead, and $10 000 for direct labour costs. The firm is asked by its agent in Smithville, a city 500 km away, if it would be prepared to accept a special order of 1 000 implements at $1 each. Such an order is within the firm's capacity (without interfering with other production) and the question is whether it should be accepted.

If the price which is offered ($1.00) is compared with the unit cost of production ($1.10), it seems to be unprofitable to accept the order. The unit-cost figure is clearly irrelevant in making the decision, however, because it includes a share of fixed manufacturing overhead, which remains unaffected by the decision. It is necessary to compare the price which is offered with the differential cost of completing the order. Provided that there is idle capacity in the plant and that there are no special costs associated with the order, and if it is assumed that the proportion of variable overhead to direct labour costs remains constant, the cost of producing the special order is given by the variable costs:

Direct material cost	$0.30
Direct labour cost	0.40
Variable overhead	0.20
Unit variable cost	$0.90

In the conditions postulated it clearly is worthwhile accepting the order, since the differential revenue associated with the order (1 000 x $1 = $1 000) exceeds the added costs which have to be incurred (1 000 x $0.90 = $900). It must be emphasized, however, that this answer depends on the existence of idle capacity in the factory, the absence of other orders which could make a greater contribution to fixed overhead and profits, and the existence of a separate market for the special order. It may not pay to accept the order if the quoted price reduction is likely to affect adversely the selling prices received on existing sales; under these circumstances the differential revenue will be less than the $1 000 which has been assumed.

The practice of accepting lower prices for special orders is described as 'dumping', and is prevalent in international trade where markets are separated by physical barriers and other factors which facilitate discrimination. Where the total revenue received from the sale of the dumped product fails to cover its total cost, dumping cannot be regarded as providing a permanent basis for pricing policy, since in the long run fixed as well as variable costs must be met if the firm is to stay in business. The more general pricing problem will be considered in the next example.

The Optimal Price

Where selling prices as well as unit costs vary with output and something is known of the way in which demand is likely to be affected by price changes, differential or marginal analysis may be applied directly to the problem of deciding the price at which profits will be maximized.

Suppose that a firm making room heaters incurs fixed costs of $4 000 per annum and variable manufacturing and selling costs of $5 per heater, and that it is faced with the following expected demand situation:

1 000 heaters can be sold if the price is	$9.00
980 heaters can be sold if the price is	9.50
940 heaters can be sold if the price is	10.00
855 heaters can be sold if the price is	10.50
750 heaters can be sold if the price is	11.00

It will be seen that, if the selling price is increased from $9 to $9.50, the differential revenue is $490 (980 units sold multiplied by the price increase of $0.50) *minus* $180 (the fall in sales volume of 20 units multiplied by the original selling price of $9), or $310. The differential cost is *minus* $100 (representing the saving in variable costs, 20 x $5), so that the net increase in income is $410. Clearly, a selling price of $9.50 is more profitable than one of $9. Differential revenues and costs resulting from changes in prices, sales and output may be recorded in a statement prepared in accordance with Table 30—6.

Table 30—6
Differential Revenues and Costs Resulting from Changes in Price

Selling price	$9.00	$9.50	$10.00	$10.50	$11.00
Quantity sold (units)	1 000	980	940	855	750
Sales revenue	$9 000	$9 310	$9 400	$8 977	$8 250
Costs—					
Fixed	4 000	4 000	4 000	4 000	4 000
Variable	5 000	4 900	4 700	4 275	3 750
Income	—	$410	$700	$702	$500
Differential revenue	—	$310	$90	−$423	−$727
Differential cost	—	−$100	−$200	−$425	−$525

It is profitable for the firm to raise its selling price at least to $10, since up to that point each price increase has the effect of increasing total revenue as well as reducing total costs. By increasing the price from $10 to $10.50, however, differential revenue is reduced by $423. This is approximately the same as the fall in differential cost, so that income is virtually unchanged. It may be concluded that the most profitable price is somewhere within the range $10 to $10.50, and that at this price the quantity sold will be between 940 and 855 units.

It will be seen that, for purposes of pricing policy, the concepts of differential revenue and differential cost are again similar in their significance to the economist's concepts of marginal revenue and marginal cost, and as a general rule it may be said that price should not be increased beyond the point where the fall in differential revenue resulting from the reduced demand exceeds the fall in differential cost resulting from the lower output. In the example, it is clearly unprofitable to increase prices from $10.50 to $11.00.

Transfer Pricing

The application of the opportunity cost principle to pricing policy may be illustrated by reference to the problem of fixing a price for work done by one department of a business for another. If it is assumed that, in order to make them fully responsible for their performance, departmental managers are given the power to formulate their own price and production policies, it is necessary to adopt pricing criteria in respect of internal transfers that have the effect of maximizing the over-all profit of the business as well as the profits of the departments concerned. This aim will be achieved in intra-firm transactions as long as two conditions are fulfilled. The first is that the price must not be so low that the revenue received by the supplying department for work done for another department is less than the costs which the supplying department can avoid by not doing the work (and in making this calculation allowance must be made for profits lost on outside orders which have to be given up in order to do the internal work). The second condition is that the price paid by the receiving department must not exceed the price it would have to pay if it had the work done externally. If, for example, the costs to department A of performing certain services for department B are represented by variable costs $800 *plus* profits forgone on outside orders $100, the minimum price which department A should charge is $900. If department B could get the services performed by an outside contractor for $950, the maximum price which department B can afford to pay department A is this figure of $950. Provided the transfer price is fixed between these limits of $900 and $950, the transaction is profitable both to the enterprise as a whole and to the two departments. One method that may be employed is to permit the departmental managers to bargain among themselves to fix prices within these limits.

Transfer pricing is a difficult and controversial issue. We have ignored complications such as the level of unused capacity and constraints on management's authority in one or both departments, as well as other purposes that transfer prices may be expected to serve. Our brief treatment is intended only to illustrate the relevance of the opportunity cost concept for decision making in this particular problem area.

Conclusion

We have now completed our study of the role which accounting can play in helping management to formulate business policy, and with it our examination of business enterprise accounting in general. It has been a major theme of this book that accounting is essentially an information system, the effectiveness of which must be judged by reference to its ability to provide information that is relevant to decision makers faced with the task of choosing among alternative courses of action. It has therefore been appropriate to conclude by examining the role of accounting in providing the information needed to guide investment, pricing and production decisions in business enterprises.

Discussion Questions

1 To what extent is the notion that different concepts of cost are relevant for different purposes consistent with the view that alternative bases of valuation should, as far as possible, be avoided in accounting measurement?

2 Opportunity cost is a concept which features widely in economic analysis. To what extent is the concept (a) useful, and (b) measurable, in relation to managerial accounting and business decisions?

3 What are the relevant costs to be considered in deciding whether to make or buy a part under the following circumstances:

(a) where plant is running below normal capacity and there are no alternative uses for the unutilized capacity;

(b) where plant is running below normal capacity but alternative uses exist within the firm for the unutilized capacity; and

(c) where plant is running at normal capacity and manufacturing the part will entail a fixed cash outlay in addition to variable costs?

4 What are the relevant cost concepts in deciding:

(a) whether to replace an asset with no alternative use;

(b) whether to sell a product prior to further processing;

(c) whether to make a part instead of obtaining it from an outside supplier;

(d) what is the most profitable output;

(e) whether to shut down an unprofitable department (i) temporarily, or (ii) permanently; and

(f) whether to accept a special order at a special price?

5 Contrast full cost and marginal cost pricing.

6 In the areas of cost accounting and managerial economics, a distinction is frequently made between short-run and long-run costs. What is the significance of such a distinction in relation to pricing and production decisions?

Exercises

1 Canterbury Products Ltd is a manufacturing enterprise engaged in the production of sun-blinds and beach umbrellas. Sales in Australia are subject to marked seasonal fluctuations, and the company is investigating the possibility of establishing an export market for its umbrellas in Singapore and Malaysia. Preliminary enquiries suggest that sales can only be made in those countries if the f.o.b. price is reduced to $A9 compared with the Australian wholesale selling price of $A11. What factors should be taken into account by the company in deciding whether or not to accept export orders at the lower price?

2 A manufacturing process yields 20 000 kg of product A and 20 000 kg of product B at a total cost of $140 000. Product A can be sold for $6 per kg and B for $3 per kg. It is possible by means of additional processing to convert 20 000 kg of product B into 16 000 kg of product C (which can be sold for $8 per kg) and 4 000 kg of waste material, which would have to be disposed of at a cost of 50c per kg. The cost of the additional processing is estimated at $32 000.

Would you advise the company to undertake further processing?

3 A company, which manufactures a range of products, applies manufacturing overhead to production at a rate of 200 per cent of direct labour cost. This rate is based on the following budgeted costs for the normal level of activity:

Budgeted fixed overhead	$64 000
Budgeted variable overhead	96 000
Budgeted direct labour cost	80 000

You have been asked to advise on the following problems:

(a) The normal selling price of product A is $24 per unit and its production cost is as follows:

Direct materials	$8
Direct labour cost	4
Manufacturing overhead	8
	$20

The company has been asked to supply a special order for 2 000 units of product A at $16 each. The order will have no effect on the normal sales of this product and the company has the capacity to produce the extra units. Should this order be accepted?

(b) The cost of manufacturing a component part of product B is:

Direct materials	$4
Direct labour cost	8
Manufacturing overhead	16
	$28

This part can be purchased from an outside source for $24. Should the company continue to make the part, or buy it from outside?

4 Reliance Manufacturing Ltd is currently operating at full capacity. It has received an order from an important customer to supply 10 000 units of a special component. These units must be supplied to maintain the company's goodwill. The company can either purchase the component from a subcontractor at $4 per unit or manufacture it in its own factory. The manufacturing operation will need additional assembly space, which can be rented for $12 000. The variable costs of manufacture will be $2.50 per unit.

Should Reliance Manufacturing Ltd buy the parts from the outsider supplier? Discuss the financial and qualitative factors in the decision.

5 What advice would you give to a manufacturer contemplating whether or not to accept a special production order (for which plant capacity is available) at a price of $3 per unit? The cost specification for the product specifies: direct materials, $1 per unit; direct labour, $\frac{1}{2}$ hour at $2.40 per hour; and an overhead absorption rate of $3 per direct labour hour. The overhead absorption rate was calculated from a manufacturing overhead budget which estimated that fixed overhead would be $10 000 and variable overhead $5 000, and that 5 000 direct labour hours would be worked.

6 A manufacturer of kitchen utensils makes a number of products on multi-purpose machines. He applies fixed manufacturing overhead to products on the basis of 50 per cent of the direct labour cost, and fixed selling and administrative expense on the basis of 10 per cent of the sales revenue.

In the year ended 31 December 1985, the factory as a whole records a satisfactory profit, but it is estimated that product X has made a loss of $1 000, calculated as follows:

Sales		$10 000
Less: Cost of goods sold—		
Direct materials	$4 000	
Direct labour	2 000	
Manufacturing overhead	2 000	8 000
Gross profit		2 000
Less: Selling and administrative expenses		3 000
Net loss		$(1 000)

The proprietor is disturbed by this result and proposes to cease making product X, although he does not contemplate the production of any alternative lines at present. He seeks your advice on:

(a) whether he should discontinue the manufacture of product X; and

(b) the likely effect on total profit if a decision is made to discontinue the manufacture of X.

7 The Vita Bakery operates a delivery service using two horse-and-cart combinations, which cost $500 each four years ago and were then believed to have a life of ten years. If sold now, it is expected that the combinations would realize $200 each.

It is decided to investigate the possibility of replacing the two teams by one motor delivery van. The van can perform the same amount of work as the two horse-and-cart teams, and no expansion in delivery services is anticipated. The cost of the van is $4 000 and its estimated life is six years, with a resale value of $1 600 at the end of this period. On the basis of the following information, would you advise the replacement of the horses and carts by the motor van?

Operating Costs Per Year	Two Horses and Carts	One Motor Van
Drivers' wages	$12 000	$8 000
Fodder, blacksmith charges, insurance, etc.	2 000	
Petrol, oil, maintenance, insurance, etc.		5 000

It may be assumed that the stables can be converted to a garage without additional cost, and that any new capital required may be obtained at 10 per cent per annum.

8 ABC Co.'s unit costs of making and selling a given item at a level of 30 000 units per month are as follows. The product is sold at $12 per unit through regular channels.

Manufacturing costs—	
Direct materials	$2.40
Direct labour	2.20
Variable overhead	1.40
Fixed overhead	0.50
Selling costs—	
Variable costs	3.00
Fixed costs	0.90

You are required to make the necessary calculations to support your answers to the various problems posed below. Treat each problem as independent of the other problems.

(a) State two alternative values at which a closing inventory of 5 000 units may be presented in the balance sheet. Give reasons for the alternative you prefer.

(b) ABC Co. recently signed a contract for the delivery of 8 000 units to a government department on the following terms: reimbursement of all manufacturing costs plus a fixed fee of $2 000. Assume that these 8 000 units would not otherwise have been produced. How much would profits have been increased by the government contract?

(c) Assume the same data as in (b) above, but the 8 000 units will displace 8 000 other units from production. Should the company have accepted the contract?

(d) The company has 5 000 units of old stock of this item. These must be sold in the market in the normal manner at drastically reduced prices. What is the unit cost that should be employed for determining a minimum selling price?

9 Platinum Ltd last year produced three joint products at a joint cost of $200 000. These products were processed further. The additional processing costs, which were all variable costs, and the sales revenues of the products after processing are as follows:

	Additional Processing Costs	Sales Revenue
Product X	$400 000	$490 000
Product Y	600 000	660 000
Product Z	200 000	350 000

The company could have sold the products at the split-off point without any further processing for the following proceeds: product X, $112 000; product Y, $56 000; and product Z, $112 000. The company expects the same levels of production and sales opportunities in the coming year.

You are required to advise the company on which product should be processed further and which should be sold at the split-off point.

10 Maya Company has developed a new product for which a growing demand is expected. During the next six years sales are expected as follows:

Year 1	40 000 units
Year 2	60 000 units
Year 3	100 000 units
Year 4	160 000 units
Year 5	160 000 units
Year 6	160 000 units

Maya Company must choose between two alternative production arrangements:

(a) Buy a big, heavy-duty machine with an annual capacity of 180 000 units and an estimated useful life of six years. This machine costs $500 000.

(b) Buy a smaller machine with an annual capacity of 100 000 units and an estimated useful life of three years. Three years from today buy two such machines to replace the one that will be worn out. The smaller machines now cost $200 000 each.

Maintenance and insurance costs are expected to be $20 000 per year for the large machine throughout the six years. Maintenance and insurance costs for the smaller machine are expected to be $10 000 per year per machine for the first three years and $12 000 per year per machine for the last three years. Variable production costs per unit will be $6.00 per unit for the large machine and $6.20 per unit for the small machine. All machines will have zero disposal values at the end of their respective lives.

The purchase prices of machinery used to produce this new product are expected to rise at the rate of 6 per cent per annum throughout the period under consideration.

Which is the more attractive alternative for Maya Company? Assume that the cost of capital is 12 per cent. For convenience of calculation assume also that all outlays other than those for the purchase of machinery take place at the end of the appropriate years.

Indexes

Index of Publications by Governments, Professional Accounting Bodies and Other Organizations

Name Index

Subject Index